OXFORD EC LAW LIBRARY

General Editor: F. G. Jacobs
Advocate General, The Court of Justice
of the European Communities

EC CUSTOMS LAW

OXFORD EC LAW LIBRARY

The aim of this series is to publish important and original studies of the various branches of European Community Law. Each work will provide a clear, concise and critical exposition of the law in its social, economic and political context, at a level which will interest the advanced student, the practitioner, the academic, and government and Community officials.

Other Titles in the Library

EC Customs Law

TIMOTHY LYONS

OXFORD
UNIVERSITY PRESS

OXFORD
UNIVERSITY PRESS

Great Clarendon Street, Oxford OX2 6DP

Oxford University Press is a department of the University of Oxford.
It furthers the University's objective of excellence in research, scholarship,
and education by publishing worldwide in

Oxford New York

Auckland Bangkok Buenos Aires
Cape Town Chennai Dar es Salaam Delhi Hong Kong Istanbul
Karachi Kolkata Kuala Lumpur Madrid Melbourne Mexico City Mumbai
Nairobi São Paulo Shanghai Singapore Taipei Tokyo Toronto

with associated company in Berlin

Oxford is a registered trade mark of Oxford University Press
in the UK and in certain other countries

Published in the United States
by Oxford University Press Inc., New York

British Library Cataloguing in Publication Data

Data available

Library of Congress Cataloging in Publication Data

Data available

ISBN 0–19–876492–8

1 3 5 7 9 10 8 6 4 2

Typeset in Photina by
Cambrian Typesetters, Frimley, Surrey

Printed in Great Britain
on acid-free paper by
TJ International Ltd, Padstow, Cornwall

To Patricia

General Editor's Foreword

This book on EC customs law is a welcome addition to the Oxford EC Law Library. Although customs law might, at first sight, seem a subject of limited academic and even practical concern, that branch of law is in fact of central importance in the European Union.

The European Community is based, as the EC Treaty states, on a customs union; and, as the author of this book admirably explains in his preface, the foundational role of the customs union ensures that customs law is intricately related to EC law and policy in a wide field. Customs law is of critical importance to the internal market, and it is fundamental also to the Union's relations with the outside world—in particular both to the common commercial policy and to the Community's development policy. Moreover, the subject has to be seen in its global setting, being governed by many international arrangements and agreements.

This book places customs law in this broader context, and then examines against that background the main branches of the subject—including, for example, rules of origin, classification under the Common Customs Tariff, valuation, customs procedures, customs debt, etc—while never losing sight of the wood for the trees.

All those concerned with trade law and with the operation of the customs union will welcome this clear, expert, and systematic exposition of the subject. Because of its focus on the guiding principles, as developed in particular in the case-law of the Court of Justice, and by its emphasis on the place of customs law within the Community legal system, the book will appeal also to an even wider readership.

Francis G. Jacobs

Author's Preface

The customs law of the EC is sometimes regarded as a specialist field, having little association with the main body of EC law and divorced from some of its most interesting developments. Nothing could be further from the truth. As the EC Treaty itself acknowledges, the EC is 'based upon a customs union'. This is true to some extent financially because customs duties form part of the Community's own resources. The foundational role of the customs union also ensures that customs law affects, and is affected by, EC law and policy in a wide range of areas. On the one hand, customs law is inextricably associated with internal elements of the Community, such as freedom of movement of goods and their free circulation. These are matters that are particularly examined in Chapters 2 and 3. On the other hand, it is fundamental to the relationship between the EC and the rest of the world, particularly, of course, in relation to trade relations and development policy. These matters are considered in Chapters 1 and 6.

As well as being at the heart of the EC's internal and external policies, customs law has also proved to be an arena in which the competences and powers of the institutions of the EC, and the relations between them, have developed. Although the competence of the Community to enter into international agreements may come immediately to mind, the exercise of discretion by the Commission and the Council may also be mentioned; a topic that is considered in Chapters 4 and 5 which deal with customs legislation and administration and the common customs tariff. Relationships between Community institutions and traders have also been examined within the context of customs law. Chapter 13 has, consequently, to consider what amounts to matters of EC administrative law in relation to claims for repayment and remission of customs duty

Even many of those aspects of customs law which, at first sight, appear most closely concerned with exclusively customs matters prove to have a wider significance. For example, the consideration of customs legislation in Chapter 4 has to cover matters such as the construction of consolidating regulations, the discussion of rules of origin in Chapter 7 has significance for many activities concerned with the regulation of markets, and the treatment of valuation in Chapter 8 is significant too beyond the field of customs duty.

Of course, there are matters which are frequently the preserve of customs lawyers and the book seeks to ensure that these are covered too. Chapter 5 is concerned with the common customs tariff and its interpretation, and seeks to outline the principles established by the numerous classification cases which the Court of Justice has had to consider. Chapters 9 to 12 are concerned with matters such as the customs declaration, customs procedures, approved treatments and uses (including, of course, the economically important matters of transit and internal and external processing), and the customs debt.

In many areas, although the customs union has been in place a long time, customs law is still developing. The law and practice on transit, for example, have recently been subjected to considerable improvement and the establishment of electronic means of information transfer is leading to important changes which are likely to prove of great assistance to customs authorities and traders alike. At a time when the role of Member States within the Community and the relationship of Member States to Community institutions give rise, in some quarters, to sustained debate, it is worth remembering that the EC customs union operates without a single customs service. Instead, the individual customs services of Member States are required to operate, so far as possible, as one. Programmes for the future of the customs union, such as Customs 2002, which is briefly considered in Chapter 14, seek, amongst other things, to enhance this co-operation.

Throughout the book I have sought to describe the guiding principles and rules of customs law, in the Community Customs Code and the Implementing Regulation, and to consider them in the context of the relevant case law of the Court of Justice, in a way which is useful to experienced customs lawyers as well as to those coming to the subject for the first time. It is true, of course, that the courts and tribunals of the Member States, just like the national customs administrations, play a vital role in the application of customs law. Following the introduction of a civil appeals procedure in the UK, as required by the Community Customs Code, lawyers in the UK are particularly aware of this. Nevertheless, although I do briefly refer to some decisions reached by courts and tribunals in the UK, and have referred briefly to the UK appeals procedure in Chapter 13, I have not attempted to incorporate the domestic case law, or statute law of the UK, or of any other Member State, into the text. To do that would require a different and much larger book.

The manuscript was completed and dispatched to the publishers on 1 May 2001. I have, however, been able to take in subsequent cases and developments, including the important Commission Regulation (EC) 993/2001 of 4 May 2001, during the publishing process. I have attempted to ensure that the book states the law as at 1 August 2001. Some developments after that date, such as the publication in the Official Journal of Guidelines concerning customs procedures with economic impact, the publication of the provisional edition of the Commission's Transit Manual and the judgment of the Court of Justice of 27 September 2001, in Case C–253/99 *Bacardi GmbH v Hauptzollamt Bremerhaven*, are referred to in footnotes where possible.

24 Old Buildings
Lincoln's Inn
London

Acknowledgements

I am immensely grateful to Advocate General Francis Jacobs for giving me the opportunity to contribute to this series of books, and for his encouragement and comments on the draft manuscript. I am indebted, as well, to two authors of other books in the EC Law Series: Mr Paul Farmer, who first suggested that I write on EC customs law and then read the completed manuscript, and Professor Takis Tridimas, who reviewed the book in draft. Mr Pinheiro de Jesus Ferreira, of the Legal affairs and enforcement of Community provisions unit in the Taxation and Customs Union Directorate General of the EC Commission, also gave generously of his time and experience in providing an analysis of the manuscript, in a depth which was both very helpful and far beyond the call of duty. I should say too how much I have benefited from hearing the views of colleagues in the Customs Practitioners Group on a wide range of customs matters. Mr David Blakemore of the World Customs Organization kindly provided the details, in Chapter 1, concerning which states have signed the revised Kyoto Convention. Mr Christopher Williams of the Treaty Section of the Foreign and Commonwealth Office kindly provided details concerning the ratification of certain of the treaties referred to on pages 46 and 47. Naturally, I alone remain responsible for the text and for any errors it may contain.

Mr John Louth and Mr Michael Watson of Oxford University Press have seen the manuscript through the publishing process with admirable efficiency. Finally, I should like to acknowledge the patience and constant encouragement of my wife Patricia.

Note
The Community Customs Code, Council Regulation (EC) 2913/1992 of 12 October 1992, [1992] OJ L302/1, as amended, is referred to as 'the CCC'. Commission Regulation (EEC) 2454/1993 of 2 July 1993, [1993] OJ L253/1, as amended is referred to as 'the Implementing Regulation'. Council Regulation (EEC) 2658/87 of 23 July 1987 [1987] OJ L256/1, as amended, is referred to as 'the Tariff Regulation'.

Contents

Contents xvii

Table of Cases from the European Court of Justice and Court of First Instance

Table of Cases

Table of Cases from the European Court of Human Rights

Table of Cases from Other Jurisdictions

Table of European Community Treaties

Table of European Community Secondary Legislation

Table of Legislation from Other Jurisdictions

Greece

United Kingdom

Table of Legislation from Other Jurisdictions

United States

Table of International Agreements, Conventions, and Treaties

1

Introduction

A study of Community customs law is, in large measure, a study of achieve-ment. The success of the European Community in establishing a customs union ahead of schedule, on 1 July 1968, may now be taken for granted and overshadowed by the more far-reaching achievement of EMU. The fact, though, that the European project has advanced a long way in more recent times should not be allowed to disguise the truths that the European Economic Community was, as the Treaty of Rome, Article 9[1] said, 'based upon a customs union' and that without a successful economic community there would have been no European Community. Neither should the achievement of a customs union be regarded as rendering irrelevant the prohibition in the EC Treaty, Article 25, of customs duties and charges having equivalent effect and the case law relating to it. One needs only to take a brief glance at the reports of cases decided by the Court of Justice to see that the prohibition is as necessary as ever it was. The debate on taxation in the EU may long ago have shifted its focus from customs duty to the more colourful arena of direct taxation, but it remains necessary, on occasions, to remind Member States of the constraints of the customs union.

Although the establishment of the customs union was a significant achievement for the Community, its customs law can be seen neither as a purely Community matter nor one of exclusively fiscal concern. The interna-tional community has always been influential in Community customs law through the medium, firstly, of GATT and now of GATT 94 and the agree-ments relating to the World Trade Organization. Moreover, the close relation-ship between customs law and trade and development policy ensures that Community customs law has to be viewed from the point of view of the devel-oping as well as of the developed world and from the perspective of exporters to the Community as well as of its importers. This can turn even the simplest dispute over tariff classification into a complex matter of international politics. As Advocate General Ruiz-Jarabo Colomer remarked in his Opinion in a classi-fication case on the unpromising subject of corn gluten feed:

> What appears on the surface to be a technical matter—the drafting of a simple note to supplement a particular tariff sub-heading—in fact conceals a delicate commercial issue, of undeniable economic importance, which has been the subject of difficult negotiations between the Commission and the Government of the United States of America. The course of the negotiations and their final result both

---

[1] Now Art 23.

led to questions being raised in the European Parliament . . . and produced reactions from the trade circles concerned.[2]

Before embarking on a consideration of the customs law that gives rise to such cases it is as well to stand back and place the subject in some historical, economic and political perspective.

A. CUSTOMS DUTIES AND CUSTOMS UNIONS: A BROADER PERSPECTIVE

Customs duties have, of course, been a significant feature of commercial life for a long time. Professor David Landes, speaking of an industrializing Europe, has said:

> A major . . . medieval legacy in restraint of trade was the extraordinarily complex array of interferences with transport and travel: river and port tolls; road fees; entrance duties at gates . . . ; customs barriers following one upon the other because of the lacework of political boundaries, including enclaves and exclaves; a multiplicity of exemptions and franchises, honored as much in the breach as in the observance.[3]

It is little wonder then that Europeans became concerned with developing customs unions, particularly in the late eighteenth and nineteenth centuries. In 1775 much of Austria was brought within a customs union. In the early part of the nineteenth century German states, with, apparently, thirty-eight separate tariff systems in 1815,[4] began to create customs unions. The move toward these began with Prussia in which internal tariffs were removed by 1818. In 1828 the Southern German states of Bavaria and Württemburg created one which was joined a year later by the Palatinate. Again in 1828, some central German states including Saxony created a customs union and on 1 January 1834 the *Deutscher Zollverein* was created. It consisted of eighteen states, with a population of 23 million people, and the Prussian Thaler subsequently became its common unit of currency. It has been said of this development, with words which have as much a contemporary as an historical resonance, that: [m]oves towards economic unification presaged the form which political unification was eventually to take'.[5] By the time the unification of Germany had been achieved, the whole of Germany was within a customs union. Austria meanwhile had created a customs union with Hungary in 1855. In the twentieth century, Switzerland and Liechtenstein formed a

---

[2] Case C–267/94 *France v Commission* [1995] ECR I–4845 at para 4.

[3] D S Landes, *The Wealth and Poverty of Nations: Why Some Are So Rich and Some So Poor* (Little, Brown and Company, London,1998) 245.

[4] I take the figure from Landes, ibid, 246.

[5] M Fulbrook, *A Concise History of Germany* (Press Syndicate of the University of Cambridge, Cambridge, 1992) 115.

customs union in 1923, having formed a currency union in 1921. Later on in 1944, a Customs Convention was concluded within the Benelux Economic Union and in 1948 customs duties were abolished between its members and a common external tariff was established. On 3 February 1958 the Treaty establishing the Benelux Economic Union was signed and was preserved by what is now the EC Treaty, Article 306.[6]

If customs unions have long been a concern of European governments there is nothing exclusively European about them. This is not the place to engage in an exhaustive review of customs unions, but it may be helpful to note how widespread they are. In Latin America, for example, the process of integration began in 1960 with the creation of the Latin American Free Trade Association, under the Treaty of Montevideo. It has so far resulted in the creation of the Southern Common market (Mercosur), established under the Treaty of Asunción signed on 26 March 1991, by Argentina, Brazil, Paraguay and Uruguay, and effective from 31 December 1994.[7] Chile and Bolivia are now associate members of Mercosur. There is also a customs union in Africa between South Africa, Botswana, Lesotho, Namibia and Swaziland. In West Africa there is the West African Economic and Monetary Union (UEMOA: *Union Economique et Monétaire Ouest-Africain*) which, on 1 January 2000, established a customs union consisting of Benin, Burkina Faso, the Ivory Coast, Mali, Niger, Senegal and Togo. The union did not, however, include the other member of UEMOA, namely Guinea Bissau. A few years before, in 1995, a customs union was created between Russia, Belarus and Kazakhstan, which Kyrgystan and Tajikistan have now joined.[8] Finally, it should be noted that the

---

[6] This states: 'The provisions of this Treaty shall not preclude the existence or completion of regional unions between Belgium and Luxembourg, or between Belgium, Luxembourg and the Netherlands, to the extent that the objectives of these regional unions are not attained by application of this Treaty.'

[7] Art 1 of the treaty states:

'This common market shall involve:
The free movement of goods, services and factors of production between countries through, inter alia, the elimination of customs duties and non-tariff restrictions on the movement of goods, and any other equivalent measures;
The establishment of a common external tariff and the adoption of a common trade policy in relation to third States or groups of States, and the co-ordination of positions in regional and international economic and commercial forums;
The co-ordination of macroeconomic and sectoral policies between the States Parties in the areas of foreign trade, agriculture, industry, fiscal and monetary matters, foreign exchange and capital, services, customs, transport and communications and any other areas that may be agreed upon, in order to ensure proper competition between the States Parties;
The commitment by States Parties to harmonize their legislation in the relevant areas in order to strengthen the integration process.'

[8] This union may provide an example of one of the disadvantages of a customs union. It has been suggested that it could lock its participants into the old technology of the Soviet Union and be unhelpful to those members whose rates of duty would be lower than those required by the common tariff: see C Michalopoulos and D Tarr, 'The Economics of Customs Unions in the Commonwealth of Independent States' (Policy Research Working Paper 1786 of the World Bank).

CARICOM countries have proceeded a long way towards putting in place a common market, including a customs union.[9]

1. *The economics of customs unions*

As we noted in relation to the customs union of which Russia is a part, customs unions are not without potential disadvantages. If free trade provides, in terms of economic theory at least, the most advantageous environment in which to conduct trade, then a geographically limited customs union is no more than 'a second-best strategy'.[10] The simple expedient of a unilateral reduction of tariffs by a group of countries may prove more attractive. It would, for example, avoid the 'trade diversion' which a customs union may induce. This may be expected to occur because the low-cost producer outside the customs union will lose trade to the high-cost producer within it. This diversion has disadvantages for the consumer within the customs union as well as for the producer outside it. There is a loss of national tariff revenue which is not passed on in full to the consumer by way of price-reduction because the goods of the high-cost producer are more expensive than those of the low-cost producer. Nevertheless, this disadvantage is offset by the fact that it is cheaper to buy the product from the high-cost producer without a tariff than from the low-cost producer with a tariff. This leads to a beneficial increase in consumption and production within the customs union. There are other economic benefits arising as between the members of a customs union, namely trade creation and trade expansion. Trade creation will occur because demand for products produced in the customs union will move to the lowest-cost producer within it. Trade expansion will occur because the fact that products may now be bought at a lower price will stimulate demand, which may be satisfied by producers either within the customs union or outside it. Trade diversion, creation and expansion are relatively short-term factors. Michael Davenport has analysed studies of trade diversion and creation in the context

---

[9] CARICOM (the Carribean Community and Common Market) was originally established by the Treaty of Chaguaramas of 1 August 1973. The Members of the Common Market are Antigua and Barbuda, Barbados, Belize, Dominica, Grenada, Guyana, Jamaica, Montserrat, St Kitts and Nevis, St Lucia, St Vincent and the Grenadines, Suriname, Trinidad and Tobago. The Bahamas is a member of the Caribbean Community but not the Common Market. Haiti is a provisional member of the Community.

[10] W T Molle, *The Economics of European Integration: Theory, Practice, Policy* (3rd edn, Ashgate Publishing Ltd, Aldershot 1997) 88 in ch 5: 'Customs Union Theory'. Readers interested in the economic theory of customs unions may also wish to refer to the early but influential works by J Viner, *The Customs Union Issue* (Stevens and Sons, London, 1950) and J E Meade, *The Theory of Customs Unions* (North-Holland, Amsterdam, 1955). There has been a substantial amount of more recent discussion. For example, Molle above and A Tovias, 'A Survey of the Theory of Economic Integration', XV *Journal of European Integration* 1, 5–23. For an accessible discussion see D Swann, *The Economics of the Common Market: Integration in the European Union* (8th edn, Penguin, London, 1995) 113–132. I have drawn heavily on Molle and Swann in writing this section.

of the Community customs union established by the original six EEC Members. From his analysis it is apparent that, if the net gain of trade creation is taken as trade creation less trade distortion, the average net gain of trade creation for the studies showing a net gain was almost \$9 billion.[11] Swann puts this at nearly 2 per cent of Community GDP or less than 1 per cent of the Member States, GNP and comments that 'We may therefore legitimately ask why so much emphasis is placed on the creation of customs unions'.[12] In answer to this question he directs attention to the long-term and broader benefits of customs unions and to political considerations.

So far as the former are concerned, there are a number of benefits to be taken into account. Producers within the union, who are no longer protected by tariffs from competition from more efficient producers, may themselves become more efficient and, to the extent that trade is created or expanded, producers may be able to achieve economies in scale that were not previously available to them. Their average size, together with the rate at which they develop, is also likely to increase making them better able to compete in the market place. The increase in competition, which arises in respect of producers within the national boundaries of members of the customs union, as well as across their national boundaries, is likely in turn to lead to more general gains, as appears to have been the case in the Community. The Community's customs union has made possible significant political gains in relation to both internal political integration and political activity on the world stage. The integration has arisen by virtue of the establishment of a body of Community customs law which replaces that of Member States and is administered by a powerful Commission. So far as external relations are concerned, the existence of a customs union has enabled the Commission to act on behalf of, and together with, the Member States in dealings with third countries, ensuring that the Community acts and negotiates as a single trading bloc in relation to third countries.

We have already seen the strong historical link between the establishment of customs and currency unions and the growth of European states. This link is likely to be important in the contemporary world as well. Swann notes that 'the process of economic integration prepares the ground for political unification'.[13] This comment properly reminds us that the Community's customs union is an important part of the entire European project and not just an end in itself. This is, indeed, apparent from the terms of the EC Treaty itself which are considered in Chapter 3 below.

---

[11] See Swann, n 10 above, 129 and 131, Table 8. The Table is taken from M Davenport, 'The Economic Impact of the EC' in A Boltho (ed), *The European Economy Growth and Crisis* (Oxford University Press, Oxford, 1982) 227, Table 8.1.

[12] Swann, n 10 above, 130.

[13] n 10 above, 130.

B. THE INTERNATIONAL DIMENSION IN COMMUNITY CUSTOMS LAW

The international community has had a long-standing interest in customs law. A treaty Concerning the Creation of an International Union for the Publication of Customs Tariffs was signed in 1896.[14] In 1923 the League of Nations sponsored a conference which gave rise to the International Convention relating to the Simplification of Customs Formalities. The Second World War not only spurred western European countries into action, it galvanised much of the developed world. So in 1945, following the Bretton Woods conference in 1944, the USA proposed an International Trade Organization. It was much less enthusiastic about the proposal later and so the ITO never came into existence, but the General Agreement on Tariffs and Trade (GATT), negotiated at Geneva in 1947, came into force on 1 January 1948. To a very large extent it took the place of the ITO although, unlike the proposed ITO, it never had legal personality.

GATT, and now GATT 94 and the agreements relating to the WTO, are, of course, of great significance in relation to customs matters and we shall return to consider them in due course, but the WTO is not the only important international forum in which customs matters are considered. The Customs Co-operation Council, known informally as the World Customs Organization (WCO) since June 1994, and established by international convention in 1950,[15] is, as its name suggests, immensely powerful. It established the Convention on Nomenclature for the Classification of Goods in Customs Tariffs of 1950, now overtaken by what is called the harmonized system as we shall see below, and a Convention on the Valuation of Goods for Customs Purposes of 1950. The Nomenclature was replaced by the WCO's Harmonized Commodity Description and Coding System[16] which became the foundation of the Community Nomenclature[17] and was applied from 1 January 1988. The Convention on Valuation was also overtaken, this time by a Customs Valuation Code of 1973 (again referred to below). More recently, the Convention on Temporary Admission, concluded in Istanbul on 26 June 1990,[18] was negotiated within the Customs Co-operation Council. As its name suggests, it is concerned with temporary importation of goods and provides for an 'ATA Carnet'. Presentation of the carnet to a customs officer brings a trader within the temporary importation procedure and enables goods to benefit from relief

[14] See A Peaslee and D Xydia, *International Governmental Organisations—Constitutional Documents* (2nd edn, Martinus Nijhoff, The Hague, 1961) 1506.
[15] International Convention establishing a Customs Co-operation Council (Brussels, 15 December 1950; TS 50 (1954), Cmd 9232).
[16] Approved by Council Decision of 7 Apr 1987 (EEC) 369/87 [1987] OJ L198/1.
[17] Brought into existence by Commission Regulation of 23 July 1987 (EEC) 2658/87 [1993] OJ L256/1: see ch 5 below.
[18] Adopted by Council Decision of 15 Mar 1993 (EEC) 329/93 [1993] OJ L130/1.

from customs duty. As well as the WCO, there is also the United Nations Economic Commission for Europe, under the auspices of which three important agreements have been negotiated. First, there was the Customs Convention on the International Carriage of Goods under cover of TIR Carnets,[19] pursuant to which goods carried internationally by road are examined for customs purposes only at the beginning and end of their journey. Secondly, there was the International Convention on the Harmonization of Frontier Controls of Goods,[20] which aims to facilitate the international movement of goods by encouraging harmonization and co-operation in relation to frontier controls. Thirdly, there was the self-explanatory International Convention on the Simplification and Harmonization of Customs Procedures[21] (known as the Kyoto Convention) which had thirty one annexes on different aspects of customs law. The Convention was accepted, together with Annex E3 on warehouses, as part of Community law in 1975; altogether twenty one of the thirty one annexes were accepted on behalf of the Community. As we will see, the Court of Justice has had regard to the Specific Annexes of the original Kyoto Convention in construing Community customs law,[22] but, apart from the annex on customs warehouses and transit, the annexes were accepted subject to various reservations.[23] Those which have been accepted are set out below:

Annex A1: Customs formalities prior to the lodgement of the customs declaration. Accepted by Council Decision of 6 June 1978.[24]

Annex A2: Temporary storage of goods. Accepted by Council Decision of 6 June 1978.[25]

---

[19] (Geneva, 14 Nov 1975: TS 56 (1983); Cmnd 9032); approved by Council Regulation of 25 July 1978 (EEC) 2112/78 [1978] OJ L252/2. The text of the Convention is annexed to the Decision. Transit and the simplification of formalities in trade in goods have been the subject of a number of international agreements. See for example, the Convention between the EEC, Austria, Finland, Iceland, Norway, Sweden and Switzerland on the simplification of formalities in trade in goods (20 May 1987; [1987] OJ L134/2), recently amended by Decision 2000/1 of the EC–EFTA Joint Committee on simplification of formalities in goods of 20 Dec 2000 [2000] OJ L9/108 and the Convention on a common transit procedure between the same parties (20 May 1987) amended by Decision 2000/1 of 20 Dec 2000 of the EC–EFTA Joint Committee on common transit: see [2001] OJ L9/1. See, more generally, Ch 10 below.

[20] (Geneva, 21 Oct 1982; Misc 8 (1984); Cmnd 9188); Council Regulation of 10 Apr 1984 (EEC) 1262/84 [1984] OJ L126.

[21] (Kyoto, 13 Mar 1973; TS 36 (1975); Cmnd 5938); approved by Council Decision of 18 Mar 1975 (EEC) 199/75 [1975] OJ L100/2. The text of the Convention is annexed to the Decision.

[22] See, eg, Case C–26/88 *Brother International GmbH v Hauptzollamt Gießen* [1989] ECR I–4253 at paras 15–21, considered in more detail in Ch 7 below.

[23] The reservations to Annexes A1, A2, B1, B2, B3, C1, D1, D2, E1, E3, E4, E5, E6, E8, F1, F2, F3 and F6 were amended by a Council Decision of 10 Mar 1994 (EC) 167/94 [1994] OJ L76/28.

[24] Council Decision (EEC) 528/78 [1978] OJ L160/13.

[25] Ibid.

Annex B1: Clearance for home use. Accepted by Council Decision of 7 March 1985.[26]

Annex B2: Relief from import duties and taxes for goods declared for home use. Accepted by Council Decision of 7 June 1988.[27]

Annex B3: Re-importation in the same state. Accepted by Council Decision of 17 March 1980.[28]

Annex C1: Outright exportation. Accepted by Council Decision of 7 March 1985.[29]

Annex D1: Rules of origin. Accepted by Council Decision of 3 June 1977.[30]

Annex D2: Documentary evidence of origin. Accepted by Council Decision of 3 June 1977.[31]

Annex E1: Customs transit. Accepted by Council Decision of 3 June 1977.[32]

Annex E3: Concerning warehouses. Accepted on conclusion of the Convention by Council Decision of 18 March 1975.[33]

Annex E4: Drawback. Accepted by Council Decision of 7 June 1988.[34]

Annex E5: Temporary admission subject to re-exportation in the same state. Accepted by Council Decision of 30 November 1987.[35]

Annex E6: Temporary admission for inward processing. Accepted by Council Decision of 3 June 1977.[36]

Annex E7: The duty-free replacement of goods. Accepted by Council Decision of 8 December 1994.[37]

Annex E8: Temporary exportation for outward processing. Accepted by Council Decision of 3 June 1977.[38]

Annex F1: Free zones. Accepted by Council Decision of 6 June 1978.[39]

Annex F2: Processing of goods for home use. Accepted by Council Decision of 24 March 1986.[40]

Annex F3: Customs facilities applicable to travellers. Accepted by Council Decision of 30 November 1987.[41]

Annex F4: Customs formalities in respect of postal traffic. Accepted by Council Decision of 8 December 1994.[42]

---

[26] Council Decision (EEC) 204/85 [1985] OJ L87/87.
[27] Council Decision (EEC) 355/88 [1988] OJ L161/3.
[28] Council Decision (EEC) 391/80 [1980] OJ L100/27.   [29] See n 26 above.
[30] Council Decision (EEC) 415/77 [1977] OJ L166/1.
[31] Ibid.   [32] Ibid.
[33] Council Decision (EEC) 199/75 [1975] OJ L100/1.
[34] Council Decision (EEC) 356/88 [1998] OJ L161/12.
[35] Council Decision (EEC) 593/87 [1987] OJ L362/1.   [36] See n 30 above.
[37] Council Decision (EC) 798/94 [1994] OJ L331/11.
[38] See n 30 above.   [39] See n 24 above.
[40] Council Decision (EEC) 103/86 [1986] OJ L88/42.
[41] Council Decision (EEC) 594/87 [1987] OJ L362/8.
[42] Council Decision (EC) 798/94 [1994] OJ L331/11.

Annex F5: Temporary admission subject to re-exportation in the same state. Accepted by Council Decision of 30 November 1987.[43]

Annex F6: Repayment of import duties and taxes. Accepted by Council Decision of 7 March 1985.[44]

The Kyoto Convention is administered by the WCO's Permanent Technical Committee and a revision group was created under its auspices. The revision of the Convention for which it was responsible has now been completed and the WTO Council adopted the Protocol of amendment which revised the Convention on 26 June 1999.[45] In its revised form, the Convention consists of Standards,[46] Transitional Standards (Standards in the General Annex to be implemented over a five-year period) and Recommended Practices[47] to be implemented by Guidelines. The aim of the revision is to encourage all 153 members of the WCO to introduce similar customs procedures and the revised Convention contains a General Annex which, by virtue of Article 12.1 of the Convention, binds all contracting parties, so preventing states accepting only certain parts of it. In addition, the revised Convention is intended to give effect to certain new governing principles. Chief among these are that customs authorities should provide transparency and predictability for those involved in international trade and that customs authorities should utilize automated systems and risk management techniques, cooperate with trade bodies and other authorities and implement appropriate international standards.

The General Annex has ten chapters dealing with matters applicable to all customs procedures such as customs clearance, the assessment, collection, payment and repayment of duties, security, customs control, the application of information technology, the decisions and rulings of, and the provision of information by, customs authorities and appeals in customs matters. These topics are then considered in detail in Guidelines. There are then ten specific annexes in Appendix III (A–K, excluding I), namely: Arrival of goods in the

---

[43] Council Decision (EEC) 593/87 [1987] OJ L362/1.

[44] Council Decision (EEC) 204/85 [1985] OJ L87/87.

[45] The Protocol together with Appendices I and II, which contain the revised Convention and the General Annex, comes into force 3 months after 40 contracting parties have signed it without reservation of ratification or have deposited their instrument of ratification or accession: see the Protocol Art 3.3. As at 30 June 2001 the following countries had so signed or deposited the relevant instruments: Algeria (26 June 1999), Australia (10 Oct 2000), Canada (9 Nov 2000), China (15 June 2000), Japan (26 June 2001), Lesotho (15 June 2000), Morocco (16 June 2000), New Zealand (7 July 2000). The following countries have signed the Protocol subject to ratification: the Democratic Republic of the Congo (15 June 2000), the Czech Republic (30 June 2000), Latvia (15 June 2000), Slovakia (15 June 2000), Sri Lanka (26 June 1999), Switzerland (29 June 2000), Zambia (26 June 1999), Zimbabwe (26 June 1999).

[46] A Standard is a provision the implementation of which is recognized as necessary for the achievement of harmonization and simplification of customs procedures and practices: Appendix I, Art I(a) of the Protocol.

[47] A Recommended Practice is a provision in a Specific Annex which is recognized as constituting progress towards the harmonization and simplification of customs procedures and practices, the widest possible application of which is desirable: Appendix I, Art 1(c) of the Protocol.

customs territory (A), Importation (B), Exportation (C), Customs warehouses and free zones (D), Transit (E), Processing (F), Temporary Admission (G), Offences (H), Special Procedures, such as those affecting travellers and postal traffic (J), and Origin (K).

According to Article 12.2, a party which accepts a Specific Annex or chapters in a Specific Annex is bound by all of the Standards in it, and by all of the Recommended Practices unless it enters a reservation in respect of one or more of them. Guidelines are also being developed for the Specific Annexes.[48] Whereas, though, contracting parties are bound by the provisions of the General Annex, by virtue of Article 4 of the Protocol, they may choose which Specific Annexes, or chapters in them, to accept.

This short review of international treaties is inevitably incomplete and a few more recent developments may be mentioned. Firstly, we may note the Convention on Customs Treatment of Pool Containers used in International Transport, made in Geneva on 21 January 1994.[49] This aims to facilitate the efficient use of containers held in a pool on the basis of equivalent compensation. Contracting parties admit into their territory, free of import duty and other prohibitions, containers forming part of a pool, for a period of up to twelve months on the basis that other containers in the pool have been or will be exported. Secondly, there is the WTO Information Technology Agreement of 13 December 1996 which entered into force on 1 April 1997. It eliminated duties on information technology products by 31 December 1999.[50] Thirdly, by virtue of a Memorandum of Understanding between the United States and the EC[51] duties on spirituous beverages, with the exception of rum which is subject to special provisions, were eliminated in four equal stages, starting on 1 July 1997 and concluding on 1 January 2000.

The width of contemporary international influences affecting customs duty and the conduct of customs authorities can be seen by the fact that the United Nations Educational Scientific and Cultural Organization (UNESCO) has also been concerned with customs duty, playing its part in establishing

---

[48] It is not proposed to review the terms of the Kyoto Convention, as originally agreed or revised. Particular attention is, however, drawn to them in the chapters dealing with customs procedures.

[49] It was approved on behalf of the Community by Council Decision (EC) 137/95 of 7 Apr 1995 [1995] OJ L91/45. The text of the Convention is annexed to the Decision.

[50] Approved on behalf of the Community by Council Decision (EC) 359/97 of 24 Mar 1997 concerning the elimination of duties on information technology products [1997] OJ L 155/1. The text of the Convention is annexed to the Decision. See also Council Regulation (EC) 2559/00 of 16 Nov 2000 [2000] OJ L 293/1, amending the Combined Nomenclature. The Convention was of particular relevance in Case C–463/98 *Cabletron Systems Ltd v The Revenue Commissioners* Judgment 1 May 2001.

[51] Approved on behalf of the Community by Council Decision (EC) 360/97 of 24 Mar 1997 [1997] OJ L155/60. The text of the Memorandum is annexed to the Decision at [1997] OJ L155/61.

duty-free movement of goods within its remit,[52] by the fact that customs authorities are helping to enforce conventions such as the Convention on International Trade in Endangered Species of Wild Fauna and Flora,[53] which places strict controls on international trade in endangered species of wild fauna and flora, and by the fact that an initiative to reduce the costs of international trade by harmonizing and simplifying data sets, message structures and customs procedures is proceeding under the aegis of the G7 countries, in which customs authorities from the UK have, of course, been involved. Finally, it should be noted that not all international agreements concerned with customs duty relate directly to its imposition. There are many bilateral agreements concerned with the facilitation of cooperation between the customs authorities as well as many specific provisions in agreements of wider significance.[54]

Of all of the international treaties and initiatives referred to above, GATT, GATT 94 and the Marrakesh Agreement setting up the World Trade Organization are worthy of particular consideration, and it is to these that we now turn.

C. GATT AND THE WTO

The achievements of the international community through the GATT are well known and they are achievements in which the European Community has shared, the EC having been represented within the GATT since the Dillon Round of 1960–61. At this round a Schedule of Concessions (Schedule XL (EEC)) was drawn up to replace the previous concessions of the Member States and a Protocol concluding the negotiations was concluded jointly by the Member States and the Community on 16 July 1962. The protocol was not, apparently, published in the Official Journal. The Kennedy Round between 1964 and 1967 achieved substantial cuts in tariff rates and the Protocol giving effect to them was ratified by a Council Decision.[55] Indeed, it was the

---

[52] Under the Agreement on the Importation of Educational, Scientific, and Cultural Materials, (Lake Success, 22 Nov 1950; TS 42 (1954); Cmnd 9185). The relief now appears in Council Regulation (EC) 918/83 of 28 Mar 1983 [1983] OJ L 105/1, as amended. See Ch 12 below.
[53] Applied in the Community by Council Regulation (EEC) 3626/82 [1982] OJ L384/1 and subsequently amended.
[54] For an example of an agreement concerned exclusively with cooperation and mutual assistance as between customs authorities see the Agreement between the European Community and Canada on Customs Cooperation and Mutual Assistance in Customs Matters of 4 Dec 1997 [1998] OJ L7/38. See also the Agreement between the European Community and the United States of America on Customs Cooperation and Mutual Assistance in Customs Matters, approved on behalf of the Community by Council Decision of 21 May 1997 (EC) 541/97 [1997], OJ L222/16. There is also, for example, a recent agreement between Chile and the EC on mutual assistance between customs authorities which will enter into force on 1 Oct 2001: see [2001] OJ L167/23 and [2001] OJ L246/33.
[55] Council Decision (EEC) 411/68 [1968] OJ L305/2.

12   EC Customs Law

success of the Kennedy Round which enabled the Community to introduce its Common Tariff eighteen months earlier than planned[56] and from the creation of the Common Customs Tariff the Community has replaced the Member States with regard to fulfilment of the obligations imposed by GATT.[57]

The Tokyo Round (1973–79) produced, amongst other things, a Protocol providing for tariff reductions and a number of multilateral agreements, including a customs valuation code, called the *Agreement on Implementation of Article VII*.[58] More recently, following the conclusion of the Uruguay Round of GATT in 1993, we have seen the Marrakesh Agreement establishing the World Trade Organization. Nearly fifty years after it was first proposed, the international community finally had its international trade organization and the Community and its Member States are parties to it.

The Marrakesh Agreement is a complex set of agreements and requires some explanation.[59] The main agreement is a mere sixteen articles long and establishes the WTO. Article III sets out its functions, which are to facilitate the objectives of the agreement and those annexed to it. There are three Multilateral Agreements (Annexes 1A–1C) and four Plurilateral Agreements (Annex 4) annexed to it. The WTO is also to administer the Understanding on Rules and Procedures Governing the Settlement of Disputes (Annex 2) which, as its name suggests, provides for a procedure for the settlement of disputes, and the Trade Policy Review Mechanism (Annex 3).

The first Annex contains the Multilateral Agreements on Trade in Goods (Annex 1A). It also contains the General Agreement on Trade in Services and Annexes ('GATS': Annex 1B) and the Agreement on Trade-Related Aspects of

[56] As the Court noted in Joined Cases 267/81 to 269/81 *Amministrazione delle Finanze dello Stato v Società Petrolifera Italiana SpA (SPI) and SpA Michelin Italiana (SAMI)* [1983] ECR 801 at 824; see paras 4 and 5.

[57] See Joined Cases 21 to 24/72 *International Fruit Company v Produktschap voor Groenten en Fruit* [1972] ECR 1219 at 1227 paras 14–18. See also Case 38/75 *Douaneagent der NV Nederlandse Spoorwegen v Inspecteur der invoerrechten en accijnzen* [1975] ECR 1439 para 16 and Case 269/81 *Amministrazione della Finanze dello Stato v SPI and SAMI* (n 56 above) at 829 para 19. It also replaced the Member States in relation to their commitments arising under the Convention on Nomenclature of 1950 and the Convention establishing the Customs Co-operation Council.

[58] The Geneva Protocol to GATT and the Agreements were approved by Council Decision of 10 Dec 1979 (EEC) 271/80 [1980] OJ L71/1. The approved texts are annexed to the Decision.

[59] The Agreements are annexed to the Council Decision pursuant to which they are approved on behalf of the EC, namely the decision of 22 Dec1994 (EC) 800/94, concerning the conclusion on behalf of the European Community, as regards matters within its competence, of the agreements reached in the Uruguay Round multilateral negotiations (1986–94) [1994] OJ L336/1. Art 1 of the Decision approves the Agreement establishing the World Trade Organization, the Agreements in Annexes 1, 2 and 3 to that Agreement, the ministerial decisions and declarations and the Understanding on Commitment in Financial Services. Art 2 provides that the plurilateral agreements in Annex 4 to the Agreement establishing the World Trade Organization are approved on behalf of the EC. The first indent of Art 1(1) of the Decision was annulled to the extent that the Council thereby approved the Framework Agreement on Bananas with the Republic of Costa Rica, the Republic of Colombia, the Republic of Nicaragua and the Republic of Venezuela, in so far as that agreement exempts certain operators from the export-licence system which it creates: Case C–122/95 *Germany v Council of the EU* [1998] ECR I–973.

Intellectual Property Rights ('TRIPS': Annex 1C). These aroused considerable controversy and extended the remit of WTO law, not without difficulty, beyond goods into the field of services and intellectual property.[60] The Multilateral Agreements on Trade in Goods contained in Annex 1A consist of the General Agreement on Tariffs and Trade 1994 ('GATT 1994') and twelve other agreements, including specific agreements on agriculture, textiles and clothing. GATT 1994 consists, as its name suggests, of the GATT agreement established in 1947 (as amended), various decisions and understandings and the Marrakesh Protocol of 15 April 1994. This Protocol provides for five further reductions in rates of customs duty. The first reduction was made on 1 January 1995 and one was made thereafter every year on 1 January for four years. The final rates are now in force. Whilst these are the terms of the general provisions, the terms of the Schedule to the Protocol may specify otherwise for a particular WTO member and particular products. The five-year period is applicable in respect of most industrial goods; a five-year period applies also to beer. A twelve-year period applies to steel, chemicals, textiles and paper.

The reductions of tariffs referred to above have resulted in the EC having a largely open market for goods, except for agricultural products, textiles and clothing, with an average Most Favoured Nation Tariff of 4.2 per cent in 1999 compared with 4.9 per cent in 1997.[61] In considering the EC's position in the global market place, the agreements which the EC has established with third countries are of great importance and these are considered in Chapter 6 below. Following the conclusion of the Uruguay Round, the EC and other WTO members attempted to launch a new comprehensive round in December 1999 in Seattle. A possible EU agenda for the Millennium Round was set out in a Commission Communication.[62] It covered many topics, including further liberalization in agriculture, services, and investment. The attempted launch of the round was, however, a well-publicized failure and, at the time of writing, the talks have not been re-launched.

---

[60] The competence of the Community to conclude agreements concerning services and the protection of intellectual property was considered by the Court of Justice in Opinion 1/94 [1994] ECR I–5267 and is considered briefly in Ch 2 below.

[61] See the Notes to Editors annexed to the WTO's Press Release of 4 July 2000 'European Union: July 2000'. The Press Release states that exclusively MFN treatment is applicable to imports from: Australia, Canada, Hong Kong, China, Japan, Republic of Korea, New Zealand, Singapore and the United States.

[62] Communication from the Commission to the Council and the European Parliament: *The EU approach to the WTO Millennium Round* COM(99)331 final, 8 July 1999.

D. GATT 94 AND EC CUSTOMS LAW[63]

It will be apparent that those elements of the multilateral agreements dealing
with goods, particularly GATT 94, are the foundations of much EC law and not
just that of relevance to customs matters.[64] A brief review of some of the articles in GATT shows this clearly. Article I contains the well-known clause
providing for general most-favoured nation treatment and Article II provides
for schedules of concessions as to the rates of customs duties and the freezing
of rates of other duties and charges.[65] Article III prohibits protective and
discriminatory internal tax and protective quantitive regulations.[66] These
prohibitions are to be found in the EC Treaty, Articles 90 and 28. Article V
provides for freedom of transit which is a part of the EC's freedom of movement of goods. Article VI permits the imposition of anti-dumping and countervailing duties and the basic EC measures on dumping state that their
provisions are in accordance with it.[67] Article VII provides that the actual
value of goods, ie the price at which they are sold or offered for sale in the ordinary course of trade under fully competitive conditions, shall be their value for
customs duty purposes.[68] This is mirrored in CCC, Article 29, which states
that the customs value shall be the price 'actually paid or payable'. Article VII
provides that fees and charges, and in particular those imposed in connection
with importation or exportation, are to correspond to the approximate cost of
the services rendered. Within the Community this limitation is observed by the
prohibition, in the EC Treaty, Article 23, on charges having equivalent effect to
customs duties. Finally, reference should be made to Article XVI which
contains provisions seeking to limit state subsidies. These are, of course,
outlawed in certain circumstances by the EC Treaty, Articles 87 and 88.

1. *The primacy of international agreements*

As we have seen, international agreements are of great significance in the

---

[63] For a consideration of the definitions of 'customs union' and 'free trade area' in GATT see Ch
3 below.
[64] In Joined Cases 21/72–24/72 *International Fruit Company v Produktschap voor Groenten en
Fruit* [1972] ECR 1219 at 1226 para 12 the Court of Justice said that the Member States' 'desire
to observe the undertakings of the General Agreement follows as much from the very provisions
of the EEC Treaty as from the declarations made by Member States on the presentation of the
Treaty to the contracting parties of the General Agreement'.
[65] Concessions may be negotiated multilaterally or bilaterally by virtue of Art XXII.
[66] The purpose of this article was stated in Case 70/87 *Fédération de l'industrie de l'huilerie de la
CEE (Fediol) v Commission* [1989] ECR 1781 at 1833 para 29 to be to avoid discrimination of
imported products in favour of domestic ones. It does not apply to differential export duties levied
on domestic products. Art XI is also concerned with the general elimination of quantitive restrictions.
[67] See Ch 2 below at 'Anti-dumping and countervailing duties'.
[68] See further Ch 8 below.

context of customs duty and their existence must always be borne in mind in considering both the validity and the interpretation of EC measures. So far as GATT and GATT 94 are concerned they clearly bind the Community[69] and the Court of Justice will take account of GATT in interpreting Community legislation 'the primacy of international agreements concluded by the Community over provisions of secondary Community legislation means that such provisions must, so far as is possible, be interpreted in a manner that is consistent with those agreements'.[70]

Furthermore, in order to ensure that GATT is interpreted consistently throughout all Member States the Court of Justice has jurisdiction to determine the scope and effect of the rules of GATT within the Community and the effect of the tariff protocols concluded within the framework of GATT.[71] As with any international agreement, GATT must be interpreted 'in good faith in accordance with the ordinary meaning to be given to the terms of the treaty in their context and in the light of its object and purpose'.[72]

Of course, from the point of view of the litigant, it is not enough simply that the Court of Justice can interpret GATT; it is necessary to be able to rely upon it. Here the situation is less straightforward. In *Germany v Council*[73] the scheme of GATT was taken to preclude its provisions having direct effect generally, but the Court noted that it could review the lawfulness of a Community act from the point of view of the GATT rules, if the Community intended to implement a particular obligation entered into within the framework of GATT, or if the act in question expressly referred to specific provisions of GATT.[74]

The case law on GATT continues to be applied in relation to GATT 94 and the WTO agreements.[75] The Court of Justice has noted that, like GATT, the

---

[69] See Joined Cases 21/72–24/72 *International Fruit Company v Produktschap voor Groenten en Fruit* (n 64 above) para 18 and, more recently, Case T–256/97 *Bureau Européen des Unions des Consommateurs (BEUC) v Commission* [2000] 1 CMLR 542 at para 65.

[70] Case C–280/93 *Commission v Germany* [1994] ECR I–4973 paras 110–111.

[71] See Case 266/81 *Società Italiana per l'Oleodotto Transalpino (SIOT) v Ministère italien des finances, Ministère della Marine Mercantile, Circoscrizione doganale di Trieste and Ente Autonomo del Porto di Trieste* [1983] ECR 731 paras 14 and 15; and Joined Cases 267/81–269/81 *Amministrazione delle Finanze dello Stato v Società Petrolifera Italiana SpA (SPI) and SpA Michelin Italiana (SAMI)* [1983] ECR 801 at para 15.

[72] Art 31.1 Vienna Convention on the Law of Treaties 1969.

[73] Case C–280/93 [1994] ECR I–4973.

[74] Ibid. 5073–5074 para 111. The Court relied upon Case 70/87 *Fédération de l'industrie de l'huilerie de la CEE (Fediol) v Commission* [1989] ECR 1781 and Case C–69/89 *Nakajima v Council* [1991] ECR I–2069 in support of this approach. See, more recently, Case C–352/96 *Italy v The Council* [1998] ECR I–6937 para 19; Case C–149/96 *Portugal v Council* [1999] ECR I–8395 para 49; Joined Cases C–300/98 and C–392/98 *Parfums Christian Dior SA v Tuk Consultancy and Assco Gerüste GmbH v Wilhelm Layher GmbH & Co KG and anr* 14 Dec 2000 paras 43 and 44 and Case T–3/99 *Banatrading GmBH v Council*, 12 July 2001, at para 49. *Portugal v Council* has also recently been followed in Case T–18/99 *Cordis Obst und Gemüse Großhandel GmbH v Commission* [2001] ECR II-913 and Case T–52/99 *T Port GmbH & Co KG v Commission* [2001] ECR II-981.

[75] See Case 149/96 *Portugal v Council* (n 74 above).

WTO agreements make no express provision for their status in domestic law
and that, so far as their structure is concerned, they continue to envisage the
negotiation of settlements to disputes. It has paid particular attention to the
fact that some of the states which are among the most important trading partners of the Community have concluded that the rules of the WTO are not
applicable by their judicial organs in reviewing the legality of their domestic
law. In the Court's view:

> To accept that the role of ensuring that [the WTO rules] comply with Community law
> devolves directly on the Community judicature would deprive the legislative and exec-
> utive organs of the Community of the scope for manoeuvre enjoyed by their counter-
> parts in the Community's trading partners.

> It follows from all those considerations that, having regard to their nature and struc-
> ture, the WTO agreements are not in principle among the rules in the light of which
> the Court is to review the legality of measures adopted by the Community institutions
> . . .

> It is only where the Community intended to implement a particular obligation
> assumed in the context of the WTO, or where the Community measure expressly refers
> to the precise provisions of the WTO agreements, that it is for the Court to review the
> legality of the Community measures in question in the light of the WTO rules.[76]

2. GATT and direct effect

Although the Court of Justice has allowed a person to rely upon GATT and the
WTO agreements, in the circumstances outlined above, it has never ruled that
any rights contained in those agreements were directly effective. In
International Fruit Company[77] a trader, who was denied import certificates in
respect of third country apples, attempted to rely upon GATT, Article XI, on
the general elimination of quantitive restrictions, in challenging the refusals.
The Court held that Article XI was not capable of conferring rights on
Community citizens upon which they could rely before the courts. A short
time later a trader attempted to rely upon Article II, pursuant to which the
schedules of duties are established. Again the Court considered that the GATT
provision did not confer rights on individuals. It relied upon the general
scheme of the GATT, ie that it was based on the principle of negotiations
undertaken on a reciprocal and mutually advantageous basis and that its
provisions allowed contracting parties considerable flexibility in applying
them, particularly in exceptional circumstances.[78] The direct effectiveness of

---

[76] Ibid., paras 46, 47 and 49.
[77] Joined Cases 21/72–24/72 *International Fruit Company v Produktschap voor Groenten en Fruit* (n 64 above).
[78] Case 9/73 *Carl Schlüter v Hauptzollamt Lörrach* [1973] ECR 1135 at 1157–1158, paras 28–30 followed by Advocate General Reischl in Case 38/75 *Douaneagent der NV Nederlandse Spoorwegen v Inspecteur der invoerrechten en accijnzen*, n 57 above, at 1457.

GATT again fell to be considered by the Court in *SIOT*[79] which was concerned, amongst other things, with whether the prohibition of certain customs and transit duties in GATT, Article V 3. could be relied upon by a trader. Again, the Court decided that it was not directly effective for the reasons given in previous cases. This position was maintained in *SPI and SAMI*[80] in which the direct effectiveness of the tariff protocols to the GATT was in question. Indeed, the Court has said that GATT does not contain *any* provisions of such a nature as to confer rights on individuals which they may invoke before national courts.[81] It has been suggested in some quarters that GATT 94 should be treated differently by the Court of Justice, given that it differs from GATT in matters such as the resolution of disputes. The comments of the Court of Justice in *Portuguese Republic v Council* quoted above, have, however, been relied upon subsequently and the Court of First Instance has recently said that:

> It is settled Community case-law that, having regard to their nature and structure, the WTO Agreement and its annexes are not in princple among the rules in the light of which the Court is to review the legality of measures of the Community institutions . . . Those texts are not such as to create rights upon which individuals may rely directly before the courts by virtue of Community law . . .[82]

In the past, at least, a certain amount of caution has been appropriate in this area. Advocate General Lenz has acknowledged that GATT may give rise to a right for traders to claim damages in certain circumstances[83] and Lord Slynn has said of the decisions on the direct effectiveness of GATT that they:

> were in part based on the specific terms of the provision in question and in part on the element of flexibility and discretion for Member States with a power of derogation and a dispute settlement procedure of its own. These latter factors may have indicated that GATT was not likely to be held to create rights for the citizens to enforce in national courts, but I do not believe that the Court ever said that it could never apply and it always seemed to me possible that one day some provisions specific enough might get through.[84]

---

[79] Case 266/81 *Società Italiana per l'Oleodotto Transalpino (SIOT) v Ministère italien des finances, Ministère della Marine Mercantile, Circoscrizione doganale di Trieste and Ente Autonomo del Porto di Trieste*, n 71 above.

[80] Joined Cases 267 to 269/81, n 56 above, at 830 particularly para 23, see n 71 above. See also Joined Cases 290/81 and 291/81 *Compagnia Singer SpA and Geigy SpA v Amministrazione delle Finanze dello Stato* [1983] ECR 847.

[81] See Case C–280/93 *Germany v Council*, n 70 above, at para 106 and Case C–469/93 *Amministrazione dell Finanze dello Stato v Chiquita Italia SpA* [1995] ECR I–4533 para 37.

[82] Case T–3/99 *Banatrading GmbH v Council*, n 74 above, at para 43. The Court relied upon Case C–149/96, *Portugal v Council*, n 74 above, at para 47, Joined Cases C–300/98 and C-392/98 *Parfums Christian Dior SA v TUK Consultancy BV and others*, 14 Dec 2000, see n 74 above, at paras 43 and 44.

[83] See Case C–469/93 *Chiquita*, n 81 above, at 4543 para 21.

[84] Lord Slynn of Hadley's Foreword to N Emilou and D O'Keefe (eds), *The European Union and World Trade Law* (John Wiley and Sons, Chichester, 1996) vii and viii. See also Ch 18 of the same work; N A E M Neuwahl; 'Individuals and the GATT: Direct Effect and Indirect Effects of the General Agreement of Tariffs and Trade in Community Law'.

In the light of its most recent statements, however, the Community courts have little room for manoeuvre.

In practice it seems that litigants are reluctant to give up the quest to obtain directly effective rights from GATT and the WTO agreements and quite recently the Court of Justice rejected a trader's contentions in support of such rights by reasoned order.[85] The reluctance stems, no doubt, from the fact that litigants are becoming used to relying upon international trade agreements entered into by the Community.[86] One may ask why the Court of Justice has refused to permit GATT to be directly effective when it has consistently upheld the direct effectiveness of other trade agreements. The arguments for treating both in the same way are considerable. They may both, for example, contain their own settlement provisions and in relation to both there may not be reciprocity between contracting parties as to the status of the agreement in domestic law.[87] There is, however, a difference in general purpose and in scale between the GATT and WTO agreements which seek to establish the legal parameters for world trade, on the one hand, and those agreements, whether bilateral or multilateral, which operate within the parameters so established. The distinction appears particularly clear when it is borne in mind that the agreements operating within the established parameters frequently seek to ensure that the third country in question joins the Community, or establishes a customs union or free trade area with it. It is not, therefore, unreasonable in principle to distinguish between the two. The distinction would not of itself, though, prevent a sufficiently specific provision from being directly effective.

E. THE EC'S CUSTOMS UNION

As we noted at the beginning of this chapter, the Community's progress in the field of customs law has been relatively fast. Shortly after the treaties establishing the European Communities had been ratified on 1 January 1958, the EC was represented at the Dillon Round of GATT. By 1 July 1968, and eighteen months ahead of the schedule set out in the Treaty of Rome, a Common Customs Tariff was in place. The Treaty of Rome, Article 23.3 had required a

---

[85] See Case C-307/99 *OGT Fruchthandelsgesellschaft mbh v Hamburg-St. Annen*, [2001] ECR I-3159, in which the Court of Justice rejected the contention that Arts I and XIII of GATT 94 were directly effective by way of a reasoned order. Recently, a trader has abandoned its contentions that provisions of GATT 1994 were directly effective: see Case T-3/99 *Banatrading GmbH v Council* (n 74 above), at paras 43 and 44 and also Joined Cases C-364/95 and C-365/95 *T Port GmbH v Hauptzollamt Hamburg-Jonas* [1998] ECR I-1023 in which the issue of the direct effectiveness of GATT was raised but not addressed by the court.

[86] See Ch 6 below 'Agreements as part of the Community's legal order'. See Case 104/81 *Hauptzollamt Mainz v Kupferberg* [1982] ECR 3641 paras 17 and 18.

[87] See Case 149/96 *Portugal v Council* [1999] ECR I-8395 para 44.

common customs tariff to be applied by the end of the twelve-year transitional period established under Article 7[88] ie by 1 January 1970. Behind the common tariff existed a customs union which has been described as 'perhaps the most cohesive customs union in existence'.[89] From the UK's point of view, the fact that it joined a customs union on its accession to the European Communities is made clear by the European Communities Act 1972, s. 5. This provides that on and after 1 January 1973 'there shall be charged, levied, collected and paid on goods imported into the United Kingdom such Community customs duty, if any, as is for the time being applicable in accordance with the Treaties'.[90]

Apart from the enlargement of the customs union with the accession of states to the EC, customs law has continued to develop and on 12 October 1992, before the expiry of the period during which the internal market was formally to be established, the Council introduced the CCC.[91] Together with its implementing regulations, this ensured that the customs union was no longer governed by increasingly fragmented legislation.

Of course, the achievements of the EC in the field of customs law are not yet complete. Indeed, the protection of the customs union itself needs constant judicial vigilance and has only in the 1990s been deepened to include the prohibition of customs duties applying to goods crossing borders within a Member State.[92] Turning from the substantive to the procedural, the mutual cooperation between the customs authorities of Member States is not always as effective as it might be. In view of the speed with which the common customs tariff was created, and the length of time it has been in place, an objective observer may, perhaps, find it a little surprising that it should be necessary for the Treaty of Amsterdam to introduce a new Title X headed 'Customs cooperation' into the EC Treaty. The new Article 135, which the title introduces into the EC Treaty, demands measures strengthening cooperation between Member States and between Member States and the Commission. The apparently anodyne statement concluding the article, to the effect that these measures shall not concern the application of national criminal law and the national administration of justice, elegantly conceals, for example, the difficulties which Member States

---

[88] Both Arts 7 and 23 were repealed by the Treaty of Amsterdam. See further Ch 2 below.

[89] JH Jackson, *The World Trading System: Law & Policy of Economic International Relations* (2nd edn, The MIT Press, Cambridge, Mass., 1997) 33.

[90] See also the Customs and Excise Management Act 1979, s 6 which gives the Commissioners of Customs and Excise, under the control of the Treasury, the duty of collecting, accounting for and otherwise managing the revenues of customs and excise. Section 9 of the 1979 Act gives the Commissioners a duty to cooperate with other customs services on matters of mutual concern. On the mutual cooperation of the Community customs services see Ch 4 below.

[91] Council Regulation (EEC) 2913/92 [1992] OJ L302/1.

[92] See, eg, Joined Cases C–485/93 and C–486/93 *Simitzi v Municipality of Kos* [1995] ECR I–2655 noted in Ch 3 below.

have in agreeing on matters such as common penalties for customs offences.[93] That there remain difficulties to be resolved in the future does not, however, detract from the great achievement which the customs union represents and its crucial role within the Community as a whole. Some of the ways in which EC customs law relates to the general body of Community law and the significance of the aims of the customs union for the Community are matters which we consider in the next chapter.

[93] The Treaty of Amsterdam also gave customs authorities an important role within the third pillar of the EU: see Ch 2 below.

2

The Customs Union in its Community Context

Until the ratification of the Treaty of Amsterdam, the EC Treaty dealt with the customs union in Articles 9–29 which constituted Chapter 1 of Title 1, devoted to free movement of goods. Many of the provisions dealt with the staged reduction of duties on imports between Member States and on the procedure by which a common customs tariff was to be established. As the customs union was created on 1 July 1968, rationalization of the customs duty provisions in the EC Treaty was clearly long overdue. It was achieved by the Treaty of Amsterdam and the basics of the customs union are now dealt with in just five articles, Articles 23–27. Articles 25–27 constitute Chapter 1 of Title 1 on the free movement of goods. Article 25 provides that customs duties on imports and exports, and charges having equivalent effect, are prohibited between Member States together with customs duties of a fiscal nature. Article 26 states that the common customs tariff is to be fixed by the Council acting by a qualified majority on a proposal from the Commission and Article 27 sets out certain matters by which the Commission must be guided in carrying out its tasks, such as the need to promote trade between Member States and third countries, and the Community's need for raw materials. Article 24 introduces us to the concept of goods in free circulation in the Community and Article 23 puts the customs union at the heart of the Community, stating that:

> The Community shall be based upon a customs union which shall cover all trade in goods and which shall involve the prohibition between Member States of customs duties on imports and exports and of all charges having equivalent effect, and the adoption of a common customs tariff in their relations with third countries.

This provision draws the distinction between the internal aspect of the customs union, concerned with the abolition of customs duties and charges having equivalent effect, and its external aspect, namely the common customs tariff and relations with third countries.[1] The elimination of customs duties and quantitive restrictions on the import and export of goods as between Member States, the creation of a common commercial policy and, originally, the establishment of a common customs tariff,[2] also appear as activities to be carried out by the Community in the EC Treaty, Article 3(a) and (b). According

---

[1] See Joined Cases 37 and 38/73 *Sociaal Fonds voor de Diamantarbeiders v NV Indiamex and Association de fait De Belder* [1973] ECR 1609 at 1622 paras 5 and 8; and Case C–126/94 *Société Cadi Surgelés v Ministre des Finances* [1996] ECR I–5647 at 5662 para 13.

[2] The reference to the establishment of a common customs tariff, achieved on 1 July 1968, was deleted by the Maastricht Treaty.

to Article 3(c), the third activity of the Community is the internal market, the creation of which also had particular implications for customs law.[3]

Given the strategic place of the customs union in the Community, it is essential to place it in its economic, legal and financial context. This chapter seeks to do that. It deals, first, with the economic and social objectives of the customs union as articulated in the EC and EU Treaties. Then it examines how the law of the customs union is related to Community law generally. After this, the impact of the EU on customs law is considered. The chapter concludes with a brief consideration of the financial significance of customs duties as part of the 'own resources' of the Community.

A. THE CUSTOMS UNION: ECONOMIC AND SOCIAL OBJECTIVES

The EC Treaty, the Treaty on European Union and the many agreements between the EC and third countries all refer to broad economic and social objectives in one way or another. The EC Treaty, Article 2, sees the customs union and the other activities of the Community as being designed:

> to promote throughout the Community a harmonious, balanced and sustainable development of economic activities, a high level of employment and of social protection, equality between men and women, sustainable and non-inflationary growth, a high degree of competitiveness and convergence of economic performance, a high level of protection and improvement of the quality of the environment, the raising of the standard of living and quality of life, and economic and social cohesion and solidarity among Member States.

The European Union now brings customs law within its scope both as a consequence of establishing the European Community as its first pillar and as a result of creating a third pillar, now appearing in the EU Treaty as Title VI (Articles 29–42) under the heading: 'Provisions on Police and Judicial Co-operation in Criminal Matters'. The first objective it has set itself is:

> to promote economic and social progress and a high level of employment and to achieve balanced and sustainable development, in particular through the creation of an area without internal frontiers, through the strengthening of economic and social cohesion and through the establishment of economic and monetary union,

---

[3] For example, it affected the administration of tariff quotas and led to Council Regulation (EC) 520/94 of 7 Mar 1994 [1994] OJ L66/1. Customs agents were affected, but failed in their claim against the Community for damages: Case T–113/96 *Edouard Dubois et Fils SA v Council and Commission* [1998] ECR II–125, applied in Joined Cases T–611/97 and T–619/97 to T–627/97 *Transfluvia v Council and the Commission* [2000] ECR II–2405, and Joined Cases T–12/98 and T–13/98 *Argon v Council and Commission* [2000] ECR II–2473. They have a role even in the single market: see, eg, Case C–35/96 *Commission v Italy* [1998] ECR I–3851 paras 49 and 50; and Case T–513/93 *Consiglio Nazionale degli Spedizionieri Doganali v Commission* [2000] ECR II–1807 para 81.

ultimately including a single currency in accordance with the provisions of this Treaty;[4]

The Treaty on European Union also makes clear, in Article 6, that:

1. The Union is founded on the principles of liberty, democracy, respect for human rights and fundamental freedoms, and the rule of law, principles which are common to the Member States.
2. The Union shall respect fundamental rights, as guaranteed by the European Convention for the Protection of Human Rights and Fundamental Freedoms . . . and as they result from the constitutional traditions common to the Member States, as the general principles of Community law.

Lest there be any question whether or not these broad statements have any practical significance for Community traders in the customs union, it should be noted that Article 6 has already been referred to by the Court of Justice in a case involving the procedures affecting remission and repayment of customs duty.[5]

There is, of course, nothing specifically European about setting the law of trade, and customs duty in particular, in a broad social and economic context. The preamble to the GATT, for example, states that the contracting parties recognized that 'their relations in the field of trade and economic endeavour should be conducted with a view to raising standards of living, ensuring full employment and a large and steadily growing volume of real income and effective demand . . .'. Furthermore the parties were 'desirous of contributing to these objectives by entering into reciprocal and mutually advantageous arrangements directed to the substantial reduction of tariffs and other barriers to trade and to the elimination of discriminatory treatment in international commerce'.[6]

B. THE LEGAL CONTEXT OF THE CUSTOMS UNION

The customs union is supported by, and supports, many other aspects of the Community and the Union. The wider realms of Community law may prove of great practical importance in determining, for example, whether a client's goods have been legally detained or inspected and whether or not a charge is legally imposed. For example, when an adviser is seeking to show that a charge or duty is illegally imposed, it must be borne in mind that not only may a

---

[4] Treaty on European Union, Art 2, first indent.
[5] See Case T–50/96 *Primex Produkte Import-Export GmbH & Co KG, Gebr Kruse GmbH, Interporc Im- und Export GmbH v Commission* [1998] ECR II–3773 at para 46. See also Ch 13 below.
[6] Art XXVI on trade and development also emphasized the social aspect of GATT by recalling that 'the basic objectives of this Agreement include the raising of standards of living and the progressive development of the economies of all contracting parties'.

charge be a prohibited customs duty or charge having equivalent effect (the nature of which is considered in Chapter 3 below), it may also be an illegal turnover tax, or illegal because it constitutes discriminatory or protective internal taxation. Alternatively, it may constitute a state aid or infringe competition law in some way.

Certain aspects of Community law, which are particularly significant in establishing the legal context in which the customs union operates, are examined below in the order in which they are addressed in the EC Treaty. They are as follows: 1 the customs union, free movement of goods and freedom of transit, 2 the Common Agricultural Policy and customs law, 3 the customs union and internal taxation, 4 the customs union and VAT and turnover taxes, 5 the customs union and state aid, 6 the customs union and competition law, 7 the common commercial policy.

1. *The customs union, free movement of goods, and transit*

The fundamental relationship between the customs union and freedom of movement of goods has frequently been noted by the Court of Justice and is confirmed, as the Court has observed,[7] by the structure of the EC Treaty. As we have noted above, all the fundamental provisions relating to the customs union are to be found in Title 1 of the Treaty, entitled 'Free Movement of Goods' and it is clear that the prohibition of customs duties is not merely necessary for a customs union, but is justified on the basis that obstacles to the free movement of goods are prohibited. As the Court of Justice has said:

> It follows from the system as a whole and from the general and absolute nature of the prohibition of any customs duty applicable to goods moving between Member States that customs duties are prohibited independently of any consideration of the purpose for which they were introduced and the destination of the revenue obtained therefrom. The justification for this prohibition is based on the fact that any pecuniary charge—however small—imposed on goods by reason of the fact that they cross a frontier constitutes an obstacle to the movement of such goods.[8]

[7] The Court of Justice has said: 'The position of these articles [23 and 25] towards the beginning of that part of the Treaty dealing with the "Foundations of the Community"—Article [23] being placed at the beginning of the Title relating to "Free Movement of Goods", and Article [25] at the beginning of the Section dealing with the "Elimination of Customs Duties"—is sufficient to emphasize the essential nature of the prohibitions which they impose.' See Joined Cases 2 and 3/62 *Commission v Luxembourg* [1962] ECR 425 at 431. See Case 266/81 *SIOT v Ministre delle Finance* [1983] ECR 731 at 777 para 16, quoted below, on the need for freedom of transit in the customs union.

[8] Joined Cases 2 and 3/69 *Sociaal Fonds voor de Diamantarbeiders v SA Ch Brachfeld & Sons and Chongal Diamond Co* [1969] ECR 211 at para 11/14. For a recent example of a charge that did not infringe the principle of free movement of goods see the Opinion of AG Fenelly in Case C–213/99 *José Teodoro de Andrae v Director da Alfândega de Leixões* 7 Dec 2000 which concerned a charge imposed automatically only on importers who failed to respect time limits for assigning a customs-approved treatment or use: see para 63 of the Opinion.

The fact that customs duties are prohibited in order to ensure free movement of goods has inevitably made it necessary to consider the relationship
between Articles 23 to 25 and Articles 28–31 (Chapter 2 of Title 1 to the EC
Treaty) which require the abolition of quantitive restrictions or their equivalent between Member States. In this regard it is worth noting that, according
to Article 23, the customs union covers 'all trade in goods'. The customs
union, therefore, 'requires the free movement of goods generally'.[9] Articles
28–31, on the other hand, are concerned, more narrowly, with prohibitions as
between Member States. The more general relationship between the specific
prohibition of customs duties, and the prohibition on quantitive restrictions,
is, however, one which came before the ECJ relatively early on. In *Carmine
Capolongo v Azienda Agricola Maya*[10] both the Commission and Advocate
General Roemer appear to have thought that Article 28, as it now is, could in
principle apply to charges equivalent to customs duties. In their view, however,
it applied only where there was some special taxation on the importer, which
was not the case in *Capolongo*. The Court of Justice found it unnecessary to
consider the matter.

A few years later, the Court dealt specifically with the role of Article 28 in
relation to customs duty.[11] Again Article 28 was relied upon by the trader. The
Commission appears to have been reluctant to concede that Article 28 had no
role to play.[12] Nevertheless, the Court was clear that it did not. Its views are
worth repeating. It said:

> However wide the field of application of Article [28] may be, it nevertheless does not
> include obstacles to trade covered by other provisions of the Treaty . . .
>
> Thus obstacles which are of a fiscal nature or have equivalent effect and are
> covered by Articles 9 to 16 and 95 of the Treaty do not fall within the prohibition in
> Article [28].[13]

The views of the Court in *Ianelli* have been repeated frequently, even in
recent times.[14] It follows from them that, in analysing any case in which the
prohibition on customs duties or discriminatory or protective internal taxation
is in issue, one must first look to the EC Treaty, Articles 25 and 90 to see if they
are applicable. Only if they are not may the provisions of Article 28 as it now

---

[9] See Joined Cases C–363/93, C–407/93, C–408/93, C–409/93, C–410/93 and C–411/93
Lancry v Direction Générale des Douanes [1994] ECR I–3957 3991 at para 29.

[10] Case 77/72 [1977] ECR 611.

[11] Case 74/76 *Iannelli & Volpi SpA v Ditta Paolo Meroni* [1977] ECR 557.

[12] Ibid, 588.

[13] Ibid, para 9. Arts 9 and 95 are now Arts 23 and 90 respectively and Art 16 has been deleted.

[14] See Case C–228/98 *Kharalambos Dounias v Ipourgos Ikonomikon* 3 Feb 2000 at para 39; Joined
Cases C–78 to 83/90 *Compagnie commerciale de L'Ouest v Receveur principal des douanes de La Pallice
Port* [1992] ECR I–1847 at para 20; and Case C–17/91 *Georges Lornoy en Zonen NV v Belgium*
[1992] ECR I–6523 at para 14. The statement of principle also appears in Case 252/86 *Bergandi
v Directeur Général des Impôts* [1988] ECR I–1343 at paras 33–34.

is, come into play.[15] In view of this, therefore, although the prohibition of quantitive restrictions is fundamental to the free movement of goods within the Community, it is not considered further in this chapter.[16] Instead, we turn briefly to one element of freedom of movement of goods which is of particular importance in relation to the customs union, namely freedom of transit.

It is plain that freedom of movement encompasses freedom of transit.[17] Freedom of transit is not, though, exclusively a Community concept. It is based on GATT, Article V. According to Article V.1, goods, vessels and other means of transport are 'traffic in transit' when the passage across the territory of a contracting party, with or without transhipment, warehousing, breaking bulk, or change in the mode of transport, is only a portion of a complete journey beginning and terminating beyond the frontier of the contracting party across whose territory the traffic passes. Article V.2 then provides that:

> There shall be freedom of transit through the territory of each contracting party, via the routes most convenient for international transit, for traffic in transit to or from the territory of other contracting parties. No distinction shall be made which is based on the flag of vessels, the place of origin, departure, entry, exit or destination, or on any circumstances relating to the ownership of goods, of vessels or of other means of transport.

The Community principle of freedom of transit, which is given effect to by the provisions in the implementing regulations on transit, has been acknowledged by the Court in the following terms:

> The Customs Union established by Part [Three], Title I, Chapter 1 of the [EC] Treaty necessarily implies that the free movement of goods between the Member States should be ensured. That freedom could not itself be complete if it were possible for the Member States to impede or interfere in any way with the movement of goods in transit. It is therefore necessary, as a consequence of the Customs Union and in the mutual interest of the Member States, to acknowledge the existence of a general principle of freedom of transit of goods within the Community. That principle is, moreover, confirmed by the reference to 'transit' in Article [30] of the Treaty.[18]

---

[15] See Case C–17/91 *Georges Lornoy en Zonen NV v Belgian State* [1992] ECR I–6523 at 6551 para 15.

[16] Indeed, regarding the customs union as no more than an area in which the free movement of goods between Member States is guaranteed would result in certain prohibited charges being permitted within the customs union. See, for example, the Opinion of Tesauro AG, not followed by the Court of Justice, in Joined Cases C–363/93, C–407/93, C–408/93, C–409/93, C–410/93 and C–411/93 *René Lancry SA v Direction Générale des Douanes and Société Dindar Confort, Christian Ah-Son, Paul Chevassus-Marché, Société Conforéunion and Société Dindar Autos v Conseil Régional de la Réunion and Direction Régionale des Douanes de la Réunion* [1994] ECR I–3957 at para 18. See further Ch 3 below.

[17] See, eg, Case 266/81 *SIOT v Ministre delle Finance* [1983] ECR 731 at 777 para 16, discussed in Ch 1 above.

[18] Ibid. The Court has referred to the need to facilitate the movement of goods in the Community as 'one of the basic principles of the common market': see Case C–117/88 *Trend-Moden Textilhandels GmbH v Hauptzollamt Emmerich* [1990] ECR I–631 at para 20; Case C–367/89

The freedom of transit is infringed if, for example, a Member State applies transit duties to goods or other charges in respect of transit, except for charges which represent the costs of transportation or of other services connected with transit, even if they are only indirectly linked with transit. It may, of course, also be infringed by the need to obtain special authorizations for transit. Authorizations may be permitted, though, if they are justified under the EC Treaty, Article 30.[19] Recently, the Court found that detention under customs control in France, of goods in transit from Spain, where they had been lawfully marketed, to Italy, where they were to be lawfully sold, constituted a breach of freedom of movement under Article 28. Attempts to justify the detention, on the basis that the action was intended to defend the rights of those entitled to a protected design, failed.[20]

Transit is a customs procedure for the purposes of the CCC[21] and is considered in Chapter 10 below.

2. The Common Agricultural Policy (CAP) and customs law

A description of this policy, which the Community is committed to amending within the framework of the WTO, is beyond the scope of this book. It is, though, important to note that, pursuant to the CAP, levies may be imposed on imported products and export refunds may be obtained in respect of exported products, so as to protect the price obtained for Community goods, and that the CAP uses the Combined Nomenclature in order to describe the products to which the relevant legislation applies. The Court has indicated that whether the headings in the common customs tariff are used to apply the rules on organization of markets, in relation to monetary compensatory amounts, or in relation to customs duty, they should receive an identical interpretation.[22]

CCC, Article 4(10) contains a definition of 'import duties' which includes agricultural levies and other import charges introduced under the CAP or under other specific arrangements. Similarly 'export duties' is defined in CCC Article 4(11) as including agricultural levies and other export charges introduced under the CAP or other specific arrangements. One important practical effect of this is that the provisions relating to incurring a customs debt in CCC, Title VII, Chapter 2 relate also to liability to agricultural levies. This does not mean, however, that the operation of the CAP is a customs matter and that

---

Criminal proceedings against Aimé Richardt and Les Accessoires Scientifiques SNC [1991] ECR I–4621 para 14; Case 237/96 *Belgian Minister for Financial Affairs v Eddy Amelynck* [1997] ECR I–5103 at para 18; and Case C–23/99 *Commission v France* [2000] ECR I–7653 at para 43.

[19] See Case 367/89, n 18 above, para 17, where the Court said that Member States were not precluded from verifying goods in transit in accordance with the provisions of the Treaty.

[20] Case C–23/99 *Commission v France*, n 18 above.

[21] CCC, see Art 4(16).

[22] Case 158/78 P *Biegi v Hauptzollamt Bochum* [1979] ECR 1103 para 18.

agricultural levies are, as a matter of general law, customs duties. This was demonstrated in *Krüger v Hauptzollamt Hamburg-Jonas*.[23] The trader relied upon CCC, Article 244 to found a claim for suspension of the authority's claim for repayment of export refunds incorrectly given. The Court, however, held that the rules relating to export refunds constituted the external part of the common pricing policy and were not customs rules to which Article 244 was applicable. The distinction between customs duty law and the CAP had been drawn almost twenty-five years earlier in *Schlüter v Haputzollamt Lörrach*[24] where the Court held that the compensatory amounts imposed on imports of cheese from Switzerland into Germany, to counteract the advantages obtained by imports as a result of currency measures, were validly imposed under the CAP and were not to be considered as unilaterally imposed levies. The imposition of them did not, therefore, contravene the provisions of the Common Customs Tariff.

3. *The customs union and internal taxation*

As is well known, the EC Treaty, Articles 90–93 are concerned with the internal taxation of Member States.[25] The objective of Article 90 is the abolition of discriminatory and protective taxation. It aims 'to guarantee the complete neutrality of internal taxation as regards competition between domestic products and imported products'.[26] Put another way, the Court has said that the objective of Article 90 is 'to ensure free movement of goods between Member States in normal conditions of competition by the elimination of all forms of protection which result from the application of internal taxation which discriminates against products from other Member States'.[27]

This is, of course, a quite distinct objective from the creation of a customs union. Yet despite having its own prescribed field of application, Article 90 has an important role to play in the context of customs law. As the ECJ said

[23] Case C–344/95 [1997] ECR I–4517.
[24] Case 9/73 [1973] ECR 1135. For an even earlier acknowledgement of the distinction between customs law and the organisation of agricultural markets see Case 92/71 *Interfood GmbH v Hauptzollamt Hamburg-Ericus* [1972] ECR 31 in which it was held that a product could be classified differently for the purposes of the two regimes.
[25] The French overseas departments are also within Art 90: see Case 148/77 *H Hansen Jun & OC Balle GmbH & Co v Hauptzollamt Flensburg* [1978] ECR 1787 1805 paras 10–12. Special provision could be made within what is now the EC Treaty, Art 299 (prior to the Amsterdam Treaty) in respect of Art 90, but not so as to permit the introduction of a charge having equivalent effect to a customs duty: Case C–212/96 *Paul Chevassus-Marché v Conseil régional de la Réunion* [1998] ECR I–743 at paras 32–37. The Treaty of Amsterdam amended Art 227 so that it now provides, as Art 299 that the entirety of the Treaty shall apply to the French overseas departments, the Azores, Madeira and the Canary Islands.
[26] Case 184/85 *Commission v Italy* [1987] ECR 2013 at 2025 para 7.
[27] See Case 168/78 *Commission v France* [1980] ECR 347 para 4.

in *Co-Frutta*[28] it is intended 'to fill in any breaches which a fiscal measure might open in the prohibitions laid down'.[29] It, therefore, supplements the abolition of customs duties and charges having equivalent effect.[30] The fact, therefore, that a charge escapes prohibition as a charge having equivalent effect to a customs duty does not mean that it is beyond all challenge. It must still be measured against the requirements of Article 90. An example of Article 90 playing its supplementary role arises in relation to the legality of charges for services, as to which the Court of Justice has said:

> the fact that a pecuniary charge constitutes consideration for a service actually supplied to traders and is of an amount commensurate with that service merely enables it to escape classification as a charge having equivalent effect within the meaning of Article [23] et seq. of the Treaty, and does not mean that it escapes the prohibition of all discriminatory internal taxation laid down in Article [90].[31]

Despite the fact that the prohibition of discriminatory or protective internal taxation plays an important role in relation to customs law, the differences between that prohibition and the prohibition of customs duties and charges having equivalent effect are considerable. A charge having equivalent effect to a customs duty is by its very nature an obstacle to trade and, therefore, it is prohibited absolutely.[32] The provisions of a state's internal taxation, on the other hand, are not by their nature an obstacle to trade. They become so if imposed in a discriminatory or protective manner. Accordingly, the prohibition of them is not absolute but conditional on discrimination or protection being established. Furthermore, the Court of Justice has made clear that the distinguishing feature of a charge having equivalent effect to a customs duty is that it applies only to imported goods to the exclusion of domestic products. An internal tax, on the other hand, is borne by both imported and domestic products and applies systematically to categories of products in accordance with objective criteria irrespective of the origin of the products.[33]

---

[28] Case 193/85 *Cooperativa Co-Frutta Srl v Amministrazione delle finance dello Stato* [1987] ECR 2085 which followed Joined Cases 2 and 3/69 *Sociaal Fonds voor de Diamantarbeiders v SA Ch Brachfeld & Sons* [1969] ECR 211.

[29] See Case 193/85, n 28 above, para 27 of the judgment. See also Joined Cases 2 and 3/62 *Commission v Luxembourg* [1962] ECR 425 at 431.

[30] See Case 168/78 *Commission v France*, n 27 above, para 4.

[31] Case 90/94 *Haar Petroleum Ltd v Åbenrå Havn, Ålborg Havn, and others* [1997] ECR I–4085, para 35. See also Case C–209/89 *Commission v Italy* [1991] ECR I–1575 para 9; and Case 46/76 *WJG Bauhuis v The Netherlands* [1977] ECR 5 para 11.

[32] This was made clear by the Court in Joined Cases 2 and 3/69 *Sociaal Fonds voor de Diamantarbeiders* (n 28 above) para 14 in relation to imports and in Case 24/68 *Commission v Italy* [1969] ECR 193 paras 6, 7 and 17 in relation to exports.

[33] See Case 90/79 *Commission v French Republic* [1981] ECR 283 at paras 13 and 14. See also Case 32/80 *Officier van Justitie v Kortmann* [1981] ECR 251 para 14; Case C–212/96 *Paul Chevassus Marché v Conseil Régional de la Réunion* (n 25 above) at I–773 para 20; Case C–109/98 *CRT France International SA v Directeur régional des impôts de Bourgogne* [1999] ECR I–2237 at paras

Despite the fact that the prohibition of customs duties and charges having equivalent effect on the one hand and that of discriminatory and protective internal taxation on the other hand, have quite different spheres of application, they frequently fall to be considered together. This is partly due to the fact that Member States who wish to justify a charge having an equivalent effect to customs duty will, not infrequently, wish to categorize it as a matter of internal taxation.[34] In seeking to escape liability to a charge, a trader, for its part, will frequently wish to put forward two contentions in the alternative. First, that the charge in question is outlawed by reason of the prohibition of customs duty or a charge having equivalent effect. Secondly, that the charge is prohibited pursuant to Article 90. Whilst, of necessity, the Court of Justice frequently considers these two matters together, conceptually, of course, they are two distinct questions and the Court has frequently found it necessary to repeat that Article 90 and the prohibition on customs duties cannot apply to the same levy.[35]

The reasons why the two prohibitions cannot overlap are simple. In the first place, the original timetable for the operation of the two sets of prohibitions was different.[36] In the second place, even given now the expiry of the respective timetables, as we have already noted, the prohibition on customs duties is absolute and that on discriminatory or protective taxation within Article 90 is limited. Only the discriminatory or protective element of internal taxation is inconsistent with the EC Treaty, not the entire tax.[37] This second distinction was highlighted in 1975 in *IGAV v ENCC*,[38] but its significance was noted as early as 1969, by Advocate General Gand who said in one Opinion:

---

11 and 13 and Joined Cases C–441 and 442/98 *Kapniki Mikhailīdis AE v Idryma Koinonikon Asfaliseon (IKA)* [2000] ECR I–7145 at para 22 (which concern a tax on exports).

[34] See, for relatively recent examples, Joined Cases C–441 and 442/98 *Kapniki Mikhailīdis AE v Idryma Koinonikon Asfaliseon (IKA)*, ibid, at paras 18–25; and Case C–109/98 *CRT France International SA v Directeur régional des impôts de Bourgogne*, n 33 above.

[35] See, eg, the judgment in Case C–212/96 *Paul Chevassus Marché v Conseil Régional de la Réunion*, n 25 above, at I–773 para 20, which relied upon Case 193/85 *Co-operativa Co-Frutta Srl v Amministrazione delle Finance dello Stato*, n 28 above, at paras 8–11. See also Case C–347/95 *Fazenda Publica v UCAL* [1997] ECR I–4911 at para 17 and the cases there referred to. The Court said, on one occasion, that the prohibition of customs duties and charges having equivalent effect and that on discriminatory and protective internal taxation could not apply to the same charge 'save in exceptional circumstances': Case 148/77 *H Hansen Jun & O C Balle GmbH & Co v Hauptzollamt de Flensburg*, n 25 above, para 22. It is hard indeed to see what those exceptional circumstances could be.

[36] As the Court pointed out in Case 10/65 *Deutschmann v Germany* [1965] ECR 469 at 473.

[37] Where the tax in question is inherently discriminatory it may not be necessary to determine whether it constitutes a prohibited customs duty or contravenes Art 90: see Case C–228/98 *Kharalambos Dounias v Ipourgos Ikonomikon* (3 Feb 2000) at para 50.

[38] Case 94/74 *Industria Gomma Articoli Vari (IGAV) v Ente nazionale per la cellulosa e per la carta (ENCC)* [1975] ECR 699 at paras 12–13. Referred to in, eg, Case 78/76 *Steinike und Weinlig v Germany* [1977] ECR 595 at para 28, Joined Cases C–78/90–C–83/90 *Compagnie Commerciale de l'Ouest v Receveur Principal des Douanes de La Pallice Port* [1992] ECR I–1847 at para 22 and *Herbert Scharbatke GmbH v Germany* [1993] ECR I–5509 para 10.

charges having equivalent effect and internal taxation constitute different fields and are not subject to the same system, in particular as regards the detailed rules and timetable laid down for their abolition or adjustment . . . [A] charge having equivalent effect is unlawful solely by virtue of the fact that it constitutes an obstacle to trade, whereas internal taxation is unlawful only, if, and to the extent to which, it is imposed more heavily on imported products than domestic products.[39]

Of course, the fact that the two prohibitions cannot be simultaneously applicable to the same charge does not prevent what appears to be one charge being, in fact, two charges, one on imports amounting to a customs duty and one internal, subject to Article 90. In pointing this out, in *Municipality of Ceuta*, the Court of Justice noted[40] that where there was clearly a tax on imports but an 'almost total absence' of tax internally three possibilities arose. The first was that, despite the exemption from tax of local products, the charge was nevertheless levied according to objective criteria which apply in the same manner to local and imported products. Such a situation results in the application of Article 90 of the Treaty.[41] The second situation is that there are two charges, as noted above. The third situation is that non-exemption of a small proportion of local production is designed to conceal a charge having equivalent effect to customs duty. Which alternative is applicable is for the national court to decide. The provisions imposing the charge and the manner in which they are applied are both to be taken into account in coming to a conclusion.[42] If, for example, there was a duty limited to specific products which had the sole purpose of financing activities for the specific advantage of taxed domestic products, so as to make good the charge upon them, the charge would be one having an effect equivalent to a customs duty.[43]

Having looked at the relationship between the prohibition of customs duties and the prohibition of discriminatory and protective internal taxation, it is proposed to look briefly at some of the learning on Article 90. This is, of course, extensive and it is not proposed here to do more than outline some of the basic elements so as to emphasize the distinction between the two prohibitions and to provide some guidance to those who are, for example, seeking to determine which of the three options referred to in *Municipality of Ceuta* are applicable in their specific case.

[39] Joined Cases 2 and 3/69 *Social Fonds voor de Diamantarbeiders v SA Ch Brachfeld and Sons* [1969] ECR 211 at 232.
[40] See Case 45/94 *Camara de Comercio, Industria y Navegación, Ceuta v Municipality of Ceuta* [1995] ECR I–4385 at paras 38–41.
[41] See also Case 78/76 *Steinike*, n 38 above, para 25.
[42] See Case 212/96 *Paul Chevassus-Marché*, n 35 above, para 24.
[43] See Case 78/76 *Steinike*, n 38 above, para 28.

3.1 *Article 90*

As we have already noted, in order for Article 90 to apply to a charge it is necessary for the charge to 'relate to a general system of internal dues applied systematically to categories of products in accordance with objective criteria irrespective of the origin of the products'.[44]

In order to fall within a general system of internal dues, the charge in question must:

> impose the same duty on national products and identical imported products at the same marketing stage and . . . the chargeable event giving rise to the duty must also be identical in the case of both products. It is therefore not sufficient that the objective of the charge imposed on imported products is to compensate for a charge imposed on similar domestic products—or which has been imposed on those products or a product form which they are derived—at a production or marketing stage prior to that at which the imported products are taxed.[45]

The concept of a general system of internal dues, although relatively wide, is clearly not without limits. For example, taxes on highly specific categories of products are unlikely to be part of such a system.[46]

So far as discriminatory taxation is concerned, the Court has to examine the taxation of similar products. Similarity between products has to be ascertained by reference to objective criteria but with some flexibility.[47] The customs duty classification of goods is, however, not necessarily relevant in ascertaining whether goods are 'similar' for the purposes of the first paragraph of Article 90. As the Court has pointed out, the customs classification is established specifically for the purposes of trade with third countries.[48] Products are similar if they have similar characteristics and meet the same needs from the point of view of consumers.[49] Once the existence of similar products is established, Article 90 will be infringed, for example, where the tax on imported products is calculated differently from that on similar domestic products and

---

[44] Case 90/79 *Commission v France*, n 33 above, para 14. See also, eg, Case 32/80 *Officier van Justitie v Kortmann* (n 33 above) para 16. For a recent adoption of the formulation see Case C–109/98 *CRT France International SA v Directeur régional des impôts de Bourgogne*, n 33 above, at para 13.

[45] Case 132/78 *Denkavit Loire Sàrl v France (Customs Authorities)* [1979] ECR 1923 para 8. See also Joined Cases C–149 and C–150/91 *Sanders Adour SNC and Guyomarc'h Orthez Nutrition Animale SA v Directeur des Services Fiscaux des Pyrenées-Atlantiques* [1992] ECR I–3899 para 17.

[46] See Case 158/82 *Commission v Denmark* [1983] 3573 (ground-nuts and brazil nuts), Case C–109/98 [1999] ECR I–2237 (CB sets) and the Opinion of Fenelly AG in Joined Cases C–441/98 and 442/98 *Kapniki Mikhailïdis AE v Iàryma Koinonikon Astaliseon (IKA)*, n 33 above, at paras 19 and 20.

[47] See Case 168/78 *Commission v France*, n 30 above.

[48] Ibid, para 35. Compare Case 45/75 *Rewe-Zentrale des Lebensmittel-Großhandels GmbH v Hauptzollamt Landau/Pfalz* [1976] ECR 181 at para 12 where a difference of classification was considered material.

[49] Case 45/75, n 48 above, at para 12. Imported used goods and those bought locally constitute similar or competing products: Case C–47/88 *Commission v Denmark* [1990] ECR I–4509 at para 17 and Case C–228/98 *Kharalombos Dounias v Ipourgos Ikonomikon*, n 37 above, at para 42.

on the basis of different criteria which lead to higher taxation on the imported products, even if only in certain cases. In *Outokumpu Oy* it did not matter that domestic electricity was taxed more heavily in some cases than imported electricity. What was significant was that imported electricity was on occasions taxed more heavily than domestic electricity. The tax burden on imported products must be compared with the lowest tax burden on similar domestic products.[50] There must be no possibility of imported products being taxed more heavily than domestic products.[51] The use to which the proceeds of a charge are put may also be relevant in determining the existence of discrimination. It may be that a charge which is imposed on both imported and domestic products, according to the same criteria, constitutes discriminatory taxation because the burden which is imposed on domestic products is neutralized by the advantages which the charge provides and only the imported product is left to bear a net burden.[52]

As in relation to other areas of Community law concerned with discrimination, Member States sometimes attempt to justify their regimes by reference to the practical difficulties which may be encountered in avoiding it. The Court of Justice has frequently made clear, however, that practical difficulties are no justification for discrimination contrary to Article 90.[53] Furthermore, a Member State must abolish even those differences between internal taxes on domestic products which are objectively justified, if that is the only way to avoid direct or indirect discrimination against imported products.[54]

While the prohibition on discriminatory taxation prevents taxation on imported products which is directly or indirectly higher than that on similar domestic products, the prohibition on protective taxation does not require similarity between competing products to be established. Instead, this limb of the prohibition applies when products are in competition with domestic products, even if the competition is partial, indirect or potential,[55] and although the strict wording of Article 90 seems to be directed to taxes on imports, the Court of Justice has made clear that the imposition of such taxation on exports is also prohibited.[56] It has also been made clear that the goods affected are not

[50] Case C–213/96 Proceedings brought by *Outokumpu Oy* [1998] ECR I–1777 at paras 34–36; see Case C–152/89 *Commission v Luxembourg* [1991] ECR I–1341 at paras 20–22; and Case C–393/98 *António Gomes Valente v Fazenda Pública*, [2001] ECR I–1327 at para 21.
[51] See Case C–68/96 *Grundig Italiana v Ministero delle Finanze* [1998] ECR I–3775 at para 12; and Case C–228/98 *Kharalombos Dounias v Ipourgos Itonomikon*, n 37 above, at para 41.
[52] See, eg, Case 73/79 *Commission v Italy* [1980] ECR 1533, at para 15; and Joined Cases C–78/90 to C–83/90 *Compagnie Commerciale de l'Ouest v Receveur Principal des Douanes de La Pallice Port* [1992] ECR I–1847 at paras 26–27. Where the charge imposed on domestic products is fully offset then a charge equivalent to a customs duty is imposed: see further Ch 3.
[53] Case C–375/95 *Commission v Greece* [1997] ECR I–5981 at para 47 and Proceedings brought by *Outokumpu Oy*, n. 50 above, para 38.
[54] Case 21/79 *Commission v Italy* [1980] ECR 1 at para 16; Proceedings brought by *Outokumpu Oy*, n 50 above, para 40.
[55] See Case 184/85 *Commission v Italy* [1987] ECR 2013 at paras 9 and 11.
[56] Case 142/77 *Statenskontrol v Larsen* [1978] ECR 1543.

just those which originate in Member States, but also those originating in third countries which are in free circulation in the Member States.[57]

The scope of Article 90 does, however, have firm limits. Firstly, it does not apply to goods which are imported directly from third countries and which are not in free circulation in a Member State[58] (although the fact that the origin of goods determines the amount of the duty does not remove it from the scope of Article 90[59]). Secondly, where a pecuniary charge is imposed at the import stage it may be classified as internal taxation only if its purpose is to put every kind of product, whatever its origin, in a comparable fiscal situation in the territory of the state imposing the tax.[60] Thirdly, it does not prohibit internal taxation on imported goods where there is no similar domestic product, or any other domestic product capable of being protected, if the tax relates to a general system of internal dues applied systematically to categories of products in accordance with objective criteria irrespective of the origin of the products.[61] The objective of Article 90 is, as we have seen, to abolish discrimination, not to place imported products in a privileged position.[62]. Fourthly, the Court has frequently held that, in its present state of development, Article 90 does not restrict the freedom of each Member State to establish a tax system which differentiates between certain products, even similar ones within the meaning of the first paragraph of Article 90, on the basis of objective criteria, such as the nature of raw materials used or the production processes employed in creating them. Such differentiation is legitimate, though, only if it pursues objectives which are compatible with the EC Treaty. It is, of course, necessary for the detailed rules governing the tax to avoid any form of direct or indirect discrimination against imports from other Member States and any form of protection of competing domestic products.[63]

4. *The customs union: VAT and turnover taxes*

The EC Treaty, Article 93, which requires the harmonization of turnover taxes,

[57] Case 193/85 *Cooperativa Co-Frutta v Amministrazione Delle Finance Dello Stato* [1987] ECR 2085.
[58] Case C–284/96 *Didier Tabouillot v Directeur des services fiscaux de Meurthe-et-Moselle* [1997] ECR I–7471 para 21. See also Case C–130/92 *OTO SpA v Ministero della Finanze* [1994] ECR I–3281 at para 18.
[59] Case C–90/94 *Haahr Petroleum*, n 31 above, para 19; and Case C–109/98 *CRT France International SA v Directeur régional des impôts de Bourgogne* [1999] ECR I–2237, para 20.
[60] Case 27/67 *Firma Frink-Frucht GmbH v Hauptzollamt München—Landsbergerstrasse* [1968] ECR 223. See also Case C–163/90 *Administration des Douanes et Droits Indirects v Léopold Legros and others* [1992] ECR I–4625 para 11.
[61] Case 27/67 *Firma Fink-Frucht GmbH v Hauptzollamt München-Landsbergerstrasse* (n 60 above) 231; Case 90/79 *Commission v France* [1981] ECR 283 para 14 and Case C–163/90, n 60 above, para 11; Case C–109/98 *CRT France International SA v Directeur régional des impôts de Bourgogne*, n 33 above, para 13.
[62] See Case 78/76 *Steinike und Weinlig v Germany*, n 38 above, at para 30.
[63] *Outokumpu Oy*, n 50 above, at paras 30–33.

is placed in the same chapter of the Treaty as the provisions on internal taxation discussed above. Article 33 of the Sixth VAT Directive[64] harmonizing VAT, allows Member States to impose taxes so long as they are not turnover taxes and do not, in trade between Member States, give rise to formalities connected with the crossing of frontiers. An adviser considering how best to attack an impost should, therefore, bear in mind that if the tax in question can be characterized as a turnover tax rather than a customs duty, or an equivalent charge, it will be invalid on account of breaching Article 33. Two cases in which the ECJ has had to consider a possible breach of Article 33 as well as the prohibition on customs duties are *Bergandi v Directeur Général des Impôts*[65] and *Fazenda Publica v UCAL.*[66] In *UCAL* the Court reiterated that the aim of Article 33 is to preclude the imposition of duties, taxes or charges in the nature of turnover taxes. These are impositions which are levied on the movement of goods and services in a way comparable to value added tax, which would compromise the functioning of the common system of value added tax and which exhibit the essential characteristics of VAT. These were identified by the Court as follows:

> VAT applies generally to transactions relating to goods or services; it is proportional to the price of those goods or services, it is charged at each stage of the production and distribution process and, finally, it is imposed on the added value of goods and services, since the tax payable on a transaction is calculated after deducting the tax paid on the previous transaction.[67]

In the light of this statement it should be readily apparent whether one is dealing with a turnover tax or a customs duty or equivalent charge.

Although customs duty and turnover taxes must be distinguished, and the territorial scope of VAT and the Community customs territory are not coincidental as we note in Chapter 3, VAT law and the laws relating to customs duty are, nevertheless, inextricably linked. This linkage is not surprising considering that, by virtue of the Sixth Directive, Article 2, the importation of goods is subjected to VAT. The importation of goods is defined in Article 7 of the Directive to cover two situations: first, entry into the Community of goods which do not fulfil the conditions laid down in the EEC Treaty, Articles 9 and 10 (now Articles 23 and 24) or, where the ECSC is concerned, are not in free circulation,[68] and, secondly, entry into the Community of goods not within the first category.[69]

---

[64] Council Directive of 17 May 1977, (EC) 388/77 [1977] OJ L145/1 as amended.
[65] Case 252/86 [1988] ECR 1343.
[66] Case 347/95 *Fazenda Publica v União das Cooperativas Abastecedoras de Leite de Lisboa, UCRL (UCAL)* [1997] ECR I–4911.
[67] Ibid, para 34. See also paras 31–33 and Joined Cases 93/88 and 94/88 *Wisselink v Staatssecretaris van Financiën* [1989] ECR 2671 paras 13 and 14; Case C–200/90 *Dansk Denkavit and Poulsen Trading v Skatteministeriet* [1992] ECR I–2217 para 10; and Case 295/84 *SA Rousseau Wilmot v Caisse de compensation de l'Organisation autonome nationale de l'industrie et du commerce (ORGANIC)* [1985] ECR 3759 para 16.
[68] Sixth Directive, Art 7.1(a).
[69] Ibid, Art 7.1(b).

The precise use which VAT law makes of customs duty law cannot be explored in great detail here but a few points may be noted.[70] For example, the Sixth Directive applies customs duty law in establishing, in respect of importations, the chargeable event, the moment when the tax becomes chargeable, and the taxable amount for the purposes of the tax. Article 10 of the Directive provides that the chargeable event occurs on importation, or when goods cease to be covered by certain customs arrangements. It is specifically provided that where imported goods are subject to customs duties, agricultural levies or charges having equivalent effect under a common policy, the chargeable event shall occur and the tax shall become chargeable, when the chargeable event occurs and chargeability arises in respect of those Community duties. Where goods are not subject to any of those Community duties, Member States are to apply the customs duty provisions relating to the chargeable event and the moment when the tax becomes chargeable.[71]

So far as the taxable amount is concerned, the Sixth Directive, Article 11B.1 provides that the primary rule governing the taxable amount for VAT is to be the value of the goods for customs purposes, although there are derogations from this in respect of works of art, collectors' items and antiques. The VAT regime is not, however, governed by reference to the 'transaction price' in exactly the same way that the customs duty regime is, with the result that the amounts on which VAT and customs duty are imposed are different. The taxable amount for VAT excludes, amongst other things, certain discounts[72] which will be taken account of in determining the price paid or payable. On the other hand, the taxable amount for VAT includes taxes, duties, levies and other charges due outside the importing Member State and those due, like customs duty, by reason of importation.[73] For customs duty purposes, import duties or other charges payable in the Community by reason of the importation or sale of goods are excluded from the price actually paid or payable, provided that they are shown separately from it.[74] Buying commissions, too, are excluded from the amount on which customs duty is charged, so long as they are shown separately from the price actually paid or payable, but are included in the taxable amount for VAT.[75]

If customs law is relevant to the charging of VAT it is also relevant in relation to exemptions from it and to the application of reduced rates. For example, no VAT is to be charged in respect of a final importation of goods

---

[70] Indeed, so far as matters within the competence of Member States are concerned, the use which is made of customs law in the administration of VAT varies as between Member States. In Italy, for example, it appears that CCC, Arts 243 and 244, concerning appeals, are applied to VAT: see Case C–1/99 *Kofisa Italia Srl v Ministero delle Finanze* (ECJ, 11 Jan 2001).

[71] Sixth Directive, Art 10.3.

[72] Ibid, Arts 11A.3 and 11B4.

[73] Ibid, Art 11B.3(a).

[74] CCC Art 33.1(f). See further Ch 8 below.

[75] See Sixth Directive, Art 11B.3(b) and (CCC, Art 33.1(e)).

qualifying for exemption from customs duties, other than as provided for in the Common Customs Tariff, although VAT may be imposed where exemption would be liable to have a serious effect on conditions of competition.[76] Exemptions from VAT are also established in respect of certain re-importations where the goods qualify for customs duties exemptions, or would do so if they were imported from a third country, and in respect of importations under diplomatic and consular arrangements which qualify for exemption from customs duties.[77] The Member States are permitted to exempt certain supplies of goods linked to international goods traffic, such as goods placed in a free zone or warehouse, or placed under customs warehousing or inward processing arrangements.[78] The provisions which apply in respect of these arrangements for customs duty purposes also apply for VAT purposes.[79] So far as concerns the application of reduced rates of VAT, it is provided that Member States may use the Combined Nomenclature to establish precisely the categories of goods, supplies of which attract such rates.[80]

Finally, it should be noted that the Sixth Directive provides that goods which enter the Community from a country which the Sixth Directive considers to be a third country are to be subject to the same entry formalities as those applicable in respect of importations into the customs territory.[81] The internal Community transit procedure is also adapted to the VAT territory.[82] So too are the customs export procedures where goods are exported for VAT purposes to a third country which is within the customs territory.[83]

5. *The customs union and state aid*

As is well known, the EC Treaty, Article 87 provides that state aids which distort or threaten to distort competition by favouring certain undertakings, or the production of certain goods, are to be incompatible with the common market in so far as they affect trade between Member States. It is, of course, possible for a tax or duty to amount to a state aid.[84] It is possible too for a

---

[76] Sixth Directive, Art 14.1(d).
[77] Ibid, Art 14.1(e) and (g).
[78] Ibid, Art 16 and Art 28c.E.
[79] Ibid, Art 33a.1(c).
[80] Ibid, Annex H. See, for example, the United Kingdom's Value Added Tax Act 1994, Sch 5A which contains a list of products, with a description and their CN Code, which are eligible, as the heading to the Schedule puts it, 'to be fiscally warehoused'. The fiscal warehousing regime provides, amongst other things, that an acquisition or supply of goods subject to the regime may be treated as taking place outside the UK: see Value Added Tax Act 1994, s 18B(3).
[81] Sixth Directive, Art 33a.1(a).
[82] Ibid, Art 33a.1(b).
[83] Ibid, Art 33.2(a). Art 33.2(b) ensures that goods which are temporarily exported outside the VAT territory are treated like goods which are temporarily exported outside the customs territory.
[84] See Case C–387/92 *Banco de Crédito Industrial SA, now Banco Exterior de España SA v Ayuntamiento de Valencia* [1994] ECR I–877. For a recent example of a UK tax provision being held to be a state aid see *R v C&E Commrs, ex p Lunn Poly Ltd* [1998] STC 649 (the provisions permitting a lower than standard rate of insurance premium tax held to constitute a state aid).

parafiscal charge which is prohibited as a charge having equivalent effect to a customs duty, or as discriminatory or protective internal taxation, to constitute a state aid by reason of the use to which the receipts of a tax or duty are put, eg for the benefit of domestic products, or by reason of the machinery for their reimbursement.[85]

The EC Treaty, Article 88 lays down the procedures to be adopted by a Member State and the Community institutions in determining the validity of state aid. Article 88.3 stipulates that the Commission must be informed of plans to grant or alter aid. If it considers that the aid is incompatible with the common market it must initiate a procedure establishing the status of the aid. So far as the Member State is concerned, Article 88 requires that it 'shall not put its proposed measures into effect until this procedure has resulted in a final decision'. In one case concerning a parafiscal charge imposed by the French authorities for the benefit of the *Fonds d'Intervention et d'Organisation des Marchés des Produits de la Pêche Maritime et de Cultures Maritime*,[86] the Court of Justice held that the provision quoted above has direct effect so that a trader may rely upon it before a national court. Failure to comply with it renders the measures giving effect to the aid invalid, although the final determination on the validity of the aid as a matter of EC law is for the Commission. The measures giving effect to the aid will, of course, often include the measures imposing the parafiscal charge in the first place. The result of this is that, even if the imposition is not prohibited by virtue of Articles 25 or 90, it may be possible to invalidate a charge until the procedures outlined in Article 88 are complied with.

6. *The customs union and competition law*

The imposition of a parafiscal charge or duty may give rise to competition law issues, in particular pursuant to the EC Treaty, Article 82. This Article prohibits an abuse by an undertaking of a dominant position within the common market or a substantial part of it. It can happen that the undertaking imposing the parafiscal charge is an undertaking in a dominant position. In

[85] Joined Cases C–78/90 to C–83/90 *Compagnie Commerciale de l'Ouest v Receveur Principal des Douanes de La Pallice Port* [1992] ECR I–1847 para 32; Joined Cases C–149/91 and C–150/91 *Sanders Adour Snc v Directeur des Services Fiscaux des Pyrénées-Atlantiques* [1992] ECR I–3899 para 24; Case C–72/92 *Firma Herbert Scharbatke GmbH v Federal Republic of Germany* [1993] ECR I–5509 para 18; Case C–17/91 *Georges Lornoy en Zonen NV v Belgium* [1992] ECR I–6523 at para 28.

[86] Case C–354/90 *Fédération Nationale du Commerce Extérieur des Produits Alimentaires and Syndicat National des Négociants et Transformateurs de Saumon v France* [1991] ECR I–5505. See also Case C–17/91 *Georges Lornoy en Zonen NV v Belgium* [1992] ECR I–6523 (concerning compulsory contributions to a fund set up to assist in the financing of compensation, allowances and other benefits for combating animal disease, improving hygiene and improving the health and quality of animals and animal products); and Case C–114/91 *Criminal proceedings against Gérard Jerôme Claeys* [1992] ECR I–6559 and *Sanders Adour Snc v Directeur des Services Fiscaux des Pyrénées-Atlantiques*, n 85 above.

Haahr Petroleum, for example, the undertaking operating certain Danish ports and its own ferry route was charged with levying a goods duty on goods passing through the ports. It did not, however, levy the duties on itself. Although the Court of Justice did not deal with the impact of the EC Treaty, Article 82 on this situation, Advocate General Jacobs agreed that it could apply.[87] If the duties charged were to yield an unreasonable profit, after payment of the operating costs of the port, there would be an abuse of a dominant position in that there would be the imposition of unfair prices within Article 82(a). The fact that the undertaking did not have to pay the duties which it imposed on others could also amount to an abuse within Article 82(c), in that it applied dissimilar conditions to equivalent transactions with other trading parties, thereby placing them at a competitive disadvantage.

It is not only the imposition of charges which may infringe competition law; the activities of, for example, customs agents may do so as well. The Court of Justice has held in *Commission v Italy*, that the activity of a customs agent falls within the concept of an undertaking for the purposes of the Community's competition rules. It held too that a decision of the National Council of Customs Agents setting tariffs for customs agents' charges constituted a decision of an association of undertakings, which restricted competition, and was capable of affecting intra-Community trade, contrary to what is now EC Treaty, Article 81. The fact that the setting of the tariff was required by law meant that Italy had failed to fulfil its obligations under the Treaty.[88]

In defeating the imposition of compulsory fees for Italian customs agents, competition law achieved what customs law could not. The Italian law relating to customs agents was questioned by a letter from the Commission to Italy on 16 December 1976 and attacked in a subsequent application to the Court dated 17 July 1978.[89] The Court held that certain elements of the law infringed the freedom of establishment. On 24 March 1992 the Commission sought a declaration that, amongst other things, Italy had infringed what are now the EC Treaty, Articles 23 and 25, by approving the tariff which amounted to a charge having equivalent effect to a customs duty. This application was unsuccessful on the basis that the use of professional customs forwarding agents was not compulsory in all circumstances.[90] On 30 June 1993, prior to bringing Case C–35/96, the Commission adopted a Decision[91]

---

[87] Case C–90/94 *Haahr Petroleum Ltd v Åbenrå Havn and others*, n 31 above, at 4125–4126 paras 133–136.

[88] Case C–35/96 *Commission v Italy* [1998] ECR I–3851. As Léger AG observed at para 63 of his Opinion in Case C–309/99 *J.C.J. Wouters and others v Algemene Raad vande Nederlandse Ordre van Advocaten*, 10 July 2001, Case C–35/96 was the first case in which the Court of Justice applied the concept of an association of undertakings to a professional association.

[89] Case 159/78 *Commission v Italy* [1979] ECR 3247.

[90] See Case C–119/92 *Commission v Italy* [1993] ECR I–393.

[91] (EEC) 438/93 [1993] OJ L203/27.

requesting that the infringement of Article 85(1), as it then was, effected by the tariff, be brought to an end. Judgment in favour of the Commission in Case 35/96 was given on 18 June 1998. Finally, on 30 March 2000, the Court of First Instance dismissed an action seeking the annulment of the Decision.[92]

7. *The common commercial policy and external affairs*

There are four articles in Title IX of the EC Treaty dealing with the common commercial policy, namely Articles 131–134.[93] The EC Treaty, Articles 131 and 133.1 give some clear guidance as to its purpose and scope. Article 131 states that 'By establishing a customs union between themselves Member States aim to contribute, in the common interest, to the harmonious development of world trade, the progressive abolition of restrictions on international trade and the lowering of customs barriers'.

Article 133.1 states that the common commercial policy is '. . . based on uniform principles, particularly in regard to changes in tariff rates, the conclusion of tariff and trade agreements, the achievement of uniformity in measures of liberalisation, export policy and measures to protect trade such as those to be taken in case of dumping or subsidies'.

The existence of such a common commercial policy is clearly essential for the operation of a customs union and indeed the customs union is essential for a common commercial policy.[94] The policy is implemented by Community legislation, such as that governing imports and exports (often referred to as 'autonomous' commercial policy) but also by agreements with third countries on trade matters (often referred to as 'conventional' commercial policy).[95] This leaves little room for action by the authorities of the Member States. The Court has said, quoting its Opinion 1/75:[96]

> 'It cannot be accepted that in a field covered by export policy and more generally by the common commercial policy the Member States should exercise a power concurrent to that of the Community, in the Community sphere and in the international sphere . . . [S]ince full responsibility in the matter of commercial policy was transferred to the Community by Article 113(1) measures of commercial policy of a national character are only permissible after the end of the transitional period by virtue of specific authorization by the Community.'[97]

[92] Case T–513/93 *Consiglio Nazionale degli Spedizionieri Doganali v Commission* [2000] ECR II–1807.
[93] Art 133 has been replaced by the Treaty of Nice, Art 2.8, which has yet to be ratified. The terms of Art 133.1, quoted below, are unaltered.
[94] As Trabucchi AG said in Case 8/73 *Hauptzollamt Bremerhaven v Massey-Ferguson GmbH* [1973] ECR 897 at 913.
[95] See ibid at 908 para 4.
[96] [1975] ECR 1355.
[97] Case 174/84 *Bulk Oil (Zug) AG v Sun International Limited and Sun Oil Trading Company* [1986] ECR 559 paras 30 and 31. The Court relied upon Case 41/76 *Donckerwolke v Procureur de la Republique* [1976] ECR 1921.

There is room, however, for debate as to the scope of the Community's commercial policy, as we shall see below.

Whatever else the common commercial policy includes, it encompasses, of course, much more than customs matters. These are, nevertheless, an important part of the policy and are strongly influenced by its imperatives, as was indicated in Joined Cases 37 and 38/73, in which the Court of Justice regarded the policy as an important consideration in determining that a charge on the importation of diamonds was contrary to Community law. It noted that the common commercial policy involved 'the elimination of all national disparities, whether in the field of taxation or of commerce, which regulate trade with third countries'.[98]

In the 1990s the breadth of the commercial policy and its capacity to develop was noted in two Opinions of the Court of Justice.[99] In the latter of them the Court approved this statement:

Article [133], empowers the Community to formulate a commercial 'policy', based on 'uniform principles' thus showing that the question of external trade must be governed from a wide point of view and not only having regard to the administration of precise systems such as customs and quantitive restrictions. The same conclusion may be deduced from the fact that the enumeration in Article [133] of the subjects covered by commercial policy (changes in tariff rates, the conclusion of tariff and trade agreements, the achievement of uniformity in measures of liberalisation, export policy and measures to protect trade) is conceived as a non-exhaustive enumeration which must not, as such close the door to the application in a Community context of any other process intended to regulate external trade. A restrictive interpretation of the concept of common commercial policy would risk causing disturbances in intra Community trade by reason of the disparities which would then exist in certain sectors of economic relations with non-member countries.[100]

The fact that the policy is broad and developing having, as the Court of Justice has put it, an 'open nature',[101] does not mean it is limitless. In Opinion 1/94, for example, the Court of Justice made clear that the policy does not cover areas which the EC Treaty treats separately, such as transport, which is dealt with in Title V of the treaty.[102] Neither does it cover trade between

---

[98] Joined Cases 37 and 38/73 *Sociaal Fonds voor de Diamantarbeiders v NV Indiamex et Association de fait De Belder* [1973] ECR 1609 at para 23.

[99] Opinion 1/94 on the competence of the Community to conclude international agreements concerning services and the protection of intellectual property [1994] ECR 5267 and Opinion 2/92 on the competence of the Community or one of its institutions to participate in the Third Revised Decision of the OECD on national treatment [1995] ECR 521.

[100] Opinion 1/78 on the International Agreement on Natural Rubber [1979] ECR 2871 para 45, approved in Opinion 1/94, n 99 above, para 39. In relation to commercial policy generally see the cases referred to in para 38. Note that the power of the Community to negotiate association agreements with third countries and international organizations arises from Art 133.

[101] Opinion 1/94, (n 99 above, para 41.

[102] Ibid, paras 48–52. The Court relied upon Case 22/70 *Commission v Council* [1971] ECR 263 at para 16. Note too that in Case C–130/92 *OTO SpA* v *Ministero delle finanze*, n 58 above, at para

Member States,[103] nor all agreements as to services, nor the harmonization of intellectual property protection.[104] Furthermore, the fact that the policy is sufficiently flexible to develop does not mean that it may be interpreted differently in different contexts; its content at any one time is the same in whatever context it is considered.[105]

It is important to note that any development which does occur need not be exclusively in the direction of the liberalization of trade. In the words of the Court:

> Although it may be thought that at the time when the Treaty was drafted liberalization of trade was the dominant idea, the Treaty nevertheless does not form a barrier to the possibility of the Community's developing a commercial policy aiming at a regulation of the world market for certain products rather than at a mere liberalization.[106]

It is understandable that the Court should seek to preserve as wide a field of action as possible for the Community. Times change and it is essential that the Community is able to change with them. As the Court itself has said, a commercial policy which was restricted to the use of instruments intended to have effect only on the traditional aspects of external trade would 'become nugatory in the course of time'.[107] Nevertheless, the liberalization of trade was not merely the dominant idea at the time the Treaty was drafted it was one of the concepts which formed, and form, the foundations of the Community. Whilst regulation of trade is clearly necessary, and properly falls within the scope of the commercial policy, regulation is not to be treated as a concept which is equal in force to that of liberalization. The terms of Article 131 and its reference to 'the progressive abolition of restrictions on international trade and the lowering of customs barriers' make that clear.

No consideration of commercial policy can be confined, though, to the issues of liberalization and regulation of trade. Issues such as environmental protection, aid and development must feature in any contemporary commercial policy. They are, to some considerable extent, of significance in the context of customs law. For example, the Community system of generalized preferences, which was established against the background of an increasingly

---

20, the Court observed that Article 133, as it now is, did not contain any provision similar to EC Treaty, Article 90 regarding domestic taxation in respect of trade with non-member countries, subject to any treaty provisions applicable as between the Community and the country of origin of a given product.

[103] Opinion 2/92 [1995] ECR 521, see note 99 above, Section IV paras 8 and 9. There remains debate as to the extent to which the policy covers services, see p 44 below.
[104] Opinion 1/94, n 99 above, paras 47 and 71.
[105] Opinion 1/75 [1975] ECR 1355 at 1362.
[106] Opinion 1/78, n 100 above, para 44.
[107] Ibid, at para 44.

strong link between trade and development, recognized by GATT and the United Nations Conference on Trade and Development, is plainly within the scope of the commercial policy, notwithstanding that the trade arrangements with developing countries may be justified on development policy grounds.[108] The special preferential tariff arrangements established pursuant to agreements with third countries also fall, of course, within the Community's commercial policy. The fact that measures in these areas are designed to implement the common commercial policy is an important consideration in applying their provisions—those relating to customs duty and cooperation between customs authorities as much as any others.

The need for a broad and adaptable commercial policy springs not just from considerations of global trade and international development. The requirements of intra-Community trade point in the same direction. To quote the Court in Opinion 1/78 again: 'A restrictive interpretation of the concept of common commercial policy would risk causing disturbances in intra-Community trade by reason of the disparities which would then exist in certain sectors of economic relations with non-member countries.'[109]

A broad conception of commercial policy may also be significant, if not desirable, for reasons of intra-Community politics, particularly in relation to the validity of Community measures and Community competence. So far as the validity of Community measures is concerned, Case C–62/88[110] is worth noting. In it, Greece sought unsuccessfully to establish that a regulation, setting radiation levels for imports from third countries following the Chernobyl disaster, ought to be made pursuant to the Community's policy on the environment and not its commercial policy. The latter is subject to different procedural requirements and qualified majority voting[111] rather than unanimity, as may be required in respect of environmental policy.[112] The scope of the commercial policy may also affect the validity of measures in the customs duty field. In Case 45/86[113] regulations governing generalized tariff preferences were held valid on the ground that they fell within the commercial policy. As we noted above, a link with development policy did not exclude them from its scope.

Turning to the issue of Community competence in relation to international agreements, we should first note that, since the establishment of the customs union, the Community has replaced the Member States with regard to the fulfilment of the obligations under the GATT.[114] The inevitable involvement of

---

[108] Case 45/86 *Commission v Council* [1987] ECR 1493 at paras 20–21.
[109] n 100 above, para 45.
[110] Case C–62/88 *Greece v Council* [1990] ECR I–1527.
[111] See EC Treaty, Art 133.2 and 4.
[112] See EC Treaty, Art 175.2.
[113] n 108 above.
[114] See Joined Cases 21 to 24/72 *International Fruit Company v Produktschap voor Groenten en Fruit* [1972] ECR 1219 at paras 14–18. See also Case 38/75 *Douaneagent der NV Nederlandse*

the Community in international negotiations means that many agreements with third countries must be concluded by the Community and the Member States jointly.[115] Clearly, these 'mixed type agreements', as they are known, are likely to prove more cumbersome to negotiate than those within the exclusive competence of the Community. Frequently, though, Member States are keen to assert the importance of their role and the dispute over competence in relation to GATS and TRIPS showed the significance which they attach to limiting the exclusive competence of the Commission.[116] So far as GATS was concerned, the Court of Justice was unwilling to exclude services from the ambit of the commercial policy as a matter of principle, but concluded that only those cross-frontier supplies of services not involving cross-frontier movement of persons fell within the common commercial policy. Only to that extent, therefore, did the Community have competence in relation to GATS. So far as TRIPS was concerned, the commercial policy of the Community covered only the provisions on the release into free circulation of counterfeit goods. In all other respects, contrary to the views of the Commission, the Member States were held to have competence. These two agreements were, therefore, mixed agreements. Unsurprisingly, perhaps, but importantly in the context of customs duty, the Court of Justice held that the Community did have exclusive competence pursuant to Article 133 to enter into GATT 94 and, consequently, to agree to the reductions in customs duty for which GATT 94 provided. It affirmed, however, that the exclusive competence of the Community arises not merely as a result of the Community's competence to lay down rules at Community level. For the Member States to lose their competence to enter into agreements with third countries it is necessary for there to be common rules which could be affected by the agreement in question.[117] In relation to the customs union that is, of course, the case. No doubt, as international agreements governing the global economy increase in scope, the issue of Community competence will fall to be considered again.

7.1 *Anti-dumping and countervailing duties*

Other important elements of commercial policy relate to the organization of markets by the imposition of anti-dumping and countervailing duties. Both these areas have been placed on a new legislative footing following the conclu-

Spoorwegen v Inspecteur der invoerrechten en accijnzen [1975] ECR 1439 para 16; and Case 269/81 *Amministrazione della Finanze dello Stato v SPI and SAMI* [1983] ECR 801 at para 19. It also replaced the Member States in relation to their commitments arising under the Convention on Nomenclature of 1950 and the Convention establishing the Customs Cooperation Council.

[115] See further Ch 6 below.
[116] For a case in which the Commission successfully defended its competence see Opinion 1/78, n 100 above.
[117] Opinion 2/92, n 99 above, Section V para 3 and Opinion 1/94, n 116 above, para 77.

sion of the Uruguay Round.[118] We cannot explore them in any detail here, but it should be noted that an anti-dumping duty may be imposed where a non-Community product is released by a trader into free circulation in the Community and causes injury. A product is to be considered as being dumped if its export price to the Community is less than a comparable price for the like product, in the ordinary course of trade, as established for the exporting country.[119] A countervailing duty, on the other hand, may be imposed to counter direct or indirect subsidies, by a government or public body, given for the manufacture, production, export, or transport of any product the release of which for free circulation in the Community causes injury.[120] The Anti-Dumping Regulation provides that no product shall be subject to both anti-dumping duty and a countervailing duty for the purpose of dealing with one and the same situation arising from dumping or from export subsidization.[121]

These duties are not, however, customs duties or charges having an effect equivalent to customs duties, nor are they import duties within the definition adopted in CCC, Article 4(10). Furthermore, it is expressly stated that anti-dumping duties are to be collected independently of customs duties.[122] Nevertheless, customs law and customs authorities play an important role in relation to the regimes established by both these regulations. The Anti-Dumping Regulation, Article 14.3 and the Countervailing Duty Regulation, Article 24.3 provide that special provisions, in particular with regard to the common definition of the concept of origin, as contained in the CCC, may be adopted pursuant to the regulation. In consequence of this provision it is usual to find that a regulation imposing an anti-dumping duty, or a countervailing duty, states that, unless otherwise specified, the provisions in force concerning customs duty shall apply.

So far we have looked at the legal context of Community customs law and the EC Treaty; now we turn to consider customs law and the EU Treaty.

C. CUSTOMS LAW AND THE EU

It is not proposed to review every element of the EU which may be relevant to the customs authorities of Member States, but the fundamental provision of

---

[118] For anti-dumping duties see: Council Regulation (EC) 384/96 of 22 Dec 1995 on protection against dumped imports from countries not members of the European Community [1996] OJ L56/1 ('the Anti-Dumping Regulation'); amended by Council Regulation (EC) 2331/96 of 2 Dec 1996 [1996] OJ L317/1 and Council Regulation (EC) 905/98 of 27 Apr 1998 [1998] OJ L128/18. For countervailing duties see Council Regulation (EC) 2026/97 of 6 Oct 1997 on protection against subsidized imports from countries not members of the European Community [1997] OJ L288/1 ('the Countervailing Duty Regulation').
[119] See the Anti-Dumping Regulation, Art 1.2.
[120] See the Countervailing Duty Regulation, Art 1.2
[121] Anti-Dumping Regulation, Art 14.1.
[122] In the Anti-Dumping Regulation, Art 14 and the Countervailing Duty Regulation, Art 24.

the Treaty on European Union which directly concerns the customs union is Article 29. It provides that:

> Without prejudice to the powers of the European Community, the Union's objective shall be to provide citizens with a high level of safety within an area of freedom, security and justice by developing common action among the Member States in the fields of police and judicial cooperation in criminal matters and by preventing and combating racism and zenophobia.

That objective is to be achieved by preventing and combating crime, trafficking in persons and offences against children, illicit drug and arms trafficking, corruption, and fraud. This, in turn is to be established by 'closer cooperation between police forces, customs authorities and other competent authorities in the Member States.'[123]

The treaty also provides that common action in the field of police co-operation is to include operational co-operation between the competent authorities of the Member States, including the police, customs, and other specialized law enforcement services, in relation to the prevention, detection, and investigation of criminal offences.[124] Of particular significance is a Convention on the Use of Information Technology for Customs Purposes,[125] drawn up on the basis of the Treaty on European Union, Article K.3, now Article 31, which provides for common action on judicial co-operation in criminal matters. Article 2 of the Convention states that:

> 1. The customs administrations of the Member States shall set up and maintain a joint automated information system for customs purposes, hereinafter referred to as the 'Customs Information System' ['CIS'].
> 2. The aim of the Customs Information System, in accordance with the provisions of this Convention, shall be to assist in preventing, investigating and prosecuting serious contraventions of national laws by increasing, through the rapid dissemination of information, the effectiveness of the cooperation and control procedures of the customs administrations of the Member States.

The CIS, managed by the Commission, is to consist of a central database of information accessible by designated authorities, including the customs

---

[123] TEU, Art 29, second para first indent.
[124] TEU, Art 30.1(a).
[125] [1995] OJ C316/34. By virtue of Art 25.4 of the Convention, it is fully in force between Austria, Denmark, Finland, Greece, Italy, Portugal, Spain, Sweden, and the UK. An agreement of 26 June 1995 permitting the provisional application of the Convention between Member States was established: see [1995] OJ C316/58. See also: (i) a Protocol, of 29 Nov 1996, on the interpretation, by way of preliminary rulings by the Court of Justice of the European Communities, of the Convention on the use of Information Technology for Customs Purposes; (ii) the Action Plan of the Council and the Commission on how best to implement the provisions of the Treaty of Amsterdam on an area of freedom, security and justice—Text adopted by the Justice and Home Affairs Council of 3 Dec 1998: [1999] OJ C19/1 paras 44–48.

authorities of all Member States. It is to contain data on a wide range of matters and persons to facilitate the fight against fraud.[126]

The EU Treaty, Article 31 has provided the basis for significant inter-governmental action to counter fraud and protect the own resources of the Community. In the context of customs duty, particular attention should be paid to the Convention on Mutual Assistance and Cooperation between Customs Administrations of 18 December 1997,[127] pursuant to which Member States will co-operate in relation to the prosecution and punishment of customs offences. The Convention is frequently known as 'Naples II' because it replaces the Convention of the Member States of the European Economic Community on the Provision of Mutual Assistance by their Customs Authorities, signed in Rome on 7 September 1967 and known as the Naples Convention.[128]

In 1999 the European Parliament deplored the delay in ratifying the Convention on the Use of Information Technology for Customs Purposes and related agreements and the Convention on Mutual Assistance and Cooperation between Customs Authorities and called on the Commission to make them Community measures.[129] The Action Plan of 1998,[130] however, called for the ratification of the "CIS" and Naples II Conventions by 31 July 2001.[131]

Although the legal context in which customs law operates is important, customs duty is significant in Community affairs, primarily because of the role which it plays in financing the Community, and we conclude this chapter by looking at customs duty as part of the Community's own resources.

---

[126] The CIS established pursuant to the Convention concerns those matters which remain within the control of Member States. A Customs Information System is already in place pursuant to Council Regulation (EC) 515/97 of 13 Mar 1997 [1997] OJ L82/1, implemented by Commission Regulation (EC) 696/98 of 27 Mar 1998 [1998] OJ L96/22. The fifth recital to the Council Regulation specifically states that it is without prejudice to the application of the Convention of 1967 referred to below, which is replaced by the 1995 Convention, in fields which remain within the sole control of Member States. Mutual assistance between customs authorities is discussed further in Ch 4, at p 106 below.

[127] See the explanatory report on the Convention at [1998] OJ C189/1. The text was approved by the Council on 28 May 1998.

[128] Co-operation between customs authorities goes back to the Recommendation on mutual administrative assistance prepared by the Customs Cooperation Council in 1953. Following the Naples Convention the Community set up a Customs Mutual Assistance Group (MAG) and a new Customs Mutual Assistance Group was set up in 1992 (MAG 92) as set out in a Declaration by the representatives of the governments of the Member States, meeting within the Council, concerning the continuing role of customs services after 1992: [1990] OJ C262/3.

[129] See Resolution on the progress made in 1998 in the implementation of co-operation in the fields of justice and home affairs pursuant to TEU, Title VI, para 24, 14 Jan 1999: [1999] OJ C104/135. Note that, by declaration, Spain and Denmark have declared an intention to include data in the CIS subject to conditions: [1999] OJ C91/7.

[130] See paras 43 and 44(e). For the Action Plan see n 125 above.

[131] As noted in 'The Prevention and Control of Organised Crime: A European Strategy for the Beginning of the New Millennium' 1 [2000] OJ C124/1, Ch 2.5, 'Existing mandates and initiatives'. At the time of writing no EC Member State has ratified Naples II. See n 125 for the position re the CIS Treaty.

EC Customs Law

D. THE FINANCIAL CONTEXT OF CUSTOMS DUTY: OWN RESOURCES

The Commission is obliged to undertake, before 1 January 2006, a general review of the own resources system, in the light of a number of matters including enlargement of the Community.[132] For the foreseeable future, however, customs duties will continue to constitute a significant proportion of the Community's own resources. The General Budget of the European Union for the Financial Year 2001 sets out total revenue and customs duties and other duties referred to in Article 2(1)(b) of the Council Decision of 31 October 1994[133] which governs the system of own resources. It shows that the Member States which contributed the most in such duties were Germany, the United Kingdom and the Netherlands. It gives the following figures in euros:[134]

	2001	2000	1999
Total revenue	92 569 368 837	89 440 586 293	86 908 069 738
Own resources	90 972 068 520	85 557 370 687	82 083 049 989
Customs duty, etc	13 657 500 000	12 961 400 000	13 006 508 622
Germany's contribution	3 178 000 000	3 016 100 000	3 026 558 598
UK's contribution	2 657 500 000	2 522 100 000	2 530 846 980
Netherlands' contribution	1 607 500 000	1 525 500 000	1 530 828 490

These figures may be compared with those which appear in the General Budget for the European Union for the financial year 1996[135] in which amounts are given in ecus:

---

[132] Council Decision of 29 Sept 2000 on the system of the European Communities' own resources [2000] OJ L253/42, Art 9.

[133] (EC) 728/94, Euratom [1994] OJ L293/9. See further p 149.

[134] Final Adoption of the General Budgetof the EU for the financial year 2001: [2001] OJ L56/1 at pp 7 and 13. Figures for 1999 ignore parts of Euros.

[135] Final adoption of the General Budget of the European Union for the financial year 1996: [1996] OJ L22. See pp 7, 20 and 21. Figures for 1994 ignore parts of Ecus.

	1996	1995	1994
Total revenue	81 888 440 991	75 438 426 452	66 002 143 762
Own resources	81 320 317 223	70 244 632 418	68 082 069 352
Customs duty, etc	14 281 000 000	14 380 100 000	12 419 982 286
Germany's contribution	3 990 000 000	3 979 500 000	3 729 460 079
UK's contribution	2 740 000 000	2 700 000 000	2 574 866 351
Netherlands' contribution	1 473 100 000	1 487 300 000	1 521 515 012

It will be apparent that the duties formed about 15 per cent of own resources for 2001 and 2000 and nearer to 16 per cent for 1999. It was a little over 17.5 per cent in 1996, nearly 20.5 per cent in 1995 and a little in excess of 18 per cent in 1994.[136]

Own resources are the sole source of financing the budget of the Communities, as is made clear by the EC Treaty, Article 201. The Communities' system of own resources is, at the moment, governed by the Council Decision of 31 October 1994.[137] Article 2 sets out what revenue is to constitute 'own resources' and Article 2.1(b) provides that Common Customs Tariff duties and other duties established by institutions of the Communities in respect of trade with non-member countries are to be included. On 29 September 2000 a further Council Decision[138] was issued on the system of the European Communities' own resources. Naturally, this continues, in Article 1(b), to treat Common Customs Tariff duties as own resources. Although the Decision is to take effect generally on 1 January 2002, when the earlier Decision will be repealed, two provisions take effect on 1 January 2001. One of these is Article 2(3) which provides that Member States are to retain, as collection costs, 25 per cent of certain amounts, including customs duty. Previously only 10 per cent could be retained to cover collection costs.[139] Both the Decisions make clear that customs duty and other funds 'shall be collected by

---

[136] In its Communication concerning a strategy for the Customs Union, to the Council, the European Parliament and the Economic and Social Committee, COM(2001)51 final, the Commission noted that, in 1997, the duties constituted 19.1% of total budgetary resources, in 1998 they constituted 17.9% of it and in 1999 17.3%. These figures demonstrate the same downward trend in customs duty receipts.

[137] See n 133.   [138] (EC) 597/2000, Euratom [2000] OJ L253/42.

[139] Art 2.3 of Decision 728/94, n 133 above.

the Member States in accordance with the national provisions imposed by law, regulation or administrative action, which shall, where appropriate, be adapted to meet the requirements of Community rules'.[140]

The national responsibility for collection of customs duty is a matter which gives rise to a number of problems, as we will see later in the book, particularly in Chapter 13 below, but the scale of the task given to national administrations should not be underestimated. In 1999–2000, HM Customs and Excise collected £20.6bn from imports, from outside the Community, valued at £97bn. Of this sum, 72 per cent consisted of VAT on imports, 18 per cent consisted of excise duty on alcohol and tobacco and 10 per cent, ie, about £2bn, consisted of customs duty.[141] On the figures noted above, the total customs duty obtained by the Community amounts to something in excess of £7bn.

1. *General obligations concerning own resources*

As well as their obligation to collect customs duty[142] the Member States also have significant general obligations in relation to the Community's own resources. These, and the general regime relating to own resources, are set out in a Council Regulation.[143] This states that Member States must keep, free of charge, an account of own resources in the name of the Commission on which the Commission may draw.[144] The Community's entitlement to customs duties is established as soon as the conditions provided for in the CCC, concerning the entry of the customs debt in the accounts and notification of the debtor, have been met, and it is the date of entry in the accounts which is 'the date of establishment'.[145] Supporting documents relating to the date of establishment and the making available of own resources must be kept by Member States for a period of three calendar years, counting from the end of the year to which the documents refer.[146] Member States must keep accounts of own resources[147] and, in the two months following the end of each quarter, must send the Commission a description of cases of fraud and irregularities detected involving entitlements of over EUR 10,000.[148] In relation to customs duties amongst other charges, entry of own resources in the account of own resources is to be made, at the latest, subject to certain exceptions, on the first working day following the nineteenth day of the second month following the

---

[140] See Art 8.1 of both Decisions.
[141] See Report by the Comptroller and Auditor General, *HM Customs and Excise Regulating Freight Imports from Outside the European Community* HC 131 Session 2000–2001: 2 Feb 2001, para 1.1., published by the National Audit Office.
[142] See CCC, Art 232.
[143] Council Regulation (EC, Euratom) 1150/2000 of 22 May 2000 [2000] OJ L130/1.
[144] Ibid, Art 9.1 and 12.
[145] Ibid, Art 2.1 and 2.
[146] Ibid, Art 3.
[147] Ibid, Art 6.
[148] Ibid, Art 6.5.

month during which the entitlement was established.[149] Delay in making the entry in the account attracts interest payable by the Member State.[150] The rate of interest is the rate applicable on the Member State's money market on the due date for short-term public financing operations, increased by two percentage points. The rate is increased by 0.25 per cent for each month of delay and the increased rate is to be applied to the entire period of delay.[151] In addition to these obligations to the Commission, Member States' failures in carrying out their obligations, whether in relation to collection or to the more general operation of the customs system, may well be exposed by the Court of Auditors.

The obligations of the Member States in relation to the protection of the Community's own resources have been strengthened by the EC Treaty, Article 280, introduced by the Treaty of Maastricht and amended by the Treaty of Amsterdam. Member States are to take the same measures to counter fraud against the financial interests of the Community as they take in relation to their own financial interests.[152] Furthermore, they are obliged to co-ordinate their action and to organize, together with the Commission, close and regular cooperation between competent authorities.[153] This obligation is, of course, as relevant to customs authorities as to others. The role of the Member States is crucial. As the Court of Justice has said 'it is quite clear from Article 209a [now Article 280] inserted into the EC Treaty by the Treaty on European Union, that it is for the Member States to combat fraud which is prejudicial to the financial interests of the Community.'[154]

Yet the amendments introduced by the Treaty of Amsterdam have ensured that it is not just the Member States which have this responsibility. The new Article 280.1 imposes upon the Community and the Member States an obligation to take measures to counter fraud and other illegal activities affecting the financial interests of the Community which are to act as a deterrent and provide 'effective protection' in the Member States. The Council too is given obligations in relation to the prevention of fraud and the fight against it to the extent that it affects the financial interests of the Community. It is obliged, after consulting the Court of Auditors, to adopt necessary measures with a view to

---

[149] Ibid, Art 6.3(a) and Art 10.1.

[150] This may prove to be a significant consideration in post-clearance recovery cases where CCC, Art 220 is in point. See generally Ch 13 below.

[151] Art 11, n 143 above. The Court of Justice has said that 'there is an inseparable link between the obligation to establish the Community's own resources, the obligation to credit them to the Commission's account within the prescribed time-limit and the obligation to pay default interest'. Furthermore, the interest is payable 'regardless of the reason for the delay in making the entry in the Commission's account': see Case 68/88 *Commission v Greece* [1989] ECR 2965 para 17; Case 303/84 *Commission v Germany* [1986] ECR 1171 para 11; and Case 96/89 *Commission v Netherlands* [1991] ECR I–2461 at para 38. In the latter case, the Court of Justice held that the Netherlands had failed to observe Community law by, amongst other things, refusing to make customs duty and interest available to the Community in respect of imports of certain products.

[152] EC Treaty, Art 280.2.　　　　　　　　　　　　　　　　　[153] Ibid, Art 280.3.

[154] Case C–476/93 P *Nutral SpA v Commission* [1995] ECR I–4125 para 21.

affording 'effective and equivalent protection in the Member States'. The measures taken, however, are not to concern the application of national criminal law or the national administration of justice.[155] To ensure democratic oversight of the effect of Article 280, measures taken in implementation of it are to be the subject of an annual report submitted to the European Parliament and to the Council by the Commission in co-operation with Member States.[156]

That the fight against fraud has become a major concern for the Community is reflected in the second recital to a recent regulation amending the CCC, which noted that 'Every revision of the Code must, without instituting any barriers to international trade, be regarded as an opportunity to introduce instruments and procedures to prevent fraud, the prevention of fraud being one of the best ways of saving taxpayers' money . . .'.[157]

The Commission's *Unité de Co-ordination de la Lutte Anti-Fraude* (UNCLAF) was the organization responsible for investigating fraud within the EU budget until 1 June 1999. As from that date a new body, known as the European Anti-fraud Office (*Office Européen de Lutte Anti-fraude*—OLAF) was set up by the Commission, to assist it in the fight against fraud and to carry out investigations independently of it and other governments, institutions and bodies.[158] Its 'Fraud Report' highlights two areas in which the protection of the Community's own resources had been improved in relation to customs duty, namely improved co-ordination between Member States in the transit system and reform of the preferential tariff arrangements.[159] In the context of customs duty, however, the need to detect and deter fraud will, inevitably, be a continuing concern of the Community.

Although, as we have seen, there is a strong relationship between the customs union, the own resources derived from customs duties and the need, therefore, to protect the customs duty regime from fraud, one should not identify the objectives of the customs union with the essential institutional requirement that own resources be preserved. When the Commission sought to do that the Court of Justice made clear that:

> the protection of the financial interests of the Community does not follow from the establishment of the customs union, but constitutes an independent objective which, under the scheme of the [EC] Treaty, is placed in Title II (financial provisions)

---

[155] EC Treaty, Art 280.4.

[156] Ibid, Art 280.5.

[157] Recital (2) to Regulation (EC) 2700/2000 of the European Parliament and of the Council of 16 Nov 2000 [2000] OJ L311/17.

[158] See Commission Decision of 28 Apr 1999 establishing the European Anti-fraud Office (OLAF), notified under document number SEC(1999) 802, (EC) 99/352, ECSC, Euratom [1999] OJ L136/20. See Art 3 in particular.

[159] See: 'Protecting the Communities' financial interests and the fight against fraud—Annual report 1998' COM(99)590 final sections 2.2.1 (preferential tariffs) and 3.1 (transit system)

of Part V relating to the Community institutions and not in Part III on Community policies, which includes the customs union and agriculture.[160]

It followed that a regulation concerned with official mutual assistance and co-operation in customs and agricultural matters[161] could not be based upon Article 100a, now Article 95, but was properly based upon Article 235, now Article 308, which requires unanimity.

---

[160] Case C–209/97 *Commission v Council* [1999] ECR I–8067 para 29.
[161] Council Regulation (EC) 515/97 of 13 Mar 1997 on mutual assistance between the administrative authorities of the Member States and cooperation between the latter and the Commission to ensure the correct application of the law on customs and agricultural matters [1997] OJ 1997 L82/1.

3

Fundamental Concepts of the Customs Union

Having placed the Community's customs union in the context of Community law generally, we now turn to consider Community customs law itself. We begin with an examination of the nature of the Community's customs union and its relationship with the European Coal and Steel Community and the European Atomic Community. Then, after mentioning briefly the common customs tariff, which is considered in more detail in Chapter 5 below, we look at three matters which are essential to the internal aspect of the EC's customs union, namely, the prohibition of customs duties and charges having equivalent effect, the nature of goods for the purposes of the customs union and the meaning of goods in free circulation. Finally, we examine the territorial scope of the customs territory of the Community and identify the customs unions of which it forms part.

A. THE NATURE OF THE COMMUNITY'S CUSTOMS UNION

The nature of the customs union created by the EC Treaty appears from Article 23.1 which introduces a number of basic customs duty concepts. As we noted in Chapter 2 above, it states that:

> The Community shall be based upon a customs union which shall cover all trade in goods and which shall involve the prohibition between Member States of customs duties on imports and exports and of all charges having equivalent effect, and the adoption of a common customs tariff in their relations with third countries.

Article 23.2 then establishes that all products originating in the Member States and all products in free circulation in them are to benefit from the customs union and the elimination of quantitive restrictions on imports. The Article raises some matters of great significance. At the outset, it makes clear, of course, that a customs union was to be created and not a free trade area.

1. *A customs union not a free trade area*

As a preliminary point it should be noted that the creation of a customs union is plainly, as the Court of Justice has said,[1] consistent with the GATT. GATT's Article XXIV.5(a) states that subject to certain provisos:

---

[1] See Case 38/75 *Douaneagent der NV Nederlandse Spoorwegen v Inspecteur der invoerrechten en accijnzen* [1975] ECR 1439 at para 14.

. . . the provisions of this Agreement shall not prevent, as between the territories of the contracting parties, the formation of a customs union or of a free-trade area or the adoption of an interim agreement necessary for the formation of a customs union or of a free trade area . . .

The main proviso in relation to customs unions is that the duties or other regulations of commerce which are imposed are not 'on the whole' higher or more restrictive than the general incidence of such duties or regulations prior to the establishment of the union. This is important because, as we noted in Chapter 1, it is possible for customs unions to cause economic damage where this is not the case.

The GATT not only permits customs unions, it defines them, and the definition it adopts demonstrates why it is correct to say that the customs union 'is technically a concept of the EC Treaty'.[2] The definition in the GATT is as follows:

A customs union shall be understood to mean the substitution of a single customs territory for two or more customs territories, so that

(i) duties and other restrictive regulations of commerce [with certain exceptions] are eliminated with respect to substantially all the trade between the constituent territories of the union or at least with respect to substantially all the trade in products originating in such territories, and,

(ii) . . . substantially the same duties and other regulations of commerce are applied by each of the members of the union to the trade of territories not included in the union;[3]

This definition requires in (i) only that duties are eliminated with respect to substantially all the trade within the customs union and the elimination may be confined to substantially all the trade in products originating within the customs union. In (ii) the treatment of trade of territories outside the union is to be substantially the same. By contrast, the Community's customs union involves the absolute prohibition of duties and charges having equivalent effect on internal trade and that prohibition is not confined to products originating in the customs territory, but applies to all goods in free circulation within it. Furthermore, the Community is subject to precisely the same external tariff. There is no question of the external tariff being substantially the same throughout the Community. So far as concerns 'other restrictive regulations of commerce' as the GATT calls them, it should be noted that although quantitive restrictions are eliminated in the customs union by virtue of Chapter 2 of Title 1 on Free Movement of Goods, the provisions on the customs union itself, in Chapter 1, are not directly concerned with the elimination of quantitive restrictions. It has been said that:

---

[2] J Usher: 'Consequences of the Customs Union', ch 8 of E Emiliou and D O'Keefe (eds.), *The European Union and World Trade Law after the GATT Uruguay Round* (Wiley, Chichester, 1996) 10.
[3] Art XXIV, para 8(a).

the concept of a customs union as exemplified in the EEC Treaty means that third country goods should receive the same customs and commercial policy treatment wherever they enter the Community . . . and that within the customs union both goods produced within the Community and goods legitimately imported from third countries should be able to move from Member State to Member State without being subject to customs duties and charges equivalent thereto . . . without being subject to quantitive restrictions or measures equivalent thereto . . . and without being subject to discriminatory or protective internal taxation . . .[4]

This definition focuses on the practical effects of the EC Treaty within the customs union. This does indeed result in the abolition of quantitive restrictions, by virtue of Articles 28–31, and discriminatory and protective internal taxation, by virtue of Articles 90–93. Both these sets of provisions fall outside the provisions of the EC Treaty on the customs union and, as we saw in Chapter 2 above, are quite distinct from the prohibition of internal customs duties.

It is, nevertheless, the case that the Community's customs union requires a greater degree of integration between its members than the notion of a customs union necessarily implies.[5] This is no doubt because the customs union is itself part of a broader process of European integration. The extent of the integration required is thrown into sharp relief if one contrasts the Community's customs union with the definition of a free trade area contained in the GATT. This states that a free trade area is:

> . . . a group of two or more customs territories in which the duties and other restrictive regulations of commerce [with some exceptions] are eliminated on substantially all the trade between the constituent territories in products originating in such territories.[6]

A free trade area, therefore, lacks a common customs tariff, applies only to trade between constituent territories, and applies only to products originating in them. The comparison between this definition and the ambitions of the Community has been highlighted by Advocate General Jacobs who, in one case, having referred to the definition, said:

---

[4] See Green, Hartley and Usher, *The Legal Foundations of the Single European Market* (Oxford University Press, Oxford, 1991), 3 and Usher, n 2 above, at 105.

[5] It is, of course, a customs union within the GATT Art XXIV 8(a) as the Court of Justice has noted: see Case 266/81 *SIOT v Ministero Delle Finanze* [1983] ECR 731 at para 12.

[6] Art XXIV para 8 (b). The Court of Justice has referred to this definition on occasions. For example, in Case 270/80 *Polydor Ltd and RSO Records Inc v Harlequin Records Shops Limited and Simons Records Limited* [1982] ECR 329 at para 11, where the Court of Justice used it in construing the scope of the Agreement between the EEC and Portugal of 22 July 1972 [1972] OJ Spec Ed, L301/167. See also Case C–163/90 *Administration des Douanes et Droits Indirects v Legros and Others* [1992] ECR I–4625 in which the Court concluded that the prohibition of customs duties and charges having equivalent effect in the EC/Sweden Agreement (Council Regulation (EEC) 2838/72 of 19 Dec 1972 [1972] OJ L300/96) was to be interpreted as broadly as the comparable provisions of the EC Treaty.

By contrast, the EEC Treaty does not seek merely to establish a free trade area in the sense understood in the context of the Agreement but to achieve economic integration leading to the establishment of an internal market and to contribute together with the other Community Treaties to making concrete progress towards European union . . .[7]

As this quotation reminds us, the nature of the Community's customs union must be understood not only in the context of integration within the EC, to which we have already referred, but also in relation to the other Communities which may be briefly mentioned here.

2. *Euratom and ECSC*

The Community and the European Atomic Energy Community ('EURATOM') are both established by treaties for an unlimited period.[8] By contrast, the European Coal and Steel Community was established for fifty years from the date of the entry into force of the ECSC Treaty.[9] Consequently, it comes to an end at midnight on 24 July 2002.[10] The ECSC is also different from the EC and Euratom in that the latter two established customs unions,[11] but the former did not, preferring to establish minimum and maximum rates of duty instead of a common tariff.[12] Furthermore, the prohibition of customs duties, charges having equivalent effect and quantitive restrictions was not absolute but only 'as provided' in the ECSC Treaty.[13] Confirmation that the ECSC had not established a customs union was provided by the Court of Justice in *Mabanaft v Hauptzollamt Emmerich*.[14] Advocate General Slynn in his Opinion in that case noted that '. . . the ECSC Treaty . . . does not create a customs union within the definition of Article XXV (8)(a) of GATT and may be nearer to the definition of a free-trade area in paragraph 8(b) . . .' He went on to observe, however, that '. . . there are features of the ECSC Treaty which, even without reliance on the EEC Treaty, seem to put it into a separate category.'[15]

The Court, noting that the ECSC provided for freedom of movement for products which were in free circulation in the ECSC, as well as for those originating

[7] See his Opinion in Case C–312/91 *Procedural issue relating to a seizure of goods belonging to Metalsa Srl* [1993] ECR I–3751 para 15.
[8] See EC Treaty, Art 240 and Euratom Treaty, Art 208.
[9] See ECSC Treaty, Art 97.
[10] It is not proposed to explore the relationship between the three communities here. Account should now be taken, though, of further developments including the Nice Treaty which amends the ECSC Treaty and adds Protocol C on the financial consequences of the expiry of the ECSC Treaty and on the research fund for coal and steel, annexed to the Nice Treaty.
[11] Customs duties, charges having equivalent effect, and quantitive restrictions on imports and exports between Member States were abolished pursuant to Euratom Treaty, Art 93, whilst a common customs tariff was created pursuant to Art 94.
[12] ECSC Treaty, Art 72.
[14] Case 36/83 [1984] ECR 2497.
[13] Ibid, Art 4.
[15] Ibid, 2534.

there, considered that '. . . the ECSC does not constitute a free-trade area in which the origin of a product is a determining factor, but is more akin in its structure to the principle of a customs union.'[16] Both the Advocate General and the Court of Justice, however, agreed that the ECSC was not a customs union.

Despite the differences between Euratom and the ECSC, products within them both are within the common customs tariff of the Community. A common customs tariff for the purposes of Euratom had been in place since 1 January 1959[17] and the Euratom tariff has always been reproduced in the Community tariff. So far as the ECSC is concerned, it decided in 1986 that 'The Community provisions to ensure the uniform application of the nomenclature of the Common Customs Tariff shall apply to the products falling within the province of the ECSC Treaty.'[18]

Having examined the nature of the Community's customs union and its relationship to the other communities, we can now look at the essential features of the Community's customs union mentioned above.

B. THE COMMON CUSTOMS TARIFF

The Common Customs Tariff was imposed on 1 July 1968[19] and, as we have seen, is required pursuant to what is now EC Treaty, Article 23. Its administration and interpretation are considered in detail in Chapter 5 below. Here we set out some fundamental provisions relating to it, concentrating in particular on the extent of the limitations which it imposes on Member States.

According to EC Treaty, Article 28 'Common Customs Tariff duties shall be fixed by the Council acting by a qualified majority on a proposal from the Commission.' Article 29 then states that the Commission shall be guided by a number of considerations in carrying out the tasks which are entrusted to it. These are:

(a) the need to promote trade between Member States and third countries;
(b) developments in conditions of competition within the Community

[16] Ibid, para 22.
[17] See the Agreements of 22 Dec 1958 between the Member States on the establishment of a Common Customs Tariff for the products contained in List A1 and A2 of Annex IV to the Treaty establishing the European Atomic Energy Community: [1959] OJ 20/406–409 and 410–416.
[18] Decision 86/98/ECSC of the representatives of the Governments of the Member States, meeting within the Council of 3 Mar 1986 [1986] OJ L81/29: Art 1. For more detailed consideration of the tariff and Euratom and the ECSC see 'Problems under the ECSC and Euratom Treaties' in J Usher, 'Consequences of the Customs Union' in Emiliou and O'Keefe (eds), *The European Union and World Trade Law After the GATT Uruguay Round*, n 3 above.
[19] See Council Regulation (EEC) 950/68 of 28 June 1968 [1968] OJ L173/1. Entry into force on 1 July 1968 was prescribed by Art 4.

insofar as they lead to an improvement in the competitive capacity of undertakings;

(c) the requirements of the Community as regards the supply of raw materials and semi-finished goods (in this connection the Commission must take care to avoid distorting conditions of competition between member States in respect of finished goods);

(d) the need to avoid serious disturbances in the economies of Member States and to ensure rational development of production and an expansion of consumption within the Community.

Although it follows from the existence of a common tariff that there must be a prohibition on Member States imposing customs duties in respect of goods coming from third countries, the Treaty does not expressly outlaw the imposition of charges having equivalent effect to customs duties on imports into the Community from third countries, as it does in relation to movements of goods between Member States.[20] The internal prohibition and the Community's relationship with third countries are not comparable; the latter falling within the scope, as we have seen of the Community's commercial policy.[21] Nevertheless, it is plain that, following the establishment of the common customs tariff, Member States cannot themselves introduce such charges on goods imported directly from non-member countries.[22] In the words of the Court of Justice:

> Both the unicity of the Community customs territory and the uniformity of the common commercial policy would be seriously undermined if the Member States were authorized unilaterally to impose charges having equivalent effect to customs duties on imports from non-member countries.[23]

Furthermore, where an agreement which the EC concludes with a third country contains a prohibition on the imposition of customs duties and charges having equivalent effect to customs duties, the latter phrase is to be construed in the same way as it is in EC Treaty, Article 25. To quote the Court of Justice

---

[20] See Joined Cases 2/69 and 3/69 *Sociaal Fonds voor de Diamantarbeiders v S.A.Ch.Brachfeld and Sons* [1969] ECR 211, paras 28–32, referred to relatively recently in Case 36/94 *Siesse—Soluções Integrais em Sistemas Software e Aplicações Ld^a v Director da Alfândega de Alcântara* [1995] ECR I–3573 para 17.

[21] This was made particularly clear in Case 70/77 *Simmenthal SpA v Amministrazione delle Finanze dello Stato* [1978] ECR 1453 at paras 20–24, where the Court of Justice refused to transpose its jurisprudence on whether a charge for a service is a charge having equivalent effect to a customs duty, discussed below, to health inspection charges imposed in relation to trade with third countries. See also Case 30/79 *Land Berlin v Firma Wigei, Wild-Geflügel-Eier-Import GmbH & Co. KG* [1980] ECR 151 in which charges for inspections of goods brought into the Community were permitted, notwithstanding that inspections had been carried out and charged for in a third country, provided that the charges were proportionate and did not clearly exceed the cost of the inspections (para 16).

[22] Joined Cases 37/73 and 38/73 *Sociaal Fonds voor de Diamantarbeiders v NV Indiamex* [1973] ECR 1609, paras 18–22. Also referred to in Case C–36/94, n 20 above, at para 17.

[23] Case C–125/94 *Aprile Srl, in liquidation v Amministrazione delle Finanze dello Stato* [1995] ECR I–2919 at para 34.

in *Aprile* again: 'Those agreements would be deprived of much of their effectiveness if the term "charge having equivalent effect" contained in them were to be interpreted as having a more limited scope than the same term appearing in the Treaty . . .'[24] Whilst Member States not infrequently seek to impose customs duties, or charges having equivalent effect as between themselves, allegations that the Common Customs Tariff has been infringed are not, perhaps, so common. One of the more recent allegations concerned a Portuguese levy imposed on importers who failed to comply with the time limits applicable to the period for which goods may be in temporary storage. The Court of Justice had no difficulty, however, in concluding that such a specific charge could not be regarded as a customs duty or charge which undermined the unicity of the Common Customs Tariff.[25] Charges for health inspections have also been challenged, for example, in *Freistaat Bayern*,[26] in which it was established that the costs charged by Member States for services relating to imports from third countries could be higher than the costs for services relating to movements of goods within the Community.[27]

C. THE PROHIBITION OF INTERNAL CUSTOMS DUTIES AND EQUIVALENT CHARGES

As we have seen, EC Treaty, Article 25 prohibits, as between Member States, customs duties on imports and exports and all charges having equivalent effect. This prohibition, for reasons we noted in Chapter 2 above, cannot simultaneously apply to charges prohibited as illegal internal taxation pursuant to Article 90.[28] Where it does apply, it governs products which are in free circulation in Member States whether they originate in the Member States or come from third countries.[29] Despite the fact that the prohibition is wide its limitation to goods in free circulation is significant. It means, for example, that the

---

[24] Case C–125/94, n 23 above, at para 40. The Court relied upon Case C–163/90 *Administration des Douanes et Droits Indirects v Léopold Legros* [1992] ECR I–4625, para 26. See also pp 185–6 below. The same approach to the phrase is also adopted, *a fortiori*, where it appears in regulations providing for common organisation of agricultural markets and governing trade with third countries: see *Aprile* at para 41.

[25] Case C–36/94, n 20 above, para 18. Note also the Commission's recent decision to commence infringement proceedings against Greece regarding a tax on pleasure craft.

[26] Case 1/83 *IFG Intercontinentale Fleischlandelsgesellschaft mbH & Co. KG v Freistaat Bayern* [1984] ECR 349.

[27] Discussed further below.

[28] See Case C–212/96 *Paul Chevassus-Marche v Conseil régional de la Réunion* [1998] ECR I–743 para 20 referring to Case 193/85 *Co-Frutta v Amministrazione delle Finanze dello Stato* [1987] ECR 2085, paras 8–11.

[29] See Joined Cases 37 and 38/73 *Sociaal Fonds voor de Diamantarbeiders v NV Indiamex and Association de fait De Belder*, n 20 above, at paras 5, 8 and Case C–126/94 *Société Cadi Surgelés v Ministre des Finances* [1996] ECR I–5647 at para 13.

prohibition does not apply to goods which are in temporary storage prior to their release.[30]

Although the prohibition is wide, it may be thought that it became only of historical interest once the customs union had been established. In fact, it remains of great importance. It has rendered invalid national[31] and regional[32] duties as well as EC legislation.[33] The Court has quite rightly referred to the internal prohibition of customs duties and charges having equivalent effect, along with Article 9, now EC Treaty, Article 23, as having 'a crucial role in the construction of the common market'.[34] It has observed, in a frequently used phrase, that:

> The abolition as between Member States of customs duties and charges having equivalent effect constitutes a fundamental principle of the [c]ommon [m]arket applicable to all products and goods with the result that . . . any possible exception, which in any event must be strictly interpreted, must be clearly laid down . . .[35]

The prohibition of customs duties and charges having equivalent effect has proved crucial too in that it led the Court of Justice to develop the concept of direct effect. As is well known, in *Van Gend en Loos v Administratie der Belastingen* the Court concluded that 'according to the spirit, the general scheme and wording of the Treaty, Article 12 [now Article 25] must be interpreted as producing direct effects and creating individual rights which

---

[30] Case C–36/94 at para 16, where the Court of Justice held that a charge imposed on goods in respect of which the time-limits on temporary storage have not been observed was not within Art 9, as it then was.

[31] For recent examples see eg Case C–272/95 *Bundesanstalt für Landwirtschaft und Ernährung v Deutches Milch-Kontor GmbH* [1997] ECR I –1905 and Case C–109/98 *CRT France International SA v Directeur régional des impôts de Bourgogne* [1999] ECR I–2237.

[32] See for example Joined Cases C–485/93 and C–486/93 *Simitzi v Municipality of Kos* [1995] ECR I–2655, Joined Cases C–363/93, C–407/93, C–408/93, C–409/93, C–410/93 and C–411/93 *René Lancry SA* [1994] ECR I–3957 and Case C–163/90 *Administration des Douanes et Droits Indirects v Legros* [1992] ECR I–4265.

[33] For example, Regulation 816/70 Art 31(2) was held to be invalid in Joined Cases 80 and 81/77 *Société Les Commissionaires Réunis Sàrl v Receveur des Douanes* [1978] 927. It permitted Member States, subject to certain conditions, to take action to limit imports of wine from another Member State. In reliance on this provision, in 1975, the French government imposed a levy on imports of wine from Italy.

[34] Case 87/75 *Conceria Daniele Bresciani v Amministrazione Italiana delle Finanze* [1976] ECR 129 para 7.

[35] See, for example, Joined Cases 90/63 and 91/63 *Commission v Luxembourg and Belgium* [1964] ECR 625 and Joined Cases 80/77 and 81/77 *Commissionnaires Réunis v Receveur des Douanes* [1978] ECR 927, para 24; Case C–426/92 *Germany v Deutsches Milch-Kontor GmbH* [1994] ECR I–2757, para 51; Case C–272/95 *Bundesanstalt für Landwirtschaft und Ernährung v Deutsches Milch-Kontor GmbH* (n 31 above) para 35. For a case in which exceptions were permitted, see the Court's ruling on the new *'octroi de mer'* arrangements in Case C–212/96 *Paul Chevassus-Marché v Conseil régional de la Réunion* (n 28 above) in which it emphasized that it could not 'on any view, authorise a system of general or systematic exemptions which would amount to the reintroduction of charge equivalent to a customs duty, contrary to Articles 9, 12 and 13 of the Treaty' (para 37).

national courts must protect.'[36] Given the power of the prohibition, its significance in Community law, and the fact that traders may seek repayment of
charges levied contrary to Community Law,[37] it is important to consider the
nature of a customs duty or charge having equivalent effect.

1. *What is a customs duty or charge having equivalent effect?*

It has been said that the fact that the Treaty prohibits the imposition of a
customs duty or a charge having equivalent effect means that 'the more
restricted notion of the customs duty as normally understood has no independent importance . . .'[38] This is not absolutely true. A customs duty is always
prohibited whatever the purpose of its imposition and whatever the destination of the revenue raised. On the other hand, the purpose of a charge and the
use of the revenue raised may be relevant to whether or not a charge is one
having equivalent effect to a customs duty, as we shall see. It is, nevertheless,
the case that the definition of a charge having equivalent effect is, these days,
the more important definition in practice. As we saw above, a customs duty is
a duty imposed by the state by reason of the fact that goods cross a frontier and
is, consequently, an obstacle to the free movement of goods. A charge having
equivalent effect is also one which is imposed by reason of the fact that goods
have crossed a frontier and is similarly an obstacle to the free movement of
goods. It follows, of course, that only imported goods bear customs duties and
charges having equivalent effects to them whilst both imported goods and
domestic products bear internal taxation.[39]

The Court of Justice set out the basic definition of a charge having equivalent effect in the 1960s in a formulation which continues to be referred to in
contemporary cases and which Advocate General Jacobs has called 'a core
definition.'[40] It said that:

---

[36] Case 26/62 [1963] ECR 1 at 13. Cited in Case 17/91 *Lornoy and Ors v Belgium* [1992] ECR
I–6523 at para 24.

[37] See Joined Cases C–441/98 and C–442/98 *Kapniki Mikhailïdis AE v Idryma Koinonikon
Asfaliseon* [2000] ECR I–7145 at paras 27–42.

[38] Weatherill & Beaumont *EC Law* (3rd edn, Penguin, London, 1999) 458.

[39] Case 90/79 *Commission v France* [1981] ECR 283, para 13. Recently cited in Case C–109/98
CRT France International SA v Directeur régional des impôts de Bourgogne (n 31 above), para 11.

[40] See para 41 of the Joined Opinion of Advocate General Jacobs in Case C–90/94 *Haahr Petroleum
Ltd v Åbenrå Havn and others* Joined Cases C–114 and C–115/95 *Texaco A/S v Middelfart Havn* and
Olieselskabet Danmark amba v Trafikministeriet, Case C–242/95 *GT-Link A/S v De Danske Statsbaner
(DSB)* [1997] ECR 1–4085. The quotation appears in Case 24/68 *Commission v Italy* [1969] ECR
193 paras 9 and 11, Joined Cases 2/69 and 3/69 *Sociaal Fonds voor de Diamantarbeiders v S.A.Ch.
Brachfield and Sons*, n 20 above, paras 18 and 20. The definition was based upon Joined Cases 2/62
and 3/62 *Commission v Luxembourg and Belgium* [1962] ECR 425, at 432; Case 10/65 *Deutschmann
v Germany* [1965] ECR 469 at 473; and Case 7/68 *Commission v Italy* [1968] ECR 423. For examples
of other recent applications of the definition see, Joined Cases C–485/93 and C–486/93 *Simitzi v
Municipality of Kos* [1995] ECR I–2655, para 15; Case C–45/94 *Cámara de Comercio, Industria y
Navegación, Ceuta v Municipality of Ceuta* [1995] ECR I–4385, para 28 and Joined Cases C–441/98
and C–442/98 *Kapniki Mikhailïdis AE v Idryma Kononikon Asfaliseon* (IKA), n 37 above.

any pecuniary charge, however small and whatever its designation and mode of application, which is imposed unilaterally on domestic or foreign goods by reason of the fact that they cross a frontier, and which is not a customs duty in the strict sense, constitutes a charge having equivalent effect . . . even if it is not imposed for the benefit of the State, is not discriminatory or protective in effect and if the product on which the charge is imposed is not in competition with any domestic product . . .

It follows from Article 95 *et seq.* that the concept of a charge having equivalent effect does not include taxation which is imposed in the same way within a State on similar or comparable domestic products, or at least falls, in the absence of such products, within the framework of general internal taxation . . .

To this core definition one should add that an imposition which is suffered solely by reason of the frontier being crossed will be a charge having equivalent effect notwithstanding that it is imposed on a product at a stage of processing or marketing subsequent to its crossing a frontier.[41] Furthermore, a charge cannot escape the prohibition by reason of being proportionate to the quantity of goods rather than their value.[42]

If it may, at first sight, seem that only a relatively narrow category of charges is likely to fall under the heading of a charge having equivalent effect to a customs duty, then it should be emphasized that the prohibition is a wide one. In the following sections we consider a number of matters which advisers should bear in mind when considering the legitimacy of charges imposed upon their clients. We look first at regional duties; secondly at the impact the purpose of a charge may have on its legality; thirdly, the relevance of the identity of the payee; and finally, we consider the circumstances in which a charge for services is prohibited.

1.1 *Regional duties*

The extent of the prohibition on charges having equivalent effect to customs duties has been illustrated in the course of litigation over dock dues (*octroi de mer*) charged on movement of goods into the French overseas departments (*départements d'outre-mer:* 'DOM'). As a matter of French law, these constitute part of France.[43] The Court of Justice first had to consider whether or not the dock dues payable on cars manufactured in Germany and Sweden, and imported into one of the DOM from France with the benefit of transit procedures, amounted to charges having equivalent effect to customs duties or

---

[41] Case 78/76 *Steinike und Weinlig v Germany* [1977] ECR 595 at para 29.

[42] Case 87/75 *Conceria Daniele Bresciani v Amministrazione Italiana delle Finanze*, n 34 above, at para 9.

[43] In this section we refer to those cases in which the *octroi de mer* regime has been ruled inconsistent with the Treaty. Council Decision (EEC) 688/89 of 22 Dec 1989, [1989] OJ L399/46, providing for exemptions to the charges survived examination in Case C–212/96 *Chevassus-Marche v Conseil Régional de la Réunion* (n 28 above). See also Joined Cases C–37 and 38/96 *Sodiprem SARL* and *Roger Albert SA v Direction générale des douanes* [1998] ECR I–2039.

contravened Article 95, as it then was. As the dues were not imposed on goods originating in the DOM they did not constitute internal taxation. The issue before the Court, therefore, was whether they amounted to prohibited charges equivalent to customs duties under the Treaty or under an EC/Sweden Agreement. It was contended that they were not prohibited because they were not imposed by reason of the fact that a national frontier had been crossed. The Court of Justice concluded in *Legros* that:

> A charge levied at a regional frontier by reason of the introduction of products into a region of a Member State constitutes an obstacle to the free movement of goods which is at least as serious as a charge levied at the national frontier . . .

> The effect of such a regional levy on the unity of the Community customs territory is not altered by the fact that it is also charged on goods from the other parts of the territory of the Member State in question.[44]

For his part, Advocate General Jacobs said:

> I consider that the customs union envisaged by Article 9 [as it then was] implies a territory in which no [customs duties or charges having equivalent effect] are imposed anywhere within its borders. It would in my view be inconsistent with the objectives of the Treaty to regard the prohibition of charges having equivalent effect as confined to charges imposed by reason of the fact that a national frontier has been crossed, to the exclusion of charges imposed when a regional frontier is crossed.[45]

The decision of the Court of Justice related, however, to a regional charge imposed on goods moving between Member States. The fact that the charge was also imposed on movements within a Member State was acknowledged by the Court but regarded as immaterial.[46]

In *René Lancry SA*[47] the Court had to consider a number of cases which raised more directly the issue whether prohibited regional charges were confined to those imposed on the movement of goods between Member States, or whether regional charges were prohibited even in relation to movements within Member States. The Court held that the prohibition extended to the latter situation. In so doing, it had regard to certain practical matters, such as the difficulties of verifying the origin of imports. The main principle underlying the Court's decision, though, was that:

> Since the very principle of a customs union covers all trade in goods, as provided for by Article [23] of the Treaty, it requires the free movement of goods generally, as

[44] Case C–163/90 *Administration des Douanes et Droits Indirects v Léopold Legros* [1992] ECR I–4625 at paras 16 and 17.
[45] See the Opinion of the Advocate General at para 26.
[46] See n 44 above, para 18 of the judgment.
[47] Joined cases C–363/93, C–407/93, C–408/93, C–409/93, C–410/93 and C–411/93 *René Lancry SA v Direction Générale des Souanes and Société Dindar Confort, Christian Ah-Son, Paul Chevassus-Marche, Société Conforéunion and Société Dindar Autos v Conseil Régional de la Réunion and Direction Régionale des Douanes de la Réunion* [1994] ECR I–3957.

opposed to inter-State trade alone, to be ensured within the union. Although Article [23] et seq. makes express reference only to trade between Member States, that is because it was assumed that there were no charges exhibiting the features of a customs duty in existence within the Member States. Since the absence of such charges is an essential precondition for the attainment of a customs union covering all trade in goods, it follows that they are likewise prohibited by Article [23] et seq.[48]

In taking this approach the Court differed from Advocate General Tesauro who governed his approach to the issue by referring to the Court's established case law under which it declined to apply the rules regarding free movement of goods in situations internal to a Member State. This approach, however, treats the customs union as no more than an area in which free movement of goods between Member States is guaranteed. As the Court indicated, it is more than that.

Whether or not the Court of Justice had, in fact, developed its views in *Lancry* was a matter which came to be considered in *Simitzi v Municipality of Kos*,[49] in which the Court applied its reasoning in *Lancry* and held that a consumption duty, charged according to the value of goods on their entry into the Dodecanese from elsewhere in Greece, was prohibited as a charge having equivalent effect to a customs duty. Advocate General Tesauro indicated that, in *Lancry* he considered that the court had departed from its earlier case law by treating internal regional duties as prohibited.[50] The Court did not say so directly, but it is clear that it did not take this view because it chose the date of its judgment in *Legros* as the date in relation to which the temporal effects of its judgment should be limited and not the date of its judgment in *Lancry*. It considered that after the judgment in *Legros* the Greek Government must have been aware that the regional consumption duty was incompatible with Community Law.[51]

1.2 *The relevance of a charge's purpose and use*

As we saw above, it is the effect of the charge having equivalent effect, namely the fact that it is an obstacle to the free movement of goods, that renders it incompatible with EC law. It follows that it is essential to establish the true economic impact of a charge in order to determine whether or not it is one having equivalent effect to a customs duty. Throughout the EC, products attract a wide range of charges to a wide variety of government departments and administrative or trade bodies. Using the receipts obtained, the entity in question then provides services which are often for the benefit of a Member

---

[48] n 47 above, at para 29.
[49] Joined Cases C–485/93 and C–486/93 [1995] ECR 1–2655.
[50] See para 19 of his Opinion.
[51] See para 33 of the judgment. Note the views of Professor Dassesse: 'Regional Customs Duties and EC Law: 'The *Lancry* and *Dodecanese* Judgments' [1995/96] 1/3 *EC Tax Journal* 177.

State's domestic trade and traders, but not for the benefit of exporters who also pay the charge. In such circumstances, what may appear as a charge imposed under a general system of internal taxation, may in fact constitute a charge having equivalent effect to a customs duty.

The facts of the case of *Herbert Scharbatke GmbH v Germany*[52] provide a typical example of this kind of situation. Scharbatke operated a German slaughterhouse. It presented a number of slaughtered pigs, which it had imported from the Netherlands, for inspection. On presentation it was required to pay a compulsory contribution to a fund, the purpose of which was to promote 'the marketing and use of German agricultural, forestry and food products by opening up and developing domestic and foreign markets through the use of modern methods and techniques'.[53] In determining whether or not the charge was prohibited under the EC Treaty, the Court of Justice said:

> if the advantages stemming from the use of the revenue from a contribution which constitutes a parafiscal charge fully offset the burden borne by the domestic product when it is placed on the market, that contribution constitutes a charge having an effect equivalent to customs duties, contrary to Articles [23] and [25] of the Treaty. If those advantages only partly offset the burden borne by domestic products, the charge in question is subject to Article [90] of the Treaty.[54]

It is, of course, usually for the national court to determine whether there has been any offsetting in fact.[55] Nevertheless, the Court of Justice has given some guidance on when the burden of a charge can be regarded as fully offset. In *CELBI v Fazenda Pùblica*,[56] for example, the Court was concerned with a charge on sales of chemical pulp, payable to a Forestry Products Institute. This was a financially autonomous body which was intended to carry out a wide variety of functions in relation to the production and marketing of wood, cork, and resins. The Court was asked if the offset was to be understood as a monetary offsetting of the charge or whether it could be interpreted more widely. In reply, it pointed out that the cases concerned with offsetting relied upon the fact that imported products were bearing a financial burden not imposed upon domestic products. Therefore, it said:

---

[52] Case C–72/92 [1993] ECR 1–5509.

[53] Ibid, para 3 of the judgment.

[54] Ibid, para 10. See also, for example, Joined Cases C–78/90 to C–83/90 *Compagnie Commerciale de l'Ouest v Receveur Principal des Douanes de La Pallice Port* [1992] ECR I–1847 para 27, and Case C–17/91 *Georges Lornoy en Zonen NV v Belgium* [1992] ECR I–6523 , para 21. In Case 77/76 *Entreprise Fratelli Gucchi v Avez SpA* [1977] ECR 987 it was contended that partial set-off was sufficient to make the charge a customs duty but the Court of Justice rejected this submission: see para 19.

[55] See *Scharbatke*, n 52 above, at para 11. See also Joined Cases C–78/90–C–83/90 *Compagnie Commerciale de l' Ouest*, n 54 above, at para 28 and Case C–17/91 *Georges Lornoy en Zonen NV v Belgium*, n 54 above, at para 22.

[56] Case 266/91 [1993] ECR 4357 followed in Case 347/95 *Fazenda Pública v UCAL* [1997] ECR 1–4911 para 25.

the criterion of whether a burden is offset, in order to be usefully and correctly applied, presupposes a check, during a reference period, on the financial equivalence of the total amounts levied on domestic products in connection with the charge and the advantages afforded exclusively to those products. Any other parameter . . . would not provide a sufficiently objective basis on which to determine whether a domestic fiscal measure is compatible with the provisions of the Treaty . . .[57]

In order for a charge to be a charge having equivalent effect to a customs duty it is, though, not enough that it is fully offset. It must also, firstly, have the sole purpose of financing activities for the specific advantage of the taxed domestic product and secondly, the taxed product and the domestic product must be 'the same'.[58] This latter requirement is not as rigorous as it at first may appear. It is true that in *Lornoy*, Advocate General Tesauro relied upon *Gucchi* and *Interzuccheri* for the proposition that the products must be identical.[59] It seems clear, though, that he did not mean absolutely identical since he refers in this context to what is now, Article 90. This requires a comparison be made 'between products which, at the same stage of production or marketing, have similar characteristics and meet the same needs from the point of view of consumers'.[60] It is, therefore, the real economic impact of the charge which is to be taken into account. Continuing this concern with economic reality the Court has made clear that it is not necessary for a charge having equivalent effect to be imposed by the state.

1.3 *Prohibited charges need not be payable to the Member State*

It may be thought that as customs duties form part of the own resources of the Community passed to it by Member States, a charge having equivalent effect to a customs duty would also be charged by the state or an emanation of it. This is not the case. The charge may be made by an entirely private concern.[61] When the 'core definition' of a charge having equivalent effect to a customs duty, quoted at pp 62–3 above, says 'any pecuniary charge' it should be understood literally. In referring to charges having equivalent 'effect', EC Treaty Article 25 clearly directs attention solely to the economic results of the charge.

---

[57] Case 266/91, n 56 above, at para 18.
[58] Case 77/76 *Entreprise Fratelli Gucchi v Avez SpA*, n 54 above, at para 19 and Case 105/76 *Interzuccheri SpA v Dicta Rezzano e Cavasa* [1977] ECR para 12.
[59] n 54 above, 6534.
[60] Ibid. This formulation is used by the Court of Justice in Case 45/75 *Rewe-Zentrale des Lebensmitte-Großhandels GmbH v Hauptzollamt Landau/Pfalz* [1976] ECR at 194.
[61] This should be compared with the narrower position under Art 90 which does not cover charges paid to private bodies for private purposes. In Case 74/76 *Ianelli & Volpi SpA v Ditta Paulo Meroni* [1977] ECR 557, para 19, however, the Court of Justice made clear that the fact that duty is collected by a body governed by public law other than the state or is collected for its benefit and is a special charge or one appropriated for a specific purpose does not prevent it falling within, what was then, Art 95: Case 74/76 *Ianelli & Volpi SpA v Ditta Paulo Meroni* [1977] ECR 557 para 19.

Were it to do otherwise, the economic objectives of the customs union would
be capable of being defeated, (particularly now that many state functions are
being privatized). Advocate General Mancini made the point plainly enough in
Commission v Denmark.[62] Having referred to the 'core definition' of charges
having equivalent effect to customs duties, identified above, he said:

> If, therefore, the designation and mode of application of the charge are irrelevant,
> the fact that, . . . the sums paid by the importer are charged by private bodies which
> do not transfer them to the public administration is also irrelevant. What is relevant
> . . . is . . . the obstructive effect, albeit minimal, which the charge has on intra-
> Community trade.[63]

The facts of the case demonstrate perhaps how powerful the economic objectives of the customs union are. The Danish government wished to ensure that
the carcinogenic substance aflatoxin was not present in discernible quantities
in imports of groundnuts, or groundnut products, intended to be, or to form
part of, foodstuffs. It therefore passed an order requiring their import to be
subject to administrative authorization, granted on production of a certificate
of analysis issued by a private Danish laboratory. The charge having an equivalent effect to a customs duty was the payment made by the importer to the
private laboratory for the analysis.

1.4 *Charges for services may be prohibited charges*

Speaking very generally, a charge which represents payment for a service actually rendered to an importer, which is in proportion to the service, is not a
charge having equivalent effect. Nevertheless, charges for services may be
prohibited as is made clear by *Commission v Denmark*.[64] Of course, even if a
charge for services is not prohibited as a charge having equivalent effect to a
customs duty, and is consistent with Community freedoms,[65] it does not follow
that the charge is legitimately imposed. It may be prohibited under Article 90
EC Treaty, as we saw in Chapter 2.[66]

It is not, however, easy for a Member State, which is in any event allowed to
retain 25 per cent of its customs duty receipts to cover costs,[67] to impose
charges for services which escape the prohibition on charges having equiva-

---

[62] Case 158/82 [1983] ECR 3573.
[63] Ibid at para 18.
[64] Case 158/82, n 62 above, paras 18 and 19, Case C–130/93 *Lamaire v NDALTP* [1994] ECR
I–3215, para 14 and Case C–109/98 *CRT France International*, n 40 above, para 19.
[65] See eg the charges in Case 266/81 *SIOT v Ministère italien des finances and others* [1983] ECR
731 at paras 20 and 21.
[66] Case 90/94 *Haahr Petroleum Ltd v Åbenrå Havn and others* [1997] ECR I–4085, para 35. See
also Case C–209/89 *Commission v Italy* [1991] ECR I–1575, para 9 and Case 46/76 *WJ G Bauhuis
v The Netherlands* [1977] ECR 5, para 11. See also the reference to the Court of Justice in Joined
Cases C–34/01 and C–38/01 *Enirisorse SpA v Ministero delle Finanze* [2001] OJ C79/19.
[67] See Ch 2 above: 'The financial context of customs duty: own resources'.

lent effect to a customs duty. It must overcome at least three hurdles. First of all, it must establish that the activity carried out by the body in question, often some form of inspection related to quality of goods, health, the prevention of disease, or organization of trade, is consistent with the internal market. If the activity is inconsistent with the internal market it follows that one is not permitted to impose a charge for it. It does not follow, however, that because an activity is permitted under Community law a charge can be imposed. A contention that it could be was rejected in *Marimex v Amministrazione Finanziaria Italiana*,[68] in which a charge for permitted veterinary inspections on meat and animals passing from Germany to Italy was struck down as equivalent to a customs duty. If the activity for which payment is required is legal as a matter of Community law, a second condition must be met, namely, that the activity must be a service to the payee. Thirdly, if the activity is such a service, the charge imposed must be of an amount permitted under Community law. Each of these three elements is considered further below.

1.4.1 *Are the activities charged for required or permitted under Community law?*

Some activities for which payment is demanded are, of course, required under Community law and these may amount to services for which charges can be imposed. An example of such services are certain health inspections carried out under Community law, in the state of origin, which are valid for the whole of the Community, and are imposed by a Member State prior to the transfer of goods to another Member State.[69] Not all the activities which Member States wish to carry out, and to charge trader for, are required, or even permitted, under Community law. An example of a case in which charges were imposed in respect of activities not permitted under Community law is provided by *Deutsches Milch-Kontor II*.[70] Samples of powdered milk for testing were taken by the authorities from every lorry-load of powdered milk destined for transportation to Italy. This was held to be an infringement of freedom of movement of goods even though the inspections were carried out away from the national border[71] and the charges for the inspections amounted to charges having equivalent effect to customs duty. This was so notwithstanding that the charge corresponded to the actual costs of inspection.

---

[68] Case 29/72 [1972] 1309, 1319, followed in Case 87/75 *Bresciani v Amministrazione Italiana delle Finanze* [1976] ECR 129, at para 5.

[69] Case 1/83 *IFG Intercontinentale Fleischhandelsgesellschaft mbH & Co. KG v Freistaat Bayern* [1984] ECR 349 at para 9 and the cases referred to in it including Case C–46/76 *Bauhuis v The Netherlands* [1977] ECR 5. See also Case 340/87 *Commission v Italy* [1989] ECR 1483, para 21.

[70] Case C–272/95 *Bundesanstalt für Landwirtschaft und Ernährung v Deutsches Milch-Kontor GmbH* [1997] ECR 1–1905.

[71] Unlike the inspections in Case C–426/92 *Germany v Deutsches Milch-Kontor GmbH* [1994] ECR 1–2527 (*Deutches Milch-Kontor I*).

1.4.2 *Is the activity a service to the payee?*

Member States have not been slow to present their activities as services to traders and have been doing so since at least the 1970s. The Court, though, has consistently denied that something which is done by a public authority for the benefit of the general public as well as the trader concerned, is a service to the trader for which a charge may be made. The Court's approach was made clear, for example, in *Cadsky*.[72] An Italian 'exporter' of salad vegetables to Germany was required to pay for a quality control inspection of the goods and for the stamp which was affixed to them if they passed the inspection. Only goods passing the inspection could be exported. The Court had no difficulty in rejecting the contention that the charge was permissible. In the first place, it said that the inspection, coupled with the prohibition on export of goods failing it, could not constitute a service to the exporter. Secondly, even if the maintenance of the standard of produce encouraged exports generally, the individual interest of each exporter was so ill-defined that the charge could not be regarded as consideration for a specific benefit 'actually and individually conferred'.[73]

Soon afterwards it was the turn of importers to challenge the legality of certain Italian charges, this time for public health inspections of raw cowhides. The Court observed that:

> The activity of the administration of the State intended to maintain a public health inspection system imposed in the general interest cannot be regarded as a service rendered to the importer such as to justify the imposition of a pecuniary charge. If . . . public health inspections are still justified at the end of the transitional period, the costs which they occasion must be met by the general public which, as a whole, benefits from the free movement of Community goods.[74]

A similar approach had been taken in *Bakker Hillegom* in which the Court held that if plant inspections carried out under an international convention were for the benefit of exporters only, exporters could be required to pay for them. If, however, products intended not for export but for the home market derived even slight benefit from the inspections the charge would be equivalent in effect to a customs duty.[75] In *Commission v Belgium*,[76] the Court made clear that Belgian charges for the storage of goods in transit in specified warehouses were charges having equivalent effect because no service at all was rendered to the importer. First, the clearance facilities in question were linked solely with the completion of compulsory customs formalities so there was no actual service provided. Secondly, the facilities were provided in the interests of the

---

[72] Case 63/74 *Cadsky v Instituto Nazionale per il Commercio Estero* [1975] ECR 281.
[73] Ibid, para 8.
[74] *Bresciani*, n 68 above, para 10.
[75] See Case 111/89 *The Netherlands v P Bakker Hillegom BV* [1990] ECR I–1735 para 19.
[76] Case 132/82 [1983] ECR 1649, paras 13 and 14.

common market completion and of traders in general so that there was no individual conferment of anything.

At a time when it is increasingly common for governments to contract out to independent providers even essential functions, it is as well to note that the Court of Justice has held that a charge for carrying out customs or public functions is prohibited whether it is imposed by the state or by private undertakings pursuant to contract. In *Dubois and Général Cargo Services*,[77] forwarding agents challenged their obligation to pay a transit charge to the managers of an international road station at which the customs authorities had an office where customs clearance operations could be carried out. The charge covered the building and maintenance of a TIR vehicle park used by the customs authorities and the expenses of the managers, which were incurred in relation to the performance by the customs authorities and veterinary services of their public functions. The Court stated that a Member State was in breach of, what are now, EC Treaty, Articles 23 and 25, if it charged economic agents the costs of customs inspections and administrative formalities. It further held that whether those charges were imposed by measures adopted by the authorities or by a series of contracts was immaterial. The forwarding agents were, therefore, not liable to the managers of the road station for the transit charge.

If an authority establishes its right to levy a charge it must then proceed to demonstrate that the level of the charge is legitimate. This is something we consider next.

1.4.3 *Is the amount of the charge legitimate?*

To be permitted, the charge must be of an amount commensurate with the service. In relation to goods which originate in the Community, or which are in free circulation, it is clear that a Member State is allowed to pass on to traders the actual cost, but no more, of the service in question, for example, carrying out phytosanitary inspections.[78] There must be a 'direct link' between the amount of the fee and the costs of the service. Consequently, costs which are related to the length of time the service takes to carry out, the number of persons required to provide it, the costs of materials used, the overheads of actually carrying out the service, and similar factors may all be passed on to the trader.[79] Fees which are related, for example, to value or weight of the goods in question are not permitted.[80]

---

[77] Case 16/94 *Edouard Dubois & Fils SA and Général Cargo Services SA v Garonor Exploitation SA* [1995] ECR 1–2421.

[78] See Case 89/76 *Commission v The Netherlands* [1977] ECR 1355 para 16. For an example of a case in which the Court decided that the charges exceeded the cost, see Case 209/89 *Commission v Italy* [1991] ECR 1–1575.

[79] See Case 209/89 *Commission v Italy* [1991] ECR 1–1575 at para 10 and Case 111/89 *The Netherlands v P Bakker Hillegom BV* [1990] ECR 1–1735 at para 12.

[80] Case 170/88 *Ford España SA v Estado Español* [1989] ECR 2305.

A relatively narrow interpretation is placed, however, on the costs of carrying out a service. Such costs do not, for example, encompass the administrative costs which are necessary to put the service-provider in a position to carry out the service, unless the goods are coming into the Community from third countries.[81] So far as intra-Community trade is concerned, there is an obvious need to limit the costs which can be charged. The costs incurred by an inefficient Member State for providing a service will be greater than those incurred by the efficient Member State so making it cheaper to move goods into the efficient Member State and introducing a distortion into the common market. Where imports from third countries are concerned, however, charges are imposed in a different context and are permitted if they are sufficiently closely related to cost and are not more favourable than those levied in intra-Community trade.[82]

D. THE NATURE OF 'GOODS'

As we saw in Chapter 1, the agreements concluded at the end of the Uruguay Round ensured that the rules of the international trading community within the WTO were extended, by means of GATS, to cover the provision of services. Prior to that agreement, concern was concentrated on what GATT called primarily 'products'.[83] In contrast, the EEC was from the outset concerned with both goods and services, although services were, naturally, not within the customs union. EC Treaty, Articles 49–55 establish, as one of the fundamental freedoms of the EC, the freedom to provide services. 'Services' for these purposes are widely defined and Article 60 states that activities of an industrial or commercial character and the activities of craftsmen and of the professions are all included.

Inevitably, the Court of Justice has been required to draw the line between goods and services for the purposes of the fundamental freedoms.[84] Once identified, however, goods enjoy the benefit of the customs union as well as of the free movement provisions in the EC Treaty. EC Treaty, Article 23.1 states that it covers 'trade in goods' and Article 23.2 which, as we noted in Chapter 2 above, appears at the beginning of Title 1 headed 'Free Movement of Goods', makes clear that the provisions in Chapter 1 on the customs union, and in Chapter 2, on the elimination of quantitive restrictions, both apply to the same goods, namely products originating in Member States and those coming from

---

[81] Case 1/83 *IFG v Freistaat Bayern* [1984] ECR 349, para 17.
[82] Ibid, at para 13.   [83] See Art II 1.(b).
[84] See eg Case C–275/92 *Her Majesty's Customs and Excise v Schindler* [1994] ECR 1–1039, referred to below, in which the Court held that the sale of lottery tickets fell within Art 59 as it then was, concerned with services and not Art 30, concerned with goods. See also Case C–124/97 *Markku Juhani Läärä v Kihllakunnansyyttäjä and Suomen Valtio* [1999] ECR I–6067.

third countries which are in free circulation in Member States.[85] One may speak, therefore, of 'goods for the purposes of the Treaty' rather than merely goods within the customs union.[86]

1. *Treaty goods*

The fact that 'goods' constitutes a concept of the Treaty does not mean, however, that customs duty is chargeable in respect of everything which may be regarded as a good. The Court of Justice has ruled that the Community customs tariff:

> can only apply to imports of the product which are intended for an authorized use. Indeed, *ad valorem* customs duty cannot be determined for goods which are of such a kind that they may not be put into circulation in any Member State but must on the contrary be seized and taken out of circulation by the competent authorities as soon as they are discovered.[87]

The limitations defining goods subject to customs duty are not, however, extensive. The Court of Justice has confirmed that customs duty is not exigible only in respect of goods which by their very nature and by virtue of their special characteristics cannot be marketed or introduced into economic channels. That was not the case in relation to ethyl alcohol imported as contraband into the Community customs territory, on which liability to customs duty, VAT and excise duty could all arise.[88] CCC, Article 212 is also material in this context. It provides that, on the one hand, a customs debt cannot be incurred on the unlawful introduction into the customs territory of counterfeit currency or of narcotic drugs and psychotropic substances which do not enter into the economic circuit, strictly supervised by the competent authorities, with a view to their use for medical and scientific purposes. On the other hand, a customs debt is to be incurred even if it relates to goods subject to measures

---

[85] See also Case 41/76 *Suzanne Criel, née Donckerwolcke and Henri Schou v Procureur de la République au tribunal de grande instance de Lille and Director General of Customs* [1976] ECR 1921 paras 14–18.

[86] See Case C–2/90 *Commission v Belgium* [1992] ECR I–4431 para 23. See also para 18 of the Opinion of Jacobs A-G.

[87] Case 50/80 *Joszef Horvath v Hauptzollamt Hamburg-Jonas* [1981] ECR 385 para 11 (which was concerned with smuggled heroin) and Case 221/81 *Wilfried Wolf v Hauptzollamt Düsseldorf* [1982] ECR 3681, especially para 9. In *Wolf* the Court applied *Horvath* and noted that the approach of the Community is in conformity with The Single Convention on Narcotic Drugs of 1961, to which all Member States are parties (see United Nations Treaty Series 520, no 7515). See also Case 294/82 *Einberger v Hauptzollamt Freiburg* [1984] ECR 1177, Case 269/86 *Mol v Inspecteur der Invoerrechten en Accijnzen* [1988] ECR 3627 and Case 289/86 *Happy Family v Inspecteur der Omzetbelasting* [1988] ECR 3655.

[88] See Case C–455/98 *Tullihallitus v Kaupo Salumets* [2000] ECR I–4993 at para 19. See also Case C–3/97 *Criminal Proceedings against Goodwin and Unstead* [1998] ECR I–3257, re counterfeit perfumes; Case C–283/95 *Karlheinz Fischer v Finanzamt Donaueschingen* [1998] ECR I–3369, re the organization of illegal games of chance; Case C–111/92 *Lange v Finanzamt Fürstenfeldbruck* [1993] ECR I–4677 re the export of computer systems in unlawful circumstances.

of prohibition or restriction, on importation or exportation, of any kind what-soever.

It is plain that the concept of goods is not necessarily confined to goods used for the purposes of trade. Goods for private use or consumption are included.[89] In the late 1960s, the Italian government had contended that 'goods' for the purposes of the customs union were 'consumer goods or articles of general use'.[90] The Court rejected such a narrow view. In issue were articles having an artistic, historic, archaeological or ethnographic value on which Italy imposed a progressive tax in the event of their export to another Member State. The Commission alleged that this constituted an infringement of the EC Treaty, Article 16, since deleted, which obliged Member States to abolish between themselves customs duties on exports and charges having equivalent effect. The Court based its reasoning on the terms of Article 23, as it now is, and stated in terms which now appear too narrow that: 'By goods, within the meaning of that provision, there must be understood products which can be valued in money and which are capable, as such, of forming the subject matter of commercial transactions'.[91] The articles formed 'part of that vast market which the Treaty is trying to harmonise between Member States'.[92] It followed that the imposition of the progressive tax constituted an infringement of the Treaty.

Of course, all judicial statements must be read in context and, as Advocate General Jacobs has said, it is doubtful that the Court intended, in making the statement quoted above, to give an exhaustive definition of the term 'goods'.[93] The statement that goods be capable of being valued in money was made, as we have seen, in refutation of the submission that the customs union was confined to consumer goods and articles of general use, not that goods could have a nil or negative value. Goods with such a value can still fall within the scope of the Treaty. In *Commission v Belgium*[94] the Court held that even waste which is not recyclable and which is a health hazard can form 'goods' within the meaning of the Treaty. In the same case Advocate General Jacobs took a more modern and wider approach to the meaning of 'goods' saying: 'In my opinion . . . "goods" for the purposes of the Treaty must be taken to include any moveable physical object to which property rights or obligations attach (and which can therefore be valued in monetary terms, whether positive or

---

[89] See Case 215/87 *Schumacher v Hauptzollamt Frankfurt am Main-Ost* [1989] ECR 617 and Case C–362/88 *GB-INNO-BM v Confédération du commerce luxembourgeois* [1990] 1–667 at para 8.

[90] Case 7/68 *Commission v Italy* Case 7/68 [1968] ECR 423 at 426 and 428.

[91] Ibid at 428. Art 23.2 EC Treaty refers to 'products' originating in Member States or third countries, but there is no distinction between 'goods' and 'products' for these purposes as can be seen from the quotation cited above in which the Court has used the terms interchangeably.

[92] *Per* the Opinion of Gand AG, n 90 above, 433.

[93] Case C–2/90 *Commission v Belgium*, n 86 above, para 12 of the Opinion.

[94] Ibid, at paras 28 and 30.

negative).'[95] It should be noted that even these wide words do not purport to provide an exhaustive definition of goods but simply identify what the term 'goods' includes. The approach of the Advocate General is consistent with the views of the Court of Justice in *Cinéthèque v Fédération Nationale des Cinémas Français*.[96] In its judgment, in holding that the production of videos did not amount to the provision of services, the Court relied upon the fact that the production resulted in the manufacture of 'a material object'.[97] It did not refer to the need for the object to be moveable, though that must be the case given that the fundamental freedom which the EC Treaty seeks to establish is freedom of movement of goods. Neither was the issue of value considered, although it did note that the objects in question were the subject of a classification in the Common Customs Tariff. In the Advocate General's formulation, value is a secondary feature flowing from the attachment to the object of rights and obligations. It would seem, therefore, that strictly, in determining what 'goods' are for the purposes of the Treaty, one can exclude any reference to value at all and concentrate simply on the fundamental requirement of something which may be the object of rights or obligations.

That thing does not need, however, to be a physical object as usually understood. This is clear from the Common Customs Tariff itself which includes, for example, 'electrical energy' at CN 3716, as the Court of Justice noted in a judgment which confirmed that electricity falls within the scope of the provisions on free movement of goods.[98] Examples of other items within the tariff which would not ordinarily be called objects are petroleum gases and other gaseous hydrocarbons at CN 2711 and hydrogen and rare gases at CN 2804. Advocate General Cosmas was undoubtedly correct to state that 'electricity and natural gas are 'goods' for the purpose of Title I of the Treaty'.[99] If a product is not just a physical object, as commonly understood, it remains necessary for it to have a physical, and not just a legal existence. In 1991, the Court of Justice confirmed that intangible property, such as software, did not fall within the scope of the tariff, although it could form part of a 'good' when it was incorporated into it.[100] More recently, the Court has held that the right to fish does

---

[95] Ibid, at para 18. [96] Cases 60 and 61/84 [1985] ECR 2605.

[97] Ibid, at para 10, referred to by the Court in Case C–275/92 *Her Majesty's Customs and Excise v Schindler* [1994] ECR I–1039 at para 18. As is well known, in *Schindler* the Court decided that the import and export of goods (lottery tickets and advertisements) for the sole purpose of providing services (the lottery) forms part of the services themselves and is outside the scope of the rules on free movement of goods. The principles applied in *Schindler* were considered in Case C–124/97 *Läärä v Kihlakunnansyyttäjä and Suomen Valtio*, n 84 above.

[98] Case C–158/94 *Commission v Italy* [1997] ECR I–5789 at para 17 following Case C–393/92 *Municipality of Almelo and others v NV Energiebedrijf Ijsselmij* [1994] ECR I–477.

[99] Case C–157/94 *Commission v The Netherlands* [1997] ECR I–5699 at para 17.

[100] Case 79/89 *Brown Boveri & Cie AG v Hauptzollamt Mannheim* [1991] ECR I–1853 at para 21. See also Case 1/77 *Robert Bosch GmbH v Hauptzollamt Hildesheim* [1977] ECR 1473, para 4, in which the Court of Justice said that the tariff applied to tangible goods and not to processes, services and know-how.

not constitute a good for the purposes of the Treaty provisions on the free movement of goods.[101] Indeed, Advocate General Fennelly, in his Opinion on the case, considered that the inclusion of electricity as a 'good' was a special case justified by the fact that it competed as an energy source with gas and oil.[102] He pointed out, too, and the Court agreed, that intellectual property rights are not themselves goods for the purposes of the EC Treaty, although they are brought within the scope of the Treaty because of their economic effects.[103]

2. Community goods

In addition to 'goods', Community customs law also employs the concepts of 'Community goods' and 'non-Community goods'. These are defined in CCC, Article 4(7) and (8). Article 4(7) establishes three categories of 'Community goods'. The first category consists of goods which are wholly obtained in the customs territory of the Community[104] and which do not incorporate goods imported from countries or territories outside it. Goods obtained from goods placed under a suspensive arrangement are deemed not to have Community status in certain cases of special economic importance. The second category of Community goods are those imported from countries or territories not within the customs territory of the Community but which have been released for free circulation. Indeed, a release for free circulation confers on non-Community goods the status of Community goods[105] although that status can be lost in specified circumstances outlined below.[106] The final category of Community goods consists of those obtained or produced in the Community customs territory either from goods in the second category or from goods in the first and second categories.[107] Having reviewed these categories, it is easy to see why the Implementing Regulation, Article 313, provides as a fundamental rule, that all goods in the customs territory of the Community are to be deemed to be Community goods unless the contrary is established. Article 313 is, however, itself subject to exceptions and is considered in more detail in Chapter 10 below where we examine the proof necessary to establish that goods are Community goods.

[101] Case C–97/98 *Peter Jäägerskiöld v Torolf Gustafsson*, [1999] ECR I–7319 paras 36–39.
[102] Ibid, para 20.
[103] See para 21 of the Opinion and para 38 of the Judgment which refer to Joined Cases C–92/92 and C–326/92 *Phil Collins v Imtrat Handelsgesellschaft mbH* and *Patricia Im-und Export Verwaltungsgesellschaft mbH and Leif Emmanuel Krauf v EMI Electrola GmbH* [1993] ECR I–5145 at para 22.
[104] As specified in CCC, Art 23.
[105] CCC, Art 79. The Court of Justice confirmed that the purpose of release for free circulation is to confer the status of Community goods on non-Community goods in Case C–66/99 *D Wandel GmbH v Hauptzollamt Bremen*, [2001] ECR I–2579, para 38.
[106] CCC, Art 83.
[107] Note that CCC, Art 4(8), provides that non-Community goods are goods which are not Community goods.

Plainly, it is important for traders to be aware of the precise time at which goods cease to be non-Community goods and become Community goods. The Court of Justice has recently spelt this out in some detail in relation to non-Community goods declared for release for free circulation. It has said:

> if Article 10 of the EC Treaty (now, after amendment, Article 24 EC) is read together with Article 74 and the second paragraph of Article 79 of the Customs Code,[108] it is apparent that non-Community goods declared for release for free circulation do not obtain the status of Community goods until commercial policy measures have been applied and the other formalities laid down in respect of the importation of goods have been completed and any import duties legally due have been not only charged but paid or secured.[109]

The Court then went on to note that the formalities in question include the lodging and immediate acceptance of the customs declaration, the application of those measures in the CCC permitting the customs authorities to examine or analyse goods when verifying declarations and the grant of release for free circulation.[110]

E. FREE CIRCULATION

It has already been seen that it is important to know which goods are in free circulation in the Community because it is in respect of goods which are in free circulation that customs duties and quantitive restrictions as between Member States are eliminated.[111] Furthermore, the entry of goods into free circulation is the time at which a customs debt is incurred.[112] EC Treaty, Article 24 states that products are to be considered to be in free circulation in a Member State 'if the import formalities have been complied with and any customs duties or charges having equivalent effect which are payable have been levied in that member-State, and if they have not benefited from a total or partial drawback of such duties or charges.' Notwithstanding this definition of free circulation, the Court of Justice has had to consider what the phrase means in a number of cases. Many years ago, in *Donckerwolcke*, it emphasized that products in free circulation are to be understood as those duly imported into any one of the Member States in accordance with the requirements of what is now Article 24.[113] The effect of entry into free circulation is dramatic as the Court made

---

[108] CCC, Arts 79 and 74 are considered in the next section on free circulation.

[109] Case C–66/99 *D Wandel GmbH v Hauptzollamt Bremen*, n 105 above, para 36. It follows that the change in status is not a consequence of acceptance of a customs declaration: see para 45.

[110] Ibid, paras 37 and 38, Case C–66/99, n 109 above. One may express the conditions which have to be met in order for non-Community goods to become Community goods as conditions to be satisfied in order for goods to enter into free circulation. See below.

[111] EC Treaty, Art 23.2.　　　　　　　　　　　　　　　　　　　[112] CCC, Arts 201 and 209.

[113] See Case 41/76, n 85 above, at para 16.

clear in that case. Products originating in a third country which enter into free circulation in the Community are 'definitively and wholly assimilated to products originating in Member States'.[114] As late as 1990, however, in *Openbaar Ministerie v Houben*,[115] the Court had again to state that goods were in free circulation in the Community once import formalities were completed and duties were paid.[116] The fact that goods may have entered the first Member State under a Community quota does not alter the position.[117] Neither is it relevant whether or not the goods have been subject to the full rate of customs duty or whether or not they have been unloaded in the first Member State.[118] The terms of EC Treaty Article 24 are unambiguous. The entry of goods into free circulation cannot be made subject to conditions not contained in it. On the other hand, the entry of goods into free circulation in the Community does not necessarily mean that the goods can be freely marketed throughout the Community. For example, the rights of trade-mark holders must be respected.[119] Furthermore, in some circumstances free circulation may be limited pursuant to EC Treaty, Article 134. This Article recognizes that execution of the common commercial policy may be obstructed by deflection of trade and may lead to economic difficulties in Member States. To take account of these matters it permits the Commission to recommend methods for co-operation between Member States, and allows both the Commission and, in cases of urgency, the Member States to take protective measures. These urgent measures are, though, subject to the approval of the Commission. Accordingly, a Member State cannot by itself apply commercial policy measures so as to limit the movement of goods in free circulation.

    The CCC and the Implementing Regulation are also much concerned with

---

[114] See, ibid, at para 17.

[115] Case C–83/89 [1990] I–1161.

[116] See, ibid, para 10. See also Case 119/78 *SA des Grandes Distilleries Peureux v Directeur des Services Fiscaux de la Haute-Saône et du Territoire de Belfort* [1979] ECR 975 para 26. See also the quotation from Case C–66/99 *D Wandel GmbH v Hauptzollamt Bremen*, n 105 above, at para 36 above where the Court considered the requirements for goods to become Community goods. These requirements included the subjection of the goods to examination in an appropriate case. Where, therefore, 'the customs authorities have been unable to carry out an examination of goods, release of the goods cannot have been granted.': see, ibid, at para 39.

[117] See Case 288/83 *Commission v Ireland* [1985] ECR 1761 at paras 24 and 25; Case 199/84 *Procuratore della Repubblica v Migliorini and Fischl* [1985] ECR 3317; and Case 51/87 *Commission v Council* [1988] 5459 para 10.

[118] Case 69/84 *Remo Padovani v Amministrazione delle Finanze dello Stato* [1985] ECR 1859 at para 18.

[119] Case 51/75 *EMI Records Ltd v CBS United Kingdom Ltd* [1976] ECR 811 at 846 para 16. See also Case 86/75 *EMI Records Ltd v CBS Grammofon A/S* [1976] ECR 871. Council Regulation (EC) 3295/94. [1994] OJ L341/8, most recently amended by Council Regulation (EC) 241/99 of 25 Jan 1999, [1999] OJ L27/1, contains measures prohibiting the release for free circulation, export, re-export or entry for a suspensive procedure of counterfeit and pirated goods. The Court of Justice confirmed its validity and stated that its provisions apply to goods in external transit in Case C–383/98 *The Polo/Lauren Company LP v PT. Dwidua Langgeng Pratama International Freight Forwarders* [2000] ECR I–2519: see also Ch 10 below on the external transit procedure.

free circulation. CCC, Article 79 states clearly, in conformity with EC Treaty, Article 10, that release for free circulation shall confer on non-Community goods the customs status of Community goods. As appeared from EC Treaty, Article 23, entry into free circulation occurs only when import formalities are complied with and customs duty is paid. The requirement for duty to be paid before goods are released into free circulation is contained in CCC, Article 74.[120] So far as other requirements are concerned one, in particular, may be noted. Where goods are subject to favourable tariff treatment by reason of their end use, release into free circulation may be subject to written authorization.[121] It should also be noted that 'the entry of an article for free circulation must in principle be of an irreversible nature'.[122]

It does not follow, though, that because goods have been released for free circulation they are always free from customs supervision. As CCC, Article 82 makes clear, where goods which are subject to a reduced or zero rate of duty are released into free circulation they remain subject to customs supervision. Such supervision ends when the conditions permitting the zero or reduced rate cease to apply, where the goods are exported or destroyed, or where the authorities permit the goods to be used for purposes inconsistent with the application of a zero or reduced rate, subject to payment of duties.

The privileged status of Community goods which release for free circulation confers can be lost in a number of circumstances set out in CCC Article 83. The first situation is where the declaration for release for free circulation is invalidated after release. The second situation is where the import duties payable on the goods are repaid or remitted under the inward processing procedure in the form of the drawback system, in respect of defective goods or goods which fail to comply with the terms of the contract.[123] Finally, the status of Community goods may be lost in situations[124] where repayment or remission of duty is conditional upon the goods being exported or re-exported or being assigned an equivalent customs-approved treatment or use.

Given the privileges that Community goods enjoy and their significance in the context of the common commercial policy, it is important, in practice, to be sure who bears the burden of proving that goods are Community goods. This issue, as noted above, is addressed in Chapter 10.

Before concluding this brief review of the nature of free circulation, it should be emphasized that it is a concept that is not relevant solely to customs duty. This appears, for example, from Article 7 of the Sixth VAT Directive

---

[120] The declarant may request that the rate of duty is the rate which is applicable after the date the customs declaration is accepted and before release for free circulation where the rate is reduced after the making of the declaration, unless the delay in releasing the goods is attributable to the declarant alone: CCC, Art 80.

[121] See Implementing Regulation, Art 292.

[122] See the third recital of Council Regulation (EEC) 1430/79 [1979] OJ L175/1, which established a Community-wide system of repayment and remission of import and export duties.

[123] Pursuant to CCC, Art 238.   [124] Specified in CCC, Art 239.

which defines 'importation of goods'. It will be recalled from Chapter 2 that Article 2 of that directive subjects importations of goods to VAT. Article 7.1 states that an importation of goods occurs where goods enter the Community which do not fulfil the conditions set out in Articles 9 and 10, now of course Articles 23 and 24, of the EC Treaty, where the goods are covered by the ECSC Treaty are not in free circulation, or where goods enter the Community from a third country and do not fall within the above two categories.

F. THE CUSTOMS TERRITORY OF THE COMMUNITY

The customs territory of the Community is defined in CCC, Article 3. According to Article 3.1, it covers the territory of the Member States, with the following exceptions: the Faroe Islands, Greenland, Heligoland and Busingen, Ceuta and Melilla, the French overseas territories, and Saint Pierre, Miquelon, and Mayotte, the municipalities of Livigno and Campione d'Italia and the national waters of Lake Lugano which are between the bank and the political frontier of the area between Ponte Tresa and Porto Ceresio. There are specific provisions relating to the Canary Islands.[125] The Channel Islands and the Isle of Man are included along with the United Kingdom. CCC, Article 3 has been amended by regulation so that the precise extent of the Community customs territory has been altered in a number of respects.[126] The Åland Islands are no longer excluded from the customs territory now that Finland has made a declaration pursuant to EC Treaty, Article 99(5) as it now is and a reference to the exclusion of Saint-Pierre, Miquelon, and Mayotte has been inserted in place of one to the exclusion of '*collectivités* territoriales', alongside the reference to France.[127]

CCC, Article 3.2(b) originally included Monaco within the customs territory. Article 1.1(b) of the amending regulation confirms its inclusion by virtue of a Customs Convention of 18 May 1963. The position of San Marino, which was also originally included in the customs territory by virtue of CCC, Article 3.2(c), also required consideration. Recital (2) of the regulation states that it cannot be considered part of the customs territory. In fact, it appears that the Code was incorrect to bring it within the customs territory in the first place.

---

[125] These are contained in Regulation (EEC) 1911/91 [1991] OJ L171/1, as amended. So far as the Common Customs Tariff is concerned, Art 6 provided that this was to be introduced by 31 Dec 2000. Art 1 of Council Regulation (EC) 1105/2001 of 30 May 2001 [2001] OJ L151/1 provides that it is now to be introduced by 31 Dec 2001. On that date the authorization expires for the imposition of a tax on production and imports (APIM) on all products entering, or produced in, the Canary Islands.

[126] See Regulation (EC) 82/97 of the European Parliament and Council of 19 Dec 1996 [1997] OJ L17/1.

[127] See ibid, Art 1.1(a).

The status of San Marino had been made clear in a Council Decision of 27 November 1992.[128] This approved on behalf of the Community the Interim Agreement on trade and customs union between the European Economic Community and the Republic of San Marino. The agreement created a customs union between the Community and San Marino in respect of products covered by Articles 1–97 of the Common Customs Tariff, and excluded those products covered by the ECSC. No doubt it would be preferable for the exclusion of San Marino to have been made clear in the body of the regulation rather than in a recital to it. Its exclusion is, however, not in doubt. CCC, Article 3.3 makes clear that the terrritorial waters, the inland maritime waters and the airspace of all territories and Member States are within the customs territory, except where excluded by Article 3.1. Free zones and free warehouses are within the customs territory, but while Community goods are within them they shall be considered for import duty purposes as not being within the customs territory provided they are not released for free circulation or subject to unapproved procedures.[129]

As well as being founded upon a customs union, the EC has joined in customs unions. The most significant is one with Turkey effective from 1 January 2001 in respect of industrial products. The foundations for this were laid by Decision 1/95 of the EC–Turkey Association Council[130] which provided, amongst other things, that customs duties and charges having equivalent effect were to be abolished as between the EC and Turkey from 31 December 1995 (the date of entry into force of the Decision). Until 1 January 2001, Turkey was permitted to retain customs duties higher than those of the Common Customs Tariff in respect of third countries, for products agreed by the EC–Turkey Association Council.[131] The Community customs territory and the customs territory of Turkey constitute 'the customs territory of the Customs Union'.[132] The EC also has a customs union with Andorra for industrial products[133] and, as noted above, one with San Marino. The Association

---

[128] Decision (EEC) 561/92 [1992] OJ L359/13.

[129] CCC, Art 166.

[130] Made on 22 Dec 1995 [1996] OJ L35/1. The progress to customs union between the EC and Turkey is the subject of further decisions. See eg Decision 1/2001 of the EC–Turkey Customs Co-operation Committee of 28 Mar 2001 [2001] OJ L98/31, amending Decision1/96 laying down detailed rules for the application of Decision 1/95 of the EC–Turkey Association Council. The EC–Turkey Association Council was established pursuant to the EC–Turkey Association Agreement of 12 Sept 1963, approved by the Community by Decision (EEC) 732/64 of 23 Dec 1964 (Collection of the Agreements concluded by the European Communities, Vol 3, p 541). Art 5 of the Agreement envisages the creation of a customs union. See also the Additional Protocol and Financial Protocol to the Agreement of 23 Nov 1970. Title 1 Chapter 1 is concerned with customs union: [1977] OJ L361/60.

[131] Art 15 of the Decision.

[132] Art 3.3 of the Decision.

[133] See Art 2 of the Agreement in the form of an Exchange of Letters between the European Economic Community and the Principality of Andorra, 26 Nov 1990 [1990] OJ L374/14. It entered into force on 1 July 1991.

Agreements with Malta and Cyprus also provide for the eventual establishment of a customs union, in two stages, again for industrial products.[134]

It will be apparent that the Overseas Countries and Territories, ie those non-European Countries and Territories which have special relations with Denmark, France, the Netherlands, and the United Kingdom and are listed in Annex II to the EC Treaty, do not form part of the customs territory. They are governed primarily by Part Four of the treaty and their position is dealt with in Chapter 6 below.

Finally, it should be emphasized that the area to which the Sixth VAT Directive applies[135] ('the VAT single market') is not coextensive with the Community customs territory. The Channel Islands and the Canary Islands are within the Community customs territory but not within the VAT single market, by virtue of the Sixth Directive, Article 3.2 and 3.3 respectively. Article 3.3 of the the Sixth Directive also excludes from the VAT single market Άγιο Όρος which is within the customs territory.[136]

---

[134] See further Ch 6.

[135] See Art 3 of Council Directive EC 388/ 77 of 17 May 1977 [1977] OJ L145/1, as amended.

[136] For completeness it should be noted that the 6th Directive, Art 3.3 excludes from the VAT single market 'the Italian waters of Lake Lugano'. As noted above, CCC, Art 3 excludes 'the national waters of Lake Lugano which are between the bank and the political frontier of the area between Ponte Tresa and Porto Ceresio'.

4

The Customs Union: Legislation and Administration

Having looked at the foundations of the Customs Union, we now turn, briefly, to some of the legal instruments and administrative arrangements at the heart of it. We look in section A at the CCC[1], its nature, its contents, issues surrounding its amendment, and its application and interpretation. In section B the Implementing Regulation[2] is examined. Sections C and D consider the different roles of the Commission and the Member States respectively in the administration of the Community's customs duties' regime and the legal bases upon which their co-operation is founded. Having established the distinct roles of the Commission and the Member States, we look, in section E, at the level of co-operation between them. The chapter concludes with section F which contains some brief observations on the relationship between the trader and both the Commission and Member States.

As will be seen from the section on amendments to the CCC particularly, both the law and administration of customs duty continue to develop. The developments are guided to a considerable extent by what was the Customs 2000 programme, now known as Customs 2002, which is noted briefly in this chapter and in Chapter 14 below.[3]

It should be emphasized that the CCC and the Implementing Regulation are not, of course, the only sources of Community customs law. The Community customs tariff is of fundamental importance and is dealt with in the next chapter. International agreements with third countries are also of great significance. These are considered in Chapter 6. In considering all these sources of customs law it is essential to bear in mind decisions of the Court of Justice, not just in relation to customs duty measures but also in relation to the general principles of community law. The principles of effectiveness and equivalence as well as those of proportionality, the protection of legitimate expectations, legal certainty,[4] equal treatment, *force majeure*, and unjust enrichment are relevant just as much in relation to customs law as elsewhere.

---

[1] Council Regulation (EC) 2913/92 [1992] OJ L302/1 as amended.

[2] Commission Regulation (EC) 2454/93 [1993] OJ L253/1 as amended.

[3] Decision (EC) 210/97 of the European Parliament and of the Council of 19 Dec 1996 adopting an action programme for customs in the Community (Customs 2000), [1997] OJ L33/24 amended by Decision 105/2000 of the European Parliament and of the Council of 17 Dec 1999 [2000] OJ L13/1.

[4] For a relatively recent case in which a regulation imposing duty was annulled because it infringed the principle of legal certainty see Case T–115/94 *Opel Austria GmbH v Council* [1997] ECR II–37. The Court of Justice stated, at para 124: 'The principle of legal certainty requires that every measure of the institutions having legal effects must be clear and precise and must be brought to the notice of the person concerned in such a way that he can ascertain exactly the time

The CCC and the Implementing Regulation constitute a massive and somewhat inaccessible body of legislation although, recently, substantial steps have been taken to rationalize the law, particularly the Implementing Regulation, and the number of its Articles and Annexes has been reduced.[5] Yet, just as EC customs law is, to a large extent, a success substantively, it has some claim to be seen as a success so far as its form is concerned. It was not always so. In recent years, concern at the political distance between the Community institutions and EU citizens has resulted in repeated expressions of intention to simplify Community law pursuant to the SLIM programme. The need for simplification led to a recognition of the need to codify the law. In 1997, for example, the Commission adopted five consolidation proposals, involving the repeal of ninety-three legislative instruments and undertook the informal consolidation of 160 basic instruments.[6] It was as long ago as 28 February 1990, however, that the Commission presented a proposal for the codification of Community customs law. Originally intended to come into force on 1 January 1993, the CCC eventually came into force on 1 January 1994, although Title VII relating to aAppeals did not apply to the UK until 1 January 1995. As noted above, the CCC has been amended somewhat since its introduction and these amendments are dealt with briefly below. The CCC is implemented by a number of Commission Regulations, the fundamental one of which is the Implementing Regulation. This extensive piece of legislation has also been much amended and is itself now subject to proposals for consolidation. The Commission recognizes the need to ensure that the Code and its implementing legislation are easy to use in practice and has stated its readiness to publish annual updates of both.[7]

A. THE CCC

The scale of the project to create the CCC, consisting of 253 Articles and nine Titles, can be quickly seen from its pre-penultimate article, Article 251, which

---

at which the measure comes into being and starts to have legal effects. That requirement of legal certainty must be observed all the more strictly in the case of a measure liable to have financial consequences in order that those concerned may know precisely the extent of the obligations which it imposes on them'. See further the second recital to an Inter-institutional Agreement on common guidelines for the quality of drafting Community legislation quoted on p 87.

[5] See particularly Commission Regulation (EC) 993/2001 of 4 May 2001 [2001] OJ L141/1 and Commission Regulation (EC) 2787/2000 of 15 Dec 2000 [2000] OJ L330/1. Recital 15 in the former makes particular mention of the aim of reducing the number of annexes, by incorporating them in the text, combining them, or deleting them altogether. Recital 3 of the latter states that it seeks to create simpler and clearer transit rules.

[6] See EU General Report 1997 paras 1119–1120.

[7] See recital 16 to Regulation (EC) 82/97 of the European Parliament and the Council of 19 Dec 1996 [1997] OJ L17/1.

shows it has repealed twenty-six Council Regulations and two Council Directives, which themselves had been amended by subsequent legislation. It is not surprising that agreement on such a large project was reached only 'after decades of endeavour',[8] particularly as twelve disparate legal systems had to be taken into account in reaching a consensus. The CCC is undoubtedly a great achievement. As the Commission has noted:

> The Community Customs Code has brought about much more transparency than there was before it was established. It has been taken as a model by many third countries in Europe, and even beyond. Its role is to underpin several Community policies and provide a common framework for the operations of the national customs administrations.[9]

Faced with such a significant achievement it is perhaps not surprising that the European Economic and Social Committee has said that: 'The Customs Code made the single market a reality in relation to customs.'[10] Yet, without diminishing the extent of the Community's achievement in creating the CCC, it may be thought that this is a somewhat exaggerated claim. Two points may be briefly highlighted. First, in customs law, as in other areas of Community action, legal structures provide only the foundation for building the single market, they do not create it. That task falls to Community traders acting in conjunction with the relevant national authorities. In the field of customs law, considerable co-operation between the customs authorities of the Member States is required as well as an ability on their part to ensure that the law is interpreted and applied in an identical fashion throughout the Community. This is a state of affairs which has yet to be achieved. The Commission is conscious of the problems, as can be seen from its action plans Customs 2000 and Customs 2002,[11] but their existence continues significantly to impede the realization of a single market. Secondly, it should be borne in mind that there is still considerable scope for the application of the national law of Member States in customs matters. This is of particular significance in relation to provisions governing the enforcement and collection of customs duties and to penalties imposed for the commission of customs offences, a matter which is considered later in this chapter. Again, it must be said that the Commission is conscious of the difficulties but has not yet been able to persuade the Member States to eliminate them.

---

[8] Opinion of the Economic and Social Committee on the 'Proposal for a European Parliament and Council Regulation (EC) amending Council Regulation (EEC) 2913/92 establishing the Community Customs Code: [1999] OJ C101/6 at para 1.1.

[9] Para 3 of the Commission's summary contained in its Proposal for a Regulation, of 3 June 1998 [1998] OJ C228/8 considered further below.

[10] The Opinion of the Economic and Social Committee on the Proposal for a European Parliament and Council Regulation (EC) amending Council Regulation (EEC) 2913/92 establishing the Community Customs Code [1996] OJ C174/14, para 1.1.

[11] See n3 above.

1. *The nature of the CCC*

Before looking at what the CCC contains one should make clear that although the legislation resulted from a programme of consolidation, the CCC is not a pure consolidation measure, at least as that term may be understood by common law lawyers. The second recital to the CCC makes this clear. It states that the CCC:

> must incorporate current customs legislation, . . . [but] it is, nevertheless, advisable to amend that legislation in order to make it more consistent, to simplify it and to remedy certain omissions that still exist with a view to adopting complete Community legislation in this area.

Some of the amendments and other new provisions were of very great importance. So far as the UK is concerned, for example, those introducing a civil appeals procedure were particularly significant and led to an extension in the jurisdiction of what were the VAT tribunals. It is better, perhaps, to think of the CCC as 're-casting' customs law, to use the words of the EC Commission.[12]

Customs lawyers no doubt welcome the fact that the law in this area has received the early attention of the Community's draftsmen. From a drafting point of view, there is, as one would perhaps expect in relation to any extensive piece of legislation, some room for improvement. For example, a lack of clarity may sometimes be caused by a failure to use consistent phraseology. In *Firma Söhl & Söhlke v Hauptzollamt Bremen*[13] the use of three German phrases corresponding to 'manifest negligence' and 'obvious negligence' in the English version of the CCC gave rise to comment. The use of a single phrase would have avoided any need for the Court of Justice to rule that the words had the same meaning in the context in which they were used. On occasions too, the language of the English version of the Code is somewhat awkward. The Community recognizes, however, the importance of good drafting. So far as customs duty is concerned the Council passed a resolution on 25 October 1996,[14] ie after the CCC was fully applicable in the Member States, on the simplification and rationalization of the Community's customs regulations and procedures. The resolution recognized that 'in the highly competitive environment in which trade and commerce operate today, customs legislation needs to be more lucid and transparent, and customs procedures less cumbersome'. Amongst other things, it invited the Commission, in Article 1, in partnership with the Member States, to draw up a plan to simplify and rationalize customs regulations and procedures. Subsequently the Member States have noted that 'the quality of the drafting of Community legislation is crucial if it

---

[12] See the fourth recital to the preamble to the Proposal for a Regulation put forward by the Commission on 6 June 1998, [1998] OJ C228/8.

[13] Case 48/98 [1999] ECR I–7877.

[14] [1996] OJ C332/1.

is to be properly implemented by the competent national authorities and better understood by the public and in business circles'.[15] The declaration from which this quotation is taken has now given rise to an Inter-institutional Agreement on common guidelines for the quality of drafting of Community legislation.[16] The second recital of this is of particular significance in relation to customs duty and states:

> according to the case-law of the Court of Justice, the principle of legal certainty, which is part of the Community legal order, requires that Community legislation must be clear and precise and its application foreseeable by individuals. That requirement must be observed all the more strictly in the case of an act liable to have financial consequences and imposing obligations on individuals in order that those concerned may know precisely the extent of the obligations which it imposes on them.

Before turning to the contents of the CCC, it should be noted that as it and the Implementing Regulation take the form of regulations, their provisions take immediate effect in the domestic law of Member States. The use of regulations in the governance of the customs union is, of course, highly desirable and is now hardly a matter for comment. That itself is a mark of progress bearing in mind that directives were used for a considerable period after the creation of the customs union. For example, inward processing was governed by directive until 1 January 1987 and outward processing was regulated by directive until 1 January 1988.[17]

2. *The contents of the CCC*

Title I (Articles 1–19) contains, as may be expected, general provisions which set out some basic definitions, specifying, for example, the extent of the customs territory of the Community (which we have already considered).[18] It also sets out the crucial principle that, save as otherwise provided, Community customs rules shall apply uniformly throughout that territory.[19] Customs rules may, of course, apply even outside the customs territory within the framework of rules governing specific fields or international conventions. The remainder of the title is concerned with certain of the rights and obligations of traders and others. Specific consideration is given to the establishment of customs representatives, and the provision of information to customs author-ities and the provision of information and the making of decisions by customs authorities.

---

[15] Declaration on the quality of the drafting of Community legislation, No 39 adopted by the Inter-governmental Conference and annexed to the Final Act of the Treaty of Amsterdam.

[16] Of 22 Dec 1998 [1999] OJ C73/1.

[17] The relevant regulations were Council Regulation (EEC) 85/99 of 16 July 1985 [1985] OJ L188/1 and Council Regulation (EEC) 2473/86 of 24 July 1986 [1986] OJ L212/1.

[18] See Ch 3 above.   [19] CCC, Art 2.

Title II (Articles 20–36) deals with factors on the basis of which customs duties are applied. So Article 20 specifies that duties are to be based on the Customs Tariff of the European Communities ('the Tariff') and goes on to provide a definition of the Tariff, which is considered further in Chapter 5 . Not surprisingly, this has the combined nomenclature of goods as its fundamental, but by no means only, component. As well as the identification and classification of goods by reference to the Tariff, the origin of goods must be established and Articles 22–27 consider non-preferential and preferential origin. The origin of goods is considered in Chapter 7. Articles 28–36 are concerned with the remaining important feature of goods—their value. Article 28 lays down the basic rule that the customs value of goods is the price actually paid or payable for the goods when sold for export to the customs territory ('the transaction value'). The ascertainment of customs value may, however, frequently be a complex matter and the remaining articles of the title provide the foundation for a considerable body of law on this topic which is considered in more detail in Chapter 8.

Title III (Articles 37–57) contains provisions governing goods which are brought into the customs territory. The presentation of goods to customs authorities and summary declarations are dealt with. In addition, it is made clear that goods brought into the customs territory are subject to customs supervision until their status is determined or, in the case of non-Community goods (ie those which, amongst other things, have not been wholly obtained or produced in the customs territory[20]) until their customs status is changed, they are put into a free warehouse or free zone, or are re-exported or destroyed.[21] It is essential, too, for goods which enter the customs territory to be assigned a customs-approved treatment or use (unless a transit procedure is applicable).[22]

Title IV logically enough, is concerned with what is a customs-approved treatment or use and sets out conditions for each of them. It is the longest of the Titles starting at Article 58 and continuing to Article 182. First of all, it provides that all goods to be placed under a customs procedure shall be covered by a declaration for that procedure[23] and specific requirements are set out in relation to declarations. Article 78 gives customs authorities the ability to amend customs declarations after release of goods and the right to conduct post-customs clearance examinations of goods which enable them to be sure that the contents of the declaration are accurate. The title then contains provisions in Articles 79–182 on each of the eight customs procedures set out in Article 4(16). These are: release for free circulation, transit, customs warehousing, inward processing, processing under customs control, temporary admission, outward processing, and, finally, exportation. These procedures are considered in Chapters 10 and 11 below. The longest title is followed by the

---

[20] Art 4(7) and (8).   [21] Art 37.   [22] Art 48.   [23] Art 59.1.

shortest, namely Title V, which consists of Article 183. It provides that goods leaving the customs territory shall be subject to customs supervision. Title VI (Articles 184–188) is another short title and is concerned with relief from duties.

Title VII (Articles 189–242) is entitled 'Customs Debt' and, as its name implies, is concerned with all aspects of the debt incurred by traders. The topic is considered in Chapter 12 below but it may be noted that Chapter 1 (Articles 189–200) deals with the provision of security in respect of the customs debt. Chapter 2 (Articles 201–216) is concerned with the incurring of the customs debt. It provides rules for determining when a customs debt is incurred on importation or exportation. It specifies the debtor, providing that, in the event of indirect representation, the person on whose behalf the declaration is made is also liable for duty and establishing that where liability for the customs duty debt is imposed on several people, the liability is joint and several.[24] Following the rules regarding the liability of the debt Chapter 3 (Articles 217–232) deals with its recovery. Articles 217–221 set out the requirements for the entry into the accounts by the customs authorities of the amount of duty due, the time limits within which entry must be made, and the necessity for the amount of duty to be communicated to the debtor by the authorities. Articles 222–232 deal with the time limits within which payment of duty must be made, the deferment of payment, the enforcement of payment and the liability to interest on sums due. Chapter 5 (Articles 233–234) describes the circumstances in which a customs duty debt is extinguished and Chapter 6 (Articles 235–242) addresses the often difficult issue of repayment and remission of duty, which is considered in Chapter 13 below along with appeals. The CCC deals with the latter subject in Title VIII (Articles 243–246). It provides that any person shall have the right to appeal against decisions taken by the customs authorities which relate to the application of customs legislation, which concern him directly and individually.

The final Title, Title IX (Articles 247–253), is entitled 'Final Provisions'. Chapter 1, namely Articles 247–249, establishes the Customs Code Committee to assist the Commission. The Committee may adopt its own rules of procedure and may examine any question concerning customs legislation which is raised by the representative of the Commission which chairs it, either on their own initiative or at the request of a Member State.[25] Article 19 of the most recent regulation to amend the CCC[26] repeals the original CCC, Articles 247–249 and replaces them with new Articles, 247, 247a, 248, 248a, and 249. Under these new articles the Commission continues to be assisted by the Customs Code Committee but the Commission and the Committee advising it

---

[24] Art 213.　　　　　　　　　　　　　　　　[25] CCC, Arts 247a, 248a and 249.
[26] Regulation (EC) 2700/2000 of the European Parliament and of the Council of 16 November 2000 [2000] OJ L311/17.

are to operate according to the provisions of Council Decision (EC) 468/99[27] in carrying out their functions. This decision lays down the procedures for the exercise by the Commission of implementing powers given to it generally. It applies, of course, in customs matters amongst many others, and deals, in particular, with the operation of the committees which support the Commission in its work. It sets out different procedures pursuant to which the Commission is to operate, involving the European Parliament.

The new Article 247 provides that, in customs matters, the Commission is, very largely, to follow the regulatory procedure set out in Article 5 of the decision, as opposed to the advisory and management procedures referred to in Articles 3 and 4 respectively of it.[28] Under Article 5 the Commission is to be assisted by a committee composed of the representatives of the Member States and chaired by a representative of the Commission. When a measure is to be taken by the Commission, the Commission representative is to submit to the committee a draft of the measure in question. The committee then delivers its opinion on the draft within a time limit which the chairman may lay down according to the urgency of the matter. The opinion is to be delivered according to weighted majority voting of the representatives of the Member States and 62 votes in favour are required (the chairman does not have a vote).[29] Except in cases where the European Parliament has called into question the Commission's power to act, if the measures envisaged are in accordance with the opinion of the committee, the Commission is to adopt them. If the measures envisaged are not in accordance with the opinion of the committee, or if it does not deliver an opinion, the Commission must, without delay, submit to the Council a proposal relating to the measures to be taken and shall inform the European Parliament. The Parliament must inform the Council if it considers that a proposal is outside the powers of the Commission. The Council, for its part, may act by qualified majority on the proposal, within three months from the date of referral to it. If, on the expiry of that period, it has neither adopted the proposal nor indicated its opposition to it, the proposal is to be adopted by the Commission. If within that period the Council has indicated by qualified majority that it opposes the proposal, the Commission must re-examine it and may then submit an amended proposal to the Council, re-submit its proposal or present a legislative proposal on the basis of the Treaty.

In relation to the implementation of CCC, Articles 11 and 12 (which concern the provision of information by customs authorities and binding tariff information) and CCC, Article 21 (which concerns favourable tariff treatment

---

[27] Of 28 June 1999 [1999] OJ L184/23.

[28] The use of the regulatory procedure is subject to Arts 9 and 10 of Council Regulation (EEC) 2658/87 of 23 July 1987 [1987] OJ L256/1 as amended, discussed in Ch 5 below. It does not apply in relation to appeals or to the implementation of CCC, Arts 11,12, and 21, considered below.

[29] See EC Treaty, Art 205.2. This provision will be amended as a result of the Inter-Governmental Conference at Nice in Dec 2000.

by reason of nature or end use), the simpler management procedure set out in Article 4 of the decision is applicable. Under this procedure, the committee gives its opinion on measures which may be adopted by the Commission. The Commission then adopts measures which are to apply immediately. If, however, the measures do not accord with the opinion of the committee then the matter is communicated to the Council, which has three months from the communication in which to take a different decision, acting by a qualified majority. The Commission may defer the application of measures which are not in accordance with the committee's opinion for a period of three months from communication to the Council.

Chapter 2 of Title IX consists of Article 250 which, broadly speaking, specifies that the acts of the customs authorities of one Member State are to be given the same force in other Member States as if they had been carried out by their own customs officers. Articles 251 and 252 are concerned with repeals and amendments and the final chapter concludes with Article 253 which provides, amongst other things, that the CCC, subject to exceptions, is to apply from 1 January 1994. From the point of view of the UK the most significant exception was that Title VIII, concerning appeals, applied to it from 1 January 1995. The delay enabled the UK to transform its VAT Tribunals into VAT and Duties Tribunals pursuant to the Finance Act 1995, so giving the citizens of the UK, as we have already noted, a civil customs duty appeals procedure. After that, the CCC was fully applicable in all Member States.

3. *Amendments to the CCC*

In general, throughout this book, the provisions of the CCC are considered in the form which they take following the latest round of amendments by Regulation (EC) 2700/2000.[30] What follows are some general comments on the substance of amendments which have been made to the CCC since its introduction and on the procedures by which they have been introduced.

As we noted above, in recent times, amendments to the CCC have come to be associated with the fight against fraud. There have been, of course, many other concerns and developments which have necessitated amendments to it and its final article, Article 253, anticipated that amendments would be necessary. It required the Council to review the CCC before 1 January 1998, on the basis of a Commission report, with a view to adapting it to the achievements of the internal market. Those adaptions were effected pursuant to Regulation (EC) 2700/2000.[31] Prior to them, however, two other amending regulations

---

[30] A regulation of the European Council and the Parliament, of 16 Nov 2000 [2000] OJ L311/17. Amendments to the CCC have been introduced by giving new articles an existing article number plus a letter, so ensuring that the original numbering is not unduly disrupted.

[31] Despite the timetable set out in the CCC, a proposal for a regulation was submitted by the Commission to the Council on 8 June 1998: see [1998] OJ C228/1.

had proved necessary, in addition to the changes necessitated by the accession to the EC of Finland, Sweden and Austria.[32] The first of these was Regulation (EC) 82/97 of 19 December 1996.[33] This changed the boundaries of the customs territory slightly and implemented a number of other more important changes, such as extending traders' rights to remission or repayment of duty in the context of the inward processing procedure.[34] Two changes which were required by the agreements which brought the Uruguay Round to an end deserve particular attention. First of all, the provisions of the CCC were amended to take account of the fact that the Agreement on Agriculture required the abolition of agricultural levies.[35] The changes were made by, amongst other things, deleting from the definition of import duties and export duties, in CCC, Article 4(10) and (11) respectively, the reference to 'agricultural levies'. Secondly, the position relating to provision of information by customs authorities was improved. The CCC had from its introduction provided, in Article 12, for the provision of binding tariff information. Article 3(f) of the Agreement on Rules of Origin[36] extended the provision of binding information to cover information as to the origin of a good and the CCC was amended accordingly. The motivation for this change is made clear in the preamble to the Agreement on Rules of Origin which noted, amongst other things, that: 'clear and predictable rules of origin and their application facilitate the flow of international trade'. It also recorded the desire of members of the WTO: 'to ensure that rules of origin are prepared and applied in an impartial, transparent, predictable, consistent and neutral manner'.

The second regulation amending the CCC, Regulation (EC) 955/99 of 13 April 1999,[37] was the first amendment to be made under the new co-decision procedure between the Council and the European Parliament, introduced by the Treaty of Amsterdam. This regulation, together with a subsequent regulation of 16 November 2000, discussed below, constitute a fundamental revision of the CCC. Regulation No 995/1999 was concerned largely with the Community's external transit procedure, which enables non-Community goods to move around the Community without the payment of import duties[38] and followed the Commission's adoption of an action plan for transit in Europe on 30 April 1997,[39] which sought both to simplify and clarify the rules applicable

---

[32] See the Act of Accession of the Kingdom of Norway, the Republic of Austria, the Republic of Finland and the Kingdom of Sweden 1994 Annex I.XIII.A. introduced by Council Decision (EC) 1/95 [1995] OJ L1/1.

[33] [1997] OJ L17/1.

[34] See CCC, Art 128, considered in Ch 11 below.

[35] See Art 4 of the Agreement on Agriculture, Annex 1A, 'Multilateral Agreements on Trade in Goods' to the Marrakesh Agreement Establishing the World Trade Organization.

[36] See Annex 1A referred to in n 35 above.

[37] A regulation of the European Parliament and Council: [1999] OJ L119/1.

[38] CCC, Art 91. See Ch 10 below.

[39] Communication from the Commission to the European Parliament and the Council: Action plan for transit in Europe—a new customs policy: COM (97)188 final, [1997] OJ C176/3.

to transit. The regulation seeks to do this by, for example, defining the concept of discharge in relation to the transit procedure, and amending certain provisions concerned with guarantees. It also specifies the place at which the customs debt is incurred and makes the customs authorities of that place responsible for collecting the customs debt.

The third regulation to amend the CCC, as we have seen, was Regulation (EC) 2700/2000.[40] As the Commission's summary of the proposed regulation makes clear, whereas some previous amendments to the Code were intended to take account of external matters such as the Uruguay Round and external transit, these proposed amendments were focused on internal matters.[41] They are aimed at simplifying the rules and making them more flexible, particularly in relation to certain customs procedures and aligning customs rules with the imperatives of the internal market. Important changes were made in relation to customs declarations in that where they are made electronically, traders are now permitted to keep records at their premises, so dispensing with the need to present documents at the border.[42] The regulation also contained provisions to increase the flexibility of inward processing relief and seeks to speed up the authorization process upon which use of the relief depends by introducing a committee procedure to determine cases where certain economic conditions are met. Improvements were made in relation to processing under customs control, temporary importation, and outward processing. Provisions were also introduced permitting the supervision of unenclosed free zones which may now be controlled in the same way as customs warehouses. The regulation also provided that the running of the three-year period, during which communication to the debtor of the debt must be made, is to be suspended for the duration of appeal proceedings.

The most controversial amendments contained in the regulation relate to the circumstances in which late entry of duty in the accounts is prohibited.[43] Much attention was paid to the plight of traders who, having acted properly and in good faith, and having relied on inaccurate certificates of origin issued by third-country authorities, were confronted by post-clearance demands, for amounts of duty which, on occasions, threatened to bring down their businesses. The issue had significant implications for the level of the Community's own resources as well as for the financial circumstances of traders. As matters now stand, in circumstances where the preferential status of goods is established on the basis of a system of administrative co-operation with third-country authorities, the fact that a certificate of origin proves to be incorrect is to

---

[40] A regulation of the European Council and the Parliament, of 16 Nov 2000 [2000] OJ L311/17.

[41] See para 5 of the Summary attached to the Commission's proposal for the regulation COM (98) 226 final—COD 1998/0134, 3 June 1998 [1998] OJ C228/8.

[42] See CCC, Art 77.2, which the amending regulation added.

[43] See Chs 12 and 13 below.

constitute an error which could not be reasonably detected by the trader. Assuming that the trader has acted in good faith and in compliance with all the legislative provisions as regards his customs declaration the duty due is not to be entered late into the accounts. The issue of the inaccurate certificate is not, however, to constitute an error where, it is based on an incorrect account of the facts provided by the exporter. This may seem largely to negate the protection given to the trader. An exception to this rule is provided, though, where, in particular, it is evident that the issuing authorities were aware, or should have been aware, that the goods did not satisfy the conditions for preferential treatment. A person may plead good faith where he has taken due care[44] to ensure that all the conditions for preferential treatment have been fulfilled, but may not do so where the Commission has published a notice in the *Official Journal* stating that there are grounds for doubt concerning the proper application of the preferential arrangements by the third country in question. So far as notifications in the *Official Journal* are concerned, the Commission has stated its intention to publish, in the *Official Journal* C Series, a notice to importers explaining that there is reasonable doubt about imports of all or some products originating in a particular country which is a party to preferential tariff arrangements. The information in question will also be passed on to the competent administrations of Member States and the relevant authorities of the beneficiary country.[45]

It is important to note that the compromise represented by these provisions was reached with some difficulty. At one stage, the Commission took the view that proposals, made in the Council Working Group and the Committee of Permanent Representatives, would facilitate fraud. On 1 December 1999, it mandated the relevant Commissioner, Mr Frits Bolkestein, to withdraw the proposal to amend the CCC should the text, which was due to be agreed by the Internal Market Council a week later, not include sufficient safeguards against fraud.[46] The political intricacies of this particular situation cannot be explored here. It is important to note, however, that amending the CCC can give rise to difficult and protracted policy debates with considerable domestic political significance for Member States as well as problems in relation to the Community's own resources. This in turn means that the process of amend-

[44] The amendment does not define 'due care', and properly so because each case must be judged on its particular facts. In the ordinary case, however, traders should be in a position to show that they are aware of the rules of origin, have addressed problems, or potential problems, of which they are aware and have obtained written assurances from suppliers that the rules have been observed.
[45] See Communication from the Commission to the Council and the European Parliament setting out conditions, in the context of preferential tariff arrangements, for informing economic operators and Member State administrations of cases of reasonable doubt as to the origin of goods COM(2000)55 final, 8 Sept 2000, which contains a list of the main circumstances liable to give rise to reasonable doubt about origin; and COM402(07) of 23 July 1997 para 9.3.2. See further Ch 13 below.
[46] See the Commission Press Release of 1 Dec 1999 IP/99/926 which was headed 'To guard against fraud, European Commission may withdraw Customs Code proposal.'

ment may sometimes be long and difficult in a fast-moving commercial world. Consequently, it may fall to the Court of Justice to protect the honest and vigilant trader and, indeed, the Court did develop the law in relation to remission and repayment of duty, during the political debates about amending the CCC to protect traders, by allowing traders to rely upon errors of administration by the Commission.[47]

Inevitably, this most recent set of amendments to the CCC will not be the last and, quite apart from the need to adapt it, amendments are likely to follow from the revision of the Kyoto Convention referred to in Chapter 1.

4. *The application and interpretation of the CCC*

So far as the application of the CCC is concerned, according to CCC, Article 253, it mostly applies, as we have already noted, from 1 January 1994. It is well settled that, whereas procedural rules apply to all cases pending at the time that they enter into force, substantive rules do not usually apply to situations which arose before they entered into force, except to the extent that, in the absence of transitional provisions, such application clearly follows from their terms, objective, or general scheme.[48] The CCC contains no transitional provisions. Consequently, in one case the Court of Justice held that CCC, Article 239 does not apply to importations made prior to 1 January 1994, when the CCC entered into force, despite the fact that the relevant notices of recovery in the case were dated after 1 January 1994.[49] Of course, the CCC contains both substantive and procedural rules. Accordingly, it is possible for cases to arise in which the substantive rules existing prior to entry into force of the CCC are applicable alongside the procedural rules contained in the CCC, and in the legislation implementing it. An example of such a case is provided by *De Haan Beheer BV*,[50] which concerned a demand for customs duty made after 1 January 1994 in respect of a situation arising before that date.

---

[47] See the judgment of the Court of First Instance, given on 19 Feb 1998 in Case T–42/96 *Eyckeler & Malt AG v Commission* [1998] ECR II–401, appealed: see [1998] OJ C258/14 as Case C–163/98 P, but removed from register on 19 May 2000. See also the later judgments in Case T–50/96 *Primex Produkte Import-Export GmbH & Co. KG, and others v Commission* [1998] ECR II–3773, appealed: see [1999] OJ C1/11 as Case C–417/98 P, but removed from register, 10 May 2000, and Case C–61/98 *De Haan Beheer BV v Inspecteur der Invoerrechten en Accijnzen te Rotterdam* [1999] ECR I–5003.

[48] Joined Cases 212/80 to 217/80 *Amministrazione delle Finanze dello Stato v Srl Meridionale Industria Salumi and others* [1981] ECR 2735 at para 9 applied in Case T–42/96 *Eyckeler & Malt AG v Commission*, n 47 above, para 55 and 56. See also Joined Cases T–10 and 11/97 *Unifrigo Gadus Srl and CPL Imperial 2 SpA v Commission* [1998] ECR II–2231 para 18.

[49] See *Eyckeler & Malt AG v Commission*, n 47 above, at para 40 and Case C–97/95 *Pascoal & Filhos Ldª v Fazenda Pública* [1997] ECR I–4209, para 25.

[50] Case C–61/98 *De Haan Beheer BV v Inspecteur der Invoerrechten en Accijnzen te Rotterdam*, n 47 above. See also Joined Cases T–186/97, T–187/97, T–190/97 to T–192/97, T–210/97, T–211/97, T–216–2128/97, T–279/97, T–280/97, T–292/97 and T–147/99, *KauFring AG and others v Commission*, 10 May 2001.

Turning now to the interpretation of the CCC, it must of course be construed in the light of GATT 94 and regard should be had to the Court's statements on this matter discussed in Chapter 1 above.[51] The Court of Justice also has regard to the other international obligations which the Community has undertaken, such as the Kyoto Convention.[52] Being a Council regulation, the CCC is subject to the same rules of interpretation that apply to any EC regulation. It is not proposed to review these here in any detail. Matters such as legislative history are, of course, as important in relation to the CCC as to other legislation. One recent case in which the history of the CCC proved to be significant was *Giloy*.[53] The Court of Justice referred to the Commission's proposal for establishing the CCC[54] and the Opinion of the Economic and Social Committee[55] on the proposal, in considering the interpretation of Article 244 CCC dealing with the circumstances in which the decision of a customs authority may be suspended.

One issue which has particular significance for the interpretation of the CCC, in view of the fact that it is a 'consolidating' measure, is the relevance of judicial decisions given in respect of the legislation which the CCC supersedes. This issue had to be confronted in the recent case of *Firma Söhl & Söhlke v Hauptzollamt Bremen*[56] which was, in part, concerned with the difficult area of post-clearance recovery of duty. The Court stated that:

> it appears that the Customs Code brought together the provisions of customs law which had previously been dispersed in a large number of Community regulations and directives. When that happened Article 13 of Council Regulation (EEC) No 1430/79 of 2 July 1979 . . . was essentially reproduced in Article 239 of the Customs Code. Therefore, the case-law of the Court concerning the former must also apply to the latter.[57]

The fact that case law established prior to the coming into effect of the CCC can be relevant to the interpretation of the CCC is, of course, no reason to regard the regulation itself as relevant to situations which arose prior to the date from which it applies, namely 1 January 1994.[58] Not surprisingly, when the Court was asked to construe Article 201.3 in relation to a situation arising prior to 1 January 1994, it pointed out that the provision was new and that the importations in question were effected before it became applicable.[59]

---

[51] p 15.
[52] See in particular Case C–26/88 *Brother International GmbH v Hauptzollamt Gießen* [1989] ECR I–4253 at paras 15–21, considered in more detail in Ch 7 below.
[53] Case C–130/95 *Bernd Giloy v Hauptzollamt Frankfurt am Main-Ost* [1997] ECR I–4291.
[54] [1990] OJ C128/1, see also the amended proposal at [1991] OJ C97/11.
[55] [1991] OJ C60/5.   [56] Case C–48/98, n 13 above.
[57] Ibid, para 53. See also Case T–195/97 *Kia Motors Nederland BV and Broekman Motorships BV v Commission* [1998] ECR II–2907 para 33 and Joined Cases T–186/97, T–187/97, and others *Kaufring AG v Commission*, n 50 above, at para 26.
[58] Art 253.
[59] Case C–97/95 *Pascoal & Filhos Ldª v Fazenda Pública*, n 49 above. See also p 95 above.

A further issue that the Court has had to address relates to the approach to be adopted to differences in different language translations of the same provision of the CCC. The problem is one which the Court of Justice faces generally in relation to Community measures. Nevertheless, in *Firma Söhl & Söhlke v Hauptzollamt Bremen*[60] the Court was given the opportunity to state the general principles in the context of the CCC. It repeated that the need for uniform interpretation of Community regulations makes it impossible for the text of a provision to be considered in isolation. Instead it must be interpreted and applied in the light of all the other language versions.[61] Having reviewed the other linguistic versions of the provisions in question it noted that five used a single term in all the relevant provisions, some used two terms, some three, and some four. It concluded, therefore, that there was no particular reason for the use of different terms and that all should be construed in the same way.

B. THE IMPLEMENTING REGULATION

Just as the CCC was a consolidating measure containing various amendments to the pre-existing legislation, so too is the implementing legislation, contained primarily in Commission Regulation (EEC) 2454/93[62] as amended.[63] Originally containing 912 Articles and with over 100 Annexes, the regulation now consists of Parts I–V, including a Part IVa, which are broken down as necessary into titles, chapters, sections, and subsections. Part I (Articles

---

[60] n 13 above.

[61] See para 46 of the judgment which relied upon Case C–296/95 *The Queen v Commissioners of Customs and Excise, ex parte EMU Tabac SARL and Others* [1998] ECR I–1605, at para 36. See also Case C–253/99 *Bacardi GmbH v Hauptzollamt Bremerhaven* Judgment 27 Sept 2001 at para 41.

[62] Of 2 July 1993, [1993] OJ L253/1.

[63] Amended most recently by Commission Regulation (EC) 993/2001 of 4 May 2001 [2001] OJ L141/1, which applies almost entirely from 1 July 2001 and by Commission Regulation (EC) 2787/2000 of 15 Dec 2000 [2000] OJ L330/1. Points 2 to 80 of Art 1 of the latter Regulation apply from 1 July 2001 with some limited exceptions. See also Commission Regulation (EC) 1602/2000 of 24 July 2000 [2000] L188/1, Commission Regulation (EC) 1662/99 of 28 July 1999 [1999] OJ L197/25, Commission Regulation (EC) 502/99 [1999] OJ L65/1, Commission Regulation (EC) 1539/99 of 13 July 1999 [1999] OJ L178/2, Commission Regulation (EC) 46/99 of 8 Jan 1999 [1999] OJ L10/1, Commission Regulation (EC) 1677/98 of 29 July 1998 [1998] OJ L212/18, Commission Regulation (EC) 75/98 of 12 Jan 1998 [1998] OJ L7/3, Regulation (EC) 1427/97 of 23 July 1997 [1997] OJ L196/31, Regulation (EC) 89/97 of 20 Jan 1997 [1997] OJ L17/28, Commission Regulation (EC) 12/97 of 18 Dec 1996 [1997] OJ L9/1, Council Regulation (EC) 2153/96, of 25 Oct 1996 [1996] OJ L289/1, Commission Regulation (EC) 1676/96 of 30 July 1996 [1996] OJ L218/1, Commission Regulation (EC) 482/96 of 19 Mar 1996 [1996] OJ L70/4, Council Regulation (EC) 1762/95 of 19 July 1995 [1995] OJ L171/8, Council Decision [EC] 95/1, n 32 above, [1995] OJ L1/1, Regulation (EC) 3254/94 of 19 Dec 1994 [1994] OJ L346/1, Commission Regulation (EC) 2193/94 of 8 Sept 1994 [1994] OJ L235/6, Council Regulation (EC) 1500/94 of 21 June 1994 [1994] OJ L162/1, Commission Regulation (EC) 655/94 of 24 Mar 1994 [1994] OJ L82/15. Commission Regulation (EC) 3665/93, of 21 Dec 1993 [1993] OJ L335/1. See also Corrigenda at [2001] OJ L257/10 [2001] OJ L175/27, [2001] OJ L163/34 [1994] OJ L268/32, [1996] OJ L180/34, [1997] OJ L156/59, and [1999] OJ L111/88.

1–307) is entitled 'General Implementing Provisions'. It consists of eight titles, the first of which, in Articles 1 to 4c, is a definition chapter followed by some general provisions. Article 4c is introduced by the amendment to the regulation, made on 15 December 2000,[64] and permits Member States to waive the value declaration and take other steps to enable them to engage in international simplification test programmes to harmonize and simplify customs procedures.[65] Title II (Articles 5–15) concerns binding tariff information. Title III (Articles 16–34) dealt with favourable tariff treatment by reason of the nature of goods and has been deleted.[66] Title IV (Articles 35–140) contains important provisions on the origin of goods, the methods of establishing origin, and the role of certificates of origin. Title V (Articles 141–181) deals with the frequently difficult area of establishing customs value. Title VI (Articles 182–197) concerns the introduction of goods into the customs territory and Title VII (Articles 198–238) deals with the customs declaration. Title VIII (Articles 239–252) is entitled 'Examination of the goods, findings of the Customs Office and other measures taken by the Customs Office'. Title IX (Articles 253–289) is entitled 'Simplified Procedures' and deals with matters such as declarations for release for free circulation, declarations for a customs procedure with economic impact and export declarations.

Part II entitled 'Customs-Approved Treatment or Use' originally contained Articles 290–843. Following the introduction of Commission Regulation (EC) 993/2001[67] the legislation has been rationalized and Articles 593–787 dealing with customs procedures and Articles 815–840 dealing with free zones and warehouses have been repealed. It contains six Titles. Title I is concerned with release for free circulation and goes on to provide regulations for situations in which goods are admitted with favourable tariff treatment, or subject to reduced or zero rates of duty, by reason of their end use. As a result of the amendment to the Implementing Regulation on 15 December 2000, Title II is to be entitled 'Customs status of goods and transit' instead of merely 'Transit' so that its scope is clearer. Significant changes are made to the Community transit regime and to the provisions governing recovery of customs debts and guarantees in respect of goods in transit. As noted above, the regulation applies largely from 1 July 2001 as does Commission Regulation (EC) 993/2001. Title III entitled 'Customs procedures with economic impact'[68] is the title from which Articles 583–787 have recently been excised. It deals with customs procedures such as customs warehousing, the suspension of import duties in respect of inward processing, processing under customs control and

[64] n 63 above.
[65] The G7 countries are currently engaged in such an initiative: see Ch 1 above.
[66] By Art 1.4 Commission Regulation (EC) 1602/2000 of 24 July 2000, n 63 above.
[67] n 63 above.
[68] This phrase refers to customs warehousing, processing under customs control, temporary importation, and inward and outward processing: CCC, Art 84.

temporary importation. It then moves on to consider the suspension of export duties in respect of outward processing. The remaining titles contain provisions relating to permanent and temporary export, along with rules governing duty free-zones and free-warehousing. Part II ends with, amongst other things, some provisions governing re-exportation, destruction, and abandonment of goods.

Part III, covering Articles 844–856 and dealing with the exemption from import duties of returned goods, is a more manageable size. Part IV (Articles 857–912g), concerned with the customs debt, is more substantial. It contains four titles. Title I (Articles 857–858) deals with security for customs debts. Title II (Articles 859–867a) contains provisions relating to the incurring of the customs debt. Title III Articles (868–876) is entitled 'Entry in the Accounts and Post-Clearance Recovery', whilst the final title, Title IV (Articles 877–912) deals with repayment or remission of import or export duties. Part IVa containing Articles 912a–912g on controls on the use and/or destination of goods was added by Regulation 1602/2000.[69] Part V (Articles 913–915) contains the final provisions. It will be apparent that the Implementing Regulation has been amended a number of times since its introduction. The most recent amendments were made in July 2001 by Commission Regulation 993/2001[70] and deal with matters such as the modernization of customs procedures with economic impact and the rules governing free zones.

The procedure of adopting a Council Regulation which is then implemented by Commission Regulation is a very familiar one. In *Söhl & Söhlke v Hauptzollamt Bremen*, however, a trader supported by the German government, contended that the Commission had no power to provide, in Article 859 of the Implementing Regulation, an exhaustive list of the circumstances which were considered to have no significant effect on the correct operation of the temporary storage of goods or customs procedure in question and which, therefore, did not result in the imposition of a customs duty liability under CCC, Article 204.1. This provided the Court with an opportunity to state the legal foundations underpinning the Implementing Regulation as a whole. It returned to EC Treaty, Article 26 which provides, as we saw in Chapter 1, that the common duties of the customs union are to be fixed by the Council acting by a qualified majority on a proposal from the Commission. It noted that, in these circumstances, the Council could confer on the Commission powers for the implementation of the rules which it lays down. This power is given to the Council in the third intent to EC Treaty, Article 202. The fourth indent to Article 211 to the Treaty gives to the Commission the power to exercise the powers of implementation conferred on it by the Council.[71]

So far as the challenge to Article 859 was concerned, the Court noted that

---

[69] n 63 above.   [70] n 63 above.
[71] See para 32 of the judgment, n 13 above.

the Council had not reserved a power to create an exhaustive list of relevant circumstances, as envisaged by CCC, Article 204. Furthermore, it observed that, with certain irrelevant exceptions, CCC, Article 249 conferred on the Commission the task of adopting, pursuant to a procedure involving the Customs Code committee, the provisions for implementing the Code.[72] This article, said the Court of Justice, 'constitutes a sufficient basis for the Commission to adopt a set of rules for the implementation of the Customs Code and Article 204'.[73] The Commission did not require specific authority to act from the Council; a general power to do so was sufficient. Having laid down the essential rules governing the matter in question, the Council could delegate to the Commission without having to specify the essential components of the delegated power.[74] With the ability of the Commission to act established, the Court turned to consider the nature of the measures that the Commission could enact. Following established case law it concluded that the Commission was authorized to adopt all the measures which are necessary or appropriate for the implementation of the CCC, provided that they are not contrary to it or to implementing legislation adopted by the Council.[75] An examination of the provisions of the Implementing Regulation in question showed that they were validly enacted.

C. THE COMMISSION: CUSTOMS LAW AND ADMINISTRATION

Although the Member States have an important contribution to make to the creation and operation of the Community's system of customs duties, it will be apparent that the Commission has a crucial role to play in the making of legislation. It has a similarly crucial role at the heart of the administration of the customs duty regime.[76] For example, by virtue of EC Treaty, Article 28, it is the Commission which proposes to the Council the Common Customs Tariff duties. Its role is much wider than that, however. The Commission itself has said:

> The European Commission's main function as regards customs activity is to manage the customs instruments needed for the application of the European Union's common policies (commercial policy, agricultural policy, environment, public health etc.) for the purposes of controlling its external frontiers and guaranteeing the security of European citizens and fair trading for businesses in the internal market and economic and monetary union. This task of managing the customs union is the basis for measures by the Taxation and Customs Union DG aimed in particular at establishing a customs nomenclature, managing databases relating to

---

[72] See para 33 of the judgment.   [73] See para 35 of the judgment.
[74] See para 34 of the judgment.
[75] See para 36 of the judgment and the cases referred to in it.
[76] See also the comments on the Commission's role in relation to the determination of origin in Ch 7 below.

tariff arrangements and rules of origin, setting up a system for the exchange of information on controls and checks to fight fraud and irregular practices. . . .[77]

In carrying out its functions and in analysing the information it receives, the Commission is subject to a duty of good administration[78] and to the duties laid down in the EC Treaty, particularly Article 211, the first part of which states that 'In order to ensure the proper functioning and development of the common market, the Commission shall:–ensure that the provisions of this Treaty and the measures taken by the institutions pursuant thereto are applied.'[79] The duties of the Commission derive not just from the basic provisions governing the Community but also from specific legislation, for example requiring information to be communicated to it by Member States, and from international agreements.[80] Frequently, it alone is in a position to detect abuse of the Community customs system. Its failure to observe its duties can, as we see in Chapter 13 below, be relied upon by traders who wish to resist post-clearance recovery of customs duty.

As well as duties in relation to the administration of customs duty, the Commission, and indeed the Council, has significant discretions which it must exercise.[81] One area in which its exercise of discretion is important is in relation to applications for remission or repayment of customs duty (considered in Chapter 13 below). Another area of discretion, which gave rise to litigation, existed as a result of the Commission's power of appraisal in relation to the applicability or otherwise of reliefs from customs duty.[82] Under the existing legislation it is for the Member States to take decisions on the availability or otherwise of reliefs (see further Chapter 12 below), but the guidance of the Court of Justice in relation to the exercise of the Commission's discretion and

---

[77] The Commission's 17th Annual Report on monitoring the application of Community law, 1999, COM(2000)92 final [2001] OJ C30/1, at para 2.1.3.5.

[78] Note that Art 41 of the Charter of Fundamental Rights contains a right to good administration stating that 'Every person has the right to have his or her affairs handled impartially, fairly and within a reasonable time by the institutions and bodies of the union'. In contrast with this duty, the duty of good administration which is applicable in this context extends to the general quality of the work carried out.

[79] See Case T–50/96 *Primex Produkte Import-Export GmbH & Co KG, and others v Commission*, n 47 above, para 143.

[80] See ibid, paras 144 and 146 in relation to tariff quotas. Member States' obligations to keep the Commission informed of trade flows arise in other areas too, eg, in relation to imports attracting preferential rates of duty. The Commission also has a duty to monitor the implementation of some international agreements, see Joined Cases T–186/97 and T–187/97 and others *Kaufring AG and others v Commission*, n 50 above, at paras 257 onwards. The duty of diligence and good administration is, of course, a general duty imposed upon the Commission and is relevant to matters such as anti-dumping duties and competition law as well as customs duty: see eg, Case T–178/98 *Fresh Marine Company AS v Commission* [2000] ECR II–3331.

[81] For a consideration of the Council's discretion in relation to the suspension of customs duty see Ch 5.

[82] Case C–269/90 *Technische Universität München v Hauptzollamt München-Mitte* [1991] ECR I–5469.

the need to apply principles such as *audi alteram partem* remains of some considerable significance.[83] The Court said:

> where the Community institutions have . . . a power of appraisal, respect for the rights guaranteed by the Community legal order in administrative procedures is of even more fundamental importance. Those guarantees include, in particular, the duty of the competent institution to examine carefully and impartially all the relevant aspects of the individual case, the right of the person concerned to make his views known and to have an adequately reasoned decision. Only in this way can the Court verify whether the factual and legal elements upon which the exercise of the power of appraisal depends were present.[84]

Important as the Commission's responsibilities are in relation to customs duty, it does not act alone in this sphere. It must work with all Member States, the customs officers of which provide the human face of the Community customs duty regime.

D. THE MEMBER STATES: CUSTOMS LAW AND ADMINISTRATION

The role of the Member States in creating, and subsequently amending, the Community Customs Code is obvious. The Member States are, however, involved not just in creating Community customs law but in administering it. In the absence of a Community customs service, the Member States' domestic law and administration are essential to the functioning of the customs union. The basic principles pursuant to which the Member States act have been frequently set out by the Court of Justice. It has said in relation to the collection of customs duties that:

> in the absence of relevant provisions of Community law, it is for national legal systems of each Member State to lay down the detailed rules and conditions for the collection of Community revenues, although such procedures and conditions may not render the system for collecting Community charges and dues less effective than that for collecting national charges and dues of the same kind, or render virtually impossible or excessively difficult the implementation of Community legislation . . .[85]

The principles of equivalence and effectiveness that this quotation embody are, of course, generally applicable in Community law and Community

---

[83] The Court of First Instance itself considered Case C–269/90 referred to in n 82 above of importance in Case T–346/94 *France-aviation v Commission* [1995] ECR II–2841 at para 26. See for a more recent reference to Case C–269/90, in a competition matter, Case T–154/98 *Asia Motor France SA v Commission*, [2000] ECR II–3453 at para 54.

[84] See para 14 of Case C–269/90 at n 82 above.

[85] Joined Cases C–153/94 and C–204/94 *The Queen v Commissioners of Customs and Excise, ex parte Faroe Seafood Co. Ltd and Others* [1996] ECR I–2465 at 2534, para 66. The judgment referring the case to the Court of Justice is reported at [1994] 3 CMLR 65.

customs law. Other formulations of the principle have been employed in other areas of customs duty. In another case, for example, the Court of Justice said that:

> in the absence of Community rules governing a matter, it is for the domestic legal system of each Member State to designate the courts and tribunals having jurisdiction and to lay down the detailed procedural rules governing actions for safeguarding rights which individuals derive from the direct effect of Community law, it being understood that such rules must not be less favourable than those governing similar domestic actions nor render virtually impossible or excessively difficult the exercise of rights conferred by Community law . . .[86]

The development of these principles by the Court of Justice has resulted in a considerable body of case law.[87] One of the most recent cases, *Aprile II*,[88] concerns the recovery by the authorities of a charge having equivalent effect to a customs duty. The charge in question was for the cost of customs inspections carried out after normal business hours. In *Aprile I*[89] the Court of Justice found that the Member States were not entitled unilaterally to impose these charges in trade with non-member countries. In *Aprile II* Aprile then claimed repayment of the charges. The administration refused its claim, relying on a law which reduced the relevant five-year period of limitation to three years. (The limitation period in relation to claims between individuals was ten years.) The Court of Justice reviewed the cases in this area and held that there was no objection to a national provision imposing a three-year limitation period provided that the time limit applies in the same way to actions based on Community law for repayment as to those based on national law. Furthermore, the Member State could rely upon a time limit under national law even if, as was the case, it had yet to amend its national rules so that they were compatible with Community law.

---

[86] Case 48/98 *Firma Söhl & Söhlke v Hauptzollamt Bremen* [1999] ECR I–7877 para 66. See also the cases referred to in the para, eg, Case C–312/93 *Peterbroeck and others v Belgium* [1995] ECR I–4599, at para 12. In *Söhl & Söhlke* the Court decided that the national court could decide whether an extension of a time limit would have been obtained if one had been applied for within Art 859.1 of Commission Regulation (EEC) 2454/93 which refers to time limits allowed for assignment of goods to one of the customs-approved treatments or uses.

[87] The case law stretches from the early decisions in Case 33/76 *Rewe v Landwirtshaftskammer für das Saarland* [1976] ECR 1989 and Case 45/76 *Comet v Productschap voor Siergewassen* [1976] ECR 2043 to modern decisions such as Case C–312/93 *Peterbroeck v Belgium*, n 86 above. Case C–228/96 *Aprile Srl v Amministrazione delle Finanze dello Stato* [1998] ECR I–7141, Case C–326/96 *Levez v Jennings (Harlow Pools) Ltd* [1998] ECR I–7835, Case C–343/96 *Dixelport v Amministrazione delle Finanze* [1999] ECR I–579 and, more recently, Case C–228/98 *Kharalambos Dounias v Ipourgos Ikonomikon*, 3 Feb 2000 at para 58 and Case C–88/99 *Roquette Freres SA v Direction des Services Fiscaux du Pas-de-Calais*, 28 Nov 2000, particularly paras 20–29. For a review of this area see Ch 8 of *The General Principles of EC Law* (Oxford EC Law Library, Oxford University Press, Oxford, 1999) by Prof Takis Tridimas.

[88] Case C–228/96, n 87 above.

[89] Case C–125/94 *Aprile Srl, in liquidation v Amministrazione delle Finanze dello Stato* [1995] ECR I–2919.

The role of Member States was again highlighted in *Dixelport*[90] which followed *Aprile II*. Although primarily concerned with the right to obtain repayment of charges which were imposed contrary to Article 95, the Court made clear that there is nothing to stop a national administration from refusing a repayment of taxes or duties where that would result in the unjust enrichment of the recipients (where, for example, the liability has been passed on to third parties). Nevertheless, a rule of evidence, such as the presumption that the burden of charges has been passed on to others, with which the Court was concerned, and which made it virtually impossible or excessively difficult to obtain a repayment was contrary to Community law.

Member States do not merely act in areas where Community law is silent, such as in relation to the collection of customs duty. They act too in areas where their involvement is specifically envisaged by Community law. So, for example, they provide binding information to traders,[91] exercise their own discretion in administering the customs system,[92] and operate their own appeal procedures.[93] The significant role which the national law of Member States plays in relation to customs duty ensures that it is not yet possible for the fifteen customs authorities to act as one. One area where the diversity of national law has attracted particular attention, and which we have already noted, is the law of penalties for customs offences.

1. *Penalties for customs offences*

The Court of Justice has had to address directly the role and nature of national penalties for breach of Community customs law provisions. In *Commission v Greece*[94] it set out some of the applicable principles as follows:

> in the absence of harmonization of Community legislation in the field of customs offences, the Member States are competent to adopt such penalties as appear to them to be appropriate . . .[95] When making use of that competence they are,

---

[90] n 87 above.

[91] See CCC, Arts 11 and 12.

[92] One example of this is the discretion given to customs authorities to authorize certain goods for temporary importation where the absence of identification measures is not liable to give rise to any abuse of the procedure: see CCC, Art 139.

[93] CCC, Art 245.

[94] Case 210/91 [1992] ECR I–6735 at paras 19 and 20. The Court held that the Commission had not established the illegitimacy of a penalty, equal to 100% of the duty and taxes due, on importation of an allegedly concealed item in the personal effects of a traveller who would ordinarily have been entitled to claim relief from duty on account of the temporary importation of personal effects. See also Case C–36/94 *Siesse—Soluções Integrais em Sistemas Software e Aplicações Ldª v Director da Alfândega de Alcântara* [1995] ECR I–3573 paras 20 and 21, Case C–213/99 *José Teodoro de Andrade v Director da Alfândega de Leixões*, 7 Dec 2000 at paras 19 and 20 and Case C–262/99 *Paraskevas Louloudakis v Elliniko Dimiosio*, 12 July 2001 at para 67.

[95] The Court here referred to Case 50/76 *Amsterdam Bulb BV v Produktschap voor Siergewassen* [1977] ECR 137, para 33, and Case 240/81 *Einberger v Hauptzollamt Freiburg* [1982] ECR 3699, para 17.

however, required to comply with Community law and its general principles, and consequently, with the principle of proportionality.

... [T]he administrative measures or penalties must not go beyond what is strictly necessary for the objectives pursued and the control procedures must not be accompanied by a penalty which is so disproportionate to the gravity of the infringement that it becomes an obstacle to the freedoms enshrined in the Treaty . . .[96]

The penalties must be governed by procedural and substantive conditions which are analogous to those imposed in respect of infringements of national law of a similar nature and importance.[97] They must be 'effective, dissuasive and proportionate'.[98] In order to be proportionate a penalty must be necessary and appropriate for its purpose and the purpose must not be attainable in a less restrictive manner. Furthermore, the advantages pursued must not be disproportionate to the measure's onerous effects.[99] All these requirements derive from the general principles of EC law developed by the Court of Justice. It is worth noting, though, that it is possible for tax or duty penalties to constitute infringements of the fundamental freedoms established under the EC Treaty in appropriate circumstances.[100]

Clearly, the existence of fifteen national penalty regimes is inconsistent with the unicity which is implicit in a customs union. Although the Commission is well aware of this the Member States have been unable to take effective joint action.[101] The nature of penalties has been the subject of particular attention in the UK where civil penalties for excise duty were introduced as from 1 January 1995 but where customs duty penalties remained part of the criminal law. There are, however, advanced plans to introduce a regime of civil penalties. At the time of writing a draft statutory instrument entitled 'The Customs (Civil Penalties) Regulations 2001' has been published. It will apply to a person in relation to any conduct in which he is, or becomes, engaged after the day that it enters into force. Draft regulations 4 and 5 impose penalties for

---

[96] The Court here referred to Case 203/80 *Criminal Proceedings Against Guerrino Casati* [1981] ECR 2595, para 27; Joined Cases 286/82 and 26/83 *Luisi and Carbone v Ministero del Tesoro* [1984] ECR 377; and Case 68/88 *Commission v Greece* [1989] ECR 2965. The general principles of Community law, of course, include fundamental rights which in turn includes the rights of defence: see the Opinion of Fennelly AG in Case C–213/99 *José Teodoro de Andrade v Director da Alfândega de Leixões*, n 94 above, at paras 52–53.

[97] Case C–5/88 *Wachauf v Bundesamt für Ernährung und Forstwirtschaft* [1989] ECR 2609 at para 19. See also Case 36/94 *Siesse—Soluções Integrais em Sistemas Software e Aplicações Ldª*, n 94 above, at paras 20 and 21 and Case C–213/99 *José Teodoro de Andrade*, n 94 above, at para 19.

[98] Case C–177/95 *Ebony Maritime and Loten Navigation v Prefetto della Provincia di Brindisi and Others* [1997] ECR I–1111 at para 35 and Case C–213/99 *José Teodoro de Andrade*, n 94 above, at para 19.

[99] Case C–213/99, *José Teodoro de Andrade*, n 94 above, para 33.

[100] See the comments of Jacobs AG on the legality of excise duty penalties under Community law in his Opinion in Case C–247/97 *Marcel Schoonbroodt, Marc Schoonbroodt and Transports AM Schoonbroodt SPRL v Belgium* [1998] ECR I–8095 at para 49.

[101] See the references to penalties in Customs 2000, Decision of the European Parliament and Council 210/97/(EC), n 3 above, at Arts 5.5 and 13.

breaches involving evasion of customs duty of the greater of £5,000 or three times the relevant value of the goods in question. Draft regulation 6 imposes a penalty of £2,500 in respect of contraventions of any Community customs provision, subject to a defence of reasonable excuse. Provision is made for appeal to the VAT and Duties Tribunal.[102]

E. CO-OPERATION BETWEEN MEMBER STATES AND WITH THE COMMISSION

Given the important roles which the Member States and the Commission play in the customs duty regime, it will be obvious that co-operation between all of them is crucial to a properly functioning system which achieves its fiscal and commercial purposes. That co-operation has two particular limbs. First there is co-operation between Member States in relation to the recovery of customs duties. Secondly, there is co-operation with the aim of ensuring the proper application of customs law. These are considered in turn below.

1. *Co-operation in relation to recovery*

The first area is dealt with by Council Directive (EEC) 308/76.[103] It is used mainly in relation to VAT and had been regarded by the Member States as unsatisfactory although, as noted below, the regime established by the Directive has been improved somewhat.[104] To date, however, no extensive alterations have been effected.

---

[102] It is understood that the introduction of a civil penalty regime has been somewhat delayed pending the resolution of litigation about whether certain VAT penalties for dishonesty amount to criminal charges within the European Convention on Human Rights, Art 6. The Court of Appeal has ruled that they do: see *Commissioners of Customs and Excise v Han and Yau* [2001] STC 1188. Leave to appeal to the House of Lords has been granted. See also the decision of the European Court of Human Rights in *Georgiou v UK*, Appl No 40042/98 [2001] STC 80.

[103] Of 15 Mar 1976, on mutual assistance for the recovery of claims relating to certain levies, duties, taxes, and other measures [1976] OJ L73/18. The Directive is implemented in the UK by the Finance Act 1977, s 11 and Finance Act 1980, s 17. It has been amended by Council Directive (EEC) 1071/79 of 6 Dec 1979, [1979] OJ L331/10, which extended the scope of the directive to cover VAT, Council Directive (EEC) 108/92 of 14 Dec 1992, [1992] OJ L390/124, which extended it to cover certain excise duties, and Council Directive (EC) 44/2001 [2001] OJ L175/1, which extended it to cover certain taxes on income and capital and taxes on insurance premiums. It also improved the mutual assistance procedure in a number of respects, making it easier to operate and more efficient. Member States have until 30 June 2002 to transpose it into domestic law. The directive was implemented by Commission Directives (EEC) 1977/794 of 4 Nov 1977 [1977] OJ L333/11, Commission Directive (EEC) 479/85 of 14 Oct 1985 [1985] OJ L285/65, and Commission Directive (EEC) 498/86 of 24 Sept 1986 [1986] OJ L283/23, which raised to ECU 1500 the size of claims subject to the mutual assistance procedure.

[104] See Communication from the Commission to the European Parliament and the Council on a strategy for the better functioning of mutual assistance on recovery including a Proposal for a European Parliament and Council Directive amending the basic directive COM(1998)364 final, 25 June 1998 para 2.2. The Commission indicated in June 1998 that, since 1993, approximately 1,000 requests had been sent every year with an estimated total value of ECU 50 million: see para 2.2 of the Communication.

Nevertheless, it is worth noting that the directive created a Committee of Recovery on which all Member States are represented and established two methods of co-operation. The first method of assistance, in Article 4, enables an applicant authority to obtain from another authority in another Member State 'any information which would be useful' to the applicant authority in the recovery of a claim for customs duty which it is making. The request may relate to the debtor, to any person liable for the settlement of the claim in the applicant's Member State, or to a third party holding the assets of either.[105] The authority in receipt of the request is to make use of the powers available in respect of similar claims arising in its own state. The recipient authority is not obliged to supply information which it would be unable to obtain for the purpose of similar recovery claims in its own state. It is also not obliged to disclose any commercial, industrial, or professional secrets. Neither is it obliged to disclose anything which would be liable to prejudice security or be contrary to public policy. The second method of co-operation is contained in Article 6. This provides that one authority may request another to recover customs duty claims, in the latter's state, which are the subject of an instrument permitting their enforcement. An authority may not make a request for recovery unless the claim and/or the instrument permitting its enforcement are not contested in the Member State in which it is situated and it has, in its own Member State, applied such recovery procedures as are available to it without full success.[106] An authority is not obliged to assist an applicant authority under this second method of co-operation if the recovery of the claim would, because of the situation of the debtor, create serious economic or social difficulties in the Member State in which the authority is situated. Neither is it obliged to assist the applicant if the latter has not exhausted the means of recovery in its own Member State.[107]

2. *Co-operation in relation to the application of customs law*

The second area of co-operation, namely mutual assistance between the Commission and Member States, and between the Member States themselves, to ensure the correct application of customs law, has been more successful. The first Community measure concerned with this was passed in May 1981.[108] The current measure was passed in March 1997.[109] This created a

---

[105] Commission Regulation (EEC) 794/77, n 103 above, Art 3.

[106] See the Directive at n 103 above, Art 7.2. Under Council Directive (EC) 44/2001, n 103 above, the terms of Art 7.2 are amended to widen the circumstances in which a request may be made.

[107] Art 14. The terms of Art 14 are narrowed by amendments introduced under Council Directive (EC) 44/2001, n 103 above.

[108] Council Regulation (EEC) 1468/81 of May 1981, [1981] OJ L144/1, amended by Council Regulation (EEC) 945/87 [1987] OJ L90/3.

[109] Council Regulation (EEC) 515/97 of 13 Mar 1997 [1997] OJ L82/1, held valid in Case C–209/97 *Commission v Council* [1999] ECR I–8067. It was implemented by Commission Regulation (EC) 696/98 of 27 Mar 1998 [1998] OJ L96/22.

new legislative foundation for mutual assistance, increased the level of information which the Commission obtained from Member States and, importantly, provided for the creation of a Customs Information System. As between Member States, the regulation provides for assistance on request (Articles 4–12: Title I) and spontaneous assistance (Articles 13–16: Title II). So far as assistance on request is concerned, the requested authority is obliged to transmit any information, or supply certain documents or information, which may enable the applicant authority to ensure compliance with the provisions of customs or agricultural legislation, and in particular with legislation on certain matters such as the application of customs duties and charges having equivalent effect. In addition, a Member State may request that a special watch be kept on persons where there are reasonable grounds for believing that they are breaching customs legislation and on certain places, movements of goods, and means of transport. A Member State may also request that an authority carry out certain administrative enquiries. Turning to spontaneous assistance, Article 14 provides that where they consider it useful for ensuring compliance with customs or agricultural legislation, each Member State's competent authorities shall, as far as is possible, keep, or have kept, the special watch described above and communicate to the competent authorities of the other Member States concerned all information in their possession concerning operations which constitute, or appear to them to constitute, breaches of customs or agricultural legislation. According to Article 15, the competent authorities of each Member State shall immediately send to the competent authorities of the other Member States concerned all relevant information concerning operations which constitute, or appear to them to constitute, breaches of customs or agricultural legislation, and in particular concerning the goods involved and new ways and means of carrying out such operations.

Relations between the Member States and the Commission are dealt with in Title III, Articles 17 and 18. The competent authorities of Member States are obliged to communicate to the Commission, as soon as it is available to them, any information they consider relevant concerning: goods which have been, or are suspected of having been, the object of breaches of customs legislation; methods and practices used or suspected of being used to breach customs legislation and requests, action taken, and information received pursuant to a request, for assistance by a Member State. The Member States are also to communicate to the Commission any information on 'shortcomings or gaps' in customs legislation. The Commission may seek information from a Member State (and does so on a regular basis). Furthermore, at the Commission's request Member States are to carry out enquiries. Articles 19–22, in Title IV, deal with relations with third countries and they empower the Commission to carry out missions to third countries. In recent years these missions have frequently been concerned to establish the accuracy or otherwise of certificates of origin issued by the authorities of third countries.

Title V of the Regulation, consisting of Articles 23–41, is concerned with the establishment of the Customs Information System (CIS). The CIS is an automated information system which is intended to assist in the prevention, investigation, and prosecution of operations which are in breach of customs legislation. It consists, essentially, of a central database facility which is to be accessible via terminals in each Member State and in the Commission. The information it contains falls within six categories, namely, commodities, means of transport, businesses, persons, fraud trends, and availability of expertise. The information which may be included under these categories is set out in Commission Regulation (EC) 696/98.[110] There are limits on the personal information which may be kept, so that data revealing racial or ethnic origin, political opinions, religious or philosophical beliefs, trade union membership, and data concerning the health or sex life of an individual are not to be included. Clearly, the collection, retention, and communication of data are sensitive activities and the regulation contains specific provisions governing these matters. It also provides for personal data protection.

The CIS facilitates the information exchange which is given such a high priority in the Customs 2002 Programme. With a view to ensuring the close co-operation which is so desirable between the authorities of Member States the Programme also seeks to facilitate the exchange of officials between Member States and more uniform and efficient training for customs officials, along the lines of arrangements established under the Mattaeus Programme.[111]

F. THE TRADER, THE MEMBER STATES, AND THE COMMISSION

The Community customs system is to some extent a two-tier system. The Commission deals with Member States in the top tier and Member States deal with traders in the bottom tier. Yet this is not entirely accurate because the Commission deals directly with traders through the Official Journal and the trader 'ignores the Journal at his peril'.[112] Furthermore, in some situations traders may make representations to the Commission about their liability, as we shall see in Chapter 13 . Nevertheless, on a day-to-day basis the customs officials with which traders come into contact are national officials and CCC, Articles 13–17 lay down a number of basic rules governing the relationship

---

[110] See n 109 above, Art 2.
[111] See, in particular, para 14a of Decision (EC) 105/2000, n 3 above. For the Mattaeus Programme see Council Decision (EEC) 341/91 of 20 June 1991 [1991] OJ L187/41.
[112] *CCE v Invicta Poultry Ltd* [1998] V&DR 128 at 130 *per* Buxton LJ. The obligation of traders to be familiar with the *Official Journal* is dealt with in Ch 13 below. In this context it should be noted that the early warning system for informing traders of cases where there is reasonable doubt as to the origin of goods is to be operated by means of notices in the *Official Journal*: Communication from the Commission to the Council and the European Parliament COM(2000)55 final, 8 Sept 2000.

between the trader and national customs authorities. The authorities may carry out all the controls they deem necessary to ensure that customs legislation is properly applied.[113] Furthermore, any person directly or indirectly involved in 'operations concerned for the purposes of trade in goods' must provide the authorities with all the requisite information and all requisite assistance at their request and by any time limit prescribed.[114] Documents are to be kept for the period specified in Community or national law and for a minimum of three years irrespective of the storage medium used.[115] The three-year period runs from the end of the year in which:

(i)   the declarations for release for free circulation or export are accepted (in the case of goods released for free circulation, not within (ii) below, or declared for export);

(ii)   the goods cease to be subject to customs supervision (in the case of goods released for free circulation at a reduced or zero rate of import duty on account of their end-use);

(iii) the customs procedure concerned is completed (in the case of goods placed under another customs procedure);

(iv)   goods which have been placed in a free zone or warehouse leave the undertaking concerned.[116]

Information which is by its nature confidential, or which is provided on a confidential basis, is covered by the obligation of professional secrecy. It is not to be disclosed by the customs authorities without the express permission of the provider of it. Communication of information is permitted, however, where the customs authorities may be obliged to communicate it pursuant, particularly, to provisions in respect of data protection or in connection with legal proceedings.[117]

---

[113] CCC, Art 13.
[114] CCC, Art 14.
[115] Where a check by the customs authorities shows that an entry in the accounts has to be corrected, documents are, subject to a limited exception, to be kept beyond the specified period for a period sufficient to permit the correction to be made and checked: CCC, Article 16 second para.
[116] CCC, Art 16.
[117] CCC, Art 15.

5

The Common Customs Tariff: Administration and Interpretation

The Common Customs Tariff ('the Tariff') came into existence on 1 July 1968 nearly eighteen months ahead of schedule. Its creation was a formidable achievement. It has been said that a total of 20,000 national tariff items were reduced to what were then 3,000 common tariff items.[1] Originally, the setting up of the Tariff was dealt with in EEC Treaty, Articles 18–27. These were repealed in the Treaty of Amsterdam and now the main provision governing the Tariff is Article 28 which states simply 'Common Customs Tariff duties shall be fixed by the Council acting by a qualified majority on a proposal from the Commission.' The obvious and central importance to customs duty of the Tariff is made plain by CCC, Article 20.1, which provides that duties legally owed where a customs debt is incurred shall be based on the Tariff.[2] It is not, however, important solely in relation to customs duty. Many kinds of measures relating to trade in the Community use the Tariff as a means of identifying the goods with which they are concerned. Indeed, CCC, Article 20.2 provides that other measures 'shall, where appropriate' use the tariff classifications of goods.

Any consideration of the Tariff is bound to require examination of a wide range of matters. This chapter is split into six sections. In the first section (A), we look at the definition of the Tariff. In the second (B), certain elements of the Tariff are examined. The Combined Nomenclature (CN) is considered first, particularly its function, history, and basis and then its exact nature. Secondly, the common features of the customs duties imposed and their different types are considered. Thirdly, the alteration and suspension of customs duties is addressed. Fourthly and finally, tariff quotas are commented upon. The third section (C) deals with the tariff *intégré de la Communauté* ('TARIC') and the role of the Commission in relation to both it and the CN. The fourth section (D) considers the role of the Court of Justice in classification matters, its general approach to classification cases, and the requirement of objectivity in classifying products. The fifth section (E) deals with aids to the interpretation of the tariff. First of all general rules of interpretation are briefly dealt with. Secondly, the uses of explanatory notes and opinions are outlined. Thirdly, some reference is made to the case law of the Court in relation to specific product groups.

---

[1] P Kapteyn and P Verloren van Themaat, *Introduction to the Law of the European Communities*: (2nd edn by L W Gormley, Kluwer Law and Taxation Publishers, London, 1989), at 365.
[2] Favourable tariff treatment of certain goods depending on their nature or end use is permitted by CCC, Art 21.

Finally, in the sixth section (F), we turn from the field of Community action to the role played by the customs authorities in Member States in the provision of tariff information.

A. WHAT IS THE TARIFF?

The definition of the Tariff formerly appeared in Article 4 of the Council Regulation on the tariff and statistical nomenclature and the common customs tariff ('the Tariff Regulation').[3] That definition has now been deleted in deference to the definition in the CCC.[4] CCC, Article 20.3 states that the Tariff is to consist of seven elements, listed at (a)–(g). First, there is the CN. Then, secondly, there is any other nomenclature which is wholly or partly based on the CN, or which adds any subdivisions to it, and which is established by Community provisions relating to specific fields with a view to the application of tariff measures relating to trade in goods. The third element consists of the rates of charge normally applicable to goods covered by the CN as regards customs duties and import charges laid down under the Common Agricultural Policy, or under certain specific arrangements applicable to goods resulting from the processing of agricultural products. The fourth and fifth elements are the preferential tariff measures contained in agreements between the Community and third countries and in unilateral Community legislation respectively. The sixth element of the Tariff consists of autonomous suspensive measures providing for a reduction in, or relief from, import duties. The preferential treatment and reductions or reliefs from duty referred to in elements four to six are stated to be applicable at the declarant's request.[5] Furthermore, they may be limited by reference to tariff quotas, in which the preferential treatment ceases once a specified volume of imports has been reached, or to tariff ceilings, in which case the preferential treatment ceases on a ruling by the Commission.[6] The seventh and final element of the Tariff is established

---

[3] Council Regulation (EEC) 2658/87 of 23 July 1987 [1987] OJ L256/1, as amended in particular by Council Regulation (EEC) 1969/93 of 19 July 1993 [1993] OJ L180/9 and Council Regulation (EC) 254/2000 of 31 Jan 2000 [2000] OJ L28/16. The latter regulation applies as from 1 Jan 2000 and was passed to implement the light of the SLIM (Simpler Legislation for the Internal Market) initiative. Other amendments to the Tariff Regulation are contained in Commission Regulation (EC) 2263/2000 of 13 Oct 2000 [2000] OJ L264/1, and Council Regulation (EC) 2559/2000 of 16 Nov 2000 [2000] OJ L293/1, Commission Regulation 1229/2001 of 19 June 2001 [2001] OJ L168/5 and Commission Regulation 1230/2001 of 21 June 2001 [2001] OJ L168/6. Commission Regulation (EC) 2031/2001 of 6 Aug 2001 [2001] OJ 279/1 replaces Annex I of the Tariff Regulation as from 1 Jan 2002. It modernizes the Annex but was published too late for comment here. Note that the Tariff Regulation was originally adopted on an erroneous legal basis because it was based on, what were then, Arts 28, 43, 113, and 235 of the Treaty. The reference in it to Art 235 (now Art 308) was removed by Council Regulation (EEC) 3528/89 of 23 Nov 1989 [1989] OJ L347/1 in the light of the decision of the Court of Justice in Case 275/87 *Commission v Council* [1989] ECR 259.

[4] See Council Regulation (EC) 254/2000, Art 1.4 and recital (9), n 3 above.

[5] CCC, Art 20.4.   [6] CCC, Art 20.5.

pursuant to a catch-all provision which provides that it includes other tariff measures provided for by other Community legislation.

It is important to emphasize at the outset that the Tariff is based not on national but Community law. The customs authorities of Member States provide traders with information about the Tariff, as we shall see, but national compilations of Community law are not authoritative sources of law. As the Court of Justice has said in relation to an official German compilation of customs law:

> the applicable Community provisions relating to the customs tariff must be published in the Official Journal of the European Communities. From the date of that publication, they constitute the sole relevant positive law, of which all are deemed to be aware. A tariff manual such as the Gebrauchs-Zolltarif, drawn up by national authorities, therefore constitutes, as is clear from the terms of its table of contents, no more than a handbook for customs clearance.[7]

B. ELEMENTS OF THE TARIFF

1. *The Combined Nomenclature:*

1.1 *Its function, history, and basis*

In any customs duty system, the nomenclature describes the goods to which a specified rate of duty is applied. The Community's CN has two basic uses. First, it is designed to serve the requirements of the Tariff. Secondly, it is intended to facilitate the gathering of the external trade statistics of the Community and other Community policies concerning the importation and exportation of goods.[8]

The basis of the first combined nomenclature in the Community was the Nomenclature Convention of Brussels of 15 December 1950 and it was contained in a Council Regulation the annex to which contained the tariff.[9] The Tariff Regulation introduced a replacement nomenclature based on the International Convention on the Harmonized Commodity Description and Coding System of 14 June 1983.[10] The Convention which, as its name

---

[7] Case 161/88 *Friedrich Binder GmbH & Co KG v Hauptzollamt Bad Reichenhall* [1989] ECR 2415 para 19.   [8] Tariff Regulation, Art 1.
[9] Council Regulation 950/68 of 28 June 1968 [1968] OJ Spec Ed (I) 275.
[10] Amended by the Protocol of Amendment to the International Convention on the Harmonized Commodity Description and Coding System of 24 June 1986. The Convention was approved on behalf of the Community by Council Decision (EEC) 369/87 of 7 Apr 1987 [1987] OJ L198/1, to which the text of the Convention is annexed at [1987] OJ L198/3. It should be noted that some agreements between third countries and the Community which are in the form of an exchange of letters, such as that with Switzerland, continued to use the Customs Co-operation Council Nomenclature. The Commission has opened negotiations with these countries to amend the agreements to reflect the new nomenclature. For the decision of the EC–Switzerland Joint Committee giving effect to the amendment see Decision 1/2000 of the EC–Switzerland Joint Committee of 25 Oct 2000 [2001] OJ L51/1.

suggests, established the harmonized commodity description and coding system, or as it is usually called 'the harmonized system', required that the customs tariffs and statistical nomenclatures of contracting parties conformed to the harmonized system. The EC as well as the Member States are contracting parties to the Convention and the harmonized system is reputed to be used by over 176 countries and economies.[11] The system is administered by the Customs Co-operation Council, informally known as the World Customs Organization (WCO) in Brussels.[12] The Convention is updated by the Harmonized System Committee which is established under Article 6 of the Convention and is composed of representatives from each of the contracting parties. Amongst other functions, the Committee proposes amendments to the Convention and prepares Explanatory Notes and Classification Opinions.[13] The notes and opinions are deemed to be approved by the WCO if no contracting party objects within a specified time period.[14]

The harmonized system contains headings and sub-headings referring to categories of goods. The former are given a four-digit numerical code and the latter a six-digit numerical code. In pursuance of the obligation to conform to the harmonized system, contracting parties undertake to use all the headings and sub-headings without addition or modification, together with their numerical codes, and to follow the numerical sequence of the harmonized system. They also undertake to apply the General Rules for the Interpretation of the Harmonized System and all the Section and Sub-heading Notes and agree not to modify the scope of the Sections and Chapters into which the harmonized system is divided.[15] The official interpretation of the harmonized system is given in four volumes of Explanatory Notes published by the WCO.

1.2 The CN: what is it?

The CN which, as we have seen, is the first of seven elements of the Tariff is itself defined in the Tariff Regulation as consisting of three elements.[16] First of all there is the nomenclature of the harmonized system.[17] Secondly, there are

---

[11] It was adopted by the USA pursuant to the Omnibus Trade and Competitiveness Act 1988 sections 1201–1217 (Pub L. 100-418; Stat.1147–1163). In tariff classification cases it is sometimes helpful to have regard to the classification of a product adopted by non-EC countries, such as the USA.

[12] 30, Rue du Marchéé, B-1210 Brussels (Belgium) Telephone: 32.2.209.92.11–Fax: 32.2.209.92.92.

[13] Art 7.1(a) and (b) of the Convention. The WCO's Harmonized System Review Sub-Committee reviews the tariff established under the harmonized system. Its last periodic review was completed in 1999 and the changes made will be implemented by 1 Jan 2002. The next review is now under way. It will be completed by spring 2004 and implemented by 2007. The nomenclature needs reviewing in a number of areas, particularly in relation to high technology products.

[14] Art 8.1.   [15] See Art 3.1(a).   [16] See Art 1. 2.

[17] Both the CN and the harmonized nomenclature are used in agreements between the EC and

the Community subdivisions to that nomenclature (where these specify a particular rate of customs duty they are called 'CN sub-headings'). Thirdly, there are preliminary provisions, additional section or chapter notes and foot-notes relating to CN headings.

The CN uses an eight-digit numerical code to identify a product, the first six digits of which are those of the harmonized system.[18] The extra two digits identify the CN sub-headings of which there are about 10,000. Where there is no Community sub-heading these two digits are '00'. There are also ninth and tenth digits which identify the TARIC sub-headings of which there are about 18,000. These are necessitated by many elements of the system of Community customs duty, such as tariff suspensions, quotas, preferences, anti-dumping and countervailing duties, valuation matters, and various restrictions and prohibitions relating to the import and export of goods. If there are no TARIC sub-headings then the ninth and tenth digits are also to be '00'. Member States may use sub-divisions which meet national requirements in accordance with the CCC.[19] An extra code of four digits exists in respect of certain matters such as complex anti-dumping and countervailing duties, pharmaceutical products listed in Part Three, Section II, of the CN, products subject to the Convention on the International Trade in Endangered Species, and the reference price for fish.

The CN is contained in Annex I to the Tariff Regulation. It is updated annually by a Commission Regulation which is to be published not later than 31 October and applies from 1 January of the following year.[20] Annex I is in three parts. Part One contains, in Section IA, general rules for the interpretation of the CN, in Section 1B general rules concerning duties, and in Section 1C general rules applicable both to the CN and to duties. Part Two contains the chapters of the harmonized system along with schedules of customs duties. Each chapter is devoted to a particular class of product and contains important Notes on interpretation at the beginning. Part Three contains tariff annexes. Section I contains the agricultural annexes. Section II contains lists of pharmaceutical substances which qualify for duty-free treatment, amongst other things. Section III contains quotas and Section IV details favourable tariff treatment by reason of the nature of goods and certain other matters.

There are, of course, many Commission regulations relating to classification matters which must be consulted in relation to any particular classification question. These are too numerous to consider here.

---

third countries. Art 6 of the recent agreement between the EC and South Africa, eg, provides that the CN is to be applied in relation to imports from South Africa and the nomenclature of the harmonized system is to be used in relation to imports into South Africa: see [1999] OJ L311/3. See also n 10.

[18] Tariff Regulation, Art. 3(1)(a).   [19] See Tariff Regulation, Arts 3.2 and 5.3.

[20] As noted above, the most recent annual amendment to the Tariff Regulation was by Commission Regulation (EC) 2031/2001 [2001] OJ 279/1 effective from Jan 2002. There are, of course, amendments to Annex 1 throughout the year as well see n 3 above.

2. *Customs duties: common features – different types*

The customs duties imposed pursuant to the CN are of differing types and are imposed at widely differing rates. One principle which is fundamental to all customs duties, however, is that their imposition must comply with the principle of legal certainty. This principle is fundamental to the Community legal order and it has an obvious application in the context of any financial obligation including customs duty. In the words of the Court the principle requires, in particular, that 'rules imposing charges on a taxpayer be clear and precise so that he may be able to ascertain unequivocally what his rights and obligations are and take steps accordingly'.[21] This is something that must be borne in mind in reviewing any provision imposing customs duty. The Court made the statement quoted above in relation to the effects of the Tariff Regulation. In the case with which it was concerned, the goods in question were treated as free of duty on importation having regard to the Tariff Regulation. Subsequently, they were classified under a different heading in reliance on a regulation that came into effect prior to the Tariff Regulation and conflicted with it. Tariff Regulation, Article 15 placed on the Commission an obligation to amend Community acts to conform to the CN. It had not amended the regulation in question and the principle of legal certainty consequently ensured that customs duty could not be charged in reliance upon it.

Turning to the differences between the duties imposed by the CN, it will be apparent that they are conventional and autonomous in nature, and charged at *ad valorem* or fixed rates, or sometimes both. The nature of these duties is set out in Part One, Section IB, of the CN which contains 'General rules concerning duties'. According to rule 1, conventional duties are, unless the context otherwise requires, applicable to goods imported from any third country and are applicable to imported goods originating in countries which are Contracting Parties to the GATT or those with which the EC has concluded agreements containing the most-favoured-nation tariff clause.[22] Autonomous duties are those shown in column 3 of the CN. These are applicable where they are less than the conventional duties. Frequently, however, they are considerably higher than conventional duties. The conventional rates of duty are shown in column

---

[21] Case C–143/93 *Gebroeders van Es Vouane Agenten BV v Inspecteur der invoerrechten en accijnzen* [1996] ECR 1–431 at 471 para 27. See also p 83 n 4 and p 87.

[22] The general most-favoured-nation clause contained in GATT 94 is set out in Art 1 and Art 1.1 and reads as follows:

> With respect to customs duties and charges of any kind imposed on or in connection with importation or exportation or imposed on the international transfer of payments for imports or exports, and with respect to all rules and formalities in connection with importation and exportation, . . . , any advantage, favour, privilege or immunity granted by any contracting party to any product originating in or destined for any other country shall be accorded immediately and unconditionally to the like product originating in or destined for the territories of all other contracting parties.

4a or 4b in the CN. Rates appearing in column 4a are applicable as from 1 January 2001. Rates appearing in column 4b are applicable as from 1 July 2001. As rule 4 makes clear, where the rates of duty are expressed as percentages, the duties are imposed *ad valorem*. In respect of many products, however, duties are expressed as euros per kg/net, for example, and are specific duties. Sometimes the total duty payable is a combination of *ad valorem* and specific duties.

According to general rule 2, conventional duties are not imposed, pursuant to general rule 1, where special autonomous duties are provided for in respect of goods originating in certain countries or where preferential duties are applicable in pursuance of agreements. Furthermore, according to general rule 3, neither rule 1 nor 2 is to preclude Member States from applying customs duties other than those of the Tariff where the application of such duties is justified by Community law. General rule 5 states that, in addition to the *ad valorem* duties, goods are chargeable with an additional agricultural component, fixed in accordance with Annex 1, where the symbol 'EA' appears. Under general rule 6 there is an additional duty, set out in Annex 1, which is imposed for certain forms of sugar and flour where the symbol 'AD S/Z' or 'AD F/M' appears. General rule 7 provides that so far as products containing alcohol are concerned, there is a specific duty, expressed in euros, calculated according to the percentage volume of alcohol per litre in accordance with the stated formula. Sometimes a minimum value is shown by 'MIN'. In these cases the duty chargeable is the higher of the duty calculated according to the formula and the minimum duty.

It is, of course, essential that both *ad valorem* and specific duties are uniformly applied throughout the Community. So far as *ad valorem* duties are concerned, uniformity of application is achieved by common rules of valuation, considered in Chapter 8 below. So far as the specific duties are concerned, uniformity is now achieved by use of the euro, and by use of standard units of measurement such as the kilogram. The use of the euro has enabled the Community to ensure uniformity of application of specific duties to a greater extent than was possible when the ecu was used, when it was necessary to convert the units of account into all the national currencies of the Member States. The inequality of application caused by the use of units of account was acknowledged by the Court of Justice in 1980 when it said 'At the present stage of integration, where Member States essentially retain their powers in monetary matters, recourse to the mechanism of specific duties in the Common Customs Tariff will inevitably lead to certain differences in the incidence of the duties charged.'[23] Complete uniformity of application will, of course, only be

---

[23] Case 248/80 *Kommanditgesellschaft in Firma Gebrüder Glunz v Hauptzollamt Hamburg-Waltershof* [1982] ECR 197 at para 22. The judgment contains a useful summary of monetary matters in relation to customs duties and points out that, originally, units of account were converted using fixed parities based on gold. From about 1974, and following the demise of the Bretton Woods Agreement, the use of these fixed parities resulted in clear inequalities in the

achieved when the customs territory and the euro-area are coterminous. For countries which are outside the euro-zone, conversion of the specific duties into their national currencies remains essential and the ecu continues to be used for this purpose with its value being fixed once a month.[24]

The uniformity with which duties are applied may be contrasted with the diversity of rates at which they are imposed, both in respect of conventional and autonomous duties. In relation to conventional duty, for example, the rate of duty on certain inactive yeasts and similar products (CN 2102 20 19) was fixed at 0.3 per cent until 30 June 2000. In contrast, the rate of conventional duties on certain sorts of apricot products (CN 2008 50 51) is put at 26.7 per cent plus a specific duty for the same period. This wide variation in rates means that the economic significance of customs duty varies greatly between different trades. Note only is the rate of duty variable as between different goods, it may also vary in respect of the same product. The duty to be charged in any particular case may, for example, be affected by the application of tariff quotas, or be altered or suspended autonomously.[25]

3. The alteration and suspension of customs duties

The alteration and suspension of duties is permitted by Article 26 of the EC Treaty which allows the Council to fix the duties of the Tariff acting on a proposal from the Commission.[26] The Court has held, however, that although the Council has a wide discretion in applying this provision, when deciding to suspend duties it must select objective and verifiable criteria, strictly limiting the scope of the suspension of duties to the products for which the user industries of the Community have clearly developed a need, and which the Council has actually been able to establish. Account must be taken too, of the requirements of legal certainty and of the difficulties confronting the national administrations. Accordingly, provisions suspending duty are to be construed strictly and may not be applied to products which they do not mention,[27] and as the Court of Justice has said:

application of customs regulations. In Nov 1978 a system of conversion using a basket of currencies was introduced.

[24] See CCC, Art 18, which contains a number of important provisions on the use and conversion of the ecu, and general rule 3 under *C General rules applicable both to nomenclature and to duties* in Annex I to the Tariff Regulation.

[25] See CCC, Art 21.

[26] The requirement of a proposal from the Commission was inserted by the Single European Act, Art 16.1.

[27] Case 58/85 *Ethicon GmbH v Hauptzollamt Itzehoe* [1986] ECR 1131 paras 12, 18–20 which refer to Case 227/84 *Texas Instruments Deutschland GmbH v Hauptzollamt München-Mitte* [1985] ECR 3639. For a case in the UK High Court in which a tariff quota was strictly construed see *CCE v Anchor Foods Ltd* [1999] V&DR 425. It concerned the availability of a quota for New Zealand butter. Dyson J said that 'if there is any relevant ambiguity in the words "directly manufactured", then they should be construed strictly, and against the party seeking to invoke the preferential

A later amendment of the description of a product on which duties have been suspended cannot retroactively affect the interpretation of the description previously applied for that purpose. . . Moreover, where a provision is ambiguous it must be interpreted according to the general scheme and purpose of the rules of which it forms part.[28]

Where necessary, it is for the importer seeking to take advantage of an exemption to submit his application to the competent authorities so that the Council may take a decision on the matter.[29]

It should be noted here that, although duties are usually suspended by regulation, Part One, Section II of the CN provides for suspension of duties in respect of goods intended for incorporation in ships, boats, vessels, and drilling or production platforms, subject to certain conditions.

4. *Tariff quotas*

Tariff quotas themselves may be 'conventional', ie derived from an agreement between the EC and a third country, or autonomous, ie derived from Community measures. To take just one example of a quota being derived from an agreement one may refer to the Agreement between the EC and Switzerland.[30] An agreement by way of an exchange of letters, relating to Protocol 2 of the Agreement, established the opening of tariff quotas from 1 April 2000 which are to be increased by 10 per cent in 2001.[31] For an example of autonomous tariff quotas one may look at the legislation in relation to oscillators. The Community's need for these products led, in July 2000, to a raising of the quota to 202,000,000 units.[32]

Both conventional and autonomous quotas are administered in accordance

tariff quota. If, however, the meaning of the words is clear, they should be given their full effect': see 432 G–H. For other authorities in the Court of Justice see: Case 247/97 *Marc Schoonbroodt, Transports A M Schoonbroodt SPRL v Belgian State* [1998] ECR I–8095 at para 23; Joined Cases C–47/95, C–48/95, C–49/95, C–50/95, C–60/95, C–81/95, C–92/95 and C–148/95 *Olasagasti & C Srl v Amministrazione delle finanze dello Stato* [1996] ECR I–6579 para 20.

[28] Case 467/93 *Hauptzollamt München–West v Analog Devices GmbH* [1995] ECR I–1403 para 8. See also Case C–338/90 *Hamlin Electronics v Hauptzollamt Darmstadt* [1992] ECR I–2333, in which the Court of Justice bore in mind that the suspension of duty was implemented because of a shortage within the Community of certain switches and a reference to reed switches 'containing not more than . . . a small quantity of mercury' was held to include those that contained none: see paras 12–15. For a more recent example of a case in which the purpose of tariff suspension was important in the construction of a regulation suspending autonomous duties see Case C–190/00 *Criminal Proceedings against Édouard Balguerie and Société Balguerie*, [2001] ECR I–3437 at para 38.

[29] Case 58/85 *Ethicon GmbH Hauptzollamt Itzehoe*, n 27 above, at para 19.

[30] See the Agreement between the EEC and the Swiss Confederation of 19 Dec 1972 [1972] OJ L300/189. The EC has recently finalized a new set of Agreements with Switzerland.

[31] [2000] OJ L76/12. See also Commission Regulation (EC) 697/2000 of 31 Mar 2000 [2000] OJ L181/49.

[32] Commission Regulation (EC) 1501/2000 of 11 July 2000 [2000] OJ L172/11, amending Council Regulation (EC) 2505/96of 20 Dec 1996 [1996] OJ L345/1.

with the regime established by Council Regulation (EC) 520/94, which must itself be read in the light of implementing and amending regulations,[33] and Articles 308a–d of the Implementing Regulation. This council regulation replaced the existing administrative regime and ensured that the relevant procedures conformed to the requirements of the internal market. There are separate measures governing the administration of quotas in relation to agricultural products and textiles and certain separate arrangements which arise from agreements between the Community and third countries.[34] The administration of the quota regime requires the participation of Member States, the Commission, and, to a significant extent, the authorities of third countries. Applications for quota are made to Member States, the Commission allocates it,[35] whilst the third country certifies that the produce exported to the EC originates in its territory. The relationship between these three parties may be a source of difficulty for traders and the Court of Justice has had to consider it, and the duties of the Commission which, in part, arise out of it, in some detail.

The Court of Justice has made clear that the Commission is subject to the principle of good administration in relation to the application of tariff quotas, as in relation to all areas of its work. The Commission must ensure that the quotas are properly applied and not exceeded. Amongst other things this requires it to check the information which it receives from the customs administrations of third countries under the relevant agreements, and collate it, so that it is possible to determine whether or not a quota is exceeded. The Commission must also ensure that it maintains efficient links with national administrations. For example, the Member States must be given copies of the specimen signatures of officials. Once the Commission has received information and analysed it in good time pursuant to a, preferably computerized, monitoring procedure, it must then react effectively to the information it has received. If it does not do these things there may be a failure to subject goods to the correct duty and post-clearance recovery may be compromised.[36]

---

[33] Council Regulation (EC) 520/94 of 7 Mar 1994 [1994] OJ L66/1. Implemented by Commission Regulation (EC) 738/94 of 30 Mar 1994 [1994] OJ L87/47 (the form for and method for making quota applications etc.) itself amended by Commission Regulation (EC) 1150/95 of 22 May 1995 [1995] OJ L116/3 and Commission Regulation (EC) 983/96 of 31 May 1996 [1996] OJ L131/47. Council Regulation (EC) 520/94 has been amended by Council Regulation (EC) 138/96 of 22 Jan 1996 [1996] OJ L21/6, and the text takes account of this.

[34] Council Regulation (EC) 520/94, n 33 above, Art 1.2.

[35] The Commission is assisted in relation to quotas by a Committee, consisting of representatives of the Member States and chaired by a Commission representative: see Art 22 of Council Regulation (EC) 520/94, n 33 above.

[36] Case T–50/96 *Primex Produkte Import-Export GmbH KG v Commission* [1998] II–3773 at paras 143–158 (under appeal as Case C–417/98 P [1999] OJ C1/112; Case T–42/96 *Eyckeler and Malt v Commission* [1998] ECR II–401, paras 163–192 (under appeal as Case C–163/98 P [1998] OJ C258/14); and Case 175/84 *Krohn v Commission* [1987] ECR 97, para 15.

4.1 *Tariff quotas: applications and licences*

The Commission is obliged to publish a notice announcing the opening of quotas in the *Official Journal*, for which the trader may then apply. The notice must state the allocation method to be used and the conditions to be met by applications, including the applicable time limit and the address to which applications must be sent.[37] Traders may make a single licence application, on specified forms,[38] in respect of each quota, or tranche of quotas, to the competent authority of the Member State, or region as the case may be. The application must be drawn up in the official language or languages of the state concerned.[39] The licences which are issued must be for economically significant quantities of the product having regard to its nature.[40]

Generally speaking, the releases for free circulation, or export, of products subject to quotas are made conditional on the presentation of the non-transferable[41] import or export licence issued by the Member States to which quota applications are made.[42] Where the allocation of quota is by reference to traditional trade flows (considered below), the Member States must issue licences immediately on verification of the Community balance of quota which is available. In other cases, the Commission is to notify the competent authorities in the Member States, within a specified period to be determined, of the quantities for which they may issue licences to the applicants. Then, the competent authorities in the Member States are to issue licences within ten working days of notification of the Commission decision, or within the time limit set by the Commission. They must inform the Commission of the issue of the licences.[43] The issue of licences may be made conditional on the lodging of security.[44] Licences are valid for a period of four months[45] throughout the Community, except where the quota is limited by reference to a region of the Community when they are valid in the region, or regions, in question. Licences or extracts from them must be returned to the competent authorities of the Member States which issued them, at the latest, within ten working days of their expiry date, except in cases of *force majeure*. If a licence has been granted on the lodging of security, the security shall be forfeit if this time limit is not complied with, again except in cases of *force majeure*.[46]

---

[37] Council Regulation (EC) 520/94, Art 3.   [38] Ibid, Art 17.4.
[39] Ibid, Art 4.   [40] Ibid, Art 5.
[41] Ibid, Art 18.
[42] Ibid, Art 2.6. An extract from the licence may be applied for and shall have the same legal effects as the licence: ibid, Art 17.3.
[43] Ibid, Art 15.   [44] Ibid, Art 16.
[45] Ibid, Art 17.2. A different period of validity may be set.
[46] Ibid, Art 19, as amended by Commission Regulation (EC) 138/96, n 333 above.

4.2 *Management of tariff quotas*

When a declaration for release for free circulation of goods is accepted by a Member State, it is to draw from the tariff quota, through the Commission, a quantity corresponding to its needs.[47] Allocations of quota by the Commission are then to be made on each working day, with some exceptions,[48] on the basis of the date of acceptance of the declaration for release for free circulation and priority is to be determined by reference to these dates.[49] The Member States are to communicate to the Commission without delay all valid requests for drawing. Their communication must include the relevant dates on which the declarations for release for free circulation were accepted and the exact amount applied for on the declarations.[50] If the quantities requested exceed the balance available the allocation is made on a pro rata basis.[51] In respect of new tariff quotas, no request for drawing is to be granted before the eleventh working day following the date of publication of the provision creating the quota in question.[52] Unused quota is to be immediately returned to the Commission by the Member States.[53] The Member States must immediately return to the Commission any quantity drawn in respect of goods in relation to which a declaration for release for free circulation has been invalidated and the request for drawing is to be completely cancelled.[54] Details of requests for drawings by a Member State are to be kept confidential by other Member States and the Commission.[55]

After the first allocation of tariff quota, the quota is regarded as 'non-critical' where (i) a quota for the same products and origins was opened in each of the last two years, for a minimum period of six months, was not exhausted before the last working day of the seventh month of the quota period during those two years and, (ii) the initial volume of the new tariff quota is not less than each of those of the last two years.[56] The quota becomes 'critical' as soon

---

[47] Implementing Regulation, Art 308a.2. The request to the Commission for quota is not to be presented to it until the requirements of Art 256.2 and 3, Implementing Regulation, have been met: Art 308a.3 above. The requirements are that the document, on which the granting of reduced or zero rates of duty is conditional, is to be presented to customs. In some circumstances the document may be presented after the expiry data of the period for which the reduced or zero rate was set.

[48] Ibid, Art 308b.

[49] Ibid, Art 308a.4. Acceptance of a declaration on 1, 2, or 3 Jan is regarded as acceptance on the third of the month, unless one of the days is a Saturday or Sunday, in which case the declaration is deemed to be accepted on the fourth: see Art 308a.8, ibid. Subject to this, allocations of quota shall take into account all unanswered requests relating to declarations for release for free circulation accepted up to and including 'the second previous day' which have been communicated to the Commission: ibid, Art 308b.2.

[50] Ibid, Art 308a.4.   [51] Ibid, Art 308.7.

[52] Ibid, Art 308a.9.

[53] Ibid, Art 308a.10. Member States need not make a return where an erroneous drawing, representing a customs debt of less than ECU 10 or less, is discovered after the first month following the end of the period of validity of the quota concerned.

[54] Ibid, Art 308a.11.   [55] Ibid, Art 308a.12.

[56] Ibid, Art 308c.1.

as 75 per cent of the initial volume of a non-critical tariff has been used, or at the discretion of the competent authorities.[57]

4.3 *Allocation of quotas*

Council Regulation (EC) 520/94, referred to above, provides that a quota must be allocated to applicants as soon as possible after it has been opened and may be allocated in tranches.[58] The Commission must adopt one of four methods of allocation, namely:

(i)   a method based on traditional trade flows;
(ii) a method based on the order in which applications are submitted;
(iii) a method based on the quantity of quota which is requested using the simultaneous examination procedure;
(iv) a combination of the above.[59]

Methods (i) to (iii) are considered in turn below.

4.3.1 *Traditional trade flows*

Where traditional trade flow is used in allocating quota, one part of the quota is to be reserved for traditional importers or exporters and the other part is to be set aside for other importers or exporters.[60] Importers or exporters are deemed to be traditional if they are able to show that, in the previous reference period, they have imported or exported products within the quota.[61] In order to qualify for quota and show that they are traditional importers or exporters, quota applicants must enclose with their licence applications a certified copy of the original of the entry for free circulation or export declaration. This must be made out in the name of the importer or exporter concerned or, where applicable, that of the operator whose activities they have taken over. Applicants may enclose such equivalent evidence as may be permitted.[62] Within a period specified in the notice opening the quota, Member States are to inform the Commission of the number and the aggregate amount of the import or export applications, broken down into those from traditional importers or exporters and other importers or exporters. They must also inform the Commission of the amount of the previous imports or exports carried out by the applicants during the reference period.[63] The Commission is then to examine this information and establish the quantitive criteria according to which applications from traditional importers and

---

[57] Ibid, Art 308c.2, in n 47 above.   [58] Ibid, Art 2.1 (see n 33 above).
[59] Ibid, Art 2.2, 3 and 4.
[60] Where no traditional importers or exporters apply, the whole quota or tranche is to go to the other applicants and be allocated on the order in which applications are submitted: see Art 12, ibid.
[61] Ibid, Art 6.   [62] Ibid, Art 7.
[63] Ibid, Art 8.

exporters are to be met. Applications are to be met in full where aggregate applications are equal to, or less than, the amount set aside for traditional importers or exporters. Where applications exceed the amount set aside for 'traditional' applicants, applications are to be met on a pro rata basis by reference to each applicant's share of the total reference imports or exports. Where this would result in an applicant being allocated more than it has applied for, the quota must be re-assigned in accordance with specified procedures.[64]

4.3.2 *Order of applications—first come first served*
Where this method is used, the Commission is given the responsibility of determining the quantity which operators are entitled to receive on making an application. This quantity is to be the same for all traders. In fixing the quantity, allowance is to be made for the need to assign economically significant quantities of the product in question. A trader who can prove that he has used his quota may make a further application.[65]

4.3.3 *Application according to quantity requested*
When this method is used, Member States are to inform the Commission of the number of licence applications they have received which comply with the requisite conditions, specifying the number of applicants and the aggregate quantities applied for. Within the specified deadlines, the Commission is then to examine the information provided by the competent authorities and determine the quantity of quota or tranches for which licences are to be issued. The applications are, of course, to be met in full where licence applications are equal to or less than the quota available. Where applications exceed quota, they are to be satisfied on a pro rata basis by reference to the amounts applied for. [66]

Quantities of goods that are not allocated, assigned, or used, are to be redistributed in time to allow them to be used before the end of the quota period.[67]

C. TARIC AND THE TARIFF REGULATION

The TARIC is established pursuant to Tariff Regulation, Article 2 and is published in all the official languages of the Community. It is designed to show

---

[64] Ibid, Arts 9, 11 and 14. For an example of regulations providing for such redistribution in relation to certain imports from China see: Commission Regulation (EC) 786/98 of 14 Apr 1998 [1998] OJ L113/17; Commission Regulation (EC) 880/99 of 28 Apr 1999 [1999] OJ L113/17 and Commission Regulation (EC) 1280/98 of 19 June 1998 [1998] OJ L176/17.

[65] Art 12 of Council Regulation (EC) 520/94, in n 33 above.

[66] Ibid, Art 13.

[67] Ibid, Art 2.5. To facilitate redistribution, Member States are to inform the Commission, immediately they are aware of the quantities of quota assigned and not used, and in no case later than 20 days after the expiry of the licences,: ibid, Art 20. The rules governing redistribution are contained in ibid, Art 14.

the rules which apply to a specific product on importation into the customs territory (or in some cases on exportation from it). It incorporates the harmonized system, the CN, and the provisions of customs legislation relating to rates of duty, suspensions of tariff, tariff quotas, and preferences, the rules regarding the generalized system of preferences, anti-dumping and countervailing duties, and many other matters relating to import and export. Although published in the Official Journal, the TARIC is a practical document which does not itself have a legal status. Its codes must, however, be used for customs declarations and statistical returns.[68] Since 4 September 2000, what is known as the DDS (Data Dissemination System) database has been available on the Europa server of the Commission. This enables TARIC, the tariff quotas and ceilings (QUOTA), and the European Communities' Inventory of Chemical Substances (ECICS) to be consulted free on the World Wide Web.[69]

As required by the Tariff Regulation, Article 6, TARIC is established, updated, managed, and disseminated by the EC Commission using computerized means wherever possible. Updates are published annually[70] although alterations are made on an almost daily basis. The Commission is obliged to integrate into the TARIC all measures in the Tariff Regulation, or shown in Annex II to it, and must attribute the TARIC codes and additional codes.[71] The day-to-day changes are recorded in a database which is continually and immediately up-dated in electronic format.[72]

The Commission was formerly assisted by the Committee on Tariff and Statistical Nomenclature ('the Nomenclature Committee'). Now its role is fulfilled by the Customs Code Committee,[73] which is considered further below. It is sufficient here to note that, by virtue of the Tariff Regulation, Articles 7 and 8, the Committee can examine any matter referred to it by its chairman, either on its own initiative or at the request of a Member State. The matter may relate to the CN, the TARIC, and any other nomenclature which is wholly or partly based on the CN, or which adds any subdivisions to it, and which is established by Community provisions with a view to the application of tariff or

---

[68] Before 1987, the Community used the Nomenclature of goods for the external trade statistics of the Community and statistics of trade between member States ('Nimexe').

[69] The address is http://europa.eu.int/comm/taxation_customs/dds/en/home.htm as noted at [2000] OJ C321/24. The Commission decided on 9 Apr 2001 to stop the Taxation and Customs Union DG managing ECICS. It was also decided to stop intervention in the management of the BTI system: see further p 152 n 208. For the tariff schedule of the USA see http:/www.usite.gov/taffairs.htm.

[70] For the most recent see [2000] OJ C119/1.

[71] Art 6(a) and (b).

[72] Art 6(c) and (d). Art 12 also provides that measures and information concerning the tariff or TARIC shall, whenever possible, be disseminated in electronic format using computerized means.

[73] Tariff Regulation, Arts 6 and 10 as amended by Regulation 254/2000, in 3 above, Art 1.6 and 1.10. Art 1.10 ensures that the Committee operates according to the management procedure set out in Art 4 of Council Decision (EC) 468/99 of 28 June 1999 [1999] OJ L184/23, discussed at pp 126–127 and pp 90–91.

other measures relating to trade in goods. One activity of particular importance which is carried out by the Committee is the publication of opinions on the Combined Nomenclature. The force of these opinions is considered later on.

1. *The Commission's discretions in applying the CN and TARIC*

The Tariff Regulation, Article 9.1(a)–(g) sets out a number of matters in respect of which measures may be adopted by the Commission. These include the application of the combined nomenclature and the TARIC and, in particular, the classification of goods in the nomenclatures, Explanatory Notes, which are considered further below, and the creation of statistical sub-headings in the TARIC for the Community's own purposes. The Commission may make amendments to the CN to take account of changes in requirements relating to statistics, commercial policy, and to technological or commercial developments, and to ensure the alignment or clarification of texts, or compliance with changes to the harmonized system. It may also make amendments to measures within Annex II incorporated into the TARIC, make adjustments to duties to ensure compliance with decisions adopted by the Council or Commission and deal with questions relating to the application and functioning, management, and implementation of the harmonized system, which are to be discussed with the Customs Co-operation Council. Article 9.2 identifies a number of matters in respect of which the Commission may not act. These include measures to alter the rates of customs duties, certain matters relating to the common agricultural policy, and quantitive restrictions.

The procedure for adopting measures within Article 9 is set out in Article 10. This requires the management procedure to be adopted within Articles 4 and 7 of Decision (EC) 468/99.[74] Pursuant to Article 4 of the Decision, the Commission is to be assisted by the Customs Code Committee which is to be composed of representatives of the Member States, and chaired by a representative of the Commission. This representative must submit to the Committee a draft of the measures to be taken. The Committee must then deliver its opinion on the draft within a time period to be established by the Committee chairman, according to the urgency of the matter. The opinion is to be delivered by majority vote, as laid down in Article 205.2 of the Treaty in respect of decisions which the Council is required to adopt on a proposal from the Commission. The votes of the representatives of the Member States within the Committee are weighted in the manner set out in that Article. The chairman does not vote. It is provided that the Council acting by a qualified majority may take a different decision within three months of receiving a communication from the Commission about the measures it proposes to adopt. Provision is made for the

---

[74] A Decision of 28 June 1999, [1999] OJ L184/23. See also the EC Commission's Code of Conduct for the management of the CN [2000] OJ L150/4.

Commission to adopt measures which apply immediately with certain safeguards. Article 7 of the Decision requires the European Parliament to be kept informed of Committee proceedings and Article 7.2 provides that the principles and conditions on public access to documents applicable to the Commission shall apply to the committees.

1.1 *Case law on the Commission's role*

The scope of Article 9, in its original form, has been considered by the Court of Justice which has noted that:

> the Council has conferred upon the Commission, acting in co-operation with the customs experts of the Member States, a broad discretion to define the subject matter of tariff headings falling to be considered for the classification of particular goods. However, the Commission's power to adopt the measures mentioned in Article 9(1)(a), (b), (d) and (e) of Regulation No 2658/87 does not authorise it to alter the subject matter of the tariff headings which have been defined on the basis of the HS established by the Convention whose scope the Community has undertaken, under Article 3 thereof, not to modify . . .[75]

The Commission's powers are also limited where the WCO, otherwise known as the Customs Co-operation Council, has given an interpretation of the nomenclature. The Court has noted that 'if the Customs Cooperation Council has not given an interpretation of the nomenclature, the Community legislature has the power to interpret, by means of regulations and subject to review by the Court of Justice, the nomenclature as it is to be applied by the Community'.[76] Where the limitations on the Commission's power are not observed, the provisions in question are *ultra vires*.[77] In determining whether or not the Commission has exceeded its powers the Court of Justice has sought to establish whether the Commission has committed 'a manifest error of assessment'.[78] The phrase is useful to the extent that it indicates that the Court

---

[75] Case C–309/98 *Holz Geenan GmbH v Oberfinanzdirektion München* Judgment of 28 Mar 2000 para 13 which refers to Case C–267/94 *France v Commission* [1995] ECR I–4845 at paras 19–21, recently quoted by Jacobs AG at para 77 in his Opinion of 1 Feb 2001 in Case C–463/98 *Cabletron Systems Ltd v The Revenue Commissioners*. In the quotation, the Court omits a reference to Art 9(1)(c) as that refers to Community measures integrated into the TARIC. See also Case C–265/89 *Gebr. Vismans Nederland v Inspecteur der Invoerrechten en Accijnzen* [1990] ECR I–3411, para 13, Case C–401/93 *Goldstar Europe v Hauptzollamt Ludwigshafen* [1994] ECR I–5587, para 19, Case C–80/96 *Quelle Schickedanz AG und Co v Oberfinanzdirektion Frankfurt am Main* [1998] ECR I–123 at para 14 and Case 259/97 *Uwe Clees v Hauptzollamt Wuppertal* [1998] ECR I–8127 at paras 22–24.

[76] Case C–401/93 *Goldstar Europe v Hauptzollamt Ludwigshafen*, n 75 above at para 18. The Court relied upon Case 233/88 *Van de Kolk* [1990] ECR I–265 at para 10.

[77] See, eg, Case C–401/93 *Goldstar Europe v Hauptzollamt Ludwigshafen*, n 75 above, and Case 309/98 *Holz Geenan*, n 75 above. See also the Opinion of Fennelly AG in Case C–80/96 *Quelle Schickedanz AG und Co. v Oberfinanzdirektion Frankfurt am Main*, n 75 above, para 12.

[78] Case C–401/93 *Goldstar Europe v Hauptzollamt Ludwigshafen*, n 75 above, at para 20.

will not intervene except when a clear case has been established.[79] It leaves unresolved, however, the requisite degree of manifestness. Advocate General Jacobs addressed this issue recently in his Opinion in *Cabletron* in a way which highlighted that the nature of the Commission's discretion is not identical in every case. He said:

> Where there is real doubt [about classification], it is important that the Commission should be able to resolve that doubt within the Community in the interests of legal certainty but it is also important that Community law should not find itself at odds with the intended tenor of the HS. The concern not to limit unduly the Commission's power to settle genuinely doubtful cases by way of regulation must be qualified by the need to control the exercise of that power where it brings the Community into conflict with the uniform international practice which the HS seeks to achieve.

Having noted that in the case with which he was concerned what was at issue was the correct classification of goods in accordance with the Community's obligation to comply with the harmonized system, he said that:

> Closer scrutiny is I consider justified in such cases, where the dispute is between headings or sub-headings whose content is established at that higher level and which fall only to be interpreted for Community purposes, than where the Commission enjoys a fuller discretionary power, for example as regards the determination of the correct eight-digit sub-heading, which is a matter of Community law alone. In the former case . . . a regulation may be invalid by reason of its failure to comply with the Community's international obligations; in the latter, it will not be invalid unless the classification was manifestly at odds with the CN.[80]

1.2 Classification regulations

Regulations which are designed to clarify what goods fall within a particular tariff heading or sub-heading are, of course, legislative in nature. They cannot, therefore, have retroactive effect. For them to do so would infringe the principle of legal certainty.[81] Nevertheless, as Advocate General Jacobs has

[79] For a recent example of a case in which the Commission made an error of assessment see Joined Cases T–133/98 and T–134/98 *Hewlett Packard France and Hewlett Packard Europe BV v Commission*, 13 Feb 2001. In this case the Court of First Instance found that the Commission made an error of assessment in deciding that certain binding tariff information should be revoked in relation to a unit designed to enable personal computers in a local network to have access to and control of printers.

[80] Opinion in Case C–463/98 *Cabletron Systems Ltd v The Revenue Commissioners*, in n 75 above, at paras 83 and 84. Jacobs AG did not accept that international uncertainty over the classification of computer network equipment in the 1990's arising out of economic considerations, namely, the EC's desire to classify the equipment under a heading that resulted in the imposition of a higher rate of duty, could be said to prevent a manifest error of assessment. He therefore considered that the Court should hold the relevant regulations to be invalid. The Court approved paras 82 to 95 of Jacobs AG's Opinion at para 20 of its judgment of 10 May 2001.

[81] Case 158/78 *P Biegi v Hauptzollamt Bochum* [1979] ECR 1103, para 11. The Court has made

pointed out, the relevant regulations generally state that classification is determined by the provisions of the general rules for the interpretation of the nomenclature and by the wording of headings and sub-headings. This suggests that the legislature takes the view that the classification enacted follows from the legislation already in force.[82] The Court of Justice has suggested a similar approach to regulations concerning rules of interpretation for the Tariff, which are designed to co-ordinate interpretative practices for the Tariff as a whole and, therefore, do not form a 'legal innovation'.[83] it should also be emphasized that the fact that a Commission regulation is made, changing the classification of a product, does not mean that an earlier classification of the product was necessarily invalid,[84] or even perhaps incorrect. 'The validity of a regulation cannot be called in question because of events which took place at a later date.'[85] An individual trader cannot normally seek the annulment of a regulation relating to the CN in reliance upon the provisions of EC Treaty, Article 230, although a challenge may of course be brought by, for example, a Member State, pursuant to the second paragraph of Article 230.[86] The regulation is usually not of 'direct and individual concern' to the trader. Rather, it is of general application throughout the Community.[87] The proper recourse for the trader is to challenge the specific decision in relation to the particular goods in question.[88] In the course of that challenge the trader can allege, and the Court may find, the regulation in question to be invalid.[89] If it does so, the Court may limit the retroactive effect of its judgment so that only those persons who had initiated proceedings, or raised a claim, prior to the

the point on a number of occasions, see, eg, Case 30/71 *Kurt Siemers & Co v Hauptzollamt Bad Reichenhall* [1971] ECR 919 at para 8 and, most recently, Case C–479/99 *CBA Computer Handels- und Beteiligungs GmbH v Hauptzollamt Aachen*, 7 June 2001 at para 31.

[82] See the Opinions of Jacobs AG in Case C–201/99 *Deutsche Nichimen GmbH v Hauptzollamt Düsseldorf* [2000] ECR I–2701at para 24 and in Case C–11/93 *Siemens Nixdorf v Hauptzollamt Augsburg* [1994] ECR I–1945 ECR 2263 para 25.

[83] Case 183/73 *Osram GmbH v Oberfinanzdirektion Frankfurt/Main* [1974] ECR 477 at para 8.

[84] See the Opinion of Jacobs AG in Case C–401/93 *Goldstar Europe GmbH v Hauptzollamt Ludwigshafen*, n 75 above, at para 22. For a case before the UK courts on this see: *General Instrument (UK) Ltd v CCE* [1999] V&DR 443, [2000] 1 CMLR 34.

[85] Joined Cases 9 and 11/71 *Compagnie d'Approvisionnement v Commission* [1972] ECR 391 para 39. See also Joined Cases C–267/88 to C–285/88 *Wéidart v Laiterie Coóóperative Eupenoise and others* [1990] ECR I–435 at para 14.

[86] Case C–267/94, *France v Commission* at n 75 above, provides an example of a challenge succeeding on the ground that the Commission had altered a tariff classification and, therefore, exceeded its powers. Note too, that the governments of regions or self-governing communities do not have *locus standi* under the second para of Art 230. They may, however, be able to bring an action under the fourth para of the Article, on the same grounds as an individual: see Joined Cases T–32/98 and T–41/98 *Netherlands Antilles v Commission*, [2001] ECR II–201.

[87] See, eg, Case C–119/99 *Hewlett Packard BV v Directeur Général des Douanes et Droits Indirects*, 17 May 2001, at para 19.

[88] Case 40/84 *Casteels PVBA v Commission* [1985] ECR 667.

[89] See for an example of this Case C–309/98 *Holz Geenan GmbH v Oberfinanzdirektion München*, and Case C–463/98 *Cabletron Systems Ltd v The Revenue Commissioners*, nn 75 and 80 above.

date of the judgment can rely upon it. The general principle, however, is that any person may in any proceedings rely upon the invalidity of the measure. A departure from the general principle must be justified by overriding considerations of legal certainty.[90]

Two final points may be made in this section. First, when the Community legislature amends the Combined Nomenclature it has a duty to protect traders who would otherwise sustain unforeseeable and irreparable damage.[91] Secondly, regulations which are made suspending duty are, of course, construed according to the general scheme and purpose of the rules of which they form part. The concepts of legal certainty and objectivity retain their significance in relation to them.[92] Regulations governing classification generally must also, of course, be construed as having regard to the reasons given for them.[93]

D. THE TARIFF, THE COURT OF JUSTICE, AND THE REQUIREMENT OF OBJECTIVITY

The determination of the classification of specific goods is, of course, primarily the responsibility of traders who have to state on their declarations the code corresponding to the product in question. In fulfilling this responsibility they may seek information from the customs authorities and obtain binding tariff information, which is discussed at the end of this chapter. Disputes over classification between the trader and the customs authorities will, of course, proceed to domestic tribunals and courts which may refer the matter to the Court of Justice under EC Treaty, Article 234.

The cases are frequently of great financial significance, not just for traders, but for the authorities of the countries concerned. As Advocate General Jacobs has said 'The main purpose, other than statistical, of customs classification is to apply different tariffs to different goods, and the main origin of classification

---

[90] For customs duty cases in which temporal limitations of judgments were considered see Joined Cases C–485/93 and C–486/93 *Maria Simitzi v Dimos Kos* [1995] ECR 1–2655 at paras 29–34, Case C–163/90 *Administration des Douanes et Droits Indirects v Léopold Legros* [1992] ECR I–4625, paras 28–36, and Case C–463/98 *Cabletron Systems Ltd v The Revenue Commissioners*, at paras 111–115 of the Advocate General's Opinion, approved by the Court of Justice at para 26 of its judgment, nn 75 and 80 above. See also Case C–212/94 *FMC and others v Intervention Board for Agricultural Produce* [1996] ECR 1–389 paras 54–66 and Joined Cases C–38/90 and 151/90 *Criminal proceedings against Lomas and Others* [1992] ECR I–1781, paras 23–30.

[91] See Case C–315/96 *Lopex Export GmbH v Hauptzollamt Hamburg-Jonas* [1998] ECR I–317 para 30, discussed further below.

[92] Case C–338/90 *Hamlin Electronics GmbH v Hauptzollamt Darmstadt*, in n 28 above.

[93] See, eg, Case C–119/99 *Hewlett Packard BV v Directeur Général des Douanes et Droits Indirects*, in n 87 above, at para 20 and Case C–67/95 *Rank Xerox Manufacturing (Nederland) BV v Inspecteur des Invoerrechten en Accijnzen* [1997] ECR I–5401 at para 26.

disputes lies in the conflicting desires of traders and exporting countries for lower tariffs and of the revenue authorities of importing countries for higher tariffs.'[94] Probably the only situation in which a trader will be prepared to pay a higher rate of duty than is attributable to a product is where a single consignment contains many different goods and the costs of declaring which individual product falls under which tariff heading are disproportionate to the duty involved. In these circumstances all the goods may be declared as within the tariff heading attracting the highest amount of duty.[95] Ordinarily, however, traders will wish to ensure that the correct amount of duty is paid and, as we noted above, the forum in which a classification dispute is resolved will be a domestic one.

1. *The role of the Court of Justice*

Even where a reference is made to the Court of Justice, the national tribunal or court will retain its role of applying the Tariff. The role of the Court of Justice is to interpret the Tariff and the CN,[96] so that it is interpreted uniformly throughout the Community.[97] Although the division between interpretation and application is clear conceptually it is not necessarily plain or helpful in practice. It takes little ingenuity to formulate a question of application as a question of interpretation. Of course, the tension between interpretation and application of Community law is apparent in a number of areas of law, but is undoubtedly pronounced in classification matters. Not that the tension is anything new. A relatively short time after the establishment of the Tariff, Advocate General Roemer noted that:

> the only task assigned to the Court is to interpret the Community concepts . . . to enable the national court to make a correct classification. However, . . . an excessive scrupulosity in this matter is misplaced. In my opinion there can be no objection if the Court resolves directly the subsumed question of classification . . . and does not limit itself to giving a circumstantial and abstract definition of the concepts which have to be interpreted by means of which the national judge then proceeds to answer the larger question.[98]

The extent to which the Court is willing to classify goods itself undoubtedly depends upon the particular circumstances of the case. As anyone reading this section of the book will see, there have been many cases on classification which at first sight appear to be inappropriate for consideration by the Court of

---

[94] Case C–339/98 *Peacock AG v Hauptzollamt Paderborn* [2000] ECR I–8947. Opinion of Jacobs AG at para 26. [95] See CCC, Art 81.

[96] Joined Cases C–106/94 and C–139/94 *Criminal proceedings against Patrick Colin and Daniel Dupré* [1995] I–4759 at para 12.

[97] Case 317/81 *Howe & Brianbridge BV v Oberfinanzdirektion Frankfurt am Main* [1982] ECR 3257, para 16. See more recently, eg, Case C–201/96 *Laboratoires de Therapeutique Moderne (LTM) v Fonds d'Intervention et de Régularisation du Marché du Sucre (FIRS)* [1997] ECR 6147 at para 25.

[98] Case 40/69 *Hauptzollamt Hamburg-Oberelle v Firma Paul G Bollman* [1970] ECR 69 at 88.

Justice. The founding fathers of the Community surely did not imagine that the Court of Justice, established to oversee the legal order of the new Community, would need to rule that, for the purpose of Community law, 'nightdresses' includes 'under garments which, by reason of their objective characteristics, are intended to be worn exclusively or essentially in bed'.[99] One needs little imagination to perceive a certain weariness at the end of the judgment when, having considered a number of matters, the Court concluded:

> Finally, it remains to point out that it is, in any event, for the national court, within the context of the dispute before it, to determine, in the light of the cut of the garments, their composition and presentation, and developments in fashion within the Member State concerned, whether those garments do have such objective characteristics or whether, on the contrary, they may be worn equally in bed and elsewhere.[100]

Classification cases cover, of course, a wide variety of products. Relatively recently, the Court of Justice has had to rule in relation to the correct classification for products as diverse as network cards for personal computers,[101] digital copiers, and fax machines,[102] consignments of dried sweet peppers cut into pieces measuring between 4 and 8 mm,[103] 'Vista' boards consisting of printed circuits,[104] sets of underwear,[105] pharmaceutical preparations for the treatment of asthenia,[106] and skimmed milk cheese.[107] It is, nevertheless, easy to see the theoretical justification for the Court considering these cases. the Tariff is a fundamental element of the Community and it must, as we have already noted, be uniformly interpreted throughout all Member States. Failure to achieve uniformity of interpretation will result in distortions of trade. Yet, at a time when the workload of the Court is so great that the time taken to dispose of references is rising and the demands of enlargement have yet to be met, it is impossible to escape the fundamental question: should the Court of Justice continue to hear apparently routine classification cases?

This question was raised by Advocate General Jacobs in his Opinion in

---

[99] Case C–338/95 *Wiener SI GmbH v Hauptzollamt Emmerich* [1997] ECR I–6495 at para 21.

[100] See ibid, at para 21. See also Joined cases C–274/95, C–275/95 and C–276/95 *Ludwig Wünsche & Co. v Hauptzollamt Hamburg-Jonas* [1997] ECR I–2091 at para 22.

[101] Case C–339/98 *Peacock AG v Hauptzollamt Paderborn*, n 94 above.

[102] Case C–67/95 *Rank Xerox Manufacturing (Nederland) BV v Inspecteur der Invoerrechten en Accijnzen*, n 93 above.

[103] Case C–143/96 *Leonhard Knubben Speditions GmbH v Hauptzollamt Mannheim* [1997] ECR I–7039.

[104] Case C–382/95 *Techex Computer + Grafik Vertriebs GmbH v Hauptzollamt München* [1997] ECR I–7363.

[105] Case C–80/96 *Quelle Schickedanz AG und Co v Oberfinanzdirektion Frankfurt am Main*, n 75 above.

[106] Case C–270/96 *Laboratoires Sarget SA v Fonds d'Intervention et de Régularisation du Marché du Sucre (FIRS)* [1998] ECR I–1121.

[107] Case C–42/99 *Fabrica de Queijo ERU Portuguesa Ld^a v Tribunal Técnico de Segunda Instância*, [2000] ECR I–7691.

Wiener, which will surely prove to be essential reading for anyone advising on a classification case. In seeking to provide an answer to the question the Opinion considers fully the law on classification under the Tariff. The general thesis for which the Opinion contends is that, in straightforward classification cases, the Court has gone as far as it can in establishing the principles which national courts should apply. The Advocate General observed that he:

> [did] not consider that it is appropriate, or indeed possible, for the Court to continue to respond fully to all references which, through the creativity of lawyers and judges, are couched in terms of interpretation, even though the reference might in a particular case be better characterized as concerning the application of the law rather than its interpretation. However, to declare more references inadmissible would not be the right answer. Where a referring court has duly translated a Community law point into a question of interpretation the Court is in principle bound to reply.[108]

He concluded that 'It seems to me that the only appropriate solution is a greater measure of self-restraint on the part of both national courts and this Court.'[109] It is important, of course, to bear in mind that it is not every classification case in which the Court is doing no more than classifying particular goods. In some cases the validity of a regulation is in issue. In others, the Court is giving general guidance on, for example, the general rules for interpreting the Tariff. These types of cases, amongst others no doubt, the Advocate General would exclude from his rubric of restraint.

The views of the Advocate General ought to attract widespread agreement. Undoubtedly, there are numerous cases in which yet another formulaic judgment on the interpretation of the Tariff is unnecessary for the proper development of Community law, and recently the Advocate General's Opinion was specifically taken into account, by a judge of the High Court, in refusing a reference requested by the Commissioners of Customs and Excise.[110] Yet one point deserves to be made, namely, that despite the extensive case law of the Court of Justice and the best endeavours of all concerned, the relevant principles are not always applied correctly in classification matters. An example arose in *Holz Geenan*.[111] It appears to have been contended that the use of the product in question could not be taken into account for classification purposes because its use or intended use was not referred to in the relevant heading of the Tariff. Yet, as the Court had previously stated, use may be taken into account if it is inherent to the product and the inherent character of the product is capable of being assessed on the basis of the product's objective characteristics and properties.[112] The Court, then, must not only state the applicable

---

[108] Opinion Case 338/95 *Wiener SI GmbH v Hauptzollamt Emmerich* at n 99 above, para 17.
[109] Ibid, para 18.
[110] *CCE v Anchor Foods Ltd*, in n 27 above.   [111] In n 75 above.
[112] See 3.7 *The intended use of products* below.

principles of law but affirm and protect them; they cannot be left to fend for themselves. As a result, it is likely to continue to receive references from national courts with which, viewed objectively, it should not be troubled.[113]

Before leaving a consideration of the role of the Court of Justice it is worthwhile emphasizing, as Advocate General Jacobs did in *Peacock*, that it is a role with clearly defined limits. The Court is, he said:

> a court of law, specifically of Community law. Its role clearly includes the task of interpreting, as a matter of law, the terms of the CN. It is not a technical body qualified to settle disputes on purely technical matters, nor should it intervene in any way in a process of technical negotiation concerning the content of various HS headings, in which those with the appropriate expert knowledge will be seeking international agreement on . . . a vexed and highly technical question. That process may involve amendments clarifying the wording of the HS [Harmonized System] and is the most appropriate means of achieving a long-term settlement of the differences of opinion involved. The Court may, however, contribute by stating how the relevant terms of the CN are to be interpreted, at a given moment, as a matter of Community law.[114]

As we noted at the beginning of this book,[115] classification cases may provide lawyers with the opportunity to play a role in relation to delicate commercial matters, sometimes of international significance. The role of lawyers and of law, however, is inevitably limited. Its fulfilment should never have the effect of excluding the technical expert, the trade diplomat and, ultimately, the elected politician from the centre of the stage.

2. *The Court of Justice's general approach and the requirement of objectivity*

The Court takes, in many respects, no different an approach to the interpretation of measures governing the classification of products than it does to any others. The context and objective of regulations amending the Tariff are to be borne in mind as they are in other fields of Community law.[116] It should be

---

[113] Recent changes in the working practices of the Court of Justice may assist the process of ensuring that the Court takes time only with significant references: see, eg, Art 104.3 of the Rules of Procedure of the Court of Justice, updated as at 1 Feb 2001 [2001] OJ C34/1, which states that: 'Where a question referred to the Court for a preliminary ruling is identical to a question on which the Court has already ruled, where the answer to such a question may be clearly deduced from existing case-law or where the answer to the question admits of no reasonable doubt, the Court may, after informing the court or tribunal which referred the question to it, hearing any observations submitted by the persons referred to in Article 20 of the EC Statute, Article 21 of the Euratom Statute and Article 103(3) of these Rules and hearing the Advocate General, give its decision by reasoned order in which, if appropriate, reference is made to its previous judgment or to the relevant case-law.'

[114] Case 339/98 *Peacock AG v Hauptzollamt Paderborn*, n 94 above. Opinion at para 37.

[115] See pp 1–2.

[116] Case 194/91 *Firma John Friedrich Krohn v Hauptzollamt Hamburg-Jonas* [1992] ECR I–6661 para 10.

noted that so far as concerns the languages of the Combined Nomenclature, although it appears in all the official languages of the Community, it may be the English and French versions which one should primarily have regard to in cases of difficulty. The reason is that, as we noted above, the Combined Nomenclature is based on the harmonized system and only the English and French versions of this are authoritative.[117]

There are a number of specific matters which must be ignored by the Court and a number which it must take into account in classification cases. As regards the former, an amendment to a heading in the Tariff was ignored where it was adopted after the case in question, as one would expect. It did not matter that the amendment had been proposed at the time of the case nor that the Nomenclature Committee of the WCO had made clear that pre-amendment classifications of the product should be different.[118] Also to be ignored are alleged trade usages of terms and differences in classification between Member States[119] along with Euronorms adopted by the European Committee for Standardization in relation to steel products.[120] Other matters are ignored where they do not comply with the requirement of objectivity and are considered below. The most important additional matters to be taken into account in classification cases are the general rules for the interpretation of the CN and various explanatory notes and opinions. These matters are considered below. The most fundamental rule in classification cases, though, is that classification must be made on the basis of the objective properties and characteristics of the goods in question. The Court of Justice regularly sets out the requirement of objectivity in classification cases and has recently described its approach as follows:

> in the interests of legal certainty and ease of verification, the decisive criterion for the customs classification of goods must be their objective characteristics and properties, as defined by the wording of the headings of the Common Customs Tariff and the notes to the sections or chapters . . . Likewise, the notes preceding the chapters of the Common Customs Tariff and the explanatory notes drawn up by the Customs Cooperation Council are important means for ensuring the uniform application of the Tariff and may be an important aid to the interpretation of the scope of the various tariff headings but do not have any legally bind force.[121]

---

[117] See Case C–143/96 *Leonhard Knubben Speditions GmbH v Hauptzollamt Mannheim*, n 103 above, at para 15. See also Jacobs AG's Opinion in *Holz Geenan GmbH v Oberhauzdirektion München*, n 75 above, at paras 41 and 42 where regard is had to all Community languages.

[118] Case C–120/90 *Ludwig Post GmbH v Oberfinanzdirektion Müchen* [1991] ECR I–2391.

[119] See, eg, Case 120/90 *Ludwig Post GmbH Oberfinanzdirektion München*, n 118 above, at para 24. Note, however, that the requirement to ignore trade usage does not mean that an internationally accepted meaning of a term *must* be accepted in preference to it: see *CEE v Anchor Foods Ltd*, n 27 above, at 437 (Dyson J, High Court).

[120] See Case 122/80 *Jepsen Stahl v Hauptzollamt Emmerich* [1981] ECR 2781, para 12 and Case 234/87 *Casio Computer Co. GmbH v Oberfinanzdirektion München* [1989] ECR 63, para 12.

[121] Case C–164/95 *Fábrica de Queijo Eru Portuguesa Ldª v Alfândega de Lisboa (Tribunal Técnico Aduaneiro de 2ª Instância)* [1997] ECR I–3441, para 13. See also Case C–479/99 *CBA Computer Handels und Beteiligungs GmbH v Hauptzollamt Aachen*, n 81 above, at para 21; Case C–288/99 *Van*

It is not just the process of classification in which objectivity is important. It is important too in drawing the distinctions between the Tariff headings. The Court has, on a number of occasions made clear that these distinctions: '. . . cannot be based on qualities which are defined essentially by reference to subjective and indeterminate criteria but must be founded on the objective criteria adopted by the Tariff for the purposes both of its effective operation and of legal certainty. . . .'[122]

2.1 *Time that objective characteristics considered*

The consideration of the objective characteristics and properties of products is generally to be carried out as at the time of their presentation for customs clearance.[123] This fact does not mean, however, that the differences between products will always be apparent at that time. Subsequent technical or scientific analysis may be necessary in order for the objective characteristics and properties of products to be ascertained.[124]

2.2 *Evidence of objective characteristics*

In determining the objective characteristics and properties of products a

De Sport GmbH Co. KG v Oberfinanzdirektion Koblenz, 10 May 2001, para 12; Case C–201/99 *Deutsche Nichimen GmbH v Hauptzollamt Düsseldorf,* 5 Apr 2001 at para 19; Joined Cases T–133/98 and T–134/98 *Hewlett Packard France and Hewlett Packard Europe BV v Commission,* n 79 above, at para 24. In the latter case the Court referred to Case C–339/98 *Peacock AG v Hauptzollamt Paderborn,* n 94 above, at para 9, Case C–11/93 *Siemens Nixdorf v Hauptzollamt Augsberg,* n 82 above, at para 11 and Case C–382/95 *Techex Computer etc v Hauptzollamt München,* n 104 above, at para 11. See also Case C–270/96 *Laboratoires Sarget SA v Fonds d'Intervention et de Régularisation du Marché du Sucre (FIRS),* n 106 above, at para 16 and the cases referred to in it namely: Case C–201/96 *Laboratoires de Therapeutique Moderne (LTM) v Fonds d'Intervention et de Régularisation du Marché du Sucre (FIRS),* in 97 above, at para 17, Case 175/82 *Hans Dinter GmbH v Hauptzollamt Kölu Deutz* [1983] ECR 963 at paras 9 and 10, Case C–459/93 *Hauptzollamt Hamburg-St. Annen v Thyssen Haniel Logistic* [1995] ECR I–1381 para 8, Joined Cases C–106/94 and C–139/94 *Colin and Dupré* [1995] ECR I–4759 para 22 and Case 35/93 *Develop Dr Eisbein GmbH & Co. v Hauptzollamt Stuttgart-West* [1995] ECR I–2655 at para 21. Statements similar to the quotation above appear in many judgments of the Court but in the early cases the statement is somewhat less developed: see, eg, Joined Cases 98 and 99/75 *Carstens Keramik GmbH and Firma August Hoff v Oberfinanzdirektion Frankfurt am Main* [1976] ECR 241 at para 8.

[122] Case C–228/89 *Farfalla Flemming und Partner v Hauptzollamt München-West* [1990] ECR I–3387 at para 12. See also see judgments in Case 23/77 *Westfälischer Kunstverein v Hauptzollamt Münster* [1977] ECR 1985, para 3, and Case C–1/89 *Ingrid Raab v Hauptzollamt Berlin-Packhof* [1989] ECR 4423, para 25.

[123] Case 175/82 *Hans Dinter GmbH v Hauptzollamt Köln-Deutz* in n 121, para 10.

[124] See Case 175/82 *Hans Dinter GmbH v Hauptzollamt Köln Deutz,* n 121 above, at para 3 in which particles of seasoning, identifiable neither organoleptically nor optically, but only microscopically, changed the classification of turkey meat. A subjective characteristic such as taste could not, at first, be considered. Subsequently, however, laboratory analysis could identify four basic flavours, sweet, acid, salt and bitter: Case C–233/88 *Gijs van de Kolk-Douane Expéditeur BV v Inspecteur der invoerrechten en accijnzen,* [1990] ECR I–265, at paras 13–16. Both cases were referred to in Case C–38/95 *Ministero delle Finanze v Foods Import Srl* [1996] ECR I–6543 para 17. See also 'Sight and sensory perception' below at 3.9, p 140.

tribunal or court is likely, in many cases to be assisted by expert evidence. Sometimes this may be derived from oral testimony and specially commissioned reports. On other occasions catalogues and learned treatises may be consulted. So far as foodstuffs are concerned, for example, the Codex Alimentarius drawn up by the Food and Agriculture Organization and the World Health Organization may be referred to.[125] More specialist works may also be useful. For example, the VAT and Duties Tribunal has had regard to a work on citrus fruit[126] and the Court of Justice has had regard to works on the classification of fish.[127]

3. *Specific considerations relating to objectivity*

In the course of considering the requirement of objectivity, the Court of Justice has commented on a number of specific matters, such as the relevance of taste and the significance of technological development. Some of these matters are set out below in alphabetical order.

3.1 *Advances in medical science*

In classifying medicaments regard must be had to medical developments.[128] This may be particularly significant, for example, where the medical properties of a product are newly established.

3.2 *Artistic merit*

One consideration which is clearly too subjective to be relevant to classification is artistic merit.[129]

3.3 *Breeding methods*

Just as the method of manufacturing an inanimate object is to be ignored, as

---

[125] See, eg, the Opinion of Fennelly AG in Case C–42/99 *Fábrica de Queijo ERU Portuguesa Ld^a v Tribunal Técnico de Segunda Instância*, n 107 above, at para 33. Also of use may be a Common Catalogue of Varieties of Vegetable Species published by the Commission. The 10th and most recent supplement to the 21st complete edition is at [2001] OJ C252A/1.

[126] The work was *Citrus Varieties of the World* by J Saunt (Sinclair International, Norwich, 1990). In *Louis Konyn & Sons Ltd v CCE* [1999] V&DR 189 the tribunal said 'We are indebted to *Saunt* for our findings of fact on the subject of limes' (at 192).

[127] See Case C–38/95 *Ministero delle Finanze v Foods Import Srl*, n 124 above, at para 16. Fennelly AG refers, at para 15 of his Opinion, to D M Cohen, T Inada, T Iwamoto and N Scialabba, FAO Species Catalogue, *Gadiform Fishes of the World* Vol. 10 (FAO, Rome, 1990) and Commission of the EC, *Multilingual Illustrated Dictionary of Aquatic Animals and Plants* (Office for Official Publications of the EC, Brussels, Luxembourg, 1993).

[128] Case C–177/91 *Bioforce GmbH v Oberfinanzdirektion München* [1993] ECR I–45 para 9 onwards (hawthorn drops).

[129] See Case 23/77 *Westfälischer Kunstverein v Hauptzollamt Münster* [1977] ECR 1985 at 1990, para 3 and Case C–1/89 *Ingrid Raab v Hauptzollamt Berlin-Packhof*, n 122 above, para 25.

we shall see below, so too is the specific method of breeding an animal. For example, the Court of Justice has held that the distinction between the meat of domestic swine and other swine-meat was to be sought in the notion of species, which identifies a category defined on the basis of objective zoological and genetic criteria, not on the basis of the specific method by which the animals are bred.[130]

3.4 *Functions which the product facilitates*

The Court of Justice distinguishes between an analysis of a product by reference to its objective characteristics and properties and an assessment of it on the basis of the functions that it enables an item, in which it is incorporated, to perform.[131]

3.5 *Geographical origin*

The Court has said that 'a product's classification may depend on the process by which it is manufactured or the geographical origin of some of its constituents, those being characteristics which are not necessarily apparent.'[132] Nevertheless, this will be so only where the Tariff refers to them.[133]

3.6 *Intention and the creation of products*

Whether or not the product in question, such as a mixture of animal foods, was intentionally created is immaterial.[134]

3.7 *The intended use of products*

The intended use of a product may constitute an objective criterion for classification if it is inherent to the product and the inherent character of the product is capable of being assessed on the basis of the product's objective characteristics and properties.[135] This test can be simply satisfied. For exam-

---

[130] Case C–393/93 *Walter Stanner GmbH & Co KG v Hauptzollamt Bochum* [1994] ECR I–4011.
[131] See Case C–339/98 *Peacock AG v Hauptzollamt Paderborn*, n 94 above, para 14. See also Case C–382/95 *Techex Computer + Grafik Vertriebs GmbH v Hauptzollamt München*, n 104 above, at para 19.   [132] Case C–38/95 *Ministero dell Finanze v Foods Import Srl*, n 124 above.
[133] See Case 40/88 *Paul F Weber (in liquidation) v Milchwerke Paderborn-Rimbeck AG* [1989] ECR 1395 paras 16 and 17.
[134] Case 36/71 *Günter Henck v Hauptzollamt Emden* [1972] ECR 187 at 200.
[135] Case C–201/99 *Deutsche Nichimen GmbH v Hauptzollamt Düsseldorf*, n 121 above. Case C–309/98 *Holz Geenan GmbH v Oberfinanzdirektion München*, in n 75 above, at para 15. See Case C–459/93 *Hauptzollamt Hamburg St. Annen v Thyssen Haniel Logistic GmbH*, n 121 above, at para 13, Case 36/71 *Günter Henck v Hauptzollamt Emden*, n 134 above, at para 4. See also Case 256/91 *Emsland-Stärke GmbH v Oberfinanzdirektion München* [1993] I–1857 at para 16, Case 114/80 *Dr Ritter GmbH & Co v Oberfinanzdirektion Hamburg* [1981] ECR 895, and Case 192/82 *Kaffee-Contor Bremen GmbH & Co KG v Hautpzollamt Bremen-Nord* [1983] ECR 1769 at para 12. For statements which do not refer to use being inherent to the product see, eg, Case 38/76 *Industriemetall Luma*

ple, in *Holz Geenan* the Court, in considering the classification of laminated window scantlings, said that 'the very wording of CN heading 4418, which refers to 'builders' goods, contains a criterion of intended use.'[136] Indeed, the fact that use could be taken into account in classification has been made clear by the Court since the decision in *Günter Henck*[137] and has been repeated subsequently in the cases referred to in footnote 135. On occasions it appears that, in relation to products which may be used in a number of different ways, the intended main use may be its only distinguishing objective characteristic. In *Neckerman* for example, the Court said:

> In the absence of . . . a definition, the objective characteristic of pyjamas, which is capable of distinguishing it from other ensembles, can be sought only in the use for which pyjamas are intended, that is to say to be worn in bed as nightwear . . . It follows that, for a garment to be classified as pyjamas for customs purposes, it does not have to be solely or exclusively meant to be worn in bed. It suffices if that is the main use for which it is intended.[138]

The fact, therefore, that the products in question could be used other than as pyjamas did not prevent them being so classified.

3.8 *Manufacturing and processing of products*

As the objective characteristics and properties of goods are fundamental for classification, the process of manufacturing is not usually relevant to it.[139] Where, however, the Tariff refers to manufacturing processes, as in *Develop Dr Eisben*,[140] they are to be taken into account. The Court has said that:

> whilst the Customs Tariff does indeed in certain cases contain references to manufacturing processes it is generally preferred to employ criteria for classification based

GmbH v Hauptzollamt Duisburg [1976] ECR 2027 at para 7 and Case 219/89 *Wesergold GmbH & Co. KG v Oberfinanzdirektion München* [1991] ECR I–1895 para 9, Case 246/90 *Parma Handelsgesellschaft GmbH v Hauptzollamt Bad Reichenhall* [1992] ECR 3467 paras 20 and 26 and, before the VAT and Duties Tribunal, *Colour Communications Incorporated v CCE* (C00083), 11 Aug 1998. For an example of a case in which use was not taken into account because it was not 'inherent' see Case 222/85 *Hauptzollamt Osnabrück v Kleiderwerke Hela Lampe GmbH & Co. KG* [1986] ECR 2449. It is, of course, true that the purpose of the product may be expressly referred to in the CN: see, for an example, Case C–218/89 *Shimadzu Europa GmbH v Oberfinanzdirection Berlin* [1990] ECR I–4391 which concerned oscilloscopes, etc, in CN 9030, and Case C–108/92 *Astro-Med GmbH v Oberfinanzdirektion Berlin* [1993] ECR I–3797 which concerned thermorecorders.

[136] n 75 above, para 18 of the judgment.
[137] Case 36/71 *Gunter Henck v Hauptzollamt Emden*, n 134 above.
[138] Case C–395/93 *Neckermann Versand AG v Hauptzollamt Frankfurt/Main-Ost.* [1994] ECR I–4027, at paras 8 and 9. The reasoning in this case was followed in Case C–338/95 *Wiener SI*, n 99 above, at paras 13–15.
[139] Case 145/81 *Hauptzollamt Hamburg-Jonas v Ludwig Wünsche & Co* [1982] ECR 2493 at paras 11 and 12.
[140] Case C–35/93 *Develop Dr Eisben GmbH & Co v Hauptzollamt Stuttgart-West* [1994] ECR I–2655. See also Case C–248/92 *Jepsen Stahl GmbH v Hauptzollamt Emmerich* [1993] ECR I–4721, Case C–338/90 *Hamlin Electronics v Hauptzollamt Darmstadt*, in n 28 above, and Case 40/80 *Weber v Milchwerke Paderborn-Rimbeck*, n 133 above.

on the objective characteristics and properties of products which can be ascertained when customs clearance is obtained. . . . Consequently, manufacturing processes are decisive only when the subheading so provides.[141]

So far as the processing of a product is concerned, this does not affect classification if the processed product contains the essential constituents of the basic product, in proportions which do not differ substantially from those which the product exhibits in its natural state.[142]

3.9 *Sight and sensory perception*

In one case, where the Tariff did not expressly or by implication refer to what may be seen, the Court said a particular classification could only be obtained if the importer:

> . . . submits his goods for customs inspection in a form which enables it to be recognized on visual inspection that they are in fact [goods within the classification]. This solution is not only in accordance with the requirement of simplicity of inspection, because it avoids metallographic analyses, but also serves to prevent the risk of frauds . . .[143]

Other matters of a perception, such as what can be seen with the naked eye,[144] what can be distinguished by taste[145] or smell[146] may be taken into account

---

[141] Case 40/88 *Paul F Weber (in liquidation) v Milchwerke Paderborn-Rimbeck AG*, n 133 above, at paras 14 and 15. The Court relied upon Case 38/76 *Industriemetall Luma v Hauptzollamt Duisburg* [1976] ECR 2027 and Case 42/86 *Directeur général des douanes et droits indirects v Artimport* [1987] ECR 4817.

[142] Case 120/90 *Ludwig Post GmbH v Oberfinanzdirektion München*, in n 118 above, para 19, Case 40/88 *Paul F Weber (in liquidation) v Milchwerke Paderborn-Rimbeck*, in n 133 above, para 19 and Case 36/71 *Gunter Henck v Hauptzollamt Emden*, in n 134 above, at para 10.

[143] See Case 111/77 *Bleiindustrie KG, formerly Jung & Lindig v Hauptzollamt Hamburg-Waltershof* [1978] ECR 659, para 7.

[144] See Note 2(a)(1) to Chapter 59 of the CN which provides that Heading No 5903 applies to 'fabrics in which the impregnation, coating or covering cannot be seen with the naked eye . . . ' Note 2(a)(3) refers to 'products in which the textile fabric is either completely embedded in plastics or entirely coated or covered on both sides with such material, provided that such coating or covering can be seen with the naked eye with no account being taken of any resulting change of colour'. In Case 317/81 *Howe & Brianbridge BV v Oberfinanzdirektion Frankfurt am Main*, n 97 above, at para 14, it was said that in order to satisfy this test the impregnation must be 'directly visible upon simple visual examination'. See also Chapter 52 (Cotton) Note 1 which refers to 'products of one and the same colour' and Chapter 63 (Other Made-Up Textile Articles . . .) note 3(b) with its reference to goods 'which show signs of appreciable wear'. For examples of the application of the naked eye test in the UK VAT and Duties Tribunal see *NDC (UK) Ltd v The Commissioners of Customs and Excise* C 00120, decision released 7 July 2000 and *Lloyd Pascal & Company Ltd v The Commissioners of Customs and Excise* C 00135, 8 Mar 2001.

[145] See Case 185/73 *Hauptzollamt Bielefeld v Offene Handelsgesellschaft in Firma H C König* [1974] ECR 607 in which the Court noted that taste was relevant to classification. The concept of 'cooking' refers to a change in taste and in the chemical properties of a product: see Case 324/89 *Nordgetranke GmbH & Co KG v Hauptzollamt Hamburg-Ericus* [1991] ECR I–1927 paras 8–9.

[146] See the references to scented products or those impregnated with perfume in Note 4 to Chapter 33 (Essential Oils etc). See also, eg, the reference to 'perfumed bath salts' at CN 3307 30 00 00.

where required by the Tariff. Such factors should be determined in an objective way where possible. Taste is one subjective matter which may be relevant in classification. For example, additional Note 6(a) in Chapter 2 in Section I of Part II states that: '"Seasoned meat" shall be uncooked meat that has been seasoned either in depth or over the whole surface of the product with seasoning either visible to the naked eye or clearly distinguishable by taste'. The Court has held this note valid. Furthermore, it did not regard the reference to taste as infringing the requirement of objectivity, stating:

> In order to apply criteria such as those set out in the note at issue, there are objective techniques of sensory analysis which have recently been developed and for which national and international standards have been laid down, for example, Standard DIN 10954 in the Federal Republic of Germany and Standard ISO 4120, which the International Organization for Standardization, Geneva, submitted to its member committees in 1982. . . . [T]hose methods of analysis allow, in particular, the goods as presented for customs clearance to be accurately assessed for the four basic flavours—sweet, acid, salt and bitter—which can be detected, even at very low levels, by a statistically significant population.[147]

The Court had earlier stated that the presence of seasoning in 'prepared meat' had to be determined by laboratory analysis[148] and that taste was irrelevant to classification as being too subjective.[149] The Court subsequently said, however, that:

> it must be pointed out that that judgment was delivered in different circumstances from those in the present case; there was no provision in a regulation on the interpretation of the Common Customs Tariff and at the time of the national authorities' inspection of the goods Standard ISO 4120 had not yet been devised.[150]

3.10 *Technological innovation*

The application of new technological innovations in a product does not in itself change its classification. In *Analog Devices*,[151] the Court noted that:

> ... it cannot be denied that the technical developments which have taken place in the industrial sector concerned, as a result of which the use of integrated circuits has become more widespread, justify the drawing up of a new customs classification.

[147] Case 233/88 *Gijs van de Kolk-Douane Expéditeur BV v Inspecteur der Invoerrechten en Accijnzen*, n 124 above, at para 13.
[148] In this context it should be noted that Art 12.3 of the Tariff Regulation, as amended by Regulation 254/2000, provides that the Commission is to promote the co-ordination and harmonization of practices in Member States' customs laboratories, using wherever possible, computerized means.
[149] Case 175/82 *Hans Dinter GmbH v Hauptzollamt Köhn-Deutz* at n 121 above, para 9.
[150] Case 233/88, *Gijs van der Kolk Douane Expediteur Bv v Inspecteur der Invoerrechten en Accijnzen*, n 124 above, para 15.
[151] Case 122/80 *Analog Devices v Hauptzollamt München-Mütte and Hauptzollamt München-West* [1981] ECR 2781.

However, if that is the case, it is for the competent Community institutions to take account of it by amending the Common Customs Tariff. Failing such an amendment, the interpretation of the tariff cannot be adapted to changing processes.[152]

It is, of course, the case that the possibilities of technological development may be encompassed within the Tariff. Again this was significant in *Analog Devices* which was concerned with the concept of miniaturization within Note 5(B)(a) and (c) to chapter 85 of the Tariff, in relation to electronic integrated circuits and microassemblies. The Court noted that 'The concept of miniaturisation constitutes a relative criterion which refers, at least indirectly, to the normal technical possibilities in existence in the electronics industry at the time of importation.'[153] Furthermore, technological developments can be taken into account in interpreting the Tariff. For example, in *Chem-Tec* the Court construed the term 'packages' 'taking into account the relevant explanatory notes, in the light of the particularly swift pace of technical development in the case of packages'.[154]

E. AIDS TO THE INTERPRETATION OF THE TARIFF

1. *General rules regarding the CN*

In Part One Section 1 of the CN at 'A' are the general rules for the interpretation of the nomenclature. They are, in fact, the general rules for the interpretation of the Harmonized System. At 'B' are general rules concerning duties which are referred to at B.2 'Customs duties: common features—different types' above. At 'C' are general rules applicable both to nomenclature and to duties. We consider the rules in 'A' and 'C' next.

1.1 *General rules for the interpretation of the CN*

These are capable of being of great importance and are not infrequently referred to by the Court of Justice. They are summarized below, but in any situation in which they are significant reference should obviously be made to the precise wording of each rule.

Rule 1[155] states that the titles of sections, chapters, and sub-chapters are

---

[152] Case 122/80 *Analog Devices*, n 151 above, para 12. See also Case C–67/95 *Rank Xerox Manufacturing (Nederland) BV v Inspecteur der Invoerrechten en Accijnen*, n 93 above, at para 22. See also Case 234/87 *Casio Computer Co GmbH Deutschland v Oberfinanzdirektion München* at n 120 above, paras 12–13.

[153] Case 122/80 *Analog Devices v Hauptzollamt München Mütte etc*, n 151 above, at para 20.

[154] Case 278/80 *Chem-Tec v Hauptzollamt Koblenz* [1982] ECR 439, at para 14.

[155] Referred to, eg, in Case C–1/89 *Ingrid Raab v Hauptzollamt Berlin-Packhof*, n 122 above, paras 12 and 24 and Case C–38/95 *Ministero delle Finanze v Foods Import Srl*, n 124 above, paras 13 and 19.

143

provided for ease of reference only and that classification of goods is to be determined according to the terms of the headings to any section or chapter notes and, in the absence of any contrary statement, to a number of other rules.[156] These are to be referred to only if the application of the first rule does not enable classification to be made.

Rule 2(a) states that any reference in a heading to an article shall be taken to include a reference to that article complete or finished, unassembled or disassembled,[157] or incomplete or unfinished, so long as it has the essential character of the complete or finished article.[158] The purpose of the rule is 'to enable two products which are extremely close to one another, to the extent that they are in substance identical from the user's point of view, to be deemed to be the same notwithstanding differences relating only to their presentation'.[159] The Court has said, in a case concerning unsterile calf foetus serum, that only a product which is so close to the finished product that it can come under the same tariff heading as the finished product can be accepted as having such character.[160] Unsurprisingly, a component within a video recorder which only represented 30 to 40 per cent of the video recorder could not be classified as a video recorder.[161] It should also be noted that the explanatory note on rule 2(a) states that it does not 'normally' apply to products in Sections I to VI, in other words Chapters 1–38, although, of course, it is capable of doing so.

According to rule 2(b), any reference in a heading to a material or substance is to include references to mixtures of them with other materials or substances and to goods consisting wholly or partly of such material or substance. The classification of goods consisting of more than one material or substance is governed by rule 3.[162] This provides, at (a), that where goods are

---

[156] Commission Regulation (EC) 2204/1999 of 12 Oct 1999 amending Annex I to the Tariff Regulation [1999] OJ L278/1, 11–13.

[157] At least at one time, the German translation of Rule 2(a) referred only to 'disassembled': Case 165/78 *IMCO - J Michaelis GmbH & Co. v Oberfinanzdirektion Berlin* [1979] ECR 1837.

[158] This rule was considered in Case 35/93 *Develop Dr Eisben Gmb and Co v Hauptzollamt Stuttgart-west*, n 140 above. The Court held that an article is to be regarded as imported unassembled or disassembled where the component parts are all presented for customs clearance at the same time and no account is to be taken in that regard of the assembly technique or the complexity of the assembly method (see para 19). see also Case 183/73 *Osram GmbH v Oberfinanzdirektion Frankfurt*, n 83 above, at paras 7 and 8 and Case C–280/97 *ROSE Elektrotechnik GmbH & Co. v Oberfinanzdirektion Köln*, [1999] ECR I–689. Where standard interchangeable parts are concerned, only those parts which may be assembled to form the finished article should be classified under the appropriate heading. The remainder are covered by the concept of 'parts and fittings': see Case 165/78 *IMCO - J Michaelis GmbH & Co. v Oberfinanzdirektion Berlin*, in n 157 above, at paras 9–10.

[159] Case 290/97 *Georg Bruner v Hauptzollamt Hamburg-Jonas* [1998] ECR I–8333 para 32.

[160] Case C–318/90 *Hauptzollamt Mannheim v Boehringer Mannheim GmbH* [1992] ECR I–3495 para 18 applied in Case 290/97 *Georg Bruner v Hauptzollamt Hamburg-Jonas*, n 159 above, para 30.

[161] Case C–401/93 *GoldStar Europe GmbH v Hauptzollamt Ludwigshafen*, n 75 above, at para 27.

[162] This rule was considered in Case 67/95 *Rank Xerox Manufacturing (Nederland) BV v Inspecteur des Invoerrechten en Accijnzen*, n 93 above, paras 30–31 in Case C–105/96 *Codiesel - Sociedade de*

classifiable under two or more headings, then the heading which provides the most specific description is to be preferred. Where two or more headings refer to part only of materials or substances contained in mixed or composite goods, or to part only of the items in a set put up for retail sale, the headings are regarded as equally specific, even if one of them gives a more complete or precise description of the goods.[163] Under rule 3(b), goods which cannot be classified under rule 3(a) are to be classified as if they consisted of the material or component which give them their essential character so far as this criterion is applicable. The essential character of the goods may be ascertained by '... determining whether the product would retain its characteristic properties if one or other of its constituents were removed from it.'[164] If neither rule 3(a) nor (b) facilitates classification, rule 3(c) requires that the goods in question are to be classified under the heading which occurs last in numerical order among those which equally merit consideration.[165]

Rule 4 requires that goods which cannot be classified under the foregoing are to be classified under the heading appropriate to the goods to which they are most akin. The Court of Justice has stated that the decision as to what goods a product is most akin is to be decided not only on the basis of physical characteristics, but also on their commercial use and value, which in the absence of special circumstances is their market price.[166] The appropriate

Apoio Técnico a Industriá Ldª v Conselho Técnico Aduaneiro [1997] ECR I–3465, para 22 onwards and in *Quelle Schickedanz AG und Co v Oberfinanzdirektion Franfurt am Main*, n 75 above, at 142–3 para 11–14. See also Case 37/88 *Rheinkrone-Kraftfutterwerk Gebr Heubers GmbH & Co KG, Wesel, v Hauptzollamt Hamburg-Jonas* [1989] ECR 3013.

[163] As well as determining whether goods are in sets it can be important to determine whether they consist of a functional unit in which case, according to the explanatory notes issued by the Customs Co-operation Council they should be classified together: see further E.3.1, Case law on specific goods and classification headings, below.

[164] Case 253/87 *Sportex v Oberfinanzdirecktion Hamburg* [1988] ECR 3351 at para 8 of the judgment applied in Case C–288/99 *VauDe Sport GmbH & Co KG v Oberfinanzdirektion Koblenz*, in n 121above, at para 25. For further examples of the application of rule 3 see: Case 278/80 *Chem-Tec v Hauptzollamt Koblenz*, n 154 above; Case 205/80 *ELBA Elektroapparate- und Maschinenbau Walter Goettmann KG v Hauptzollamt Berlin-Packhof* [1981] ECR 2097; Case 60/83 *Metro International Kommanditgesellschaft v Oberfinanzdirektion München* [1984] ECR 671; Case C–191/91 *Abbott GmbH v Oberfinanzdirektion Köln* [1993] ECR I-867; Case 256/91 *Emsland-Stärke GmbH v Oberfinanzdirektion München* [1993] I–1857; Case 356/93 *Techmeda Internationale Medizinisch-Technische Marketing- und Handels- GmbH & Co KG v Oberfinanzdirektion Köln* [1994] ECR I–2371. Case 253/87 was referred to in Case C–151/93 *Criminal proceedings against M. Voogd Vleesimport en-export BV* [1994] ECR I–4915 and Case C–150/93 *Directeur Général des Douanes et Droits Indirects v Société Superior France SA and Danzas SA* [1994] ECR I–1161. See also Joined Cases 59 and 64/94 *Ministre des Finances v Société Pardo & Fils and Camicas SARL* [1995] ECR I–3159 and Case C–121/95 *VOBIS Microcomputer AG v Oberfinanzdirektion München* [1996] ECR I–3407. The appearance of an article may be a decisive criterion: Case 192/82 *Kaffee-Contor Bremen GmbH & Co KG v Hauptzollamt Bremen-Nord* [1983] ECR 1769 para 10.

[165] For recent examples of the application of rule 3(c) see Case C–80/96 *Quelle Schickedan AG und Co v Oberfinanzdirektion Frankfurt am Main*, n 93 above, paras 13 and 14 and Case C–67/95 *Rank Xerox Manufacturing (Nederland) BV v Inspecteur der Invoerrechten en Accijnzen*, n 75 above.

[166] See Case 40/69 *Hauptzollamt Hamburg-Oberelle v Firma Paul G Bollmann* [1970] ECR 69 at 80, para 12.

heading must be selected on the basis of the essential characteristics and the particular nature of the product in question. A detailed technical examination of a product is, therefore, frequently necessary.[167]

Rule 5(a) states that cases for cameras, musical instruments, guns, drawing instruments, necklaces, and other similar containers, which are specifically shaped or fitted to contain an article or a set of articles, which are suitable for long-term use and are presented with the articles for which they are intended, are to be classified with such articles when normally sold with them. This rule does not apply, however, where the container gives the whole its essential character. Subject to this, rule 5(b) provides that packing materials and containers, as specifically defined, and except those clearly suitable for repetitive use, which are presented with the goods in question, are to be classified with them if they are of a kind normally used for packing such goods.[168] The final rule, rule 6, relates to sub-headings in the CN and provides that the classification of goods in the sub-headings of a heading is to be determined according to the terms of those sub-headings, and any related sub-headings, and the previous rules are to apply in relation to them. It also specifies that only sub-headings at the same level may be compared and that the relative section and chapter notes are to apply unless the context otherwise requires.[169]

1.2 General rules applicable to both nomenclature and duties

The first of these is that, unless otherwise provided, the provisions relating to customs value are applied to determine the values by reference to which the scope of certain headings or sub-headings is defined, as well as the customs value for the purposes of *ad valorem* customs duties. The second rule specifies the meaning of 'gross weight' and 'net weight' (or simply weight) where goods are chargeable by weight and where weight is used to define the scope of certain headings or sub-headings. 'Gross weight' is the aggregate weight of the goods and of all the packing materials and packing containers and 'net weight', or 'weight' without qualification, is the weight of the goods themselves without packing materials and packing containers of any kind. The third rule relates to rates of exchange and provides that the equivalent in

---

[167] See Case 223/84 *Telefunken Fernseh und Rundfunk GmbH v Oberfinanzdirektion München* [1985] ECR 3335, para 25.

[168] Rules 5(a) and (b) should be read subject to Part One Section IIE of the CN. See Case 357/87 *Firma Albert Schmid v Hauptzollamt Stuttgart-West* [1988] ECR 6239, in which it was held, in relation to a phrase that now appears substantially in a footnote to rule 5(b), that the term 'packings' refers to containers which are suitable for transporting and storing and marketing products. It therefore included beer barrels, beer bottles and plastic crates for beer bottles even where they are to be returned to the seller of the beer in another country: see paras 8–9.

[169] For an example of a case in which the Court chose between two sub-headings in the Tariff on the basis of rule 3(a) which applied by virtue of rule 6 see Case C–164/95 *Fabrica de Queijo Eru Portuguesa Ldª Alfândega de Lisboa etc*, n 121 above, at para 14.

national currencies to the Euro, for Member States other than participating Member States, is fixed in accordance with CCC Article 18.[170]

2. *Notes and Opinions of the WCO and the Community*

The explanatory notes and opinions issued by the WCO are of considerable significance in interpreting the meaning and scope of tariff headings. The Court of Justice regards the notes and opinions as an authoritative source of interpretation where no explanatory notes have been issued by the Community, as the Court noted in a number of early cases, such as, *Bakels*.[171] So far as the WCO's explanatory notes are concerned, the Court has said 'The explanatory notes drawn up, as regards the CN, by the Commission and, as regards the HS, by the Customs Co-operation Council . . . , may be an important aid to the interpretation of the various tariff headings but do not have legally binding force . . .'[172] So far as opinions of the WCO are concerned, the Court has said:

> It is true that classification opinions do not bind contracting parties but they have a bearing on interpretations which is all the more decisive because they emanate from an authority entrusted by the contracting parties with ensuring uniformity in the interpretation and application of the nomenclature.

> When, furthermore, such an interpretation reflects the general practice followed by the contracting parties, it can be set aside only if it appears incompatible with the wording of the heading concerned or goes manifestly beyond the discretion conferred on the Customs Co-operation Council (WCO).[173]

The limitation referred to in the last paragraph should not be regarded as the expression of a mere formality. Where necessary the Court will, indeed, consider whether the content of opinions and explanatory notes from the WCO is in accordance with the provisions of the tariff and whether it alters the meaning of its provisions.[174] The Court will also take account of the different

---

[170] There are special rules in relation to agriculture.

[171] Case 14/70 *Deutsche Bakels GmbH v Oberfinanzdirektion München* [1970] ECR 1001 at paras 9–10. See also Case 77/71 *Gervais-Danone AG v Hauptzollamt München-Schwanthalerstraße* [1971] ECR 1127 at para 5 and Case 30/71 *Kurt Siemers & Co v Hauptzollamt Bad Reichenhall*, n 81 above.

[172] Case C–309/98 *Holz Geenan GmbH v Oberfinanzdirektion München*, n 75 above, at para 14. The statement is supported by a reference to Case C–405/97 *Mövenpick Deutschland GmbH für das Gastgewerke v Hauptzollamt Bremen*, [1999] ECR I–2397, at para 18 and was followed in Case C–228/99 *VauDe Sport GmbH & Co. KG v Oberfinanzdirektion Koblenz*, in n 121 above, at para 13.

[173] Case 38/75 *Douaneagent der NV Nederlandse Spoorwegen v Inspecteur der Invoerrechten en Accijnzen* [1975] ECR 1439 paras 24 and 25, applied in Case C–233/88 *Gijs van de Kolk-Douane Expéditeur BV v Inspecteur der Invoerrechten en Accijnzen*, n 124 above, at para 18. A classification opinion of the WCO was considered for the first time by the VAT and Duties Tribunal in *Higher Nature Limited v CCE* (C00099), 13 July 1999.

[174] See Case 798/79 *Hauptzollamt Köln-Rheinau v Chem Tec* [1980] ECR 2639 in which the Court of Justice refused to follow an opinion of the Customs Co-operation Council. The UK VAT and

language versions of Explanatory Notes from the WCO.[175] It should be noted too that as well as Opinions and Explanatory Notes from the Harmonized System Committee of the WCO, the Court will have regard to, for example, the views of the WCO's Scientific Sub-Committee.[176]

Turning to consider material emanating from the EC, the Court of Justice has regard to the Explanatory Notes adopted by the Commission[177] and Opinions of the Customs Code Committee, formerly the Nomenclature Committee. (One must, of course, distinguish between explanatory notes adopted by the EC Commission from the notes which introduce the chapters of the CN. These latter notes are an integral part of the Tariff and cannot be modified by explanatory notes.)[178] In many cases, the approach of the Court of Justice to these 'internal' explanatory notes and opinions is the same as its approach to those of the WCO as appears from the quotation given above from the judgment in *Holz Geenan*.[179]

In relation to Explanatory Notes the Court has said:

> the interpretation given by a judgment of the Court to a provision concerning tariff classification cannot be altered by the Commission's adoption of explanatory notes. While such notes constitute an important means of ensuring the uniform interpretation of the CN by the customs authorities of the Member States, they do not have legally binding force . . . The issue is whether the notes in question correspond to the principles established by the Court's case-law concerning the interpretation of the relevant tariff provision.[180]

In relation to Opinions of the Committee, the Court of Justice has said in *Dittmeyer*,[181] in which it did not follow an Opinion, that:

> The opinions of the Committee on Common Customs Tariff Nomenclature constitute an important means of ensuring the uniform application of the Common Customs Tariff by the customs authorities of the Member States and as such they may be considered as a valid aid to the interpretation of the tariff. Nevertheless such opinions do not have legally binding force so that, where appropriate, it is necessary

---

Duties Tribunal refused to follow an opinion of the WCO in *Smithkline Beecham plc v CCE* [2000] V+DR 24. See also *Develop Dr Eisben*, n 140 above, at para 21 and Case C–280/97 *ROSE Elektrotechnik GmbH & Co v Oberfinanzdirektion Köln*, n 158 above, particularly at paras 23 and 24, in which the Court of Justice refused to follow an Explanatory Note of the WCO on the ground that it was contrary to the wording of the relevant heading and altered its meaning.

[175] See for examples of a case in which the German version of the Explanatory Note was not followed: Case 50/81 *Paul Kaders GmbH v Hauptzollamt Hamburg-Ericus* [1982] ECR 1941 at para 9.
[176] See Case 14/91 *SuCrest GmbH v Oberfinanzdirektion München*, [1992] ECR I–441 at para 11.
[177] Published at [2000] OJ C199/1.
[178] Case 183/73 *Osram GmbH v Oberfinanzdirektion Frankfurt/Main*, n 83 above, at para 12. Case 149/73 *Otto Witt KG v Hauptzollamt Hamburg-Ericus* [1973] ECR 1587 at para 3.
[179] See p 146, n 172.
[180] Case 259/97 *Uwe Clees v Hauptzollamt Wuppertal*, n 75 above, para 12.
[181] Joined Cases 69 and 70/76 *Firma Rolf H Dittmeyer v Hauptzollamt Hamburg-Waltershof* [1977] ECR 231. For an example of a case in which the Court of Justice followed an Opinion of the Nomenclature Committee see Case C–267/94 *France v Commission* [1995] ECR I–4845 at para 37.

to consider whether their content is in accordance with the actual provisions of the Common Customs Tariff and whether they alter the meaning of such provisions.[182]

The relationship between the EC Explanatory Notes and Opinions and those of the WCO is not entirely clear. On the one hand the EC material does not emanate from an authority entrusted with ensuring uniformity in the harmonized system by the contracting parties to it. It may be thought therefore, that it is, to that extent, less authoritative than the material issued by the WCO. On the other hand, as we noted above, the Court has specifically stated that the WCO is an authoritative guide where there is no explanatory material from the EC. In one case, although it did not have to decide the question whether the EC Notes should be preferred to the WCO Notes, the Court observed that in the notice preceding the Community's Explanatory Notes it was stated that they were not intended to replace the WCO Notes but only to supplement them.[183] Given that the Explanatory Notes and Opinions of the WCO emanate from an authority entrusted by the contracting parties with ensuring uniformity in the interpretation and application of the nomenclature, as the Court of Justice has noted,[184] they should prevail over the internal pronouncements of the EC. It is most unlikely, however, that the Court of Justice will need ever to establish the formal relationship between the different kinds of explanatory notes and opinions, because, as we have seen, all are weighty and none is binding. The task of interpreting the Tariff belongs to the Court of Justice and ultimately to it alone.

3. *Case law generally*

In carrying out its interpretative functions the Court has regard, in an appropriate case, not only to its previous decisions on the present nomenclature, but also to decisions handed down prior to the introduction of the harmonized system.[185] The Court does, however, draw a distinction between the Combined Nomenclature itself and regulations or directives which may refer to the CN for convenience. The case law interpreting the latter is not usually useful in construing the CN.[186] Case law interpreting the Tariff, even if for purposes other than the imposition of customs duty, is, however, important.

---

[182] n 181 above, para 4.

[183] Case 11/79 J *Cleton en Co. BV v Inspecteur des droits d'entrée et accises à Rotterdam*, [1979] ECR 3069, at paras 12–13.

[184] See the quotation from Case 38/75 *Douaneagent der NV Nederlandse Spoorwegen v Inspecteur der invoerrechten en accijnzen*, n 173 above.

[185] See, eg, Fennelly AG's approach in Case C–80/96 *Quelle Schickedanz AG und Co. v Oberfinanzdirektion Frankfurt am Main*, n 75 above, at paras 25 and 30. He followed the Court's interpretation of 'goods put up in sets' in Rule 2(b) of the General Rules of Interpretation contained in Case 163/84 *Hauptzollamt Hannover v Telefunken* [1985] ECR 3299 at para 35.

[186] See case C–201/96 *LTM v FIRS*, in n 97 above, at para 27. As already noted the CN is widely used in relation to measures governing the organization of markets. See re countervailing charges, eg, Case C–370/96 *Covita AVE v Elliniko Dimsoio* [1998] ECR I–7711.

The Court has said that it would be inappropriate for Tariff headings to be applied differently for one and the same product depending on whether the classification is for the imposition of customs duties, the application of rules governing the organization of markets, or in respect of the system of monetary compensatory amounts.[187] In doubtful cases, the Court will bear in mind these wider uses of the Tariff in construing it.[188] The decisions of other customs authorities or tribunals in other jurisdictions may also be of some assistance in some cases.

3.1 Case law on specific goods and classification headings

In the course of considering the classification of particular products, the Court has, in some areas, developed a body of case law dealing with specific goods and classification headings to which reference must be made. There is insufficient space to consider all of these in detail, but a number of examples may be examined. They are mostly concerned with scientific or technological products, but sometimes familiar products and familiar processes give rise to some case law. The Court has, for example, had to consider the freezing of food and the nature of fresh goods and has concluded that irreversible changes to the structure of flesh which occurred after thawing goods prevented them from being fresh.[189]

Turning to more technical matters, the nature of medicaments has also given rise to litigation, particularly in relation to the construction of heading 30.04 of the CN which covers 'Medicaments . . . consisting of mixed or unmixed products for therapeutic or prophylactic uses, put up in measured doses or in forms or packings for retail sale.' The Court has ruled that, in order to fall within this heading, the product must have 'clearly defined therapeutic and, above all, prophylatic characteristics the effect of which is concentrated on precise functions of the human organism'.[190] Laws J has said that, in adopting this formulation, the Court of Justice has provided a 'tight, certain

---

[187] Case 158/78 *P. Biegi v Hauptzollamt Bochum*, n 81 above, at para 18, but see also Case 169/80 *Administration des douanes v SA Gondrand Frères and SA Garancini* [1981] ECR 1931 paras 13–15.

[188] Case 36/71 *Günther Henck v Hauptzollamt Emmerich*, n 134 above, at para 9.

[189] See Case 120/75 *Riemer v Hamptzollamt Lübeck-West* [1976] ECR 1003 para 4 and Case 405/97 *Mövenpick Deutschland GmbH für das Gastgewerbe v Hauptzollamt Bremen*, n 172 above, at para 22. See also Case C–338/95 *Wiener S I GmbH*, n 99 above, and Case C–395/93 *Neckerman Versand*, in n 138 above (nightwear) and Case 259/97 *Uwe Clees v Hauptzollamt Wuppertal*, n 75 above and Case 200/84 *Daiber v Hauptzollamt Reutlingen* [1985] ECR 3363 (motor vehicles within heading no 7095 of the CN, covering collections and collectors' pieces of historical or ethnographic interest).

[190] Case C–177/91 *Bioforce GmbH v Oberfinanzdirektion München*, n 128 above, at para 12, cited in Case C–201/96 *LTM v FIRS*, in n 97 above, at para 29, Case C–270/96 *Laboratoires Sarget SA v FIRS*, n 106 above, at I–1142 para 28. See also Case C–328/97 *Glob-Sped v Hauptzollamt Lörrach* [1998] ECR I–8357.

and focussed approach'.[191] The VAT and Duties Tribunal has noted that the formulation of the Court means that the item in question must have a specific medicinal use rather than being generally beneficial to health.[192]

Heading 3003, which covers certain medicaments not put up in measured doses or in forms or packings for retail sale, has also been the subject of litigation. The Court has said that it covers a product consisting of sugar, but above all of active flavouring agents with medicinal properties in such a proportion that the product is used only for therapeutic and prophylactic purposes. Nevertheless, where the proportion of flavouring agents in the composition of each product does not enable it to be used only for therapeutic or prophylactic purposes, it cannot be regarded as a pharmaceutical product falling under that heading.[193] The Court has also held that powdered sterile mixtures of amino acids may be regarded as medicaments within CN 3003.[194]

Other technical matters which have come before the Court concern, the distinction between foodstuff and chemical products[195] and the distinction between 'residue' and 'waste' from processing products.[196] Unsurprisingly, advances in the fast-moving world of computer technology and electronics have also led to cases before the Court of Justice which has had to consider, for example, 'electronic micro circuits'[197] 'sound cards',[198] 'vista boards' capable of being used as 'graphics cards',[199] and technology relevant to computer networks.[200] It should also be noted that a number of cases clarify a 'functional unit' test, contained in explanatory notes of the WCO, pursuant to which, if a separately presented item is by virtue of its function intended

[191] *HM Customs and Excise v Cedar Health Ltd*, 21 May 1998, followed in *Unigreg Ltd v CCE Customs and Excise* [1998] 3 CMLR 128, see para [6].

[192] *SmithKline Beecham plc v CCE* [2000] V&DR 24, in which the tribunal (chaired by Dr J F Avery Jones) held that nicotine patches designed to cure nicotine addiction was a medicament within CN 3004. The tribunal was uninfluenced by the fact that the product was licensed by the Medicines Control Agency as the definition of 'medicinal product' for the purposes of that legislation is widely drawn, although the objective characteristics of the product as set out in the licence application are relevant evidence: see the tribunal's decision at 7 where it founded its approach on *Unigreg Ltd v CCE Customs and Excise*, n 191 above.

[193] See Joined Cases 106 and 139/94 *Criminal proceedings against Patrick Colin and Daniel Dupré* [1995] ECR I–4759.

[194] See Case C–459/93 *Hauptzollamt Hamburg-St. Annen v Thyssen Haniel*, n 121 above, at para 11 and Case C–270/96 *Laboratoires Sarget SA v FIRS*, n 106 above, at para 48.

[195] See Case C–14/91 *SuCrest GmbH v Oberfinanzdirektion München*, n 176 above, at para 6.

[196] See Case 268/87 *Cargill BV v Inspecteur der invoerrechten en accijnzen.* [1988] ECR 5151 at para 11 and Case 129/81 *Fratelli Fancon v Società Industriale Agricole Tresse (SIAT)* [1982] ECR 697 para 14.

[197] See Case 122/80 *Analog Devices v Hauptzollamt München Mütte*, n 151 above.

[198] Case C–479/99 *CBA Computer Handels- und Beteiligungs GmbH v Hauptzollamt Aachen*, n 81 above.

[199] Case 382/95 *Technex Computer + Grafik Vertriebs GmbH v Hauptzollamt München*, at n 104 above.

[200] See Case C–339/98 *Peacock AG v Hauptzollamt Paderborn*, n 94 above, and Case C–463/98 *Cabletron Systems Ltd v the Revenue Commissioners* at n 75 above, and Joined Cases T–133/98 and T–134/98 *Hewlett Packard France and Hewlett Packard Europe BV v Commission*, n 79 above.

exclusively for particular equipment, then it is to be classified within the same tariff heading as the equipment in question.[201]

F. THE PROVISION OF INFORMATION BY CUSTOMS AUTHORITIES

It was emphasized by the Court of Justice a long time ago that national administrations could not issue binding rules of interpretation in relation to the Tariff.[202] To permit them to do so would, it was thought, destroy the necessary uniform interpretation of the Tariff. Nevertheless, given the important role of national authorities in the administration of the customs union it is essential that traders are able to rely upon their statements and the CCC and the Implementing Regulation now give national customs authorities the power to issue binding information to traders.

CCC, Article 11 makes clear that any person can request information concerning the application of customs legislation from the customs authorities. The width of this provision is limited only by the requirement that the request may be refused where it does not relate to an import or export operation actually envisaged. Information is to be provided free, although charges of 'the relevant amount' may be imposed if special costs are incurred by the customs authorities, in particular as a result of analyses or expert reports on goods, or as a result of the return of goods to the applicant. Although important, Article 11 does not permit the giving of information by which the customs authorities are bound. That is left to CCC, Article 12 which contains distinct provisions governing the provision of binding information originally in relation to tariffs but now, as we have seen, in relation to origin as well.

1. *Issuing binding information*

The provision of binding information by customs authorities is plainly of great importance to traders and in the following section some of the important features of the regime under which the information is provided are examined.[203] CCC, Article 12 specifies that the customs authorities have an obligation to issue binding tariff or origin information on written request.[204] The

---

[201] See Case 60/77 *Fritz Fuss KG, Elektrotechnische Fabrik v Oberfinanzdirektion de Munich* [1977] ECR 2453 at para 5; Case 163/84 *Hauptzollamt Hannover v Telefunken Fernseh und Rundfunk GmbH*, n 185 above, at paras 30–34; Case 57/85 *Senelco GmbH v Oberfinanzdirektion München* [1986] ECR 821 at paras 11–14; Case 60/83 *Metro International Kommanditgesellschaft v Oberfinanzdirektion München* [1984] ECR 671 at para 10.

[202] Case 40/69 *Hauptzollamt Hamburg-Oberelle v Firma Paul G Bollmann* [1970] ECR 69 at paras 8 and 9.

[203] The legislation is contained in CCC, Art 12 and Implementing Regulation, Arts 5 to 15.

[204] Art 12.1. Note that there is no provision for the provision of binding information by a court or tribunal. In a complex area of classification, a trader who establishes a specific classification of goods in litigation in one Member State is, therefore, left without the benefit of binding information. For an example in the UK see *SmithKline Beecham plc v CCE*, n 192 above, at 32.

information is binding on the customs authorities of all the Member States when the procedural conditions set out in Articles 6 and 7 of the Implementing Regulation are met.[205] Article 6 specifies the form to be used for applying for binding tariff information, which is contained in Annex 1B to the Implementing Regulation. It sets out what information must be supplied to the customs authority and gives it power to seek further information before responding. The customs authority must notify the applicant that the application has been received and state from what date the relevant time limits governing the provision of information run.[206] These time limits are set out in the Implementing Regulation, Article 7. This specifies that, in relation to tariff matters, if the customs authority has not provided the applicant with binding information within three months of accepting the application, then it should notify the applicant of the reason for the delay and indicate when it expects to be able to provide the information. Binding origin information must be provided within 150 days from acceptance of the application. A refusal to provide binding information may be appealed against.[207]

The regime governing the provision of binding information throws into sharp focus what may be thought of as one of the most significant challenges of the customs union, namely that a Community regime is operated by national authorities and the national authorities may provide information which is binding on all Member States' customs authorities. In these circumstances it is only to be expected that a Member State should have the obligation to transmit binding information to the Commission.[208] Article 8.1 of the Implementing Regulation provides that a copy of the application for binding tariff information, a copy of the notification of binding information (copy No 2 of Annex 1 to the Implementing Regulation) and the facts (copy No 4 of Annex 1) are to be transmitted to the Commission 'without delay' by the customs authorities of the Member State and by electronic means. In relation

[205] Implementing Regulation, Art 5. In *Niko Surgical Limited v CCE* (C00118), 6 June 2000, a VAT and Duties Tribunal held that binding tariff information provided by Danish customs authorities in 1991 was binding on the UK authorities, notwithstanding that it was provided to the 'sister company' of the appellant before the tribunal and that a provision equivalent to Art 5 was not applicable in relation to information provided before 1 Jan 1993.
[206] Implementing Regulation, Art 6.4. The form of the notification is set out in Implementing Regulation, Annex 1 in relation to binding tariff information, and in Annex 1A in relation to binding origin information: See Art 7.2.
[207] Implementing Regulation, Art 7.2 and CCC, Art 243. Note that these provisions follow Art 2(h) of the Agreement on Rules of Origin, Annex 1A to the Final Act of the Uruguay Round, discussed in Ch 7 below.
[208] The information received by the Commission is used to maintain a European Binding Tariff Information database. The Commission decided on 26 July 2000 to stop all intervention of DG TAXUD in the management of the BTI system by 2002. Unsurprisingly, this decision has attracted criticism from representatives of trade organizations and customs authorities. Clearly, the operation of customs authorities as one requires the maintenance and increased accessibility of the existing system. The Commission appears to be better placed than Member States to operate the BTI system and it is understood that its decision is being reconsidered.

to binding origin information a copy of the binding origin information notified and the facts must be transmitted. Any failure by a Member State to comply with their obligations is likely to threaten the unicity of the customs union and could cause other customs authorities and traders throughout the Community considerable hardship. There is no room here to place any gloss upon the words 'without delay' so as to take account of the convenience of a customs administration. The phrase is to be contrasted with that applicable in relation to the obligations of the Commission which require it to act 'as soon as possible' in communicating to Member States the dates upon which it has adopted measures which render binding information invalid.[209]

2. Relying upon binding information

Binding information may be relied upon by the holder of the information only in respect of tariff classification or determination of origin of goods and only in respect of those goods in respect of which specified customs formalities were completed after the date on which the information was supplied.[210] Customs authorities may require the holder of the information to inform them that he is in possession of binding information.[211] In order to be able to rely on the information which has been supplied, the holder of the information must be able to prove, in relation to tariff information, that the goods declared correspond in every respect to those described in the information. So far as origin is concerned, the holder must be able to prove that the circumstances determining the acquisition of origin correspond in every respect to the goods and the circumstances described in the information.[212] There is no margin for error here on the part of the holder. The need to provide accurate and complete information to the customs authorities is emphasized by the fact that binding information is annulled where it is based on inaccurate and incomplete information from the applicant. The error or inadequacy in question must, though, relate to information upon which the binding information is based.[213] Customs authorities cannot, therefore, rely upon immaterial errors in order to escape from the constraints of binding information.

---

[209] Implementing Regulation, Art 12.3. Member States have a similar obligation to notify the Commission where binding information they have supplied is void or ceases to be valid within CCC, Art 12.4 or 5 (see Implementing Regulation, Art 13).

[210] CCC, Art 12.2 and Implementing Regulation, Art 11 provides that binding tariff information supplied by the customs authorities of a Member State since 1 January 1991 is binding on the competent authorities of all the Member States under the same conditions. Note that it is only the holder of the information who may rely upon it. There is no provision for corporate affiliates of the holder to rely upon the information.

[211] Implementing Regulation, Art 10.2.

[212] CCC, Art 12.3.

[213] CCC, Art 12.4.

3. *The uses of binding information*

The uses to which binding information may be put are set out in CCC, Article 12.7. It may be used solely for the purpose of determining import or export duties, calculating export refunds and amounts granted for imports and exports within the common agricultural policy, and using import, export, or advance-fixing certificates for acceptance of the customs declaration, providing that such certificates were issued on the basis of the information concerned.

4. *Binding information: validity and invalidity*

Binding information is valid for a limited period only. The maximum period of validity is six years in the case of tariff information and three years in the case of origin information.[214] In each case the period runs from the date of issue. In many cases, however, as we shall see below, the periods will be much shorter than this. There are a number of express rules regarding the period for which binding information may be relied upon and they cannot be circumvented by use of the principle of legitimate expectations or the principle of legal certainty. Neither does binding information provide protection against legislative changes. The Court of Justice made clear in *Lopex Export* that:

> the aim of binding tariff information is to enable the trader to proceed with certainty where there are doubts as to the classification of goods in the existing customs nomenclature, thereby protecting him against any subsequent change in the position adopted by the customs authorities with regard to the classification of goods. However, such information is not aimed at, nor can it have the effect of, guaranteeing that the tariff heading to which the trader refers will not subsequently be amended by a measure adopted by the Community legislature.[215]

No doubt a similar approach is applicable in relation to origin information. Nevertheless, the principles of legal certainty and legitimate expectations do combine to impose upon the Community legislature an obligation to protect traders from harm caused by amendments to the CN. It must protect, by means of appropriate measures, those traders who would otherwise sustain unforeseeable and irreparable damage, whether or not they are the addressees of binding tariff information.[216]

---

[214] CCC, Art 12.4. It has been suggested that the CCC should be amended to include a requirement that the customs authorities notify an importer when binding information becomes invalid by virtue of a regulation as HM Customs and Excise do as a matter of practice at the moment. It appears that the Commission's Customs Code Committee (Binding Tariff Information Sector) does not intend to make notification of the importer in such circumstances a requirement within the Community: see A Hart, *De Voil Indirect Tax Intelligence* (2000) 53: 13.

[215] Case C–315/96 *Lopex Export GmbH v Hauptzollamt Hamburg-Jonas*, n 91 above, at para 28.

[216] Ibid, at paras 29–30.

Binding information may either be invalid from the time of its provision or it may become invalid subsequently. The UK's VAT and Duties Tribunal has held binding information to be invalid where the information given is consistent with an incorrect opinion of the WCO.[217] So far as subsequent invalidity is concerned, CCC, Article 12.5(a)(i)–(iii)[218] sets out three situations in which this arises in relation to tariff information. The first of these was at issue in *Lopex Export*[219] and is simply where a regulation is adopted and the information in question no longer conforms to the law which it lays down. The second situation is where the information is no longer compatible with the interpretation of one of the nomenclatures forming part of the Tariff, whether by virtue of amendments to the explanatory notes to the Combined Nomenclature, a ruling of the Court of Justice, or at international level, by virtue of a classification opinion of the WCO, or an amendment to the explanatory notes to the nomenclature of the harmonized system. The information ceases to be binding on the date of the publication of the Community measures, or the date on which an international measure is published, in the *Official Journal* 'C' Series. The third situation in which binding tariff information ceases to be valid is where the holder of the information is notified of the withdrawal or amendment of the binding information in accordance with CCC, Article 9. This provides for decisions to be revoked or annulled where conditions for their issue are not complied with or fulfilled. It is important to note that in both the second and third situations, the binding information in question may be relied upon for up to six months after the date of its publication or notification as the case may be, although that is subject to the conditions laid down in CCC, Article 12.6 discussed below.[220]

CCC, Article 12.5(b)(i)–(iii) provide a similar set of rules in relation to binding origin information. So far as the first situation is concerned, in addition to changes by way of regulations, changes by the conclusion of an agreement are included. So far as concerns the second situation, reference is made to the incompatibility of the information with the explanatory notes and opinions adopted for the purposes of interpreting the rules, in place of the reference to the Combined Nomenclature, and at the international level compatibility is to be judged by reference to the Agreement on Rules of Origin established in the

---

[217] See *SmithKline Beecham plc v CCE*, n 192 above, at 32.

[218] Implementing Regulation, Art 12 provides that on adoption of one of the acts or measures referred to in CCC, Art 12.5, the customs authorities are to take the necessary steps to ensure that binding information is subsequently issued only in conformity with the act or measure in question. The dates to be taken into account are set out in Implementing Regulation, Art 12.2. The Commission is to communicate the dates of adoption of the act or measure to the customs authorities 'as soon as possible': Art 12.3, ibid.

[219] Case C–315/96 *Lopex Export GmbH v Hauptzollamt Hamburg-Jonas* at n 91 above.

[220] For a recent example of a decision directed at the UK which required its customs authorities to revoke binding tariff information which it had given see: Commission Decision (EC) 4/2000 of 29 Dec 1999 [2000] OJ L13/27.

WTO or to the explanatory notes or an origin opinion adopted for the interpretation of the Agreement. Binding origin information ceases to be valid on
the date indicated when the measures are published, or, in relation to international measures, the date shown in the communication by the Commission in
the Official Journal 'C' Series. The third situation is identical to that existing in
relation to tariff information.

Except where information is rendered invalid pursuant to CCC, Article 9, as
noted above, CCC, Article 12.6 permits the holder of binding information to
rely upon it for six months from the date of its publication or notification, if he
had concluded binding contracts for the purchase or sale of the goods in question on the basis of the binding information and before the tariff measure was
adopted.[221] Where an import, export, or advance-fixing certificate is submitted when customs formalities are carried out, the six-month period is replaced
by the period for which the certificate is valid. So far as changes by way of
regulations and agreements are concerned, Article 12.6 permits a regulation
or agreement to lay down a period within which a holder of information is
protected subject to the rules set out above. So far as regulations are
concerned, a period of three months is generally established.[222]

As one would expect, provision is made for the Commission to be informed
by the customs authorities where void binding information is supplied or
where it becomes invalid in certain circumstances.[223]

5. *The UK and binding information*

In a book devoted to Community law there is insufficient room to look at the
domestic law and practice of the UK in any detail. It may be noted, however,
that HM Customs and Excise publish public Tariff Notices on the classification
of products and offer advice on classification via Customs and Excise Inland
Advice Centres and, in more complicated cases, over a helpline.[224] Binding
information is available free of charge, apart from the costs of, for example,
obtaining expert advice or analysis. If, however, the information is provided
pursuant to the fast-track binding information service, a charge is made.[225]
The authorities aim to provide the information within forty-eight hours of
accepting the request which is to be made on a specified form. If the information is provided late the charge is waived.

---

[221] The holder of binding information who wishes to rely upon CCC, Art 12.6 must notify the
customs authorities providing any necessary supporting documentation enabling his entitlement
to do so to be checked: see Implementing Regulation, Art 14.
[222] See, eg, Commission Regulation (EC) 289/2000 of 3 Feb 2000 [2000] OJ L33/3, Art 2.
[223] Implementing Regulation, Art 13.
[224] Telephone number (00 44) (0)1702 366077. Information about binding tariff information
is also available on the web-site of HM Customs and Excise at www.hmce.gov.uk/bus/tso/class5.
htm.
[225] Initially this was put at £200 plus VAT.

Appeals to the VAT and Duties Tribunals are dealt with generally in Chapter 13. It should be noted here that the category of decisions of which it is possible to seek a review, pursuant to the Finance Act 1994, section 14, was enlarged by the Customs Reviews and Appeals (Tariff and Origin) Regulations 1997[226] so as to take account of the Community regime governing binding information on tariff and origin of goods. Regulation 3 establishes that a review may be sought of any decision by Customs and Excise on, first, the tariff classification or determination of the origin of goods; secondly, any decision on whether binding information of either type is to be supplied; and, thirdly, any decision on whether such information is to be annulled, withdrawn, or revoked. Regulation 5 permits reviews of any decision, not within regulation 3, which is made for the purposes of preferential tariff measures applicable to the export of goods, first, on the determination of the origin of goods and, secondly on whether there is sufficient evidence to determine the origin of goods.

These decisions may be appealed to the VAT and Duties Tribunal pursuant to the Finance Act 1994, section 16 with the burden of proof resting upon the appellant.[227] Only in respect of the first-mentioned decisions in regulations 3 and 5, ie those in respect of tariff classification and origin, may the tribunal quash or vary the decision or substitute its own decision.[228] In respect of the other decisions the tribunal has a limited jurisdiction. It may act only if it considers that the decision could not reasonably be arrived at. If this is established it has three options. First, it may direct that, so far as the decision remains in force, it shall cease to have effect from a specified date. Secondly, it may require the Commissioners to carry out another review of the decision, and thirdly, where the decision has already been acted upon or taken effect and cannot be remedied by further review, it may declare the decision unreasonable and give directions to secure that repetitions of the unreasonableness do not occur in future comparable circumstances.[229]

---

[226] SI 1997/534.
[227] Finance Act 1994, s 16(6). Any necessary reference to the Court of Justice may, of course, be made by the tribunal. Note that in Case C–134/97 *Proceedings for a preliminary decision brought by Victoria Film A/S* [1998] ECR I–7023 at para 17, the Court of Justice observed that, in giving binding rulings in relation to VAT, the Swedish Skatterättsnämnden was in a comparable position to national customs authorities giving binding tariff information. Consequently, it could not make a reference to the Court for a preliminary ruling.
[228] Finance Act 1994, s 16(5).
[229] Ibid, s 16(4).

6

International Arrangements and Agreements

In the previous two chapters we have looked at the basic sources of customs law created autonomously by the Community which are central to the customs union. We now turn to those sources of customs law which have been established or negotiated by the Community to govern its relationship with third countries—arrangements, agreements, and conventions which, as well as being concerned with customs law, implement the Community's external relations policy, particularly in relation to trade and development.

External trade, in the words of the preamble to the CCC, is of 'paramount importance' for the Community. The EC's interests are truly global and are furthered by a variety of different types of agreement. The scope of the EC's interests is apparent when one reviews its recent activity in relation to trade and development.[1] In 2000 it began negotiations with MERCOSUR and Chile for a free trade agreement[2] with the former Yugoslav Republic of Macedonia[3] for a stability and association agreement and with Turkey, with a view to liberalizing trade in services and the mutual opening of procurement markets. An association agreement with Egypt was signed on 25 June 2001[4] and negotiatons are continuing with Algeria, Lebanon, and Syria for the establishment of Euro-Mediterranean Association Agreements which are designed to replace the existing association and co-operation agreements between the EC and countries bordering the Mediterranean and in the Middle East.[5] In addition, a co-operation and free trade agreement is being negotiated with the Gulf Co-operation Council (Bahrain, Kuwait, Oman, Qatar, Saudi Arabia, and the UAE). On 1 January 2000, some elements of the trade, development, and co-operation agreement between the EC and South Africa[6] entered provisionally

---

[1] For a list of some of the EC's regional trade agreements and the status of negotiations with third countries see: 'EC Regional Trade Agreements' available on the website of the EC Commission's Directorate General for Trade at http://europa.en.int/comm/dgs/trade/index_en.htm.

[2] Relations between the EU and MERCOSUR are based on the Interregional Framework Co-operation Agreement of 1995 (see [1996] OJ L69/4) approved on behalf of the EU by a Council Decision of 22 Mar 1999 (see [1999] OJ L112/65). The agreement seeks the establishment of an inter-regional association.

[3] An interim agreement entered into force on 1 June 2001: [2001] OJ L149/1.

[4] See Press Release IP/01/892, Brussels, 25 June 2001.

[5] For other Euro-Mediterranean Agreements see: Israel ([2000] OJ L147/3) Jordan, signed on 24 Nov 1997; Morocco ([2000] OJ L70/2) the Palestinian Liberation Organization for the benefit of the Palestinian Authority of the West Bank and the Gaza Strip ([1997] OJ L187/3) and Tunisia ([1998] OJ L97/3). The measure approving the agreements on behalf of the Community appears immediately before them in the *Official Journal*.

[6] [1999] OJ L311/3. This agreement, like all the modern agreements entered into by the EU contains, in Art 2, express acknowledgement that respect for democratic principles and fundamental human rights together constitutes an essential element of them.

into force.[7] It should also be noted that on 1 July 2000, the Economic Partnership, Political Co-ordination and Co-operation Agreement (Global Agreement) between the EC and Mexico, concluded on 8 December 1997,[8] came into force. It seeks to establish a free trade area between the EC and Mexico over a transitional period of no longer than ten years. The greater part of the dismantling of tariff barriers will, however, be completed long before then. For example, by 2003, when industrial products will be fully liberalized in NAFTA, all Mexican exports will enter the EU duty free and there will be a maximum tariff barrier to EU exports of 5 per cent. By 2007 96 per cent of EU–Mexican trade will be liberalized.[9]

The EU's policy towards developing countries is clearly inseparable from its trade policy. In acknowledgement of this the EU is pressing to ensure that development issues are fully considered in what has been called the Millennium Round. It has also established its 'Everything but arms' package[10] for the world's forty-eight poorest countries.[11] In addition, a new partnership between the EU and the African, Caribbean, and Pacific (ACP) countries was established by the Cotonou Agreement of 23 June 2000, much of which came into force on 2 August 2000.[12] Finally, it should be noted that the EU continues to take a close interest in the affairs of the overseas countries and territories (OCTs) which are considered below.

As was indicated above, the EC's relations with third countries are not governed exclusively by negotiated agreements. Sometimes they are governed by autonomously established measures. We consider some of these in section A of the chapter, paying particular attention to the generalized system of

---

[7] See the exchange of letters at [1999] OJ L311/29.

[8] See [2000] OJ L276/45. Agreement approved on behalf of the Community by Council Decision of 28 Sept 2000 [2000] OJ L276/44. See also Decision No 2/2000 of the EC–Mexico Joint Council of 23 Mar 2000 [2000] OJ L157/10 implementing the interim agreement between the EC and Mexico. The date of 1 July 2000, as the date the agreement enters into force is specified in Art 49 of the Decision.

[9] See the Commission's Press Release: 'Entry into force of the EU–Mexico Free Trade Agreement signals start of new era in Europe's relations with Mexico' IP/00/703. The EU has, of course, had regard to the position of the USA and Canada in negotiating with Mexico and Commissioner Lamy said, on the completion of the free trade agreement in services, that: 'This will put the EU on a level footing with the US and Canada in the Mexican market.': see Press Release, 'Lamy welcomes completion of EU–Mexico Free Trade Agreement' 27 Feb 2001. The EC's activities in Latin America have, inevitably, attracted some attention in the USA. One commentator, after noting some criticism within the USA of the fact that, in contrast to the EC, the USA has only two free trade agreements, the agreement establishing NAFTA and one with Israel, has said that 'the EU is encroaching on U.S. turf by striking a deal with Mexico and negotiating with Mercosur, the South American trade bloc led by Brazil, offering Brazil the possibility of playing Europe off against the United States'. See, 'Bush Needs to Look Beyond a Regional Trade Accord', R Dale, *International Herald Tribune* 27 Feb 2001, 11.

[10] See Council Regulation (EC) 416/2000 of 28 Feb 2001 [2001] OJ L60/43, amending Regulation (EC) 2820/98, of 21 Dec 1998 [1998] OJ L357/1.

[11] Listed at n 340 below.

[12] See below for more detailed discussion.

160   EC Customs Law

preferences and the arrangements with the OCTs. Negotiated agreements are dealt with in section B. The EEA Agreement, then the Europe Agreements and other association agreements, co-operation agreements and conventions, including those with the ACP countries, are also looked at. Finally, partnership and co-operation and trade and co-operation agreements are referred to. The third section, section C, is concerned with the interpretation and application of agreements and with the rights of traders under them. The chapter concludes with section D which looks, briefly, at the impact of international law on agreements with third countries in the context of Community customs law.

A. AUTONOMOUS COMMUNITY MEASURES

The relationships with third countries which are established pursuant to autonomous measures are inevitably significantly different from those created by virtue of international agreements. This has considerable implications for customs law. For example, the nature of the relationship between the respective customs authorities of the relevant countries differs depending upon whether a regulation or an international agreement is in issue, particularly so far as concerns the ascertainment of the origin of goods.[13] Furthermore, whereas it appears to be taking a considerable amount of litigation to establish the direct effect of provisions, including provisions relating to customs law, in international agreements, no such difficulty arises in relation to autonomous Community measures. That is not to say, of course, that autonomous measures are never the subject of litigation. It can frequently be important to establish whether or not they contain provisions of 'direct and individual concern' to traders who seek to annul them, and whether or not there are grounds upon which they may be annulled or which found a claim for non-contractual damages.[14]

The fact that autonomous measures can have features which are quite distinct from conventional agreements does not, of course, prevent them

[13] Joined Cases C–153/94 and C–204/94 *The Queen v Commissioners of Customs & Excise, ex p Faroe Seafood Co Ltd, Føroya Fiskasøla L/F* [1996] ECR I–2465 at para 24.

[14] These areas of law have been considered in litigation over the regulation of the market in bananas. See, eg, Case C–280/93 *Germany v Council* [1994] ECR I–4973 which held, among other things, that it was not possible to rely upon GATT to defeat a Community regulation unless: it imposed an obligation which was directly applicable in the domestic legal system, the EC intended to implement a particular obligation or the regulation specifically referred to it: see paras 110–1. See also Case 466/93 *Atlanta Fruchthandelsgesellschaft mbH and others v Bundesamt für Ernährung und Forstwirtschaft* [1995] ECR I–3799. A claim for non-contractual damages was rejected in Case T–521/93 *Atlanta AG and others v Council and Commission* [1996] ECR II–1707, appealed as Case C–104/97 P, [1997] OJ C142/11 removed from the register on 12 June 2001. The validity of regulations has also been considered in relation to the OCTs: see, eg, Joined Cases T–32/98 and T–41/98 *Netherlands Antilles v Commission* [2001] ECR II–201 now under appeal: see [2000] OJ C233/22.

playing an important role in the context of customs law. As we have already mentioned, they have been used to establish the system of generalized preferences and to determine the relationship between the EC with the overseas countries and territories (OCTs). We consider each of these in turn below.

1. *The generalized system of preferences (GSP)*

The basic function of the GSP has been described by the Court of Justice as follows:

> The system of tariff preferences granted by the Community . . . is one of the measures adopted by the Community as part of the trade policy of development aid agreed upon by the United Nations Conference on Trade and Development for the adoption of a policy of development cooperation on a world-wide scale comprising in particular the improvement of tariff preferences with the aim of achieving a steady increase in imports of manufactured products from developing countries.[15]

A little earlier the Court had put it more shortly, saying that the GSP 'is based on the principle of the unilateral grant by the Community of tariff advantages in favour of products originating in certain developing countries with the aim of facilitating the flow of trade with those countries'.[16]

Although the use of a system of generalized preferences is not confined to the EC it does operate: 'the largest scheme of generalised preferences . . . in the world, mainly benefiting the countries of Asia and Latin-America'.[17] It first granted generalized preferences to some third countries in 1971, in accordance with an offer made within the United Nations Conference on Trade and Development. The preferences were granted in respect of certain agricultural and industrial products for a period of ten years which ended on 31 December 1980. The scheme was renewed for a further ten years to 31 December 1990 and then kept in force up to 31 December 1994 when the Community made a new offer for the period 1995 to 2004. In late 1994, a Council Regulation[18] was made applying a four-year scheme of generalized tariff preferences up to 31 December 1998. This was subsequently extended to 30 June 1999.[19] In 1996, a Council Regulation[20] was made applying generalized tariff preferences to agricultural products up to 30 June 1999. The generalized system of preferences was, most recently, continued for the period 1 July 1999 to 31

---

[15] Case 231/81 *Hauptzollamt Würzburg v H. Weidenmann GmbH & Co* [1982] ECR 2259 at para 7.

[16] Case 827/79 *Amministrazione delle Finanze v Ciro Accampora* [1980] ECR 3731 at para 5. The question when a product originates in a GSP country is considered in Ch 7 below.

[17] Communication from the Commission on the Management of Preferential Tariff Arrangements COM(97)402 final, 23 July 1997, 9 para 2.1.

[18] Council Regulation (EC) 3281/94 of 19 Dec 1994 [1994] OJ L348/1

[19] Art 34.2 of Council Regulation (EC) 2820/98 of 21 Dec 1998 [1998] OJ L357/1. Corrigendum at [1999] OJ L184/50

[20] Council Regulation (EC) 1256/96 of 20 June 1996 [1996] OJ L160/1.

December 2001 by another Council Regulation[21] ('the GSP Regulation'). On 12 June 2001, the Commission presented a proposal for a Council Regulation applying a scheme of generalized tariff preferences for the period from 1 January 2002 to 31 December 2004.[22] The renewal of the GSP arrangements for limited periods is not borne out of a reluctance to assist beneficiary countries. Rather, as the quotations from the judgments of the Court of Justice make clear, the GSP is development-oriented and, consequently, transitional in nature. It will be phased out when it is no longer needed.[23]

The states which benefit, in some way, from the generalized preferences at the moment are set out in the footnote below[24] and appear in Annex III to the GSP Regulation. Countries may be removed from the list, or find that their benefit under the system is limited in certain circumstances considered below. Many of them are also ACP countries.

---

[21] Council Regulation (EC) 2820/98, n 19 above, as amended by Council Regulation (EC) 1763/1999 of 29 July 1999 [1999] OJ L211/1, by Commission Regulation (EC) 1310/2000 of 20 June 2000 and by the regulation establishing the 'Everything but arms' package. Council Regulation (EC) 416/2000 at n 10 above. Corrigendum at [2001] OJ L65/20.

[22] [2001] OJ C 270 E/24. The cut-off date of 31 Dec 2004 is inapplicable in relation to the special arrangements for Least Developed Countries: see Art 40.2 of the proposed regulation.

[23] See also the GSP Regulation recital (6).

[24] The following lists contain countries with widely varying levels of development. Some are exceedingly poor and have little or no financial or industrial infrastructure. The countries are as follows: Part A: Afghanistan, Albania, Algeria, Angola, Antigua and Barbuda, Argentina, Armenia, Azerbaijan, Bahamas, Bahrain, Bangladesh, Barbados, Belarus, Belize, Benin, Bhutan, Bolivia, Bosnia and Herzegovina, Botswana, Brunei, Burkina Faso, Burundi, Cambodia, Cameroon, Cape Verde, Central African Republic, Chad, Chile, China, Colombia, Comoros, Congo, Democratic Republic of Congo, Costa Rica, Côte d'Ivoire, Croatia, Cuba, Cyprus, Djibouti, Dominica, Dominican Republic, Ecuador, Eritrea, Ethiopia, Egypt, Equatorial Guinea, Fiji, Gabon, Gambia, Georgia, Ghana, Grenada, Guatemala, Guinea-Bissau, Guinea, Guyana, Haiti, Honduras, India, Indonesia, Iran, Iraq, Jamaica, Jordan, Kazakhstan, Kenya, Kiribati, Kuwait, Kyrgyzstan, Laos, Lebanon, Lesotho, Liberia, Libya, Former Yugoslav Republic of Macedonia, Madagascar, Mali, Malaysia, Marshall Islands, Mauritius, Mauritania, Malawi, Maldives, Mexico, Federated States of Micronesia, Moldova, Mongolia, Morocco, Mozambique, Myanmar, formerly Burma (this country has temporarily lost the benefits of the system: see Art 34.4 of the Regulation and Art 39.2 of the proposed regulation) Nauru, Nepal, Nicaragua, Namibia, Niger, Nigeria, Oman, Pakistan, Panama, Papua New Guinea, Paraguay, Peru, Philippines, Qatar, Russia, Rwanda, St Kitts and Nevis, St Lucia, St Vincent, Samoa, São Tomé and Príncipe, Saudi Arabia, Senegal, Seychelles and dependencies, Sierra Leone, Solomon Islands, Somalia, South Africa, Sri Lanka, Sudan, Suriname, Swaziland, Syria, Tajikistan, Tanzania, Thailand, Togo, Tonga, Trinidad and Tobago, Tunisia, Turkmenistan, Tuvalu, Uganda, Ukraine, United Arab Emirates, Uruguay, Uzbekistan, Vanuatu, Vietnam, Venezuela, Yemen, Zambia, Zimbabwe. Palau Part B. Countries and territories dependent or administered or for whose external relations Member States of the Community or third countries are wholly or partly responsible: American Oceania, Anguilla, Aruba, Australia Oceania (Christmas Island, Cocos (Keeling) Islands, Heard and McDonald Islands, Norfolk Island) Bermuda, British Indian Ocean Territories, British Virgin Islands, Cayman Islands, Falkland Islands, French Polynesia, Gibraltar, Greenland, Macao, Mayotte, Montserrat, Netherlands Antilles, New Caledonia and dependencies, New Zealand Oceania (Tokelau and Niue Islands, Cook Islands) Pitcairn, Polar Regions (French Southern and Antarctic Territories, Australian Antarctic Territories, British Antarctic Territories, South Georgia and South Sandwich Islands), St Helena dependencies, St Pierre and Miquelon, Turks and Caicos Islands, Virgin Islands of the United States, Wallis and Futuna.

1.3 *The benefits of the GSP*

The essential objective of the generalized preference regime is to provide for reductions of customs duty, charged under the Tariff, in relation to specified products according to what is called a 'modulation mechanism'[25] which replaced reliance upon the use of quotas and ceilings. The products which are affected are listed in Annex I to the GSP Regulation. All the products identified in the Annex are referred to both by their description and a CN code. The preferential scheme is, however, to be determined by the coverage of the codes. The description is stated to have no more than 'indicative value'. Sometimes 'ex' is placed before a code. In such cases the identity of the products referred to is to be determined by the CN code and the description together. Products which qualify for exemption or total temporary suspension of the tariff duties are included within Annex I for the purposes of simplification only.[26]

The Annex is divided into four parts. Part 1 lists 'very sensitive products' subject to a preferential duty, which is to be 85 per cent of the tariff duty applicable to the product concerned. These products include some fish, fruit, and vegetables as well as some fabrics, clothes, and floor-coverings. Part 2 lists 'sensitive products' subject to a preferential duty which is to be 70 per cent of the applicable tariff duty. The list includes some live animals, some meat, fruit, vegetables and other edible foods, spirits, and cigarettes. Part 3 lists 'semi-sensitive products' in respect of which the preferential duty is to be 35 per cent of the applicable tariff duty. These products range from, amongst other things, fish, to certain machinery and electrical apparatus. Part 4 lists 'non-sensitive products' in respect of which customs duty under the Tariff is to be suspended. Again the products concerned are very varied and range from foodstuffs and live animals to aircraft and tanks. It will be apparent that, generally speaking, agricultural products benefit from lower reductions of duty than other products and preferential reduction is limited to *ad valorem* duty in relation to products falling within Chapters 1–24 of the CN.[27]

The rate of duty by reference to which the preferential duties are calculated is, generally speaking, the lowest rate of duty appearing in column 3 (autonomous duty) or 4 (conventional duty) of the Tariff. Consequently, the benefits of the system of general preferences are linked to the EC's most-favoured-nation rate. It is not possible to review the proposed regulation continuing the scheme of generalized tariff preferences in detail. It would, however, replace the four categories of product referred to above with just two: 'non-sensitive' products which will enjoy duty-free access as at the moment, and 'sensitive products' which will cover all other products. To take account of

---

[25] See GSP Regulation, Art 2, which sets out the reductions of duty outlined above and refers to the reductions as a 'modulation mechanism'.
[26] See n 3 to Annex I Part 1, of the GSP Regulation.
[27] See Art 29 and n 1 to Annex I Part 1, of the GSP Regulation.

the erosion of the value of preferences, *ad valorem* duties on sensitive products
are to be reduced by 3.5 per cent and specific duties on them are to be reduced
by 30 per cent.[28]

It should be noted that, currently, the preferential rates are themselves
reduced by between 10 and 35 per cent of the customs duty rate pursuant to
certain special incentives relating to labour rights and environmental protection which may be granted by the Commission.[29] Furthermore, the countries
of the Andean Group[30] and the Central American Common Market[31] benefit
from special arrangements supporting measures to combat drugs.[32] These
special incentive arrangements are complex and have not enjoyed as much
success as was hoped for at the time of their introduction. Amongst other
changes, therefore, the recently proposed regulation provides for an additional
reduction of a further 3.5 per cent in relation to *ad valorem* duties and a further
30 per cent in relation to specific duties.

The most favourable treatment of all, though, is reserved, by virtue of the
GSP Regulation, Art 6,[33] for the least-developed countries listed in Annex IV.[34]
According to the EC Commission's DG for Trade, in 1998 the EU imported 56
per cent, and the USA 36 per cent, of the total exports of these countries.[35]
The new 'Everything but arms' package[36] gives them immediate duty-free
access to the EU, without quantitive restrictions, in respect of products within
chapters 1 to 97 of the common customs tariff (except for products within
chapter 93, ie arms and ammunition) and provides for progressive opening of
markets for sugar, rice, and bananas. Full liberalization will be achieved for
sugar and rice as from 1 July 2009 and 1 September 2009 respectively and for
bananas as from 1 January 2006.

---

[28] See Art 7 of the proposed regulation.
[29] See Arts 8 and 9, of the GSP Regulation.
[30] Colombia, Venezuala, Ecuador, Peru, and Bolivia.
[31] Guatemala, Honduras, El Salvador, Nicaragua, Costa Rica, and Panama.
[32] See Art 7 and Annex V of the GSP Regulation.
[33] See the GSP Regulation as amended by Council Regulation (EC) 416/2000 of 28 Feb 2001
[2001] OJ L60/3.
[34] The 48 least-developed developing countries are: Afghanistan, Angola, Bangladesh, Benin,
Bhutan, Burkina Faso, Burundi, Cambodia, Cape Verde, Chad, Central African Republic, Comoros,
Democratic Republic of Congo, Djibouti, Equatorial Guinea, Eritrea, Ethiopia, Gambia, Guinea,
Guinea-Bissau, Haiti, Kiribati, Laos, Lesotho, Liberia, Madagascar, Mali, Malawi, Maldives,
Mauritania, Mozambique, Myanmar (formerly Burma) Nepal, Niger, Rwanda, Samoa. Sierra
Leone, São Tomé and Príncipe, Solomon Islands, Somalia, Sudan, Tanzania, Togo, Tuvalu,
Uganda, Vanuatu, Yemen, Zambia. The nine non-ACP countries in the above are Afghanistan,
Bangladesh, Bhutan, Cambodia, Laos, Maldives, Myanmar, Nepal and Yemen, The list of the least-
developed landlocked and island States for the purposes of the Cotonou Agreement is somewhat
different and is given below.
[35] See a Trade DG Press Release of 20 Sept 2000 and a Press Briefing of 17 Jan 2001 on the
'Everything but arms' (EBA) package.
[36] Implemented by Council Regulation (EC) 416/2000, n 33 above, and maintained in the
proposed regulation.

1.2 *Loss of benefits*

A country may be removed from the list of beneficiary countries if two conditions are met.[37] These are, first, that the country has a per capita gross national product exceeding US$8,210 for 1995, according to the most recent World Bank figures, and secondly, a development index, calculated in accordance with the formula and figures given in Part 2 of Annex II, greater than 1. It is possible for states to lose entitlement to the advantages of the general system of preferences in relation to specified products pursuant to a 'graduation mechanism'.[38] This uses a development index to measure a country's overall level of industrial development compared to that of the EU and a specialization index which is derived from the relationship between the proportion of imports in a particular sector from a particular country, compared to the total amount of Community imports in the sector, and the country's share of Community imports.[39] The proposed regulation continuing generalized tariff preferences amends the graduation mechanism with a view to the new regime coming into force as from 1 January 2003. Under the new rules the list of beneficiary countries is to be established on a yearly basis and a country is to cease to be a beneficiary country where, during three consecutive years, it is classified by the World Bank as a high-income country and satisfies the rules relating to the development index.[40] The benefits granted by the system of generalized preferences may be withdrawn at any time in the event of certain circumstances arising, such as the use of slave or prison labour, failings in relation to drugs control and money laundering, fraud and unfair trading. The proposed regulation includes serious and systematic violation of core labour standards and significant detrimental effects on the environment arising from the production of certain products as reasons for temporary withdrawal of GSP benefits.

The GSP Regulation also contains a safeguard clause.[41] It ensures that where a product is imported on terms which cause, or threaten to cause, 'serious difficulties'[42] to a Community producer of like or directly competing products, customs duties on that product may be reintroduced at any time at the request of a Member State or on the Commission's own initiative. In exceptional circumstances, a procedure providing for the implementation of measures with immediate effect is available.

---

[37] See GSP Regulation, Art 1.4.

[38] The states and products are listed in Annex II Part 1 of the GSP Regulation.

[39] The indices are defined in Annex II Part 2, ibid.

[40] Art 3, proposed regulation. Provision is also made for countries which lose beneficiary status to regain it: Art 3.2, ibid.   [41] See Art 28.

[42] In examining the existence of serious difficulties the Commission must take account of the factors set out in Annex VI of the GSP Regulation, where the information is available. These are: reduction in the market share of Community producers, reduction in their production, increase in their stocks, closure of their production capacity, bankruptcies, low profitability, low rate of capacity utilization, employment, trade, prices.

1.3 *Administrative matters*

Within six weeks of the end of each quarter Member States are required to inform the Commission of their statistical data on goods admitted for free circulation during the quarter under the system of generalized preferences.[43] There is also a Generalized Preferences Committee which may examine any matter relating to the application of the regulation establishing the system of generalized preferences.[44] Similar obligations to report to the Commission and comparable committees are established under the agreements which the EC enters into with third countries and which are discussed below.

2. *Overseas Countries and Territories*[45]

The OCTs have a special relationship with the EC, as appears from the fact that Article 3(s) of the EC Treaty provides that the activities of the Community shall include 'the association of OCTs in order to increase trade and promote jointly economic and social development'. The application of the Council Decision which contains the details of the relationship between the EC and the OCTs was extended first to 28 February 2001 and more recently to 1 December 2001.[46] The relationship between the OCTs and the EC, which has always been the product of 'a dynamic and progressive process'[47] is, however, set to

---

[43] Art 30, GSP Regulation.

[44] Art 31, GSP Regulation. The Committee was created by reg 17 of Council Regulation (EC) 3281/94, n 18 above.

[45] These are set out in Annex 1 of Council Decision (EEC) 482/91 of 25 July 1991 [1991] OJ L263/1 and are as follows: 1. Country with special relations with Denmark—Greenland. Overseas territories of the French Republic: New Caledonia and Dependencies, French Polynesia, French Southern and Antarctic Territories, Wallis and Futuna Islands. 3. Territorial collectivities of the French Republic: Mayotte, Saint Pierre and Miquelon. 4. Non-European countries of the Kingdom of the Netherlands: Aruba, Netherlands Antilles: Bonaire, Curaçao, Saba, Sint Eustatius, Sint Maarten. 5. Overseas countries and territories of the United Kingdom of Great Britain and Northern Ireland: Anguilla, Cayman Islands, Falkland Islands, South Georgia and the Sandwich Islands, Montserrat, Pitcairn, Saint Helena and Dependencies, British Antarctic Territory, British Indian Ocean Territory, Turks and Caicos Islands, British Virgin Islands. Note that the list of OCTs in Annex II to the EC Treaty contains Bermuda, however, it does not appear in the list of OCTs in Annex 1 to Council Decision 482/91. This is because the UK did not request its inclusion, notwithstanding that the UK is responsible for its external relations. For the same reason it is not included in the list of countries and territories referred to in Article 362 of the Fourth Lomé Convention which permits OCTs which become independent to request accession to the Convention: See Written Question (E–425/95) to the Commission on the status of Bermuda and Answer: [1995] OJ C175/42.

[46] See Council Decision (EC) 169/2000 of 25 Feb [2000] OJ L329/50, and Council Decision (EC) 161/2001 of 26 Feb 2001 [2001] OJ L58/21 extending Council Decision of 25 July 1991 (EEC) 482/91, n 45 above. This latter decision originally applied for 10 years from 1 Mar 1990: see Art 240/1. It was amended, in mid-term, by Council Decision (EC) 803/97 of 24 Nov 1997 [1997] OJ L329/50.

[47] Case 17/98 *Emesa Sugar (Free Zone) NV v Aruba* [2000] ECR I–675 at para 28. See also Case C–310/95 *Road Air v Inspecteur der invoerrechten en accijnzen* [1997] ECR I–2229, para 40, and Case C–390/95 P *Antillean Rice Mills v Commission* [1999] ECR I–769, para 36.

change. Declaration Number 36 on the OCTs, adopted by the conference which agreed the Amsterdam Treaty, noted that the circumstances then surrounding the OCTs were considerably different from those existing in 1957. It stated that whereas the arrangements were intended for numerous countries and territories, there are now only twenty of them. They are scattered island territories with a population of under 1 million facing severe geographical and economic handicaps, and the original arrangements can no longer deal with the challenges they are facing. It concluded by saying that:

> The Conference invites the Council, acting in accordance with the provisions of Article 136 [now 187] of the Treaty establishing the European Community, to review the association arrangements by February 2000, with the fourfold objective of:
> — promoting the economic and social development of the OCTs more effectively;
> — developing economic relations between the OCTs and the European Union;
> — taking greater account of the diversity and specific characteristics of the individual OCTs, including aspects relating to freedom of establishment;
> — ensuring that the effectiveness of the financial instrument is improved.

For its part, the Commission has subsequently made clear that it is engaged in a 'root and branch' revision of the existing arrangements with a view to taking account of the progress of European integration over the last ten years and of the new objectives and aspirations of the territories.[48] At the present time, however, it is Part Four of the EC Treaty, Articles 182–188, which is devoted to the association of the OCTs and which is considered below.

These provisions of the Treaty clearly confer a privileged status on the OCTs. Nevertheless, they are not part of the EC and, indeed, in many respects they are in the same situation as non-member countries.[49] The approach of the EC to them is comparable in particular to that adopted in respect of the ACP countries discussed below. The arrangements with both groups of countries are the result of the Community's efforts:

> to contribute towards international cooperation and to the solution of international problems of an economic, social and cultural nature, in conformity with the aspirations of the international community towards a new, more just and more balanced international economic order . . .[50]

These high aims are translated into the relevant provisions of the EC Treaty. Article 182 of the Treaty states that the purpose of the association of OCTs with the Community is the promotion of the OCT's economic and social development and the establishment of close economic relations between them and the Community as a whole. This economic relationship is intended to lead the

[48] IP/00/171, 16 Feb 2000.
[49] Case 17/98 *Emesa Sugar (Free Zone) NV v Aruba*, n 47 above, para 29. See also Opinion 1/78 [1979] ECR 2871, para 62, and Opinion 1/94 [1994] ECR I–5267, para 17.
[50] See the second recital to Council Decision(EEC) 482/91, n 45 above.

OCTs, in the words of Article 182 to 'the economic, social and cultural development to which they aspire'.[51] EC Treaty, Article 183 then sets out a number
of objectives of the association concerned with trade, investment and freedom
of establishment.

Customs duties are mentioned specifically in Article 184.1, which provides
that customs duties on imports into the Community from goods originating in
the OCTs are to be prohibited in conformity with the prohibition of customs
duties which the Treaty requires as between Member States. Article 184.2 then
states that customs duties on imports into the OCTs from the Member States are
to be prohibited in accordance with Article 25 of the Treaty, discussed in Chapter 3 above.[52] By virtue of Article 184.3, however, the OCTs may levy customs
duties which meet the needs of their development and industrialization or
produce revenue for their budget. The duties must not exceed the level of those
imposed on imports of products from a Member State with which each OCT has
special relations. The Article concludes by providing, in paragraph 5, that any
change in, or introduction of, customs duties imposed on imports into an OCT
must not give rise, either in law or fact, to any direct or indirect discrimination
between imports from the various Member States. The scope of what is now
Article 184 was considered in *Leplat*,[53] in which it was decided that although
the Article referred only to customs duties, it also encompassed charges having
equivalent effect. In justifying its conclusion the Court of Justice said:

> An interpretation of Article [184] restricting its scope to customs duties in the
> narrow sense would render the arrangements established by that article nugatory
> and would deprive them of their practical effect in so far as it would be possible to
> avoid their application by introducing charges which, while not customs duties in
> the strict sense, none the less had the same effects on trade between the Member
> States and the countries and territories. Such an interpretation, moreover, would
> be contrary to the objectives defined in the part of the Treaty dealing with the
> association of the countries and territories.[54]

The Court went on to confirm that the terms of the Article permitted the OCTs
to levy, and introduce, customs duties and charges having equivalent effect on
imports from Member States, provided that the requirements of the Treaty
were met. The Court ended its judgment by noting that, originally, Article 133
of the EC Treaty, as Article 184 then was, had provided for staged reductions
in customs duties during the transitional period and that the obligation to
reduce duties was satisfied on entry into force of a Council Decision in 1964.[55]

---

[51] Art 182, third para.
[52] Art 184.2 does not apply to countries and territories which already apply a non-discrimina-
tory customs tariff, by reason of the particular international obligations by which they are bound:
see Art 184.4.
[53] Case C–260/90 *Bernard Leplat v Territory of French Polynesia* [1992] ECR I–643.
[54] Ibid, para. 18.
[55] See Council Decision (EEC) 349/64 [1964] OJ 93/1472.

Turning to the remaining provisions of the Treaty relating to OCTs, Article 185 permits Member States to ask the Commission to propose action to remedy situations in which the level of duties, payable in respect of goods entering an OCT from a third country, is liable to cause deflections of trade prejudicial to Member States. Article 186 is concerned with freedom of movement for workers and Article 188 is concerned exclusively with the position of Greenland.[56] Article 187 is of more general importance. It authorizes the Council, acting unanimously, to lay out the detailed rules and procedures governing the association between the EC and the OCTs. It has done so by way of Council Decision and in particular the Council Decision (EEC) 482/91 which is noted by the title to this section ('the OCT Decision').

2.1 *The OCT Decision*

As one would expect, the OCT Decision is very broad in its scope and the provisions it contains concerning customs duties are a small part of it. They are contained in Part Three ('The Instruments of EC–OCT Cooperation') and Title 1 ('Trade Co-operation'). The Decision follows the EC Treaty in stating, in Article 101.1, that products originating in the OCTs shall be imported into the Community free of import duties.[57] As may be expected it also provides that the Community, subject to certain caveats relating to various matters of public policy or interest, shall not apply to imports of products originating in the OCT any quantitative restrictions or measures having equivalent effect.[58]

So far as customs duties are concerned, Article 101.2 goes on to provide that products not originating in the OCT, but which are in free circulation in one of the OCTs and are re-exported as such to the Community, shall be accepted for import into the Community free of customs duties and taxes having equivalent effect. This advantage is subject to a number of requirements being met. The first is that in the OCT concerned, customs duties or taxes having equivalent effect have been paid at a level equal to, or higher than, the customs duties applicable in the Community on import of the same products originating in third countries and eligible for the most-favoured-nation clause. Secondly, the goods must not have been the subject of a full or partial exemption from, or refund of, customs duties or taxes having equivalent effect. Finally, the goods must be accompanied by an export certificate. The advantages permitted under Article 101.2 do not, however, apply in relation to certain agricultural products, or in relation to those which, on import into the

---

[56] It provides that Arts 182–187 of the Treaty are to apply to Greenland, subject to the Protocol on special arrangements for Greenland annexed to the Treaty. The position of Greenland is also referred to in Art 105 of Council Decision (EEC) 482/91 at n 45 above.

[57] Prior to its amendment in 1997 it referred to customs duties and charges having equivalent effect.

[58] Arts 102 and 103.

Community, are subject to quantitative restrictions, limitations, or anti-dumping duties.[59]

So far as customs duties imposed by the OCT are concerned, Article 106.1 provides that the relevant authorities may retain or introduce, in respect of imports of products originating in the Community or in other OCTs, such customs duties or quantitative restrictions as they consider necessary. Special provision is made in relation to the origin of products and for administrative cooperation between the respective customs authorities.[60]

The OCTs have not always been uncritical of their treatment by the EC and the Court of Justice has had to consider a number of legal challenges to the OCT Decision and other legislation. In one case, for example, a sugar producer challenged Article 108b of the OCT Decision. This was introduced by the mid-term amendment to the OCT Decision in November 1997, and provided, among other things, for a limited quantity of sugar to be imported into the EC annually without customs duty being paid.[61] The limit was challenged on a number of grounds. The ability of the EC to amend the OCT Decision in mid-term, the compatibility of the 1997 Decision with the EC Treaty, and its proportionality were all questioned. The provision survived unscathed.[62] The Netherlands Antilles, however, succeeded in obtaining the annulment of Commission regulations which provided, amongst other things, that no more import licences for rice within CN Code 1006 should be granted.[63] The regulations were made under the safeguard provisions contained in Article 109 of the OCT Decision, in its original form.[64] Broadly speaking, the safeguard clause provides that the Commission may authorize a Member State to take safeguard measures in certain unusual situations. These are: where the application of the OCT Decision causes serious disturbances to occur in a sector of the economy of the Community, or one or more of its Member States, or their external financial stability is jeopardized, or if difficulties arise which may result in a deterioration in a sector of the Community's activity or in a region of the Community. The Netherlands Antilles first established that it had *locus standi* to challenge the regulation, because the measure was 'of direct and indi-

---

[59] See Art 101.3

[60] See Arts 108, 108a and 108b, and Annex II of the OCT Decision. See Ch 7 below in relation to the origin of goods.

[61] It also amended the definition of customs value to conform with the WTO Agreement of 1994: see Ch 8 below.

[62] Case C–17/98 *Emesa Sugar (Free Zone) NV v Aruba*, n 47 above.

[63] Joined Cases T–32/98 and T–41/98 *Netherlands Antilles v Commission* [2001] 2 CMLR 14 and now under appeal: see OJ C233/22.

[64] Safeguard measures continue to be important. They were recently extended to 31 Dec 2001 with regard to imports of sugar by Commission Regulation (EC) 1325/2001 of 29 June 2001, and widened in scope by Commission Regulation (EC) 1476/2001 of 18 July 2001 [2001] OJ L195/29. Note that the Court of First Instance rejected a request for interim relief against safeguard measures in relation to sugar sector products in Case T–350/00 R *Free Trade Foods NV v Commission* [2001] OJ C161/18.

vidual concern' to it under, what is now, EC Treaty, Article 230.4.[65] It then obtained the annulment of the regulations[66] on the basis that, despite having a wide discretion in relation to the existence of the conditions justifying safeguard measures and the principle of adopting them, the Commission had to show the existence of a causal link between the application of the OCT Decision and the emergence of disturbances in the Community market[67]. It had made no attempt to do so and so the regulations it had passed were annulled.

B. AGREEMENTS

In Chapter 1 we observed the importance of international treaties, particularly multilateral treaties, in the global and Community law relating to trade and customs matters and noted the significance of issues such as Community competence. In this section we turn our attention from the Final Act of the Uruguay Round and the other multilateral international conventions which together lay the foundations of international customs law, to some of those treaties which seek to implement more specific elements of the EC's external policy.[68]

It has been said that the agreements entered into by the Community should be seen as a series of concentric circles[69] with the outermost agreements providing for the loosest relationships. Adopting this plan, the EEA is at the centre and is considered first. Next to it are the wide-ranging Europe Agreements which are another group of mixed agreements designed to assist East European states in achieving membership of the EC. Then there are other association agreements. These are followed by agreements with the ACP countries and co-operation agreements. Finally, there are partnership and co-operation agreements and trade and co-operation agreements.

Given that the external policy of the EC must vary as between different third countries and regions of the world, the agreements are bound to differ

---

[65] Joined Cases T–32/98 and T–41/98 *Netherlands Antilles v Commission*, at n 63 above, and paras 44–62.

[66] The Regulations in question were Commission Regulation (EC) 2352/97 of 27 Nov 1997 introducing specific measures in respect of imports of rice originating in the overseas countries and territories [1997] OJ L326/21 and Commission Regulation (EC) 2494/97 of 12 Dec 1997 [1997] OJ L343/17 on the issuing of import licences for rice falling within CN code 1006 and originating in the overseas countries and territories under the specific measures introduced by Regulation (EC) 2352/97.

[67] As the Court of Justice made clear in Case C–390/95 *Antillean Rice Mills v Commission*, n 47 above, at para 47 and in Joined Cases T–32/98 and T–41/98 *Netherlands Antilles v Commission*, n 63 above, at para 77f.

[68] Treaties on transit are considered in Ch 10 below.

[69] P Kapteyn and P VerLoren van Themaat, *Introduction to the Law of the European Communities* (3rd edn by L Gormley, Kluwer International, London, 1998), 1328.

significantly from each other. Although, in relation to certain matters, third countries may sometimes disapprove of this, it is unexceptional and not of itself a ground of complaint. This state of affairs has, of course, implications for Community traders too. It should, therefore, be noted that the Court of Justice has on more than one occasion said that:

> there is no general principle of Community law obliging the Community, in its external relations, to accord third countries equal treatment in all respects. Therefore, . . . if different treatment of third countries is compatible with Community law, then different treatment accorded to traders within the Community must also be regarded as compatible with Community law where that different treatment is merely an automatic consequence of the different treatment accorded to third countries with which such traders have entered into commercial relations.[70]

It may be, nevertheless, that Community traders can show that the different treatment of them is illegal by reference to some general principle of law, as they did, at least to some extent, in *Germany v Council*,[71] from the judgment in which the above quotation is taken. The traders relied upon the second paragraph of Article 34.2 of the EC Treaty which provides that the common organization of agricultural markets 'shall exclude any discrimination between producers or consumers within the Community'. This provision the Court held, perhaps unsurprisingly, was 'a specific enunciation of the general principle of equality, one of the fundamental principles of Community law'.[72]

With this general proposition in mind, we now turn to specific agreements. It is impossible to review these in detail. What follows is intended to make clear, very briefly, the broad purposes of the agreements which the EC has entered into. Clearly, in advising on any specific case, the terms of the relevant agreement will have to be considered in detail.

1. *The EEA Agreement*

The historical background to this agreement is that Austria, Denmark, Finland, Portugal, Sweden, Switzerland, and the UK were originally members of the European Free Trade Area (EFTA) pursuant to the Stockholm Convention which entered into force on 3 May 1960. Iceland joined EFTA on 1 March 1970, Finland on 1 January 1986, and Liechtenstein on 1 September 1991. Denmark and the UK withdrew on joining the EEC on 1 January 1973 and Portugal withdrew when it joined the EC on 1 January 1986. Austria, Finland, and Sweden withdrew in January 1995 when they joined the EC.

---

[70] Case C–122/95 *Germany v Council* [1998] ECR 973 at para 56. See also Case C 52/81 *Faust v Commission* [1982] ECR 3745 para 25.

[71] Ibid.

[72] Ibid, para 64.

Prior to the creation of the EEA, the EC had established free trade agreements with the countries of EFTA.[73] These were all similar in form and contained specific provisions governing customs law which, as we will see later have required consideration by the Court of Justice.

The EEA Agreement was intended as an introduction to the EC for EFTA members and functioned as such for Austria, Finland, and Sweden. It was signed in Oporto on 2 May 1992 by the EC, the ECSC, and the then twelve Member States of the EC, together with the then states of the European Free Trade Area, namely Austria, Finland, Iceland, Liechtenstein, Norway, Sweden, and Switzerland. The Swiss voted against the EEA Agreement in December 1992. Consequently, the non-EU states in the EEA are now Iceland, Liechtenstein, and Norway. The states within EFTA are those three states plus Switzerland. The free trade agreement between Switzerland and the Community, which came into force on 1 January 1973 continues in effect.[74] Recently, seven agreements have been negotiated between Switzerland and the EC in relation to different economic sectors. These are: free movement of persons, air transport, land transport, agriculture, research, public procurement and technical barriers to trade. The Agreements were signed on 21 June 1999 and have been approved in a referendum in Switzerland in May 2000. They are likely to enter into force in 2001.[75]

In general terms, the EEA Agreement involves, as the Court of Justice has made clear: 'a high degree of integration, with objectives which exceed those of a mere free-trade agreement'.[76] Among other things, it extends the geographical reach of the four fundamental freedoms of the EC to the EEA. The agreement does not, however, deal with many other matters including agriculture and fiscal harmonization. Neither is the EEA bound by the EC's common commercial policy. Perhaps most significantly, the agreement does not aim to establish a new legal community as the EC Treaty does. Its objective is simply to establish legal obligations binding upon the contracting parties in the usual manner of an international treaty. It does not involve the transfer of any sovereign rights.[77]

---

[73] The agreements are published in the *Official Journal*, following their implementing regulations, as follows: Austria [1972] OJ L300/2, Finland [1973] OJ L328/2, Iceland [1972] OJ L301/2, Norway [1973] OJ L171/2, Portugal [1972](OJ L301/165, Sweden [1972] OJ L300/97, Switzerland, and Liechtenstein, which have a customs union between themselves [1972] OJ L300/189.

[74] Like all the other free trade agreements with the EFTA countries, n 73 above, the one with Switzerland contains its own provisions on origin. These have been considered by the Court of Justice in Case 218/83 *Les Rapids Savoyards and Others v Directeur Général des Douanes et Droits Indirects* [1984] ECR 3105, I–2465. See further Ch 7 below.

[75] Copies of the agreements and ratification details are available at: www.europa.admin.ch/e/index.htm.

[76] See Case T–115/94 *Opel Austria GmbH v Council* [1997] ECR II–39 at para 107.

[77] See Opinion 1/91 [1991] ECR I–6079 at para 20. The Opinion contains a useful analysis of the EEA in comparison with the EC.

Turning to matters relating to customs duty, free movement of goods is dealt with in Part II of the EEA Agreement and Chapter 1 (Articles 8–17 inclusive). These provisions mirror those to be found in the EC Treaty on customs duties and internal taxation. Article 10 is of particular importance. It was held in *Opel*[78] to have direct effect and to be identical in substance to, what was then, Articles 12 (now Article 25), 13, 16 and 17 (now repealed) of the EC Treaty. It states that 'Customs duties on imports and exports, and any charges having equivalent effect, shall be prohibited between the Contracting Parties. Without prejudice to the arrangements set out in Protocol 5, this shall also apply to customs duties of a fiscal nature'. In reaching its conclusion on direct effect, the Court was greatly assisted by the terms of EEA, Article 6 which requires provisions which are identical in substance to the EEC Treaty, and the ECCS Treaty, to be interpreted in conformity with the relevant rulings of the Court of Justice given prior to the date of signature of the EEA Agreement. It should be borne in mind, though, that despite containing some similar provisions on customs duties to the EC Treaty, the EEA agreement does not constitute a customs union. As a result, rules of origin are necessary and these are set out in Protocol 4, chapter 3 of which provides for co-operation in customs-related matters.

2. *The Europe Agreements*

The ten Europe Agreements are wide-ranging in scope and, like all the agreements with which we are concerned, create their own institutional structure with Association Councils and other bodies.[79] The agreements are not identical to each other, but there is a great degree of similarity between them. For convenience, reference is made in the discussion below to the agreement with the Czech Republic.

The fundamental intention of the agreement can be seen from its second recital which states that 'the Community and the Czech Republic wish to strengthen [their] links and to establish close and lasting relations, based on reciprocity, which would allow the Czech Republic to take part in the process of European integration'. Article 1.2 is even more explicit stating that one of the aims of the agreement is 'to provide an appropriate framework for the Czech Republic's gradual integration into the Community'. Broadly speaking, this aim is intended to be achieved at the end of a ten-year transitional period

---

[78] Case T–115/94 *Opel Austria GmbH v Council*, n 76 above, at para 110.

[79] There are Europe agreements with: Bulgaria [1994] OJ L358/2 the Czech Republic [1994] OJ L360/2; Estonia [1998] OJ L68/3; Hungary [1993] OJ L347/2; Latvia [1998] OJ L26/3; Lithuania [1998] OJ L51/3; Poland [1993] OJ L348/2; Romania [1994] OJ L357/2; the Slovak Republic [1994] OJ L359/2; and Slovenia [1999] OJ L51/3. The Decisions which approve the agreements on behalf of the Community appear immediately before the agreements in the *Official Journal*. The agreements have been amended from time to time.

which started when the agreement entered into force. As is well known, though, the timing of the accession to the EC of the states which are parties to the Europe Agreements is a matter of some debate.

So far as the free movement of goods is concerned, the Community and the Czech Republic are, according to Article 8 of the agreement, to establish a free trade area in a ten-year transitional period and the CN is to be applied in respect of trade between the parties. In respect of most industrial products Community customs duty is not applicable in respect of imports from the Czech Republic. In respect of some products tariffs were reduced over a period of not more than three years from entry into force of the agreement.[80] Duties imposed on imports into the Czech Republic of goods of Community origin are to be reduced over longer periods of either five or nine years.[81] It will be apparent that rules of origin are necessary in order to apply the agreement and these are set out in a separate Protocol. Finally, it may be noted that the provisions concerning the abolition of customs duties on imports apply also to customs duties of a fiscal nature.[82] Furthermore, the Community and the Czech Republic were required to abolish upon entry into force of the agreement any charges having an effect equivalent to customs duties on imports in trade between themselves.[83]

3. *Association agreements*

Association agreements do not expressly aim at bringing the third country into the EC, but are mostly focused on commercial relations. Some aim at deeper relationships than others and some seek a customs union, at least in respect of industrial products. This is true of the association agreement with Turkey (referred to at p 81 above), which, as we have seen, has now given rise to the intended customs union for industrial products between the EC and Turkey. The agreements with Cyprus[84] and Malta[85] also seek a customs union which has yet to be concluded. The intention to create one is, however, clearly stated in the agreements. The third paragraph of the preamble to the agreement with Cyprus states that:

> the object of this Agreement is the progressive elimination of obstacles to trade between the European Economic Community and Cyprus, and . . . it provides that, eighteen months before the expiry of the first stage, negotiations may be opened

---

[80] Art 10 of the Agreement.   [81] Ibid, Art 11.

[82] Ibid, Art 12.   [83] Ibid, Art 13.

[84] See [1973] OJ L133/2, Council Regulation (EEC) 1247/73 [1973] OJ L133/1. Cyprus is, of course, now negotiating for entry into the EU and Turkey has been informed that it is, in principle, welcome.

[85] See [1971] OJ L61/2. See Art 2.3 of the Agreement. See also Council Regulation (EEC) 429/71 [1971] OJ L61/1.

with a view to determining the conditions under which a customs union between the Community and the Republic of Cyprus could be established,[86]

The first stage of the agreement was extended from 30 June 1977 to 31 December 1980 by a Protocol[87] to the Agreement. Customs union with Cyprus is now to be achieved by the end of the second phase of the second stage, which may be either 2004 or 2005.[88] So far as Malta is concerned, customs union is again linked to the first stage of the agreement which was extended to 31 December 1991, continuing after that from year to year until it is denounced by one of the parties by 1 July in any year.[89]

Cyprus, Malta and Turkey are, of course, countries within the Euro-Mediterranean Partnership launched by the Barcelona conference of 1995. Nine other countries are included within the Barcelona process, namely, Egypt, Israel, Jordan, the Palestinian Authority, Lebanon and Syria ('Mashrek') and Morocco, Algeria, Tunisia ('Maghreb'). Libya has observer status at certain meetings. The Euro-Mediterranean Agreements that have yet to be concluded replace either existing association agreements or co-operation agreements. The terms of the Euro-Mediterranean Agreements vary considerably between themselves. For example, the agreement with Israel seeks to strengthen the free trade area which exists between the parties.[90] The agreements with Morocco and Tunisia seek to establish a free trade area over a period of not more than twelve years[91] while the agreement with the Palestinian Authority seeks to establish a free trade area by 31 December 2001.[92] Taken together, however, the agreements will lead to, amongst other things, the creation of a Euro-Mediterranean Free Trade Area by 2010.

4. Co-operation, trade, and development agreements: Yaoundé, Lomé, and Cotonou

One recently concluded and important co-operation, trade, and development agreement is that with South Africa which was referred to at the beginning of this chapter. The agreement is likely to prove of considerable commercial importance. It seeks to establish a free trade area between the EC and South Africa, taking a maximum period of twelve years, from entry into force of the Agreement, on the South African side and a maximum period of ten years on the EC side.[93] Customs duties are to be progressively reduced so as to meet the

---

[86] See also Art 2.3 of the Agreement.
[87] [1987] OJ L393/2, Regulation (EEC) [1987] OJ L393/1.
[88] See Arts 1 and 31 of the Protocol.
[89] Art 1 of the Protocol to the Agreement: [1991] OJ L116/67.
[90] See Art 6 and n 5 above.
[91] Ssee Art 6 in both cases and n 5 above.
[92] See Art 3 and n 5 above.
[93] See Art 5 and n 6 above.

time limits.[94] Important though this agreement is, the agreements with the ACP countries have attracted rather more attention and we turn now to consider these.

The two Yaoundé Conventions, which were mixed agreements, established the relationship between the EEC, certain African countries, and Madagascar. These had been overseas countries and dependencies, but had since attained independence. The first Yaoundé Convention was signed on 20 July 1963,[95] the second Yaoundé Convention terminated on 31 March 1976.[96] It was replaced by the First Lomé Convention.[97] The parties to the this Convention were not only African but also Caribbean and Pacific countries. They were consequently known as the 'ACP' countries.[98] The Lomé Convention then went through four 'editions'. The life of the Fourth and final Lomé Convention was due to end on 28 February 2000. The ACP–EC Committee of Ambassadors decided, however, that it should remain in force from 1 March 2000[99] to 1 August 2000.[100] During that period, on 23 June 2000, a new agreement between the EC and the ACP countries was signed in Cotonou, Benin. Negotiations for this new partnership agreement had begun on 30 September 1998 and concluded on 3 February 2000. The Cotonou Agreement, as it is known, will come into force once it has been ratified by the European Parliament and national parliaments. No doubt, bearing in mind the lengthy delays in the ratification of amendments to the Fourth Lomé Convention, the ACP–EC Council of Ministers has decided[101] that, as from

---

[94] See ibid, Art 7.

[95] The agreement is available at [1964] OJ 93/1431, but not in English.

[96] The agreement is available at [1970] OJ L282/2 , but not in English.

[97] See Council Regulation 199/76, of 30 Jan 1976 [1976] OJ L25/1. It was signed on 28 Feb 1975 and expired on 1 Mar 1980. The Second Lomé Convention was signed on 31 Oct 1979 [1979] OJ L347/147. It expired on 28 Feb 1985. The Third Lomé Convention was signed on 8 Dec 1984 [1986] OJ L86/3. It expired on 28 Feb 1990. The Fourth Lomé Convention was signed on 15 Dec 1989 [1991] OJ L229/3. It was amended by an Agreement signed in Mauritius on 4 Nov 1995 [1998] OJ L156/3. It did not enter into force until 1 June 1998 due to delays in the ratification procedure: see the Answer to Question (E–0212/98) to the Council on this matter: [1998] OJ C223/138.

[98] The current ACP countries are: Angola, Antigua and Barbuda, The Bahamas, Barbados, Belize, Bénin, Botswana, Burkina Faso, Burundi, Cameroon, Cape Verde, The Central African Republic, The Comoros, The Congo, The Côte D'Ivoire, Djibouti, Dominica, The Dominican Republic, Ethiopia, Fiji, Gabon, Gambia, Ghana, Grenada, Guinea, Guinea-Bissau, Equatorial Guinea, Guyana, Haïti, Jamaica, Kenya, Kiribati, Lesotho, Liberia, Madagascar, Malawi, Mali, Mauritius, Mozambique, Niger, Nigeria, Uganda, Papua New Guinea, Rwanda, St.Christopher and Nevis, St. Lucia, St.Vincent and the Grenadines, Western Samoa, São Tomé and Príncipe, Senegal, Seychelles, Sierra Leone, The Solomon Islands, Somalia, Sudan, Suriname, Swaziland, Tanzania, Chad, Togo, Tonga, Trinidad and Tobago, Tuvalu, Vanuatu, Zaire, Zambia, Zimbabwe. South Africa acceded to Lomé IV on 24 Apr 1997. South Africa has a customs union with four ACP states, namely Botswana, Lesotho, Swaziland, and Namibia.

[99] According to Art 366, the Convention was to last for a period of 10 years expiring on 28 Feb 2000.

[100] Decision 1/2000 of 28 Feb 2000 [2000] OJ L56/47.

[101] By Decision 1/2000 of 27 July 2000 [2000] OJ L195/46. The Decision applies until the

2 August 2000, the provisions of the Cotonou Agreement are to be put into early application except for Annex I, containing the Financial Protocol, Annex II, chapter 1, which deals with investment financing and Annex IV, chapter 3, Articles 17–19 and chapters 4–6, which concern certain aspects of implementation and management procedures. Certain provisions of the Lomé Convention are to remain in force until the coming into force of the Agreement.[102]

The Fourth Lomé Convention is a co-operation convention and is, of course, as much concerned with development as with trade.[103] Given that the convention will retain its importance to practitioners for a while yet, it is worthwhile briefly reviewing its terms. It contains a wide range of provisions affecting commercial, political, cultural, and development issues. Following the amendments to this Convention in 1995, the focus of these objectives is identified in Article 5.1 which states that:

> Cooperation shall be directed towards development centred on man, the main protagonist and beneficiary of development, which thus entails respect for and promotion of all human rights. Cooperation operations shall thus be conceived in accordance with this positive approach, where respect for human rights is recognised as a basic factor of real development and where cooperation is conceived as a contribution to the promotion of these rights.

The promotion of trade is, of course, an essential part of the co-operation established by the Convention which is intended to assist in the development of the economies of the ACP countries so as to make them self-reliant and to integrate them into the world economy.[104] Clearly customs duties will be significant in this context. Article 25 provides that the general trading arrangements are, as a general rule, to be based, with exceptions for agriculture,[105] on the principle of free access to Community markets for products originating in the

Agreement enters into force, but no longer than 1 June 2002, though it may be extended by the Council of Ministers. The Agreement is annexed to the Decision: see [2000] OJ L317/3.

[102] Art 2 of Decision 1/2000, n 101 above. The main provisions are as follows: Part 3 Title II Chapter 1 and Chapter 3 are extended to 31 Dec 2000 for certain purposes. Part 3 Title III Chapter 3, Sections 3 and 4 remain applicable until funds are exhausted and Part 3 Title III Chapter 5 Sections 1–6 (subject to certain qualifications for Section 1) remain applicable until the entry into force of the Agreement.

[103] The level of imports of goods into the EU from the ACP countries is small and appears to be diminishing somewhat rather than growing. Imports from ACP states as a percentage of total EU imports were 1.7% in 1988 and 1.3 per cent for 1995 to 1997. The same is true in relation to exports from the EU to the ACP countries. In 1988 exports to the ACP states were 1.5% of all EU exports. For 1994 to 1997 they fell to 1.1% of all EU exports: *Eurostat Yearbook 2000, A statistical eye on Europe, Data 1988–98*, 466.

[104] Arts 6 and 6a, of the Convention, n 97 above.

[105] It should be noted that the Court has specifically stated that the provisions of the Lomé Convention must be taken account of by Community institutions in formulating Community policy, particularly agricultural policy: see Case C–280/93 *Germany v Commission*, n 14 above, para 56. No doubt Community institutions must always take account of the EC's international agreements in formulating policy.

ACP states. There is no need, however, for reciprocal treatment of the EC by the ACP states. In the context of customs duties, this means that the EC does not impose customs duties or charges having equivalent effect on goods imported from ACP states[106] or quantitive restrictions or measures having equivalent effect,[107] whilst the ACP states may maintain their duties.[108] It should be noted that there are specific protocols for bananas, beef and veal, rum, and sugar. Products within the ECSC are also dealt with separately.

The necessary rules regarding origin of goods are set out in a Protocol and discussed in Chapter 7 below. These are more favourable than those applicable in respect of the system of generalized preferences.[109] The Convention contains special provisions for the least developed ACP countries[110] for which there are specific rules on origin.

Turning to the new Cotonou Agreement, it should first be noted that there was considerable concern among the ACP countries that the Agreement would require them to come within the ambit of the generalized system of preferences. As we have seen, unlike the Lomé Convention this does not provide for free access to the EC's markets but establishes reductions in duty according to a 'modulation mechanism'.[111] In the event, the fears of the ACP countries were not realized and they have obtained an agreement which is to last for twenty years from 1 March 2000,[112] with provision for revision of the financial protocols every five years.[113] Its fundamental aim is encapsulated in Article 1 which states that it is entered into:

in order to promote and expedite the economic, cultural and social development of the ACP States, with a view to contributing to peace and security and to promoting a stable and democratic political environment.

The partnership shall be centred on the objective of reducing and eventually eradicating poverty consistent with the objectives of sustainable development and the gradual integration of the ACP countries into the world economy.

The Agreement is built on five linked pillars. The first is political, with emphases on political dialogue, peace-building policies, human rights and

---

[106] Art 168 of the Convention, n 97 above.   [107] Art 169, ibid.

[108] Art 174, ibid.   [109] Also discussed in Ch 7 below.

[110] As from 1 Jan 1996 the following countries graduated from the list of least developed ACP countries: Antigua and Barbuda, Belize, Botswana, Dominica, Grenada, St Kitts and Nevis, St Lucia, St Vincent and the Grenadines, Seychelles, Swaziland, and Tonga. The following countries were added to the list: Angola, Liberia, Madagascar, Zaïre, and Zambia: see Decision 5/1995 of the ACP-EC Council of Ministers of 3 Nov, 1995 [1995] OJ L327/31.

[111] Had the ACP states transferred to preferential treatment under the generalized system of preferences, it has been suggested that: '[t]he resulting transfer of revenue from the ACP export chain to the EU treasury (following the increase in tariffs) would be equivalent to a large proportion of aid (based on 1994 disbursements from the European Development Fund).' Institute of Development Studies Research Paper for Oxfam GB, Nov 1997, by Jane Kennan and Christopher Stevens.

[112] Art 95.1 of the Agreement, n 101 above.

[113] Art 95.2 of the Agreement, n 101 above.

democracy, and good governance.[114] The second is called the 'participatory approach' which is intended to promote a wider involvement in matters relating to the ACP/EC partnership. The third is the creation of development strategies, with poverty reduction as its central objective. The fourth consists of the establishment of new trading arrangements, pursuant to Part 3 Title II of the Cotonou Agreement. The fifth is reformed financial co-operation which is concerned with cooperation in relation to development finance.[115]

Negotiations for the new trading arrangements of the fourth pillar are to start in September 2002. The new arrangements are to be introduced gradually over a preparatory period. This period is to end by 31 December 2007 at the latest and the new trading arrangements are to enter into force by 1 January 2008 unless earlier dates are agreed by the parties.[116] During the preparatory period, the non-reciprocal trade preferences permitted under the Fourth Lomé Agreement are to be maintained, but under the conditions contained in Annex V to the Cotonou Agreement.[117] As a general principle, the Annex provides that products originating in the ACP states are to be imported into the Community free of customs duties and charges having equivalent effect.[118] In relation to certain specified products the Community is to provide more favourable treatment than that given to countries benefiting from most-favoured-nation treatment in respect of the same products.[119] As well as the prohibition of duties on imports, the Community agrees not to apply quantitive restrictions or measures having equivalent effect.[120] So far as the least developed countries are concerned, the agreement provides that they should have duty-free access to the EC market for essentially all products by

---

[114] Some concern within the Community with the internal policies of some of the ACP states is inevitable. Sometimes it is the success of certain economic policies which give rise to concern not only on the part of the Community but on the part of the developed world in general including, eg, the OECD. The Report to the 2000 Ministerial Council Meeting and Recommendations by the OECD's Committee on Fiscal Affairs entitled *Progress in Identifying and Eliminating Harmful Tax Practices* (published the day before the Cotonou Agreement was signed) listed certain ACP countries as jurisdictions which meet the 'tax haven criteria' in the OECD's report: *Harmful Tax Competition: An Emerging Global Issue* (1998). The countries named were: Antigua and Barbuda, The Bahamas, Barbados, Belize, Dominica, Grenada, Liberia, St. Christopher and Nevis, St. Lucia, St. Vincent and the Grenadines, Seychelles, Tonga, Vanuatu, and Samoa. The list of 35 areas meeting the criteria included six OCTs.

[115] The European Development Fund consists of 13.5 bn euros. This makes the EU the world's main provider of official development assistance. The Commission has recently engaged in radical reform of its management . This has included setting up a new office to manage most of the external aid it provides—the EuropeAid Co-operation Office—which started work on 1 Jan 2001 (see Press Release, of 21 Dec 2000, IP/00/1535). The Commission's reforms are a swift response to the criticism made of it in some quarters: see, eg, the comments of the UK's Secretary of State for International Development, Ms Clare Short MP, in the *Financial Times*, 23 June 2000.

[116] Art 37.1 of the Agreement, n 101 above.   [117] Ibid, Art 36.3.

[118] Annex V, Art 1.

[119] The products are those listed in Annex 1 to the EC Treaty where they come under common organization of a market within Art 34 of the Treaty and products which are subject to specific rules on importation into the Community by reason of the common agricultural policy.

[120] Annex V to the Agreement, n 101 above, Art 2.

2005.[121] Continuing the approach of the Fourth Lomé Convention, the ACP states are not required to give reciprocal treatment to goods originating in the Community, but are not to give such goods treatment which is less favourable than most-favoured-nation treatment, although the most-favoured-nation treatment is not to apply as between ACP states themselves or as between them and other developing countries.[122]

The agreement continues to permit the taking of some safeguard measures by the Community where there is caused, or threatened, serious injury to domestic producers, serious disturbances in any sector of the economy, or difficulties which could bring about serious deterioration in the economic circumstances of a region.[123] The parties have agreed however, that every effort should be made to avoid having recourse to safeguard measures.[124] Finally, it should be noted that the definition of originating products is contained in Protocol 1 to Annex V and is considered further in Chapter 7 below. In Chapter 2 of Annex V there are special provisions in respect of beef, veal, sugar and bananas.

5. *Co-operation agreements*

In many cases the Euro–Mediterranean Agreements referred to above have replaced, or will replace, co-operation agreements. Most co-operation agreements do not aim to create a customs union or free trade area. They do provide, however, amongst other things, for reductions in customs duty rates, especially on the part of the Community. One important example of a co-operation agreement is the one concluded with the ASEAN countries[125] and which Brunei Darussalam[126] and Vietnam[127] have subsequently joined.

6. *Partnership and co-operation agreements*

The next circle of agreements between the EC and third countries is constituted by the Partnership and Co-operation Agreements with the countries

---

[121] Art 37.9, n 101 above. The list of the ACP least-developed, landlocked and island states for the purposes of the Cotonou Agreement is given in Annex VI, Article 1, as follows: Angola, Benin, Burkina Faso, Burundi, Republic of Cape Verde, Central African Republic, Chad, Comoros Islands, Democratic Republic of Congo, Djibouti, Ethiopia, Eritrea, Gambia, Guinea, Guinea (Bissau), Guinea (Equatorial), Haiti, Kiribati, Lesotho, Liberia, Malawi, Mali, Mauritania, Madagascar, Mozambique, Niger, Rwanda, Samoa, São Tome and Príncipe, Sierra Leone, Solomon Islands, Somalia, Sudan, Tanzania, Tuvalu, Togo, Uganda, Vanuatu, Zambia. The Annex contains separate lists of landlocked and island states in respect of which there are distinct provisions.

[122] Annex V, Art 5 of the Agreement, n 101 above.

[123] Annex V, Arts 8 and 9, ibid, n 101 above.

[124] Annex V, Protocol 2, Art 1, ibid, n 101 above.

[125] See [1980] OJ L144/2.

[126] The Protocol extending the agreement with the ASEAN to Brunei Darussalam is at [1985] OJ L81/2.

[127] The Protocol extending the agreement with the ASEAN to Vietnam is at [1999] OJ L117/31.

which are the former members of the USSR, for example, Russia,[128] Kazakhstan,[129] Armenia,[130] Georgia,[131] the Kyrgyz Republic,[132] and the Ukraine[133] and countries such as India.[134] These aim to liberalize trade in goods, to facilitate their transit, establish co-operation between customs authorities, and create the conditions for bringing about freedom of establishment of companies, of cross-border trade in services, and of capital movements. Unlike other agreements which have been mentioned so far, Co-operation and Partnership Agreements are established not pursuant to Article 310, formerly 238 (which gives the Community power to conclude international associations) but pursuant to more general provisions including those in the well-known Article 235, now Article 308.

7. *Trade and co-operation agreements*

The final circle of agreements consists of trade and co-operation agreements with a wide variety of other countries throughout the world. These again are not based on Article 310 of the EC Treaty, but on Articles relating to commercial policy, ie Articles 133 and 134. They cover countries in, for example, the Americas[135] and Asia.[136] The agreements seek to enhance economic and commercial co-operation between the parties but at a relatively general level.

C. APPLYING AND INTERPRETING INTERNATIONAL AGREEMENTS

1. *Agreements as part of the Community legal order*

In approaching any international agreement between the Community and a third country, it is important to bear in mind the legal basis upon which it has been negotiated. As we noted above, the agreements establishing the closest co-operation between the parties are based upon EC Treaty, Article 238, now Article 310.[137] This states that 'The Community may conclude with one or

---

[128] [1997] OJ L327/3.   [129] [1999] OJ L196/3.
[130] [1999] OJ L239/3.   [131] [1999] OJ L205/3.
[132] [1999] OJ L196/48.   [133] [1998] OJ L49/3.
[134] [1994] OJ L223/24.

[135] See, eg, the Framework Co-operation Agreement between the European Economic Community and the Republics of Costa Rica, El Salvador, Guatemala, Honduras, Nicaragua and Panama of 22 Feb 1993 [1999] OJ L63/39, under which the parties agree to grant each other most-favoured-nation treatment: see Art 4, and develop trade co-operation: see Arts 5 and 6.

[136] See, for a recent example, the Co-operation Agreement between the European Community and the People's Republic of Bangladesh of 22 May 2000, which came into force on 1 Mar 2001: [2001] OJ L118/48. The agreement seeks to establish more extensive co-operation than the agreement it replaces (see OJ L319/2, 19.11.76) and includes, amongst many other things, a commitment to improve co-operation in customs matters: Art 4.4(b).

[137] Other possible bases for agreements are those Arts in the EC Treaty concerned with the EC's commercial policy (Arts 133 and 134) and the general empowering provision of Art 308 EC Treaty.

more States or international organisations agreements establishing an association involving reciprocal rights and obligations, common action and special procedure'. It is clearly established that when an agreement, in accordance with the provisions of the EC Treaty, is concluded by the Council with a non-member country it is, so far as concerns the Community 'an act of one of the institutions of the Community . . . and, as from its entry into force, the provisions of such an agreement form an integral part of the Community legal system'.[138] It is not just the agreement that forms an integral part of the Community legal system, but also the measures adopted by institutions created under the agreement. Therefore, the decisions of, for example, association councils are also part of the Community legal system. The reasons these agreements and measures form part of the Community legal system were reiterated by the Court of Justice when it had to consider provisions governing internal taxation in the association agreement between the EEC and Portugal.[139] It said:

> In ensuring respect for commitments arising from an agreement concluded by the Community institutions the Member States fulfil an obligation not only in relation to the non-member country concerned but also and above all in relation to the Community which has assumed responsibility for the due performance of the agreement. That is why the provisions of such an agreement . . . form an integral part of the Community legal system.[140]

2. The Court as interpreter of the agreements

One obvious result of an agreement becoming part of the Community legal system is that the Court of Justice is the interpreter of it and questions on its interpretation and status may be referred to the Court of Justice from courts and tribunals of Member States. As late as 1987, however, in the *Demirel* case, which concerned an association agreement between the EEC and Turkey,[141] Member States were contending that the Court of Justice had no jurisdiction to interpret so-called 'mixed' agreements, ie those agreements to which both the EC and Member States were parties.[142] These contentions were decisively dismissed by the Court of Justice.[143] Since then the Court of Justice has regularly interpreted

---

[138] Case 12/86 *Meryem Demirel v Stadt Schwäbisch Gmünd* [1987] ECR 3719 para 7, which applied Case 181/73 *R&V Haegeman v Belgium* [1974] ECR 449 and Case 101/81 *Hauptzollamt Mainz v Kupferberg & Cie* [1982] ECR 3641. See also *Opel Austria GmbH v Council*, n 76 above, at para 101 and Case C–162/96 *A. Racke GmbH & Co. v Hauptzollamt Mainz* [1998] ECR I–3655 at para 41.

[139] n 73 above.

[140] Case 104/81 *Hauptzollamt Mainz v C A Kupferberg & Cie*, n 138 above, para 13.

[141] Signed on 12 Sept 1963, concluded approved and confirmed in the name of the Community by Decision of 23 Dec 1963 ([1973] OJ C113/1).

[142] All the agreements referred to in section 2 of this chapter are 'mixed agreements'.

[143] See Case 12/86 *Meryem Demirel v Stadt Schwäbisch Gmünd* at n 138 above, paras 6–12

and given effect to the terms of agreements and, on quite a number of occasions, has been concerned with provisions in them relating to customs matters, as we shall see.

In interpreting international agreements with third countries the Court will have regard to 'the purpose and the objective of the agreement and . . . its context'.[144] As a result of this, identical phrases in the EC Treaty and in agreements may be given different interpretations. For example, in *Polydor* the prohibition of quantitive restrictions on imports and of 'any measures having an effect equivalent to quantitive restrictions' in Article 14(2) of the association agreement between the EEC and Portugal was held not to prohibit reliance on a UK copyright to prevent importation into the UK of gramophone records lawfully made and sold under licence in Portugal.[145] Reliance on a copyright to achieve these ends would have been 'a measure having an effect equivalent to quantitive restrictions' within what was then EEC Treaty, Article 30. In the Court's view this did not matter. The difference in treatment was justified because the EC Treaty aimed at a single market whereas the association agreement did not.[146] More recently in *Metalsa*, the Court refused to apply its jurisprudence on what was then EC Treaty, Article 95, now Article 90, in the interpretation of similar provisions of the EEC/Austria agreement. It said:

> It is clear . . . that the extension of the interpretation of a provision in the Treaty to a comparably, similarly or even identically worded provision of an agreement concluded by the Community with a non-member country depends, *inter alia*, on the aim pursued by each provision in its particular context and that a comparison between the objectives and context of the agreement and those of the Treaty is of considerable importance in that regard.[147]

In relation to some association agreements, however, the Court of Justice has interpreted prohibitions of discriminatory internal taxation in conformity with the EEC Treaty. This occurred, for example in relation to the agreement

---

[144] See Case C–163/90 *Administration des Douanes et Droits Indirects v Léopold Legros* [1992] ECR I–4624 at para 23, (concerning the EEC/Sweden Agreement); Case T–115/94 *Opel Austria GmbH v Council*, n 76 above, at para 106 (concerning the EEC/Austria Agreement). See also Case C–312/91 *Procedural issue relating to a seizure of goods belonging to Metalsa Srl* [1993] ECR I–3751 paras 11 and 12 (concerning the EEC/Austria Agreement) and Case 270/80 *Polydor Ltd and RSO Records Inc. v Harlequin Record Shops Ltd and Simons Records Ltd* [1982] ECR 330 at para 8 (concerning the EEC/Portugal Agreement). This approach is consistent with Art 31.1 of the Vienna Convention on the Law of Treaties of 23 May 1969 referred to below in section D.
[145] Case 270/82 *Polydor Ltd and RSO Records Inc. Harlequin Record Shops Ltd and Simons Records Ltd*, n 144 above.   [146] Ibid, para 18.
[147] Case C–312/91 *Procedural issue relating to a seizure of goods belonging to Metalsa Srl*, n 144 above, para 11. See also Case 104/81 *Hauptzollamt Mainz v CA Kupferberg & Cie*, n 138 above, at para 30 in which the Court of Justice reached the same conclusion in relation to the EEC/Portugal Agreement. Note too that the Court of Justice takes a different approach to provisions dealing with the determination of the origin of goods depending upon whether they appear in an agreement with a third country or in an autonomous Community measure: Joined Cases C–153/94 and C–204/94 *The Queen v Commissioners of Customs and Excise, ex p Faroe Seafood Co Ltd Føroya Fiskasøla L/F* at n 13 above, paras 22–24.

with Greece in *Pabst & Richarz*.[148] The Court noted that the provision in that agreement:

> fulfils, within the framework of the Association between the Community and Greece, the same function as that of Article [90]. It forms part of a group of provisions the purpose of which was to prepare for the entry of Greece into the Community by the establishment of a customs union, by the harmonization of agricultural policies, by the introduction of freedom of movement for workers and by other measures for the gradual adjustment to the requirements of Community law.[149]

At first sight it may appear anomalous that the Court of Justice was prepared to construe the provisions in the agreement with Greece relating to discriminatory internal taxation in conformity with what was then EC Treaty, Article 95 but was not prepared to do so in the case of the agreement with Portugal. The apparent anomaly is, however, explained by the Advocate General who noted that the Preamble to the agreement showed that the agreement 'constitutes much more than a free-trade agreement of the classical type with other non-member countries'.[150] This explicitly envisaged the establishment of 'ever closer bonds between the Greek people and the peoples brought together in the European Economic Community' with a view to the eventual accession of Greece to the Community.

2.1 *Charges having equivalent effect*

The problems surrounding the interpretation of phrases in bilateral agreements which are similar to those in the EC Treaty arise specifically in relation to the prohibition of customs duties and charges having equivalent effect. We have already noted in chapter 3 that the prohibition on customs duties and charges having equivalent effect is interpreted similarly wherever it is found. This is because the broad objectives pursued by EC Treaty, Article 23 and the EEA Agreement or other bilateral agreements, are sufficiently similar to justify a similar interpretation of the prohibition.[151] As the Court said in *Aprile I*: 'The purpose of such agreements is to consolidate and extend the economic relations existing between the parties and, in pursuit of that aim, to eliminate obstacles to trade, including import customs duties and charges having equivalent effect.'[152] Accordingly, there was, in its view:

---

[148] Case 17/81 *Pabst & Richarz KG v Hauptzollamt Oldenburg* [1982] ECR 1331.
[149] Ibid, para 26.
[150] Ibid, para 4.
[151] The fact that the more specific objectives of the EEA are different from those of the EC is therefore immaterial: *Opel Austria GmbH v Council*, n 76 above, para 109. The differences were noted by the Court of Justice in Opinion 1/91, n 77 above at paras 13–29.
[152] Case C–125/94 *Aprile Srl, in liquidation v Amministrazione delle Finanze delo Stato* [1995] ECR I–2919 at para 40.

no reason to interpret the prohibition of charges having an effect equivalent to customs duties differently depending on whether the trade concerned is conducted within the Community or with non-member countries under the abovementioned agreements or regulations governing particular sectors.[153]

Indeed, the Advocate General made clear that it was not just the interpretation of the phrase that was to be the same. The trader had to have the same right to decline to pay the charges having an equivalent effect to customs duties as he had in respect of such charges which were outlawed by the EC Treaty.[154] The statements of the Court of Justice in *Aprile I* are broad and unconditional, and it seems most unlikely that any agreement could be discovered in which a less rigorous interpretation of the phrase 'charges having an effect equivalent to customs duties' would be justifiable. The Court will be astute to avoid giving a meaning to the words which may render prohibition of customs duties themselves meaningless.

Consistency of interpretation in relation to provisions prohibiting customs duties and charges having equivalent effect had, in fact, been demonstrated a long time before *Aprile I*, in *Bresciani*,[155] in which the prohibition in Article 2(1) of the First Yaoundé Convention was in issue. The Court of Justice noted that, like the Lomé Conventions which succeeded it, the Yaoundé Convention prohibited the imposition of customs duties and charges having an equivalent effect only by Member States and not by the third countries which were parties to the Convention. This imbalance between the obligations of the contracting parties did not, however, change the Court's approach to the effect of the phrase. Nor did it prevent the prohibition from being directly effective. In the light of the principles outlined above, and the fact that the EEA Agreement aimed at closer integration than the agreements it replaced and certainly at closer integration than the Yaoundé Convention, it is somewhat surprising that it was contended, in *Opel Austria GmbH*, that the prohibition of customs duties and charges having equivalent effect should be construed differently in the EEA Agreement than in the EC Treaty and the EEC/EFTA agreements. Predictably, the Court of Justice gave the same interpretation to the prohibition, contained in EEA Agreement, Article 10 as it had given to the identical provisions in Article 12 of the EC Treaty.[156]

---

[153] Ibid, para 39 of the judgment. See also the judgment in Case C–163/90 *Administration des Douanes et Droits Indirects v Léopold Legros*, n 144 above, at para 26 in which the agreement between the EEC and Sweden was interpreted in a similar way.

[154] See Case 125/94 *Aprile Srl. in liquidation v Amministrazione delle Finanze delo Stato* at n 152 above. See para 44. For the rights of traders to a refund of charges levied in breach of Community Law see Joined Cases C–397/98 and C–410/98 *Metallgesellschaft Ltd and Others v Inland Revenue Commissioners and Attorney General* [2001] STC 452 at para 84 of the judgment and the cases referred to there.

[155] Case 87/75 *Conceria Daniele Bresciani v Amministrazione Italian delle Finanze* [1976] ECR 129.

[156] See *Opel Austria GmbH v Council*, n 76 above, para 105.

3. *Traders' directly effective rights*[157]

If the ascertainment of the purpose of agreements is important in interpreting them generally, it is of particular importance in determining whether or not traders have directly effective rights. The Court of Justice has made quite clear that 'the question of the direct effect of provisions contained in an agreement concluded by the Community with non-member countries invariably involves an examination of the spirit, general scheme and terms of that agreement'.[158] If the issue of direct effect, in this context, involves an examination of the terms of the agreement, it is because the application of the doctrine of direct effect is designed to do no more than achieve the full implementation, or bona fide performance, of the terms of the agreement. As is well known, the doctrine of direct effect has proved to be extremely valuable in preserving the integrity of the Community legal order in relation to directives. A similar concept has proved very valuable in relation to international agreements and the direct effectiveness of many of the provisions in agreements with third countries is now well established.[159] In the field of Community customs law, provisions relating to the prohibition of customs duties and charges having equivalent effect[160] and those relating to the determination and proof of origin of goods have been held to have direct effect.[161] So too has the prohibition of discriminatory internal taxation.[162]

There may be said to be two fundamental reasons why the Court applies the doctrine of direct effect in relation to international agreements. One flows

---

[157] The question of the direct effectiveness of provisions of GATT and GATT 94 has been addressed in Ch 1 above at D. 2.

[158] See Case 469/93 *Amministrazione delle Finanze delo State v Chiquita Italia SpA* [1995] ECR I–4533 at para 26 (in which a provision of Protocol No 5 to the Fourth Lomé Convention was held to be directly effective) and Joined Cases 21/72, 22/72, 23/72 and 24/72 *International Fruit Company and Others v Produktschap voor Groenten en Fruit* [1972] ECR 1219 para.

[159] See *Opel Austria GmbH v Council*, n 76 above, para 101. There has been some discussion whether direct effect in relation to international agreements is the same as direct effect in relation to other areas of Community law. The result of direct effect in both cases is the same, namely that the trader has an enforceable right. The criteria to be satisfied in order to attain direct effect are, however, different. The debate and papers formulating opposing positions are noted in J Bourgeois, 'The European Court of Justice and the WTO' in JHH Weiler (ed), *The EU, the WTO and the NAFTA Towards a Common Law of International Trade* (Oxford University Press, Oxford, 2000) 100–101 and n 104

[160] See, eg, Case 87/75 *Conceria Daniele Bresciani Amministrazione Italian delle Finanze*, n 155 above, para 25 (Yaoundé). In Case C–163/90 *Administration des Douanes et Droits Indirects v Léopold Legros*, n 144 above, which concerned the prohibition in the EEC/Sweden Agreement, it was not suggested that the prohibition was not directly effective: see para 6 of the Opinion of Jacobs, AG. This appears also to have been the case in Case 125/94 *Aprile Srl, in liquidation v Amministrazione delle Finanze delle Stato*, n 152 above.

[161] See Case C–432/92 *The Queen v Minister of Agriculture, Fisheries and Food ex p S P Anastasiou (Pissouri) Ltd* [1994] ECR I–3087 at para 26 and the cases referred to in it.

[162] Case 17/81 *Pabst & Richarz KG v Hauptzollamt Oldenburg*, n 148 above, at para 27 (Greece/EEC); Case 104/81 *Hauptzollamt Mainz v Kupferberg & Cie*, n 138 above, para 23 (Portugal/EEC).

from international law and the other from Community law. The one derived from international law has already been alluded to and it is that there must as a matter of international law be bona fide performance of every agreement and the doctrine of direct effect is the Community's means of ensuring bona fide performance.[163] The second reason is that the agreement is part of the Community's internal legal order and two of the characteristics of that order are that it has primacy over the law of the Member States and that many of its provisions have direct effect.[164] It is unsurprising, therefore, to see the Court of Justice continuing to affirm the direct effectiveness of provisions in the agreements, as it did relatively recently in *Opel Austria*. It may be surprising to some that the issue of direct effectiveness has been so strongly contested for so long.[165] The opportunity to contest the issue continues to arise, however, because agreements themselves are silent on the matter.[166]

In support of the contention that provisions are not directly effective, reliance has been placed upon a number of matters including the fact that agreements have different objectives from the EC Treaty, the fact that the agreements contain their own procedures for dispute resolution, and upon the fact that many, but not all, agreements are based upon the principle of reciprocity and the other contracting party may not permit direct effectiveness even if the EC does.[167] The Court of Justice, however, has not been persuaded by any of these reasons.

On occasions the grounds for contesting direct effectiveness have been based on policy as much as law. This was particularly true in *Anastasiou*.[168] This case concerned the association agreement between the EEC and Cyprus. Traders and producers in the Republic of Cyprus objected to the UK's practice of allowing certain fruit and vegetables into the UK with certificates of origin issued by that part of Cyprus under Turkish control, and without the necessary certificates of origin and phytosanitary certificates issued by the Republic of Cyprus as required under Community law.[169] The UK contended that the provisions of the relevant Protocol to the association agreement were not directly effective. Instead, it said, their purpose was the establishment of an

---

[163] See Case 104/81 *Hauptzollamt Mainz v Kupferberg & Cie*, n 138 above, para 18.

[164] Opinion 1/91, n 77 above, para 21.

[165] Such submissions have been advanced by Community institutions as well as the Member States: see, eg, Case T–115/94 *Opel Austria GmbH v Council*, n 76 above, at paras 62 and 74.

[166] See Case 104/81 *Hauptzollamt Mainz v Kupferberg & Cie*, n 77 above, at para 17.

[167] See, eg, ibid, at para 16 and also Case C–37/98 *The Queen v Abdulnasir Savas* [2000] ECR I–2927 and [2000] 3CMLR 729 where the lack of reciprocity in a non-customs duty context was not considered to prevent a provision being directly effective.

[168] Case C–432/92 *The Queen v Minister of Agriculture, Fisheries and Food ex p S P Anastasiou (Pissouri) Ltd*, n 161 above. As a result of the decision in this case, exporters in the north of Cyprus routed their produce via Turkey: see Case C–219/98 *R v Minister of Agriculture, Fisheries and Food, ex p S P Anastasiou (Pissouri) Ltd*: [2000] ECR I–5421.

[169] Pursuant to the 1977 Protocol to the 1972 Association agreement between the EEC and Cyprus and Directive (EEC) 93/77 of 21 Dec 1976 respectively.

administrative system for verifying the origin of products and for enabling effective administrative co-operation between Cyprus and the importing state, in this case the UK. This amounted to a denial that the relevant Protocol was part of the Community's system of law. The Court re-stated the position it had taken, a few years before, in *Demirel*, and has repeated since. It said, in words which are similar to those with which this section commenced:

> a provision in an agreement concluded by the Community with non-member countries must be regarded as having direct effect when, regard being had to its wording and the purpose and nature of the agreement itself, the provision contains a clear and precise obligation which is not subject, in its implementation or effects, to the adoption of any subsequent measures . . .[170]

The Advocate General put the point more shortly. Noting the UK's contention that the provisions in question could not have direct effect, he responded with a short paragraph: 'That view is mistaken.'[171] The UK and the Commission were strongly influenced in making their submissions by the fact that the Turkish occupation of Cyprus was not internationally recognized and their view that the benefits of the agreement should be available to all Cypriots. The policy considerations upon which they relied, however, were no more effective in preventing the application of the doctrine of direct effect than the strictly legal justifications, which we outlined above and which were advanced, for example, in *Kupferberg*.[172]

In concluding this section it should be noted that the issue of direct effectiveness may be closely linked to the principle of the protection of legitimate expectations. This principle, together with the principle of direct effect, may assist a trader even prior to the entry into force of an agreement. As the Court of Justice has said:

> In a situation where the Communities have deposited their instruments of approval of an international agreement and the date of entry into force of that agreement is known, traders may rely on the principle of protection of legitimate expectations in order to challenge the adoption by the institutions, during the period preceding the entry into force of that agreement, of any measure contrary to the provisions of that agreement which will have direct effect on them after it has entered into force.[173]

---

[170] Case C–432/92 *The Queen v Minister of Agriculture, Fisheries and Food ex p S P Anastasiou (Pissoui) Ltd*, n 168 above, at 3127, para 23. This wording is taken from Case C–12/86 *Meryem Demirel v Stadt Schwäbisch Gmünd*, n 138 above, at para 14. See also Case T–115/94 *Opel Austria GmbH v Council*, n 76 above, at para 101 and Case C–162/96 *A Racke GmbH & Co v Hauptzollamt Mainz* at n 138 above, at para 31 in which the same wording is adopted. See more recently in a non-customs duty context Case C–37/98 *The Queen v Abdulnasir Savas*, n 167 above, at paras 39 and 41.

[171] para 36 of the Opinion of Gulmann AG. See n 170 above

[172] Case 104/81 *Hauptzollamt Mainz v CA Kupferberg & Cie* at n 138 above, para 52. See also Case C–469/93 *Amministrazione delle Finanze dello Stato v Chiquita Italia SpA*, n 158 above, at para 34.

[173] *Opel Austria GmbH v Council*, n 76 above, at para 94.

The principle of the protection of legitimate expectations has its corollary in public international law in the principle of good faith[174] and it is to international law which we now turn.

D. THE ROLE AND INFLUENCE OF INTERNATIONAL LAW

As we noted above, one of the justifications for requiring the direct effectiveness of provisions in an international agreement is derived from international law. This alone shows that the fact that international agreements are part of the legal order of the Community does not mean that international law is rendered irrelevant. On the contrary, it has a significant role to play in informing Community law, including Community customs law. Its exact relationship with Community law is not, however, always easy to define. Indeed, in the recent case of *Racke*, Advocate General Jacobs spoke of the Court of Justice being 'in uncharted waters'.[175] Nevertheless, there are some areas in which the role of international law is clear. For example, it is plain that the Court of Justice may, in certain circumstances, review the validity of a measure adopted by a Community institution by reference to international law. According to the judgment in *International Fruit*,[176] there are two conditions to be satisfied for such a review to take place. First, the Community must be bound by the relevant provision of international law. Secondly, the provision must be capable of conferring rights on citizens of the Community which they can invoke before the courts.

In other areas, international law and Community law are complementary. This is particularly so in relation to the interpretation and application of treaties. We have already noted that Community law requires the Court of Justice to look to the purpose, objective, and context of the treaty provision in question. As the Court has noted,[177] Article 31.1 of the Vienna Convention on the Law of Treaties of 23 May 1969, which entered into force on 27 January 1980, imposes a similar requirement. It requires that 'A treaty shall be interpreted in good faith in accordance with the ordinary meaning to be given to the terms of the treaty in their context and in the light of its object and

---

[174] Case 162/96 *A Racke GmbH & Co v Hauptzollamt Mainz* at n 138 above, para 93.

[175] Ibid, para 76 *per* Jacobs AG.

[176] Joined cases 21–24/72 *International Fruit Company NV v Produktschap voor Groenten en Fruit*, n 158 above, at paras 7 and 8. The Court concluded that Art XI of the GATT, concerning the general elimination of quantitive restrictions, was not capable of conferring rights on citizens which they could invoke before the courts. In Case C–286/90 *Auklagemyndigheden v Poulsen and Diva Navigation Corp* [1992] ECR I–6019 the Court of Justice held that a regulation governing the fishing industry must be interpreted and its scope limited in the light of the international law of the sea. This included the United Nations Convention on the Law of the Sea, which had not entered into force, because its provisions expressed the current state of customary international maritime law (see para 10).

[177] See, eg, Opinion 1/91, n 77 above, at para 14.

purpose.' Not all Member States have ratified the treaty but the Court is still able to look to it for guidance on the basis that 'It is generally recognised that the ... Vienna Convention codifies certain universally binding rules of customary international law and that hence the Community is bound by the rules codified by the Convention.'[178] Of course, the Vienna Convention on the Law of Treaties is not the only element of international law of importance in this area. Other conventions, such as the Vienna Convention on the Law of Treaties between States and International Organizations of 21 March 1986, which is not yet in force, are also referred to by the Court.[179] In *Opel Austria*, the Court referred to Article 18 of both Vienna Conventions. Both Articles impose on a state an obligation not to defeat the object and purpose of a treaty which it has signed prior to its entry into force.[180] In so doing they give effect to the customary international law principle of good faith.[181] These principles, together with the principle of legal certainty, were important in *Opel Austria* because the regulation requiring payment of a duty which was under attack was adopted after, not merely the signature, but the ratification of the EEA Agreement and less than two weeks before it, together with its prohibition of customs duties and charges having equivalent effect in Article 10, came into force. This state of affairs led to an infringement of the principle of legal certainty because a situation had been created in which there would be competing rules of law, one in the contested regulation imposing a charge and one in Article 10 of the EEA Agreement prohibiting it. Furthermore, the principle of legitimate expectations was infringed. This was because, as we noted above, where the Communities have deposited their instruments of approval of an international agreement, and the date of entry into force of that agreement is known, traders may rely on the principle of legitimate expectations in order to challenge the adoption of any measure contrary to the provisions of the agreement which will have direct effect on them after it has entered into force.[182]

In summary, therefore, we may say that international law reinforces the purposive approach to the interpretation of international agreements, gives additional force to the Community principle of legitimate expectations (and

---

[178] Case T–115/94 *Opel Austria GmbH v Council*, n 76 above, at para 77.

[179] Ibid, at paras 77–78.

[180] Art 18 of the Vienna Convention on the Law of Treaties 1969, states:
A state is obliged to refrain from acts which would defeat the object and purpose of a treaty when:
(a) it has signed the treaty or has exchanged instruments constituting the treaty subject to ratification, acceptance or approval, until it shall have made its intention clear not to become a party to the treaty; or
(b) it has expressed its consent to be bound by the treaty, pending the entry into force of the treaty and provided that such entry into force is not unduly delayed.

[181] Case T–115/94 *Opel Austria GmbH v Council*, n 76 above, para 90. As we noted above, this principle is the international law corollary of the principle of legitimate expectations.

[182] Ibid, para 94.

thereby to the principle of legal certainty), and, as we noted earlier, undergirds the principle of direct effectiveness with the doctrine of bona fide performance. Furthermore, it is capable of protecting directly effective Community rights, enabling them to be maintained in circumstances where, without its intervention, they would be lost. This is particularly apparent from *Racke*[183] which we noted at the beginning of this section and to which we return in conclusion.

In *Racke* the general relationship between international law and Community law had to be considered. The facts were, briefly, that between 1990 and 1992 a trader imported wines into the Community and sought to rely upon a preferential tariff established under the Co-operation Agreement with Yugoslavia of 2 April 1980. Customs duty was demanded in May 1992 following the release of the goods into free circulation. The Co-operation Agreement had been suspended by a Council regulation of 1991 due to the hostilities within, and the disintegration of, Yugoslavia. The importer contended that the suspension was invalid as a matter of international law and that it should obtain the benefit of the preferential tariff contained in the Co-operation Agreement. In formulating its case, the importer relied upon Articles 26, 62, 65, and 67 of the Vienna Convention on the Law of Treaties 1969. Article 26 contains the *pacta sunt servanda* principle, which the Court of Justice described as a fundamental principle of any legal order and which, in an international context, requires that any treaty be binding on the parties to it and be performed by them in good faith.[184] An exception to this principle is provided by the *rebus sic stantibus* rule which permits the termination or suspension of a treaty in the event of a fundamental change of circumstances. It is codified in Article 62 of the Vienna Convention.[185] Articles 65 and 67 contain procedural requirements in case of reliance on Article 62.

The Court made clear that the rules of customary international law relating to the *rebus sic stantibus* exception are binding upon Community institutions and form part of the Community legal order, but noted that their direct effect was not

---

[183] Case C–162/96, *A Racke GmbH & Co v Hauptzollamt Mainz* at n 138 above.

[184] Ibid, para 49. Art 26 states: 'Every treaty in force is binding upon the parties to it and must be performed by them in good faith.' As we have noted, the principle was referred to in Case 104/81 *Hauptzollamt Mainz v CA Kupferberg & Cie*, at n 138 above, at para 18 but without reference to Art 26.

[185] So far as relevant this states:

'1. A fundamental change of circumstances which has occurred with regard to those existing at the time of the conclusion of the treaty, and which was not foreseen by the parties, may not be invoked as a ground for terminating or withdrawing from the treaty unless:

(a) the existence of those circumstances constituted an essential basis of the consent of the parties to be bound by the treaty; and

(b) the effect of the change is radically to transform the extent of the obligations still to be performed under the treaty.

2 . . .

3. If, under the foregoing paragraphs, a party may invoke a fundamental change of circumstances as a ground for terminating or withdrawing from a treaty it may also invoke the change as a ground for suspending the operation of the treaty.

in issue. The trader wished to rely upon rights under the Co-operation Agreement, not rights provided by international law whether arising under custom or the Vienna Convention of 1969.[186] It decided that the trader could challenge the regulation on the basis of Article 62 of the Convention, but because of the complexity and imprecision of the rules of customary international law it was necessary to show that the Council made 'manifest errors of assessment' concerning the conditions for applying them.[187] It concluded that no such errors were present. It also said that even if Article 65 had been infringed, the procedural requirements it contains do not form part of customary international law and so could not be relied upon by the trader. As the Advocate General noted, there were good reasons for not allowing individuals to challenge decisions such as the one in issue here in reliance on the law of treaties.[188] Nevertheless, both he and the Court of Justice decided to permit traders to make such a challenge in appropriate cases. No doubt those with the greatest chance of success will be those who can rely also on Community law by, for example, establishing a breach of legitimate expectations.[189] That is only to be expected given that, in the majority of cases, the role of international law is to potentiate existing Community rights, not to create new ones.

---

[186] *A Racke GmbH & Co v Hauptzollamt Mainz* at n 138 above, paras 46–7. There is surely little doubt that the Court would have refused to find that the provisions of the Vienna Convention were directly effective: see paras. 82 and 83 of the Opinion of Jacobs AG.

[187] See ibid, para 52.

[188] See Jacobs AG's Opinion, at para 86.

[189] Ibid, para 89.

7

The Origin of Goods

The ability to determine the origin of goods is obviously essential for the operation of the EC's customs union and the application of the Tariff. Indeed. it is also essential for the operation of a free trade area and other preferential arrangements, and many of the international agreements which were considered in the previous chapter contain extensive provisions dealing with the determination and proof of the origin of goods. The determination of origin is important too not just for customs matters but for many activities concerned with the regulation of markets. The Court of Justice has highlighted this, saying:

> A common definition of the concept of the origin of goods constitutes an indispensable means of ensuring the uniform application of the common customs tariff, of quantitive restrictions and all other measures adopted, in relation to the importation or exportation of goods, by the Community or by the Member States.[1]

Prior to the creation of the customs union, the Member States of the Community applied their own domestic rules in many circumstances in relation to the determination of origin. In 1968 it became necessary to establish Community rules of origin and these were, at first, contained in Council Regulation (EEC) 802/68 of 27 June 1968.[2] This regulation was repealed upon the passage of the CCC[3] and the rules now contained in the CCC and the Implementing Regulation are considered below.

In the first section of this chapter, A, we consider what rules of origin are concerned with and their function. The second, B, deals with certain multilateral international agreements relating to the harmonisation of rules governing non-preferential origin. The third section, C, is concerned with the rules governing non-preferential origin of goods originating in only one country (at C.1), and then (at C.2) in more than one country. The fourth section, D, considers preferential origin. It deals at (D.1) with the rules applying to the Generalized System of Preferences, at (D.2) with the rules applying to the Overseas Countries and Territories, at (D.3) with autonomous provisions in relation to certain other countries, and at (D.4) with the provisions contained in some of the agreements that were outlined in Chapter 6 above. The chapter concludes, at E, with some consideration of the rules governing the proof of

---

[1] Case 49/76 *Gesellschaft für Überseehandel mbH v Handelskammer Hamburg* [1977] ECR 41 para 5.
[2] OJ L148/1. On the same day the Council passed a regulation establishing the Community rules of valuation for customs purposes: see Ch 8 below.
[3] Art 251.1, first indent.

origin, the necessary administrative cooperation in this area and the obligations of the Commission and the importer. It will be obvious that in a chapter this size it is impossible to discuss the topic fully. It is hoped, nevertheless, to enable a reader to approach this area with a general guide to the applicable concepts, and at the same time to highlight matters of particular interest.

A. RULES OF ORIGIN: WHAT THEY CONCERN AND THEIR FUNCTION

Two fundamental points should be emphasized at the outset. First, customs duty's concern with the origin of goods is not to be confused with concern about the identity of the seller of the goods, the location of the seller's establishment, or the place at which the contract of sale is made, although these matters may have great significance for the application of direct and indirect taxation. Consequently, although the introduction of intermediaries, who do nothing in relation to the goods but buy and sell them, may be of great significance for direct and indirect taxation, the position is different so far as customs duty is concerned. The Court of Justice has had to consider the re-invoicing of goods in relation to the common requirement that, in order to benefit from preferential tariff rates, goods must be directly transported from the country of export to the Community. It concluded that

> A commercial operation such as the re-invoicing of goods which are under the surveillance of the customs authorities of the country of transit cannot in itself have any effect in relation to the destination of the goods or their origin.[4]

The country of origin of goods is, instead, to the use the definition employed in both Annex D1 of the Kyoto Convention and Specific Annex K of the revised Convention

> the country in which the goods have been produced or manufactured, according to the criteria laid down for the purposes of application of the Customs tariff, of quantitative restrictions or of any other measure related to trade.[5]

As we shall see, the main distinction which the Convention draws is between goods which are wholly produced in one country and goods in the production of which two or more countries have taken part. In the measures and agreements affecting the Community's definition of originating products, the term 'obtained' rather than 'produced or manufactured' is used. Consequently, the

---

[4] Case 156/85 *Procureur de la République v Perles Eurotool* [1986] ECR 1595 para 9.

[5] See the definitions in Chapter 1 of Specific Annex K to the revised International Convention on the Simplification and Harmonization of Customs Procedures and paragraph (a) of the definition clause of Annex D1 to the original version of the Convention concluded at Kyoto on 13 Mar 1973 TS 36 (1975) Cmnd 5938. Approved by Council Decision of 18 Mar. 1975, (EEC) 199/75 [1975] OJ L100/2. Annexes D1 and D2 were accepted by Council Decision of 3 June 1977: (EEC) 415/77 [1977] OJ L 166/1.

fundamental division is that between goods which are and which are not 'wholly obtained' in one country or territory.

The second point, which follows from the first, is that although origin cannot be altered by factors relating to the identity of the seller it may be altered by factors relating to the production or manufacture of the goods. It is possible, therefore, for traders to influence, at least to some extent, the origin of the goods which will enter the customs territory of the Community. For example, the place in which goods with one origin are processed or worked will become the place of origin of the ultimate product, provided that the working or processing is extensive enough. Accordingly, the rate of customs duty applicable in respect of imports from a particular country may be a material consideration in selecting the country in which the working or processing is to be carried out and, indeed, the nature and extent of the working or processing. Another example of the way in which the origin of goods may be deliberately influenced concerns the origin of fish. The nationality of a percentage of the crew of a fishing vessel can affect the origin of fish caught by the vessel on which they work. The selection of crew members may, therefore, be influenced by rules governing the origin of fish.

Turning now to consider the function of rules of origin, it is necessary to distinguish between 'non-preferential' and, the more desirable, 'preferential' origin. Non-preferential origin is defined in CCC, Articles 22–26. By virtue of CCC, Article 27, preferential origin is defined in community measures, such as the Implementing Regulation[6] which concern the generalized system of preferences, and in international agreements such as were considered in the previous chapter. The rules of non-preferential origin apply to goods which are subject to the rules of the WTO and facilitate the application of the Tariff, the application of the outward processing procedure,[7] and commercial measures, such as those of relevance in the context of anti-dumping. The rules of preferential origin, on the other hand, are designed to determine whether or not a particular product is subject to the preferential measures negotiated between the Community and a third country or group of countries.

Like so much of the Community law relating to customs duty, some of the basic concepts which are employed in relation to the origin of goods are set out in multilateral international agreements which bind the Community and it is to these that we now turn.

---

[6] See Arts 35–140. It should be noted that, whereas prior to the introduction of the CCC the Commission was assisted in matters relating to origin by the Committee on Origin (set up pursuant to reg 12 of Council Regulation (EEC) 802/68 of 27 June 1968 on the common definition of the concept of the origin of goods: [1968] OJ L148/1), it is now assisted by the Customs Code Committee, created under Art 247 of the CCC. See further Ch 4 above.

[7] See eg CCC, Art 147.2.

B. MULTILATERAL INTERNATIONAL AGREEMENTS AND NON-PREFERENTIAL ORIGIN

One of the most important recent multilateral agreements is the Agreement on Rules of Origin in Annex 1A to the Final Act of the Uruguay Agreement which, as we have already noted, has led to the provision of binding origin information by customs authorities.[8] The main purpose of the Agreement on Rules of Origin was to achieve a harmonization of non-preferential rules of origin. It established a Committee on Rules of Origin, to work in conjunction with a Technical Committee on Rules of Origin set up under the auspices of the WCO.[9] This latter committee was charged with carrying out the technical work required by Part IV of the Agreement which established a work programme in relation to non-preferential rules of origin. The work programme was to be completed within three years following the entry into force of the Final Act, ie by 20 July 1998. That ambitious deadline could not be met, but the work is now advanced and the WCO's Origin Project has been holding workshops on the new rules of origin which have been established.

By virtue of Article 2 of the Agreement on Rules of Origin, the parties have subjected themselves to certain binding disciplines prior to harmonization of the rules. It is possible here to refer briefly only to some of these. At the outset, Article 2 provides that WTO members must clearly state the requirements to be fulfilled when they issue administrative determinations of general application in relation to rules of origin.[10] The Article then states that notwithstanding the element of commercial policy to which the rules are linked, WTO members must not use rules of origin to pursue trade objectives either directly or indirectly,[11] their rules must not themselves create restrictive, distorting, or disruptive effects on international trade,[12] and they must neither be more stringent in respect of imports and exports than in respect of domestic goods, nor be discriminatory in relation to other WTO members.[13] Furthermore, the rules must be administered in a consistent, uniform, impartial and reasonable manner,[14] be based on positive standards,[15] be publicly available,[16] and not retroactive.[17] Article 2 also requires the contracting parties to provide binding origin information upon the request of an exporter, importer, or any person with a justifiable cause.[18] Finally, there are provisions requiring judicial appeals to be available against any administrative action taken in relation to

---

[8] Considered in Ch 5 above at F.
[9] See Part 3, Art 4 of the Agreement on Rules of Origin.
[10] Ibid, Art 2(a).
[11] Ibid, Art 2(b).
[12] Ibid, Art 2(c).
[13] Ibid, Art 2(d).
[14] Ibid, Art 2(e).
[15] Ibid, Art 2(f).
[16] Ibid, Art 2(g).
[17] Ibid, Art 2(i).
[18] Ibid, Art 2 (h)f. For convenience, the Community provisions dealing with binding origin information, introduced in compliance with this Art are dealt with in Ch 5 above, along with the provision of binding tariff information.

the determination of origin,[19] and requiring information which is by nature confidential, or disclosed on a confidential basis for the purpose of applying the rules, to be treated as confidential except to the extent that it may be required to be disclosed in judicial proceeding.[20] These disciplines, like other provisions of the Final Act, do not as the law now stands give rise to directly effective obligations. Nevertheless, they should be borne in mind in construing the relevant provisions of EC customs law.[21] It should also be noted that although the Agreement was primarily concerned with non-preferential rules of origin, in Annex II to the Agreement, WTO members agreed to ensure that certain of these disciplines, broadly speaking, those consistent with a preferential regime, were applied in respect of preferential rules of origin.

Another multilateral treaty of great significance in the context of rules of origin is the Kyoto Convention, referred to above. Two annexes of particular significance are Annex D1 'Rules of origin' and Annex D2 'Documentary evidence of origin'. The revised Kyoto Convention has placed its harmonizing standards in relation to origin in the three chapters of Specific Annex K to the Convention. One chapter concerns the non-preferential rules of origin, one relates to documentary evidence of origin, and one deals with the control of that documentary evidence. The terms of these chapters are not, in many respects, different in substance from the provisions of Annexes D1 and D2 .

1. *Kyoto: Annex D1 and Specific Annex K*

The provisions of Annex D1 by which the EC is bound are, first of all, standard 1, which is a formal provision requiring compliance with the provisions of the Annex. Then follow the two fundamental standards, Standards 2 and 3. Standard 2 identifies what products are to be considered to be produced wholly in a given country. Standard 3 deals with the origin of products not produced wholly in one country. Recommended Practices 4 and 5 and Standard 6 address this criterion in more detail. Standard 9 provides that, for the purpose of determining origin, packings shall be deemed to have the same origin as the goods they contain unless the national legislation of the country of importation requires them to be declared separately for tariff purposes, in which case their origin shall be determined separately from that of the goods. Standard 11 states that, for the purpose of determining the origin of goods, no account shall be taken of the origin of the energy, plant, machinery, and tools used in the manufacturing or processing of the goods. Recommended Practice 12 states that where provisions requiring the direct transport of goods from the country of origin are laid down, derogations from them should be allowed, in

---

[19] Ibid, Art 2(j).
[20] Ibid, Art 2 (k).
[21] The direct effect of GATT 94 is considered in Ch 1 above at D.2. Direct effect in relation to other international agreements is considered in Ch 6 at C.2.2.

particular for geographical reasons (for example, in the case of landlocked countries) and in the case of goods which remain under customs control in third countries (for example, in the case of goods displayed at fairs or exhibitions or placed in customs warehouses). Standard 13 requires the competent authorities to ensure that rules of origin and any changes to them and interpretative information are readily available to any person interested in them,[22] whilst Standard 14, the final provision of the annex, states that changes in the rules of origin, or in the procedures for their application, shall enter into force only after sufficient notice has been given to enable the interested persons, both in export markets and in supplying countries, to take account of the new provisions.

So far as concerns the provisions which the EC did not accept, and non-acceptance of which was maintained in 1994,[23] there is first of all Standard 7. This provides that accessories, spare parts, and tools for use with a machine, appliance, apparatus, or vehicle, shall be deemed to have the same origin as the machine, appliance, apparatus, or vehicle, provided that they are imported and normally sold with it and correspond, in kind and number, to its normal equipment. Standard 8 states that an unassembled or disassembled article which is imported in more than one consignment because it is not feasible, for transport or production reasons, to import it in a single consignment shall, if the importer so requests, be treated as one article for the purpose of determining origin. Recommended Practice 10 provides that in determining origin, where packings are deemed to have the same origin as the goods, account should be taken, in particular where a percentage method is applied, only of packings in which the goods are ordinarily sold by retail. Provisions equivalent to all of these appear in Specific Annex K, as Recommended Practices 7, 8, and 10. As these are not Standards, the EC may again enter reservations against them, as it did in relation to Annex D1.[24]

1.1 *Criteria for establishing origin*

In the introduction to Annex D1 to the Kyoto Convention it is noted that there are two basic criteria used in establishing origin. The first is that of goods which are 'wholly produced' in a single country. This, as the introduction says, 'applies mainly to "natural" products and to goods made entirely from them so that goods containing any parts or materials imported or of undetermined origin are generally excluded from its field of application'. The second criterion is necessary where more than one country is involved in the production of the goods and is based upon the notion of the 'substantial transformation' of goods. This criterion is defined in both Annex D1 and Specific Annex K as 'the

---

[22] This does not appear in Specific Annex K, but, as was noted above, is now contained in the Agreement on Rules of Origin.

[23] See the Annex to Council Decision of 10 Mar 1994 (EEC) 167/94 [1994] OJ L76/28.

[24] See Art 12.2 of the revised Kyoto Convention.

criterion according to which origin is determined by regarding as the country of origin the country in which the last substantial manufacturing or process-ing, deemed sufficient to give the commodity its essential character, has been carried out'.

The Introduction to Annex D1 and Standard 3, Note 1, states that the crite-rion of 'substantial transformation' can be employed by means of three meth-ods of application used cumulatively or alternatively. As we shall see the Community makes use of all three methods. The first of these is a rule, less popular than formerly, requiring, subject to lists of exceptions, a change of tariff heading in a specified nomenclature. Standard 3.2 of Annex D1, which is not reproduced in Specific Annex K provides that, under this general rule, the product obtained is considered to have undergone sufficient manufactur-ing or processing if it falls in a heading of the tariff which is different from the headings applicable to each of the materials utilized. The lists of exceptions may cite (a) manufacturing or processing operations which, although they entail a change in the tariff classification heading, are not regarded as substantial, or are regarded as substantial only under certain conditions and (b) manufacturing or processing operations which, although they do not entail a change in the tariff classification heading, are regarded as substantial under certain conditions. It is then provided that the conditions referred to in (a) and (b) may relate either to a type of treatment undergone by the goods or to an *ad valorem* percentage rule. Recommended Practice 4, provides that in applying the substantial transformation criterion, use should be made be made of the Brussels Nomenclature. Recommended Practice 4 of Specific Annex K, requires the use of the Harmonized System which came into being after the conclusion of the Kyoto Convention.[25]

The second method of application of the substantial transformation crite-rion is the use of lists of manufacturing or processing operations which do, or do not, confer upon goods the origin of the country in which those operations were carried out. This simpler method is widely considered the best available. The third method makes use of an *ad valorem* percentage rule, which requires either the values of the materials utilized or the percentage of the value added by manufacturing or processing to be used to determine origin. So far as the utilization of material is concerned, origin in a particular country is retained only if the value of utilized materials of foreign or unknown origin does not exceed a specified percentage of the value of the finished product. In relation to added value by virtue of manufacturing or processing, if the value added equals a specified percentage then the origin of the goods is the country in which the activity was carried out. Standard 3.3 states that the *ad valorem* percentage requirement may be expressed in the form of a general rule laying down a uniform rate, without a list of individual products. Recommended

---

[25] See further Ch 1 above at B.

Practice 5 provides that where the *ad valorem* percentage rule is used, the values to be taken into consideration should be, in respect of materials imported, the dutiable value at importation or, in the case of materials of undetermined origin, the first ascertainable price paid for them in the territory of the country in which manufacture took place. In respect of goods produced, the values taken into consideration should be either the ex-works price or the price at exportation, according to the provisions of national legislation.

Standard 6 has general application and provides that operations which do not contribute, or which contribute only to a small extent, to the essential characteristics or properties of the goods, are not to be regarded as constituting substantial manufacturing or processing. Consequently, the operations cannot affect the origin of goods. Operations which do not constitute substantial manufacturing or processing are stated, in particular, to be those confined to one or more of the following, namely: (a) operations necessary for the preservation of goods during transportation or storage; (b) operations to improve the packaging or the marketable quality of the goods or to prepare them for shipment, such as breaking bulk, grouping of packages, sorting and grading, and repacking; (c) simple assembly operations; (d) mixing of goods of different origin, provided that the characteristics of the resulting product are not essentially different from the characteristics of the goods which have been mixed.

The Introduction to Annex D1 sets out the advantages and disadvantages of each of the three methods of application referred to above from the point of view of the authorities and the user.[26] So far as the first (change of tariff heading) is concerned, the advantages are that the origin of goods is determined by precise and objective criteria and, furthermore, proof of origin is unlikely to cause difficulty. The disadvantages are that it is necessary to maintain lists of circumstances in which a change of tariff heading is not decisive or does not impose further conditions and descriptions of manufacturing processes in such lists cannot be unduly complicated otherwise errors in good faith may be committed. It is necessary, too, for the countries of exportation and importation to use the same nomenclature and apply it uniformly. The same advantages and disadvantages are stated to apply in respect of the second method, namely the use of lists of manufacturing processes, although as the lists in question are more detailed the disadvantages in relation to them are heightened. The third method (the *ad valorem* percentage rule) is considered to have the advantage of simplicity and precision, with the necessary information being obtainable from commercial records. There are, however, a number of major difficulties. Borderline cases may present particular difficulty and determining costs, whether of manufacture or of products may prove troublesome

[26] The Community makes use of all three methods: see Title IV, Chapter 1 of the Implementing Regulation.

in practice. Furthermore, costs and therefore origin may be affected by fluctuations in prices for particular goods.

Having noted that the international community has taken a close interest in rules of origin, which clearly are capable of having a significant impact on a country's trading position, we turn to consider the rules which the Community has established, contained, in particular in the CCC. We look first at non-preferential and then at preferential origin.

C. THE CCC AND NON-PREFERENTIAL ORIGIN

1. *Origin in only one country*

The fundamental rule is contained in CCC, Article 23.1 which states that goods originating in a country shall be those wholly obtained or produced in that country. Article 23.2 provides a definition of what 'goods wholly obtained in a country' means in ten lettered paragraphs. The terms of these provisions are very similar to Standard 2 in the Kyoto Convention, Annex D1. They refer mainly to natural products, although the Convention refers to goods being 'wholly produced' in a given country whereas the CCC refers to goods being 'wholly obtained or produced'. In the context of the provisions, nothing appears to turn on the distinction.

The ten lettered paragraphs of Article 23.2 refer to: (a) mineral products extracted within the country in question; (b) vegetable products harvested within it; (c) live animals born and raised in it; (d) products derived from live animals raised in it; (e) products of hunting or fishing carried on in it; (f) products of sea-fishing and other products taken from the sea, outside its territorial sea, by vessels which are registered or recorded in the country concerned and flying that country's flag;[27] (g) goods obtained or produced on board factory ships, from the products referred to in (f) originating in the country in question, provided that such factory ships are registered or recorded in that country and fly its flag; (h) products taken from the seabed or subsoil beneath the seabed outside the territorial sea of the country in question provided that that country has exclusive rights to exploit that seabed or subsoil; (i) waste and scrap products derived from manufacturing operations and used articles, if they were collected in the country in question and are fit only for the recovery of raw materials; and finally (j) goods which are produced in the country in

---

[27] As a matter of international law a vessel has the nationality of the state in which it is registered: see Geneva Convention on the High Seas of 29 Apr 1958 Arts 5 and 6 (UNTS 463, p 366), United Nations Convention on the Law of the Sea Arts 91 and 92 and Case 286/90 *Anklagemyndigheden v Poulsen and Diva Navigation Corp* [1982] ECR 6019 para 13. In Case C–280/89 *Commission v Ireland* [1992] ECR I–6185 at para 14, the Court of Justice noted that the equivalent of this provision prior to the introduction of the CCC meant that fish caught by British boats were British wherever caught. For the United Nations Convention see p 203 and n 28.

question exclusively from goods referred to in (a)–(i) above or from their derivatives, at any stage in production.

1.1 *Maritime matters*

1.1.1 *Territorial sea: CCC, Article 23.2 and 23.3*

It is specifically provided, in Article 23.3, that the reference to 'country' in Article 23.2 covers the country's territorial sea. This provision means, of course, that disputes over the extent of a country's territorial sea may be incorporated into customs law and introduces into Community law certain aspects of international maritime law. Both the notion of territorial sea and the right to exploit a seabed, or subsoil, are considered in the United Nations Convention on the Law of the Sea of 10 December 1982 (UNCLOS).[28] Its terms, in many respects, contained accepted norms of international law even before it came into force.[29] Some of its provisions are to be found in the Convention on the Territorial Sea and the Contiguous Zone of 29 April 1958 which entered into force on 10 September 1964 and to which the UK is a party.

Article 2 of UNCLOS provides that a state's sovereignty extends beyond its land territory, internal waters and archipelagic waters to an adjacent belt of sea described as the territorial sea, the airspace above it and the seabed and subsoil below it. The limits of the territorial sea are then set out in Section 2. Whereas a specific limit was not specified in the Convention on the Territorial Sea and the Contiguous Zone, Article 3 of Section 2 of UNCLOS states that 'Every State has the right to establish the breadth of its territorial sea up to a limit not exceeding 12 nautical miles, measured from baselines determined in accordance with this Convention'.[30] Article 5 goes on to indicate that the normal baseline is, generally speaking, the low-water line along the coast as

---

[28] The text of the Convention is available at [1998] OJ L179/3. It came into force, for the EC, on 1 May 1998. The EC approved the Convention and the Agreement relating to the Implementation of Part XI of the United Nations Conventions on the Law of the Sea of 10 Dec 1982 (28 July 1984) by Council Decision of 23 Mar 1998 [1998] OJ L179/1. It formally confirmed both on 1 April 1998. The preamble to the Decision makes clear that the Community had been applying the Convention provisionally since 23 Nov 1994 when the Convention came into force generally. The Agreement came into force on 28 July 1996. The EC made a declaration on ratifying the Convention and, amongst other things, said that 'By virtue of its commercial and customs policy, the Community has competence in respect of those provisions of Parts X and XI of the Convention and of the Agreement of 28 July 1994 which are related to international trade'. Part X is headed 'Right of Access of Land-locked States to and from the Sea and Freedom of Transit'. Part XI is headed 'The Area' ie the area over which the International Sea-Bed Authority has control. The UK acceded to the Convention and the Agreement on 25 July 1997. There are 135 parties to the Convention. Of the EC member states Denmark has not ratified the Convention or the Agreement and, outside Europe, neither has the USA.

[29] As the Court of Justice has noted in Case 286/90 *Auklagemyndigheden v Poulsen and Diva Navigation Corp*, n 27 above, at para 10.

[30] The limits actually adopted by states vary widely. A limit of 12 nautical miles is adopted by the UK for all purposes: see the Territorial Sea Act 1987 s. 1(1)(a).

marked on large-scale charts officially recognized by the coastal state. A number of other provisions deal with matters such as straight baselines, reefs, bays, and ports.

1.1.2 *Products taken from the sea: Article 23(f)*

As was noted above, CCC, Article 23(f) treats as wholly obtained or produced in a country, products taken from the sea, outside its territorial sea, by specified vessels. The phrase 'taken from the sea' is one which has somewhat different meanings in different Community languages and the Court of Justice has had to consider the phrase in some detail. *Commission v United Kingdom*[31] concerned a predecessor of Article 23(f).[32] The case concerned joint fishing operations in international waters in the Baltic Sea some forty to eighty miles off the Polish coast and in a zone over which Poland claimed exclusive fishing rights. In an attempt to gain access to Polish waters and circumvent the Polish claim, British trawlers cast empty trawl nets into the sea which were taken over and trawled by Polish vessels. On completion of the trawl, British trawlers drew alongside the Polish ones and took back control of the nets. British fishermen then lifted the nets onto the British boats. The question was whether or not the fish were of Community origin, and therefore free of customs duty. If they were 'taken from the sea' by British boats they were of Community origin and if they were 'taken from the sea' by Polish boats they were of Polish origin. The Court of Justice decided the latter was the case. In construing the provision in question, the Court derived no help from a comparison of its different language versions. Instead, noting that the provision envisaged the origin of fish being determined on the basis of the flag or registration of the vessel catching them, it gave the provision a purposive construction and concluded that:

> the origin of the fish must be made to depend on the flag flown by the vessel which performed the essential part of the operation of catching them. In that connection it appears consonant with actual fact to take the view that the vessel that locates the fish and separates them from the sea by netting them performs the essential part of that operation.[33]

The United Kingdom's contention that the phrase 'taken from the sea' should be construed as 'complete removal from the water' was, therefore, rejected.

1.1.3 *Exclusive rights to exploit the seabed: Aarticle 23(h)*

It will be recalled that Article 23(h) provides that products taken from the seabed, or subsoil beneath the seabed, outside the territorial sea are goods wholly obtained in the country which has exclusive rights to exploit the seabed

---

[31] Case 100/84 [1985] ECR 1169.
[32] Namely, Art 4(2)(f) of Council Regulation (EEC) 802/68 of 27 June 1968 on the common definition of the concept of origin of goods [1968] OJ Spec Edn 165.
[33] See Case 100/84 *Commission v United Kingdom*, n 31 above, para 19.

or subsoil. The reference to a country which has 'exclusive rights to exploit' the seabed outside its territorial sea has now to be viewed against a background of developments in the international law of the sea, particularly the coming into force of UNCLOS. This convention gives effect to the concept of the common heritage of mankind, a concept introduced into the UN General Assembly in 1967.[34] It requires exploitation to be performed only on receipt of permission from the International Sea-Bed Authority.[35] Such permission may be granted to a country but may equally well be granted to a commercial entity. Furthermore, UNCLOS envisages that the Authority enjoys overall control over what it calls 'the Area', namely, the sea-bed, ocean floor, and subsoil beyond the limits of national jurisdiction. The Area and its resources are to constitute the common heritage of mankind[36] and activities in the Area are to be carried out for the benefit of mankind as a whole.[37] The Convention also provides that there shall be no discrimination between minerals derived from the Area and from other sources and that there shall be no preferential access to markets for such minerals, or for imports of commodities produced from such minerals, in particular by the use of tariff or non-tariff barriers or on the basis of nationality.[38] The important developments contained in UNCLOS clearly have wide-ranging implications in many fields of law. Customs duty in general and CCC, Article 23(h) are not exempt.

2. *Origin in more than one country*

The Community provisions governing non-preferential origin in more than one country are primarily contained in CCC, Article 24. The Article does not

[34] See Rosalyn Higgins QC, *Problems & Process: International Law and How We Use It* (Oxford University Press, Oxford, 1994, repr 1999) at 130. The author comments in relation to the concept that: 'it [i]s interesting to see how, in a short space of time, this notion was widely perceived as having a normative quality' (131).
[35] See Art 153 of UNCLOS, n 28 above, and Annex III Art 3.
[36] Art 136 of UNCLOS, n 28 above, states: 'The Area and its resources are the common heritage of mankind.' Art 137 says:

1. No State shall claim or exercise sovereignty or sovereign rights over any part of the Area or its resources, nor shall any State or natural or juridical person appropriate any part thereof. No such claim or exercise of sovereignty or sovereign rights nor such appropriation shall be recognized.
2. All rights in the resources of the Area are vested in mankind as a whole, on whose behalf the Authority shall act. These resources are not subject to alienation. The minerals recovered from the Area, however, may only be alienated in accordance with this Part and the rules, regulations and procedures of the Authority.
3. No State or natural or juridical person shall claim, acquire or exercise rights with respect to the minerals recovered from the Area except in accordance with this Part. Otherwise, no such claim, acquisition or exercise of such rights shall be recognized.

These articles have, of course, to be read as part of the Convention as a whole and a full discussion of the Area and its significance is clearly beyond the scope of this book.
[37] See Arts 140 and 153 of UNCLOS, n 28 above.
[38] S 6 of the Agreement relating to the Implementation of Part XI of UNCLOS, n 28 above.

refer to particular products or classes of products, but there are specific provisions governing the non-preferential origin of textiles, textile articles and certain other products in the Implementing Regulation, Article 35 onwards. These are dealt with briefly at the end of this section.

In considering the provisions of the Kyoto Convention which determine the origin of products produced in more than one country we noted that it employed the test of 'substantial transformation'. CCC, Article 24 does not use that precise phrase. Instead, it provides that goods, the production of which involved more than one country, are to be given a deemed origin, and states that:

> Goods whose production involved more than one country shall be deemed to originate in the country where they underwent their last, substantial, economically justified processing or working in an undertaking equipped for that purpose and resulting in the manufacture of a new product or representing an important stage of manufacture.

It will be apparent that this definition contains considerable similarities to the definition of the substantial transformation criterion referred to above. This has not, however, avoided the necessity for judicial consideration of its terms. Although it may seem self-evident, the Court of Justice has found it necessary to make clear that the provision does not apply to any situation in which more than one country is involved. Rather, it applies only where there is 'economically justified processing or working'.[39] The Court of Justice has also commented on the reference to the 'last' working or processing and considered what constitutes 'substantial' working or processing. These two matters are considered in turn below.

2.1 *'Last' processing or working*

The importance of referring to the place of 'last' processing or working is shown by two cases called *Yoshida*.[40] It was contended that the origin of slide fasteners should depend upon matters related to the initial manufacture of the goods. The Court of Justice held, however, that Community origin was conferred upon the goods by virtue of the 'last' processes carried out in the Community which consisted of a number of operations which were essential for the creation of individual slide fasteners from the manufactured material. Whether or not a process was the last relevant process was a technical question to be examined by reference to the definition of the product in question and of the various operations resulting in its formation.[41]

---

[39] This was emphasized by the Court of Justice in Case 100/84 *Commission v United Kingdom* [1985] ECR 1169 at para 14.

[40] Case 114/78 *Yoshida GmbH v Industrie-und Handelskammer Kassel* [1979] ECR 151 and Case 34/78 *Yoshida Nederland BV v Kamer van Koophandel en Fabrieken voor Friesland* [1979] ECR 115.

[41] Case 114/78 *Yoshida GmbH v Industrie-und-Handelskammer Kassel*, n 40 above, para 9.

2.2 'Substantial' processing or working

As we have noted, the EC employs, to a greater or lesser extent, all three methods of applying the substantial transformation criterion set out in the Kyoto Convention. The Court of Justice has, however, adopted a cautious approach in relation to the use of tariff headings. It has noted, having regard to the need for origin to be defined by objective criteria and to the importance of ensuring that origin is not determined by way of non-substantial processes or operations, that:

> it would not seem sufficient to seek criteria defining origin of goods in the tariff classification of the processed products, for the Common Customs Tariff has been conceived to fulfil special purposes and not in relation to the determination of the origin of products.

> In order to meet the purposes and requirements of regulation No.802/68,[42] the determination of the origin of goods must be based on a real and objective distinction between raw material and processed product, depending fundamentally on the specific material qualities of each of those products.[43]

A process or operation was, therefore, only 'substantial' within Article 5 of the Regulation 'if the product resulting therefrom has its own properties and a composition of its own, which it did not possess before that process or operation'.[44] It followed, in the Court's view, that cleaning and grinding, sorting and packing, raw casein which was imported from a third country did not constitute a 'substantial' process. The processes changed the presentation of the goods for future use. They did not affect the goods' substantial properties. Applying the same test, the Court has also held that processing meat by boning it, trimming it and drawing its sinews, cutting it into pieces and vacuum packing it, did not result in the acquisition of origin where the processes where carried out. The processes facilitated the marketing of the meat and did not result in any substantial change in its properties and composition.[45]

It is not the case, however, that all use of the tariff in the determination of origin is forbidden. In one case, the Commission was held not to have exceeded its powers where it made a regulation concerning origin which took the change of tariff heading as a basic rule and then supplemented that basic rule with the use of lists of processes which did and did not result in a change of origin.[46] In coming to its conclusion the Court had regard to the need for legal

---

[42] The regulation which contained the predecessors to CCC, Arts 23–25. See n 32 above.

[43] Case 49/76 *Gesellschaft für Überseehandel mbH v Handelskammer Hamburg* [1977] ECR 41 at para 5. See also Case 162/82 *Criminal proceedings against Paul Cousin* [1983] ECR 1101 at para 16.

[44] Case 49/76 *Gesellschaft für Überseehandel mbH v Handelskammer Hamburg* at n 43 above, para 6.

[45] Case 93/83 *Zentralgenossenschaft des Fleischergewerbes eG (Zentrag) v Hauptzollamt Bochum* [1984] ECR 1095, paras 13 and 14.

[46] Case 162/82 *Criminal proceedings against Paul Cousin*, n 43 above, at para 17. See also Art 37 of the Implementing Regulation.

certainty and the difficulty of definition 'in multiple economic circumstances'.[47]

2.3 Assembly operations

In *Brother International*,[48] the Court had to confront the question whether or
not the assembly of typewriters in a 'screwdriver factory' in Taiwan resulted in
the typewriters obtaining Taiwanese as opposed to Japanese origin. In emphasizing that the decisive criterion in answering this question was the identity of
the 'last substantial process or operation' within Article 5 of Regulation (ECC)
802/68, noted above, the Court referred to the Kyoto Convention. It noted that
its approach was supported by Rule 3 of Annex D.1 to the Convention. It also
observed that the Convention was more detailed than Regulation (EEC)
802/68, in that the latter did not specify to what extent assembly operations
could constitute a substantial process or operation. Standard 6 in the
Convention, however, states, as we have seen, that operations which do not
contribute, or which contribute to only a small extent, to the essential characteristics or properties of the goods, are not to be regarded as constituting
substantial manufacturing or processing. This is expressed to be true in particular in relation to a number of specified operations including, at (c), 'simple
assembly operations'. The Convention contains no definition of this phrase,
but in the view of the Court of Justice, it means:

> operations which do not require staff with special qualifications for the work in
> question or sophisticated tools or specially equipped factories for the purposes of
> assembly. Such operations cannot be held to be such as to contribute to the essential
> characteristics or properties of the goods in question.[49]

The Court noted, however, that the Convention provides no more than that
simple assembly operations cannot result in goods obtaining origin in the place
where they are carried out. It does not go further and state in what circumstances assembly operations constitute a substantial process or operation. The
Court, therefore, said that:

> An assembly operation may be regarded as conferring origin where it represents
> from a technical point of view and having regard to the definition of the goods in
> question the decisive production stage during which the use to which the compo-
> nent parts are to be put becomes definite and the goods in question are given their
> specific qualities.[50]

---

[47] Case 162/82 *Criminal proceedings against Paul Cousin*, n 43 above, at para 17.
[48] Case C–26/88 *Brother International GmbH v Hauptzollamt Gießen* [1989] ECR 4253. The case
concerned the acquisition of origin in the context of anti-dumping duties but, as was noted at the
beginning of this chapter, the concept of origin is the same whether used in relation to customs
duties or other regulations affecting the organization of markets.
[49] Ibid, at para 17.
[50] Ibid, at para 19.

It acknowledged, of course, that there were situations in which a consideration of technical criteria would not be decisive. In such circumstances it said
that the value added by the assembly could be used as an ancillary criterion.[51]
In support of this proposition it again cited the Kyoto Convention which, as we
have seen, permits the 'substantial transformation' criterion to be expressed in
terms of added value. In the Court's view, for value to be added, it was necessary for the assembly operations as a whole to involve an appreciable increase
in the commercial value of the finished product at the ex-factory stage. In
determining whether the value added by assembly conferred on the products
origin in the country of assembly, it was necessary in each case to compare the
amount of the value added in the country of assembly with the value added in
other countries. The Court stated that, where only two countries are
concerned, if the value added in the country of assembly is appreciably less
than the value added in the other country, then the resulting goods do not
obtain the origin of the country of assembly. Furthermore, value added of less
than 10 per cent, which was the estimate of added value put forward by the
Commission in the case, could not, in any event, result in origin of the country of assembly being obtained. Not surprisingly, the Court rejected the
contention that the 'intellectual' contribution made in any country should be
taken into account in determining origin.[52]

3. *CCC, Article 25 and origin shopping*

The use of a screw-driver factory in *Brother International*[53] provides a good
example of what may be called 'origin shopping', whereby attempts are made
to ensure that goods attain a favourable origin by means of as limited an activity as possible. Clearly, the terms of the substantial transformation test, and the
other provisions of the Kyoto Convention, together with the terms of CCC,
Article 24 and the jurisprudence of the Court of Justice, have been established
with a view to preventing origin shopping, but CCC, Article 25 addresses the
issue specifically.

The Article provides that where it is established, or where the ascertained
facts justify the presumption, that any processing or working had, as its sole
object, the circumvention of Community provisions relating to goods from
specific countries, the processing or working is under no circumstances to
result in the goods in question obtaining the origin of the place where it is
carried out. This may appear a relatively narrow provision given that processing or working has to have circumvention of Community provisions as its 'sole
object' not its main object. The provision will naturally, though, be given a
purposive construction which is likely to ensure that abuse is prevented.

---

[51] Ibid, at paras 20 and 21.   [52] Ibid, paras 21–24.
[53] Case C–26/88 *Brother International GmbH v Hauptzollamt Gießen*, at n 48 above.

Consequently, no trader should assume that the presence of an insignificant subsidiary object will enable the provision to be avoided. The provision is plainly inapplicable, however, where the operations in question have a number of reasonable objects. This was demonstrated in *Brother International* itself which was concerned with the predecessor of CCC, Article 25. The Court was asked whether the transfer of assembly from the country of manufacture of the component parts to a country where use is made of already existing factories in itself brings the presumption into operation. It held that the mere transfer, in such circumstances, was no ground for the presumption as there may be other grounds for the transfer. In at least one circumstance, however, the burden of proof will fall on the trader to show that the presumption is inapplicable. The Court said that where the transfer of the assembly coincides with the entry into force of the rules which are avoided, the trader concerned must prove that there were reasonable grounds for carrying out the assembly operations in the country from which the goods were exported, other than the avoidance of the consequences of the provisions in question.[54] In many cases, however, moving production to a particular location will be attractive not merely for customs duty reasons, but because of lower production, and particularly labour, costs.

4. *Special rules for particular products*

Chapter 1 (Articles 35–65) of Title IV of the Implementing Regulation is concerned with the non-preferential origin of textiles and textile articles falling within Section XI of the CN and of certain other products. It is designed to establish their origin by indicating when the criteria for the attainment of origin within CCC, Article 24 are satisfied. So far as concerns textiles and textile articles, the requirements of Article 24 are met where the working or processing to which they are subject constitutes a complete process.[55] A complete process is generally defined in Article 37 as working or processing as a result of which the products obtained receive a classification under a heading of the CN which is different from the various non-originating materials used. For certain products, listed in Implementing Regulation, Annex 10, however, only the processes listed in column 3 of the Annex are regarded as complete whether or not they involve a change of heading.[56] Furthermore, Article 38 lists a number of processes which are always to be considered as insufficient to confer the status of originating products, whether or not there is a change of heading. The specified processes are not fully listed here, but include, operations to keep products in good condition during transport and storage, simple operations such as dust-removal, screening, classifying, washing, changing packing, affixing marks, and the simple assembly of parts.

---

[54] Ibid, at para 28.   [55] Implementing Regulation, Art 36.
[56] The method of applying the rules in Annex 10 is described in Annex 9.

Article 39 provides that in respect of other goods falling within Section XI of the CN, the processes which confer originating status on goods, within CCC, Article 24, are set out in Annex 11 which is in the same format as Annex 10. The lists in both Annex 10 and Annex 11 provide, in respect of some products, that origin is conferred if the value of the non-originating materials used does not exceed a given percentage of the ex-works price of the products obtained. Article 40 provides specific definitions for 'value', 'ex-works price' and 'value acquired as a result of assembly operations'.

Articles 41 to 46 deal with accessories, spare parts, or tools delivered with any piece of equipment, machine, apparatus, or vehicle which, subject to a number of qualifications, are deemed to have the same origin as the goods with which they are delivered.

D. PREFERENTIAL ORIGIN

CCC, Article 27 is the only Article in the CCC dealing with preferential origin. Essentially, it specifies only that the rules on preferential origin, contained in international agreements and autonomous legislation, lay down the conditions governing acquisition of origin which goods must fulfil in order to benefit from the relevant provisions. under the agreements with third countries or autonomous legislation.

In a book of this size it is impossible to review all the preferential regimes which exist. Instead, it is proposed to highlight some of the features of the regimes. It should be noted at the outset that the rules on preferential origin follow the structure and approach of those governing non-preferential origin to a considerable extent. Therefore, many comments on non-preferential origin above are equally relevant to preferential origin. It should also be noted that since the European Council at Essen, the last European Council which Jacques Delors attended as President of the Commission, the Community has been committed to unifying its preferential rules of origin, particularly in relation to the EEA states, the EFTA states, the Central and Eastern European Countries, and the Baltic countries. This has resulted in amendments to the rules of origin established under many agreements. There has, for example, been a move away from the use of tariff headings and towards the use of lists for determining what is insufficient working or processing to establish origin. Other matters covered in amendments have included provisions permitting accounting segregation in respect of identical and interchangeable originating and non-originating materials, regional cumulation, the introduction of a common provisions relating to units of qualification, and new provisions to take account of the euro. The move to harmonize preferential rules of origin has also led to some amendments to the provisions governing the generalized system of preferences which we consider next.

1. *The generalized system of preferences (GSP)*

Chapter 2 of Title IV of the Implementing Regulation deals with preferential origin and section 1 is concerned with origin in relation to the GSP.[57] The rules in section 1 are less favourable to beneficiary countries than those contained in specific international agreements, a fact that the ACP countries were very conscious of in negotiations leading to the recent Cotonou Agreement discussed in Chapter 6. The Court of Justice has also shown itself to be aware of the fact and has held that, where appropriate, the Commission may apply the concept of origin in a different and stricter manner in relation to the GSP than in relation to non-preferential origin and that such a course of action may be necessary to achieve the objectives of the GSP.[58]

As one would expect, products originate in a GSP country, or in the Community[59] as the case may be, if they are wholly obtained there[60] or if they have undergone sufficient working or processing there.[61] Before looking at these two categories of products two preliminary matters may be mentioned. First, there are certain matters which are expressly stated to be irrelevant to the ascertainment of origin in the context of the generalized system of preferences. These are the origin of the energy and fuel, plant, equipment, machines, and tools used in the manufacture of the product, together with any goods used in manufacture which do not enter, and which are not intended to enter, into the final composition of the product.[62] Secondly, the conditions governing the acquisition of originating status are to be satisfied 'without interruption' in the beneficiary country or in the Community.[63] If originating goods which are exported from the beneficiary country, or from the Community, are returned, they must be considered as non-originating unless two matters can be demonstrated 'to the satisfaction of the competent authorities'. The first is that the goods returned are the same as the goods exported. The second is that the goods have not undergone any operations beyond what is necessary to preserve them in good condition while abroad or being exported.[64] There are also provisions governing in what circumstances goods are to be considered as transported

---

[57] Ch 2 (Arts 66–123) was recently replaced by Commission Regulation (EC) 1602/2000 of 24 July 2000 [2000] OJ L188/1. The replacement was effected largely in the interests of clarity: see recital (8) to the regulation.

[58] Case 385/85 *S R Industries v Administration des douanes* [1986] ECR 2929 para 7: the case concerned the validity of a Commission regulation governing the origin of certain products produced by developing countries.

[59] For the purposes of the generalized system of preferences 'Community' does not include Ceuta and Melilla: see the Implementing Regulation, Art 96.

[60] See Implementing Regulation, Art 67.1(a). Art 68, defines what goods are wholly obtained in a territory and is considered below.

[61] Ibid, Art 67.1(b) above. What constitutes sufficient working or processing is specified in Art 69, and is considered below.

[62] Ibid, Art 75.

[63] Ibid, Art 77, first para.

[64] Ibid, Art 77, second para.

directly from a beneficiary country to the Community or *vice versa*.[65] Goods sent from a beneficiary country to another country for the purposes of exhibition are subject to particular provisions.[66]

1.1 *Origin in a single country*

Implementing Regulation, Article 68 contains a list of products which are considered to be wholly obtained in a beneficiary country or in the Community. It is very like the list which exists for non-preferential goods in Article 23 of the CCC in that it contains animal, vegetable, and mineral products. There are, however, some differences in drafting. The main difference concerns the definition of vessels and factory ships of a beneficiary country or the Community which is narrower than the definition used in relation to non-preferential origin.[67] A vessel must be registered or recorded in, and sail under the flag of, the beneficiary country or Member State, as required by CCC, Article 23. It must, however, satisfy further conditions. First, it must be owned, as to at least 50 per cent, by nationals of the beneficiary country or Member States, or by a company having its head office in the beneficiary country, or in one of those Member States of which the manager or managers, chairman of the board of directors, or of the supervisory board, and the majority of the members of such boards are nationals. Secondly, in the case of companies, at least half the capital must belong to the relevant beneficiary country, or the Member States, or to public bodies or nationals of them. Thirdly, at least 75 per cent of the crew[68] of the vessel must be nationals of the beneficiary country or of the Member States.[69] A vessel operating on the high seas, including factory ships on which the fish caught is worked or processed, is to be considered to be part of the territory to which it belongs provided that it satisfies the conditions relating to a vessel set out above.[70]

Difficulties have also arisen in relation to fish of different origins being processed together. It had been contended that so long as the fish of different

---

[65] Ibid, Art 78.   [66] Ibid, Art 79.

[67] Ibid, Art 68.2.

[68] 'Crew' 'does not include persons not forming part of the vessel's normal complement who are engaged in addition thereto on a particular voyage or part of a voyage to work as trainees or as unskilled hands below decks, particularly for training purposes, in order to comply with a joint venture agreement entered into with an undertaking in a non-member country for the purpose of enabling the vessel to fish inside the exclusive economic zone of that country, whether those persons are paid either by the operator of the vessel or by the undertaking in the non-member country': Joined Cases C–153/94 and C–204/94 *The Queen v Commissioners of Customs & Excise, ex p Faroe Seafood Co. Ltd, Føroya Fiskasøla L/F and others* [1996] ECR I–2465 at para 47. The observations of the Court of Justice were made in relation to Commission Regulation (EEC) 3184/74 [1974] OJ L344/1, but they are equally applicable in relation to the GSP.

[69] The conditions are cumulative: see Case C–153/94 and C–204/94 *The Queen v Commissioners of Customs & Excise, ex p Faroe Seafood Co Ltd, Føroya Fiskasøla L/F and another*, n 68 above, at para 41.

[70] Implementing Regulation Art 68.4.

origins were separated according to 'book-keeping principles' it did not matter that they were physically mixed for the purposes of processing. The Court of Justice, however, has held that in order to enjoy preferential customs treatment prawns of differing origins had to be kept physically separate during process-ing. This could give rise to practical difficulties and in some circumstances, perhaps, render the preferential treatment impossible to obtain. No doubt mindful of this, the Court has indicated that in the interests of fairness, where no separation occurs, the customs authorities of the Member State may, with the agreement of the EC Commission, levy duty in an amount equal only to that which would have been payable if the origins of the goods in the consign-ment in question had corresponded, proportionally, to the origins of the raw materials brought into the factory in the year in which the import occurred.[71] This approach avoids considerable logistical difficulties for traders, not just in relation to fish, but in relation to many kinds of products. Indeed, many rules of origin have been amended so as to permit, what is called 'accounting segre-gation'. Where this is permitted, stocks of originating and non-originating products which are identical and interchangeable may, with the authorization of customs authorities be stored together. So far the GSP rules of origin have not been amended to permit this.

1.2 *Origin in two or more countries*

The general rule is, as one would expect, that products which are not wholly obtained in a country, or in the Community, obtain origin in the country in which they are worked or processed provided that non-originating materials used in manufacturing the products have undergone sufficient working or processing.[72] This rule does not apply, however, where the non-originating materials used in a product's manufacture have a total value which does not exceed 10 per cent of the ex-works price of the final product and so long as the specific percentages given for the maximum value of non-originating materials, in respect of the products listed in Annex 15 of the Implementing Regulation, are not exceeded. This provision is known as the 'general tolerance rule' and similar rules are found in all the régimes governing origin.[73] It used to be the case that the test of a change of tariff-heading was the primary test in deter-mining whether a product was sufficiently worked or processed. It used to be necessary, therefore, for the product obtained by the working or processing in question to be in a different classification heading from all the non-originating materials used in its manufacture. As part of the plan to harmonize

---

[71] Joined Cases C–153/94 and C–204/94 *The Queen v Commissioners of Customs & Excise, ex p Faroe Seafood Co Ltd, Føroya Fiskasøla L/F and others*, n 68 above, para 58.

[72] Implementing Regulation, Art. 69.

[73] Implementing Regulation, Art 71. It does not apply to products falling within Chapters 50–63 of the Harmonized System (textiles and textile articles): see ibid, Art 71.2.

Community rules of preferential origin, the Implementing Regulation now provides, as we have seen, that the test of sufficient working or processing is to be applied by the more certain means of testing compliance with conditions set out in a list in Annex 15 to the Implementing Regulation.[74] There remain, of course, some operations which are considered to constitute insufficient working or processing to confer originating status on products.[75] These include operations designed to preserve products in good condition during storage or transport, and a number of uncomplicated operations, including simple assembly,[76] and the slaughter of animals.

1.2.1 *Unit of qualification, accessories and sets*

Implementing Regulation, Article 70a.1 sets out the general rule that the unit of qualification, for the application of the provisions relating to the GSP, is the product which is the basic unit when determining classification using the nomenclature of the harmonized system. It also states that where the harmonized system would treat an assembly of articles, or a product with its packaging, as a single unit, that single unit is to be the unit of qualification for the purposes of the GSP rules and that consignments of a number of identical products must be taken separately in applying the provision.[77]

There are specific provisions regarding accessories, spare parts, and tools dispatched with a piece of equipment, machine, apparatus, or vehicle, which are part of the normal equipment in question. If they are included in the price, or are not separately invoiced, they are to be regarded as one with the product with which they are dispatched.[78] So far as sets[79] of goods are concerned, these are to be treated as originating sets when the components of them are treated as originating products. There is, however, a tolerance to this rule. When a set is composed of articles of mixed origin, the set as a whole is to be regarded as originating so long as the value of the non-originating articles does not exceed 15 per cent of the ex-works price of the set.[80]

1.2.2 *Norway and Switzerland*

Norway and Switzerland apply similar rules of origin for the purposes of GSP to the EC and have entered into an agreement with the Community in relation to the GSP regime.[81] Amongst other things it provides that, if industrial products

---

[74] See also the second recital to Regulation (EC) 46/99 of 8 Jan 1999 [1999] OJ L10/1.
[75] Implementing Regulation, Art 70 .
[76] See the comments on assembly operations at C.2.3 above.
[77] Implementing Regulation, see Art 70a.1, second and third paras respectively, and Art 70a.2
[78] Ibid, Art 73.
[79] As defined in General Rule 3 of the Harmonized System.
[80] Implementing Regulation, Art 74.
[81] For the agreement with Norway see the letters at [2001] OJ L38/29–32, and for the agreement with Switzerland see the letters at [2001] OJ L38/25–28.

originating in the EC, Norway, or Switzerland are subject to sufficient processing in a beneficiary country, then they are to be considered by the contracting
parties to be originating in that beneficiary country. The agreement also
provides for administrative assistance between the customs authorities of the
parties to the agreement and for the acceptance of replacement certificates
issued by the parties in place of a beneficiary country's Form A (which certifies origin).[82]

1.2.3 *Regional cumulation*

There are particular provisions governing what is known as 'regional cumulation' in the Implementing Regulation, Articles 72–72b. Regional cumulation
applies in relation to four regional groups of countries namely: the Association
of South East Asian Nations ('ASEAN')[83], the Central American Common
Market ('CACM'),[84] the Andean Community,[85] and the South Asian
Association for Regional Co-operation ('SAARC').[86] In order for it to apply the
rules regulating trade between the countries of the regional group must be
identical to those set out in the section of the Implementing Regulation
concerned with the GSP, and the countries in question must have undertaken
to comply with them and provide administrative co-operation within the
regional group and in relation to the EC.[87]

Regional cumulation occurs when a product is manufactured and has its
origin in one beneficiary country and is used in further manufacture in
another country of the regional group. When this happens the product is
treated as if it originated in 'the country of further manufacture'.[88] The
attainment of origin in that country is, however, subject to some conditions.
The value added in that country[89] must be greater than the highest customs
value of the products used and originating in any one of the other countries of
the regional group.[90] Furthermore, the working or processing must exceed
that set out in Implementing Regulation, Article 70, outlined above and, in
relation to textile products, the operations set out in Annex 16.[91] It must, of
course, be possible to prove that the goods have originated in the first country

---

[82] See also Implementing Regulation Arts 67.4 and 5.
[83] These are Brunei, Darussalam, Indonesia, Laos, Malaysia, Philippines, Singapore, Thailand,
and Vietnam. The ASEAN was founded on 8 Aug 1967 by Indonesia, Malaysia, Philippines,
Singapore, and Thailand. Brunei Darussalam joined on 8 Jan 1984, Vietnam joined on 28 July
1995, Laos and Myanmar on 23 July 1997, and Cambodia on 30 Apr 1999.
[84] Costa Rica, Honduras, Guatemala, Nicaragua, and El Salvador.
[85] Bolivia, Colombia, Ecuador, Peru, and Venezuela.
[86] Bangladesh, Bhutan, India, Maldives, Nepal, Pakistan, Sri Lanka.
[87] Implementing Regulation, Art 72b.
[88] Ibid, Art 72a.1.
[89] 'Added value' means the ex-works price minus the customs value of each of the products
incorporated which originated in another country of the regional group: see ibid, Art 72a.3.
[90] Ibid, Art 72a.1(a).
[91] Ibid, Art 72a.1(b).

of the regional group. This proof is to be provided by a certificate of origin in Form A issued by that country.[92]

1.2.4 *The least-developed countries*

In Chapter 6 we noted that the GSP contained a list of the least-developed countries which were given particularly favourable treatment by the EC. They can also submit to the EC a request for a derogation from the provisions governing origin in the GSP.[93] The Commission is to pass the derogation request on to the Customs Code Committee and it is to be decided upon using the committee procedure.[94]

A derogation may be made when the development of existing industries or the creation of new industries justifies it.[95] There are a number of matters which are required to be taken into account in examining a request for a derogation. These are, first, cases where the application of the existing rules of origin would significantly affect an existing industry's ability to continue exporting to the Community, particularly where this could lead to the closure of businesses. Secondly, account must be taken of cases in which it can be clearly demonstrated that significant investment in industry could be deterred by the rules of origin and of cases where a derogation encouraging an investment programme would enable the rules to be satisfied in stages. Thirdly, the economic and social impact of the decision to be taken must be taken into account, especially in relation to employment, both in the Community and in the beneficiary countries.[96]

The request for a derogation must be supported by the 'fullest possible information' which should comprise a number of specified matters. These include: the description of the finished product, the nature and quality of the materials originating in a third country, the manufacturing process, the value added, the number of employees in the enterprise concerned, and the anticipated volume of exports to the Community.[97]

2. *The Overseas Countries and Territories*

The rules governing the origin of goods and procedures for administrative

---

[92] Ibid, Art 72a.4–6.
[93] Ibid, Art 76.
[94] Ibid, Art 76.4.
[95] Implementing Regulation, Art 76.1.
[96] Ibid, Art 76.2(a)–(c).
[97] Ibid, Art 76.3. For an example of a recent derogation see Commission Regulation (EC) 1537/99 of 13 July 1999 [1999] OJ L178/26, derogating from Regulation (EEC) 2454/93 in respect of the definition of the concept of originating products used for the purposes of the scheme of generalized preferences to take account of the special situation of Laos regarding certain exports of textiles to the Community. This permitted raw materials used in Laos to originate in countries of the South Asian Association for Regional Co-operation or in countries subject to the Lomé Convention, in respect of imports into the Community between 15 July 1999 and 14 July 2000, subject to certain annual quantitive limits. See similar measures in respect of Cambodia in Commission Regulation (EC) 1538/99 of 13 July 1999 [1999] OJ L178/34, and in respect of Nepal in Commission Regulation (EC) 1539/99 of 13 July 1999 [1999] OJ L178/42.

co-operation are contained in Annex II to the OCT Decision.[98] There is a very considerable similarity between these rules and those governing the ACP states discussed below. Like the ACP states the OCTs are treated as a single territory. The treatment of the ACP states is, however, somewhat more favourable than that for OCTs. For example, the general tolerance rule is applied by reference to a figure of 15 per cent in relation to ACP states rather than 10 per cent for the OCTs.[99] Nevertheless, the OCTs are treated more favourably, in some respects, under the OCT Decision than they would be under the provisions governing the GSP. For example, the definition of the OCTs vessels and factory ships, which is similar to that applicable in relation to the ACP states considered below, is more generous than that under the GSP rules. Furthermore, the tolerance rule operated by reference to a figure of 5 per cent rather than 10 per cent until 2000.[100]

The mid-term amendment of the OCT Decision was designed, in part, to deal with difficulties arising in relation to the Common Agricultural Policy. Amongst other things, it placed quotas on cumulation of origin in relation to rice and sugar and gave rise to a considerable amount of litigation discussed in the previous chapter. It also contained provisions establishing cumulation of origin between the OCTs and the ACP countries.[101] Consequently, when products wholly obtained in the Community, or in the ACP States, undergo working or processing in the OCTs, they are to be considered as having been wholly obtained in the OCTs. Conversely, when working and processing is carried out in the Community or in the ACP States, it is to be considered as having been carried out in the OCTs when the materials undergo working or processing in them. It is also worth noting that Article 7 of the OCT Decision provides that originating products made up of materials wholly obtained or sufficiently processed in two or more OCTs, or in one or more ACP States and in one or more OCT, are to be considered as products originating in the OCT or ACP states where the last working or processing took place. The working or processing must, however, exceed that referred to in the list of operations contained in Article 3(3).

3. *Other Community measures governing origin*

Although Bosnia-Herzegovina and Croatia, the Federal Republic of Yugoslavia, the former Yugoslav Republic of Macedonia, and Albania are covered by the generalized system of preferences, there are specific rules

---

[98] 482/91 OJ of 25 July 1991[1991] L263/1, as amended by Council Decision (EC) 803/97 of 24 Nov 1997 [1997] OJ L329/50 and extended to 1 Dec 2001 by Council Decision of 26 Feb 2001 (EC) 161/2001 [2001] OJ L58/21.

[99] Implementing Regulation, Art 5, and see below for further examples.

[100] Commission Regulation (EC) 1602/2000 see n 57 above.

[101] See the OCT Decision Art 6, Annex II, n 98 above, as amended.

governing the determination of the origin of certain products exported from them[102] and certain applicable autonomous measures in addition to those contained in the Implementing Regulation.[103] There are also autonomous Community measures in relation to areas such as the Canary Islands and Ceuta and Melilla.[104] The rules of origin in the Implementing Regulation no longer apply to the territories of the West Bank and the Gaza Strip because these benefit from conventional preferential tariff measures.[105] Autonomous measures in relation to the Faroe Islands have also been replaced by conventional measures.[106]

4. *Preferential origin under international agreements*

We now turn to consider briefly, the rules of origin contained in the main agreements referred to in Chapter 6 above. Once again, it should be noted that to the extent that the provisions in the agreements follow those which apply in relation to non-preferential origin, or the provisions in autonomous Community measures, reference should be made to the earlier discussion in this chapter.

4.1 *The EEA*

The rules of origin in the EEA Agreement are contained in Protocol No 4.[107] For the purposes of the Agreement, the EC and the EEA are considered as a single territory with certain exceptions for Liechtenstein until 1 January

---

[102] See Arts 98–122.

[103] eg, in relation to Albania see also Council Regulation (EC) 1763/99 of [1999] OJ L211/1. Measures relating to the Republics of Bosnia and Herzegovina and Croatia and to imports of wine originating in the Former Yugoslav Republic of Macedonia and the Republic of Slovenia are contained in Council Regulation (EC) 6/2000 of 17 Dec 1999 [2000] OJ L2/1.

[104] These appear in the Implementing Regulation at Arts 123–140: see particularly Art 140.

[105] See recital (5) to Commission Regulation (EC) 1602/2000 of 24 July 2000 [2000] OJ L188/1, and the Agreement between the EC and the Palestinian Liberation Organization for the benefit of the Palestinian Authority of the West Bank and the Gaza Strip [1997] OJ L187/3.

[106] In Case C–153/94 *The Queen v Commissioners of Customs & Excise, ex p Faroe Seafood Co. Ltd, Føroya Fiskasøla L/F and others*, at n 68 above, the provisions concerning the origin of products from the Faroe Islands were autonomous. They are now contained in Decision 1/99 of the EC/Denmark–Faroe Islands Joint Committee of 22 June1999. This replaced Protocol 1 of the Agreement concerning the tariff treatment and arrangements applicable to certain fish and fishery products released for free circulation in the Community or imported into the Faroe Islands: [1999] OJ L178/58, which replaced the Agreement between the EC, of the one part, and the Government of Denmark and the Home Government of the Faroe Islands, of the other part of 6 Dec 1996: [1997] OJ L53/27. Protocol 3 Title II deals with originating products and administrative co-operation.

[107] See [1994] OJ L1/54. Amended by the Decision of the EEA Council 1/95 (see below), Decision of the EEA Joint Committee 71/96 of 22 Nov 1996 [1997] OJ L21/12, the Decision of the EEA Joint Committee No 114/98 of 27 Nov 1998 [2000] , OJ L266/53.

EC Customs Law

2000^{108} and Austria until 1 January $1997.^{109}$ As noted in Chapter 6 above, Switzerland remains a member of EFTA but not the $EEA.^{110}$

As one may expect, products which originate in the EEA are either those which are wholly obtained in the EEA or those which are sufficiently worked, or processed, in the EEA to have originating status conferred on them. Products which are wholly obtained are defined in Article 4. This is in similar terms to the Implementing Regulation, Article 68. The definitions of EEA or EC vessels or factory-ships also follow the terms of the Implementing Regulation, Article 68.2, discussed above. The only difference appears to be that the requirement as to the ownership of the capital of companies is extended to partnerships.

The rules regarding sufficient working and processing are set out in Article 5 and Annex II, which specifies operations which are sufficient to confer originating status, and Article 6 which lists the operations which are not sufficient to do so, in terms which are similar to those of Article 70 of the Implementing Regulation. As with the GSP rules, they operate not by reference to a change of tariff classification, but by reference to a list of processes which are considered to confer originating status relating to specific products in Annex II. There is, however, a general tolerance rule in Article 4.2 which is in similar terms to that operating in relation to the GSP. Except in relation to products within chapters 50–63 of the Harmonized System (ie textiles and textile articles) which have their own rules, the Protocol permits non-originating materials to be used to a limit of 10 per cent of the ex-works price of the product (as defined). The Protocol also contains provisions equivalent to Articles 73, 74, and 75 of the Implementing Regulation.[111]

Article 11 of the Protocol provides that working or processing outside the EEA is to be ignored on goods exported from the EEA and subsequently re-imported into it, provided that certain conditions are met. In particular, prior to their exportation, the goods must be wholly obtained in the EEA or have undergone working or processing going beyond that listed in Article 6. Furthermore, it must be demonstrated to the customs authorities' satisfaction that the reimported goods result from the working or processing of exported

---

[108] See Decision 1/95 of the EEA Council of 10 Mar 1995 on the entry into force of the Agreement on the European Economic Area for the Principality of Liechtenstein [1995] OJ L86/58.   [109] See Art 1.2, Protocol 4, n 107 above.

[110] Provisions on origin relating to goods passing between Switzerland and the EC are contained in Protocol 3, to the Agreement, signed on 22 July 1972, between the European Economic Community and the Swiss Confederation, concerning the definition of the concept of 'originating products' and methods of administrative cooperation, and amended on a number of occasions but most substantially by Decision 1/96 of the EC–Switzerland Joint Committee of 19 Dec 1996 No L195/1. See also the Decision 1/99 of the EC-Switzerland Joint Committee of 24 June 1999, OJ L249/25, and Decision 2/99 of 29 Nov 1999 [1999] OJ L323/14.

[111] These concern accessories, spare parts and tools dispatched with a product and sets (Arts 8 and 9), and provide a list of items the origin of which is irrelevant in determining the origin of a product (Art 10).

materials and that the total added value acquired outside the EEA does not exceed 10 per cent of the ex-works price of the final product in question. Article 12 limits preferential treatment to those goods transported directly within the EEA or those countries in respect of which cumulation is permitted.[112] Article 13 deals with products sent for exhibition in a third country and subsequently imported into a contracting party and Article 14 provides that non-originating materials, used in the manufacture of products originating in the EEA, are not subject to any drawback or exemption from customs duties of any kind.

4.1.1 *Regional cumulation*

We have already noted that Article 2 of Protocol No 4 treats the EEA as a single territory. Unlike the free trade agreements which the EEA replaced, Protocol 4 has wide cumulation provisions. Article 3 provides, in addition, for regional, or 'diagonal' cumulation.[113] The regional cumulation provisions permit products, which incorporate materials from certain other European countries, to be considered as originating in the EEA if the products are treated as originating in the EEA pursuant to the agreement between the contracting parties to the EEA and the European countries in question.[114] The materials may originate in the Community, Bulgaria, Poland, Hungary, the Czech Republic, the Slovak Republic, Romania, Lithuania, Latvia, Estonia, Slovenia, Iceland, Norway, Switzerland (including Liechtenstein with which it has a customs union), or Turkey (for industrial products). In order to be originating in the EEA, it is necessary for the product to be worked or processed in the EEA beyond the level described in Article 6 of the Protocol, which lists the operations which cannot confer originating status as we noted above. Where the working or processing does not exceed the prescribed level, Article 3.2 of the Protocol provides that a product may still be regarded as of EEA origin, but only where the value added there is greater than the value of the materials used which originate in any one of the countries listed above. If the value added is not greater than that, the product is considered to originate in the country which accounts for the highest value of originating materials used in manufacture in the EEA.

---

[112] The countries are listed below. Arts 11 and 12 are similar to the Implementing Regulation Arts 77 and 78.

[113] The present form of this Art is inserted by Decision of the Joint Committee of the EEA, No 45/99 of 26 Mar 1999 with effect from 1 Jan 1999: [2000] OJ L266/53. Somewhat more limited cumulation provisions were introduced into the EEA Agreement by the Joint Committee's Decision 71/96 of 22 Nov 1996, which took effect from 1 Jan 1996, n 107 above. The original EEA Agreement did not contain diagonal cumulation provisions. The term 'bilateral cumulation' is sometimes used in contrast to diagonal cumulation. It occurs when a product originating in one party's territory is treating as originating in the other's following working or processing.

[114] These rules in these agreements must be the same as those contained in Protocol No 4: see Art 3.4.

4.2 *The Europe Agreements*

As we noted in Chapter 6 above, the Community has entered into a number of
'Europe Agreements' with Central and Eastern European Countries and the
Baltic states. As in that chapter, we take as an example the Agreement between
the EC and the Czech Republic.[115] In many respects, in structure and
substance, the provisions are similar to those contained in the EEA agreement
considered above. For example, the general tolerance provision operates by
reference to a figure of 10 per cent,[116] and the definition of vessels and factory
ships includes a reference to the ownership of capital of partnerships as well
as companies.

The original provisions on origin of goods were contained in Protocol 4 to
the Agreement which was replaced by a Decision of the Association Council in
1998.[117] The amendments made in 1998 were designed to ensure the proper
operation of the extended regional cumulation system introduced in 1996.[118]
The cumulation provisions provide, in Articles 3 and 4, that goods originate in
the EC or the Czech Republic as the case may be, if the products are obtained
there, incorporating materials which, according to the agreement between the
EC and the following countries originate in the Community: Bulgaria, Poland,
Hungary, the Czech Republic, the Slovak Republic, Romania, Lithuania,
Latvia, Estonia, Slovenia, Iceland, Norway, Switzerland (and Liechtenstein), or
Turkey, in respect of industrial products. The working or processing must
exceed the minimum prescribed in Article 7. The Protocol was amended again
in 1999[119] to take account of the introduction of the euro. The most recent
amendments to the Protocol are contained in Decision 2/2001 of the EU
Czech Republic Association Council.[120] The Decision contains, amongst other
things, amendments providing for a list of operations which are considered
insufficient to confer originating status on products and for accounting segre-
gation of stocks of identical and interchangeable originating and non-originating products.

4.3 *Agreements with EFTA*

The only EFTA agreement with which practitioners are likely to be concerned,
frequently, is that between the EC and Switzerland. The provisions on origin in

---

[115] See [1994] OJ L360/24.
[116] See Art 6.2.
[117] See Decision 6/98 of the EU/Czech Association Council of 21 Dec 1998 [1999] OJ L35/32.
[118] See Decision 3/96 of the EU/Czech Republic Association Council of 29 Nov 1996 [1996] OJ
L343/1. The original agreement provided, in Art 2 and 3 for bilateral cumulation and cumulation
with Poland, Hungary, and the Slovak Republic.
[119] See Decision 3/99 of the EU/Czech Republic Association Council of 15 Dec 1999 [2000] OJ
L28/42.
[120] OJ of 23 Jan 2001, [2001] OJ L64/36.

the Agreements with the EFTA states were contained in Protocol No. 3. In the case of Switzerland this was replaced by Decision 1/96 of the EC–Switzerland Joint Committee,[121] which modernized the terms of the Protocol in a number of respects, introducing an extended system of cumulation, a changed definition of origin with provisions governing vessels and factory ships, a change to the use of lists of operations which do not give originating status in place of reference to a change of tariff heading, and an increase in the percentage governing the general tolerance rule to 10 per cent.

4.4 *Euro-Mediterranean Agreements*

Within the scope of this chapter it is impossible to consider these agreements in detail. The provisions on origin follow a form which is very similar to the Europe Agreements and departs from them only in some limited respects such as regional cumulation. The agreement with Morocco,[122] for example, is drafted so as to regard, in certain respects as least, Algeria, Tunisia and Morocco as a whole.

4.5 *The ACP states*

The rules of origin in the Cotonou Agreement, contained in Protocol 1 to Annex V of the Agreement, along with many other of its provisions, came into force on 2 August 2000.[123] The structure of the rules is similar to that of those already discussed. They substantially follow those contained in the Fourth Lomé Convention, as amended, in accordance with the new, generally applied format for preferential origin. There are, though, some significant features of the rules. In this section, attention is drawn only to some points which are of particular importance to the ACP countries. The rules in the Lomé Convention are mentioned first, then those contained in the Cotonou Agreement.

In the Lomé Convention,[124] the concept of origin is applied to the ACP states as a whole and they are treated as a single territory.[125] As was noted

---

[121] Of 19 Dec 1996 [1997] OJ L195/1. See also Decision 1/99 of the EC–Switzerland Joint Committee of 24 June 1999 [1999] L249/25, Decision 2/99 of the Joint Committee of 29 Nov 1999 [1999] OJ L323/14, and Decision 1/2001 of the EC–Switzerland Joint Committee of 24 Jan 2001 [2001] OJ L51/40.

[122] Approved by Council and Commission Decision (EC, ECSE) 204/2000 of 24 Jan 2000 [2000] OJ L70/1.

[123] See Decision 1/2000 of the EC–ACP Council of Ministers of 27 July 2000 [2000] OJ L195/46. The Decision applies until the Agreement enters into force, but no longer than 1 June 2002, though it may be extended by the Council of Ministers.

[124] The Fourth Lomé Convention was signed on 15 Dec 1989 [1991] OJ L229/3. It was amended by an Agreement signed in Mauritius on 4 Nov 1995 [1998] OJ L156/3. The rules of origin are contained in Protocol 1 to the Convention and references to Arts are to Arts in the protocol. See also Ch 6, n 97.

[125] Ibid, Art 6.1.

above, the rules are considerably more generous than those which apply in the context of the GSP. The reference to countries' vessels encompasses those which are registered, recorded, or sail under the flag of a Member State, an ACP state, or an OCT. As in the GSP rules the ownership of the vessel must be as to 50 per cent by nationals of the ACP country, OCT, or Member States as the case may be. Unlike the GSP rules, a country's vessels include those which are chartered by the ACP states, or an OCT, in certain circumstances where the EC does not take up an ACP state's offer to negotiate a fisheries agreement with it. Furthermore, whereas Article 68 of the Implementing Regulation requires 75 per cent of the crew to be nationals of relevant countries, the figure for the ACP states is 50 per cent.[126] So far as concerns products which are obtained in the ACP states by virtue of working or processing, the test of tariff change plus reference to lists of products or operations is utilized.[127] The general tolerance rule is operated by reference to a figure of 15 per cent, following the amendment of the Convention[128] as compared with 10 per cent for the GSP regime[129] and 10 per cent for the OCTs.

The cumulation rules, contained in Article 6, are also favourable to the ACP states. Products which are wholly obtained in the Community or in the OCTs are considered to be wholly obtained in the ACP states if they undergo working or processing there. Working or processing which is carried out in Member States, or in the OCTs, is considered to be carried out in the ACP states when the materials in question undergo working or processing in the ACP states. These rules apply to any working or processing in the ACP states. Although Article 3.3 indicates what is insufficient working or processing to confer originating status, its restrictions do not apply in this context. Where products are made up of materials wholly obtained or sufficiently processed in two or more ACP states they are considered to originate in the ACP state where the last working or processing took place provided that this exceeded certain levels.[130] Following the amendment of the Lomé Convention, the cumulation rules were further relaxed in relation to some goods to provide that, following a request from the ACP states, goods originating from non-ACP countries were subsequently to be regarded as originating in one of them in certain circumstances. The non-ACP country must be a neighbouring developing country, other than an ACP state, which belongs to a coherent geographical entity, and the goods in question must undergo further working or processing in excess of the operations listed in Article 3.3. The request is to be decided upon by the ACP–EC Council of Ministers on the basis of a report drawn up by the ACP–EC Customs Co-operation Committee.[131]

---

[126] See Art 5.2 and 3.
[127] Art 3, Art 4 contains a list of neutral elements which is in some respects wider than that contained in Implementing Regulation, Art 75.
[128] Art 5.   [129] Implementing Regulation, Art 71.
[130] Art 7, Protocol 1.   [131] Ibid, Art 6.5.

Finally it should be noted that derogations from the Protocol may be obtained on request by an ACP state.[132] The derogations are granted by the Customs Co-operation Committee, generally for an initial period of five years. For a request to be made, the derogation must be justified by the development of existing industries or the creation of new ones. It is specifically provided that the Community is to respond positively to all requests for derogations which are so justified and which cannot cause serious injury to an established Community industry.[133]

The rules contained in the Cotonou Agreement are similar in many respects to those discussed above. It should be noted, though, that Protocol 1 to Annex V of the Cotonou Agreement commences with a definition Article which, amongst other things, specifies that customs value is to be determined in accordance with the WTO agreement on customs valuation.[134] The protocol goes on to provide, in the usual way, that goods originate in the ACP if they are wholly obtained there or sufficiently worked or processed there. The definition of wholly obtained products is largely the same as before save that there is an amendment to the provision dealing with used articles,[135] and a new provision governing products extracted from marine soil or subsoil outside territorial waters which are wholly obtained by the entity which has the sole right to work that soil or subsoil.[136] The requirement of sufficient working or processing is to be applied by reference to lists of operations unrelated entirely to change of tariff heading.[137] Also added are provisions governing cumulation affecting South Africa, under which materials originating in South Africa are considered to originate in the ACP states when incorporated into a product which is wholly obtained there. This cumulation provision does not contain a requirement that there be sufficient working or processing. It is, however, required that the value added in the ACP states should exceed the value of the originating materials used in South Africa. These provisions are limited by reference to lists of products, which set out those products to which these rules apply after three years, those to which they apply after six years, and those to which they do not apply or apply conditionally.[138] Protocol 1 also contains a provision that defines the unit of qualification for the application of the Protocol, which, as in other agreements, is to be the particular product which is considered as the basic unit when determining classification using the nomenclature of the harmonized system.[139]

---

[132] See Art 31, n 124 above. A derogation is possible not just from the rules governing originating products but also from the rules governing proof of origin and methods of administrative co-operation.

[133] Ibid, Art 31.1.   [134] Art 1(e).

[135] There is a reference to used tyres fit only for re-treading or use as waste in Art 2(h) which is not in the Lomé Agreement, Art 2(h) which states that used articles fit only for the recovery of raw materials are wholly obtained where they are collected.

[136] Art 1(j).   [137] Art 4.

[138] Art 6.3–10.   [139] Art 7.

E. PROOF OF ORIGIN, CUSTOMS AUTHORITIES,
THE COMMISSION, AND THE TRADER

The rules governing proof of origin and the administrative co-operation between the customs authorities of exporting and importing states are contained either in the relevant regulations or international agreements. As with the substantive rules of origin, it is impossible in a book of this size to consider the relevant provisions in detail. We turn to consider proof of origin first of all.

1. *Proof of origin*

Proof of origin has always been of the utmost importance to traders, as well as to the authorities of the Community and its trading partners and, particularly in recent years, there have been many disputes over post-clearance demands for customs duty issued following the discovery that certificates of origin, in reliance on which preferential rates of duty have been applied, are inaccurate. In this section, after examining the provisions of the Kyoto Convention, the rules relating to the GSP are explained as these contain many of the basic elements of the provisions applicable in other situations. There follows a short section on proof of origin and international agreements. In any specific situation the rules contained in Community measures or international agreements must, of course, be consulted.

1.1 *Proof of origin and the Kyoto Convention*

Like Annex D1 which is concerned with the substantive rules of origin, Annex D2 of the Kyoto Convention, concerning documentary evidence of origin, was accepted on behalf of the Community by Council Decision (EEC) 415/77.[140] Three recommended practices were, however, not accepted. These were: number 3, which sets out certain situations in which documentary evidence should not be required, number 10, which permits the authorities of a country through which imports pass to issue certificates of origin, and number 12, which specifies certain instances in which a declaration of origin, rather than a certificate of origin, should be accepted.

The link between certificates of origin and preferential duty rates, referred to above, is made plain by Standard 2 of the Annex which states that documentary evidence of origin may be required only when it is necessary for the application of preferential customs duties, of economic or trade measures adopted unilaterally or under bilateral or multilateral agreements, or of measures adopted for reasons of health or public order. Standard 5 confirms

[140] OJ L 166/1 of 3 June 1977.

this link by stating that documentary evidence may be required from the country of origin whenever the customs authorities of the country of importation have reason to suspect fraud. The Convention then moves on to deal with more administrative matters, for example, setting out a model form of certificate of origin in recommended practice 6, requiring certificates to be in English or French as well as the language of the country of exportation, in recommended practice 7, and providing that the country of importation shall not require a translation of the certificate as a matter of course where the certificate is not in its language. Recommended practice 11, which provides that those issuing certificates should retain copies of them, and applications for them, for not less than two years, is also of some significance. Appendix II sets out specific requirements on the nature of the certificate and its completion requiring, for example, that it should be ISO size A4. Appendix III sets out certain rules for the 'establishment' of certificates of origin requiring, for example, that they may be completed by any process provided that the entries are indelible and legible.

The revised Kyoto Convention contains, in Chapters 1 and 2 of Specific Annex K, provisions similar to Annex D1 and Annex D2 of the Convention. The revision of the Convention contains in Chapter 3 of Specific Annex K, a new set of rules governing administrative assistance to be provided by customs authorities to each other in relation to checking certificates of origin. Whereas standard 5 of Annex D2 required some co-operation in cases of fraud, as we have seen, Chapter 3, recommended practice 3, envisages co-operation where there are reasonable grounds to doubt the authenticity of the document or of the accuracy of the particulars in it, and on a random basis. According to standard 4, requests for control on a random basis are, however, to be kept to a minimum. The chapter goes on to set out the manner in which co-operation between customs authorities is to be effected.

1.2 *Proof of origin and the GSP*

The Implementing Regulation contains provisions governing certificates of origin and administrative co-operation between the authorities of exporting and importing countries in relation both to non-preferential and preferential origin. They are, as may be expected, more detailed than those contained in the Kyoto Convention. The provisions on non-preferential origin are contained in Articles 47–65. The provisions on preferential origin are to be found in Articles 80–95 which is concerned with the GSP. In determining, however, the arrangements which apply to any particular state benefiting from the GSP it is important to look beyond the provisions of the Implementing Regulation. Specific arrangements may be made in relation to particular states. For example, following the discovery by the EC's anti-fraud service that imports of Vietnamese footwear were effected on the basis of fraudulent certificates of origin between 1994 and 1997, more rigorous administrative systems were put in place in relation to such products.[141]

Article 80 provides that products originating in a beneficiary country benefit from preferential tariffs on submission of either a certificate of origin Form A, the form of which is specified in Annex 17, or in certain cases on submission of an invoice declaration, ie a declaration of origin in a specified form, on an invoice, a delivery note, or any other commercial document which describes the product in sufficient detail to enable it to be identified. The text of the necessary declaration is set out in Annex 18 of the Implementing Regulation.

1.2.1 *Certificate of origin form A*

Certificates of origin are issued on the written application of the exporter, or his authorized representative, and are to be made available to the exporter as soon as the export has taken place or is ensured.[142] Exceptionally, a certificate of origin may be issued after the exportation of goods. This is permitted, for example, where there have been errors or accidental omissions or in special circumstances.[143] One case in which an exceptional circumstance was found to exist was where Indian traders bought goods from a country outside the EC and paid for them in kind rather than in cash. The certificate of origin issued in relation to the goods provided as consideration by the Indian traders stated their destination and gave it as a non-EC country. According to Article 81.8 it should have indicated either 'European Community' or one of the Member States if GSP treatment was to be forthcoming. GSP treatment was, therefore, denied. As the payee had no use for the goods, however, they were sold within the EC. The Court of Justice held that, although treatment according to the GSP regime was correctly denied, provided that the goods in question satisfied the origin criteria, a fresh certificate of origin, giving the destination as an EC state could be retrospectively issued.[144]

1.2.2 *The obligations of the competent authorities*

A certificate of origin Form A is to be issued by the competent authorities of the beneficiary country only if the products to be exported can be considered products originating in that country in accordance with the rules of origin

---

[141] See Council Regulation (EC) 1/2000 of 17 Dec 1999 [2000] OJ L1/1.

[142] Implementing Regulation Art 81.3 and 5. For a discussion of the difference between certificates of origin and certificates of authenticity see Case C–253/99 *Firma Bacardi GmbH v Hauptzollamt Bremerhaven*: Opinion of Jacobs AG of 25 Jan 2001, paras 84–88; Judgment 27 Sep 2001.

[143] Ibid, Art 86. Art 86, contains provisions for the issue of duplicates in the event of theft, loss, or destruction of the certificate. Ibid, Art 88, permits the issue of replacement certificates issued for the purpose of sending goods elsewhere in the Community or in Norway or Switzerland.

[144] Case C–368/92 *Administration des Douanes v Solange Chiffre* [1994] ECR I–605 paras 26–30.

discussed above.[145] The exporter must provide the authorities of the exporting country with the proof that the goods originate in the exporting country.[146] Those authorities have the right to call for documents or carry out such checks as they consider appropriate[147] and the due completion of the applications and certificates are its responsibility.[148] It is the responsibility of the competent authorities of the exporting country to take any necessary steps to verify the origin of the product and to check the other statements on the certificate.[149] So far as the customs authorities of the Member States are concerned, they may require the proof of origin to be translated and may also require the import declaration to be accompanied by a statement from the importer that the goods meet the conditions required for the application of the GSP.[150]

1.2.3 *Invoice declarations*

Invoice declarations are dealt with in Implementing Regulation, Articles 89–92. Generally speaking, they offer reliable exporters a simplified method of establishing origin. An invoice declaration may be made out by two categories of person. First, and most usually, one may be made out by an approved Community exporter. Secondly, an invoice declaration may be made out by any exporter for any consignment consisting of one or more packages the total value of which does not exceed EUR 6000, provided that the authorities of the beneficiary country assist the Community by allowing the authorities of the Member States to verify the authenticity of the document or the accuracy of the information regarding the true origin of the products in question.[151] The declaration must be in English or French and in a specified form.[152] An approved exporter is one who makes frequent shipments of Community goods[153] and who offers to the satisfaction of the customs authorities all the guarantees necessary to verify the originating status of the products as well as the fulfilment of the other administrative requirements.[154] The status of an approved exporter is given by the customs authorities of the Community on any conditions which they consider appropriate.[155] The customs authorities must

---

[145] Implementing Regulation, Art 81.5.

[146] Ibid, Art 81.4. It is for the exporter to be in possession of documents evidencing origin not the importer: see Case C–12/92 *Criminal Proceedings against Edmond Huygen* [1994] ECR I–6381, para 34. Note that the obligation resting on the exporter to obtain a certificate of origin is not to be confused with the obligation to pay the customs duty, even in a case where the certificate of origin is inaccurate: see Case C–97/95 *Pascoal & Filhos Ld[a] v Fazenda Pública* [1997] ECR I–4209 para 47.

[147] Implementing Regulation, Art 81.6. Note that this provision does not mean that the authorities must call for the documents and the importer cannot resist a post-clearance demand on the grounds of *force majeure* by virtue of their failure to do so: see Case C–97/95 *Pascoal & Filos Ld[d] v Fazenda Pública*, n 146 above, paras 65–66.

[148] Implementing Regulation, Art 81.7. [149] Ibid, Art 83.

[150] Ibid, Art 84, and CCC Art 62. [151] Ibid, Art 89.1 and 81.1.

[152] Ibid, Art 89.4. [153] As defined in Implementing Regulation, Art 67.2.

[154] Ibid, Art 90.1. [155] Ibid, Art 90.2.

monitor the use of the authorization given to the authorized exporter.[156] They may withdraw it at any time and must do so where the exporter in question no longer offers the necessary guarantees, does not comply with any conditions which have been imposed, or makes improper use of the authorization in any manner whatever.[157]

1.2.4 *Single or global proofs of origin?*

In some cases there is a certificate or declaration of origin for every imported item, but, in certain circumstances, a single certificate or declaration of origin may be submitted where, for example, the same importer is importing goods within the same CN code from the same exporter over a period of time, not exceeding three months, or where sets of goods are imported.[158] A single proof of origin is also permitted where, at the request of the importer and on the conditions laid down by the authorities of the importing country, dismantled or non-assembled products, within the meaning of General Rule 2a of the Harmonized System and falling within Sections XVI or XVII, or heading numbers 7308 and 9406 of the Harmonized System, are imported by instalments. The proof of origin must be presented on importation of the first instalment.[159]

1.2.5 *Presentation of the proof of origin*

A proof of origin is valid for ten months from the date of issue in the exporting country and must be presented within that period to the customs authorities of the importing country. The authorities of the Member State may accept it later in exceptional circumstances[160] or where the products have been presented to them within the ten-month period.[161] If a certificate is presented within the ten-month period, then the importer will benefit from any applicable suspension of duty notwithstanding that it has expired by the time of presentation.[162] In justifying this position the Court of Justice noted that the GSP was established in the context of the United Nations Conference on Trade and Development and said:

> Considered in that context, the system of tariff preferences, whilst it may involve the requirement of a certificate of origin in order to justify the application of preferential rates, must not be understood as authorizing excessively restrictive administrative measures in the actual machinery for checking the origin of the goods.[163]

The situation is different, however, where customs duties have been re-

---

[156] Implementing Regulation, Art 90.4.
[157] Ibid, Art 90.5.
[158] Ibid, Art 90b.4.
[159] Ibid, Art 82.
[160] Ibid, Art 90b.1and 2.
[161] Ibid, Art 90b.3.
[162] Case 231/81 *Hauptzollamt Würzburg v H Weidenmann GmbH & Co* [1982] ECR 2259 para 7.
[163] Ibid, para 8.

introduced and late production of the certificate can result in the breach of any ceiling on the quantity of imports which are duty-free. In such a case it is necessary for the certificate of origin to be produced before the re-imposition of duty.[164]

1.2.6 *Errors in certificates and declarations*

Slight discrepancies between the information contained in certificates of origin, in an EUR 1, or in an invoice declaration and the information in documents produced to customs authorities for the purpose of carrying out the formalities for importing the products, are not *ipso facto* to render the certificate or declaration null and void, provided that it is duly established that the document corresponds to the products in question.[165] Furthermore, obvious formal errors in certificates or declarations declaration will not cause the documents to be rejected if the errors do not create doubts as to the correctness of the statements made in the documents.[166]

1.2.7 *Transactions for which certificates of origin are unnecessary*

Certificates of origin in Form A and invoice declarations are unnecessary in relation to small packages not exceeding EUR 800 sent between private persons and products not exceeding EUR 1200, forming part of travellers' personal baggage, provided that such imports are not imported by way of trade and have been declared, as meeting the above conditions, without their being any doubt about the veracity of the declaration.[167] Imports which are occasional and consist exclusively of products for the personal use of the recipients or travellers, or their families, are not to be considered as imports by way of trade if it is evident from the nature and quantity of the products that no commercial purpose is in view.[168]

1.2.8 *Evidence of the status of Community goods*

Just as certificates of origin or invoice declarations are required to establish the origin of goods in relation to exporting countries, so also evidence is required to establish the originating status of Community goods. It is provided in the form of an EUR 1 movement certificate, a specimen of which is set out in Annex 21 to the Implementing Regulation, or by an invoice declaration as required by Article 89 of the Implementing Regulation referred to above.[169] The provisions concerning the issue, use, and subsequent verification of certificates of origin apply *mutatis mutandis* to EUR 1 certificates and, in relation to use and verification, to invoice declarations.[170] There are specific provisions relating to products originating in Norway and Switzerland.[171]

---

[164] Case 321/82 *Volkswagenwerk AG v Hauptzollamt Braunschweig* [1983] ECR 3355 paras 8–10.
[165] Implementing Regulation, Art 92 para 1.   [166] Ibid, Art 92 para 2.
[167] Ibid, Art 90c.1, and 2.   [168] Ibid, Art 90c.2.
[169] Ibid, Art 90a.   [170] Ibid, Art 90a.3.
[171] Ibid, Art 67.4 and 5, Arts. 88, 91 and 95.

1.3 *Proof of origin and international agreements*

It is not proposed to review the requirements relating to proof of origin in relation to the individual agreements between the EC and third countries. The
broad outline of the requirements is similar to that applicable in respect of the
GSP, with certificates of origin being required and declarations being accepted
in respect of certain classes of exporters. It is, however, important to highlight
the approach of the Court of Justice to the requirements relating to proof of
origin in agreements with third countries. In considering the agreement
between the EEC and Austria, for example, the Court noted that the need to
prove origin by production of the required documentation has to be strictly
observed to ensure the 'unity and security' of the agreement.[172] Where,
through circumstances beyond the control of the importer and exporter, the
required documentation could not be obtained, and the origin of the goods
could be established by other means, then the requirement that origin be
proved by means of the appropriate documentation may be dispensed with.[173]
The existence of this exceptional treatment should not, however, be regarded
as lowering the standards of conduct which are expected of importers. They
may avoid disadvantages flowing from the conduct of others, but cannot gain
advantage by their own lack of due care.[174]

Of course, the nature of the proof of origin which is required by the agreements is inseparable from the nature of the co-operation between the customs
services in the Community and in the third country concerned. The Court of
Justice noted this when it had to consider the Co-operation Agreement
between the EEC and Yugoslavia. It observed that:

> the system whereby movement certificates are regarded as evidence of the origin of
> products is founded on the principle of mutual reliance and cooperation between
> the competent authorities of the exporting State and those of the importing State. A
> system of that kind cannot therefore function properly unless the procedures for
> administrative cooperation are strictly complied with.[175]

---

[172] See Case C–334/93 *Bonapharma Arzneimittel GmbH v Hauptzollamt Krefeld* [1995] ECR I–319
para 16.
[173] See Case C–334/93 *Bonapharma Arzneimittel GmbH v Hauptzollamt Krefeld*, n 172 above, paras
16–24 and Case C–12/92 *Criminal Proceedings Against Edmond Huygen* [1993] ECR I–6381. In the
former case the relevant circumstances were that an illegal concerted practice ensured that the
certificates of origin were unavailable. In the latter case, the inability of the customs authorities of
the exporting state to establish the origin of the goods through their own negligence permitted the
importer to rely upon the doctrine of *force majeure*. This was defined as 'abnormal and unforeseeable
circumstances beyond the control of the trader concerned, whose consequences could not have
been avoided despite the exercise of all due care': see ibid, para 31. See also Ch 13 n 17.
[174] The ability of Community traders to avoid customs duty liabilities where, for example, an
exporter has behaved fraudulently or the relevant authorities have not fulfilled their obligations is
discussed in Ch 13 below.
[175] See Case C–230/98 *Amministrazione delle Finanze dello Stato v Schiavon Silvano (an insolvent
firm)* [2000] ECR I–3547 at para 53, where the Court relied upon Case C–432/92 *The Queen v
Minister of Agriculture, Fisheries and Food, ex p Anastasiou* [1994] ECR I–3087, paras 38 and 40.

It is, therefore, vital for the body issuing the certificate of origin to be the body which is authorized to issue certificates of origin for the period during which the relevant importations were made.[176]

2. Administrative co-operation

In this section we look first of all at the administrative co-operation which is necessary for the operation of the GSP. The provisions of the Implementing Regulation serve as a guide to administrative co-operation more generally, although clearly, as with substantive rules of origin, in any specific case the rules of the relevant regulation or agreement must be addressed. Then we move on to consider some cases before the Court of Justice dealing with administrative co-operation between exporting and importing countries. The chapter concludes with a brief look at the responsibilities of the Commission and the importer in relation to the origin of the imported goods.

2.1 Administrative co-operation and the GSP

The countries benefiting from the GSP are to inform the Commission of the names and addresses of their governmental authorities which are empowered to issue certificates of origin in Form A. They are also to provide specimens of stamps used by those authorities and the names and addresses of the governmental authorities responsible for the control of the certificates of origin and invoice declarations. The stamps are valid as from the date they are received by the Commission.[177] Furthermore, for the purpose of tariff preferences, every beneficiary country is to comply, or ensure compliance, with the rules concerning the origin of goods, the completion and issue of certificates of origin of Form A, the conditions for the use of invoice declarations, and the conditions concerning methods of administrative cooperation.[178] The Commission is, in turn, to forward the information it has received to the customs authorities of the Member States, indicating the date of entry into use of the stamps. Although the information passed on to the Member States is for official use only, the importer or his representative may consult the specimen impressions of the stamps.[179] The Commission is also to send to the beneficiary countries specimens of the stamps used by Member States to issue EUR 1 movement certificates.[180]

---

[176] See Case C–230/98 *Amministrazione delle Finanze dello Stato v Schiavon Silvano*, n 175 above, at para 54.
[177] Implementing Regulation, Art 93.1.
[178] Ibid, Art 93a.
[179] Ibid, Art 93.1.   [180] Ibid, Art 93.3.

2.1.1 *Subsequent verification of origin*

Article 94 of the Implementing Regulation goes on to deal with the sometimes difficult issue of the verification of certificates of origin issued by a beneficiary country, ie the Form As and the invoice declarations. As the Court of Justice has noted, verification is essential: 'The benefit of [the] preferential system is . . . linked to the origin of goods and the verification of that origin is therefore a necessary element of the system.'[181] Verification is economically as well as administratively important. The Report of OLAF for 1998 highlighted the fact that the losses to the Community's own resources by virtue of the abuse of the system of preferential tariffs, for example, by misdescription of the origin of goods, are 'substantial and increasing'.[182] As an example of abuse the report noted that 18.5 million T-shirts said to originate from one beneficiary country, the Maldives, had never even entered that territory.[183] The abuse is, naturally, not confined to countries benefitting from GSP. For example, one very significant example of abuse arose from the false attribution of Hungarian origin to cars made by a Japanese car manufacturer and imported from Hungary between 1994 and 1997. This cost the Community 32 million ECU.[184]

Notwithstanding the administrative and economic importance of verification, clearly it would not be practicable to verify the origin of all imported products. That would result in excessive delay to customs transactions and render international trade virtually impossible. Instead, the Implementing Regulation provides that subsequent verification is to be carried out at random, or whenever the customs authorities in the Community have 'reasonable doubt' about the authenticity of the documents, the originating status of the products concerned, or the fulfilment of the other requirements of Chapter 2, Section 1, of the Implementing Regulation, which is concerned with GSP.[185] The authorities in the Community may suspend tariff preferences pending verification, but if they do they must offer to release the products to the importer subject to any precautionary measures judged necessary.[186]

In order to facilitate verification by the exporting countries, copies of Form A certificates and any export documents referring to them are to be kept for three years by the competent governmental authorities of the exporting beneficiary country.[187] Where subsequent verification is to take place, the customs authorities in the Community are to return the certificate of origin, Form A, and the invoice if it has been submitted, the invoice declaration, or a copy of these documents, to the competent government authorities in the exporting

---

[181] Case 827/79 *Amministrazione delle Finanze v Enterprise Ciro Acampora* [1980] ECR 3731 at para 5.
[182] See: 'Protecting the Communities' financial interests and the fight against fraud—Annual report 1998'. COM(99)590 final, 17 Dec 1999, at 2.2.1.
[183] See para 2.2.1.3.   [184] See ibid, para 2.2.1.1.
[185] Art 94.1.   [186] Ibid, Art 94.2.
[187] Ibid, Art 94.7.

country. Where appropriate, they are to give their reasons for their enquiry. Any documents and information obtained suggesting that the information given on the proof of origin is incorrect is also to be forwarded in support of the request for verification.[188] The results of subsequent verification, which must be such as to establish whether the proof of origin applies to the goods in question and whether the products can be considered as products originating in the beneficiary country or in the Community, must be communicated to the customs authorities in the Community within six months along with certain documentation.[189] There are specific rules governing the situation when the six-month period is not complied with which give the authorities a further four-month period following a second communication from the Community customs authority. If the real origin of the products is not determined within this period the application of preferential tariff measures is to be refused, save in exceptional circumstances.[190] Where the verification procedure or any other available information, 'appears to indicate' that the provisions governing the GSP are being contravened, the exporting beneficiary country must, either on its own initiative or at the request of the Community, carry out appropriate inquiries or arrange for such enquiries to be carried out with due urgency to identify and to prevent cont raventions. For this purpose the Community may participate in inquiries.[191]

2.2 Case law on relations between importing and exporting states

In *Pascoal & Filhos Ld*[a] [192] the Court set out the basic elements of the relationship between importing and exporting states in relation to the verification of origin. It referred to a number of previous cases[193] and said:

> It follows from that case-law that determination of the origin of goods is based on an allocation of responsibilities as between the authorities of the exporting country and those of the importing country, origin being established by the authorities of the exporting country, if necessary at the request of the authorities of the importing country, and the proper working of that system being monitored jointly by the authorities concerned on both sides. That system is justified by the fact that the

---

[188] Ibid, Art 94.2.   [189] Ibid, Art 94.3.
[190] Ibid, Art 94.5.   [191] Ibid, Art 94.6.
[192] Case C–97/95 *Pascoal & Filhos Ld*[a] *v Fazenda Pública*, n 145 above.
[193] Case 218/83 *Les Rapides Savoyards v Directeur Général des Douanes et Droits Indirects* [1984] ECR 3105, I–2465 (concerning the Agreement on free trade between the EEC and the Swiss Confederation, Case C–12/92 *Criminal proceedings against Edmond Huygen*, n 172 above (concerning the free trade agreement between the EEC and Austria), Case C–432/92 *The Queen v Minister of Agriculture, Fisheries and Food ex p Anastasiou*, n 174 above (concerning the association agreement between the EEC and Cyprus) and in Joined Cases C–153/94 and C–204/94 *The Queen v Commissioners of Customs and Excise ex p Faroe Seafood Co Ltd, Føroya Fiskasøla L/F and another*, n 68 above, (concerning the definition of 'originating products' and methods of administrative cooperation in relation to arrangements with the Faroe Islands).

authorities of the exporting country are in the best position to verify directly the facts which determine origin . . .

In the same judgments, the Court also considered that that mechanism can function only if the customs authorities of the importing country accept the determinations legally made by the authorities of the exporting country. . . .

The Court held that once the state of exportation has carried out its verification the authorities in the state of importation may rely upon the results of that verification and demand duty, if the verification has shown that the statements of origin were inaccurate.[194] The fact that there was a mechanism in the relevant legislation for reconciling differences between the state of importation and the state of exportation did not alter this conclusion.[195]

Although it is possible for the state of importation to rely upon the statements of the state of exportation, it is not inevitable that the two states will agree with each other. Where the results of the verification by the exporting state indicate that the certificate of origin was inaccurate, the importing state may take account of other evidence relating to the origin of goods which supports the certificate of origin.[196] Sometimes the opposite situation occurs and the importing country concludes that the certificate of origin was wrongly issued and the authorities in the exporting country disagree. This was the case in *Faroe Seafood*[197] in which the state of exportation maintained that its certificates of origin were accurate, even in opposition to the views of the Commission which were supported by the findings of a mission which it had sent to examine the origin of certain goods. The Court of Justice, therefore, had to decide whether the principles outlined above applied in such circumstances. It noted that recognition of the decisions of the authorities of the exporting country by the customs authorities of the Member States is necessary in order that the Community can, in turn, demand that the authorities of countries with which it has concluded agreements accept the decisions, taken by the customs authorities of the Member States, regarding the origin of products exported from the Community to those non-member countries. The Court also pointed out that the functioning of that system did not encroach on the fiscal autonomy of the Community and its Member States, or of the non-member

[194] *Pascoal & Filhos Ldª v Fazenda Pública*, n 145 above, para 37.

[195] Ibid, para 38. Where there are mechanisms for reconciling differences it is nevertheless important that they are not ignored: see Joined Cases T–186/97, T–190/97–T–192/97, T–210/97, T–211/97, T–216/97–T–218/97, T–279/97, T–280/97, T–293/97, and T–147/99 *Kaufring AG and others v Commission*, 10 May 2001 at para 270.

[196] Case C–12/92 *Criminal proceedings against Edmond Huygen and others*, n 173 above, at paras 19–28. The authorities in the country of export (Austria) concluded that a product was not of Austrian origin, but had not made contact with its Austrian purchaser. The authorities in the country of import (Belgium) held an invoice showing that the machine had been purchased by the Austrian purchaser. In these circumstances, it was clearly just to permit the Belgian authorities to take account of the invoice.

[197] Joined Cases C–153/94 and C–204/94 *The Queen v Commissioners of Customs and Excise ex p Faroe Seafood Co Ltd, Føroya Fiskasøla L/F and another*, n 68 above.

countries concerned, because the rules laid down in the agreement in question were established on the basis of reciprocal obligations placing the parties on an equal footing in their dealings with each other.[198] The Court concluded, however, that the need for mutual recognition of decisions did not arise in the same way where the preferential system was based, as it was in *Faroe Seafood*, on a unilateral Community measure and not an international agreement.[199] That there was no need for recognition of the views of the exporting country was made even clearer in that case by the fact that the competent authorities of the exporting country were not disputing the facts found by the mission, but the mission's assessment of the facts in the light of the relevant customs rules of the Community. As the Court said: 'There is nothing to suggest that the authorities of the non-member country have the power to bind the Community and its Member States in their interpretation of Community rules of the kind at issue in this case.'[200] The Court also noted that there was no procedure for settling disputes over origin in the regulation, for example, by a joint customs committee and that such a procedure had been present in cases such as *Les Rapides Savoyards*, in which the Court had concluded that recognition by the importing country of the exporting country's determinations was necessary.[201] It followed, therefore, that in *Faroe Seafood*, the customs authorities of the importing Member State could proceed with post-clearance recovery of the duty notwithstanding that the customs authorities of the exporting country disagreed with them over the question of the origin of the goods.

2.3 The Commission and subsequent verification

The role and duties of the Commission have been considered generally in Chapter 4, however, it should be noted here that the role of the Commission is frequently crucial in effecting subsequent verification. In the first place, Member States communicate information to it regarding the origin of goods and the quantities of imports pursuant to their obligations of mutual assistance and co-operation[202] and pursuant to other more specific regulations.[203]

---

[198] Ibid, at para 22 and Case 218/83 *Les Rapides Savoyards v Directeur Général des Douanes et Droits Indirects*, n 192 above, at paras 27 and 29.

[199] n 68 above, para 24.   [200] Ibid, para 25.

[201] Joined Cases C–153/94 and C–204/94 *The Queen v Commissioners of Customs and Excise ex p Faroe Seafood Co Ltd, Føroya Fiskasøla L/F and another*, n 68 above at para 26.A settlement procedure was also contained in the agreement which replaced the regulation governing relations with the Faroe Islands at paras 27 and 28. The free trade agreement which replaced the regulation is referred to above.

[202] Council Regulation (EC) 515/97 of 13 Mar 1997 [1997] OJ L82/1 corrigendum [1998] OJ L288/55. See Arts 17 and 18.

[203] The Implementing Regulation,Art 308d, provides that where Community surveillance of preferential imports is to be made, the Member States are to provide to the Commission once each month, or more frequently if the Commission requests, details of quantities of products put into free circulation with the benefit of preferential tariff arrangements during the previous months.

In the second place, expert representatives of the Commission not infrequently visit beneficiary countries on missions to establish the origin of products. Such missions may be carried out under the regulation providing for mutual assistance between the customs authorities of Member States and their co-operation with the EC Commission.[204] Articles 19–22 deal with relations with third countries and Article 20 permits the EC Commission to carry out missions in third countries in co-ordination and close co-operation with the competent authorities of the Member States.

The Commission has not only powers in relation to the verification of origin, but also duties. This was made clear in *Eyckeler & Malt* [205] in which the Court of First Instance pointed out that the Commission was obliged to ensure that quotas relating to products with a particular origin were properly applied and not exceeded. The duty of good administration was considered in more detail in chapter 4. As was explained there, it is a general duty, not confined to the Commission's conduct in relation to quotas. A duty to check the application of a quota arises, in part, as the corollary of the Member States' obligation to transfer information on imports to the Commission. As the Court said in *Eyckeler & Malt*, the requirement to communicate information 'would have been meaningless if it had not been coupled with the obligation, on the Commission to check that the quota was properly applied'.[206] It is not, of course, only in relation to quotas that the lack of any obligation on the part of the Commission would render meaningless a requirement to communicate information to it.

2.4 *The importer and subsequent verification*

When verification shows that a certificate of origin is inaccurate, the importer will be likely, subsequently, to be faced with a claim for post-clearance recovery of customs duty. The circumstances in which this may be resisted are explored in Chapter 13 below. This section is concerned with the formal responsibilities of the importer in relation to the verification of origin and an explanation of why it is that responsibilities are imposed upon him or her.

The total quantities put into free circulation since the first day of the period concerned are to be reported. The transmission of the 'surveillance reports' to the Commission is to be made no later than the 15th day of the month following the end of the period in respect of which the report is made. Information within the reports is to be treated as confidential. The information is nevertheless to be made available to litigants who are, eg, disputing post-clearance recovery demands.

[204] As noted above.

[205] Case T–42/96 *Eyckeler & Malt AG v Commission* [1998] ECR II-401 paras. 165–166. The case was appealed: see [1998] OJ C258/14 as Case C–163/98 P. It was removed from the register on 19 May 2000. See also Case T–50/96 *Primex Produkte Import-Export GmbH & Co. KG, Gebr Kruse GmbH, Interporc Im-und Export GmbH v Commission* [1998] ECR II 3773, para 75. The case was appealed: see [1999] OJ C1/11 as Case C–417/198 P. It was removed from the register on 10 May 2000.

[206] See n 204 above, para 166.

At the outset it must be emphasized that the importer bears the burden of proving the origin of goods and that burden is not completely discharged by the presentation of the certificate or statement of origin. Where subsequent verification casts doubt on the certificate or statement the importer must be able to provide further evidence if preferential treatment is to be obtained.[207] If he cannot do so, then the goods will be regarded as of unknown origin.[208] Furthermore, the possibility of verification after presentation of the certificate or statement of origin prevents an importer from being able to establish a legitimate expectation that future certificates or statements will be accepted.[209]

The Court of Justice noted in *Acampora* that an importer can suffer problems where he has acted in good faith and a certificate of origin is subsequently found to be false. In an important passage it stated that:

> It must be recognised that the possibility of checking after importation without the importer's having been previously warned may cause him difficulties when in good faith he has thought he was importing goods benefiting from tariff preferences in reliance on certificates which, unbeknown to him, were incorrect or falsified. It must however be pointed out that in the first place the Community does not have to bear the adverse consequences of the wrongful acts of the suppliers of its nationals, in the second place the importer can attempt to obtain compensation from the perpetrator of the fraud and in the third place, in calculating the benefits from trade in goods likely to enjoy tariff preferences, a prudent trader aware of the rules must be able to assess the risks inherent in the market which he is considering and accept them as normal trade risks.[210]

The Court of Justice has observed that permitting an importer to escape liability to customs duty in the circumstances outlined above would give him or her an incentive to refrain from verifying the accuracy of information supplied by the exporter and from verifying the exporter's good faith.[211] It has also noted that: 'it is the responsibility of traders to make the necessary arrangements in their contractual relations in order to guard against the risks of an action for

[207] Case C–97/95 *Pascoal & Filhos Ld³ v Fazenda Pública*, n 145 above, para 39. See also Joined Cases 121/91 and 122/91 *CT Control (Rotterdam) BV and JCT Benelux BV v Commission* [1993] ECR I–3873 at para 39.
[208] Case C–12/92 *Criminal Proceedings Against Edmond Huygen*, n 172 above, paras 16–18.
[209] Case C–97/95 *Pascoal & Filhos Ld³ v Fazenda Pública*, n 145 above, at para 40. See also Joined Cases C–153/94 and C–204/94 *The Queen v Commissioners of Customs & Excise, ex parte Faroe Seafood Co. Ltd Føroya Fiskasøla L/F and another* at n 68 above, at para 93, and Joined Cases 98/83 and 230/83 *Van Gend & Loos and Expeditiebedrijf Wim Bosman v Commission* [1984] ECR 3763, para 20.
[210] Case 827/79 *Amministrazione delle Finanze v Enterprise Ciro Acampora* at n 181 at para 8. See also Case C–97/95 *Pascoal & Filhos Ld³ v Fazenda Pública*, n 145 above, at para 59 and Joined Cases T–10/97 and T–11/97 *Unifrigo Gadus Srl and CPL Imperial 2 SpA v Commission* [1998] ECR II–2231 at para 62.
[211] C–97/95 *Pascoal & Filhos Ld³ v Fazenda Pública*, n 145 above, at para 57.

post-clearance recovery'.[212] A further justification for imposing the risk of fraud on the trader was given in a report presented by the Commission in 1998. It said:

> Although the Commission has negotiated administrative co-operation arrange-ments with all the beneficiary countries to which it accords preferential tariffs, each country retains control of the legal system in which inquiries involving contentious transactions are conducted. When collecting evidence, Community investigators are very much at the mercy of external factors such as political or commercial inter-est, the effectiveness of the local legal system and the effectiveness and goodwill of the local administration.
>
> For this reason, the Commission has always insisted on the fact that importers should be entirely responsible for the accuracy of the import declarations made in their name, holding them financially liable for any payments evaded at the expense of the Community budget.[213]

Traders may not always find convincing these justifications for placing the risks inherent in the preferential tariff regime entirely on them. Indeed, recently, the Court of First Instance has made it clear that the risks which the traders must take are not unlimited and has said in a case in which an associ-ation agreement was not properly implemented that: '. . . in the absence of clear and precise information on the part of the national or Community authorities as to the nature of the irregularities in the operation of the agree-ment, a diligent importer cannot be required to remedy the deficiencies of the parties to the agreement.'[214]

This recognition that the risks imposed on traders cannot be unlimited is welcome. In some cases it may be possible for importers to protect themselves by appropriately drafted contracts. They may, for example, be able to agree with the exporter that the purchase price of goods is not to be paid until after the issue of a customs duty assessment so that duty due may be deducted from the purchase price.[215] In many cases, however, the possibility of obtaining contractual protection is more apparent than real. In the first place, depending upon the market in question, an importer may well take the view that it must accept the trading terms offered or be obliged to obtain products from another source. Secondly, even if some contractual protection is negotiated, it may

---

[212] C-97/95 *Pascoal & Filhos Ldᵃ v Fazenda Pública*, n 145 above, at para 60, Joined Cases C-153/94 and C-204/94 *The Queen v Commissioners of Customs & Excise, ex parte Faroe Seafood Co. Ltd Føroya Fiskasøla L/F and another*, at n 68, at para 114, and Joined Cases T-10/97 and T-11/97 *Unifrigo Gadus Srl and CPL Imperial 2 SpA v Commission*, n 210 above, at para 63.

[213] Protecting the Communities' financial interests and the fight against fraud: Annual Report 1998 COM/1999/590 final at 2/.2.1 para [37].

[214] Joined Cases T-186/97, T-187/97 and others *Kaufring AG and others v Commission*, n 195 above, at para 300.

[215] Case T-75/95 *Günzler Aluminium GmbH v Commission of the European Communities* [1996] ECR II-497, para 48. In that case, the trader's failure to abide by its contract meant that it did not show the degree of care required by a trader within Art 220.2(b) CCC. See further Ch 13.

easily be rendered ineffective, either because the supplier chooses to use a special purpose vehicle which is easily liquidated, or simply because obtaining contractual remedies is impractical. An example of a case, in which contractual protection proved worthless has come before the Court of Justice in *Günzler*.[216] In this case a provision in an importation contract requiring a Yugoslavian exporter to pay customs duty proved worthless in the turmoil resulting from the break-up of the Yugoslavian republic. If the Commission is 'at the mercy of external factors', as OLAF put it, so too is the trader.

The difficulties which traders face have, however, been acknowledged by the Community institutions and recent amendments to CCC, Article 220, discussed in Chapter 4, do indeed take greater account of the trader's position. Furthermore, attempts have been made to ensure that the preferential regime is more secure. In 1997, the Commission set out to simplify the rules of origin, provide programmes of technical assistance for the beneficiary countries, better analysis of risk in sensitive areas, and tighter application of the preferential arrangement.[217] So far as concerns the GSP, the Community has greater scope for action against fraud than before with amongst other things power to withdraw, or suspend, preferential treatment in the event of fraud or the failure to provide administrative co-operation for the verification of certificates of origin in Form A.[218] Furthermore, the Commission is working on a programme for the renewal of all preferential arrangements. It is intended to improve administration and the prevention of fraud, to clarify the responsibilities of operators and customs authorities, and to harmonize procedures relating to verification, acceptance of guarantees, and the recovery of duty. It is also intended to increase the role of the Community in the issuing of certificates of origin and the responsibility of the customs authorities of beneficiary countries for the prevention of fraud.[219]

---

[216] Ibid, paras 3 and 8. See also Joined Cases 98/83 and 230/83 *Van Gend en Loos and Another v Commission* [1984] ECR 3763, para 16, where it is indicated that the customs agents could not recover the customs duty in question from their client because they had gone into liquidation.

[217] See Annual Report 1997, COM(97)402 final, Chapter 2, point 2.2.1, at 27.

[218] See Council Regulation (EC) 2820/1998 of 21 Dec. 1998 [1998] OJ L357/1and Art 22—especially Art 22.1(d)–26.

[219] See COM(99)590 final, 17 Dec 1999, n 213 above, para 3.2 at 3.2 paras [65] and [66].

8

The Valuation of Goods

Customs duties, as we saw in Chapter 5, may be specific or imposed on an *ad valorem* basis. Uniformity of treatment has been achieved in relation to specific duties by use of supplementary units, units of account, and now the euro. In relation to *ad valorem* duties, however, uniformity of treatment is ensured by establishing a uniform basis for valuing the goods in question. As the Court of Justice put it soon after the UK joined the Community:

> The functioning of a customs union requires of necessity the uniform determination of the valuation for customs purposes of goods imported from third countries so that the level of protection effected by the Common Customs Tariff is the same throughout the whole Community.[1]

Later on the Court expanded its reasoning, saying that the measures imposing rules for the valuation of goods were established:

> in order to ensure that the value for customs purposes is determined in a uniform manner in Member States so that the level of protection given by the Common Customs Tariff is the same throughout the Community and any deflection of trade and activities and any distortion of competition which might arise from differences between national provisions is thereby prevented and that equal treatment of importers as regards the collection of common customs tariff duties is ensured.[2]

As well as being essential for the imposition of *ad valorem* duty, the provisions relating to customs value are, unless otherwise provided, used to determine the values to which certain headings or sub-headings in the CN refer, and in relation to non-tariff measures of the Community governing specific fields relating to trade in goods.[3] They are also relevant for value added tax.

The Community's own measures on valuation have, of course, existed since the creation of the customs union.[4] At the present time, the relevant provisions are contained in CCC, Title II Chapter 3 (Articles 28–36) in Title V of the Implementing Regulation (Articles 141–181a) and Annexes 23–29.[5]

---

[1] Case 8/73 *Hauptzollamt Bremerhaven v Massey-Ferguson GmbH* [1973] ECR 897 at para 3.

[2] Case 248/80 *Kommanditgesellschaft in Firma Gebrüder Glunz v Hauptzollamt Hamburg-Waltershof* [1982] ECR 197 at para 10. This formulation is an adaptation of recitals 6 to 8 in Council Regulation (EEC) 803/68 of 27 June 1968 on the valuation of goods for customs purposes [1968] OJ L148/6.

[3] See CCC, Article 28 and Rule 1 in 'C General rules applicable both to nomenclature and to duties' in Annex 1 to Council Regulation (EEC) 2658/87 introduced by Commission Regulation (EC) 2204/99. See, eg, Case 91/74 *Hauptzollamt Hamburg-Ericus v Hamburger Import-Kompanie GmbH* [1975] ECR 643.

[4] See Regulation (EEC) 803/68, n 2 above.

[5] Annex 23, which contains Interpretative Notes on Customs Value to Arts of the CCC and the Implementing Regulation and Annex 24, which concerns the use of generally accepted account-

At the outset of any consideration of valuation matters it is important to note that the responsibility for valuing particular goods rests with the customs authorities of Member States. This means that companies can, on occasions, be faced with divergent valuations of identical transactions in different areas of the Community. There is no way, of course, that the customs administrations of Member States can be made to follow each other's decisions[6] and the Commission's role in this context is 'to narrow down as much as possible the scope of divergent or incorrect application by agreeing on common rules or guidelines in the Customs Code Committee'.[7] This Committee has a customs valuation section which can offer Member States a platform for doing this. It attempts to establish rules and guidelines without examining specific cases. It also deals with the co-ordination of valuation issues dealt with in the WTO and WCO.[8]

As the latter comment indicates, international agreements in relation to valuation are of great importance in Community customs law. These are considered in section A. Section B puts the topic of valuation in a Community context, whilst section C is concerned with the use of the transaction value as the primary criterion for valuation. The first part considers which sale is relevant in determining the transaction value and the second discusses what is meant by the price actually paid or payable. The third part concerns the limitations on the use of the transaction value. In section D, the alternatives to the use of transaction value are discussed. In section E those items which are to be excluded from the calculation of customs value are considered and the chapter concludes with by examining declarations of value in section F.

A. CUSTOMS VALUATION AND INTERNATIONAL AGREEMENTS

A fundamental provision relating to valuation in relation to customs duty is Article VII of GATT 1947, now GATT 1994. Article VII provides that:

The value for customs purposes of imported merchandise should be based on the

ing principles for the determination of customs value, are both of general significance in relation to the basis of valuation. Reference is made to both of these annexes in this chapter but, inevitably, their contents cannot be fully considered. Practitioners should consult them carefully in considering any specific case. See also the Compendium of Customs Valuation texts of the Customs Code Committee which includes the texts of commentaries and conclusions of the Committee on various matters and summaries of various judgments.

[6] As the Commission pointed out in its replies to paras 41–43 of the Court of Auditors Special Report 23/2000 concerning valuation of imported goods for customs purposes (customs valuation) [2001] OJ C84/1. The Report and the Commission's replies raise certain specific valuation issues such as the impact of manufacturers' guarantees, air transport costs, and royalties and licence fees, and examine the more general problems which arise in co-ordinating the valuation activities of the Member States. See also p 293 n 9.

[7] See the Commission's replies to paras 23–26 of the Special Report, n 6 above.

[8] See the Commission's replies to paras 5, 23–26, and 29 of the Special Report, n 6 above.

actual value of the imported merchandise on which duty is assessed or of like merchandise, and should not be based on the value of merchandise of national origin or on arbitrary or fictitious values.[9]

'Actual value' is defined as the price at which the merchandise or similar merchandise is sold, or offered for sale, in the ordinary course of trade under fully competitive conditions. The time and place of sale are matters to be determined by domestic legislation. To the extent that the price of goods is governed by its quantity, the price to be considered is to be uniformly related either to comparable quantities, or to quantities which are not less favourable to the importers than those in which the greater volume of the merchandise is sold in the trade between the exporting and importing countries.[10] Where the value of goods is not ascertainable in this way then, it should be based on the nearest ascertainable equivalent of such value.[11] Article VII states that, in determining value, one should not include the amount of any internal tax, applicable within the country of origin or export, from which the imported product has been exempted or has been or will be relieved by means of refund.[12] It contains specific provisions relating to currency conversions.[13] The article concludes by stating that the bases and methods for determining value should be stable and publicised sufficiently to enable traders to estimate, with a reasonable degree of certainty, the customs value of goods.

The principles of valuation set out in Article VII and the interpretative notes annexed to the Agreement had to be incorporated into the domestic law of Member States by virtue of the Brussels Convention on the Valuation of Goods for Customs Purposes, which was signed by all Member States on 15 December 1950 and entered into force on 25 July 1953. As was noted in the preamble to Regulation (EEC) No 803/1968,[14] and by the Court of Justice,[15] this was an inadequate basis for the determination of valuation in a customs union, notwithstanding the fact that all the original Member States were parties to it, because it gave the contracting parties some discretion about exactly what was incorporated into domestic law. It followed that a Community statement of the principles of valuation was necessary. The regulation provided this, stating that the fundamental basis for valuing goods for the purposes of Community customs law was the 'normal price'.

1. *The normal price and the transaction value*

The 'normal price' was defined in Article 1 of the regulation as 'the price which [the goods] would fetch, at the time [specified] . . . , on a sale in the open

---

[9] Art VII para 2(a).   [10] Ibid, Para 2(b).
[11] Ibid, Para 2(c).   [12] Ibid, Para 3.
[13] Para 4(a)(b).   [14] Of 27 June 1968 [1968] OJ L148/6.
[15] Case 8/73 *Hauptzollamt Bremerhaven v Massey-Ferguson GmbH*, n 1 above, at para 3.

market between a buyer and a seller independent of each other'. In Article 1(2) it stated that the 'normal price' of any imported goods was to be determined on the assumption that the goods were delivered to the buyer at the port or place of introduction into the country of importation. Furthermore, it was to include all costs incidental to the sale and delivery of the goods at the port or place of introduction, but was to exclude any duties or taxes applicable in the country of importation.

The concept of the normal price was, however, replaced following further work carried out by the international community in the Tokyo Round of trade negotiations in 1973–1979. The negotiations produced an Agreement on the Implementation of Article VII of GATT to which the EC was a party.[16] This Agreement established that the fundamental basis for customs value was to be the 'transaction value'. The Community, therefore, repealed Council Regulation (EEC) 803/68 and introduced the criterion of 'transaction value' into domestic Community law in Council Regulation (EEC) 1224/80.[17] The introduction of the concept of transaction value into customs valuation was of great importance. In the words of the Commission it:

> . . . had the probably intended effect of inverting the "balance of power" between the operators and the customs administrations in this field. No longer is it in principle the declarant's burden to prove that the paid price is in agreement with the notion of a 'normal price', but the price indicated by the declarant is in principle the correct one unless challenged by customs.[18]

Following the conclusion of the Uruguay Round, the contracting parties annexed to it an amended Agreement on Implementation of Article VII of the General Agreement on Tariffs and Trade 1994 to the Marrakesh Agreement.[19] It contains twenty-four Articles and three annexes. The first of the annexes consists of interpretative notes. The second establishes, under the auspices of the WCO, the technical committee on customs valuation. The committee's purpose is to ensure uniformity in the interpretation and application of the Agreement on Implementation[20] and the statements by, and explanatory notes of, the valuation committee are frequently important in considering

---

[16] Implemented by Council Decision 271/80 [1980] OJ L71/1. The Court of Justice has referred to the Agreement for assistance on a number of occasions see: Case 17/89 *Hauptzollamt Frankfurt am Main-Ost v Deutsche Olivetti GmbH* [1990] ECR I–2301 paras 17 and 18; Case 290/84 *Hauptzollamt Schweinfurt v Mainfrucht Obstverwertung GmbH* [1985] ECR 3909 para 29 and cases noted under 'Simple equitable and commercial—not arbitrary or fictitious' below.

[17] Of 28 May 1980 [1980] OJ L134/1; see in particular Art 3. This regulation as amended, was repealed on the introduction of the Community Customs Code: see CCC, Article 251.1.

[18] See the Court of Auditor's Special Report No 23/2000, n 6 above and the Commission's replies to para 7.

[19] See Annex 1A to the Final Act of the Uruguay Round [1994] OJ L336/119 implemented into Community law by Council Decision (EC) 800/94 of 22 Dec 1994 [1994] OJ L336/1.

[20] Art 1, Annex II to the Agreement on Implementation. Its role is an advisory one: see Annex II Art 2(a), ibid.

valuation matters.[21] The third annex contains specific provisions for developing countries.

Although the Agreement is said to elaborate the provisions of Article VII, it does rather more than that. Article 1 sets out that, subject to certain provisos, 'The customs value of imported goods shall be the transaction value, that is the price actually paid or payable for the goods when sold for export to the country of importation adjusted in accordance with the provisions of Article 8'. Article 8 provides that there is to be added to the price actually paid or payable for imported goods a number of costs to the extent that they are incurred by the buyer and are not included in that price. Articles 2–7 set out alternative ways of establishing the value of goods if value cannot be determined under Article 1. The alternatives are, to use:

(i)   the value of identical goods sold for export to the same country of importation and exported at about the same time as the goods in question;[22] or

(ii)   the value of similar goods sold subject to the same conditions;[23] or

(iii)   the unit price of the goods, identical or similar goods;[24] or

(iv)   a computed cost based on the costs of materials and production, profits, general expenses and certain other specified items;[25] or finally,

(v)   a reasonable means consistent with the Agreement and Article VII on the basis of data available in the country of importation.[26]

Having outlined the terms of the Agreement, we can now turn to the Community law on valuation for customs duty purposes.

B. VALUATION AND COMMUNITY LAW

1. *Simple, equitable, and commercial—not arbitrary or fictitious*

As we have seen, the Agreement on the Interpretation of Article VII of GATT is one of the foundations of Community law in this area. The Court of Justice has, on occasions, had recourse to the Agreement in articulating the basic requirements of Community valuation. In *Olivetti*, for example it observed that 'It is evident from the fifth recital in the preamble to the Agreement that the criteria adopted for determining the customs value must be simple, equitable and consistent with commercial practices'.[27] Earlier the Court of Justice had

---

[21] The opinions of the committee are not binding but the Court of Justice does have regard to them: see, in relation to the original agreement, Case 183/85 *Hauptzollamt Itzehoe v H J Repenning GmbH* [1986] ECR 1873 at para 13 and Case 7/83 *Ospig Textilgesellschaft KG W Ahlers v Hauptzollamt Bremen-Ost* [1984] ECR 609 paras 16 and 17.

[22] Art 2 of the Agreement on Implementation.   [23] Ibid, Art 3.

[24] Ibid, Art 5.   [25] Ibid, Art 6.

[26] Ibid, Art 7.

restated the fourth recital to the Agreement, noting that '. . . the objective of the Community rules on customs valuation is to introduce a fair, uniform and neutral system excluding the use of arbitrary or fictitious customs values'.[28] This objective is a powerful one. In one case, it required the Court of Justice to provide for the reduction in the customs value of damaged goods, even where, at the relevant time, there was no regulation in place permitting such a reduction.[29] For the most part, of course, the objective is achieved by the customs authorities of the Member States operating within the tightly controlled limits set by the bases of valuation in the CCC and certain other fundamental rules, such as the requirement that they must utilize information prepared in a manner consistent with the generally accepted accounting principles in the country which is appropriate for the article in question.[30]

1.1 *Rates of exchange*

In determining a fair and commercial valuation of products, an appropriate rate of exchange must be used where a relevant currency differs from that of the Member State in which the valuation is made. The CCC requires the competent authorities of Member States to publish the rate of exchange to be used in the valuation process. In the absence of any such rate, the rate of exchange is to be determined according to the committee procedure. The rate is to reflect as accurately as possible the current value of the foreign currency in commercial transactions in the Member State's currency.[31]

---

[27] Case 17/89 *Hauptzollamt Frankfurt am Main-Ost v Deutsche Olivetti GmbH*, n 16 above, at para 18.

[28] See Case C–11/89 *Unifert v Hauptzollamt Münster* [1990] ECR I–2275 at para 35 and Case C–15/99 *Hans Sommer GmbH & Co KG v Hauptzollamt Bremen*, 19 Oct 2000, para 25. See also Case 183/85 *Hauptzollamt Itzehoe v H J Repenning GmbH*, n 21 above, at para 14 and Case 7/83 *Ospig Textilgesellschaft-KG W Ahlers v Hauptzollamt Bremen-Ost*, n 21 above, at para 17.

[29] See Case 183/85 *Hauptzollamt Itzehoe v H J Repenning GmbH*, n 28 above. The goods in question were consignments of meat which had been damaged in the country of export and lost value accordingly. See now Implementing Regulation, Art 145, discussed below.

[30] See Implementing Regulation, Annex 24 para 2. 'Generally accepted accounting principles' are defined in Annex 24 para 1 as referring to 'the recognised consensus or substantial authoritative support within a country at a particular time as to which economic resources and obligations should be recorded as assets and liabilities, which changes in assets and liabilities should be recorded, how the assets and liabilities and changes in them should be measured, what information should be disclosed and how it should be disclosed, and which financial statements should be prepared. These standards may be broad guidelines of general application as well as detailed practices and procedures'. As Annex 24 para 2 makes clear, it follows from the foregoing that sometimes the accounting standards of the country of production may be used and sometimes the standards of the country of importation. For examples, see nn 116, and 130 below.

[31] CCC, Art 35. See also Implementing Regulation, Arts 168 (which contains certain definitions) to 172. Art 169 states that where factors used to determine value are not expressed in the currency of the Member State carrying out the valuation, the rate of exchange shall be that recorded on the second-last Wednesday of a month and published on that or the following day. Such

2. Valuation for customs duty purposes only

The fact that a valuation of goods for customs purposes is intended to comply with the requirements set out above and is to avoid fictitious and arbitrary valuation, does not mean that the value which is established for customs purposes is applicable generally for other purposes.[32] As we shall see, there are a number of adjustments to be made to the transaction value in determining the customs value of a product. Furthermore, where there are a number of sales for export from which customs value may be deduced, a declarant may choose which value should be declared for customs duty purposes. As a result, the price attributed to products for the purposes of tax on income, by virtue of, say, transfer pricing provisions in a double tax treaty or domestic legislation, may be quite different from the transaction value which is relevant for customs duty. As the Court of Justice put it in *Chatain*: 'the determination of the value for customs purposes in accordance with the rules . . . cannot have the effect of requiring the fiscal and financial authorities of the Member States to accept that valuation for purposes other than the application of the Common Customs Tariff'.[33] Consequently, a Member State is, as one would expect, free to apply legislation in areas other than customs duty so as to reduce the value placed upon a transaction for purposes other than those of customs duty.[34] From the point of view of the importer, it should be noted that a large disparity between the prices attributable to the same transaction, for the purposes of, say, customs duty and income or corporation tax, may prove difficult to justify.

---

a rate shall ordinarily be used for the following calendar month unless superseded by a rate established under Art 171 (see below). Where such a rate is not so recorded, or if recorded is not so published, the last rate recorded for the currency in question, published within the preceding 14 days, shall be deemed to be the rate recorded on that Wednesday. Where a rate of exchange cannot be determined under Art 169, the rate of exchange shall reflect as effectively as possible the current value of the currency in question in commercial transactions in terms of the currency of that Member State (Art 170). Art 171 provides at 1. that where the rate of exchange recorded on the last, as opposed to the second-last, Wednesday of the month and published on that or the following day, differs by 5% or more from the rate established under Art 169, it shall replace that rate from the first Wednesday of the following calendar month. Where a rate, recorded on a Wednesday and published on that or the following day, differs by 5% or more from the rate being used, it shall replace the rate being used for the remainder of the month, unless itself superseded (Art 171.2). If a rate of exchange is not recorded, or if recorded not published as provided above, then the rate recorded shall for the purposes of Art 171.1 and 2 be the rate most recently recorded and published prior to the Wednesday in question (Art 171.3). Where customs authorities authorize a declarant to supply certain details in the form of a periodic declaration, the authorization may, if the declarant requests, provide that a single exchange rate be used, being the rate, established as above, which is applicable on the first day of the period covered by the declaration in question (Art 172).

[32] Case 65/79 *Procureur de la République v René Chatain* [1980] ECR 1345 applied in Case 54/80 *Procureur de la République v Samuel Wilner* [1980] ECR 3673.

[33] Case 65/79 *Procureur de la République v René Chatain*, n 32 above, para 16.

[34] See Case 65/79 *Procureur de la République v René Chatain*, n 32 above, at paras 17 and 18 and Case 54/80 *Procureur de la République v Samuel Wilner*, n 32 above, at paras 6–9.

3. *The transaction value and alternatives to it*

According to the fifth preamble to the Agreement on the Impementation of Article VII of the GATT 94, the 'transaction value' should be used 'to the greatest extent possible' in ascertaining the customs value of goods. This primary basis for the valuation of imported goods for customs purposes is introduced into Community law by CCC, Article 29 which defines it as the price actually paid or payable for the goods when sold for export to the customs territory of the Community, subject to specific qualifications.[35]

Four alternative methods of establishing the customs value are provided, in CCC, Article 30, as we shall see below. These are to be employed where the transaction value cannot be utilised. To the extent that the customs value of goods cannot be ascertained by these alternative methods, it is to be determined on the basis of data available in the Community, using reasonable means consistent with the principles and general provisions of the Agreement on the Implementation of Article VII of GATT 94 and Article VII itself.[36] There are, in addition, specific provisions relating to the valuation of particular products. CCC, Article 34 provides that specific rules may be established in relation to the customs value of carrier media for use in data processing equipment and bearing data or instructions[37] and CCC, Article 36 allows for the customs value of perishable goods, which are usually delivered on consignment to be determined under simplified rules at the request of the declarant.[38]

Article 36 also provides that the rules in the CCC are without prejudice to the provisions, regarding the determination of the value for customs purposes, of goods released for free circulation after being assigned a different customs-approved treatment or use. Specific provisions were introduced in relation to

---

[35] CCC, Art 29.1. Note that the customs value need not be the transaction value where goods are used in a third country between the time of sale and the time of entry into free circulation: Implementing Regulation, Art 147.2.

[36] CCC, Art 31.1.

[37] Implementing Regulation, Art 167, provides that, notwithstanding CCC, Arts 29–33, the customs value of imported carrier media bearing data, or instructions for use in data processing equipment, is to be determined taking into account only the cost or value of the carrier medium itself. The cost or value of the data or instructions is excluded, provided that they are distinguished from the cost or value of the carrier medium in question. 'Carrier medium' excludes integrated circuits, semiconductors, and similar devices or articles incorporating such circuits or devices and data or instructions does not include sound, cinematographic, or video recordings: Art 167.2. The provisions on carrier media were introduced in 1985 following a Decision by the Committee on Customs Valuation set up by Art 18 of the Agreement on the Implementation of Art VII of GATT: see Case 79/89 *Brown Boveri & Cie AG v Hauptzollamt Mannheim* [1991] ECR I–1853. The Court stated that under the Decision, exclusion of the cost or value of data or instructions was permitted, although neither the Decision, nor the Community regulation which was passed consequent upon it, was retroactive. It has been suggested that there is now no need for Art 167 as, from 1 Jan 2000, most carrier media bearing data or instructions can be imported free of customs duty.

[38] These are contained in Implementing Regulation, Arts 173–177 and are considered below.

processing under customs control pursuant to this Article, although they have been repealed as from 1 July 2001 by Commission Regulation (EC) 993/2001.[39] These provided that where processed products were released for free circulation, their customs value had to be one of four values chosen by the person concerned on the date of acceptance of the declaration for release for free circulation. The four options were, first, the customs value, at or about the same time, of identical or similar goods produced in any third country. The second option was the selling price, provided this was not influenced by a relationship between buyer and seller. The third was the selling price in the Community of identical or similar goods, subject to the same caveat as the second option. The final option was the customs value of the import goods plus processing costs.[40]

C. DETERMINING THE TRANSACTION VALUE

1. *Which sale is relevant?*

The use of the transaction value means that 'The customs value must . . . be calculated on the basis of conditions on which the individual sale was made, even if they do not accord with trade practice or may appear unusual for the type of contract in question'.[41] The requirement to have regard to the individual sale affecting the goods in question clearly goes a long way to clarifying which transaction, and therefore which transaction value, is relevant. It is not at all unusual, however, for goods to be the subject of a number of sales and, in these circumstances, it is necessary to determine which sale is the relevant one.

As we noted above, CCC, Article 29 requires that the transaction value is 'the price actually paid or payable for the goods when sold for export to the customs territory of the Community'. The fact that goods are declared for free circulation is to be regarded as an 'adequate indication' that they were sold for export to the customs territory. Where goods have been subject to a series of sales prior to valuation, only the last sale which led to the introduction of the goods into the Community customs territory, or a sale taking place in the Community customs territory before entry into free circulation, is to constitute

---

[39] Of 4 May 2001 [2001] OJ L141/1, Art 1.28.   [40] Implementing Regulation, Art 666.
[41] Case 65/85 *Hauptzollamt Hamburg-Ericus v Van Houten International GmbH* [1986] ECR 447 at para 13. See also Case C–15/99 *Hans Sommer GmbH & Co KG v Hauptzollamt Bremen*, 19 Oct 2000, para 22. In the latter case, governed by pre-CCC legislation, honey satisfying certain contractual quality requirements was sold. The sellers' costs of analysing the honey to ensure that the requirements were met were invoiced separately to the buyer, but they were, nevertheless, to be included in the transaction value. Note too that where the individual sale is made subject to discounts, it is, as one would expect, the actual or discounted price which is relevant: see, eg, *Cray Research France v Administration des Douanes et Droits Indirects*, before the Cour de Cassation, Commercial Division, France [1994] 1 CMLR 465.

such an indication.[42] Where a price is declared which relates to a sale prior to the last sale, on the basis of which goods were introduced into the Community customs territory, it must be shown to the satisfaction of the customs authorities that this sale took place for export to the customs territory in question.[43] Indications that a sale took place for export to the Community customs territory may include the fact that goods are manufactured according to EC specifications, were produced or manufactured for, or shipped directly to, a buyer in the EC, or are in some way identified as goods to be used in the EC.

Where more than one sale satisfies the requirements of Article 29 the importer may choose which sale to use for the purposes of valuation.[44] The choice of value is frequently a matter of particular significance where a group of companies is importing goods and the Court of Justice has said that 'Any undertaking . . . may legitimately base its customs value declaration on the price actually paid for the imported goods by the member of the group entrusted with the purchase from the supplier in the non-member country'.[45] Although the declarant has a choice of what sale price to declare in certain circumstances, not every transaction can be taken into account. As noted above, Advisory Opinion 14.1 of the WCO Technical Committee on Customs Valuation, states that 'only transactions involving an actual international transfer of goods may be used in valuing merchandise under the transaction value method'. There are other limitations to be observed. For example, where a buying agent acted in his own name in buying goods for export, his transfer of the goods to the buyer, on terms agreed between them, could not be regarded as a transaction for the purposes of valuation. In the words of the Court of Justice:

> Since such an agent acts on behalf of the importer, his function in relation to the purchase of goods is only one of representation and he bears no financial risks in the purchase. Consequently, even if he acts in his own name, his function is limited to participation as indirect representative in a contract of sale concluded in fact between his principal and the supplier.[46]

[42] Implementing Regulation, Art 147.1 para 1.
[43] Ibid, Art 147.1 para 2. Art 1 of the Agreement on Implementation of Art VII, provides that the customs value of goods is the transaction value, being the price actually paid or payable for goods 'when sold for export to the country of importation'. Advisory Opinion 14.1 of the WCO Technical Committee on Customs Valuation, says of this Art that: 'there is no need that the sale takes place in a specific country of exportation. If the importer can demonstrate that the immediate sale under consideration took place with the view to export the goods to the country of importation then Article 1 can apply. It follows that only transactions involving an actual international transfer of goods may be used in valuing merchandise under the transaction value method.'
[44] Case C–11/89 *Unifert Hauptzollamt Münster*, n 28 above, at para 21. But note that, once chosen, the customs value declaration cannot be changed after the goods have been released into free circulation. See the comments on the customs value declaration below.
[45] Ibid, at para 26.
[46] Case C–299/90 *Hauptzollamt Karlsruhe v Gebrüder Hepp GmbH & Co KG* [1991] ECR I–4301 at para 13.

Article 29 contains no requirements, however, about the residence of the seller. It is possible, therefore, for the sale for export to take place between two companies which are resident in the Community. The Court of Justice put it this way:

> The criterion which emerges from the term 'sold for export' relates to the goods and not to the situation of the seller. Placed in its proper context, the term suggests that it is agreed, at the time of sale, that the goods originating in a non-member country will be transported into the customs territory of the Community. Therefore, there is nothing to prevent both parties to such a sale from being established in the Community.[47]

A buyer, however, must be established in the Community either by being resident there or by having a genuine place of business there. It is not necessary, though to have a registered office there. It is enough if the buyer has an establishment which carries on such activities as may be exercised by an independent undertaking in the same sector and has its own accounts which allow the customs authorities to carry out the necessary checks and inspections.[48]

Having established which sale is to be used to determine the transaction value, one has to ascertain what precisely is the price actually paid or payable within CCC, Article 29.1 and this is considered in the next section

2. *What is 'the price actually paid or payable'?*

As we shall see, the price actually paid or payable is the total payment made, or to be made, by the buyer to or for the benefit of the seller for the imported goods. On occasions the need to refer to the total payment made may result in the buyer becoming liable for customs duty in respect of a larger quantity of goods than has been delivered. This may occur, for example, where the buyer of a specified quantity of goods agrees to pay a fixed price for them so long as the quantity delivered falls within certain tolerances. In the event of a delivery of a quantity less than that ordered but within the agreed tolerances, there is no reduction in the price paid or payable for customs duty purposes.[49] Where, however, the goods declared for free circulation are part of a larger quantity of goods purchased in one transaction, the total price of the quantity of goods declared is to be apportioned in relation to the total quantity of goods purchased. Similar apportionments are required when part of consignment is lost or where the goods valued have been damaged before entry into free circulation.[50]

---

[47] Case C–11/89 *Unifert Hauptzollamt Münster, n 28* above, at para 11.
[48] Case 111/79 *SA Caterpillar Overseas v Belgian State*, [1980] ECR 773, para 14.
[49] Case 11/89 *Unifert v Hauptzollamt Münster*, n 28 above, at para 36.
[50] Implementing Regulation, Art 145. These deductions are allowed because they are unforeseeable reductions in the value of goods after they have been purchased but before they have been released into free circulation: Case 11/89 *Unifert v Hauptzollamt Münster*, n 28 above, at para 35

According to CCC, Article 29.3(a), the price actually paid or payable includes all payments made, or to be made, by the buyer to the seller as a condition of sale of the imported goods, or payments so made by the buyer to a third party to satisfy an obligation of the seller.[51] Where the price has not actually been paid when the goods are valued for customs purposes, it is the price payable for settlement at the time of valuation which, as a general rule, is taken as the basis for customs value.[52] As may be expected, in order for there to be a payment it is expressly provided that there need be no transfer of money. It may be made by way of letters of credit or negotiable instrument and may be made directly or indirectly.[53]

Activities which are undertaken by the buyer on his own account, including marketing activities, are not to be considered an indirect payment to the seller, except where an adjustment is specifically provided for in CCC, Article 32 considered below. This is so even though the activities may be regarded as of benefit to the seller or have been undertaken by agreement with the seller.[54] For these purposes 'marketing activities' is defined to mean all activities relating to advertising and promoting the sale of the goods in question and all activities relating to warranties or guarantees in respect of them.[55]

In order to form part of the price paid or payable, a flow of funds, or payment, between the buyer and seller must relate to the purchase in question. Accordingly, as an interpretative note makes clear, the flow of dividends or the existence of other payments between buyer and seller that do not relate to the imported goods is not part of the customs value.[56] Also excluded from the

---

and Case 183/85 *Hauptzollamt Itzehoe v H J Repenning GmbH*, n 21 above, at para 18. As will be apparent from the legislation, the time at which risk passes to the buyer is irrelevant: Case C–59/92 *Hauptzollamt Hamburg-St Annen v Ebbe Sonnischen GmbH* [1993] ECR I–2193.

[51] It includes, therefore, payments for certificates of authenticity in relation to the goods which are exported, issued by the exporting authorities and necessary to obtain the benefit of tariff quotas. The certificates relate specifically to the goods in question and not, like export quotas, to the general right to export: Case C–219/88 *Malt GmbH v Hauptzollamt Düsseldorf* [1990] ECR I–1481: see para 13. Payments in respect of warranties on imported cars were held to be payments made as a condition of sale and not within Art 33.1(b) in *Daihatsu (UK) Ltd v CCE* [1996] V&DR 192. The tribunal held that there was no need for a condition to be a condition precedent of the sale, following dicta in *BSC Footwear Supplies Ltd v CCE*, 8 June 1995, of Robert Walker J, as he then was. See also at 2.1 and section F.

[52] Implementing Regulation, Art 144.

[53] The Interpretative Note to Art 29.3(a) in Annex 23 to the Implementing Regulation states that an example of an indirect payment would be the settlement by the buyer, whether in whole or in part, of a debt owed by the seller.

[54] Art 29.3(b). It follows that the buyer's costs of weighing goods on arrival are not to be included in the price paid or payable unless weighing is carried out pursuant to the sale contract: see Case 65/85 *Hauptzollamt Hamburg-Ericus v Van Houten International GmbH*, n 41 above, at para 14.

[55] Implementing Regulation, Art 149. Art 149.2 specifically states that a buyer is regarded as carrying out such activities on his own account even if they are performed in pursuance of an obligation imposed upon him following an agreement with the seller.

[56] See the Interpretative Note to CCC, Art 29(1) in Annex 23 to the Implementing Regulation.

customs value of goods are amounts in respect of any internal tax applicable in the country of origin or export, even where they are within the price paid or payable, provided that the customs authorities are satisfied that the goods have been or will be relieved from the tax for the benefit of the buyer.[57]

2.1 Additions to the price actually paid or payable

As we noted above, there are a number of required additions to the price actually paid or payable when customs value is determined under CCC, Article 29 and these are listed in CCC, Article 32. They are designed, of course, to prevent the undervaluation of goods and so protect the customs duty revenues of the Community.[58] No additions are to be made except as provided in Article 32[59] and those that are made are to be made only on the basis of objective and quantifiable data.[60] Where no such data exists, then the transaction value cannot be determined under Article 29.[61] The required additions are as set out below.

(i)   Commissions and brokerage, but not buying commissions,[62] the cost of containers which are treated as one, for customs purposes, with the goods in question[63] and the cost of packing whether for labour or

---

[57] Implementing Regulation, Art 146.

[58] Case 65/79 *Procureur de la République v René Chatain*, n 32 above, paras 8 and 16.

[59] Art 32.3. For an example of a case in which an addition (a payment for export quota) was rejected because it did not appear in the list of specified additions see Case 7/83 *Ospig Textilgesellschaft-KG W Ahlers v Hauptzollamt Bremen-Ost*, n 21 above, at paras 12–15. Such a payment remains excluded where the trade in export quotas is illegal in the country of export: Case C–29/93 *KG in Firma OSPIG Textil-Gesellschaft W Ahlers GmbH & Co. v Hauptzollamt Bremen Freihafen* [1994] ECR I–1963. A payment to the seller for export licences allocated to the seller, free of charge in respect of own quotas, is not excluded from customs value: Case C–340/93 *Klaus Thierschmidt GmbH v Hauptzollamt Essen* [1994] ECR I–3905.

[60] CCC, Art 32.2. The customs authorities may at the request of the person concerned, authorize derogations from Art 32.2, and permit certain elements to be added to the price actually paid or payable, although not quantifiable at the time the customs debt is incurred. These are to be determined on the basis of appropriate and specific criteria and subject to certain specific conditions, including the existence of valid reasons for considering that the amount of import duty to be charged in the period covered will not be lower than that which would be otherwise levied and that competitive conditions amongst operators are not distorted: Implementing Regulation, Art 156a.

[61] Implementing Regulation, Annex 23, Interpretative Note to CCC, Art 32.2. The note gives as an example of a situation in which no objective or quantifiable data exists a case in which a royalty, required to be added to the price paid under CCC, Art 32.1(c), is based partially on the imported goods in question and partially on factors which have nothing to do with them (such as when the imported goods are mixed with domestic ingredients and are no longer separately identifiable, or when the royalty cannot be distinguished from special financial arrangements between the buyer and the seller). It confirms that, if the royalty is based only on the imported goods and can readily be quantified an addition to the price actually paid or payable can be made.

[62] CCC, Art 32.1(a)(i).

[63] Ibid, Art 32.1(a)(ii). Where containers are to be the subject of repeated importations, the declarant may request that their cost shall be apportioned, as appropriate, in accordance with generally accepted accounting provisions: Implementing Regulation, Art 154.

materials[64] are to be added to the extent that they are incurred by the buyer but are not included in the price actually paid or payable.[65] The term 'buying commission' means fees paid by an importer to his agent for the service of representing him in the purchase of the goods being valued.[66] It does not include, therefore, an amount paid by the buyer to the seller if it is calculated in such a way as to permit the seller to cover his administrative costs and other general costs not directly related to the sale in question.[67]

(ii)   The value of certain goods and services is to be added to the price actually paid or payable, apportioned as appropriate, where they are supplied directly or indirectly by the buyer, free of charge or at reduced cost, for use in connection with the production and sale for export of the imported goods. The goods and services in question are:

- materials, components, parts, and similar items incorporated in the imported goods;[68]
- tools dies, moulds, and similar items used in the production of imported goods;[69]
- materials consumed in the production of imported goods;[70] and finally,
- engineering, development, artwork, design work, and plans and sketches undertaken outside the Community and necessary for the

---

[64] CCC, Art 32.1(a)(iii).

[65] CCC, Art 32.1(a). In Case 357/87 *Firme Albert Schmid v Hauptzollamt Stuttgart-West* [1988] ECR 6239, it was held that packing (namely beer barrels, beer bottles, and plastic crates for beer bottles) retained by the importer was subject to customs duty and the additional amounts of duty could be obtained by post-clearance recovery. No additional duty was payable where the importer paid the exporter compensation for the retained packing.

[66] CCC, Art 32.4. The fact that the agent acts in his own name does not alter the position, neither does the fact that he is misdescribed in the valuation declaration: Case C–299/90 *Hauptzollamt Karlsruhe v Gebrüder Hepp GmbH & Co KG* [1991] ECR I–4301 at paras 14 and 18.

[67] See Case 11/89 *Unifert v Hauptzollamt Münster*, n 28 above, para 24.

[68] CCC, Art 32.1(b)(i). There is no requirement that the goods or services are produced or provided outside the Community: see Case C–116/89 *Baywa AG v Hauptzollamt Weiden* [1991] ECR I–1095 at para 15, in which the Court of Justice required certain licence fees attributable to seeds to be added to their customs duty value.

[69] CCC, Art 32.1(b)(ii). Interpretative Note 1 to this provision, in the Implementing Regulation Annex 23 states that the apportionments necessitated by the addition of these elements should be made in a reasonable manner appropriate to the circumstances and in accordance with generally accepted accounting principles. Interpretative Note 2 states that if the buyer acquires the item from an unrelated seller, the value of the item is the cost of acquisition. If the item was produced by a person related to the buyer or a person related to him, its value is the cost of its production. Previous use of the item by the buyer must be reflected in a downwards adjustment in value. Interpretative Note 3 provides that the method of apportioning value to imported goods will depend upon the documentation provided by the buyer and gives three examples of different methods.

[70] CCC, Art 32.1(b)(iii).

production of the imported goods (excluding research and preliminary design sketches).[71]

(iii) Royalties and licence fees, including amongst other things payments
in respect of patents, designs, trade marks, and copyrights,[72] related
to the goods being valued[73] and that the buyer must pay, either
directly or indirectly, as a condition of their sale, are to be added to
the price paid or payable, to the extent that they are not already
included.[74] Where the method of calculating the royalty or fee
derives from the price of the imported goods it is assumed, in the
absence of contrary evidence, that the royalty or fee is related to the
goods to be valued.[75] There are, however, limitations to the provisions relating to royalties and licence fees. Charges for the right to
reproduce imported goods in the Community are not to be added and
payments made by the buyer for the right to distribute, or resell, the

---

[71] Ibid, Art 32.1(b)(iv), and Implementing Regulation, Art 155. There are a number of
Interpretative Notes to Art 32.1(b)(iv). Note 1 provides that additions for elements specified in Art
32.1(b)(iv) must be based on objective and quantifiable data and data readily available in the
buyer's commercial record system should be used in so far as possible. Note 2 provides that where
the elements supplied by the buyer are purchased or leased by him, the addition shall be the cost
of purchase or leasing. No addition is to be made for elements available in the public domain, other
than the cost of obtaining copies. Note 4 states that where a firm maintains the records of its
design centre outside the country of importation, in such a way as to show accurately the costs
attributable to a specific product, a direct adjustment may be made under CCC, Art 32. According
to Note 5, however, where the costs are shown as a general overhead expense, an appropriate
adjustment may be made by apportioning total design centre costs over total production benefiting from the design centre and adding such apportioned cost, on a unit basis, to imports. In determining the proper method of allocation variations in the above circumstances will require
different factors to be considered: see Note 6. Where the production of the item in question
involves a number of countries over a period of time, the adjustment should be limited to the value
actually added to the item outside the Community: see Note 7.

[72] See the Interpretative Note to CCC, Art 32.1(c), and the definition of royalties and licence
fees in Implementing Regulation, Art 157.1. See also Case 1/77 *Robert Bosch GmbH v Hauptzollamt
Hildesheim* [1977] ECR 1473 and Case 135/77 *Robert Bosch GmbH v Hauptzollamt Hildesheim*
[1978] ECR 855.

[73] Where imported goods are an ingredient in, or component of, goods manufactured in the
Community the royalty or fee must relate to the imported goods. Where the royalties or fees relate
partly to post-importation additions, activities or services there is to be an apportionment: see the
Implementing Regulation, Art 158.1 and 3 and the Interpretative Note to CCC, Art 32.2, in the
Implementing Regulation, Annex 23. Royalties or licence fees may relate to goods being valued
which are imported unassembled or which have to undergo minor processing before resale, such
as diluting or packing: Implementing Regulation, Art 158.2.

[74] CCC, Art 32.1(c). See also Implementing Regulation, Art 157.2. A payment is not regarded
as related to the goods being valued, nor as made as a condition of sale of the goods, where the
buyer pays royalties or licence fees to a third party, unless the seller, or a person related to him,
requires the buyer to make the payment: Implementing Regulation, Art 160. The country in
which the recipient of the royalty or fee is resident is not a material consideration in applying CCC,
Art 32.1(c), Implementing Regulation, Art 162.

[75] Implementing Regulation, Art 161. This provision makes clear, however, that where the
price of the imported goods is disregarded in the calculation, the royalty or fee in question may
nevertheless be related to the goods to be valued.

imported goods are not to be added if they are not a condition of the sale for export of the goods to the Community.[76] There are specific limitations too where the royalty or licence fee is in respect of a right to use a trade mark.[77]

(iv) The value of any part of the proceeds of any subsequent resale, disposal, or use of the imported goods that accrue directly or indirectly to the seller are to be added to the price payable or paid.[78]

(v) The cost of transport and insurance of the imported goods, and the cost of loading and handling charges associated with the transport of the imported goods, to the place of introduction into the customs territory of the Community are to be added.[79] The term 'cost of transport':

> must be interpreted as including all the costs, whether they are main or incidental costs, incurred in connection with moving the goods to the customs territory of the Community. Consequently, demurrage charges, which consist in compensation provided for in the shipping contract to compensate the shipowner for any delays arising during the loading of the vessel, must be considered to be covered by the term 'cost of transport'.[80]

It should be noted that where the customs value of goods is based on a price actually paid or payable, and this includes the cost of warehousing and of preserving goods while they remain in the warehouse, these costs need not be included in the customs value if they are shown separately from the price actually paid or payable.[81]

[76] CCC, Art 32.5.
[77] Implementing Regulation, Art 159.
[78] CCC, Art 32.1(d).
[79] Ibid, Art 32.1(e). This provision governing the transport costs which may be added should be read in conjunction with CCC, Art 33.1(a), which excludes charges for the transport of goods after their arrival in the Community and is discussed below. The place of introduction into the customs territory of the Community is specifically defined in the Implementing Regulation, Art 163, to which reference should be made in any specific case. For goods carried by sea, the place of introduction includes the port of unloading or transhipment; for goods carried by road, rail, or inland waterway, it is the place where the first customs office is situated; and for other goods, it is the place where the land frontier of the Community customs territory is crossed. Where goods enter the territory and then pass through certain other countries, or are unloaded in other countries, on their way to another part of the customs territory, the place of introduction is the first place of introduction. For an example of a case in which transport costs from the border of the Community customs territory to the purchaser were not included in the customs value see Case 290/84 *Hauptzollamt Schweinfurt v Mainfrucht Obstverwertung GmbH* [1985] ECR 3909.
[80] Case 11/89 *Unifert v Hauptzollamt Münster*, n 28 above, para 30.
[81] See CCC, Art 112, which contains a number of other provisions relating to valuation and warehousing. See also Case 38/77 *Enka BV v Inspecteur der Invoerrechten en Accijnzen Arnhem* [1977] ECR 2203. See Implementing Regulation, Art 178.1 in relation to the costs of warehousing or preservation while goods remain in a free zone or warehouse.

2.2 *Exclusions from the price actually paid or payable*

The list of additions to the price actually paid or payable should be read in conjunction with the list of matters which may be excluded from the customs value of products. These are mostly contained CCC, Article 33 which is dealt with in section E below.

3. *Limitations on the use of the transaction value*

As one would expect, the customs authorities are not compelled to use the transaction value as a basis of customs valuation if, on the basis of reasonable doubts, they are not satisfied that the declared value represents the total amount paid or payable. Where the customs authorities do have reasonable doubts about the declared value, they may ask for additional information. If the authorities continue to have reasonable doubts, before reaching a final decision on the matter, they must notify the person concerned of the grounds for them, in writing if requested, and provide the person with a reasonable opportunity to respond. Once a final decision has been reached it must be communicated in writing to the person concerned.[82]

In order for the transaction value to be the basis of customs valuation certain other requirements, contained in CCC, Article 29, must be satisfied. First, generally speaking, there must be no restriction on the disposal or use of the goods by the buyer. Restrictions which are imposed or required by law, or by public authorities in the Community are, however, permitted. So too are those which limit the geographical area in which the goods may be sold and those which do not substantially affect the value of the goods.[83] Secondly, the sale and the price must not be subject to some condition or consideration for which a value cannot be determined with respect to the goods in question.[84] An example of such a condition is where the seller establishes the price of the imported goods on condition that the buyer will also buy other goods in speci-

---

[82] Implementing Regulation, Art 181a. See also the Decision Regarding Cases Where Customs Administrations Have Reasons to Doubt the Truth or Accuracy of the Declared Value of the Trade Negotiations Committee on 15 Dec 1993 and adopted on signing the Final Act Embodying the Results of the Uruguay Round.

[83] CCC, Art 29.1(a). An example of a restriction which does not substantially affect the value of goods is where a seller requires an automobile seller not to sell or exhibit them prior to the beginning of the model year: see Implementing Regulation, Annex 23: Interpretative Note No 2 to CCC, Art 29.1(a).

[84] Ibid, Art 29.1(b). Where there is such a condition or consideration, and its value can be determined with respect to the goods being valued, the value is to be regarded as an indirect payment by the buyer to the seller and part of the price actually paid or payable except where the condition or consideration relates to two matters. These are, first, activities, including marketing activities, undertaken by the buyer on his own account other than those for which an adjustment is provided in CCC, Art 32, and, secondly, a factor in respect of which an addition is to be made to the price actually paid or payable under the provisions of CCC, Art 32: see ibid, Art 29.3(b).

fied quantities.[85] Thirdly, no part of the proceeds of any subsequent re-sale, disposal, or use of the goods by the buyer must accrue to the seller unless permitted by Article 32.[86] Finally, the buyer and the seller must not be related or, where they are related, further conditions must be satisfied.[87]

3.1 *Related sellers and buyers*

The definition of related persons is apparently very wide. Article 143(a)–(h) of the Implementing Regulation provides that persons shall be deemed to be related in eight situations. These are where:

(i)   they are officers or directors of one another's businesses;

(ii) they are legally recognized partners in business;

(iii) they are employer and employee;

(iv) any person directly or indirectly owns, or controls, or holds, 5 per cent or more of the outstanding voting stock, or shares, of both of them;

(v) one of them directly or indirectly controls the other;[88]

(vi) both of them are directly or indirectly controlled by a third person;

(vii) together they directly or indirectly control a third person; or

(viii) they are members of the same family.

So far as category (viii) is concerned, persons are members of the same family if they are in any one of the following relationships to each other, namely, husband and wife, parent and child, brother and sister (whether whole or half blood), grandparent and grandchild, uncle and nephew, aunt and niece, parent-in-law and son- or daughter-in-law, and finally, brother-in-law and sister-in-law.[89]

It will be obvious that it is not necessary for there to be any direct relationship at all between the buyer and seller for them to be related. It is enough if they indirectly control an entity which is not involved in the transaction in question. The provisions are not, however, without limits. Persons who are associated in business with each other in that one is the sole agent, sole distributor, or sole concessionaire,[90] however described, of the other, are to be deemed to be related only if they fall within the criteria set out in (i) to (viii)

---

[85] See Implementing Regulation, Annex 23, Interpretative Note 3, which gives other examples and provides that conditions or consideration relating to the production or marketing of the goods are not to result in the rejection of the transaction value.

[86] CCC, Art 29.1(c).   [87] Ibid, Art 29.1(d).

[88] One person is deemed to control another when the former is legally or operationally in a position to exercise restraint or direction over the latter: Implementing Regulation, Annex 23, Interpretative Note to Art 143.1(e).   [89] See Art 143.1(h).

[90] In relation to earlier legislation on valuation, the Court of Justice said that the terms 'sole agent' and 'sole concessionaire' should be construed widely not technically nor as referring to mutually exclusive legal categories: see Case 82/76 *Farbwerke Hoechst AG v Hauptzollamt Frankfurt-am-Main* [1977] ECR 335 para 12.

above.[91] Furthermore, whilst members of the same family are related, there is no provision that ensures that all spouses of relatives are within the same family. To a common law lawyer it will be apparent that there is no specific mention of trustees, which one would expect in statutory provisions dealing with related persons in common law jurisdictions. Consequently, although, for example, a trustee of shares in a company may well be related to the company by virtue of category (iv) above, there is no provision that a settlor of a trust and a trustee are related.

The fact that a buyer and a seller are related is not of itself a sufficient ground for regarding the transaction value as unacceptable for the purposes of CCC, Article 29.1. Where necessary, that is to say where there are doubts about the acceptability of the price,[92] the circumstances surrounding the sale are to be examined and the transaction value is to be accepted 'provided that the relationship did not influence the price'.[93] If the customs authorities have grounds for considering that the relationship did influence the price, whether from information provided by the declarant or otherwise, they are to communicate the grounds to the declarant, who is to be given a reasonable opportunity to respond. If the declarant so requests, the communication must be in writing.[94] Where the customs authorities cannot accept the transaction value without further inquiry, the declarant must be given an opportunity to supply such further detailed information as may be necessary to enable them to examine the circumstances surrounding the sale. The customs authorities should be prepared to examine relevant aspects of the transaction, such as how the price was arrived at and how the parties organize their commercial relations.[95] Three examples of the price being uninfluenced by the relationship are given in the interpretative notes. The first example is that the seller settles prices with the buyer consistently with the normal pricing practices of the industry. The second is that the price is settled consistently with the way in which prices are settled with unrelated buyers. The third example is that the price ensures recovery of costs plus a profit which is representative of the firm's overall profit over a representative period (say a year) for sales of goods of the same class or kind.[96]

A different means of establishing the acceptability of the transaction value is provided by CCC, Article 29.2(b).[97] This states that, in a sale between related persons, the transaction value is to be accepted wherever the declarant

---

[91] Implementing Regulation, Art 143.2.
[92] See Interpretative Note No 2 on CCC, Art 29.2, in the Implementing Regulation, Annex 23.
[93] CCC, Art 29.2.
[94] Ibid, Art 29.2(a).
[95] Implementing Regulation, Annex 23, Interpretative Note No 3 to CCC, Art 29.2.
[96] Implementing Regulation, Annex 23, Interpretative Note No 3 to CCC, Art 29.2.
[97] The fact that CCC, Art 29.2(a) and (b) provide different means of establishing the acceptability of the transaction value is plain from a reading of the provisions but is also made clear by Interpretative Note No 1 to CCC, Art 29(2) in Implementing Regulation, Annex 23.

demonstrates that it 'closely approximates'[98] to one of three values occurring at or about the same time. These are, first, the transaction value in sales between unrelated buyers and sellers of identical or similar goods for export to the Community. The second value is the customs value of identical or similar goods determined under CCC, Article 30.2(c). The third value is the customs value of identical or similar goods determined under CCC, Article 30.2(d). The two provisions of Article 30 referred to deal with the unit price of goods and their computed value respectively and are considered below.[99] These tests are to be used at the initiative of the declarant and only for comparison purposes. They do not permit the establishment of substitute values.[100]

Where customs authorities have sufficient information to be satisfied that a test can be met there is no reason for them to require the declarant to demonstrate the fact. Furthermore, where one of the tests is met, it is not necessary to examine whether the relationship between the buyer and the seller influenced the price within Article 29.2(a).[101]

D. ALTERNATIVES TO THE TRANSACTION PRICE

We noted earlier that the transaction price was not the only method of valuation permitted by the Agreement on the Implementation of Article VII of GATT. In conformity with the Agreement, CCC, Article 30 provides four alternative measures of value where customs value cannot be determined by reference to the transaction value pursuant to CCC, Article 29. Neither a declarant nor a customs authority may choose which alternative applies. Instead, it is necessary to proceed sequentially through the alternatives, only moving on to consider applying a subsequent alternative where the customs value cannot be determined by a prior one. The only liberty given to a declarant is that of being able to request the application of the third and fourth alternatives in reverse order.[102] The alternatives to the transaction price set out in CCC, Article 30.2(a)–(d) are as follows:

[98] Some of the factors to be taken into account in determining whether one value 'closely approximates' to another are listed in Interpretative Note to CCC, Art 29(2)(b), Implementing Regulation, Annex 23. They include: the nature of the imported goods and of the industry itself, the season in which the goods are imported, and whether the difference in values is commercially significant. No percentage difference is provided because in one case a small difference may be unacceptable and significant and in another case a large difference may be acceptable.

[99] In applying these three 'tests' due account is to be taken of demonstrated differences in commercial levels, quantity levels, the elements enumerated in CCC, Art 32, and costs incurred by the seller in sales in which he and the buyer are not related and, where such costs are not incurred by the seller, where he and the buyer are related: CCC, Art 29.2.(b).

[100] CCC, Art 29.2(c).

[101] Implementing Regulation, Annex 23, Interpretative Note No 4 to CCC, Art 29(2).

[102] CCC, Art 30.1.

   (i)   the transaction value or, where there is more than one, the lowest transaction value,[103] of identical goods sold for export to the Community and exported at or about the same time as the goods being valued;

   (ii) the transaction value of similar goods sold for export to the Community and exported at or about the same time as the goods being valued;

   (iii) the value, based on the unit price, at which the imported goods, or identical or similar imported goods, are sold within the Community in the greatest aggregate quantity to buyers who are not related to the sellers;

   (iv) the computed value. This consists of three main elements. First, there is the cost or value of materials and fabrication,[104] or other processing, employed in producing the imported goods. Secondly, there is an amount for profit and general expenses, equal to that usually reflected in sales of goods of the same class or kind as the goods being valued[105] and made by producers in the country of exportation for export to the Community. Finally, there is the cost or value of transport and insurance of the imported goods and loading and handling charges associated with the transport of the imported goods to the place of introduction into the customs territory of the Community.

There is a final alternative, which applies where none of the others can be used. It is known as the default method and is contained in CCC, Article 31.1.

The Implementing Regulation contains specific provisions on each of these five alternative bases of valuation which are considered below.

1. *The value of identical goods*

'Identical goods' means goods produced (ie grown, manufactured, or mined[106]) in the same country and, where possible, by the same person,[107] which are the same in all respects, including physical characteristics, quality, and reputation (although minor differences in appearance are not to preclude goods from conforming to the definition).[108] The transaction value of the

---

[103] Implementing Regulation, Art 150.3.

[104] Implementing Regulation, Art 153.2, specifies costs which are included in this category, namely the costs of packing etc identified in CCC, Art 32.1(a)(ii) and (iii) and referred to above. Also included is the value, duly apportioned, of any product or service specified in CCC, Art 32.1(b), which has been supplied directly or indirectly by the buyer for use in connection with the production of the imported goods. The value of elements specified in CCC, Art 32.1(b)(iv), (engineering, development, artwork etc.) are included only to the extent that they are charged to the producer.

[105] The Implementing Regulation defines 'goods of the same class or kind' as goods which fall within a group or range of goods produced by a particular industry, or industry sector, and includes identical or similar goods: see Art 142.1(e).

[106] Implementing Regulation, Art 142.1(b).

[107] Ibid, Art 150.4.   [108] Ibid, Art 142.1(a).

identical goods is to be determined in a sale at the same commercial level and in substantially the same quantity as the goods being valued. Where there is no such sale, sales at a different commercial level and/or of different quantities are to be used, with adjustments for the differences, provided that the adjustments can be made on the basis of demonstrated evidence which clearly establishes the reasonableness and accuracy of the adjustment.[109] Adjustments must also be made to take account of significant differences between certain specified costs incurred as between the imported goods and the identical goods. The costs in question are those of transport and insurance, and loading and handling charges associated with transporting the goods, to the place of introduction into the Community customs territory. The adjustments are to be made, however, only where the significant differences in question arise from differences in distances and modes of transport.[110] If, in applying Implementing Regulation, Article 150 to obtain a value for identical goods, more than one transaction value is found, the lowest value is to be chosen.[111]

2. The value of similar goods

'Similar goods' is defined in Implementing Regulation, Article 142 as meaning goods grown, manufactured, or mined in the same country, which although not alike in all respects, have like characteristics and like component materials which enable them to perform the same functions and be commercially interchangeable. It is specifically provided that the quality of the goods, their reputation, and the existence of a trade mark are among the factors to be considered in determining whether goods are similar. Goods which incorporate or reflect engineering, development artwork, design work, and plans and sketches undertaken in the Community[112] are not similar goods.[113] The valuation of similar goods is to be carried out according to Implementing Regulation, Article 151 which contains similar provisions as Article 150 considered in relation to identical goods. It should also be noted that the Interpretative Notes in Annex 23 to the Implementing Regulation which are relevant to identical goods are also relevant to similar goods.

3. The value based on unit price: the deductive method

The unit price in question here is that at which the goods actually imported, or

---

[109] Ibid, Art 150.1. Attention should also be paid to the Interpretative Notes on Art 30.2(a) and (b) in Implementing Regulation, Annex 23. These provide, amongst other things, an example of an adjustment the reasonableness and accuracy of which is acceptable by reference to price lists.
[110] Implementing Regulation, Art 150.2.   [111] Ibid, Art 150.3.
[112] And in respect of which, therefore, there has been no addition to the price paid or payable pursuant to CCC, Art 32.1(b)(iv), described above.
[113] Implementing Regulation, Art 142.2.

similar or identical goods, are sold in the Community, in the greatest aggregate quantity, to persons not related to the sellers.[114] Once a unit price is obtained, there are three sets of specified deductions to be made from it in establishing a customs value.[115] The first of these consists of the commissions usually paid or agreed to be paid, or the additions usually made for profit and general expenses,[116] in connection with sales in the Community of imported goods of the same class or kind. The second consists of the usual costs of transport and insurance and associated costs incurred within the Community.[117] The third consists of import duties and other charges payable in the Community by reason of the importation or sale of the goods.[118] If neither the imported goods nor the identical or similar goods are sold, at or about the time of impor-tation of the goods being valued, the customs value of the goods is to be subject to an additional requirement. The customs value is to be based on the unit price at which the goods, or the identical or similar goods, are sold in the Community in the condition as imported at 'the earliest date' after the impor-tation in question, and before the expiration of ninety days after it.[119] The earliest date is the date by which sales of the imported goods, or of identical or similar goods, are made in sufficient quantity to establish the unit price.[120]

Where neither the imported goods, nor identical nor similar goods, are imported and sold in the Community in the condition as imported, the importer may request a special basis of customs valuation. This is the unit price at which the imported goods, after further processing, are sold in the greatest aggregate quantity to persons in the Community who are not related to the persons from whom they buy the goods. Due allowance is to be made for the value added by processing and the three sets of deductions outlined above.[121] The unit price at which imported goods are sold in the greatest

---

[114] See Implementing Regulation, Art 152.1(a).

[115] See ibid, Art 152.1(a)(i)–(iii).

[116] These are to include the direct and indirect costs of marketing the goods in question. According to Interpretative Note 1 in Implementing Regulation, Annex 23 regarding Art 152.1(a)(i), the words 'profit and general expenses' are to be taken as a whole. The figure for the deduction is to be determined consistently with the generally accepted accounting principles of the country of importation (Implementing Regulation, Annex 24). It is to be based on information supplied by the declarant, unless his figures are inconsistent with those obtaining in sales in the country of importation of imported goods of the same class or kind when other information may be used. Interpretative Note 2 on the provision states that in determining either the commissions or the usual profits or general expenses, the question whether or not goods are 'of the same class or kind' is to be determined on a case-by-case basis by reference to the circumstances involved. Sales in the country of importation of the narrowest group or range of imported goods of the same class or kind, which includes the goods being valued, and for which the necessary informa-tion can be provided, should be examined. Goods imported from the same country as the goods being valued are included as goods 'of the same class or kind' as well as goods imported from other countries.

[117] Implementing Regulation, Art 152.1(a)(ii).   [118] Ibid, Art 152.1(a)(iii).

[119] Ibid, Art 152.1(b).   [120] Ibid, Art 152.5.

[121] Ibid, Art 152.2. Interpretative Note No 1 in Implementing Regulation, Annex 23, to this provision makes clear that, in using this method of valuation, deductions for the value added by

aggregate quantity is defined as follows. It is the price at which the greatest number of units is sold, at the first commercial level after importation, to persons who are not related to the persons from whom they buy such goods.[122] Interpretative Notes 1 to 3 to this provision, in Implementing Regulation, Annex 23, give three examples of this. The first of these is that goods are sold from a price list which grants price reductions on the unit price in bands according to the amounts sold. In such a circumstance, the unit price in the greatest aggregate quantity is the unit price attributable to the band in respect of which the most sales occur.

Certain sales are not to be taken into account in determining the unit price of goods. These are sales in the Community to a person who supplies, directly or indirectly, and free of charge or at reduced cost, certain items for use in connection with the production and sale for export of the imported goods. The items in question are those specified in CCC, Article 32(1)(b) giving rise to additions to the price paid or payable,[123] for example, materials incorporated in the imported goods and engineering, artwork and designwork.[124]

4. The computed value

The use of the computed value is generally limited to cases where the buyer and seller are related and the producer of the goods in question is prepared to give the authorities of the country of importation the requisite costings, and to provide facilities for subsequent verification where necessary. Although the information required to use the computed value method is generally readily available in the Community, it may be necessary to examine the costs of production outside the Community, amongst other things.[125] In this regard it should be noted that the customs authorities may not require or compel any person not resident in the Community to produce for examination, or allow access to, any account or other record for the purposes of determining value. The customs authorities of the Member State may, however, verify information supplied by the producer of goods, for the purposes of determining, in a non-Community country, their computed customs value. For such verification to occur, the producer must agree, the

---

further processing are to be based on objective and quantifiable data relating to the cost of such work. Accepted industry formulas, recipes, methods of construction, and other industry practices would form the basis of the calculations. Interpretive Note 2 states that this method would not normally be applicable when, as a result of further processing, the imported goods lose their identity, although it may be used in some circumstances. It is also possible for the imported goods to retain their identity but form such a minor element in the goods sold in the country of importation that the use of this valuation method is unjustified. Each situation must be considered on a case-by-case basis.

[122] Implementing Regulation, Art 152.3.
[123] Discussed at p 255 above.   [124] Implementing Regulation, Art 152.4.
[125] Ibid, Annex 23, Note No 1 to CCC, Article 30.2(d).

verifying authorities must give sufficient advance notice to the authorities of the non-Community country, and those authorities must not object to the investigation.[126] Where the customs authorities use information which is not supplied by, or on behalf of, the producer for the purposes of determining a computed value, they must inform the declarant of the source of the information, the data used and the calculations based on the data, if the declarant so requests.[127]

4.1 *The elements of computed value*

There are three elements set out in CCC, Article 30.2(d) of which the computed value is to consist (with, as one would expect, no cost or value being counted twice[128]). The first element to be considered is the cost or value of materials and fabrication, or other processing, employed in producing the imported goods. This is to be determined on the basis of information relating to the production of the goods being valued, supplied by or on behalf of the producer, and on the basis of his commercial accounts. In order to be usable, though, the accounts must be consistent with the generally accepted accounting principles applied in the country of production.[129]

The second element, is 'the amount for profit and general expenses' equal to that usually reflected in sales of goods, of the same class or kind as the goods being valued,[130] which are made by the producers in the country of exportation for export to the Community. This element is to be determined on the basis of information supplied by or on behalf of the producer, unless his figures are inconsistent with those usually reflected in sales of goods of the same class or kind as those being valued[131] and made by the producers in the country of exportation for export to the country of importation.[132] Interpretative Note

---

[126] Implementing Regulation, Art 153.1.

[127] This obligation is subject to CCC, Art 15 which provides that information which is by nature confidential or which is provided on a confidential basis is covered by an obligation of professional secrecy. It can be disclosed by a customs authority only with the express permission of the person or authority providing it. Nevertheless, communication of the information is permitted where customs authorities are obliged or authorised to do so pursuant to the provisions in force, particularly in respect of data protection or in connection with legal proceedings.

[128] Implementing Regulation, Annex 23, Note 4 to CCC, Article 30.2(d).

[129] Ibid, Annex 23, Note 2 to Art 30.2(d).

[130] Whether goods are 'of the same class or kind' is to be determined on a case-by-case basis with reference to the circumstances involved. As noted above, the Implementing Regulation defines 'goods of the same class or kind' as goods which fall within a group or range of goods produced by a particular industry or industry sector and includes identical or similar goods: see ibid, Art 142.1(e). In determining usual profits and general expenses, sales for export to the country of importation of the narrowest range of goods, which includes the goods being valued, should be examined.

[131] See n 30 above.

[132] Implementing Regulation, Annex 23, Note 3 to CCC, Art 30.2(d). The information utilized in determining usual profit and general expenses should be prepared in a manner consistent with the generally accepted accounting principles of the country of production: Implementing Regulation, Annex 24.

No 5 to CCC, Article 30.2(d) in the Implementing Regulation, Annex 23, states that one has to take the 'amount for profit and general expenses' as a whole. It may be that profit figures are low and general expenses are high, for example, where a product is being launched in the Community. The producer's figures may, nevertheless, be accepted where the figures are consistent with those usually reflected in sales of goods of the same class or kind. Furthermore, a producer must show that valid commercial reasons justify its low profits and that its pricing policy reflects the usual pricing policies of the branch of industry in question.[133] Where the producer's own figures for profit and general expenses are not consistent with those usually reflected in the sales of goods of the same class or kind as those in issue, made by producers in the country of exportation for export to the country of importation, relevant information other than that supplied by or on behalf of the producer may be used.

The third element consists of the cost or value of the items referred to in CCC, Article 32.1(e), namely, the cost of transport and insurance of the imported goods to their place of introduction into the customs territory of the Community, and the loading and handling charges associated with such transport.

5. *The default method*

Where the customs value of goods cannot be determined by reference to the transaction price, or any of the four alternatives examined above, there is a final alternative available in CCC, Article 31.1. This is to determine customs value on the basis of data available in the Community, using reasonable means consistent with the principles and general provisions of the Agreement on Implementation of Article VII of GATT 94, Article VII itself, and the provisions of Chapter 3 of Title II CCC (Articles 28–36). There are limits, however to the scope of this Article. It is specifically provided that no customs value shall be determined on the basis of seven matters.[134] These are: the selling price in the Community of goods produced in the Community, a system which provides for the acceptance of the higher of two alternative values, the price of the goods on the domestic market in the exporting country, the cost of production (other than computed values determined for identical or similar goods in accordance with Article 30.2(d)), the prices for export to a country outside the Community customs territory, minimum customs values, and, finally, arbitrary or fictitious values.

The Interpretative Notes to Article 31.1 state that values determined under the default method should, to the greatest extent possible, be based on previously

---

[133] See Note 5 for an example.
[134] See CCC, Art 31.2.

determined customs values.[135] The methods of valuation employed in using
the default method should be the transaction value and the four alternative
methods discussed above, but applied with a reasonable flexibility.[136]
Interpretative Note 3 provides a number of examples of reasonable flexibility.
In relation to identical and similar goods, the requirement that the goods
should be exported at or about the same time as the goods being valued could
be flexibly interpreted. Furthermore, recourse may be had to values of goods
exported from countries other than the country of exportation, and customs
values of identical imported goods already determined under the unit price
method, or the computed value method, may be utilized. In relation to the unit
price or deductive method, the requirement that the goods should be sold in
the condition as imported may be flexibly interpreted and the ninety-day
period, within which a sale must take place, may also be applied flexibly.[137]

6. *Simplified procedures for certain perishable goods*

Implementing Regulation, Annex 26[138] contains a list of fruit and vegetables,
defined by classification heading, for which the Commission establishes a unit
value per 100kg net, expressed in the currencies of the Member States and,
now, the euro. The unit values apply for periods of fourteen days, each period
beginning on a Friday[139] and are established by the Commission on alternate
Tuesdays. The values are established on the basis of two elements in relation
to each classification heading, supplied to the Commission by the Member
States. The first element is the average free-at-frontier unit price of the goods
which are not cleared through customs. The second element is the quantities
of the goods entered into free circulation over the period of a calendar year
with payment of import duties.[140] So far as the first element is concerned,

---

[135] Implementing Regulation, Annex 23, Interpretative Note 1.
[136] Ibid, Interpretative Note 2.
[137] Implementing Regulation, Art 152.1(b) is considered at p 264 above.
[138] Amended in accordance with Annex IV to Commission Regulation (EC) 1602/2000 [2000]
OJ L188/1.
[139] Implementing Regulation, Art 173.1. For the rates of exchange into and from the ECU see Art
175.2. The last published unit values remain applicable until new ones are published. New values
may be determined on the basis of actual prices at the time of fixing the values in the case of major
fluctuations in price: ibid, Art 175.3. At the time of writing the most recent regulation governing
unit values is Commission Regulation (EC) 1877/2001 of 26 Sept 2001 [2001] OJ L258/3. Note
that the proper basis for the valuation of fruit and vegetables listed in the Annex to Commission
Regulation (EC) 3223/94 [1994] OJ L337/66, as amended, has been the subject of a reference to
the Court of Justice: see Case C–422/00 *Capespan International plc v Commissioners of Customs and
Excise* [2001] OJ C28/18. The Court is asked, among other things, whether the listed products
should be valued in accordance with the CCC and the Implementing Regulation or in accordance
with Art 5 of Commission Regulation (EC) 3223/94, or in some other way.
[140] Implementing Regulation, Art 173.2. Average unit prices are to be notified to the
Commission not later than 12 noon on the Monday of the week during which unit values are
established pursuant to Art 173 and, if that is not a working day, notification is to be made on the

according to Implementing Regulation, Article 173.2(a), the unit price is to be calculated on the basis of prices for undamaged goods[141] in specified marketing centres,[142] during a reference period,[143] and must be calculated on the basis of the gross proceeds of sales made between the importers and wholesalers.[144] From the figures obtained there are four deductions to be made.[145] First, a marketing margin is to be deducted, which is 8 per cent except for marketing centres in London, Milan, and Rungis, in respect of which it is 15 per cent. Secondly, the costs of transport and insurance within the customs territory are to be deducted.[146] Thirdly, there is a standard deduction of an amount of 5 ECU to represent all the other costs which are not to be included in the customs value.[147] Fourthly, import duties and other charges which are not to be included in the customs value are deducted.

A person joins the simplified procedure system for a calendar year in relation to products by declaring, or causing to be declared, the customs value of products by reference to the unit values determined in accordance with the simplified procedures set out in Implementing Regulation, Articles 173–177 considered above.[148] If, once a person has joined the system, he requires the use of a method of valuation other than the simplified system, the customs

---

working day immediately preceding that day. Quantities entering into free circulation during a calendar year for each classification are to be notified to the Commission before 15 June the following year: ibid, Art 174.2 and 3.

[141] Goods are treated as damaged where, at the material time for valuation for customs purposes, (i) consignments contain not less than 5% of produce unfit in its unaltered state for human consumption or, (ii) consignments have depreciated by not less than 20% in relation to average market prices for sound produce: ibid, Art 176.1. Consignments which are damaged may be valued (i) by applying unit values to the sound portion the remainder being destroyed under customs supervision, or (ii) by application of unit values established for the sound produce after deduction of a percentage from the weight of the consignment, equal to the percentage of damaged goods assessed by a sworn expert, and accepted by the customs authorities, or (iii) by application of unit values established for sound produce, reduced by the percentage assessed as damaged by a sworn expert and accepted by the customs authorities: ibid, Art 176.2.

[142] The centres are listed in Implementing Regulation, Annex 27, amended by Annex V to Commission Regulation (EC) 1602/2000 of 24 July 2000 [2000] OJ L188/1. The marketing centres to be taken into account vary according to the product in question. The centres are Athens, Barcelona, Brussels, Cologne, Frankfurt, Hamburg, Le Havre, Marseilles, Milan, Munich, Perpignan, Rungis, Rotterdam, Vienna.

[143] The reference period is the period of 14 days ending on the Thursday preceding the week during which the new unit values are to be established: Implementing Regulation, Art 174.1.

[144] Ibid, Art 173.3. In respect of the marketing centres in London, Milan, and Rungis, the gross proceeds are to be those recorded at the commercial level at which those goods are most commonly sold at those centres.

[145] See ibid, Art 173.3 second para.

[146] Standard amounts may be fixed by Member States in respect of transport and insurance costs, but the amounts and the methods for calculating them must be made known to the Commission immediately: ibid, Art 173.4.

[147] The amount of the total deduction is then converted into the currencies of the Member States on the basis of the latest rates in force and established in accordance with CCC, Art 18.

[148] Implementing Regulation, Art 177.1.

authorities of the Member State in question are entitled to notify him that he will not be allowed to benefit from the simplified system for the remainder of the current calendar year in relation to the products concerned. This exclusion can be extended to cover the following calendar year.[149]

E. ITEMS EXCLUDED FROM CUSTOMS VALUE

CCC, Article 33 states that, provided certain costs are shown separately from the price actually paid or payable, they are not to be included in the customs value of products. In determining what costs may be deducted it is essential to bear in mind that, in respect of goods which are declared for direct entry into free circulation, the date in relation to which goods are valued is the date on which the customs authorities accept the declarant's statement of intention that goods should enter into free circulation.[150] In *Boveri*, therefore, failure to distinguish assembly costs from the transaction price in the valuation declaration meant that the assembly costs could not be deducted from the value on which customs duty was chargeable, notwithstanding that assembly costs are deductible in accordance with, what is now, Article 33.[151] The costs which are deductible from the price actually paid or payable are set out below.

(i)   Charges for the transport of goods after their arrival at the place of introduction into the customs territory of the Community.[152] Where goods are carried by the *same* mode of transport to a point beyond the place of introduction into the Community, transport costs are to be assessed in proportion to the distance covered outside and inside the Community, unless evidence is produced showing the costs that would have been incurred under a general compulsory schedule of freight rates for the carriage of goods to the place of introduction.[153] Where *different* means of transport are used and an all-inclusive price

---

[149] Implementing Regulation, Art 177.2. A notified exclusion must be communicated without delay to the Commission, which in turn must immediately inform the customs authorities of the other Member States: see ibid.

[150] Case 79/89 *Brown Boveri & Cie AG v Hauptzollamt Mannheim* [1991] ECR I–1853 at para 26, considered further below.

[151] The judgment in *Brown Boveri & Cie AG v Hauptzollamt Mannheim*, at n 150 above, should not, however, be regarded as prohibiting an amendment to the relevant declaration after the release of goods, facilitating a repayment of duty pursuant to CCC, Art 236. Such an amendment was not in point in that case. The possibility of making amendments subsequent to release was made clear in Case 84/79 *Richard Mayer-Uetze KG v Hauptzollamt Bad Reichenhall* [1980] ECR 291, at para 14 and Case 290/84 *Hauptzollamt Schweinfurt v Mainfrucht Obstverwertung GmbH*, n 16 above, at para 34 onwards. At the present time a post-release amendment may be made pursuant to CCC, Art 78. This permits an amendment to be made on the initiative of the customs authorities or at the request of the declarant. See further n 159 below re Case C–379/2000 *Overland Footwear Ltd (formerly Overland Shoes Ltd) v CCE* [2000] OJ C355/28.

[152] CCC, Art 33.1(a). The place of introduction into the customs territory of the Community is specifically defined in Implementing Regulation, Art 163.

[153] Implementing Regulation, Art 164(a).

paid, one must either deduct from the price actually paid or payable the cost of transport within the customs territory of the Community, on the basis of the schedule of freight rates normally applied, or determine the cost of transport to the place of introduction into the customs territory of the Community directly on the basis of the rates normally applied. It is for the national authorities to choose the criterion which is more likely to avoid arbitrary and fictitious values.[154]

(ii) Charges for construction, erection, assembly, maintenance, or technical assistance, undertaken after importation of imported goods such as industrial plant, machinery, or equipment.[155]

(iii) Charges for interest under a financing arrangement entered into by the buyer and relating to the purchase of imported goods, irrespective of whether the finance is provided by the seller or another person, provided that three conditions are fulfilled.[156] The first is that the financing arrangement has been made in writing. The second is that, where required, the buyer can demonstrate that the goods are actually sold at the price declared as the price actually paid or payable. Thirdly, the buyer must be able, where required, to demonstrate that the claimed rate of interest does not exceed the level for such transactions prevailing when, and in the country where, the finance was provided.[157]

---

[154] Case C–17/89 *Hauptzollamt Frankfurt am Main-Ost v Deutsche Olivetti GmbH* [1990] ECR I–2301 paras 24 and 25. Art 164(b) of the Implementing Regulation provides that transport costs within the Community are not to be deducted from the uniform free domicile price which corresponds to the price at the place of introduction into the Community. Their deduction is permitted if evidence is produced showing that the free-frontier price would be lower than the uniform free domicile price. In Case 84/79 *Richard Meyer-Uetze KG v Hauptzollamt Bad Reichenhall*, at n 151 above, the Court of Justice held that the uniform free domicile price did not have to be the same for all destinations within the Community (para 10) and that it was for the national court to decide what evidence the importer must produce bearing in mind that the objective of the provisions is to ensure that only transport costs within the Community are deducted (para 13). By virtue of Implementing Regulation, Art 164(c), where transport is free or provided by the buyer, transport costs to the place of introduction, calculated in accordance with the schedule of freight rates normally applied for the same modes of transport, are included in the customs value. Ibid, Art 165 permits customs value to include post charges excluding supplementary postal charges levied in the country of importation (with exceptions for certain express postal services). Ibid, Art 166, provides that air transport costs are included in the customs value of goods by applying the rules and percentages set out in Annex 25 to the Implementing Regulation.

[155] CCC, Art 33.1(b).

[156] A financing arrangement includes an agreement to permit deferred payment for a consideration: see Case 21/91 *Wünsche Handelsgesellschaft International GmbH & Co KG v Hauptzollamt Hamburg-Jonas* [1992] ECR I–3647. The arrangement does not need to be specifically agreed: see paras 18 and 19. See also Case C–93/96 *Indústria e Comércio Têxtil SA (ICT) v Fazenda Pública* [1997] ECR 2281 at paras 16 and 17. A reference to the Court of Justice for a preliminary ruling on when interest forms part of the customs value of goods has been made in Case C–152/01 *Kyocera Electronics Europe GmbH v Hauptzollamt Krefeld* [2001] OJ C184/4. See also n 159 below.

[157] CCC, Art 33.1(c). Implementing Regulation, Art 156 states that this provision shall apply *mutatis mutandis* where the customs value is determined by applying a method other than the transaction value.

    (iv)   Charges for the right to reproduce imported goods in the Community.[158]

    (v)   Buying commissions, defined as set out above in relation to CCC, Article 32.[159]

    (vi)   Import duties or other charges payable in the Community by reason of the importation or sale of goods.[160]

The customs authorities may at the request of the person concerned, authorize derogations from CCC, Article 33 and permit certain deductions in cases where the amounts relating to the elements in question are not shown separately at the time the customs debt is incurred. These are to be determined on the basis of appropriate and specific criteria and subject to certain specific conditions. The conditions include the existence of valid reasons for considering that the amount of import duty to be charged in the period covered will not be lower than that which would be otherwise levied and that competitive conditions amongst operators are not distorted.[161]

F. DECLARATIONS OF VALUE

Subject to the qualifications set out below, where it is necessary to establish a customs value for the purposes of the CCC a person, established in the Community and in possession of the relevant facts, must make a declaration of particulars relating to customs value, which must accompany the customs entry.[162] The making of the declaration is of great significance as we have seen. The Court of Justice has said:

---

[158] CCC, Art 33.1(d).

[159] Ibid, Art 33.1(e) and Art 32.4. A preliminary ruling has been sought from the Court of Justice by the UK's VAT and Duties Tribunal in relation to CCC, Art 33: see Case C–379/2000 *Overland Footwear Ltd (formlery Overland Shoes Ltd) v CCE*, n 151 above. For the judgment of the referring tribunal see C00113: LON/99/7025. The trader in question did not show buying commissions separately and paid duty on them. On receiving advice the trader subsequently claimed repayment of the duty paid on the buying commission. The tribunal asks whether in these circumstances the commission is dutiable and whether the declaration may be amended and whether the duty on the commissions should be repaid. It is suggested that even if the commissions are dutiable if not separately shown, there is no reason why the relevant declarations should not be amended, having regard to the terms of CCC, Art 78, and the duty repaid, so long as the customs authorities are satisfied about the accuracy of the amendment.

[160] CCC, Art 33.1(f).

[161] Implementing Regulation, Art 156a.

[162] Ibid, Art 178.1 and 2. It is not necessary, of course, where the simplified procedure system is used: ibid, Art 178.5. Note that customs authorities are authorized to waive the requirement of a declaration under Art 178.1, among other things, for the purposes of test programmes designed to evaluate possible simplifications, for the period necessary to carry out the programme. The information is to be available, however, in the framework of a control operation: see Implementing Regulation, Art 4c, inserted by Commission Regulation (EC) 2787/2000 of 15 Dec 2000 [2000] OJ L330/1.

once the importer, in his customs value declaration, has chosen the price which will be used as the basis for determining the customs value, he may not correct his declaration or, consequently, the statements relating to customs value after the customs authority has released the goods for free circulation.[163]

Applying this principle the Court has also said:

> once an importer has omitted in his customs declaration to distinguish the assembly costs from the price actually paid or payable, he may not amend his declaration or, consequently, the particulars regarding the customs value, after the customs authority has released the goods for free circulation—that is, after the material time for valuation for customs purposes.[164]

The result of a failure to distinguish different kinds of costs may be that customs duty is paid on a higher value than is necessary. As we noted above, however, CCC, Article 78 permits declarations to be amended after release of goods by the customs authorities on their own initiative or at the request of the declarant and a repayment of duty may follow such as amendment.[165]

The form on which the declaration is made should correspond to the specimen form (D.V.1) contained in Implementing Regulation, Annex 28. The lodging of a declaration of particulars is said to be 'equivalent to the engagement of responsibility' by the declarant in respect of the accuracy and completeness of the particulars in the declaration, the authenticity of the documents produced to support the particulars, and the supply of any additional information or document necessary to establish customs value.[166] Where computerized systems are used, or where the goods concerned are within a general, periodic, or recapitulative declaration, the customs authorities may authorize variations in the form in which data is presented for the purposes of determining customs value.[167]

The declarant must supply the customs authorities with a copy of the invoice on the basis of which the value of the goods is declared, and where the value is declared in writing, the authorities are to retain a copy of it.[168] Where the invoice is made out to a person established in a Member State other than that in which the customs value is declared, two copies of the invoice must be supplied. One copy is to be retained by the authorities, the other is to be returned to the declarant for forwarding to the person to whom the invoice is

---

[163] Case 11/89 *Unifert v Hauptzollamt Münster* at n 28 above, at para 18.

[164] Case 79/89 *Brown Boveri & Cie KG v Hauptzollamt Mannheim* at n 150 above, at para 29. The Court cited in support Case C–11/89 *Unifert v Hauptzollamt Münster* at n 28 above. Both these cases were applied by the German Bundesfinanzhof in *Re Imports of Tapioca Pellets* (Case VII R–66/89 [1993] 2 CMLR 158.

[165] See n 151 above and Ch 9. [166] Implementing Regulation, Art 178.4.

[167] Ibid, Art 180.

[168] The declarant has no obligation to declare charges, such as quota charges, which are not part of the customs value of goods: see Case C–340/93 *Klaus Thierschmidt GmbH v Hauptzollamt Essen* at n 59 above, at paras 23–28.

made out. This copy is to bear the stamp of the office in question and the serial number of the declaration at the office. If they wish, customs authorities may apply the rules regarding two copies of the invoice to situations in which the person to whom the invoice is made out is established in the Member State in which the declaration is made.[169]

Although the obligation to make a declaration is expressed as generally applicable, it is an obligation which may or must be waived in a number of situations. The customs authorities may waive the requirement to make a declaration where the value of the goods in question cannot be determined in accordance with CCC, Article 29 which, as noted earlier, establishes the trans-action value, ie the price actually paid or payable, as the primary method of valuation. Where a waiver is given, the customs authorities must be supplied with such other information as they may request for determining the value of the goods under another Article of the CCC and the information is to be supplied in such form and manner as they may prescribe.[170] The requirement that all particulars be furnished in support of each declaration may be waived where there is continuing traffic in goods supplied by the same seller to the same buyer under the same commercial conditions. Particulars may instead be provided whenever circumstances change but at least once every three years.[171]

The customs authorities must waive the requirement to make all or part of the declaration in the following situations, except where it is essential for the correct application of import duties:

(i)   where the customs value of the goods in a consignment does not exceed ECU 5,000,[172] provided that there are not split or multiple consignments from the same consignor to the same consignee;

(ii) where the importations concerned are non-commercial,

(iii) where the submission of the particulars in question is not necessary for the application of the Community Customs Tariff, or where the customs duties provided for in the Tariff are not chargeable, pursuant to specific customs provisions.[173]

A waiver granted in any of the three circumstances set out above may, of course, be withdrawn and a value declaration required where it is discovered that a condition necessary for the waiver was not, or is no longer, met.[174]

---

[169] Implementing Regulation, Art 181.

[170] Implementing Regulation, Art 178.3. A declarant does not fail in his duty, however, when he accurately answers a specified questionnaire but does not provide information which customs authorities could have requested of him but did not: Case 65/79 *Procureur de la République v René Chatain*, n 32 above, para 24.

[171] Implementing Regulation, Art 179.3.

[172] The conversion of this value into national currency is provided for in ibid, Art 179.2.

[173] Ibid, Art 179.1, (a)–(c).

[174] Ibid, Art 179.4.

9

Customs Entry and Declaration

So far in this book we have looked at the legal concepts which underlie Community customs law. Now we turn to consider customs entry and the making of the customs declaration with the aim of stating the broad outlines of the general administrative framework within which these crucial events take place. At the outset it should be noted that the customs declaration is of the greatest importance because a customs debt is incurred at the time a declaration is accepted.[1] Administratively, the receipt of declarations is a huge task, as can be seen from the fact that in 1999–2000, HM Customs and Excise processed some 7.1 million individual import declarations.[2]

In the first section, A, we look at entry of goods into the customs territory, customs supervision, the duty to convey and present goods to the customs authorities, the summary declaration and temporary storage of goods. In the next section, B, we consider the declarant and customs declarations together with certain relevant rights and duties of the trader and the customs authorities.

This area of law, like so many others in the customs field, is addressed by international conventions and in particular the Kyoto Convention of 1974 and the Revised Kyoto Convention. Specific Annex A Chapter 1 of the revised convention is concerned with formalities prior to the lodgement of the goods declaration, and Chapter 2 is concerned with the temporary storage of goods. So far as the original Kyoto Convention is concerned, Annex A1, concerned with customs formalities prior to the lodgement of the customs declaration was accepted by a Council Decision of 6 June 1978 subject to certain reservations.[3] Annex A.2 which deals with the temporary storage of goods was accepted by the same decision, again with reservations.[4] It is not proposed to review the contents of these annexes in any detail, but they are referred to at various points throughout this chapter.

---

[1] CCC, Art 201. A customs debt arises in other circumstances too, such as the unlawful removal from customs supervision of goods liable to import duties: see CCC, Art 203.1, considered further in Ch 12 at p 379.

[2] See the Report by the Comptroller and Auditor General, *HM Customs and Excise Regulating Freight Imports from Outside the European Community,* HC 131 Session 2000–2001: 2 Feb 2001, para 1 of the executive summary. It is interesting to note, however, that although these declarations were made by 80,000 separate importers, some 250 importers were responsible for just over half the value of the imports: see ibid, at Part 1, para 1.2.

[3] Council Decision (EEC) 528/78 [1978] OJ L160/13. The reservations were amended by a Council Decision of 10 Mar 1994, (EEC) 167/94 [1994] OJ L76/28.

[4] See n 3 above,

A. ENTRY OF GOODS INTO THE CUSTOMS TERRITORY

1. *Customs supervision*

From the moment that goods enter into the customs territory of the Community, they are subject to the supervision of the customs authorities and may be subject to customs control.[5] 'Supervision by the customs authorities' means action taken, in general by those authorities, with a view to ensuring that customs rules and, where appropriate, other provisions applicable to goods subject to customs supervision are observed.[6] 'Control by customs authorities' means the performance of specific acts such as examining goods, verifying the existence and authenticity of documents, examining the accounts of undertakings and other records, inspecting means of transport, inspecting luggage and other goods carried by or on persons, and carrying out official inquiries and other similar acts, with a view to ensuring that customs rules, and other provisions applicable to goods subject to supervision, are observed.[7]

1.1 *The duration of supervision*

Goods which enter the Community customs territory remain under customs supervision for as long as is necessary to determine their customs status. Non-community goods remain under supervision until either their customs status is changed,[8] they enter a free zone or a free warehouse, or they are re-exported or destroyed in accordance with CCC, Article 182.[9] Where goods are released for free circulation with a favourable tariff treatment, or at a reduced rate of duty or a zero rate on account of their end use, they remain under customs supervision. The supervision lasts until the goods are first assigned to the prescribed end use or are exported, destroyed, or used otherwise in accordance with Implementing Regulation, Articles 298 and 299. Customs supervision may, however, continue for a period not exceeding two years after the date of being assigned to end use, where the goods are suitable for repeated use and the customs authorities consider it appropriate in order to avoid abuse.[10] Unlawful removal of goods from customs supervision gives rise to a liability to import duties.[11]

---

[5] CCC, Art 37.1. The same is true of goods outside the customs territory which are subject to the control of the customs authorities of a Member State by virtue of an agreement with a third country: ibid, Art 38.3.

[6] Ibid, Art 4(13).   [7] Ibid, Art 4(14).

[8] As defined in ibid, Art 4(7) and (8).   [9] Ibid, Art 37.2.

[10] Implementing Regulation, Art 300. This Art also provides that waste and scrap which result from working or processing of goods, and losses due to natural wastage, shall be considered as goods having been assigned to the prescribed end-use. In relation to waste and scrap resulting from the destruction of goods, supervision shall end when they have been assigned a permitted customs-approved treatment or use: see ibid, Art 300.2 and 3.

[11] See further Ch 12 at p 378.

2. *Duty to convey goods to a customs office*

In general, goods which are brought into the customs territory[12] must 'without delay' be conveyed either to (i) the customs office designated by the customs authorities or to any other place designated or approved by the customs authorities,[13] or to (ii) a free zone, so long as the goods are brought into the free zone directly, by sea, air, or by land (and in the latter case without passing through another part of the Community customs territory, where the free zone adjoins the land frontier between a Member State and a third country).[14] The person responsible for conveying the goods to the specified places is the person who brings them into the Community or any person who assumes responsibility for the carriage of goods, whether or not as a result of transhipment, after they have been brought into the customs territory of the Community.[15] The customs authorities are to be informed without delay where unforeseeable circumstances or *force majeure* mean that the obligation to convey goods cannot be complied with. They are then to determine the measures to be taken in order that the goods are conveyed as required.[16]

3. *Presentation of goods to customs authorities*

Once goods arrive at the customs office or other designated place, they are to be presented to customs by the person who brought the goods into the customs territory or the person who assumes responsibility for carriage of the goods after entry.[17] After presentation, goods may, with the permission of the customs authorities, be examined or sampled in order that they may be assigned a customs approved treatment or use.[18] Save in the event of imminent danger, they are to be unloaded or transhipped solely with the permission of the customs authorities and only in places designated or approved by them.

---

[12] But not, subject to certain conditions, goods which temporarily leave the customs territory while moving between points within it (CCC, Art 38.5), nor goods on board vessels or aircraft crossing the territorial sea or airspace of the Member States without having as their destination a port or airport situated in the Member States.

[13] There are exceptions to this rule for tourist traffic, frontier and postal traffic etc: ibid, Art 38.4.

[14] Ibid, Art 38.1.

[15] Ibid, Art 38. 2.

[16] Ibid, Art 39.

[17] 'Presentation of goods to customs' is defined in ibid, Art 4(19).

[18] Ibid, Arts 40 and 42. Further provisions regarding examination of goods are contained in Art 182 of the Implementing Regulation. A customs-approved treatment or use of goods is defined as meaning: the placing of goods under a customs procedure, the entry of goods into a free-zone or warehouse, the re-exportation of goods from the Community customs territory, the destruction of goods, and the abandonment of goods to the Exchequer (see CCC, Art 4(15)). In certain circumstances goods presented to customs authorities may be destroyed or sold (ibid, Arts 56 and 57). There are specific provisions regarding the presentation of goods brought into the customs territory from a third country by sea or air and in respect of the cabin and hold baggage of travellers: Implementing Regulation, Arts 189–197.

They may not be removed from their original position without the permission of the customs authorities, who may at any time require them to be unloaded or unpacked.[19]

Certain goods, such as those of a non-commercial nature in travellers' personal luggage, are deemed to have been presented to the customs authorities and, where not expressly declared to customs, are deemed to have been declared for release for free circulation. The declaration is deemed to have been accepted and the release is deemed to have been granted.[20]

4. *Summary declaration*

Following presentation of the goods to the customs authorities, they are to be covered by a summary declaration. The customs authorities may permit this to be lodged within a period which is not to extend beyond the first working day following the day on which the goods are presented.[21] This may now be made in computerized form. The customs authorities may permit, as a written declaration, any commercial or official document which contains the necessary particulars, but the summary declaration for goods which have been moved under transit before presentation must take the form of the copy of the transit document intended for the customs office of destination.[22] The person who must lodge the declaration is the person who brought the goods into the customs territory, or any person who assumes responsibility for carriage of the goods following entry, or the person in whose name either of the foregoing acted.[23]

5. *Temporary storage*

Goods which are presented to the customs authorities must be assigned a customs-approved treatment or authorized use.[24] During the period between presentation and assignation of a customs-approved treatment or authorized use, the goods are known as 'goods in temporary storage'.[25] Goods are placed in storage on the basis of the summary declaration[26] and remain under customs supervision until their customs status is changed.[27]

---

[19] CCC, Arts 46 and 47.   [20] See Implementing Regulation, Arts 230 and 234.
[21] CCC, Art 43. The requirement to make a summary declaration may be waived where, prior to the expiry of the period referred to, there have been carried out the formalities necessary for the goods to be assigned a customs-approved treatment or use. This is without prejudice to the provisions governing goods imported by travellers and consignments by letter and parcel post. Ibid, Art 45.
[22] Ibid, Art 44.1, and Implementing Regulation, Art 183.3.
[23] CCC, Article 44.2. Further provisions regarding the summary declaration and presentation of goods are contained in Implementing Regulation, Art 183–184.
[24] CCC, Art 48.   [25] Ibid, Art 50.
[26] Implementing Regulation, Art 186.
[27] CCC, Art 37.2; applied in Case C–66/99 *D Wandel GmbH v Hauptzollamt Bremen* [2001] ECR I-2579 para 35.

Goods in temporary storage are to be stored only in such places and subject to such conditions as the authorities specify, and security may be required for the customs debt arising in respect of them.[28] They are to be subject only to such forms of handling as are designed to ensure their preservation in an unaltered state, without modifying their appearance or technical characteristics.[29] The Implementing Regulation contains further detailed provisions regarding temporary storage, including the requirement that the storage facilities be double locked with one key held by the customs authorities.[30]

Where goods are covered by a summary declaration, the formalities for assigning them a customs-approved treatment or use must, according to CCC, Article 49, be carried out within specified time limits. These limits are, therefore, limits upon the period in which the goods are kept in temporary storage. In the case of goods carried by sea the limit is forty-five days from the date on which the summary declaration is lodged. In the case of goods carried in any other way the time period is twenty-days from the date of lodging the summary declaration.[31] Where 'circumstances' warrant, customs authorities may shorten these periods and, where genuine requirements justify it, lengthen them.[32] CCC, Article 53 provides that where the formalities for assignment have not been initiated within these time limits, customs authorities are, without delay, to take all measures necessary, including the sale of goods, to regularize the situation.[33] They may, at the risk and expense of the person holding the goods, have them transferred, pending regularization, to a special place which is under their supervision.[34] It will be apparent that Member States are given a choice as to the measures which are to apply in the event of the time limits not being met and, unsurprisingly perhaps, the Court of Justice has held that the application of an automatic sale procedure in respect of goods which are overdue for clearance is consistent with Article 53.[35] It has also held that the application of such a procedure, avoidable only by payment of an *ad valorem* surcharge, is consistent with the principle of proportionality. The surcharge, however, must be determined under conditions which are comparable to those applicable under national law to infringements of the same nature and gravity. In *José Teodoro de Andrade* it was for the national court to determine whether a 5 per cent *ad valorem* penalty was consistent with these principles.[36]

It will be apparent that goods may be kept in temporary storage only for

---

[28] CCC, Art 51.
[30] Implementing Regulation, Art 185.2(a).
[32] Ibid, Art 49.2.
[34] Ibid, Art 53.2.
[35] Case C–213/99 *José Teodoro de Andrade v Director da Alfândega de Leixões*, 7 Dec 2000, at para 13.
[36] Ibid, at paras 24 and 25. The Court applied Case C–36/94 *Siesse-Soluções Integrais em Sistemas Software e Aplicações Ld^a v Director da Alfândega de Alcântara* [1995] ECR I–3573 at paras 21 to 24.

[29] Ibid, Art 52.
[31] CCC, Art 49.1.
[33] Ibid, Art 53.1.

relatively short time periods, but, as the Court of Justice has noted, these short periods, imposed by CCC, Article 49.1, are deliberately established to ensure that goods are quickly assigned a customs approved treatment or use.[37] The Court has, however, had to consider what circumstances would warrant the extension of the time limits.

5.1 *Extending the time of temporary storage*

As we have seen, according to CCC, Article 49.2, the time limits may be shortened or extended where circumstances warrant. The Court of Justice has stated that:

> The objective of Article 49(1) of the Customs Code would not be achieved if traders were able to rely on circumstances which were in no way exceptional in order to obtain an extension. Such an interpretation of the term 'circumstances' contained in that provision would lead to the result that temporary storage could be regularly extended and the temporary storage procedure might, in time, be transformed into a customs warehousing procedure.

> Therefore, the term `circumstances' within the meaning of Article 49(2) of the Customs code must be interpreted as referring to circumstances which are liable to put the applicant in an exceptional situation in relation to other traders carrying on the same activity.

> Exceptional circumstances which, although not unknown to the trader, are not events which normally confront any trader in the exercise of his occupation, may constitute such circumstances.[38]

The Court went on to say that it is for the national authorities, courts, and tribunals to determine whether such circumstances exist and that, in the instant case, a backlog of work due to a changeover to an electronic accounting system and staff shortages due to illness did not constitute exceptional circumstances.[39]

Clearly, changes in systems and staff illness are not exceptional occurrences in commercial life and it was, no doubt, in the light of this that the Court stated that the events justifying an extension 'must not normally confront any trader'. Nevertheless, what is exceptional for a small or medium-sized business may not be so for a much larger operation. The reference to what is normal for any trader should perhaps be understood, therefore, as a reference to any trader of a comparable nature to the trader in question. The Advocate General noted that the extraordinary circumstances, being those literally 'outside the ordinary',[40] should be specific to the undertaking. This is a safeguard both for

[37] Case 48/98 *Firma Söhl & Söhlke v Hauptzollamt Bremen* [1999] ECR I–7877 at para 71.
[38] Ibid at paras 71–74.
[39] Ibid at paras 75 and 76.
[40] Ibid the Opinion of Advocate General Jacobs at para 50.

the customs authorities and for the trader. On the one hand the trader cannot obtain an extension where general difficulties have not specifically affected it. On the other hand, specific difficulties which have not been generally experienced may justify an extension.

In considering the circumstances in which an extension should be made available, it must be borne in mind that it is undoubtedly essential to ensure that temporary storage remains precisely that. It should be noted, however, that the Kyoto Convention, in both its original and revised form, is concerned to ensure that the period of temporary storage is adequate. Standard 14 of Annex A.1 to the Kyoto Convention, and Standard 9 in Chapter 2 of Specific Annex A to the revised Kyoto Convention, state that 'Where national legislation lays down a time limit for temporary storage, the time allowed shall be sufficient to enable the importer to complete the necessary formalities to place the goods under a Customs procedure.' The note to this standard, which is not reproduced in Specific Annex A to the revised Kyoto Convention, observes that the time limit which is laid down may vary according to the mode of transport and in the case of goods imported by sea 'may well be of considerable duration'.[41] The first recital to Annex A.2 to the Kyoto Convention also acknowledges that the period of temporary storage may be significant, stating that 'For a variety of reasons some time may elapse between the arrival of the goods and the lodgment of the relevant Goods declaration'.

Finally, it is also worth noting recommended practice 15 of Annex A1 to the Kyoto Convention and recommended practice 10 in Chapter 2 of Specific Annex A to the revised Kyoto Convention. They both state 'At the request of the person concerned, and for reasons deemed valid by the Customs authorities, the latter should extend the period initially fixed.'

5.2 *Global applications for extension*

So far as concerns the formalities of applying for extensions, the Court of Justice has ruled that it is possible to make one application, for an extension of time for assigning goods to a customs-approved treatment or use, in relation to a number of summary declarations.[42] In the case before the Court the summary declarations in question had been made over a period of months.[43] As the Court recognized, to require a multiplicity of applications would have been merely to introduce unnecessary administrative complexity into the system. It was not prepared to do this, particularly bearing in mind that the sixth recital to the CCC states that 'customs formalities and controls should be abolished or at least kept to a minimum'. Nevertheless, an application for

---

[41] As we have seen, the CCC does indeed provide for a longer period (45 days), in relation to goods carried by sea, as opposed to 20 days for those carried by land and air.

[42] Case 48/98 *Firma Söhl & Söhlke v Hauptzollamt Bremen* at n 37 above, at para 80.

[43] Ibid, para 78.

extension must be made 'in time'.[44] It follows that it must be made before the time limit governing the assignment to a customs-approved use or treatment expires.[45]

B. THE DECLARANT AND CUSTOMS DECLARATIONS

1. *The declarant*

The general rule is that a customs declaration may be made by any person who is able to present the goods in question to customs, or to have them presented to the customs authority, together with all necessary documents.[46] This rule is subject to the provisions of CCC, Article 5 which permits both direct and indirect representation, subject to restrictions imposed by Member States and certain other qualifications. Direct representation is where the representative acts in the name and on behalf of another person. Indirect representation is where the representative acts in his own name on behalf of another person.[47] The representative must state that he is acting on behalf of the person represented, must specify whether the representation is indirect or direct, and must actually be empowered to act as a representative. He must also be established in the Community.[48] Member States have the power to restrict the right to make a customs declaration, whether by direct representation or by indirect representation, so that the representative is a customs agent carrying on business in the territory of the Member State.[49] That is, however, the sole limitation which Member States may impose. A Member State may not, however, reserve one type of representation for a certain group of persons.[50]

The lodging with the customs office of a declaration signed by the declarant or his representative imposes a serious responsibility on him, quite apart from considerations of criminal law. The declarant is responsible for the accuracy of the information in the declaration, the authenticity of any documents attached to it, and compliance with all obligations relating to entry of the goods in respect of the procedure in question.[51] Furthermore, the declarant is one of the persons who may be made liable for the customs debt.[52]

---

[44] Implementing Regulation, Art 859.1.

[45] Case 48/98 *Firma Söhl & Söhlke v Hauptzollamt Bremen* at n 37 above, para 82.

[46] CCC, Art 64.   [47] Ibid, Art 5.2, first para.

[48] Ibid, Art 5.3 and 5.4. The requirement of establishment does not apply in relation to declarations for transit or temporary importation, or to persons who act on an occasional basis (provided the authorities consider this justified): ibid, Art 64.1 and 2. There is also provision for the application of bilateral agreements and customary practices: see ibid, Art 64.3.

[49] Ibid, Art 5.2, second para. The legislation of Member States in this area must, of course, respect the fundamental freedoms of the EC Treaty: see Case 159/78 *Commission v Italy* [1979] ECR 3247.

[50] Case C–323/90 *Commission v Portugal* [1992] ECR I–1887 and Case C–119/92 *Commission v Italy* [1994] ECR I–393 both of which concern the somewhat different legislation in place prior to the Code.

[51] Implementing Regulation, Art 199.1.   [52] Ibid, Art 201.3.

2. *The declaration*

2.1 *The purpose of the declaration*

All goods intended to be placed under a customs procedure[53] are to be governed by a declaration for that procedure and goods declared for transit, customs warehousing, export, or outward processing are to be subject to customs supervision from the time of the acceptance of the declaration in respect of the procedure until they leave the customs territory, are destroyed, or the customs declaration is invalidated.[54] The customs declaration is therefore 'the act whereby a person indicates in the prescribed form and manner a wish to place goods under a given customs procedure'.[55] A glance at a declaration will quickly show that it is more than the mere indication of a wish. The definition of 'Goods declaration', contained in Chapter 2 of the General Annex to the revised Kyoto Convention, gives a rather better impression of what a declaration is stating that it is 'a statement made in the form prescribed by Customs, by which the persons interested indicate the particular Customs procedure to be applied to the goods and furnish the particulars which the Customs require to be declared for its application'.[56] As we noted at the beginning of this chapter, the acceptance of the declaration also marks a crucial point in time so far as the imposition of customs duty is concerned because it is the time at which the customs debt is frequently incurred.[57]

3. *The form of the standard declaration*

The customs declaration may be made in writing, or using a data-processing technique,[58] or by means of a 'normal declaration or other act' whereby the declarant expresses the wish to place the goods under a customs procedure.[59] There are extensive provisions governing written declarations which apply

[53] There are eight customs procedures. They are: release for free circulation, transit, customs warehousing, inward processing and processing under customs control, temporary admission, outward processing, and exportation (see CCC, Art 4(16)). See further Chs 10 and 11.

[54] CCC, Art 59.

[55] Ibid, Art 4(17).

[56] Definition (c) in the definitions section in Annex A.2 to the Kyoto Convention is in similar terms.

[57] CCC, Art 201.2. The acceptance of the declaration may also be important for the imposition of other levies imposed by reference to the day of importation. This is the day on which the import declaration is accepted by the customs authorities. If there has been a delay in transporting goods to the customs office or place designated by them, beyond the control of the declarant, that may not alter the day of importation: See Case 113/78 *NGJ Schouten BV v Hoofdproduktschap voor Akkerbouwprodukten* [1979] ECR 695.

[58] Implementing Regulation, Art 4a–4c enables customs authorities to provide that formalities may be carried out by a data-processing technique.

[59] CCC, Art 61.

mutatis mutandis to declarations made by a data-processing technique[60] and to oral declarations.[61] Deemed declarations may also be made, along with deemed presentation of goods to the customs authorities. Deeming provisions apply in relation to goods of a non-commercial nature contained in travellers' personal luggage,[62] as noted above, and certain postal consignments.[63]

The official model form for written declarations to customs by the normal procedure to be used for the purposes of placing goods under a customs procedure, or re-exporting them, is the Single Administrative Document (SAD).[64] The SAD is to be presented in sub-sets containing the requisite number of copies for the completion of formalities relating to the customs procedure under which the goods are to be placed. The full set of subsets is contained in Annex 31 to the Implementing Regulation.[65] The SAD must be completed in accordance with the detailed explanatory notes in Annex 37 to the Implementing Regulation which Member States may expand upon.[66] The form itself must conform to the specimens contained in Annexes to the Implementing Regulation. The completed forms provide comprehensive information about the goods, their origin, the transaction in question, their transport and so on.

4. *Documents accompanying the declaration*

Specified documents are to accompany the declaration.[67] In relation to the release for free circulation, they are: the invoice on the basis of which the customs value of the goods is declared, any declaration of particulars for the

---

[60] CCC, Art 77. Art 77.2 was added by Regulation (EC) 2700/2000 [2000] OJ L311/17 and provides that where customs declarations are made electronically, traders are now permitted to keep records at their premises, so dispensing with the need to present documents at the border. For detailed rules on customs declarations made using a data-processing technique see Implementing Regulation, Arts 222–224. The UK Customs and Excise Commissioners have developed Customs Freight Simplified Procedures in order to facilitate paperless customs clearance for many goods imported from third countries. For more information on this see: http://www.hmce.gov.uk/bus/customs/index.htm. Traders who are authorized under the CSFP may use a paperless Local Clearance Procedure and, from Mar 2001, a Simplified Declaration Procedure. HM Customs and Excise also have a computerized system for import entry processing called 'CHIEF' (Customs Handling of Import and Export Freight). It is planned to extend the system to control and clear declarations for export under the 'New Export System', which at the time of writing is expected to be fully operational by 31 Dec 2001.

[61] For the rules in relation to oral declarations see Implementing Regulation, Arts 225–238.

[62] Ibid, Arts 230 and 234.

[63] Ibid, Art 237.

[64] Ibid, Art 205. Other forms may be used in certain circumstances as the Article permits. See also CCC, Art 62.1.

[65] Implementing Regulation, Art 208.1 and 3.

[66] Ibid, Art 212. Customs administrations may, for the purpose of completing export or import formalities, dispense with the production of one or more copies of the SAD provided that the information is available on other media: ibid, Art 207.

[67] See CCC, Art 62.1.

assessment of customs value, discussed in the previous chapter, the documents required for the application of preferential tariff arrangements, or other measures derogating from the applicable legal rules, and all other documents required for the application of the provisions governing the release for free circulation of the goods declared.[68] Transport documents or documents relating to previous customs procedures may also be required.[69] There are particular requirements relating to the transit declaration,[70] the declaration for a customs procedure with economic impact,[71] and export or re-export declarations.[72]

5. *Incomplete and simplified procedures*

It is not proposed to consider the provisions governing incomplete and simplified procedures in detail. It should be noted, however, that the customs authorities may accept declarations which do not contain the required information or which are not accompanied by the necessary documentation, under the rules relating to incomplete declarations. A declaration for release for free circulation, for example, need not contain all the particulars and documents referred to in Annex 37, although certain information, for example, in relation to identification, classification, and valuation is required.[73] The declarant may be allowed one month from the date of acceptance to provide necessary documents, although in certain circumstances this period may be extended by an additional period of not more than three months.[74]

The benefit of tariff quotas or preferential tariff measures is only to be granted after presentation to the customs authorities of the document on which the availability of the zero or reduced rate is conditional. The document must be presented before the tariff quota is exhausted or the reintroduction of normal duties.[75] Subject to the rules set out above, though, the presentation of the necessary documents may be made after the expiry date of the period for which the reduced or zero rate was set, provided that the declaration was accepted before that date.[76] (As we noted in Chapter 5, save as otherwise provided, quotas are to be managed in accordance with the chronological order of dates of acceptance of the declarations.[77])

---

[68] Implementing Regulation, Art 218.1. The first three of these additional documents need not be required where the goods attract the flat rate of duty or relief from import duties unless they are necessary for applying provisions relating to release for free circulation: ibid, Art 218.3.

[69] Ibid, Art 218.2.   [70] Ibid, Art 219.

[71] Ibid, Art 220. Customs procedures with economic impact are: customs warehousing, inward processing, processing under customs control, temporary importation, and outward processing: CCC, Art 84(b).

[72] Implementing Regulation, Art 221: see also ibid, Art 4c.

[73] See ibid, Art 254.

[74] See ibid, Art 256.1. See also ibid, Art 268.2 and Art 280.4 which apply some of the provisions relating to declarations for free circulation to other declarations.

[75] Ibid, Art 256.2.   [76] Ibid, Art 256.3.

[77] Ibid, Art 308a.1.

The Implementing Regulation contains detailed provisions governing simplified procedures in respect of declarations for release for free circulation (Articles 254–267), in respect of declarations for a customs procedure with economic impact, as defined above (Articles 268–278) and export declarations (Articles 279–289). Each of these groups of provisions establishes a local clearance procedure as well as a simplified declaration procedure and contains certain provisions governing the use of incomplete declarations.[78] It is not proposed to consider these in detail, but it may be noted that, in relation to the declaration for release for free circulation, following a written request, a declarant may make a declaration in simplified form.[79] It may be in the form of an incomplete SAD or of an administrative or commercial document accompanied by a request for release for free circulation.[80] It must contain the particulars necessary for the identification of the goods.[81] A local clearance procedure is also established in relation to the release for free circulation which allows an authorized person to have goods released for free circulation at his premises or at other places designated or authorized by the customs authorities.[82]

Finally, it should be noted that the simplified procedures in respect of declarations may be applied where the declaration is to be made using data-processing techniques.[83]

6. *Importers' obligations as regards the customs declaration*

It is frequently essential for importers to establish that they have complied with all the provisions laid down by the legislation in force as regards customs declarations so that they may resist a claim for the post-clearance recovery of customs duty.[84] The Court of Justice has said:

> It is settled case-law that the person making the declaration must supply the competent customs authorities with all the necessary information as required by the Community rules, and by any national rules supplementing or transposing them, in relation to the customs treatment requested for the goods in question. . . . [T]his obligation may not go beyond production of the information that the person making the declaration may reasonably be expected to possess and obtain, with the result that it is sufficient for such information, even if incorrect, to have been provided in good faith . . .[85]

---

[78] See, eg, ibid, Arts 254–259 re declarations for release for free circulation and ibid, Arts 280–281 re export declarations.

[79] Ibid, Art 260.1 and 3.   [80] Ibid, Art 260.2.

[81] Ibid, Arts 260–262. See also CCC, Art 76.

[82] Implementing Regulation, Arts 263–267.

[83] See, eg, ibid, Art 253a.   [84] See CCC, Article 220.2(b).

[85] Joined cases C–153/94 and C–204/94 *The Queen v Commissioners of Customs & Excise, ex p Faroe Seafood Co Ltd, Føroya Fiskasøla L/F and others* [1996] ECR I–2465 paras 108 and 109. In relation to the first proposition the Court relied upon Case 378/87 *Top Hit Holzvertrieb v Commission* [1989] ECR 1359 para 26. In relation to the second it relied upon Case C–348/89 *Mecanarte v Chefe do Serviço da Conferência Final da Alfândega, Oporto* [1991] ECR I–3277 para 29 and Case C–250/91 *Hewlett Packard France v Directeur Général des Douanes* [1993] ECR I–1819 para 29.

As we have seen, the legislation seeks to ensure that the administrative burdens which would otherwise rest upon an importer are relieved to some extent. Provision is therefore made for simplified declarations, incomplete declarations, paperless declarations, and local clearance. A further attempt to relieve the burden of compliance is made by CCC, Article 81. This states that where a consignment is made up of goods falling within different tariff classifications and dealing with each of the goods in accordance with its tariff classification, for the purpose of drawing up the declaration, would entail a burden of work and expense disproportionate to the import duties chargeable, the customs authorities may agree, at the request of the declarant, that duty is to be charged on the whole consignment on the basis of the tariff classification which attracts the highest rate of import duty.

7. *Lodging and acceptance*

The declaration is to be lodged at the customs office where the goods were presented and lodging is permitted as soon as presentation has taken place.[86] The customs authorities may, however, permit a declaration to be lodged before presentation and at a place other than the office of presentation.[87] The date on which a declaration is accepted is to be noted on it.[88] Declarations which satisfy the requirements governing their form, and are accompanied by the prescribed documents, must be accepted immediately by the customs authorities provided that the goods to which they refer are presented to customs.[89]

8. *Amending and invalidating the declaration*

Once made and accepted by the customs authorities, a declaration may be amended with their consent, although not so as to include additional goods under the coverage of the declaration. If the declaration is to be amended then it must be before the declarant has been informed that the authorities intend to examine the goods, before it has been established that the particulars in question in the declaration are incorrect, and before the goods have been released.[90] As well as being amended, a customs declaration which has been accepted may also be invalidated at the request of the declarant. For invalidation to take place, the declarant must provide proof that goods were declared in error for the customs procedure covered by that declaration, or that, as a result of special circumstances, the placing of the goods under the customs

---

[86] Implementing Regulation, Art 201.1.　　　　　　　　　　　　[87] Ibid, Art 202.2.

[88] Ibid, Art 203. The date of acceptance is the date on which the customs duty liability arises, see n 1 above. See also CCC, Art 67 which states that the date to be used for the purposes of all provisions governing the customs procedure for which the goods are declared shall be the date of acceptance of the declaration by the customs authorities.

[89] CCC, Art 63.　　　　　　　　　　　　[90] Ibid, Art 65. See also section 11 below.

procedure for which they were declared is no longer justified.[91] A request for invalidation, which is made after the customs authorities have informed the declarant of their intention to examine the goods is not to be accepted until after the examination has taken place.[92] Furthermore, a declaration cannot be invalidated after the goods have been released except in certain cases specified in the Implementing Regulation.[93] These permit, subject to certain conditions, invalidation within three months of the acceptance of the declaration, where goods have been declared in error for a customs procedure entailing payment of duties instead of another procedure. The three-month period may be extended in duly substantiated exceptional cases. Invalidation is also permitted within the same time limit, in certain circumstances, where goods have been declared in error instead of other goods and where mail order goods have been returned.[94] Invalidation of declarations for export may also be invalidated in certain circumstances.[95] When invalidation does take place it is effected without prejudice to the application of any penal provisions in force.[96]

9. *Examination of the declaration and the goods*

The customs authorities for their part may examine the declaration and the documents accompanying it for the purpose of verifying the declaration which they have accepted. They may call for further documents to verify the accuracy of the declaration and examine the goods and take samples of them for analysis and verification.[97] The declarant is responsible for the transport of the goods to the place where they are to be examined, and where samples are to be taken, and for all handling necessitated by the examination or sampling. The declarant is also responsible for the costs incurred in the transport and handling.[98] The declarant is entitled to be present when the goods are examined or samples are taken. Indeed, when they deem it appropriate, the customs authorities are entitled to require the declarant to be present, or be represented, at such times in order to provide them with necessary assistance.[99] The customs authorities are liable for the costs of their analysis and examination. They are not, however, liable for payment of compensation provided that the samples are taken in accordance with the provisions in force.[100] Where only some of the goods covered by the declaration are examined, the results of the examination will be applied to all the goods in question, unless the declarant requests a further

---

[91] CCC, Art 66.1, first para.   [92] Ibid, second para.
[93] CCC, Art 66.2.   [94] Implementing Regulation, Art 251.1.
[95] Ibid, Art 251.2.   [96] CCC, Art 66.3.
[97] Ibid, Art 68. See further Implementing Regulation, Arts 239–247.
[98] CCC, Art 69.1.   [99] Ibid, Art 69.2.
[100] Ibid, Art 69.3.

examination, which he may do if he considers that the results of the partial examination are not valid for the unexamined goods.[101]

10. *Release of goods*

Subject to the satisfaction of the conditions for the customs procedure in question and certain other conditions, the customs authorities must release the goods as soon as the declarations in respect of them have been verified or as soon as the declaration has been accepted without verification. All goods covered by the same declaration are to be released at the same time, although a declaration which covers two or more items is deemed to constitute a separate declaration.[102] The granting of a release gives rise to the entry in the accounts of the duties determined according to the particulars in the declaration.[103] Where the acceptance of a customs declaration gives rise to a customs debt then, except in relation to the temporary importation procedure with partial relief from duty, the goods covered by the declaration are not to be released unless the customs debt has been paid or secured.[104] If, however, security is required under provisions relating to any customs procedure, then the goods in question are not to be released until the security is provided.[105]

The customs authorities are entitled to take any necessary measures, including confiscation and sale, in relation to goods which are not removed within a reasonable time after their release,[106] or which cannot be released because of certain specified reasons. These reasons are as follows: (i) it has not been possible to undertake or continue examination of the goods within the period prescribed by the customs authorities for reasons attributable to the declarant; (ii) the documents to be produced before the goods can be placed under a customs procedure have not been produced; (iii) payments have not been made, or security has not been provided, within the specified period; (iv) the goods are subject to bans or restrictions.[107]

11. *Post-clearance examination of declarations*

Notwithstanding the obligation of the customs authorities to release goods where declarations are accepted, they do have powers to examine and amend

---

[101] CCC, Art 70.1. For these purposes, the particulars relating to each item are to be treated as a separate declaration: ibid, Art 70.2.

[102] Ibid, Art 73.

[103] Implementing Regulation, Art 248. Although the English version of Art 248.1 appears to require, where the amount of customs duty ultimately payable may be higher than that which would be chargeable by reference to the particulars in the declaration, security in respect of the possible excess, this is less clear in other language versions: see *Shaneel Enterprises Ltd v CCE* [1996] V&DR 23 at 47 para 103.

[104] CCC, Art 74.1.   [105] Ibid, Art 74.2.

[106] Ibid, Art 75(b).   [107] Ibid, Art 75(a).

declarations following the clearance of the goods. These are exercisable on the authorities' own initiative or at the request of the declarant. Where it is still possible, the goods themselves may also be inspected. If the inspection brings irregularities to light then the customs authorities may take measures necessary to regularize the situation taking account of the new information.[108]

---

[108] CCC, Art 78. The significance of Art 78 has already been considered in Ch 8 at n 159.

10

Customs Procedures and Approved Uses and Treatments

As we noted in the previous chapter there are eight customs procedures. They are:

   (i)   release for free circulation,
   (ii)   transit,
   (iii)   customs warehousing,
   (iv)   inward processing,
   (v)   processing under customs control,
   (vi)   temporary admission/importation,
   (vii) outward processing, and
   (viii) exportation.[1]

There are five customs-approved treatments or uses, namely:

   (i)   the placing of goods under a customs procedure,
   (ii)   the entry of goods into a free-zone or warehouse,
   (iii)   the re-exportation of goods from the Community customs territory,
   (iv)   the destruction of goods, and
   (v)   the abandonment of goods to the Exchequer.[2]

In this chapter it is proposed to comment on all of the procedures, except inward and outward processing, which are considered in Chapter 11,[3] and on the customs-approved treatments and uses. The procedures and approved activities demand considerable activity on the part of the customs authorities of Member States and require that they are able easily to identify 'Community goods'. In view of this, the chapter commences, in section A, with some brief comments on national controls in a customs union. In section B some of the formalities governing the procedures for proving that goods are Community goods are considered. Section C contains a short discussion of some of the newly-rationalized general rules governing customs procedures with economic impact. The chapter then moves on to consider certain specific matters. Section D deals with release for free circulation and end-use, section E deals with transit procedures, and section F is concerned with customs warehousing. Section G is concerned with processing under customs control, whilst section H deals with temporary admission. The consideration of customs

---

[1] CCC, Art 4(16).
[2] Ibid, Art 4(15).
[3] Note however that the rules governing procedures with economic impact, which are considered in section C below, include within their scope inward and outward processing.

procedures is concluded by section I on exportation. We then turn in section J to customs-approved treatments or uses, dealing with free zones and free warehouses, and concluding with re-exportation, destruction, and abandonment.

A cursory glance at the relevant parts of the CCC and the Implementing Regulation will show that there are a great many detailed regulations in place governing all of these matters. An outline rather than a detailed review is all that can be attempted here, particularly in relation to transit procedures. It should also be noted that, although certain provisions concerning the giving of security and guarantees in relation to customs procedures are considered in this chapter, the general topic of security for a customs debt is dealt with in Chapter 12.

A. NATIONAL CUSTOMS CONTROLS IN A CUSTOMS UNION

In 1979, before the introduction of the single market, the Court of Justice put customs controls in their true context and said:

> it should be emphasised that customs controls properly so-called have lost their *raison d'être* . . . Frontier controls remain justified only in so far as they are necessary either for the implementation of the exceptions to free movement referred to in Article [30] of the Treaty; or for the levying of internal taxation with the meaning of Article [90] of the Treaty . . .; or for transit controls; or . . . when they are essential in order to obtain reasonably complete and accurate information on movement of goods within the Community. These residuary controls must nevertheless be reduced as far as possible so that trade between Member States can take place in conditions as close as possible to those prevalent on a domestic market.[4]

It is not only controls on borders between Member States which are regarded as undesirable. The sixth recital to the CCC states in general terms that 'in view of the paramount importance of external trade for the Community, customs formalities and controls should be abolished or at least kept to a minimum'. Inevitably some controls must exist in relation to goods both entering and leaving the customs territory.[5] Indeed, whilst the requirements of external trade may place pressure on the authorities to keep formalities and controls to a minimum, there is a significant and growing pressure to maintain controls flowing from the need to detect and deter fraud. This pressure is, at least in part, produced by the political demands upon the Community, and particularly the Commission, to manage and account for its resources efficiently.[6] Yet there is a

---

[4] Case 159/78 *Commission v Italy* [1979] ECR 3247 at para 7.

[5] For example, CCC, Art 183 specifically provides that goods are to be subject to customs supervision and checks and are to leave the customs territory using, where appropriate, the route determined by the customs authorities and in accordance with the procedures laid down by those authorities.

[6] See further Ch 2 section D: 'The financial context of customs duty: own resources'

balance to be struck between the needs of free trade and the prevention of fraud as the Commission itself has noted.[7]

If the Community customs territory is truly to replicate a domestic market it must not only have residual internal controls and a necessary minimum of external border controls, it will also ensure that the controls which do exist are operated in a uniform manner by the customs authorities. As the Commission has said in its action plan for transit in Europe:

> Bearing in mind that a single customs code would appear to imply a single customs service, it is important that the 15 customs administrations function as if they were one, as proposed in the Customs 2000 programme and called for by Parliament's Committee of Inquiry.[8]

The need for the fifteen services to act as one is important for traders who, reasonably, require a single approach to the administration of the customs union.[9] It is also important for the Community as a whole because it is when the respective customs authorities act as one that the fraudulent exploitation of customs procedures may be combatted most efficiently. Of course, it is not merely the CCC which implies a single customs service. The concept of a customs union itself implies a single service. It is clear, however, that Community customs legislation does indeed require the fifteen different customs services to operate as one in relation to customs procedures. For example, the first indent of CCC, Article 250 provides that, where a customs procedure is used in several Member States, the decisions or identification measures taken or agreed upon, and the documents issued by, the customs authorities of one Member State, are to have the same legal effects in other Member States as they do in the Member State in which they are taken, agreed upon, or issued. Furthermore, the second indent of CCC, Article 250 provides that the findings made at the time controls are carried out by the customs authorities of one Member State are to have the same conclusive force, in the

---

[7] See recital (10) to Commission Regulation (EC) 1602/2000 of 24 July 2000 [2000] OJ L188/1. It states: 'As part of the simplification and rationalisation of customs regulations and procedures it is desirable to increase the flexibility of end-use customs supervision to meet the needs of the diversifying internal market, making it a useful instrument for several sectors. This flexibility needs to be balanced by an increased efficiency of customs supervision to prevent fraud and misuse of favourable tariff treatments as well as reduced duty rates on account of the end-use of certain goods.'

[8] Communication from the Commission to the European Parliament and the Council: Action plan for transit in Europe—a new customs policy: COM/1997/0188 Final [1997] OJ C176/3 para 6.1.

[9] It is not just in relation to customs procedures that uniformity of action by the 15 customs services is necessary. It is also desirable in relation to matters such as valuation. This is emphasized in the Court of Auditors' Special Report 23/2000 concerning valuation of imported goods for customs purposes (customs valuation), together with the Commission's replies [2001] OJ C84/1, at para 8. The Commission's replies indicate the need for realism. It says: 'The Commission is acting, within the means at its disposal, to attain that the Member States' customs authorities act uniformly in their treatment of imported goods' (reply to para 91).

other relevant Member States, as if they had been made by the customs authorities of those states.[10] In addition, a recent amendment to the Implementing Regulation provides that the customs administrations of Member States are to assist one another in checking the authenticity and accuracy of documents, and in verifying that the procedures to prove the customs status of goods, have been correctly applied.[11] Yet it is much easier to articulate the objective that there should be, in effect, a single customs service than it is to achieve it. Just how formidable is the task of co-ordinating all the customs authorities in the Member States may be seen from the fact that, in 1999–2000, the customs authorities in the UK alone had the equivalent of 1,060 staff involved in the regulation of imports spread about the country.[12]

B. PROVING THE EXISTENCE OF COMMUNITY GOODS

In Chapter 3 the concept of 'a good' and the nature of Community goods was considered. In this section we are concerned not with the nature of a good but with the proof that something is a Community good. This is dealt with in Implementing Regulation, Articles 313–336.[13] Article 313.1 provides that, subject to certain exceptions, all goods in the Community customs territory shall be deemed to be Community goods, unless it is established that they do not have Community status. The exceptions to this rule are set out in Article 313.2(a)–(c) and the goods falling within them are deemed not to be Community goods unless the contrary is established.[14] The first exception covers goods brought into the customs territory of the Community remaining subject to customs supervision in accordance with CCC, Article 37.[15] The

---

[10] See also the CCC provisions governing binding information discussed in Ch 5, section F.

[11] See the Implementing Regulation, Art 314a. The procedures in question are those used in accordance with Title II of the Implementing Regulation ('Customs status of goods and transit'). This new heading is introduced by Commission Regulation (EC) 2787/2000 of 15 Dec 2000 [2000] OJ L330/1 which amends the Implementing Regulation. The regulation introduced a number of changes in relation to the customs status of goods and transit. Note that chapter 3 of Title II is now the first chapter in the Title as the Regulation deleted the first two chapters.

[12] See the Report by the Comptroller and Auditor General, (head of the National Audit Office) *HM Customs and Excise: Regulating Freight Imports from Outside the European Community*, HC 131 Session 2000–2001: 2 Feb 2001, para 1.9. The report deals with risk management on the part of HM Customs and Excise and minimization of the burden on importers.

[13] In Part II of Title II. Note that this Part has been much amended by Commission Regulation (EC) 2787/2000 of 15 Dec 2000 [2000] OJ 330/1. The amendments are applicable as from 1 July 2001: see ibid, Art 4.2. This section is intended to reflect the law applicable as from that date.

[14] See Implementing Regulation, Art 313.2, first para.

[15] Nevertheless, and in accordance with CCC, Art 38.5, Article 313.2(a) provides that goods brought into the Community customs territory are deemed to be Community goods, unless the contrary is established, where, (i) if carried by air, the goods have been loaded or transhipped at a Community airport, for consignment to another airport in the customs territory, and carried under cover of a single transport document drawn up in a Member State; or (ii) if carried by sea, the goods have been shipped between ports in the customs territory by a regular shipping service authorised in accordance with the Implementing Regulation, Arts 313a and 313b.

second exception covers goods in temporary storage or in a free zone of control-type I, ie based on the existence of a fence, or free warehouse, and the third exception covers goods placed under a suspensive procedure,[16] or in a free zone of control-type II, ie based on formalities carried out in accordance with the customs warehousing procedure.[17]

Where goods are not deemed to be Community goods under Article 313 their status as such may not be established unless one of three conditions are fulfilled.[18] The conditions are that the goods: (i) must have been brought from another Member State without crossing the territory of a third country on the way, (ii) must have been brought from another Member State through the territory of a third country and carried under cover of a single transport document issued in a Member State, or (iii) subject to the satisfaction of certain additional requirements, must have passed from the Member State of departure to the Member State of destination having been transhipped in a third country.[19]

Recent amendments to the legislation have increased the use of commercial documents for the purpose of proving that goods have the status of Community goods. Nevertheless, without prejudice to the internal transit procedure, proof of Community status may be provided only in the ways contained in Article 314c.[20] Broadly speaking, these are:

(i) by means of a T2L document, or in certain circumstances, an invoice or transport document marked T2L;[21]

(ii) by means of a T2LF document, if the goods are consigned from a part of the customs territory outside the area covered by the Sixth VAT Directive;[22]

(iii) where the simplified Community transit procedures are used,[23] by

---

[16] As to which see CCC, Art 84 and following.

[17] See Implementing Regulation, Art 799.

[18] In accordance with ibid, Art 314c.1, considered below.

[19] Ibid, Art 314.1.

[20] Note that it is not contrary to what is now EC Treaty, Arts 23 and 24 to require, as the Implementing Regulation does, that proof of the Community status of goods be provided exclusively in certain specified ways. See Case C–117/88 *Trend-Moden Textilhandels GmbH v Hauptzollamt Emmerich* [1990] ECR I–631 paras 9–11 and 20; Case 237/96 *Belgian Minister for Financial Affairs v Eddy Amelynck* [1997] ECR I–5103 at paras 10, 15, and 16f and Case C–83/89 *Openbaar Ministerie and the Minister for Finance v Vincent Houben* [1990] ECR I–1161 at paras 13 and 14. See also Case 99/83 *Claudio Fioravanti v Amministrazione delle Finanze dello Stato* [1984] ECR 3939 at para 11.

[21] Implementing Regulation, Arts 314c.1(a), 315.1 and 317. Document T2L is made out on a form corresponding to Copy 4 or Copy 4/5 of the specimen in Annexes 31 and 32 to the Implementing Regulation: see ibid, Art 315.3. Provision is also made for continuation sheets and loading lists drawn up in accordance with Annex 45 to be used instead of continuation sheets as the descriptive part of the T2L: ibid, Art 315.5.

[22] Ibid, Arts 314c.1(a) and 315.2.

[23] See Implementing Regulation, Arts 444 and 448.

entering the letter 'C', which is equivalent to T2L, alongside the relevant items on the manifest;[24]

(iv) by production of a shipping company's manifest with each item marked 'C' for goods having Community status and 'F' for goods consigned to or from a part of the customs territory outside the scope of Directive (EC) 388/77;[25]

(v) by entering 'T2L' on a TIR[26] or ATA[27] carnet[28] (goods transported under cover of a TIR or ATA carnet are deemed to be non-Community goods unless their Community status is duly established[29]);

(vi) by the accompanying document provided for in Commission Regulation (EEC) 2719/92 of 11 September 1992;[30]

(vii) by the T2M document which is used in relation to products of sea fishing and certain goods obtained from such products;[31]

(viii) by a label in the form set out in Implementing Regulation, Annex 42b affixed to goods carried by post to or from a part of the customs territory to which the Sixth VAT Directive does not apply;[32]

(ix) by a form, conforming to the model contained in Annex 109 to the Implementing Regulation, by which the customs authorities certify goods which are placed in a free zone or free warehouse as Community, or non-Community, goods;[33]

(x) by the T5 control copy (which is used to prove the end-use or destination of goods).[34]

---

[24] Ibid, Arts 314c.1(a) and 317b.

[25] Ibid, Arts 314c.1(a) and 317a.

[26] The arrangements governing the TIR ('*Transports internationaux routiers*') carnet are considered under 'Transit Procedures' at E 2.1 and 2.2 below.

[27] The arrangements governing the ATA ('*Admission temporaire-Temporary Admission*') carnet are considered under 'Temporary Admission' at H below.

[28] See Implementing Regulation, Arts 314c.1(b) and Art 319.

[29] Ibid, Art 453.

[30] [1992] OJ L276/1. This provides for an accompanying document for the movement under duty-suspension arrangements of products subject to excise duty. See Implementing Regulation, Art 314c.1(c).

[31] See ibid, Arts 314c.1(d) and 325.

[32] See ibid, Arts 314c.1(e) and 462a.2.

[33] See ibid, Arts 314c.1(f), and Art 816, and CCC, Art 170.4. A form conforming to the model in Implementing Regulation, Annex 109 is to be used: ibid, Art 812.

[34] See ibid, Arts 314c.1(g) and 843. A T5 control copy is defined in Art 912a.1(c), as 'a T5 original and copy made out on forms corresponding to the specimen in Annex 63 accompanied where appropriate by either one or more original and copy forms T5 bis corresponding to the specimen in Annex 64 or one or more original and copy loading list T5 corresponding to the specimen in Annex 65. The forms shall be printed and completed in accordance with the explanatory note in Annex 66 and, where appropriate, any additional instructions laid down in other Community rules'. Provision is now made for replacement of T5 by electronic loading lists, etc. Article 912a.3 states that: 'All goods entered on a given T5 control copy shall be loaded on a single means of transport within the meaning of the second subparagraph of Article 347(2), intended for a single consignee and the same use and/or destination.' See generally Part IVa of the Implementing Regulation: Arts 912a–912g.

Specific provisions have recently been introduced governing the way in which an authorized consignor may provide proof of Community goods.[35] Such a person may now be authorized to use the T2L document, or a manifest, pursuant to (iii) and (iv) above, without having to present them for endorsement to the authorities.[36] There are particular provisions in relation to the customs status road vehicles, rail wagons and packaging.[37] In relation to goods in passenger-accompanied baggage, the Implementing Regulation, Article 323 provides that, if it is necessary to establish the Community status of such goods, they shall be considered to have Community status so long as they are not intended for commercial use[38] and there is no doubt about the truthfulness of the declaration of them as Community goods. Where there is doubt about this, recourse must be had to other documentary evidence. The Court of Justice has stated that the doubt must have an objective basis, such as the particular circumstances of the importation or information received by the customs authorities concerning it. The mere fact that the goods in question were manufactured in a third country cannot be enough to raise a doubt. Neither can subjective considerations on the part of officials.[39]

It should be noted that Community goods must be distinguished from import goods which are dealt with in the following section.

C. RULES GOVERNING CUSTOMS PROCEDURES WITH ECONOMIC IMPACT

Customs warehousing, inward processing, processing under customs control, temporary importation, and outward processing are known as customs procedures with economic impact.[40] The term 'import goods' is frequently used in relation to these procedures and means goods placed under a suspensive procedure. The definition is somewhat extended in relation to the inward processing procedure.[41]

The use of any of the procedures set out above depends upon authorisation being issued by the customs authorities.[42] General provisions relating

---

[35] Implementing Regulation, Arts 324a–324f.   [36] Ibid, Art 324a.1.

[37] Ibid, see Arts 320–322.

[38] The definition of 'goods of a non-commercial nature' in the Implementing Regulation, Art 1.6 states that they are goods which are entered into the relevant customs procedure on an occasional basis and whose nature and quantity indicate that they are intended for private, personal or family use of the consignees or carriers, or which are clearly intended as gifts.

[39] See Case 83/89 *Openbaar Ministerie and the Minister for Finance v Vincent Houben*, n 20 above, at para 20.

[40] CCC, Art 84.1(b). Guidelines on customs procedures with economic impact were published by the Commission in [2001] OJ C 269/1 on 24 Sept 2001. See also information on the Taxation and Customs DG's web site.   [41] Ibid, Art 84.2.

[42] Ibid, Art 85. See also the Implementing Regulation, Arts 497–508. As noted in Ch 9 it is also necessary for goods to be declared for a particular customs procedure. See section 2.1 'The purpose of the declaration', p 283.

to authorizations, those governing the application for authorization, the economic conditions which must be examined prior to authorization, the decision on authorization, and the period for which authorizations are effective are each considered below. The section concludes with a brief summary of other provisions which relate to customs procedures with economic impact.

1. *General provisions relating to authorizations*

The authorization is to set out the conditions under which the procedure in question is to be used.[43] The holder of the authorization must notify the customs authorities of all factors arising after the granting of the authorization which may influence its continuation or content.[44] The authorization is to be granted only to those who offer every guarantee necessary for the proper conduct of the operations and only where the customs authorities can supervise and monitor the procedure without having to introduce administrative arrangements disproportionate to the economic needs involved.[45]

The customs authorities may make the placing of goods under suspensive arrangements conditional upon the provision of security in order to ensure payment of any customs debt which may be incurred in respect of the goods. Specific provisions are permitted in respect of specific suspensive arrangements.[46] A suspensive arrangement with economic impact is discharged when a new customs-approved treatment or use is assigned, either to the goods placed under that arrangement or to compensating or processed products placed under it.[47] Where goods obtained from goods placed under a suspensive arrangement are not deemed to have Community status they may be considered as being placed under the same arrangement.[48] It should be noted that, subject to conditions laid down by the customs authorities, the rights and obligations of the holder of a customs procedure with economic impact may be transferred successively to other persons who fulfil any conditions laid down in order to benefit from the procedure.[49]

There are other general provisions governing matters such as the application of commercial policy measures,[50] the transfer of goods under suspensive

---

[43] CCC, Art 87.1.

[44] Ibid, Art 87.2. Note that the Court of Justice has confirmed in relation to the pre-consolidation provisions equivalent to CCC, Art 87 that they apply to conditions affecting the use and functioning of the procedure and not merely to those relating to the issue of an authorization: Case C–187/99 *Fazenda Pública v Fábrica de Queijo Eru Portuguesa Ldª*, [2001] ECR I-1429.

[45] CCC, Art 86.

[46] Ibid, Art 88. The amount required as security is considered in Ch 12, section A.

[47] Ibid, Art 89.1. Compensating products are all products resulting from processing operations: ibid, Arts 114.1(d) and 145.

[48] Ibid, Arts 87a and 4(7).   [49] Ibid, Art 90.

[50] The Implementing Regulation, Art 509.

arrangements,[51] the keeping of records by the holder of the authorization, the operator, or the designated warehouse-keeper,[52] the rate of yield and calculation formula for the purposes of inward and outward processing and processing under customs control,[53] compensatory interest on customs debts,[54] the discharge of procedures where import or temporary export goods have been entered under two or more declarations for the arrangements by virtue of one authorization, and where goods under arrangements are totally destroyed or irretrievably lost,[55] and, finally, administrative co-operation between the customs authorities of Member States and between those authorities and the Commission.[56] Particular attention is paid to rates of yield and calculations in Chapter 11.

2. *Applications for authorization*

An application for authorization to carry out a customs procedure with economic impact is to be made in writing using the model set out in Annex 67.[57] The Annex contains model forms for particular types of applications, the layout of which is not binding but which require the provision of information such as the period of validity in question, a description of the goods to be placed under the procedure, the compensating or processed products in question, the planned activities and the economic conditions.[58] The use of the forms is not always necessary. An application may be made by means of a customs declaration in writing or by means of a data-processing technique using the normal procedure in five groups of situations. The first of these consists of inward processing not involving equivalent goods, where the economic conditions are deemed to be fulfilled pursuant to Article 539 of the Implementing Regulation.[59] The second covers processing under customs control where the economic conditions are deemed to be fulfilled pursuant to

---

[51] The Implementing Regulation, Arts 511–514. Transfer between different places designated in the same authorization may be undertaken without any customs formalities: ibid, Art 512.1.

[52] Ibid, Arts 515–516.

[53] Ibid, Arts 517–518. These provisions are dealt with in Ch 11 in the discussion of inward processing.

[54] Ibid, Art 519.

[55] Ibid, Arts 520–521.

[56] Ibid, Arts 522–523 and Annex 71.

[57] Ibid, Art 497.1. Renewals of or modifications to an authorization may be permitted to be made by simple written request: ibid, Art 497.2. Applications for a single authorization, except for temporary importation, must be mde in writing using the model set out in Annex 67. A single authorization means an authorization involving different customs administrations covering entry for and/or discharge of the arrangements, storage, successive processing operations, or uses. See ibid, Arts 497.4 and 496(c).

[58] Additional information may be sought by customs authorities where they consider any of the information given inadequate: see ibid, Art 499, which contains detailed provisions on the information to be provided.

[59] Ibid, Art 497.3(a).

Article 522(1) of the Implementing Regulation.[60] The third covers temporary importation, including the use of an ATA or CPD carnet.[61] The fourth situation is outward processing where the processing operation concerns repairs and includes situations where the standard exchange system without importation is used.[62] The fifth and final situation is free circulation after outward processing (i) using the standard exchange system with prior importation or (ii) without prior importation where the existing authoriziation does not cover such a system and the customs authorities permit its modification and (iii) where the processing operation concerns goods of a non-commercial nature.[63]

2.1 *Where to apply*

The customs authorities to which an application must be submitted are specified in the Implementing Regulation, Article 498(a)–(d). An application for customs warehousing must be submitted to the customs authorities for the place to be approved as a customs warehouse, or for the place where the applicant's main accounts are held.[64] In relation to inward processing and processing under customs control, the specified customs authorities are those for the place where the processing operation is to be carried out. For temporary importation, the customs authorities are those for the place where the goods to be declared for temporary importation are located. Finally, for outward processing the customs authorities are those where the goods are to be used.[65]

3. *Single authorizations*

A single authorization means an authorization involving different customs administrations covering entry for and/or discharge of the arrangements, storage, or successive processing operations or uses.[66] Generally speaking, an application for single authorization in relation to temporary importation is to be submitted to the customs authorities of the place of first use. In other cases, it is to be submitted to the customs authorities of the place where the applicant's main accounts which facilitate audit-based controls of the arrange-

---

[60] The Implementing Regulation, Art 497.3(b).

[61] Ibid, Art 497.3(c), but see Art 497.4 and 5. An application may also be made by means of a customs declaration, including an oral declaration, for temporary importation in certain circumstances: see ibid, Art 497.3 second sub-para. See section H 'Temporary Admission' at p 330 below for reference to ATA and CPD carnets.

[62] Ibid, Art 497.3(d), first sub-para.

[63] Ibid, Art 497.3(d)(i)–(iii).

[64] Accounts means the holder of the authorization's commercial, tax, or other accounting material, or such data held on the holder's behalf: ibid, Art 496(i) and (d).

[65] This is without prejudice to ibid, Art 580.1, second sub-para, concerning the use of ATA/CPD carnets.

[66] Ibid, Art 496(c).

ments[67] are held, and where at least part of the storage, processing, or temporary export operations covered by the operations are conducted.[68] These authorities are then to communicate the application and draft authorization to the other customs authorities concerned who must acknowledge the date of receipt within fifteen days. These authorities have thirty days from receipt to notify objections. The application is to be rejected where objections have been duly notified and no agreement between customs authorities has been reached.[69] An authorization is to be issued if no objections are received within the thirty-day period and a copy of the authorization is to be sent to all customs authorities concerned.[70] This procedure requiring 'prior agreement' between customs authorities may be replaced by a notification procedure where the criteria and conditions for granting single authorizations are generally agreed upon between two or more customs administrations.[71]

4. *The examination of economic conditions*

Certain 'economic conditions' are to be satisfied before authorization in relation to inward and outward processing and processing under customs control is given.[72] They are deemed to be fulfilled in certain circumstances which are referred to in the discussion of each procedure.[73] Where the economic conditions are not deemed to be fulfilled, the Commission may become involved in examining them. An examination of them involving the Commission may take place where the customs authorities concerned consult with the Commission before or after issuing an authorization, if another customs administration objects to an issued authorization, or on the initiative of the Commission.[74]

5. *Decisions on authorizations*

According to the Implementing Regulation, Article 505, an application for authorization in writing using the model application in Annex 67 to the Regulation[75] is to be granted using the model, again set out in Annex 67. An application under Article 497.3 of the regulation is to be granted by acceptance of the customs declaration and an application for renewal or modification of an

---

[67] 'Arrangements' means a customs procedure with economic impact: Implementing Regulation, Art 496(a).

[68] Ibid, Art 500.2. [69] Ibid, Art 500.3.

[70] Ibid, Art 500.4. [71] Ibid, Art 501.2 and 3.

[72] CCC, Arts 117(c), 148(c), and 133(e) discussed in relation to each procedure.

[73] Implementing Regulation, Art 539 (inward processing), Art 552 (processing under customs control), and Art 585 (outward processing). See also Commission Regulation (EC) 1448/2001 [2001] OJ L196/9, regarding the placing of basic products in Annex I to the EC Treaty under inward processing arrangements without prior examination of the economic conditions.

[74] Implementing Regulation, Art 503. The procedure governing the Commission's examination is set out in ibid, Art 504.

[75] ie under ibid, Art 497.1.

authorization is to be granted by any appropriate act. An applicant must be
informed that an authorization has been granted, or of the reasons for its
rejection, within thirty days of lodging the application or of the receipt by the
customs authorities of requested information. The time period is sixty days in
relation to customs warehousing arrangements.[76] These time periods also
apply in relation to single authorizations where the notification procedure is
applied.[77]

6. *The period for which authorizations are effective*

Generally speaking, an authorization takes effect on the date of its issue or any
later date given in it, but retroactive authorizations may be issued except in relation to customs warehousing.[78] Retroactive authorizations take effect at the
earliest date on which the application was submitted.[79] An application for the
renewal of an authorization of the same kind of operation and goods as was
previously authorized may, however, be granted with retroactive effect from the
date the original authorization expired.[80] In exceptional circumstances an
authorization may be retroactive up to one year before the date the application
was submitted. For such retroactivity to be available, however, specific requirements must be met. First, a proven need must exist and the application must not
be related to attempted deception or to obvious negligence. Secondly, the specified limits on the periods of validity of the authorization must not be exceeded.
Thirdly, the applicant's accounts must confirm (i) that all the requirements of
the arrangements can be deemed to be met, where appropriate, and (ii) that the
goods can be identified for the period involved. The accounts must also allow the
arrangements to be controlled. Fourthly, all the formalities necessary to regularize the situation of the goods must be able to be carried out, including the
invalidation of the declaration where necessary.[81]

D. RELEASE FOR FREE CIRCULATION AND 'END USE'

Free circulation itself is not a mere customs procedure; it is a concept which
lies at the heart of the customs union. The nature of free circulation has been
dealt with in Chapter 3. Some provisions related to it appear in CCC, Articles
79–83 and 88 and 90.[82] This section looks briefly at some regulations
contained in Part II, Title I of the Implementing Regulation, headed 'Release

---

[76] Implementing Regulation, Art 506.   [77] Ibid, Art 506, second sub-para.
[78] Ibid, Arts 507.1 and 508.1.   [79] Ibid, Art 508.1, second sub-para.
[80] Ibid, Art 508.2.   [81] Ibid, Art 508.3(a)–(d).
[82] Arts 79–83 are dealt with in Ch 3, in section E 'Free calculation' at p 77, except for Art 81
which is dealt with in Ch 5 at p 131. Arts 88 and 90 are considered in section C.1 'General provisions relating to authorizations' at p 298.

for Free Circulation', and particularly those in Chapter 2, headed 'End Use'. Other regulations governing the release for free circulation of goods which have been subject to customs procedures are noted in the discussion of the relevant procedure.

As we have seen, CCC, Article 82 provides that where goods are released for free circulation, at a reduced or zero rate of duty on account of their end use, they are to remain under customs supervision. This is to end when the conditions for granting the zero or reduced rate cease to apply, where the goods are exported or destroyed, or where the use of the goods, for purposes other than those laid down for application of the reduced or zero rate, is permitted subject to payment of duties due. The rules implementing CCC, Article 82 are now made applicable also to the circumstances dealt with in CCC, Article 21, by virtue of an amendment to the Implementing Regulation.[83] (CCC, Article 21 permits regulations to be made allowing goods to benefit from favourable tariff treatment, that is to say, a reduction in or suspension of customs duty on imports, by reason either of their nature or their end use.) As a result, Implementing Regulation, Articles 291–308, concerned with the admission of goods with favourable tariff treatment by reason of their end-use have been replaced with a chapter entitled simply 'End use' consisting of Articles 291–300. The change was made as part of the simplification and rationalization of customs procedures and so as to increase the flexibility of end-use customs supervision to meet the needs of the diversifying internal market.[84]

1. *Authorization for favourable treatment*

According to Implementing Regulation, Article 292.1, the granting of favourable tariff treatment in accordance with CCC, Article 21, in respect of goods that are subject to end-use supervision is to be subject to written authorization. Written authorization is also required for the purposes of end-use customs supervisions where goods are released for free circulation, at a reduced or zero rate of duty, on account of their end use and customs supervision under CCC, Article 82 is necessary. The authorization is to be issued at the written request of the person concerned, who must use the model form set out in Annex 67.[85] The declaration for free circulation, whether in writing or by means of a data-processing technique, may constitute the application where the application involves only one customs administration, the applicant wholly assigns the goods to the prescribed end use, and the proper conduct of operations is safeguarded.[86] In such a case the authorities are to require certain

---

[83] Commission Regulation (EC) 1602/2000 of 24 July 2000 [2000] OJ L188/1.
[84] Ibid, Recital No (10).
[85] Implementing Regulation, Art 292.2.
[86] Ibid, Art 292.3.

specified information from the declarant, unless it is deemed unnecessary or is entered on a customs declaration. The information is as follows:

(i)   the name and address of the applicant, the declarant, and the operator;
(ii)   the nature of the end use;
(iii) a technical description of the goods, the products resulting from the their end-use, and the means of identifying them;
(iv)   the estimated rate of yield or method by which that rate is to be determined;
(v)   the estimated period for assigning the goods to their end use;
(vi)   the place where the goods are put to their end use.[87]

An authorization involving different customs administrations may, of course, be applied for. The application is to be made to one of two authorities: either the customs authorities where the applicant's main accounts are kept, facilitating audit-based controls, and where at least part of the operations covered by the authorization are carried out; or, the authorities where the goods are assigned to their end use. A procedure for consultation between the customs authorities covered by the authorization exists, but this may be replaced by notification by agreement between administrations.[88]

An authorization under the Implementing Regulation, Article 292 must be granted to persons established in the customs territory of the Community provided that five conditions are met. These are:

(i)   the activities envisaged are consistent with the prescribed end-use and with the provisions for transfer of goods in accordance with the Implementing Regulation, Article 296, and proper conduct of operations is ensured;
(ii)   the applicant offers every guarantee necessary for the proper conduct of operations and undertakes to fulfil certain obligations to ensure this;
(iii) efficient customs supervision is ensured and administrative arrangements by the authorities are not disproportionate to the economic needs involved;
(iv)   adequate records are made and retained;
(v)   security is provided as necessary.[89]

2. *The contents and duration of an authorization*

The authorization is to contain prescribed information which enables the authorization holder and the goods to be identified and the assignment to end

---

[87] Implementing Regulation, Art 292.4.   [88] Ibid, Art 292.6.
[89] Ibid, Art 293.1.

use to be properly effected.[90] An authorization is to take effect on the date of issue or any later date given in the authorization.[91] Retroactive authorizations may be issued which may take effect on the date the application was submitted. If the application is a renewal of authorization for the same kind of goods and operations it may take effect from the date the previous authorization expired. In exceptional circumstances, provided a proven economic need exists, the retroactive effect of an authorization may be extended beyond the dates set out above, but not to more than one year before the date the application was submitted. Any such application must not be related to attempted deception or obvious negligence and must satisfy certain other requirements.[92]

As one may expect, the expiry of an authorization does not affect goods which were in free circulation by virtue of the authorization before it expired.[93]

3. *The transfer of goods subject to an authorization*

Goods which are designated in the same authorization may be transferred without any customs formalities.[94] The T5 control copy specified in Annex 63 to the Implementing Regulation is to be used where goods are transferred between two holders of authorizations established in different Member States, if the relevant customs authorities have not agreed simplified procedures or if they have not agreed to waive its use.[95] The T5 control copy is to contain specified information and the transferor must send the complete set of T5 control copies to the transferee. The transferee is to attach the original commercial document to these, showing the date of receipt, and submit them to the customs office specified in his authorization. He must also inform it of any excess, shortfall, substitution, or other irregularity. The customs authorities, the transferor, and the transferee have specified responsibilities in relation to the forms.[96] The transferor is to be discharged from his obligations where two conditions are fulfilled: first, where the transferee has received the goods and was informed that the goods are subject to customs supervision; secondly, where customs control has been taken over by the transferee's customs authority. This shall be when the transferee has entered the goods in his records.[97] There are specific provisions

---

[90] Ibid, Art 293.3 contains a list of 12 items of information to be included in the authorization unless the information is deemed unnecessary.

[91] Implementing Regulation, Art 293.4. [92] Ibid, Art 294.

[93] Ibid, Art 295. [94] Ibid, Art 296.1.

[95] Ibid, Arts 296.2 and 3. Transfers of goods between authorized holders within a single Member State are subject to national rules: ibid, Art 296.4.

[96] Ibid, Art 296.2.

[97] Ibid, Art 296.6. Conversely, upon receipt of the goods, the transferee become the holder of the obligations in respect of them: ibid, Art 296.5.

governing the transfer of materials for the maintenance or repair of aircraft.[98] Customs authorities may agree that use of the goods in question, otherwise than as provided for in the authorization, is justified. Where they do, the use results in a customs debt arising, except where exportation or destruction occurs.[99]

E. TRANSIT PROCEDURES[100]

The need for freedom of transit of goods within the Community and its relationship with freedom of movement have already been considered.[101] Given the need for freedom of transit, a Community transit procedure is essential to the customs union and one was first established in 1969.[102] Now, detailed transit procedures, based on Community legislation and international agreements, which make provision for everything from the sealing of the goods in transit to ensuring that guarantees are in place to cover any potential customs duty liability which may arise on breach of transit obligations, have become of enormous practical importance within the Community. It was said in 1999, in relation to the reform of the Common transit system, that the customs administrations were then processing some 20 million transit operations a year on the basis of standard administrative documents.[103] The Commission was not exaggerating, therefore, when it said in one Communication that:

> Customs transit is one of the cornerstones of European integration and an issue of vital interest to European businesses. It enables goods to move much more freely and makes customs clearance formalities much more accessible by providing for the temporary suspension of duties and taxes normally applied to imported goods moving inside the Community (Community transit), or between the Community and its EFTA and Visegrad partner countries (via the Common Transit Convention), or among the 59 States that are now contracting parties to the TIR Convention.[104]

[98] Implementing Regulation, Art 297.
[99] Ibid, Art 299 and CCC, Art 208 apply.
[100] Significant changes have been and are being effected by the Community within the field of transit. The Commission has produced a 'Transit Manual'. The provisional edition of Sept 2001 is available on the web-site of the Taxation and Customs Union DG at http://europa.eu.int/comm/taxation_customs/publications/info_doc/customs/transit/transitmanual_en.htm. It was published too late for consideration here. I have drawn on the booklet 'New customs transit systems for Europe' in writing this section, which is also available on the web-site.
[101] See Ch 2. Section B.1: 'The customs union, free movement of goods, and transit' at p 24.
[102] See Council Regulation (EEC) 542/69 of 18 Mar 1969 [1969] OJ Spec Ed 125.
[103] Council Resolution of 21 June 1999 on the reform of the customs common transit system [1999] OJ C193/1 at recital (2). The Commission's introduction to its booklet, see n 100 above, also notes that one million TIR carnets are issued in Europe every year. The TIR regime is considered at 2.1 and 2.2 below.
[104] See Communication from the Commission to the European Parliament and the Council: Action plan for transit in Europe—a new customs policy: COM/1997/0188 FINAL [1997] OJ C176/3 para 1.1. As at Jan 2001 there were sixty-four states which were parties to the TIR Convention.

Yet in the same document, the Commission went on to speak of a crisis in the transit system and large-scale fraud and associated problems. The existence of large-scale fraud by international criminal organizations engaged in smuggling heavily taxed goods has proved of considerable concern.[105] The Court of Auditors has also referred to the transit system as 'long considered to be one of the customs union's high risk areas' and said that 'shortcomings are still obvious—despite undoubted improvements'.[106] The most obvious victim of fraud within the transit procedure is the Community itself which loses its own resources where customs duty is evaded. The loss of resources has been put at in excess of ECU 1.27bn, or £960m, for the period 1990–1996 by the Commission.[107] Those involved in the transit procedure, such as customs agents, may also suffer. In one recent case innocent customs agents found themselves facing a liability of NGL 2,463,318 following an abuse of the external transit system.[108] It is widely hoped that the New Computerised Transit System (NCTS) scheduled for operation by 30 June 2003,[109] and which represents 23% of the total budget of Customs 2000,[110] will lead to considerable improvements. This paperless system is to be used for common transit and internal and external Community transit, considered below. It will not, at first, cover simplified procedures governing transportation by rail, air, sea, or pipeline. In these cases, though, commercial documentation is used. In addition to the introduction of the NCTS, the common transit and Community transit systems are being reformed in two other areas. First, by ensuring that the quality of the transit legislation is improved.[111] Secondly, by making the implementation of transit

[105] See the reference to this in recital (3) to the Council Resolution, n 103 above.

[106] Special Report 8/99 of 16 Dec 1999, on securities and guarantees provided for in the Community Customs Code to protect the collection of traditional own resources together with the Commission's replies: [2000] OJ C70/1.

[107] See the National Audit Office Press Notice 21/98 and the Report by the Comptroller and Auditor General, *Customs and Excise: Reform of Customs Transit in the European Community*, HC 566 1997/98, 27 Feb 1998. The National Audit Office noted that the Community transit systems were not designed, originally, for the number of countries covered, nor for the resulting volume of transactions. Although computerization will considerably enhance the abilities of customs authorities, the enlargement of the Community, and of the area covered by the customs union, is likely to add to the pressures on them.

[108] Case C–61/98 *De Haan Beheer BV v Inspecteur der Invoerrechten en Accijnzen te Rotterdam* [1999] ECR I–5003. The customs agents, however, were held to be in a special situation within Art 13, Council Regulation (EEC) 1430/79 of 2 July 1979 [1979] OJ L175/1: because they were not informed that fraud was suspected. The demands of counter-fraud operations sometimes require that the existence of an investigation is kept secret and the ECJ's ruling facilitates this. Within the UK, however, there has been official criticism of certain authorities for permitting frauds to continue so as to improve the chances of catching fraudsters. See further Ch 13.

[109] See Decision (EC) 210/97 of the European Parliament and of the Council of 19 Dec 1996 [1997] OJ L33/4, Art 8 para 3, as amended by Decision (EC) 105/2000 of the European Parliament and of the Council of 17 Dec 1999 [2000] OJ L13/1. The decisions established Customs 2000 and Customs 2002 respectively.

[110] See recital (4) to Decision 105/2000, n 109 above.

[111] See the amendments to the external Community transit regime introduced by Commission Regulation (EC) 502/99 of 12 Feb 1999. See also Commission Regulation (EC) 2787/2000 of 15 Dec 2000 [2000] OJ L330/1.

rules more effective and uniform. The manner in which these reforms have been effected is contained in the Commission's Explanatory Booklet referred to above, but one important development is the making of a clear distinction between regular and the simplified procedures, granted to authorized persons, which apply to a number of elements of the transit regimes.

Yet the difficulties that the transit system faces are in part, at least, not capable of solution by the Community institutions acting alone. In this area, as in so many others, it is essential that the customs authorities of the Member States work together as much like a single customs administration as possible. Furthermore, it has to be borne in mind that transit is, as we have already noted, the subject of many international agreements binding many parties outside the Community. In the remainder of this section we look first at the Kyoto Convention, then at international agreements setting up transit regimes, and finally at Community transit. The international and Community regimes are not mutually exclusive, as is noted in the discussion of the Community's external and internal transit procedures.

1. *The Kyoto Convention*

Transit is dealt with in Annex E1 to the Kyoto Convention.[112] Its provisions are very broad and leave considerable scope for national regulation. They are intended to facilitate international transit rather than form the basis of a specific transit system. It is not proposed to review the provisions of the Annex in any detail here but, of the thirty-three main paragraphs which are either standards or recommended practices, standards 2 to 4 inclusive deserve noting. Standard 2 provides that national legislation is to specify the conditions to be fulfilled and the formalities to be satisfied for the purposes of customs transit. Standard 3 then specifies that customs authorities are to allow goods to be transported under 'customs transit' as it is called, in four circumstances: first, from an office of entry to an office of exit; secondly, from an office of entry to an inland customs office; thirdly, from an inland customs office to an office of exit; fourthly, from one inland customs office to another. Standard 4 provides that goods carried under customs transit must not be subject to the payment of import or export duties provided that the requirements of the customs authorities are complied with. The Revised Kyoto Convention deals with transit in Specific Annex E and has twenty-six main paragraphs which are either standards or recommended practices. Standards 2, 3, and 4 noted above are retained. Chapter 2 of the Annex deals with transhipment, which is the transfer, under customs control, from the importing to the exporting means of transport within the area of one customs office. This

---

[112] It was accepted on behalf of the Community by Council Decision (EEC) 415/77 of 3 June 1977 [1977] OJ L166/1. See further Ch 1 at p 68.

process is to be free of duty so long as the requirements of the authorities are complied with. Chapter 3 of the Annex deals with the carriage of goods coastwise. This procedure concerns goods in free circulation and those which are imported, and undeclared, on condition that they are transported in a vessel other than the one in which they arrived in the customs territory. It provides for them to be loaded on board a vessel in the customs territory, and for them to be transported to another place in the same customs territory, where they are unloaded.

2. *International agreements creating transit regimes*

As the quotation from the Commission's Communication at the beginning of this section on transit makes clear, there are operating within the Community a number of different transit regimes with their own extensive substantive and procedural rules. Quite apart from Community transit procedures, attention should be paid to the well-known transit system established pursuant to the Customs Convention on the International Transport of Goods (*The transports internationaux routiers* or TIR Convention) of 14 November 1975,[113] and to the Common Transit Convention. We turn first, briefly, to the TIR Convention.

2.1 *The TIR Convention*

According to the Court of Auditors' Special Report 8/99,[114] the most significant transit movements for the Community are made under the TIR Convention and the Community's external transit procedure.[115] The EC and forty-two other states were initial signatories to the Convention; those states included all the current Member States, Switzerland, certain countries of Eastern Europe, and the Soviet Union, as it then was, and countries as diverse as Iran, Korea, and the United States of America. As at January 2001, there were sixty-four contracting parties to the Convention, which is equally authentic in English, French, and Russian. It is, of course, designed to facilitate the international carriage of goods by road vehicle.[116] It does so by requiring the use of a 'TIR carnet'.[117] Lorries carrying out a TIR operation carry plates bearing the letters 'TIR' on the front and rear of the vehicle.[118] Two of the most important Articles in the Convention are Articles 4 and 5. Article 4 provides that 'Goods carried under the TIR procedure shall not be subjected to the payment or deposit of import or export duties and taxes at customs offices en route'. Article 5.1 states: 'Goods carried under the TIR procedure in sealed

---

[113] The Convention was approved on behalf of the Community by Council Regulation (EEC) 2112/78 of 25 July 1978 [1978] OJ L252/1 and is reproduced at [1978] OJ L252/2.

[114] See n 106 above.　　　　　　　　　　　　　　　　[115] Ibid, at para 20.

[116] Ibid, recital 1 and Art 3.　　　　　　　　　　　[117] Ibid, Art 3 and Annex 1.

[118] Ibid, Art 16 and Annex 5.

road vehicles, combinations of vehicles or containers shall not as a general rule be subjected to examination at customs offices en route.' Article 5.2 permits, in exceptional cases, examination so as to prevent abuse and particularly where irregularity is suspected. In order to protect the customs duty chargeable in respect of the goods in transit, the TIR system provides, in Chapter II (Articles 6–11), for the provision of guarantees by guaranteeing associations. The guarantee is intended to cover the duties, taxes, and interest which become due to a country in which an irregularity has been noted in connection with a TIR operation. The system of guarantees is organized by the International Road Transport Union (IRU) which is also responsible for printing and issuing the TIR carnets. Other official bodies which are an essential part of the TIR system are the TIR Administrative Committee (which elects an Executive Board) and the Working Party, both of which administer the TIR system, supported by the UN/Economic Commission for Europe Working Party on Customs Questions affecting Transport.

Although the TIR Convention is of great importance in Community transit, there are a number of difficulties in relation to the operation of its provisions.[119] This is particularly the case in relation to the enforcement of guarantees, provided by guaranteeing associations. Indeed, as a result of the difficulties which have been encountered it has now become impossible to move alcohol and tobacco under TIR or to move certain agricultural products under TIR into or out of the Community. The Convention has recently been the subject of a number of revisions, and further revisions are planned, particularly in relation to the computerization of the system.

2.2 *TIR and ATA procedures and the Implementing Regulation*

There are specific provisions in the Implementing Regulation relating to transport under the TIR or ATA carnet[120] which are not reviewed here. Suffice it to say that customs controls and formalities are to be carried out where the goods leave and re-enter the Community customs territory.[121] The goods carried

---

[119] It has recently been suggested that lorries using the TIR procedure have become 'the means of transport preferred by illegal immigration networks'. The issue has been discussed by Member States, the Commission, and the United Nations Economic Commission for Europe Working Party on Customs Questions affecting Transport. It has been agreed that there is no need to take any action in relation to the TIR. Indeed, according to the Commission, the lorry involved in an incident in which 58 immigrants were found dead at Dover was engaged in internal Community transport and was not using the TIR procedure. The Commission has emphasized that seals on the lorry should be broken by the carrier only in the presence of customs, or other authorities, except in an emergency: see Written Question E–2262/00 by Brice Hortefeux to the Commission and Answer by Mr Bolkestein: [2001] OJ C72 E/190.

[120] Implementing Regulation, Arts 451 to 470. The ATA carnet is concerned with temporary admission: see section H at p 330 below.

[121] Ibid, Art 452.

under cover of these carnets are deemed to be non-Community goods, unless their Community status is duly established.[122]

There are provisions dealing with the discovery of irregularities.[123] Where they occur in a particular Member State that state is responsible for the recovery of duties and charges.[124] If it is not possible to determine where the irregularity was committed it is deemed to be committed in the Member State in which it was discovered, unless proof of where it was committed is provided to the customs authorities within a specified time.[125] There is no Community law limit on the nature of the evidence which is to be taken into account in determining where the offence was committed and whether or not the location of the offence has been proved is a matter for national law.[126] Where the presumption that the offence took place in the state in which the offence is discovered is rebutted subsequently, so that the state in which the offence actually took place has jurisdiction to recover the duty, compensation arrangements come into operation between the two states.[127] These also apply where the Member State which has recovered the duty did not have competence to do so, but wrongly took the view, at the outset, that the evidence of where the offence was committed was insufficient.[128] The time limit for the production of evidence of where the offence was committed used to be one year,[129] and is now three months in relation to the TIR Convention and six months in relation to the ATA Competition.[130]

2.3 The Convention on Common Transit

So far as European countries are concerned, there is a system of transit based on the Convention on a Common Transit Procedure of 15 June 1987 agreed between, what were then, the European Economic Community and the countries within EFTA.[131] The parties also ratified the Convention on the

---

[122] Ibid, Art 453.1.   [123] Ibid, Art 454.

[124] Ibid, Art 454.2. The imposition of a customs debt is dealt with in Ch 12.

[125] Ibid, Art 454.3.

[126] See Joined Cases C–310/98 and C–406/98 *Hauptzollamt Neubrandenburg v Leszek Labis trading as 'Przedsiebiorstwo Transportowo-Handlowe (Met- Trans) and another* [2000] ECR 1-1797at paras 29–33.

[127] Implementing Regulation, Art 454.3 and 4.

[128] Joined Cases C–310/98 and C–406/98 *Hauptzollamt Neubrandenburg v Leszek Labis trading as 'Przedsiebiorstwo Transportowo-Handlowe (Met- Trans) and another*, at n 126 above, at paras 38–40.

[129] This follows from the terms of Art 454.3, and Art 455.1 of the Implementing Regulation and Art 11.1 of the TIR Convention: see Joined Cases C–310/98 and C–406/98, n 126 above, at para 44 onwards.

[130] See the amendments made to the Implementing Regulation, Art 454.3 and Art 455.1 by Commission Regulation (EC) 2787/2000, n 111 above, Art 1.54 and 55

[131] [1987] OJ L226/2. Approved on behalf of the Community by Council Decision (EEC) 415/87 of 15 June 1987 [1987] OJ L226/1. For the two most recent amendments see Decisions 1/2000 and 1/2001 of the EC/EFTA Joint Committee on Common Transit of 20 Dec 2000 [2001] OJ L9/1 and of 7 June 2001 [2001] OJ L165/54.

Simplification of Formalities in Trade in Goods 1987[132] which introduced the single administrative document for their use as from 1 January 1988. The EFTA States governed by these agreements now are Iceland, Norway, Switzerland, and Liechtenstein.[133] The four Visegrad countries (the Czech Republic, Hungary, Poland, and the Slovak Republic) acceded to both conventions on 1 July 1996 consequent upon entering into the Europe Agreements. These required customs co-operation in a number of respects including the interconnection between the transit systems of the Community and the contracting country.[134] As a result of this, it is intended that the common transit system be extended to further countries in due course. This objective has to be viewed against the background of concern over fraudulent use of the system which it is hoped to combat more effectively with computerised procedures, as we have already noted.[135]

It is not proposed to review the Common Transit Convention here. It is similar in many respects to the Community transit procedure, considered below, and faces many of the same challenges particularly in relation to fraud. Indeed, as we noted above, on 20 December 2000, the Convention was modernized and its provisions extensively recast with similar objectives to the recent modernization of the Community transit regime. It may be noted, however, that it makes provision for two procedures, T1 and T2. The T1 procedure is used in respect of goods, irrespective of their kind or origin, which are in transit, and goods transhipped, reconsigned, or warehoused irrespective of their kind or origin.[136] The T2 procedure is used in respect of such goods in the Community only when they are in free circulation within it and certain other conditions are satisfied. It is used in an EFTA country only when the goods have arrived in that country under the T2 procedure and are reconsigned under conditions set out in the Convention.[137]

---

[132] Adopted by Council Decision (EEC) 267/87 of 28 Apr 1987 [1987] OJ L134/2. The Convention has been amended by Decision 1/89 of the EEC–EFTA Joint Committee: [1989] OJ L200/3, implemented by Council Regulation (EEC) 2011/89 of 19 June 1989 [1989] OJ L200/1 and by Decision 2/95 of the EC–EFTA Joint Committee of 26 Oct 1995 [1996] OJ L117/18. See also Decision 1/2000 of the EC–EFTA Joint Committee of 20 Dec 2000 [2001] OJ L9/108.

[133] The agreements apply to Liechtenstein by virtue of its customs union with Switzerland.

[134] See further Mr Month's answer to written question E 1581/96 [1996] OJ C 385/17 and Decision 1/95 of the EC–EFTA Joint Committee of 26 Oct 1995 [1996] OJ L117/13. Art 91 of the Europe Agreement between the EC and Poland ([1993] OJ 1993 L348/2, as amended) which provides for co-operation so as 'to guarantee compliance with all the provisions scheduled for adoption in connection with trade and to achieve the approximation of Poland's customs system to that of the Community, thus helping to ease the steps towards liberalization planned under this Agreement.' It goes on to state that co-operation 'shall include the following in particular—the introduction of the single administrative document and of an interconnection between the transit systems of the Community and Poland—the simplification of inspections and formalities in respect of the carriage of goods.' Note too, eg road transit agreements between Bulgaria and Hungary respectively and the EC [2001] OJ L108/6 and L108 28, and Regulation (EC) 685/2001 of the European Parliament and of the Council of 4 Apr 2001 [2001] OJ L108/1.

[135] See also the Resolution of the EC–EFTA Joint Committee on Common Transit of 2 Dec 1999 [2000] OJ C42/4.

[136] Art 1.1 and Art 2 of the Convention.   [137] Art 2 of the Convention.

3. *Community transit*

Community transit is, of course, concerned with the transit of goods within the Community and, for those goods covered by the relevant customs union, with Andorra, San Marino, and Turkey.[138] It has two elements, external transit (dealt with in CCC, Articles 91–97) and internal transit (dealt with in CCC, Articles 163–165) which are considered below.

The provisions of the CCC are supplemented by provisions in the Implementing Regulation, Part II, Title II which have been recently amended as part of a process of reform.[139] Title II, Chapter 4 deals with Community transit. Section 1 (Articles 340a–344) contained general provisions applicable to external and internal Community transit. Section 2, subsection 1 (Articles 345–348) deals with individual guarantees. Subsection 2 (Articles 349–354) covers means of transport and declarations. Subsections 3, 4, and 5 deal with formalities at the office of departure, formalities en route, and formalities at the office of destination (see Articles 355–364). Sub-section 6 (Articles 365–366) deals with checking the end of the procedure, and the final subsection (Articles 367–371) deals with exchange of information using computer networks and information technology. Section 3 concerns simplifications regarding, for example, the use of a comprehensive guarantee, guarantee waivers, the use of special loading lists and seals, the transfer of goods carried by rail, sea, air, or pipeline, and authorized consignor and authorized consignee status. Section 4 deals with customs debt and recovery. The other provisions of Title II deal mainly with transport under the TIR and ATA carnet procedure and contain a specific procedure for postal consignments.[140]

In the remainder of this section we consider briefly the nature of external and internal transit procedures and then move on to consider some aspects of the administrative operation of the procedure. In relation to these, it should be borne in mind that CCC, Articles 92 and 94–97, which are concerned with the external transit procedure, apply also to internal transit movements taking place under Community transit procedures.[141]

3.1 *The external transit procedure*

The external transit procedure is generally, but not exclusively, concerned with

---

[138] See 'The Customs Territory of the Community' in Ch 3, section F, p 80. Note that the Community transit procedure is compulsory in respect of goods carried by air only if they are loaded or re-loaded at an airport in the Community and it is compulsory for goods carried by sea if they are carried by a regular shipping service: Implementing Regulation, Art 340e.

[139] See Commission Regulation (EC) 2787/2000 of 15 Dec 2000 [2000] OJ L330/1. Note that according to Art 4, points 2 to 80 of Art 1, which contain the main amendments, apply as from 1 July 2001.

[140] As regards the latter see Implementing Regulation, Art 462a.

[141] CCC, Art 163.2(a) and .3.

goods which do not satisfy the conditions of what are now EC Treaty, Articles 23 and 24, ie goods that come from non-Member States and are not in free circulation. Its aim, like that of all transit procedures, has been said to be to facilitate the movement of goods within the Community and to simplify the formalities to be undergone.[142] The Court of Justice has said that it is based on a legal fiction, noting that:

> Goods placed under this procedure are subject neither to the corresponding import duties nor to the other measures of commercial policy; it is as if they had not entered the Community territory. In reality, they are imported from a non-member country and pass through one or more Member States before being exported to another non-member country.[143]

The external transit procedure permits two specific kinds of movement. First of all, it allows the movement between points in the Community customs territory of non-Community goods without the goods being subject to import duties and other charges, or to commercial policy measures. Secondly, it also allows such movement in respect of certain categories of Community goods.[144] In this regard it should be noted that Community goods, which are exported to an EFTA country or transit the territory of one or more EFTA countries, subject to the provisions of the Convention on common transit, are required to be placed under the Community external transit procedure in four alternative situations related to the common agricultural policy, repayment or remission of import duty and the inward processing procedure.[145]

As CCC, Article 91.2 makes clear, the movement of goods under the external transit procedure may take place under the external Community transit procedure, but it may also take place pursuant to other procedures. One of these is the TIR procedure. This applies provided that the movement of the goods began or is to end outside the Community; or that it relates to consignments of goods which must be unloaded in the customs territory of the Community and which are conveyed with goods to be unloaded in a third country; or that it is effected between two points in the Community through the territory of a third country. The movement of goods is also permitted under cover of an ATA carnet used as a transit document, by post, including parcel post, and pursuant to provisions of the Convention for the Navigation of the Rhine and the Convention between the Parties to the North Atlantic Treaty regarding the Status of their Forces. The external transit procedure can apply

---

[142] Case 136/80 *Hudig en Pieters BV v Minister van Landbouw en Visserij* [1981] ECR 2233, para 2. Note that it applies without prejudice to the provisions applicable in respect of customs warehousing, inward and outward processing, processing under customs control and temporary importation.
[143] Case C–383/98 *The Polo/Lauren Company, LP v PT Dwidua Langgeng Pratama International Freight Forwarders* [2000] ECR I-2519 at para 34.
[144] See CCC, Art 91.1(a) and (b).
[145] See Implementing Regulation, Art 340c.3.

to goods passing through the territory of a third country if provision is made for that to occur in an international agreement. It is also applicable if carriage through the third country is effected under cover of a single transport document drawn up in the customs territory of the Community. In this latter case the operation of the external Community transit procedure is suspended in the territory of the third country.[146]

The Member States have the right to establish between themselves, bilaterally or multilaterally, simplified external transit arrangements but these must be communicated to the Commission. The implementation of Community measures applying to goods must, of course, be guaranteed.[147]

3.2 *The internal transit procedure*

The internal transit procedure is concerned with goods which satisfy the requirements of EC Treaty, Articles 23 and 24, and, therefore, either originate in a Member State or are in free circulation. It allows Community goods to pass through the territory of a third country on their way from one point to another within the Community customs territory and still remain Community goods.[148] This movement of goods may take place under Community transit procedures so long as such a possibility is provided for in an international agreement; under cover of a TIR carnet, pursuant to the TIR Convention; under cover of an ATA carnet; under cover of a Rhine Manifest, pursuant to the Revised Convention for the Navigation of the Rhine; pursuant to the North Atlantic Treaty signed on 19 June 1951, or by post including parcel post.[149] In all but the case where transit takes place pursuant to an international agreement, the goods are to retain their status under the conditions and in the form prescribed by provisions contained in the Implementing Regulation.[150]

Implementing Regulation, Article 340c.1 provides that Community goods are to be placed under the internal transit procedure in a number of situations. The first of these is where goods are consigned from one point in the customs territory where the Sixth VAT Directive applies to a part where it does not apply.[151] The second situation is the reverse of the first, that is where goods are

---

[146] CCC, Art 93 and Implementing Regulation, Art 340d.

[147] CCC, Art 97. See also Case 105/83 *Pakvries BV v Minister for Agriculture and Fisheries* [1984] ECR 2101 in which it was held that the rules governing which state could take action to recover customs duty under a Benelux agreement could be applied by way of derogation from those set out in the transit procedure. The Court paid particular attention to what is now Art 306 of the EC Treaty which provides that: 'The provisions of this Treaty shall not preclude the existence or completion of regional unions between Belgium and Luxembourg, or between Belgium, Luxembourg and the Netherlands, to the extent that the objectives of these regional unions are not attained by application of this Treaty'.

[148] CCC, Art 163.1, which is without prejudice to the application of CCC, Art 91.1(b).

[149] Ibid, Art 163.   [150] Ibid, Art 163.4. See also ibid, Art 164.

[151] For the difference between the Community customs territory and the area covered by the 6th VAT Directive see Ch 3, p 82.

consigned from a part of the Community customs territory to which the Sixth
VAT Directive does not apply to a part where it does. The third situation is
where goods are consigned between parts of the Community customs territory
to which the Sixth VAT Directive does not apply. The fourth situation is where
the goods are consigned between points in the Community customs territory,
through the territory of one or more EFTA countries, pursuant to the
Convention on common transit (otherwise than entirely by sea or air).[152] As
noted above, in certain limited circumstances Community goods which are
exported to an EFTA country, or transit the territory of an EFTA country,
subject to the terms of the Convention on common transit, are to be placed
under the external Community transit procedure.[153] The Implementing
Regulation also provides that goods may pass through a third country other
than an EFTA country under the Community transit procedure, provided that
the transport through the third country is effected under cover of a single
transport document drawn up in a Member State. When this occurs, the transit procedure is suspended in the territory of the third country.[154]

3.3 *Simplifications*

The standard rules for the transit procedure may be subject to simplification in
relation to persons who satisfy certain conditions.[155] Broadly speaking, they
must be established in the Community, regularly use the transit arrangements,
or be known to be able to meet their obligations, and they must not have
committed any serious or repeated offences against customs or tax legislation.
The person concerned is subject to certain requirements as to record-keeping
and the customs authorities must be able to control and supervise the procedure. Simplifications are available in relation to a wide range of matters
including: the use of the comprehensive guarantee or guarantee waiver,
special loading lists, seals, a required itinerary, authorized consignor[156] and
consignee[157] status, and in relation to goods carried by rail or large container,
air, sea, or by pipeline.

3.4 *The responsibilities of the principal/holder*

In relation to the Community transit procedure, as in relation to other customs

---

[152] Implementing Regulation, Art 340c2.
[153] Ibid, Art 340d.
[154] Ibid.
[155] An authorized consignor may be relieved of the duty to present goods and documents to the customs authorities: Implementing Regulation, Art 398.
[156] An authorized consignee may receive goods at their premises, or another specified place, without presenting to the office of destination the appropriate copies of the transit declaration: the Implementing Regulation, Art 406.
[157] See generally the Implementing Regulation, Chapter 4, Section 3, Art 372 onwards.

procedures, there is a 'holder of the procedure'. This is the person on whose behalf the customs declaration was made or the person to whom the rights and obligations in respect of the procedure have been transferred.[158] As principal, the holder is responsible for the production intact of the goods in question at the customs office of destination, within the prescribed time limit, and with due observance of the measures adopted by the customs authorities to ensure identification. The principal is also responsible for the observance of the provisions relating to the Community transit procedure.[159] Notwithstanding the principal's responsibility for the production of the goods, a carrier or recipient of the goods may also be responsible for their production. To attract this responsibility the goods must be accepted in the knowledge that they are moving under Community transit.[160]

3.5 *The transit declaration and formalities on departure, en route, and at destination*

The transit declaration must be made in accordance with detailed requirements, but may be made by data-processing technique so long as the provisions in the Implementing Regulation, Annex 37a are observed.[161] It must include only the goods loaded, or to be loaded, on a single means of transport for carriage from one office of departure to one office of destination. Where the goods carried are dispatched together, a single means of transport includes a road vehicle accompanied by its trailer(s) or semi-trailer(s), a set of coupled railway carriages or wagons, boats constituting a single chain, and containers loaded on a single means of transport.[162] Proof of the destination of goods is provided by the T5 form,[163] considered in relation to the release for free circulation at D.3 above.

Goods placed under the Community transit procedure are to be carried to the office of destination along an economically justified route.[164] Furthermore, the office of departure is to set a time limit within which the goods are to be presented at the office of destination.[165] Subject to certain qualifications, or to a waiver, goods must be sealed in order to be released.[166] Turning to formalities en route, goods placed under Community transit must be carried

---

[158] CCC, Art 4(21).   [159] Ibid, Art 96.1.

[160] Ibid, Art 96.2.   [161] Implementing Regulation, Arts 350–354.

[162] Implementing Regulation, Art 349. Note that loading lists drawn up in accordance with Annex 44a may be used instead of continuation sheets as the descriptive part of the transit declaration: ibid, Art 350.

[163] Ibid, Art 912a onwards, introduced by Commission Regulation (EC) 1602/2000 of 24 July 2000 [2000] OJ L188/1.

[164] Implementing Regulation, Art 355. The obligation to follow a prescribed itinerary may not be applied where a principal ensures that the customs authorities are able to ascertain the location of the relevant consignments at all times: ibid, Art 387.

[165] Ibid, Art 356.   [166] Ibid, Art 357.

under cover of copies Nos 4 and 5 of the transit declaration returned to the principal by the office of departure.[167] These must then be presented to the customs authorities at the office of destination. A receipt is to be issued on request for these documents. Copy No 5 is then sent by the customs authorities at the office of destination to customs authorities at the office of departure.[168]

3.6 *The end and discharge of the procedure*

If copy No 5 of the transit declaration is not returned to the customs authorities in the state of departure within two months of the acceptance of the declaration, those authorities are to inform the principal and ask for proof that the procedure has ended, that is to say that the goods have been presented to the customs authorities at the office of destination. This may be provided by way of a certificate from the authorities in the state of destination, or by way of certain other documents from the customs authorities of third countries indicating that the goods have been entered for a customs-approved treatment or use. An enquiry procedure is to be initiated if proof that the procedure has ended is not received within four months of the acceptance of the transit declaration.[169]

The transit procedure ends and the obligations of the holder are met when the goods placed under it, and the required documents, are produced at the customs office of destination. When the customs authorities are in a position to establish that the procedure has ended correctly, on the basis of a comparison of data held by the offices of departure and destination, they are to discharge it.[170]

3.7 *The principal's guarantee*[171]

We have already noted, in relation to other transit procedures, that the provision of a guarantee to cover customs duties and other charges which may become due is a fundamental element of the procedure. This is true also in relation to Community transit which assumes that most movements must be covered by a guarantee of some kind.[172] The obligation to provide a guarantee falls on the principal.[173] The guarantee may be comprehensive (in which case

---

[167] Implementing Regulation. Arts 359–360. [168] Ibid, Arts 361–363.
[169] Ibid, Arts 365 and 366.
[170] CCC, Art 92. See also Implementing Regulation, Art 374.
[171] The provisions of the CCC in relation to the customs debt, and security for it, are considered in detail in Ch12.
[172] No guarantees need to be furnished in respect of a number of operations, for example: journeys by air, carriage by pipeline and operations carried out by the railway companies of the Member States: CCC, Art 95. [173] Ibid, Art 94.1.

it covers more than one transit operation and is provided by a guarantor)[174] or individual.[175] Where it is individual it may also be in the form of guarantee vouchers, with each voucher providing for a liability of up to EUR 7000 per voucher.[176] The principal may also use a guarantee waiver up to a reference amount. This amount is to be the same as the amount of the customs debt which may be incurred in respect of goods subject to Community transit during a period of at least a week.[177] The guarantee furnished by the principal is to be valid throughout the Community and must correspond to the model forms annexed to the Implementing Regulation.[178] Comprehensive guarantee, or guarantee waiver, certificates must be presented to the office of departure, except where guarantee data are exchanged between offices using information technology and computer networks.[179] They are valid for a period of two years and their validity may be extended for a further two years.[180]

It is clearly of great importance to the guarantor that he should know when he is released from his guarantee and this is a matter on which there has been some litigation.[181] CCC, Article 199 provides that security is not to be released until such time as the customs debt in respect of which it was given is extinguished or can no longer arise, but once these conditions are satisfied it is to be released forthwith. Partial release is to take place on the request of the person concerned, unless the amount involved does not justify such action. Implementing Regulation, Article 450c provides, in addition, that a guarantor is to be released from his obligations where he has not been notified (i) within twelve months of the date of acceptance of the transit declaration that the procedure has not been discharged; or (ii) within three years of the date of acceptance of the transit declaration that he is or may be liable to pay the debt for which he is liable. Where either of the notifications has been issued, the

---

[174] Implementing Regulation, Arts 379 and 382. In order to be able to furnish a comprehensive guarantee the person concerned must be established in the Community, regularly use Community transit arrangements and not have committed any serious or repeated offences against customs or tax legislation: ibid, Art 373. In order to be able to use a guarantee in relation to the transit of goods involving a higher risk of fraud more stringent requirements must be met: ibid, Arts 345–7 and 381. According to ibid, Art 340c the goods in this category are listed in Annex 44c. They include live animals, meat, spirits, and cigarettes containing tobacco.

[175] Ibid, Art 345f.   [176] Ibid, Art 345.3.

[177] Ibid, Art 379.2. In order to obtain a guarantee waiver, the principal must demonstrate that he maintains the specified standards of reliability, is in command of transit operations, and has sufficient financial resources to meet his obligations: ibid, Art 380.3.

[178] Ibid, Art 342.

[179] Ibid, Art 383.2.   [180] Ibid, Art 383.

[181] See Case C–328/89 *Berner Allgemeine Versicherungsgesellschaft v Amministrazione delle Finanze dello Stato* [1991] ECR I–2431. The regulations then in force required a guarantor to be informed of the non-discharge of the transit procedure by the 'office of departure'. The Court held that notification by a superior customs office was unacceptable having regard to the requirement of legal certainty.

guarantor is to be informed of the recovery of the debt or the discharge of the procedure.[182] The liability of the principal remains.[183]

3.8 Irregularities and the customs debt

There are specific provisions dealing with the customs debt and its recovery in the context of the transit procedure.[184] A customs debt may be incurred where there is a failure to comply with the conditions governing the placing of the goods under the transit procedure and as a result of various other acts, such as the unlawful introduction of goods into the Community.[185] It is, of course, essential to determine where the debt was incurred because it is the Member State in which the debt was incurred, or deemed to have been incurred, which is responsible for effecting recovery.[186] CCC, Article 215 provides, therefore, that a customs debt is to be incurred at the place where the events from which it arises occur. If it is not possible to determine that place, then the debt arises at the place where the customs authorities conclude that the goods are in a situation in which a customs debt is incurred. If the goods have been entered for a customs procedure which has not been discharged and the place cannot be determined according to the above rules, within ten months from acceptance of the transit declaration,[187] the debt is to be incurred at the place where the goods were either placed under the transit or other procedure or introduced into the Community customs territory under that procedure.[188]

Against this background, the Implementing Regulation provides that where, following the initiation of proceedings, the customs authorities responsible for effecting recovery under CCC, Article 215 obtain evidence, by whatever means, regarding the place where the events giving rise to the customs

---

[182] The notification must state the number and date of the declaration, the name of the office of departure, the principal's name and the amount involved. Art 450c is applicable from 1 July 2001 see n 184 below.

[183] See Case 136/80 *Hudig en Pieters BV v Minister van Landbouw en Visserij* [1981] ECR 2233.

[184] Implementing Regulation, Arts 450a–450d applicable as from 1 July 2001: see Art 4.2. The provisions appear in Part II 'Customs Status of Goods and Transit', Title II, Chapter 4, Section 4.

[185] See CCC, Arts 202 and 216 dealt with in Ch 12.

[186] See ibid, Arts 215.3 and 217.1. Although it is impossible for two states to enforce a customs duty liability, because: 'the very concept of a customs union, . . . precludes the double taxation of goods in connection with their entry into the Community customs territory' criminal proceedings may be commenced in a state other than the state entitled to enforce the debt: see Case 252/87 *Hauptzollamt Hamburg-St Annen v Wilhelm Kiwall KG* [1988] ECR 4753 at para 11 (the case concerned the internal transit procedure). See also Case 99/83 *Claudio Fioravanti v Amministrazione delle Finanze dello Stato* [1984] ECR 3939 at para 23.

[187] Implementing Regulation, Art 450a.

[188] The customs authorities may be able to establish that the customs debt was already incurred when the goods were in another place at an earlier date. If so, the customs debt is deemed to have been incurred at the place which may be established as the location of the goods at the earliest time when the existence of the customs debt may be established: CCC, Art 215.3. See pp 385–6 below.

debt occurred, they must immediately send all the necessary documents, including an authenticated copy of the evidence, to the authorities competent for that place (known as the 'requested authorities'). These authorities must acknowledge receipt of the documents and indicate whether or not they are responsible for recovery. If no response is received within three months, what are known as the 'requesting authorities' are to resume recovery immediately. Where the requested authorities are responsible for collection, they must initiate new proceedings for recovery of other charges at the conclusion of the three-month period referred to above, and on condition that the requesting authorities are immediately informed. Uncompleted proceedings by the requesting authorities are to be suspended. Once the requested authorities provide proof that they have recovered the sums in question, the requesting authorities must repay charges already collected and cancel the recovery proceedings.[189]

F. CUSTOMS WAREHOUSING

Annex E3 to the Kyoto Convention concerning customs warehouses was accepted by the Community, along with the Convention itself, by way of a Council Decision in 1975.[190] The Annex deals with the administrative matters in relation to customs warehousing but sets out the purposes of customs warehousing in the introduction, as follows:

> It is in the nature of international trade practice that in a great many cases it is not known at the time of importation how imported goods will finally be disposed of. This means that the importers are obliged to store the goods for more or less long periods.
>
> Where it is intended to re-export the goods, it is in the importer's interest to place them under a customs procedure which obviates the need to pay import duties and taxes.
>
> When goods are intended for outright importation, it is again in the importer's interest to be able to delay payment of the import duties and taxes until the goods are actually taken into home use.
>
> In order to make these facilities available to importers, most countries have provided in their national legislations for the customs warehousing procedure.

As the Annex makes clear, this is not a complete summary of all the cases in which warehousing is useful. It may be attractive in relation to goods which are not imported and, as we shall see, certain Community goods may be stored in a customs warehouse.

---

[189] Implementing Regulation, Art 450b. See also Case C–233/98 *Hauptzollamt Neubrandenburg v Lensing Brockenhausen GmbH* [1999] ECR I–7349 at paras 65–72 and *PSL Freight Ltd v The Commissioners of Customs and Excise* 31 July 2001 (High Court).
[190] Council Decision (EEC) 199/75 of 18 Mar 1975 [1975] OJ L100/1.

Turning briefly to the provisions of the Annex,[191] it establishes a distinction between public and private warehouses and sets down standards for their establishment, management and control. There are also provisions governing matters such as the admission, removal, handling, and transfer of ownership of warehoused goods. Standard 19 of the Annex provides that customs authorities are to fix an authorized maximum duration of storage, which is to be not less than one year. Standard 11 of Annex D1 to the Revised Convention prescribes that this maximum is to apply in the case of non-perishable goods. As we shall see, Community customs law does contain provisions for a time limit to be set, but generally speaking customs warehousing in the Community is for an indefinite period.

1. *Community legislation*

The Community legislation on customs warehousing is contained in CCC, Articles 98–113 and in addition to the general provisions referred to at C above, Implementing Regulation, Articles 524–535. CCC, Article 98.1 sets out the basic purpose of the customs warehousing procedure, which is to allow the storage in a customs warehouse of non-Community goods without such goods being subject to import duties or commercial policy measures.[192] Community goods may also be stored in a customs warehouse in limited circumstances, as we shall see. Operators who do not know what customs treatment will finally apply to non-Community goods, or who do not yet wish such treatment to be applied to goods may, therefore, store goods in a customs warehouse without their being subject to the payment of import duties or the application of commercial policy measures. In this way the procedure 'ensures the promotion of Community activities relating to foreign trade and, in particular, the distribution of goods within the Community and elsewhere and . . . therefore, the customs warehousing procedure is an essential instrument of the Community's commercial policy'.[193]

---

[191] The provisions of Specific Annex D Chapter 1 in the revised Kyoto Convention are similar to those of Annex E3.

[192] CCC, Art 98.1(a). Where import goods, defined in CCC, Art 84.2 (see n 196) are released for free circulation in accordance with simplified procedures, the nature of the goods, the customs value of them, and the quantity to be taken into account in assessing the duty is to be that applicable at the time when the goods were placed under the warehousing procedure, provided that the rules of assessment relating to the goods were ascertained or accepted at the time when the goods were placed under it. The time when the customs debt is incurred may be used at the declarant's request: see Implementing Regulation, Art 112.3. Specific provisions exist in relation to the goods which have undergone the usual forms of handling: ibid, Art 112.2.

[193] Council Regulation (EEC) 2503/88 of 25 July 1988 on customs warehouses [1988] OJ L225/1, recital 1. See also the recitals to Annex E3 to the Kyoto Convention.

1.1 *Goods capable of being stored*

Non-Community goods and Community goods may be stored in a customs warehouse, but in the latter case only where Community legislation provides that the placing of the goods in a customs warehouse is to attract the application of measures normally attaching to the export of the goods.[194] Where an economic need exists, and customs supervision is not adversely affected by it, the customs authorities may relax these requirements. They may permit other Community goods to be stored in the warehouse, and they may also permit non-Community goods to be processed on the premises under the inward processing procedure or under the procedure for processing under customs control. Such goods are not to be subject to the customs warehousing procedure and may be required to be entered into stock records.[195]

1.2 *Storing and handling the goods*

Import goods, ie in this context goods subject to customs warehousing,[196] may, subject to authorization,[197] undergo 'the usual forms of handling intended to preserve them, improve their appearance or marketable quality, or prepare them for distribution or resale'.[198] This general rule is subject to certain variations in respect of goods subject to the agricultural policy of the Community. The Court of Justice has emphasized, however, that 'The essential purpose of customs warehouses is to provide for the storage of goods'.[199] It followed in the case in question that customs warehousing did not allow for the packing of butter into small packages ready for sale. As the Court made clear, the permitted operations are not intended, in principle, to permit the goods to pass from one stage of marketing to another. An express provision is required for any exceptions to this rule.[200] The Implementing Regulation now makes

---

[194] CCC, Art 98.1(b). Specific provisions govern agricultural products: CCC, Art 108.2 and Implementing Regulation, Arts 529–534.

[195] CCC, Art 106.

[196] Defined in CCC, Art 84.2 as meaning 'goods placed under a suspensive procedure and goods which, under the inward processing procedure in the form of the drawback system, have undergone the formalities for release for free circulation and the formalities provided for in Article 125.'

[197] See Implementing Regulation, Art 533.

[198] CCC, Art 109.1 and 4. The usual forms of handling are those listed in Implementing Regulation, Annex 72. The Annex states that the usual forms of handling may not give rise to a different 8-digit CN Code. Furthermore, the usual forms of handling are not to be permitted if, in the opinion of the customs authorities, the operation is likely to increase the risk of fraud. They include operations to preserve goods such as drying, simple cleaning, simple repair of transit damage, and certain kinds of temperature and electronic treatment. They also include operations affecting the presentation or marketability of goods, such as packing, unpacking, and changing packing, even if a change of CN Code results. See Case 276/84 *Gebr. Metelmann GmbH & Co KG v Hauptzollamt Hamburg-Jonas* [1985] ECR 4057, in which it was said that re-packaging in different units was not permitted: para 9. See also the Guidelines at n 40 above, Ch. 2

[199] Case 49/82 *Commission v The Netherlands* [1983] ECR 1195 para 10.

[200] Ibid, para 10.

clear that an authorization for customs warehousing may be granted only if any of the intended usual forms of handling, inward processing, or processing under customs control of the goods, do not predominate over the storage of the goods.[201] Furthermore, authorizations are not to be granted if the premises of the customs warehouses or storage facilities are used for the purpose of retail trade sale.[202]

Goods subject to the customs warehousing procedure may be temporarily removed from the warehouse for a period not exceeding three months. This period may be extended where circumstances so warrant.[203] and subject to prior authorization by the customs authorities and the conditions they set. Once outside the warehouse, the goods may undergo the handling referred to above.[204] Goods subject to the warehousing procedure may also be transferred between customs warehouses.[205]

So far as storage is concerned, both Community goods and non-Community goods may be stored together. Specific methods of identifying Community goods may be laid down with a view, in particular, to distinguishing them from goods entered for the customs warehousing arrangements. Common storage of goods, except prefinanced goods,[206] may be permitted by the customs authorities where it is impossible to identify at all times the customs status of each type of goods, but the goods in common storage must share the same eight-digit CN code and have the same commercial quality and characteristics.[207]

Generally speaking, there is no limit to the length of time for which goods may remain under the customs warehousing procedure. In exceptional cases, however, the customs authorities may set a time limit by which the depositor must assign the goods to a customs-approved treatment or use. Specific time limits may be set for Community goods which are covered by the Community agricultural policy.[208]

---

[201] Implementing Regulation, Art 527.1. Where inward processing and customs control are carried out additional provisions apply: see ibid, Arts 534 and 535.

[202] Ibid, Art 527.2. Nevertheless, an authorization may be granted where goods are retailed with relief from import duties to travellers in traffic to third countries, under diplomatic or consular arrangements, and to members of international organizations or NATO forces: ibid, Art 527.2(a)–(c).

[203] CCC, Art 110 and Implementing Regulation, Art 532.   [204] CCC, Art 110.

[205] Ibid, Art 111.

[206] 'Prefinanced goods' means Community goods, intended for export in the unaltered state, which are the subject of the payment of an amount equal to an export refund before the goods are exported, where such payment is provided for in Council Regulation (EEC) 565/80 on the advance payment of export refunds in respect of agricultural products [1980] OJ L62/5: see Implementing Regulation, Art 524.

[207] Implementing Regulation, Art 534.1 and 2. See also the Guidelines at n 40 above, Ch 2.

[208] CCC, Art 108.

1.3 *Customs warehouses*

These are defined as any place approved by and under the supervision of the customs authorities where goods may be stored under the conditions laid down.[209] They may be either public or private. A public warehouse is one which is available for the use of any person for the warehousing of goods. A private warehouse is reserved for the warehousing of goods by the warehouse-keeper, who is the person authorized to operate the customs warehouse. The person who deposits the goods in the warehouse, or the person to whom the rights and obligations of the depositor have been transferred, is the person bound by the declaration placing the goods under the customs warehousing procedure.[210] The Implementing Regulation establishes six types of customs warehouse. There are three types of public warehouse, namely types, A, B, and F. Type A consists of warehouses where the responsibility lies with the warehouse-keeper. Type B covers warehouses where responsibility lies with the depositor and type F covers warehouses operated by the customs authorities.[211] There are also three types of private warehouse. The classification applies in respect of private warehouses where responsibility lies with the warehouse-keeper, who is the same person as the depositor, but not necessarily the owner of the goods. Type D exists where release for free circulation is made by way of the local clearance procedure and may be granted on the basis of the nature, the customs value, and the quality of the goods to be taken into account at the time of their placement under the arrangements. Type E covers warehouses where the customs warehousing arrangements apply but the goods need not be stored in a place approved as a customs warehouse.[212] Type C applies where Types D and E do not.[213] A location may not be approved as more than one customs warehouse at any one time.[214]

The operation of a customs warehouse is subject to authorization by the customs authorities unless they operate the warehouse. Any person wishing to operate a customs warehouse must show that an economic need for warehousing exists. An authorization must specify the conditions applicable and may be issued only to persons established in the Community.[215]

1.4 *Responsibilities of warehouse-keeper and depositor*

The depositor is responsible at all times for fulfilling the obligations arising from the placing of goods under the customs warehousing procedure.[216] The

---

[209] Ibid, Art 98.2.
[210] CCC, Art 99.   [211] Implementing Regulation, Art 525.1.
[212] An authorization for a Type E warehouse may provide for the procedures laid down for Type D to be applied: ibid, Art 525.3.
[213] Ibid, Art 525.2.
[214] Ibid, Art 526.2.
[215] CCC, Art 100.1–3.   [216] Ibid, Art 102.2.

warehouse-keeper, who may be asked to provide a guarantee,[217] is responsible for three matters. First, for ensuring that while the goods are in the customs warehouse, they are not removed from customs supervision; secondly, for fulfilling the obligations that arise from the storage of goods covered by the warehousing procedure; and, thirdly, for satisfying the particular conditions set out in the authorization.[218] In relation to public warehouses, the authorization may provide that the first and/or second of the responsibilities referred to above may devolve exclusively upon the depositor.[219] With the agreement of the customs authorities, the rights and obligations of the warehouse-keeper may be transferred to another person.[220]

A person designated by the customs authorities is to keep stock records of all the goods placed under the customs warehousing procedure in a form approved by the authorities.[221] Stock records are not necessary, though, where a public warehouse is operated by the customs authorities. Furthermore, they may be dispensed with where, first, the depositor is exclusively responsible for fulfilling the responsibilities that arise from storage and/or for compliance with the authorization requirements, as set out above, and, secondly, where the goods are placed under the procedure on the basis of a written declaration under the normal or a simplified procedure.[222] Where necessary, the supervising office of the customs authorities is to require an inventory to be kept.[223]

1.5 *Authorization*

We noted in section C above that authorization in relation to customs procedures with economic impact is to be granted only to those who offer every guarantee necessary for the proper conduct of the operations, and only where the customs authorities can supervise and monitor the procedure without having to introduce administrative arrangements disproportionate to the economic needs involved.[224] When examining whether the administrative costs of customs warehousing are disproportionate to the economic needs involved, customs authorities are to take account, *inter alia*, of the type of warehouse and the procedure which may be applied in it.[225]

---

[217] CCC, Art 104.   [218] Ibid, Art 101.
[219] Ibid, Art 102.1.
[220] Ibid, Art 103.
[221] The goods are to be entered into stock records as soon as they are brought into the customs warehouse: CCC, Art 107. Implementing Regulation, Arts 528–530, cover the maintenance of stock records in more detail specifying that the warehouse-keeper is the person who is required to keep the records, except for Types B and F (Arts 28) and stating what the records are to contain (Art 529).
[222] CCC, Art 105.
[223] Implementing Regulation, Art 527.
[224] CCC, Art 86.
[225] Implementing Regulation, Art 527.3.

When granting authorizations, the customs authorities are to define the premises, or other location, approved as a customs warehouse of type A, B, C, or D. They may also approve temporary storage facilities as such types of warehouse or operate them as a type F warehouse.[226] Where goods present a danger, are likely to spoil other goods, or require special facilities for other reasons, authorizations may specify that they may only be stored in premises specially equipped to receive them.[227] It should be noted that single authorizations may be granted for private customs warehouses only.[228]

G. PROCESSING UNDER CUSTOMS CONTROL

Annex F2, to the Kyoto Convention, which deals with the processing of goods for home use states that:

> The purpose of the customs procedure of processing of goods for home use is to provide for the possibility where it is in the national economic interest, of processing certain imported goods under customs control to such an extent that the amount of the import duties and taxes applicable to the products thus obtained is lower than that which would be applicable to the imported goods.[229]

As the introduction to Annex F2 makes clear, and as Community legislation indicates in CCC, Article 133, the economic objective of the relief is to ensure that processing is carried out in the importing state and not lost to another country, in circumstances where the imposition of duty on the imported product may have made the 'overall commercial operation unprofitable'. Annex F2 goes on to provide that authorization for the procedure must depend upon the customs authorities being able to satisfy themselves that the processed product results from the imported product.[230] Furthermore the original state of the goods must be incapable of recovery after processing.[231] Standard 6 envisages that goods may be subject to processing if they have been imported directly from abroad but also if they have come from the transit procedure, or from a customs warehouse or free zone (the revised Kyoto convention refers merely to 'another customs procedure'[232]). Standard 5 of Annex F2 and Standard 3 of

---

[226] Ibid, Art 526.1. Type A, C, D, and E warehouses may be approved as victualling warehouses within the meaning of Art 40, Commission Regulation (EC) 800/99 of 15 Apr 1999 [1999] OJ L102/11, which lays down detailed rules for the application of the system of export refunds for agricultural products.

[227] Implementing Regulation, Art 526.3.   [228] Ibid, Art 526.5.

[229] Annex F to the revised Convention is concerned with processing generally. Chapter 1 deals with inward processing, chapter 2 with outward processing, and chapter 4 with processing of goods for home use. The definition of the procedure in Specific Annex F Chapter 4, of the revised Convention is similar to that quoted above.

[230] Standard 3 (Standard 2: revised Convention).

[231] Standard 4 (Standard 2: revised Convention).

[232] See Standard 4.

the revised Convention envisage that national legislation is to specify the categories of goods and operations allowed.

1. *Community legislation*

Processing under customs control is dealt with in CCC, Articles 130–136 and, in Articles 551 and 552 of the Implementing Regulation, in addition to its general provisions dealt with above. It permits non-Community goods to be used in the customs territory of the Community in operations which alter their nature, or state, without becoming subject to import duties or commercial policy measures. It also permits the products which result from such operations, so-called 'processed products', to be released for free circulation at the rate of import duty appropriate to them.[233] It is provided that the arrangements for processing under customs control are to apply to goods the processing of which leads to products which are subject to a lower amount of import duties than that applicable to the import goods. They also apply for goods which have to undergo operations to ensure their compliance with technical requirements for their release for free circulation.[234]

2. *Authorization*

Authorization for the procedure is to be granted at the request of the person who carries out the processing or arranges for it to be carried out.[235] The category of persons who may be granted authorization is limited. Authorization may be granted only where a series of conditions are satisfied. The persons authorized must be established in the Community, the imported goods must be capable of identification in the processed products, the goods must be incapable of being restored to their description or state prior to being placed under the procedure, and the use of the procedure must not permit the circumvention of the effect of the rules of origin and quantitive restrictions applicable to the imported goods. Finally, authorization is to be granted only where the necessary conditions are fulfilled for the procedure to help create or maintain a processing activity in the Community without adversely affecting the essential interests of Community producers of similar goods.[236]

These economic conditions, as they are called, are deemed to be fulfilled for the types of goods and operations mentioned in the Implementing Regulation,

---

[233] CCC, Art 130. In order to determine the customs value of processed products declared for free circulation, the declarant may choose any of the methods referred to in CCC, Art 30(2)(a), (b), or (c) or the customs value of the import goods plus the processing costs: Implementing Regulation, Art 551.3.

[234] Implementing Regulation, Art 551.1.

[235] CCC, Art 132.

[236] Ibid, Art 133 and Implementing Regulation, Art 502.3.

Annex 76 Part A.[237] This provides that goods of any kind may be processed into samples presented as such or put up in sets. They may be reduced to waste and scrap or destroyed. They may be denatured. Their parts or components may be recovered, damaged parts may be destroyed or separated, and they may be processed to correct the effects of damage which they have suffered. They may also be subjected to all usual forms of handling permitted in customs warehouses or free zones.[238] Other procedures are listed in respect of limited categories of goods. In respect of other types of goods and operations where the economic conditions are not deemed to be fulfilled, the conditions must be examined. In relation to the goods and operations mentioned in Annex 76 Part B but not in Part A, the economic conditions are to be examined in Committee.[239] The goods referred to in Part B are all goods subject to an agricultural measure or provisional or definitive anti-dumping, or countervailing, duty and the operation to which it refers is any form of processing.

3. *Operation of the procedure*

So far as the operation of the procedure is concerned, the customs authorities are to specify the time within which goods which are processed are to be assigned to a customs-approved treatment or use.[240] The time period may be extended where circumstances so warrant.[241] The customs authorities are also to set the rate of yield of the operation (which may be an average rate) or, where appropriate, the method by which the rate is to be determined.

According to the CCC, the rate is to be determined on the basis of the actual circumstances in which the processing operation is, or is to be, carried out[242] and the Implementing Regulation provides that, so far as possible, the rate is to be based on production or technical data or, where these are not available, data relating to operations of the same type.[243] In particular circumstances the customs authorities may establish the rate of yield after the goods have been entered for the arrangements, but not later than when they are assigned to a

---

[237] Implementing Regulation, Art 552.1, first sub-para. The cases in which the economic conditions are deemed to have been fulfilled may be determined in accordance with the committee procedure following an amendment to CCC, Art 133(e) by Regulation (EC) 2700/2000 of the European Parliament and Council of 16 Nov 2000 [2000] OJ L311/17. As a result of Commission Regulation (EC) 993/2001 of 4 May 2001 [2001] OJ L141/1, the Implementing Regulation provides that the economic conditions are deemed to be fulfilled, in relation to processing under customs control, in accordance with Art 552. See also the Guidelines at n 40 above, Ch 4.

[238] See Implementing Regulation, Annex 76, Orders Nos 1 to 7.

[239] Ibid, Art 552. In relation to the examination in committee ibid, Art 504.3 and 4 are applied.

[240] CCC, Art 134 and Art 118.1.2 and 4, and Implementing Regulation, Arts 554.2 and 543.

[241] Ibid, Art 542.1.

[242] CCC, Arts 134 and 119.1. The rate of yield is the quantity or percentage of compensating products obtained from the processing of a given quantity of import goods: ibid, Art 114.2(f). Import goods is defined in ibid, Art 84.2.

[243] Implementing Regulation, Art 517.1.

new customs-approved treatment or use.[244] Standard rates of yield are set in Annex 69 to the Implementing Regulation in respect of the operations listed there.[245] They are to apply only to import goods of sound, genuine, and merchantable quality which conform to any standard quality laid down in Community legislation and on condition that the compensating products are not obtained by special processing methods in order to meet specific quality requirements.

4. *Calculating the customs debt*

In two situations the customs debt is to be determined on the basis of elements appropriate to the import goods[246] at the time that the declaration relating to processing under customs control was accepted. These are, first, where a customs debt is incurred in respect of goods in the unaltered state[247] and, secondly, where a customs debt is incurred in respect of products that are at an intermediate stage of processing as compared with that provided for in the authorization.[248]

Where import goods qualified for preferential tariff treatment when they were placed under the procedure and preferential tariff treatment is available to processed products released for free circulation, then the import duties imposed in respect of the processed products are to be calculated by applying the rate of duty applicable under that preferential treatment.[249] Where the preferential treatment is subject to tariff quotas or ceilings, then the application of the preferential treatment is subject to an additional condition. This is that the preferential treatment must be applicable to the import goods at the time of acceptance of the declaration for release for free circulation. The quantity of import goods actually used in the manufacture of the processed products released for free circulation is to be charged against the quotas or ceilings in force at the time of the acceptance of the declaration of release for free circulation. No quantities are to be counted against the quotas or ceilings opened in respect of products which are identical to the processed products.[250]

---

[244] Implementing Regulation, Art 517.2.

[245] Ibid, Art 517.3, and CCC, Art 119.2.

[246] As noted above, 'import goods' means goods placed under a suspensive procedure and which under the inward processing procedure in the form of the drawback system have undergone requisite formalities for release for free circulation and those provided for in CCC 125: CCC, Art 84.2.

[247] 'Goods in the unaltered state' means import goods which, under inward processing or processing under customs control, have undergone no form of processing: CCC, Art 84.3.

[248] Ibid, Art 135.   [249] Ibid, Art 136.1.

[250] Ibid, Art 136.2.

H. TEMPORARY ADMISSION

The temporary admission or importation procedure has been the subject of a number of international treaties with provisions which are not always mutually compatible. Of particular importance are Annex E5 to the Kyoto Convention,[251] Specific Annex G of the revised Kyoto Convention, and the extensive Convention on Temporary Admission of 26 June 1990 ('the Istanbul Convention') which entered into force generally on 27 November 1993.[252] The latter Convention provides for a common document, the ATA[253] Carnet, to be used in respect of temporary duty-free importation or transit and contains models for both ATA Carnets[254] and CPD Carnets[255] (which are used in relation to the temporary admission of means of transport). Like the TIR Convention it also provides for guarantees to be given, by guaranteeing associations, to cover the import duty to which the importations will be subject in the event of a breach of the conditions of the temporary importation.[256] All Member States and the EC have ratified the Istanbul Convention and references to 'ATA Carnet' in the Implementing Regulation are references to the model form in the Istanbul Convention.[257] The Customs Convention on the ATA Carnet for the Temporary Admission of Goods 1961, which entered into force generally on 30 July 1963, should also be mentioned. All Members States have ratified it. This Convention is currently applied by sixty-one contracting parties and the Istanbul Convention by thirty-four contracting parties.

The revised Kyoto Convention has taken account of the Istanbul Convention in certain respects[258] but, in Specific Annex G, it reproduces almost exactly the definition of temporary admission which appeared in the original Kyoto Convention, saying that it is:

> the Customs procedure under which certain goods can be brought into a Customs territory conditionally, relieved totally or partially from payment of import duties and taxes; such goods must be imported for a specific purpose and must be intended for re-exportation within a specified period and without having undergone any change except normal depreciation due to the use made of them.[259]

---

[251] Entitled: 'The temporary admission of goods subject to re-exportation in the same state'. It was accepted by the Community by a Council Decision of 30 Nov 1987: Council Decision (EEC) 593/87 [1987] OJ L362/1.

[252] It is reproduced at [1993] OJ L130/4 and was accepted on behalf of the European Community, with certain reservations, by Council Decision (EEC) 329/93 of 15 Mar 1993 [1993] OJ L130/1.

[253] '*Admission temporaire*—Temporary Admission'.   [254] Annex A, Appendix I.
[255] Annex A, Appendix II.   [256] Annex A, Art 8.
[257] See the Implementing Regulation, Art 1.2 and 1.11.

[258] Note that Recommended Practice 22, concerning the categories of goods subject to temporary admission procedures, is drafted by reference to the goods referred to in the Annexes to the Istanbul Convention.

[259] In Annex E5, noted above, definition (a) contains exactly the same wording except that it concludes with 'the goods' instead of 'them'.

Given that the Istanbul Convention noted that 'the present situation regarding the proliferation and dispersed nature of international Customs Conventions on temporary admission is unsatisfactory', it is, perhaps, surprising that it contained its own definition of the procedure when the definition in the original Kyoto Convention was available for adoption.[260]

As Annex E5 to the Kyoto Convention says, there are many reasons why a country should encourage the temporary stay of goods. The justification of the temporary importation procedure is that:

> when goods have to stay only temporarily in the customs territory of a State, to require final payment of the import duties and taxes applicable to them would as a rule be unjustified since the effect would be, for example, to subject goods to payment of import duties and taxes every time they were imported, on a temporary basis, into one country or another.[261]

The Annexes governing temporary admission in the Kyoto Conventions are lengthy and it is not proposed to review them here, but Standard 4 in both of them states that temporary admission is not to be limited to goods imported directly from abroad, but is to be granted for goods already placed under customs procedures. Recommended practice 5 states that it should be granted without regard to the country of origin of the goods, the country from which they arrived or their destination. The provisions regarding the extension of time for which goods may remain in the importing country should also be borne in mind and are considered below.

1. *Community legislation*

The Community rules governing temporary admission or importation are dealt with in CCC, Articles 137–144 and Implementing Regulation, Articles 553–584.[262] So far as Community customs law is concerned, the procedure allows non-Community goods, intended for re-export from the Community customs territory without having undergone any change except normal depreciation due to use, to be used for a specific purpose in the Community customs territory with total or partial relief from import duty and without

---

[260] The definition of 'temporary admission' in Istanbul Convention, Art 1(a) states that it is: 'the Customs procedure under which certain goods (including means of transport) can be brought into a Customs territory conditionally relieved from payment of import duties and taxes and without application of import prohibitions or restrictions of economic character; such goods (including means of transport) must be imported for a specific purpose and must be intended for re-exportation within a specified period and without having undergone any change except normal depreciation due to the use made of them.'

[261] The Introduction to Annex E5.

[262] Reference should also be made to the Guidelines, n 40 above, Ch 5, which consider matters relating to the ATA Carnet and contain illustrative lists of goods attracting relief from duty. Lists appeared in Annexes to the Implementing Regulation until its most recent amendment.

being subject to commercial policy measures.[263] Entry of goods for the temporary importation procedure is normally subject to the provision of security[264] Authorization for temporary importation is to be granted at the request of the person who uses the goods or arranges for them to be used.[265] Where it is impossible to ensure that the import goods can be identified, the customs authorities are to refuse the authorization, except where, in view of the nature of the goods or the operations to be carried out, the absence of identification measures is not liable to give rise to any abuse of the procedure.[266]

2. Period of temporary importation

The customs authorities are to determine the period within which the import goods must be re-exported or assigned a new customs-approved treatment or use. The period must be long enough for the objective of the authorized use to be achieved.[267] The maximum period for which goods may remain under the arrangements, for the same purpose and under the responsibility of the holder, is twenty-four months[268] and this is the period which is usually applied.[269] Shorter periods of temporary importation may be determined with the agreement of the person concerned and the twenty-four month period may be extended for the time during which the goods are not used in accordance with the conditions laid down by the customs authorities. Furthermore, the maximum period and the other agreed periods may be extended where exceptional circumstances warrant it in order to permit the authorized use. The extension is to be made at the request of the person concerned and within reasonable limits.[270] For these purposes, 'exceptional circumstances' means any event as a result of which the goods must be used for a further period in order to fulfil the purpose of the temporary importation operation.[271]

[263] CCC, Art 137. Implementing Regulation, Art 553.4 confirms that the goods placed under temporary importation arrangements must remain in the same state. Repairs and maintenance, including overhaul and adjustments, or measures to preserve the goods or to ensure their compliance with the technical requirements for their use under the arrangements, are permitted, see second sub-para.

[264] Implementing Regulation, Art 581. Annex 77 lists the cases in which security is unnecessary.   [265] CCC, Art 138.

[266] CCC, Art 139.   [267] Ibid, Art 140.1.

[268] Ibid, Art 140.2 and Implementing Regulation, Art 553.2. Specific periods are laid down in the Implementing Regulation, Arts 555–578.

[269] The Court of Auditors has found considerable problems in relation to the temporary importation procedure, noting, eg, that in one jurisdiction a major trader had 470 temporary importation declarations uncleared after 2 years: see Special Report No 8/99, n 106 above, at para 15. It said that 'It is incumbent on the customs authorities of the Member States to treat the two-year limit allowed for temporary importation as that and to recognise that failure to carefully monitor goods introduced into the Community under this procedure can result in major delays in giving the Community benefit of the duties involved.' (para 16). It may be doubted whether the Court of Auditors was absolutely correct to regard the two-year period with such strictness given that extensions are permitted.

[270] CCC, Art 140.2 and 3.   [271] Implementing Regulation, Art 553.3.

Extensions of the time period for temporary importation are considered in the international conventions considered above. Recommended practice 20 of Annex E5 states that 'At the request of the person concerned, and for reasons deemed to be valid, the customs authorities should extend the period initially fixed'.[272] The Istanbul Convention, Article 7.2 states that 'The Customs authorities may either grant a longer period than that provided for in each Annex, or extend the initial period'. Extensions of time for which goods may remain under the temporary importation procedure have proved of considerable importance in the Community. The general rule, referred to above is that the period of temporary importation should be for two years but capable of extension in 'exceptional' circumstances. It is noteworthy that neither the Kyoto Convention nor the Istanbul Convention refers to the need for exceptional circumstances. Their provisions appear to concentrate on ensuring that the purpose for which the goods have been imported is achieved. Following the passage of Commission Regulation (EC) 993/2001[273] that approach is adopted by the Community. The regulation introduces Article 553.3 into the Implementing Regulation which, as we noted above, provides that 'exceptional circumstances', in this context, means any event as a result of which the goods must be used for a further period in order to fulfil the purpose of the temporary importation operation.

3. Total relief from import duty

The cases and special conditions under which the procedure may be used with total relief from import duties are to be determined by the Implementing Regulation.[274] It provides that total relief is to be granted for specified categories of goods subject to varying conditions.[275] These include: means of road, rail, air, sea, and inland waterway transport,[276] pallets,[277] containers,[278] personal effects, and goods for sports purposes,[279] disaster relief material, medical, surgical, and laboratory equipment, animals,[280] and goods for use in frontier zones,[281] sound, image, or data-carrying media, publicity material,

---

[272] Recommended practice 14 of the revised Convention is in similar terms.

[273] Of 4 May 2001 [2001] OJ L141/1.   [274] CCC, Art 141.

[275] Implementing Regulation, Arts 555–578. The provisions governing the goods which are subject to total relief were significantly rationalized by Commission Regulation (EC) 993/2001. See n 273. As noted above, reference should be made to the Guidelines, for illustrative lists of goods: n 40 above.

[276] Implementing Regulation, Arts 558–562, which include certain limited reliefs for private use of means of transport.

[277] Ibid, Art 556.   [278] Ibid, Art 557.

[279] Ibid, Art 563.

[280] Unless animals are of negligible commercial value, animals born of animals placed under the arrangements are considered to be non-Community goods and themselves placed under those arrangements: ibid, Art 553.1.

[281] Ibid, Arts 565–567.

professional and scientific equipment, and pedagogic material,[282] items such as packings and mouldings, and certain tools and replacement means of production,[283] goods for exhibition, sale by auction, and certain works of art and antiques,[284] and certain spare parts, accessories, and other goods.[285] Total relief is also available where goods which are not listed in the Implementing Regulation, or do not satisfy the requisite conditions, are imported either occasionally and for a period not exceeding three months, or in particular situations having no economic effect.[286]

4. *Partial relief from import duty*

The use of the procedure with partial relief from import duties is to be granted in respect of goods which are not covered by provisions adopted in relation to total relief,[287] or which are covered by them but do not fulfil all the applicable conditions.[288] The CCC provides that the list of goods in respect of which the temporary importation procedure with partial relief from import duties may not be used, and the conditions subject to which the procedure may be used, is to be determined in accordance with the committee procedure.[289] The Implementing Regulation now provides that partial relief is not to be granted for consumable goods.[290]

For every complete or incomplete month that partial relief is given, the goods are subject to 3 per cent of the customs duty which would have been payable had the goods in question been released for free circulation on the date on which they were placed under the temporary importation procedure.[291] The amount of duty charged is not to exceed what would have been payable had the goods been released for free circulation instead of being placed under temporary importation, ignoring any interest applicable.[292] Where rights and obligations under the temporary importation procedure are transferred, it is

---

[282] Ibid, Arts 568–570.
[283] Ibid, Arts 571–575.   [284] Ibid, Art 576.
[285] Ibid, Art 577.
[286] Implementing Regulation, Art 578.
[287] Pursuant to CCC, Art 141.
[288] CCC, Art 142.1, introduced by Art 1.9, Regulation (EC) 2700/2000, n 237 above. The earlier version of Art 142.1 provided that the goods had to remain the property of a person outside the Community.
[289] Prior to Commission Regulation (EC) 993/2001, n 273 above, Annex 95 to the Implementing Regulation excluded from entitlement to partial relief all consumable products and goods the use of which is liable to injure the economy of the Community, in particular because of the length of their useful life in relation to the intended length of stay. The Annex was now been repealed by the regulation and partially incorporated in Art 554, Implementing Regulation.
[290] Implementing Regulation, Art 554.
[291] CCC, Art 143.1. The entry for a customs-approved treatment or use of goods subject to the temporary importation procedure with partial relief is subject to payment of any amount due under CCC, Art 143: Implementing Regulation, Art 703.
[292] CCC, Art 143.2.

not necessary for the same relief arrangements to apply in respect of different periods of use.[293] The initial holder of an authorization is liable for import duties for the whole of the month in which the transfer occurs.[294]

5. *ATA Carnet*

Declarations for entry for temporary importation using ATA/CPD carnets are to be accepted, subject to certain conditions. These include a requirement that they are issued in a country which is a contracting party to the ATA Convention or a contracting party to the Istanbul Convention, having accepted the Customs Co-operation Council Recommendations of 25 June 1992, concerning acceptance of the carnet, and other matters.[295] There are further specific provisions relating to goods moving under an ATA carnet. Amongst other things, these preserve provisions relating to ATA carnets in relation to goods within the temporary importation regime.[296]

6. *The customs debt*

Where a customs debt is incurred in respect of import goods, it is to be determined on the basis of the taxation elements appropriate to the goods at the time the declaration placing goods under the temporary importation procedure is accepted. The conditions governing total relief from import duties may provide, however, that the debt is to be determined by reference to the taxation elements appropriate to the goods at the time the customs debt is incurred.[297] Where a customs debt is incurred in respect of goods under the temporary importation procedure, for a reason other than the placing of goods under it with partial relief, the amount of the customs debt is equal to the difference between two elements. These are, first, the amount of the debt payable pursuant to the provisions of CCC, Article 144.1, just discussed and, secondly, the amount payable under CCC, Article 143, discussed at 4 above.[298]

7. *Discharge of the procedure*

In addition to the general provisions, there are limited specific provisions governing the discharge of the procedure in relation to the necessary indica-

---

[293] CCC, Art 143.3.
[294] Ibid, Art 143.
[295] Implementing Regulation, Art 580.
[296] Ibid, Arts 580–581 and 583.
[297] Or such other time as is prescribed by CCC, Art 214: see CCC, Art 144.1. See also Implementing Regulation, Art 582, which applies in respect of goods attracting total relief from import duties where the goods are to be exhibited or used at public events, etc.
[298] CCC, Art 144.2.

tions which should appear on relevant documentation and to the use of means of rail transport.[299]

I. EXPORT[300]

There are limited provisions governing export in the CCC (Articles 161–162) and the Implementing Regulation (Articles 788–798) and it is not proposed to consider them in any detail. As is obvious from its name, the export procedure allows Community goods to leave the customs territory of the Community.[301] The procedure entails the application of exit formalities including commercial policy measures and, where appropriate, export duties.[302] In general, all goods intended for export are to be placed under the export procedure with the exception of goods placed under the outward processing procedure or the internal transit procedure pursuant to Article 163.[303] Goods intended for export are to be subject to an export declaration.[304] The export declaration may be made on the basis of the Single Administrative Document.[305] It must be lodged at the customs office responsible for supervising the place where the exporter is established or where the goods are packed, or loaded, for export shipment.[306] The exporter is the person on whose behalf the export declaration is made and who is the owner of the goods, or has a similar right of disposal over them at the time when the declaration is accepted. Where ownership or a similar right of disposal over the goods, pursuant to the contract on which the export is based, belongs to a person established outside the Community, the exporter is considered to be the contracting party established in the Community.[307]

---

[299] Implementing Regulation, Arts 583 and 584.

[300] Annex C.1 of the Kyoto Convention deals with exportation and was accepted by the Community by means of Council Decision (EEC) 204/85 of 7 Mar 1985 [1985] OJ L87/8. Exportation is dealt with in Specific Annex C of the Revised Kyoto Convention.

[301] Goods dispatched to Heligoland are not considered to be exports from the customs territory of the Community, notwithstanding that Heligoland is outside the customs territory: see CCC, Art 161.3 and Art 3.1 third indent.

[302] CCC, Art 161.1.

[303] Ibid, Art 161.2.

[304] Ibid, Art 161.4. This may be made orally at the office of exit in relation to goods of not more than ECU 3000, per consignment per declarant: Implementing Regulation, Art 794. Export declarations may be made retrospectively: ibid, Art 795.

[305] Implementing Regulation, Art 793.

[306] CCC, Art 161.5. Where, for administrative reasons the requirement as to where the declaration is to be lodged cannot be applied, the declaration may be lodged with any customs office in the Member State concerned, which is competent for the operation in question: Implementing Regulation, Art 790. In cases involving sub-contracting, the export declaration may be lodged at the customs office responsible for the place where the sub-contractor is established: ibid, Art 789. Acceptance of a declaration at a customs office other than that specified in CCC, Art 161.5 or Implementing Regulation, Art 790, is permitted where there are 'duly justified good reasons': ibid, Art 791.

[307] Ibid, Art 788.

Release for export is to be granted on condition that the goods in question leave the customs territory of the Community in the same condition as when the export declaration was accepted.[308] Where goods released for export do not leave the Community, the exporter must immediately inform the customs office of export.[309]

The possibility of using an ATA Carnet to facilitate temporary exportation is dealt with in Implementing Regulation, Articles 797 and 798.

It should be borne in mind that the CCC contains relief from import duty in respect of goods which have been exported and are then returned. It is possible to obtain documentation which will facilitate the application of the relief at the time of exportation. This is considered briefly in Chapter 12.

J. CUSTOMS-APPROVED TREATMENTS AND USES WHICH ARE NOT CUSTOMS PROCEDURES

CCC, Title IV, Chapter 3 (Articles 166–182) contains provisions on types of customs-approved treatment or use which do not fall within the category of customs procedures. These are the use of free zones and warehouses, re-exportation, destruction, and abandonment. The relevant provisions in the Implementing Regulation are contained in Part II, Title V, chapters 1 and 2 (Articles 799–842). We deal with each of these treatments or uses in turn.

1. *Free zones and warehouses*

By a Council Decision of 6 June 197,[310] the Community adopted Annex F1 to the Kyoto Convention which concerned free zones. The Revised Kyoto Convention deals with free zones in Specific Annex D, Chapter 2. The Annexes deal, amongst other things, with the establishment and control of such zones and warehouses, the admission of goods to them, what may be done with goods in them, for how long they may stay there, their removal, the charge to duty, and the closure of them.

As the preamble to Council Regulation (EEC) 2504/88[311] noted, free zones and free warehouses are parts of, or premises within, the Community customs territory, but separated from it, and in which there is generally a concentration of activities related to external trade. As a result of the customs facilities available in them:

these free zones and free warehouses ensure the promotion of the aforesaid activi-

---

[308] CCC, Art 162.
[309] Implementing Regulation, Art 796.1.
[310] Council Decision (EEC) 528/78 of 6 June 1978 [1978] OJ L160/13.
[311] Of 25 July 1988 [1988] OJ L225/8, first recital.

ties and, in particular, that goods are redistributed within the Community and elsewhere . . . therefore, the provision concerning them forms an essential instrument of the Community's commercial policy.

Although free zones and warehouses are either parts of the customs territory or premises situated within it, for the purposes of import duties and commercial policy measures, Community goods within them are treated as not being in the Community customs territory provided certain conditions are satisfied.[312] These are that they are not released for free circulation, or placed under another customs procedure, or used or consumed under conditions other than those provided for in customs regulations.[313] By virtue of being placed in a free zone or warehouse, Community goods may qualify for measures normally attaching to the export of goods.[314] Goods which present a danger or are likely to spoil other goods, or which for other reasons require special facilities, may be required to be placed in premises specially equipped to receive them.[315]

Customs authorities are obliged to certify the Community or non-Community status of goods placed in a free zone or warehouse at the request of the person concerned.[316] The certificate may be used as proof of the status of goods where they are brought into or returned to another part of the customs territory, or placed under a customs procedure. It is, though, possible to prove the status of goods by other means. Where the status of goods is not proved, they are considered to be Community goods for the purposes of applying export duties and in relation to export licences and export measures laid down under the commercial policy. In all other cases they are to be treated as non-Community goods.[317]

1.1 *The designation of free zones and warehouses*

Member States must designate the zones or warehouses[318] and define both

---

[312] The definition of 'free zone' in Specific Annex D, Chapter 2, of the revised Kyoto Convention, states that it is: 'a part of the territory of a Contracting Party where any goods introduced are generally regarded, insofar as import duties and taxes are concerned, as being outside the Customs territory'.

[313] CCC, Art 166(a).

[314] Ibid, Art 166(b).

[315] Ibid, Art 169.

[316] Ibid, Art 170.4.

[317] Ibid, Art 180. Commercial policy measures provided for in Community acts are to be applicable to non-Community goods placed in a free zone or free warehouse only to the extent that they refer to the entry of goods into the customs territory of the Community: Implementing Regulation, Art 808.

[318] CCC, Art 167.1. The addresses, fax, and telephone numbers of free zones within the Community (not the Community customs territory) notified to the Commission are set out in a Commission communication at [1999] OJ C345/3. They are located in Copenhagen, Bremen, Bremerhaven, Cuxhaven, Deggendorf, Duisberg, Emden, Hamburg, and Kiel. Member States are to

entry and exit points for free zones and warehouses.[319] Generally speaking, the perimeters of free zones and warehouses and their entry and exit points are subject to supervision by customs authorities and checks may be imposed on those leaving and entering them.[320] It was previously the case that all free zones had to be enclosed; now, however, it is possible for customs authorities to designate free zones in which customs checks and formalities are to be carried out and applied in accordance with the customs warehousing procedure.[321] The usual rules for free zones do not apply to such designated zones and the perimeters, and entry and exit points, of such designated free zones do not have to be subject to customs supervision.[322] These latter type of free zones are referred to in the Implementing Regulation and below as 'control type II'.[323] The other free-zones are referred to as 'control type I'.

Any person may apply to the relevant customs authorities for a part of the customs territory of the Community to be designated a free zone or for a free warehouse to be set up.[324] An application for an authorization to build in a free zone, or to convert a building in a free zone, or to convert a free warehouse is to be made in writing. It must specify the activity for which the building will be used and other information which will enable evaluation of the grounds of the application. An authorization is to be granted where the application of the customs rules would not be impeded.[325]

1.2 *Entry to a zone or warehouse*

Entry to a zone or warehouse may be refused to those who do not provide the guarantees necessary for compliance with the CCC.[326] The goods entering, leaving, or remaining in, the zone or warehouse may be checked and a copy of the transport document accompanying goods is to be handed to, or kept at the disposal of, the customs authorities.[327] Generally speaking, goods entering a free zone or warehouse do not need to be presented to customs authorities, nor does a customs

---

communicate to the Commission the free zones in existence and in operation in the Community for publication in the *Official Journal*: Implementing Regulation, Art 802. The same communication obligation exists in relation to the customs authorities designated by the Member State to receive application for approval of stock records pursuant to ibid, Art 804.

[319] CCC, Art 167.3.

[320] CCC, Art 168.1 and 2. See also Implementing Regulation, Art 805 which makes further provision for controls in relation to free zones of control-type I (defined at p 295) and free warehouses.

[321] See CCC, Art 168a inserted by Regulation (EC) 2700/2000, n 237 above.

[322] Art 168a. 1 and 2 provide that CCC, Arts 170, 176, and 180 do not apply to free zones so designated and that references to free zones in CCC, Arts 37, 38 and 205 do not apply to designated free zones.

[323] The Implementing Regulation, Art 813 provides that without prejudice to the provisions of Arts 799–804, and 814, the provisions laid down for the customs warehouse arrangements are to be applicable to the free zone of control type II.

[324] Ibid, Art 800.   [325] Ibid, Art 801.
[326] CCC, Art 168.3.   [327] Ibid, Art 168.4.

declaration need to be lodged in respect of them.[328] Goods are required, however, to be presented to the customs authorities and to undergo the prescribed customs formalities in three situations.[329] These are, first, where they have been placed under a customs procedure which is discharged when they enter a free zone or warehouse.[330] Secondly, where the goods have been placed in the zone or warehouse on the authority of a decision to grant repayment or remission of import duties and, thirdly, where the goods qualify for measures normally attaching to the export of goods. Furthermore, goods which are subject to export duties, or to other export provisions, may need to be notified to the customs authorities.[331]

1.3 Use of goods and activity within free zones and warehouses

Except in respect of goods in free zones or warehouses which qualify for measures normally attaching to the export of goods and which are covered by the common agricultural policy, goods may remain in free zones or warehouses for an unlimited time.[332] Any industrial, commercial, or service activity, subject to the conditions laid down in the CCC, is permitted in a free zone or warehouse.[333] The activities must be notified in advance to the customs authorities,[334] who may impose certain restrictions or prohibitions on them, having regard to the nature of the goods concerned or the requirements of customs supervision. Those who do not provide the necessary guarantees of compliance with the provisions of the CCC may be prohibited from carrying on an activity in a free zone or warehouse.[335]

According to CCC, Article 173, non-Community goods in a free zone or warehouse may be released for free circulation subject to the relevant conditions,[336] may undergo the usual forms of handling permitted under CCC, Article 109,[337] may be placed under the inward processing

---

[328] Ibid, Art 170.1.   [329] Ibid, Art 170.2 (a) to (c).

[330] But presentation is not required where the procedure in question permits exemption from it.

[331] CCC, Art 170.3.   [332] Ibid, Art 171.

[333] A victualling warehouse may be set up in a free zone or free warehouse in accordance with Art 40 of Commission Regulation (EC) 800/99, [1999] OJ L102/88, which lays down detailed rules for the application of the system of export refunds on agricultural products: Implementing Regulation, Art 810.

[334] The notification is considered to be effected by the necessary application for approval of stock records: Implementing Regulation, Art 804.2.

[335] CCC, Art 172. Community goods covered by the common agricultural policy which qualify for measures normally attaching to the export of goods within CCC, Art 166(b), are to undergo, without prior authorization, only the forms of handling expressly prescribed for such goods in conformity with CCC, Art 109.2: CCC, Art 174.

[336] The Community status of the goods is to be certified, using a form conforming to the model in Implementing Regulation, Annex 109, where non-Community goods are declared for release for free circulation under this provision, including where the inward processing or processing under customs control procedures are being discharged: Implementing Regulation, Art 812 second sub-para.

[337] The usual forms of handling are referred to in CCC, Art 109.2 and are set out in the Implementing Regulation: see Art 531 and Annex 72. There are specific provisions in relation to certain goods covered by the Common Agricultural Policy: CCC, Art 174.

procedure,[338] the procedure for processing under customs control, the temporary importation procedure, be abandoned pursuant to CCC, Article 182 or be destroyed (provided in the latter case that the person concerned supplies the customs authorities with all the information they judge necessary). The placing of the goods under the respective procedures is subject to the usual conditions applicable in respect of each procedure. The control arrangements in respect of inward processing, processing under customs control, and temporary importation may, however, be adapted in so far as it is necessary to take account of the conditions relating to the operation and supervision of free zones and warehouses.

Where CCC, Article 173 is inapplicable, non-Community goods and certain Community goods[339] are not to be consumed or used in free zones or warehouses. Where the relevant procedure provides, though, this limitation shall not preclude the use or consumption of goods, where their release for free circulation, or temporary importation, would not entail the application of import duties or measures under the common agricultural policy or the common commercial policy. No declaration for release for free circulation or temporary importation is necessary in these circumstances unless the goods are to be charged against a quota or ceiling.[340]

Everyone carrying on an activity involving the storage, working, processing, sale, or purchase of goods in a free zone or warehouse, must keep stock records in a form approved by the customs authorities and which enables the goods to be identified and their movements recorded. Goods must be entered in the stock records as soon as they are brought into the premises of such a person.[341] The carrying on of activities by any person involving the storage, working, processing, sale or purchase of goods in a free zone or warehouse is subject to the written approval by the authorities of stock records.[342] Approval is to be accorded only to persons offering all the necessary guarantees concerning the application of the provisions on free zones or warehouses.[343] Documents relating to the transhipment of goods within a free zone are to be kept at the disposal of the customs authorities.[344]

---

[338] CCC, Art 173 provides that processing operations within the old free port of Hamburg, in the free zones of the Canary Islands, the Azores, and Madeira, and in the overseas departments are not to be subject to economic conditions. In relation to the old free port of Hamburg, however, the Council may, by qualified majority on a proposal from the Commission, decide that economic conditions shall apply, if conditions of competition in a specific economic sector in the Community are affected as a result of the derogation. Specific provisions relating to inward processing and processing under customs control in a free zone or warehouse are contained in Implementing Regulation, Art 807.

[339] That is, those within CCC, Art 166(b) referred to above.   [340] CCC, Art 175.

[341] Ibid, Art 176.1. The particular requirements for stock records kept in relation to a free zone of control types I and II and to free warehouses are contained in the Implementing Regulation, Art 806.

[342] Implementing Regulation, Arts 803.1 and 799.

[343] Ibid, Art 803.2. The requirements governing applications for approval are set out in ibid, Art 804.   [344] CCC, Art 176.2.

1.4 *Removal of goods from free zones or warehouses*

Goods which leave a free zone or warehouse may be exported or re-exported from the Community customs territory or taken into another part of it. The customs authorities must satisfy themselves that the rules governing exportation or re-exportation are respected.[345] Where non-Community goods are brought into another part of the customs territory CCC, Articles 37–54,[346] which govern such matters as the entry of goods into the customs territory, their presentation, and temporary storage, are to apply. Community goods are also subject to them, except for Articles 48–53, which govern assignment of the goods to a customs-approved treatment or use and temporary storage.[347] Specific rules govern Community goods covered by the Community agricultural policy which qualify for measures normally attaching to the export of goods by virtue of being placed in a free zone or warehouse.[348]

1.5 *Valuation*

There are specific provisions relating to customs valuation and free zones and warehouses. If the costs of warehousing or preserving goods whilst they are in the free zone or warehouse are shown separately, they are not included in the price actually paid or payable.[349] Where the goods have undergone one of the usual forms of handling, as defined above, in the free zone or warehouse, their nature, customs value, and the quantity of them to be taken into consideration in determining the amount of import duties, are to be those which would have been taken into account at the time the customs debt was incurred, had they not undergone handling. The declarant must, however, request this treatment and the handling in question must have been authorized.[350]

2. *Re-exportation, destruction, and abandonment*

Non-Community goods may be re-exported from the customs territory of the Community, destroyed, or abandoned to the exchequer, where national legislation makes provision to that effect and in accordance with national

---

[345] CCC, Art 181. Where non-Community goods which are not unloaded or which are only transhipped are placed under the free zone using the local clearance procedure, the customs authorities may lift the obligation to inform the customs authorities of each arrival or departure of such goods. Short-term storage of goods in connection with the transhipment is considered to be an integral part of the transhipment: Implementing Regulation, Art 814.

[346] See Ch 9.

[347] CCC, Art 177. [348] Ibid, Art 179.

[349] Ibid, Art 178.1. See Ch 8.

[350] Pursuant to CCC, Art 109.3. Where the elements for assessment of the customs debt to be taken into consideration are those applicable before the goods have undergone usual forms of handling, Information Sheet INF8 may be issued in accordance with Implementing Regulation, Art 523: ibid, Art 809.

provisions.[351] Re-exportation is, where appropriate, subject to the formalities for goods leaving the Community, including commercial policy measures.[352] These may prohibit exportation of the goods.[353] Where the goods which are intended for re-exportation are placed under an economic customs procedure when on the Community customs territory, a customs declaration is to be lodged.[354] Prior to re-exportation or destruction of goods the customs authorities must be notified.[355]

Destruction and abandonment must not entail any expense for the Exchequer.[356] So far as destruction is concerned, any waste or scrap resulting from it is to be assigned a customs-approved treatment or use prescribed for non-Community goods. It is to remain under customs supervision for as long as is necessary to determine its customs status and, until its customs status is changed, it enters a free zone or free warehouse, is exported, or is itself destroyed.[357]

Non-Community goods which have been abandoned to the Exchequer, or seized or confiscated, are to be regarded as having been entered for the customs warehousing procedure. They may be sold, according to the procedures in force in the Member States, by the customs authorities only on the condition that the buyer immediately carries out the formalities to assign them to a customs-approved treatment or use. If the sale is inclusive of import duties, it is to be considered as equivalent to release for free circulation, and the customs authorities must calculate the duties and enter them in the accounts. Where the goods in question are not sold by the customs authorities, but are dealt with in another way, the customs authority must immediately carry out the formalities to assign them to a customs procedure, as defined in CCC, Article 4(16), to place them in a free zone or free warehouse, to re-export them from the Community customs territory, or to destroy them.[358]

---

[351] CCC, Art 182.1 and 3.   [352] Ibid, Art 182.2.
[353] Ibid, Art 182.3.
[354] Ibid, Art 182.3.
[355] Ibid, Art 182.3, but this is not the case in relation to re-exporation of non-Community goods which are not unloaded or which are trans-shipped: Implementing Regulation, Art 811.
[356] CCC, Art 182.4.
[357] Ibid, Art 182.5. See also Implementing Regulation, Art 842.
[358] Implementing Regulation, Art 867a.1–3.

11

Inward and Outward Processing

Inward and outward processing are customs procedures of considerable economic importance to the Community, as can be seen from the fact that the Annexes to the Kyoto Convention which deal with them (E6 and E8 respectively) were amongst some of the earliest accepted by it in 1977.[1] The Community legislation on the procedures is extensive, but has been considerably simplified by Commission Regulation (EC) 993/2001.[2] Inward processing is dealt with in CCC, Articles 114–129 and Implementing Regulation, Articles 536–550. Outward processing is dealt with in CCC, Articles 145–160 and Implementing Regulation Articles 585–592. Inevitably, the consideration of the Community legislation in this chapter is not comprehensive, but is intended to establish the general framework under which these customs procedures operate. Section A deals with the inward processing procedure and section B covers the outward processing procedure. Regard should also be paid to section C of Chapter 10 which deals with general rules governing customs procedures with economic impact. Of particular importance are the rules relating to authorizations for entry into the procedures.

A. THE INWARD PROCESSING PROCEDURE

1. *What it is and why it is necessary*

According to the revised Kyoto Convention, inward processing is:

> the Customs procedure under which certain goods can be brought into a Customs territory conditionally relieved from payment of import duties and taxes, on the basis that such goods are intended for manufacturing, processing or repair and subsequent exportation.[3]

The Introduction to Annex E6 to the original Convention, gives the main economic purpose of inward processing as being 'to make it possible for

---

[1] See Council Decision (EEC) 415/77 of 3 June 1977 [1977] OJ L166/1.

[2] [2001] OJ L141/1. The amendments are effective from 1 July 2001: see Art 2.2. In particular, the provisions governing authorizations, the 'economic conditions', the rate of yield, and the necessary calculations have been simplified and the number of Annexes reduced. Attention should also be paid to the Commission's Guidelines on customs procedures with economic impact [2001] OJ C269/1 which contain a considerable amount of material on inward and outward processing, and give useful worked examples of the application of the rules.

[3] See the Revised Kyoto Convention, Specific Annex F, 'Processing' Chapter 1, Inward Processing, Definitions. The definition in Annex E6 to the original Kyoto Convention is similar, but refers to the goods being re-exported within a specified period.

national enterprises to offer their products or services on foreign markets at competitive prices and thereby to help to provide more employment opportunities for national labour'. The procedure is a necessary accommodation by customs territories to the reality of international product and labour markets. Nevertheless, it is not intended to distort the internal economy of a customs territory. Accordingly, Annex E6 to the original Kyoto Convention provides that the relief may be made subject to the condition that the proposed operations are to be beneficial to the national economy and are not to conflict with the interests of national producers of goods identical, or similar, to those in respect of which admission is requested.[4] (In Community customs duty law these conditions are known as the 'economic conditions'.[5]) The Convention also makes clear that, although the relief generally involves total conditional relief from duty, import duties and taxes may be charged on the waste deriving from the processing or manufacturing of the goods.[6]

2. *Inward Processing: a Community procedure*

Once the Community's customs union had come into existence, there was clearly no room for the inward processing regimes of Member States to be applied in respect of goods coming from within the Community customs territory.[7] A Community-wide inward processing system did not, however, come into effect until 1 October 1969, a little while after the customs union had come into existence.[8] As has been noted above, its objective is to ensure that Community exporters are not put at a disadvantage, as against their foreign competitors, and are enabled to acquire raw materials under the same conditions as are applicable to those competitors. In the words of the Court of Justice:

> the inward processing relief arrangements were established so as not to put at a disadvantage internationally Community undertakings which use goods from non-member countries in order to manufacture products for export by giving them the possibility of acquiring such goods under the same conditions as undertakings from non-member countries.
>
> . . . Thus, that system allows goods imported from non-member countries to escape customs duties if they undergo certain working or processing operations in the

---

[4] See Standard 2 and the Introduction, 4th para. The Kyoto Convention in its original and revised forms contains extensive provisions in relation to inward and outward processing. It is not proposed to review them in this chapter.

[5] See in particular CCC, Art 117(c), Implementing Regulation, Art 539, and Commission Regulation (EC) 1448/2001 of 19 July 2001 [2001] OJ L96/9.

[6] See Standard 3. See Standard 2 of the revised Convention.

[7] Case 260/78 *Maggi GmbH v Hauptzollamt Münster* [1979] ECR 2693 at para 5.

[8] See Council Directive (EEC) 73/69 of 4 Mar 1969 [1969] OJ L58/1. This Directive permitted considerable diversity in the practices of Member States. A Regulation introducing a harmonized inward processing system was subsequently brought into force: see Council Regulation (EEC) 1999/85 of 16 July 1985 [1985] OJ L188/1.

Community and are then re-exported as compensating products outside the Community.[9]

The Court has also said that:

> such arrangements are aimed at promoting exports from Community undertakings, under the international division of labour, by enabling them to import goods from non-member countries without paying import duties where they are to be exported from the Community after processing, but without adversely affecting the essential interests of Community producers.[10]

3. The suspension system and the drawback system

CCC, Article 114 provides that the Community's inward processing procedure operates in two basic ways. First, it ensures that import duties and commercial policy measures do not apply when non-Community goods, which are intended for re-export from the Community customs territory in the form of 'compensating products', are used in the customs territory of the Community in one or more processing operations.[11] 'Compensating products' are all products resulting from processing operations.[12] In this context, the relief generally operates by way of the 'suspension' system.[13] Secondly, it ensures that import duties and commercial policy measures do not apply when goods released for free circulation, with repayment or remission of the import duties chargeable on them, are exported from the Community customs territory in the form of compensating products.[14] In this context, the procedure generally operates by way of the 'drawback' system.[15] The holder of the authorization may ask for import duty to be repaid or remitted where he can establish to the satisfaction of the customs authorities one of a number of alternative situations. These are: that import

---

[9] Case C–437/93 *Hauptzollamt Heilbronn v Temic Telefunken Microelectronic GmbH* [1995] ECR I–1687 paras 18–19; applied in Case C–187/99 *Fazenda Pública v Fábrica de Queijo Eru Portuguesa Ldª* [2001] ECR I-1429.

[10] See also Case 325/96 *Fábrica de Queijo Eru Portuguesa Ldª v Subdirector-Geral das Alfândegas, and Ministério Público* [1997] ECR I– 7249 at para 3.

[11] CCC Art 114.1(a). Commercial policy measures are applicable on entry into inward processing only to the extent that they refer to the entry of goods into the customs territory of the Community. Where compensating products, other than those mentioned in Annex 75 to the Implementing Regulation, are released for free circulation, the commercial policy measures applicable to the release for free circulation of the import goods are to be applied: Implementing Regulation, Art 509.1 and 2.

[12] CCC, Art 114(d). They are subdivided into 'main compensating products' which are the products for which the arrangements were authorized and 'secondary compensating products' which are necessary by-products of the processing operation other than the main compensating products specified in the authorization: see Implementing Regulation, Art 496(i) and (l).

[13] CCC, Art 114.2(a). Note too that the suspension procedure applies so that compensating products may qualify for exemption from the export duties to which identical products, obtained from Community goods instead of import goods, would be liable: CCC, Art 129. 'Import goods' is defined in CCC, Art 84.2, see n 16 below.

[14] Ibid, Art 114.1(b).

[15] Ibid, Art 114.2(b).

goods,[16] released for free circulation under the drawback system in the form of compensating products, or goods in their unaltered state[17] have been exported,[18] or placed under one of the following procedures, namely, transit, customs warehousing, temporary importation, inward processing (suspensive arrangement), or placed in a free zone or free warehouse. The conditions for use of the procedure must also have been fulfilled.[19] The period within which a repayment claim is to be lodged is six months from the date on which the compensating products were assigned one of the customs-approved treatments or uses referred to above.[20] For the purpose of placing goods under these procedures, compensating products or goods in the unaltered state are to be considered non-Community goods.[21]

CCC, Article 124[22] provides that the drawback system may be used for all goods, but is not usable where, at the time the declaration of release for free circulation is accepted, certain conditions exist. These are, first, that the import goods[23] are subject to quantitive import restrictions; secondly, that a tariff measure within quotas is applied to the import goods; thirdly, that the import goods are subject to presentation of an import or export licence, or certificate, in the framework of the Common Agricultural Policy; or, fourthly, that an export refund or tax has been set for the compensating products. Furthermore, no reimbursement of import duties under the drawback system is possible if the third or fourth condition is fulfilled at the time the export declaration for the compensating products is accepted.[24]

The declaration of release for free circulation must indicate that the drawback system is being used and must provide particulars of the relevant authorization. If the customs authorities so request, the authorization is to be attached to the declaration of release for free circulation.[25]

---

[16] Import goods means 'goods placed under a suspensive procedure and goods which, under the inward processing procedure, in the form of the drawback system, have undergone the formalities for release for free circulation and the formalities provided for in Art 125 CCC'.: CCC, Art 84.2.

[17] Goods in the unaltered state means import goods which, under the inward processing procedure or the procedures for processing under customs control, have undergone no form of processing: see CCC, Art 84.3.

[18] Temporary exportation of compensating products carried out under CCC, Article 123.1, is not exportation, except where the products are not re-imported into the Community within the period prescribed: CCC, Art 127.

[19] Ibid, Art 128.1.   [20] Ibid, Art 128.3.

[21] Ibid, Art 128.2.

[22] Replaced by Regulation (EC) 2700/2000, of the European Parliament and the Council of 16 Nov 2000 [2000] OJ L311/17, Art 1.6.

[23] Defined in CCC, Art 84.2, as noted at n 16 above.

[24] CCC, Art 124.1 and 2 as varied by Regulation (EC) 2700/2000, in n 22 above, Art 1.6. CCC, Art 124.3 provides that derogations from ibid, Art 124.1 and 10, may be laid down in accordance with the committee procedure.

[25] Ibid, Art 125.

4. The equivalent compensation and prior exportation systems

4.1 *The equivalent compensation system*

As well as obtaining compensating products from the goods introduced into the customs territory, it is also possible to obtain them from equivalent goods.[26] This is effected pursuant to the equivalent compensation system, which is a derogation from the main inward processing regime.[27] Equivalent goods are Community goods which are used to obtain compensating products instead of the import goods.[28] To avoid abuse of the system, the equivalent goods must fall within the same eight-digit sub-heading of the CN, be of the same quality, including commercial quality, and have the same characteristics, including technical characteristics, as the import goods.[29] In some cases the equivalent goods may be permitted to be at a more advanced stage of manufacture than the import goods.[30] This is so, however, only where the essential part of the processing to which such equivalent goods are subject is carried out in the undertaking of the holder of the authorization, or in the undertaking where the operation is being carried out on his behalf, save in exceptional cases.[31] The authorization must specify whether and under which conditions equivalent goods may be used for the processing operation.[32] Where compensating products are obtained from equivalent goods, the equivalent goods are to be regarded as import goods and the import goods are to be regarded as equivalent goods.[33] The use of equivalent goods is not subject to the formalities for entry of goods for the arrangements.[34] The equivalent goods and compensating products made from them become non-Community goods and the import goods become Community goods at the time the declaration discharging the arrangements is accepted. Where import goods are put on the market before the arrangements are discharged, they change their status at the time they are put on the market. In exceptional cases and at the request of the holder, where the equivalent goods are expected not to be present at that

---

[26] Art 115.1(a). Art 1.4 of Regulation (EC) 2700/2000, see n 22 above, provides that measures aimed at prohibiting, imposing certain requirements for, or facilitating recourse to Art 115.1, may be adopted in conformity with the committee procedure, ie in practice by amendment to the Implementing Regulation. See Implementing Regulation, Art 545 referred to below.

[27] Case C–103/96 *Directeur général des douanes et droits indirects v Eridania Beghin-Say SA* [1997] ECR I–1453 at para 24.

[28] CCC, Art 114.2(e). There are special provisions concerning equivalent goods in relation to rice, wheat, sugar, live animals and meat, maize, olive oil, and milk and milk products: Implementing Regulation, Art 541.3 and Annex 74.

[29] CCC, Art 115.2. In using the equivalent compensation system, the trader takes a risk that tariff classifications may change and render the system inapplicable: see Case C–103/96 *Directeur Général des Douanes et Droits Indirects v Eridania Beghin-Say SA*, n 27 above, at paras 34–40.

[30] CCC, Art 115.2.

[31] Implementing Regulation, Art 541.2.   [32] Ibid, Art 541.1.

[33] See Arts 115.3 and 126 which provide that Art 115.3 does not apply in relation to the drawback system *supra*.

[34] Implementing Regulation, Art 545.1.

time, the customs authorities may allow them to be present at a later, reason-able, time to be determined by them.[35] Compensating products or goods in the unaltered state become Community goods when put on the market.[36]

4.2 *The prior exportation system*

The prior exportation system is the system whereby compensating products obtained from equivalent goods are to be exported before the import goods are entered for the arrangements using the suspension system,[37] ie before impor-tation of the import goods.[38] It is unavailable in conjunction with the draw-back system.[39] Security must be provided where the prior exportation system is used and the compensating products would be liable to export duties if they were not being exported, or re-exported, under an inward processing opera-tion. The security is to ensure payment of the export duties should the import goods not be imported within the time prescribed.[40] Compensating products become non-Community goods on acceptance of the export declaration on condition that the goods to be imported are entered for the arrangements. Import goods become Community goods at the time of their entry for the arrangement.[41]

5. *Triangular traffic system*

The triangular traffic system is a system under which the office of discharge of the procedure is not the same as the office of entry to it. The specific limitations on the user of the system, which used to exist, have been repealed.[42]

6. *Permitted processing operations*

According to CCC, Article 114.2(c), the processing operations to which the goods introduced into the Community customs territory may be subjected, consist of the following:

- working the goods, including erecting or assembling them, or fitting them to other goods;
- processing the goods;
- repairing the goods, including restoring them and putting them in order.

---

[35] Implementing Regulation, Art 545.2.
[36] Ibid, Art 546, third sub-para.
[37] Ibid, Art 536(a).   [38] CCC, Art 115.1(b).
[39] Ibid, Art 126.   [40] Ibid, Art 115.5 and Art 126.
[41] Implementing Regulation, Art 545.3.
[42] See Commission Regulation (EC) 993/2001, at n 2 above, Art 1.26 and the former Art 600 of the Implementing Regulation, which confined the triangular traffic system to the prior expor-tation system.

Subject to certain limited exceptions, it is also possible to use goods which are not found in the compensating products, but which allow or facilitate the production of them, even if they are entirely or partially used up in the process.[43]

7. *Authorization*[44]

7.1 *The form of the application*

Authorization to carry out inward processing is to be issued at the request of the person who carries out the processing operations or who arranges for them to be carried out.[45] The application, which may be for a single authorization (ie one involving different customs administrations[46]) is to be made in accordance with the rules governing applications for authorizations for customs procedures with economic impact dealt with in Chapter 10.[47] An authorization for inward processing can be granted only where the applicant has the intention of re-exporting or exporting the main compensating products.[48]

7.2 *Conditions for authorization*

There are three essential requirements to be met if authorization is to be granted. First, the authorization must be granted to persons established in the Community. It may be granted to persons established outside the Community only in respect of imports of a non-commercial nature.[49] These are goods which are entered for the inward processing procedure on an occasional basis, the nature and quantity of which indicate that they are intended for the private, personal, or family use of the consignees or persons carrying them, or which are clearly intended as gifts.[50] Secondly, authorization is to be granted only where, without prejudice to the carrying out of the processing operations permitted under the inward processing procedure, the import goods can be identified in the compensating products. Where compensating products are obtained from equivalent goods it is to be granted only where it is possible to verify compliance with the conditions laid down in respect of equivalent goods.[51] Thirdly, authorization is to be granted only where the inward processing procedure can help create the

---

[43] See CCC, Art 114.2(c). The goods outside the scope of this rule are fuels, energy sources other than those needed for the testing of compensating products or for the detection of faults in import goods needing repair; lubricants, other than those needed for the testing, adjustment or withdrawal of compensating products, equipment and tools: Implementing Regulation Art 538.

[44] See generally, Ch 10, section C, where the rules governing authorization of customs procedures with economic impact, including inward processing, are referred to.

[45] CCC, Art 116.

[46] See Implementing Regulation, Art 496(c) for the full definition.

[47] See p 297 onwards.   [48] Implementing Regulation, Art 537.

[49] CCC, Art 117(a).   [50] See Implementing Regulation, Art 1.6.

[51] CCC, Art 117(b).

most favourable conditions for the export or re-export of compensating products, provided that the essential interests of the Community producers are not
adversely affected. The conditions to be satisfied in this regard are known as
the economic conditions.[52]

7.3 *Economic conditions*

The Implementing Regulation used to contain an extensive list of situations in
which the economic conditions were considered to be satisfied with a code for
each one. The applicant had to state which situations he relied upon. Now,
Article 539 of the Implementing Regulation provides that the economic
conditions are to be deemed to be fulfilled except where the application
concerns import goods mentioned in Annex 73, which covers mostly agricultural products. Even if the application concerns such import goods the
economic conditions will still be deemed to be fulfilled provided that certain
conditions are met.[53] The application must concern:

- operations involving goods of a non-commercial nature;[54]
- operations carried out under a job-processing contract:[55] 'job processing'
  means any processing of import goods directly or indirectly placed at the
  disposal of the holder which is carried out according to the specifications
  on behalf of a principal established in a third country, generally against
  payment of processing costs alone;[56]
- the processing of compensating products already obtained by processing
  under a previous authorization the granting of which was subject to an
  examination of the economic conditions;[57]
- usual forms of handling as set out in Annex 72 of the Implementing
  Regulation;[58]
- repair[58a]
- the processing of durum wheat within CN code 1001 10 00 to produce
  pasta within specified CN codes.[59]

The economic conditions will also be deemed to be fulfilled in two other situations: first, where the aggregate value of the import goods per applicant and

---

[52] CCC, Art 117(c). In the UK, the economic conditions are applied either by the Department of
Trade and Industry or by the Department of the Environment, Farming, and Rural Affairs.

[53] Implementing Regulation, Art 539, para 2.

[54] Implementing Regulation, Art 539(a)(i). Goods of a non-commercial nature are those in
respect of which entry for the customs procedure is on an occasional basis and whose nature and
quantity indicate that they are intended for the private, personal or family use of the consignees
or persons carrying them, or which are clearly intended as gifts: see ibid, Art 16.

[55] Ibid, Art 539(a)(ii).   [56] Ibid, Art 536(b).

[57] Ibid, Art 539(a)(iii).   [58] Ibid, Art 539(a)(iv).

[58a] Ibid, Art 539(a)(v).

[59] Ibid, Art 539(a)(vi).

per calendar year for each eight-digit CN code does not exceed 150,000 euro,[60] secondly, where in accordance with Article 11 of Council Regulation (EC) 3448/93,[61] import goods referred to under Part A of Annex 73 are concerned, and the applicant presents a document issued by a competent authority permitting entry of those goods for the arrangements, within the limits of a quantity determined on the basis of a supply balance.[62]

Where the economic conditions are not deemed to be fulfilled, they must be examined by the customs authorities. The examination must establish the economic unviability of using Community sources.[63] It must take account, in particular, of the following matters:

- the unavailability of Community-produced goods sharing the same quality and technical characteristics as the goods intended to be imported for the processing operations envisaged;[64]
- differences in price between Community-produced goods and those intended to be imported;[65]
- contractual obligations.[66]

The details of these matters are laid down in Annex 70 in the Implementing Regulation. As noted in Chapter 10, the examination of the economic conditions may involve the Commission.[67]

7.4 *Content of authorization*

An authorization must specify the means and methods of identifying the import goods in the compensating products and lay down the conditions for the proper conduct of operations using equivalent goods. These methods and conditions may include examination of records.[68] There are other matters which the authorization must specify. It must state whether compensating products or goods in the unaltered state may be released for free circulation without customs declaration, without prejudice to prohibitive or restrictive measures. In this case they shall be considered to have been released for free circulation if they have not been assigned a customs-approved treatment or use on expiry of the period for discharge.[69] It must state the rate of yield,[70] and

---

[60] Ibid, Art 539(b).

[61] The regulation concerns the trade arrangements applicable to certain goods resulting from the processing of agricultural products. (See also Commission Regulation (EC) 1488/2001 [2001] OJ L196/9, particularly Art 1.2. The regulation lays down rules for the application of Council Regulation (EC) 3448/93 [1993] OJ L318/18, Art 11 of which permits certain basic products to be placed under inward processing arrangements without prior examination of the economic conditions.)

[62] Ibid, Art 539(c).

[63] Ibid, Art 502.2.

[64] Ibid, Art 502.2(a).

[65] Ibid, Art 502.2(b).

[66] Ibid, Art 502.2(c).

[67] See p 301.

[68] Ibid, Art 540.

[69] Ibid, Art 546, second sub-para.

[70] Ibid, Art 517.1.

period for discharge, although this period may be extended even after the expiry of the period originally set.[71] The period for discharge is defined as the time by which the goods or products must have been assigned a new permitted customs-approved treatment or use[72] and is referred to further in the next section.

8. The rates of duration and yield of the procedure

The customs authorities must set requirements as to both the duration and the yield of the inward processing procedure and these two elements are considered in turn below.

8.1 *The duration of the procedure and the period for discharge*

The customs authorities are to specify the period within which compensating products are to be exported, or re-exported, or assigned another customs-approved treatment or use. In setting that period they must take account of the time required to carry out the processing operations and dispose of the compensating products. The period runs from the date on which non-Community goods are placed under the inward processing procedure. It may be extended on receipt of a duly substantiated request from the holder of the authorization.[73] It may be decided that a period which commences in the course of a calendar month or quarter is to expire on the last day of a subsequent calendar month or quarter during which it would expire.[74] This is known as monthly or quarterly aggregation.

Where the prior exportation system is used, the authorization must specify the period within which the non-Community goods are to be declared for the inward processing procedure. In setting the period, the customs authorities must take account of the time required for the procurement and transport to the Community of the import goods.[75] The period is not to exceed six months, except in relation to goods which are subject to a common market organization in respect of which the period is three months. The six-month period may be extended where the holder of the authorization submits a reasoned request, but an extension must not take the total period beyond twelve months. An extension may be allowed even after the original period has expired where circumstances so warrant.[76]

---

[71] Implementing Regulation, Art 542.

[72] Ibid, Art 496(m). The definition includes the time by which a new customs-approved treatment or use is to be assigned in order to claim repayment of import duties after inward processing under the drawback system.

[73] CCC, Art 118.2 first sub-para.   [74] Ibid, Art 118.2.

[75] CCC, Art 118.3 and Implementing Regulation, Art 543.1. CCC, Art 118.3 does not, of course, apply in relation to the drawback procedure: ibid, Art 126.

[76] Implementing Regulation, Art 543.2.

As noted above, the Implementing Regulation provides that the authorization is to specify the period for discharge which may be extended even after the expiry of the original period, where circumstances so warrant.[77] Where the period for discharge expires on a specific date for all the goods placed under the arrangements in a given period, the authorization may provide for an automatic extension for all goods under the arrangements on that date. The customs authorities may, however, require that the goods be assigned a new permitted customs-approved treatment or use within a specified period.[78] Irrespective of whether or not aggregation is employed or extensions are given, the periods for discharge for certain agricultural and animal products which constitute compensating products, or goods in the unaltered state, are limited, in the first instance, to periods of between two and six months. Where successive processing operations are carried out, or where exceptional circumstances so warrant, the periods may be extended on request, but the total period must not exceed twelve months.[79] These shorter periods are set so as to make more difficult the application of the inward processing procedure to agricultural products in the light of the particular problems facing the market in them.[80]

8.2 *Rates of yield*

The customs authorities must set either the rate of yield of the operation, an average rate, or, where appropriate, the method of determining the rate of yield.[81] The rate of yield is the quantity or percentage of compensating products obtained from the processing of a given quantity of import goods.[82] It must be determined on the basis of the actual circumstances in which the processing operation is, or is to be, carried out.[83] Standard rates of yield are set on the basis of actual data previously ascertained. These may be set where the circumstances warrant it and, in particular, in the case of processing operations customarily carried out under clearly defined technical conditions, involving goods of substantially uniform characteristics, and resulting in the production of compensating products of uniform quality.[84] It should be noted that the customs authorities may unilaterally alter the rate of yield fixed by them at the time when the authorization was issued where, while the arrangements are

---

[77] Ibid, Art 542.1.
[78] Ibid, Art 542.2.
[79] Ibid, Art 542.3.
[80] See Case C–325/96 *Fábrica de Queijo Eru Portuguesa Lda v Subdirector-Geral das Alfândegas, and Ministério Público*, n 10 above, at para 19.
[81] Implementing Regulation, Art 517.
[82] CCC, Art 114.2(f).
[83] Ibid, Art 119.1. So far as possible the rate should be set on the basis of production or technical data or, where these are not available, data relating to operations of the same type: Implementing Regulation, Art 517.1.
[84] CCC, Art 119.2. See the standard rates of yield shown in Annex 69 of the Implementing Regulation and Art 517.3.

being used, the actual rate proves to be higher than the rate fixed in the authorization.[85] It is not possible to rely upon the principle of legitimate expectations to prevent any correction in the rate of yield, even if the customs authorities have at all material times been supervising the procedure.[86]

9. *Movement of goods within the procedure*

Some or all of the compensating products or goods in the unaltered state may, if the relevant customs authority authorizes, be temporarily exported for the purpose of further processing outside the customs territory of the Community. Where this occurs the conditions laid down in accordance with the outward processing provisions are applicable.[87] The temporary exportation of compensating products is not to be considered as exportation for the purposes of seeking repayment or remission of duty, except where the products are not reimported into the Community within the prescribed period.[88]

Products or goods within the suspension system may, of course, need to be moved within the customs territory of the Community. They may be moved under specific transfer procedures set out in the Implementing Regulation.[89] Under these, transfer of goods between different places designated in the same authorization may be undertaken without any customs formalities. Transfer of goods from the office of entry to the facilities, or place of use, of the holder or operator may be carried out under cover of the declaration for entry for the arrangements. Transfer to the office of exit, with a view to re-exportation, may take place under cover of the arrangements. The arrangements are not, in such an event, to be discharged until the goods or products declared for re-exportation have actually left the customs territory of the Community.[90] There are also provisions permitting the transfer of goods between holders of authorizations which, so far as inward processing is concerned, may be effected only where the transferee holder enters the transferred goods or products under an authorization to use the local clearance procedure.[91] Transfers involving goods with increased risks of fraud, as set out in Annex 44C to the Implementing Regulation, are to be covered by a guarantee under conditions equivalent to those provided in the transit procedure.[92] Such goods include certain animals, meat, dairy products, sugar, bananas, alcohol, spirits, and cigarettes.

---

[85] See Case C–187/99 *Fazenda Pública v Fábrica de Queijo Eru Portuguesa Ld*ᵃ, n 9 above, at para 27.

[86] See ibid., paras 35 and 36 and Case C–325/96 *Fábrica de Queijo Eru Portuguesa Ld*ᵃ *v Subdirector-Geral das Alfândegas, and Ministério Público*, n 10 above, para 22.

[87] CCC, Art 123.1.

[88] Ibid, Art 127.

[89] See Arts 511–514.

[90] Implementing Regulation, Art 512.

[91] Ibid, Art 513 and Annex 68.

[92] Ibid, Art 514.

10. *The customs debt*

Generally, where a customs debt is incurred, its amount is to be determined on the basis of the taxation elements appropriate to the import goods at the time of acceptance of the declaration placing them under the inward processing procedure. If at that time they qualified for preferential tariff treatment within tariff quotas or ceilings, then they are to be eligible for preferential treatment applicable to identical goods at the time of acceptance of the declaration of release for free circulation.[93] The cases in which, and the conditions under which, goods in the unaltered state or compensating products are to be considered to have been released for free circulation may be determined pursuant to the committee procedure.[94]

The general rules applicable in relation to a customs debt are, however, varied in relation to compensating products in respect of which there are specific provisions.[95] Where they are released for free circulation and appear on the list of products in Annex 75 to the Implementing Regulation,[96] they are to be subject to import duties appropriate to them, in proportion to the exported part of the compensating products not included in the list.[97] The holder of the authorization may, however, ask for the general rules discussed above and contained in CCC, Article 121 to be applied.[98]

Where compensating goods are placed under a suspensive arrangement, or in a free zone or warehouse, they are to be subject to import duties calculated in accordance with the rules applicable to the customs procedure in question, or to free zones and free warehouses as the case may be.[99] Again, however, the person concerned may request that duty is assessed in accordance with the general rules in Article 121 and, in cases where compensating products have been assigned a customs-approved treatment or use other than processing

---

[93] CCC, Art 121.1 and 2. These provisions are inapplicable under the drawback procedure: ibid, Art 126.

[94] Ibid, Art 120; inapplicable under the drawback procedure: ibid, Art 126.

[95] Ibid, See Art 122. Note too that where a customs debt is incurred in respect of compensating products or import goods, compensatory interest is to be paid on import duty except in specified circumstances: Implementing Regulation, Art 519.

[96] Introduced by ibid, Art 548.1. Annex 75 contains 150 categories of product, ranging from animal and food products to textile and metal products. Where compensating products other than those mentioned on the list are destroyed they are to be treated as if they had been re-exported, Art 548.2.

[97] They are also subject to import duties appropriate to them where the goods are subject to charges established under the Common Agricultural Policy and provisions adopted in accordance with the committee procedure so provide: CCC, Art 122(a), second indent. This provision is inapplicable under the drawback procedure: ibid, Art 126.

[98] CCC, Art 122(a) first indent. This is applicable *mutatis mutandis* in determining the amount of duty to be repaid or remitted under the drawback system: ibid, Art 128.5.

[99] Ibid, Art 122(b). Without prejudice to this provision, where compensating products or goods in the unaltered state which are placed under a customs procedure or in a free zone or free warehouse, pursuant to CCC, Art 128.1, are released for free circulation, the amount of import duties repaid or remitted shall be considered to constitute the customs debt: ibid, Art 128.4.

under customs control, the amount of duty payable is to be no less than that due pursuant to that Article.[100] Where compensating goods could have been placed under the procedure of processing under customs control, they may be made subject to the rules governing assessment of duty in relation to that procedure.[101] So far as reliefs from duty are concerned, compensating goods obtain favourable tariff treatment on account of the special use for which goods are intended, where such relief is available in respect of imported goods which are identical to them.[102] Furthermore, compensating goods are to be admitted free of import duty where duty-free provision is made for identical goods imported in accordance with CCC, Article 184.[103]

Compensating products may be temporarily exported pursuant to the outward processing procedure. Where this occurs a customs debt may arise in respect of the re-imported products. Import duties are to be charged on the compensating goods, or goods in their unaltered state, in accordance with the provisions contained in CCC, Articles 121 and 122, discussed above.[104] Where products are re-imported after processing outside the Community customs territory, import duties on them are to be calculated in accordance with the provisions governing outward processing and in accordance with the conditions which would have applied had the products been exported under the outward processing procedure, and released for free circulation, before the export took place.[105]

In order to calculate the amount of import duty due, it is necessary to calculate the proportion of import goods incorporated in compensating products and it is to this that we now turn.

11. *Calculating the proportion of import goods in compensating products*

The proportion of import goods incorporated in compensating products has to be calculated so that the amount of duty on the import goods can be determined, and so that commercial policy measures may be applied.[106] The calculations are to be effected in accordance with two specified methods, or where neither of these can be used, by any other reasonable method giving similar

---

[100] See the proviso to ibid, Art 122(b).
[101] CCC, Art 122(c), inapplicable under the drawback procedure: ibid, Art 126.
[102] Ibid, Art 122(d).
[103] Ibid, Art 122(c). CCC, Art 184, provides that the Council is to determine the cases in which, on account of special circumstances, goods which are released for free circulation or are exported are to be relieved from import or export duties. See also Ch 12.
[104] CCC, Art 123.2(a).
[105] Ibid, Art 123.2(b).
[106] Implementing Regulation, Art 518, first sub-para. For the purposes of the calculations, compensating products include processed or intermediate products: ibid, Art 518, second sub-para.

results.[107] The two specified methods are known as: (i) the quantitive scale method and (ii) the value scale method. The different methods are discussed briefly below.

11.1 *The quantitative scale method*

The quantitive scale method is available in two situations and in two forms. The first of these is where only one kind of compensating product is derived from the processing operations. In this case, the quantity of import goods deemed to be present in the compensating products in respect of which a customs debt has been incurred ('the dutiable products') is to be proportional to the dutiable products as a percentage of the total quantity of compensating products.[108] The second situation in which the quantitive scale method is applicable is where several kinds of compensating products are derived from the processing operations and all elements of the import goods are found in each of the compensating products. In such a situation it is necessary to determine the quantity of import goods deemed to be present in a specific quantity of a specific compensating product for which a customs debt has been incurred. This is determined by using the ratio between the specific compensating product (irrespective of whether a customs debt has been incurred in relation to it) and the total quantity of all compensating products, to determine the quantity of import goods in the totality of the specific compensating products. The ratio between the quantity of the specific compensating product in question and the total quantity of the specific compensating product[109] is then used to ascertain the quantity of import goods in the specific quantity of the specific compensating products in question. The amount of customs duty attributable to that quantity of import goods may now be determined.[110]

In deciding whether the conditions for applying the two kinds of quantitive scale method are fulfilled, 'losses' are not to be taken into account. 'Losses' means the proportion of import goods destroyed and lost during the processing operation, in particular, by evaporation, dessication, venting as gas, or leaching.[111]

---

[107] Ibid, Art 518.1 final sub-para and Art 518.4. For examples of calculations see the Guidelines referred to at n 2 above, section 6.
[108] Implementing Regulation, Art 518.2(a).
[109] The legislation refers to the total quantity of compensating products 'of the same kind'.
[110] Implementing Regulation, Art 518.2(b).
[111] Ibid, Art 518.2. This definition is without prejudice to the terms of ibid, Art 862, which provides that quantities which are lost solely because of natural wastage and not from any negligence or manipulation on the part of the person concerned are to be taken into account at the request of that person.

11.2 *The value scale method*

The value scale method is to be applied when the quantitive scale method is inapplicable.[112] This specifies that the quantity of import goods in a specific quantity of a specific compensating product incurring a customs debt, as in the second situation in which the quantitive scale method is applied, is determined in two stages. First, the value of the import goods in the totality of the specific compensating product is determined. This is achieved by applying to the import goods the percentage which the value of the specific compensating product, irrespective of whether a customs debt is incurred, bears to the total value of all compensating products.[113] Secondly, the value of the import goods in the specific quantity of the specific compensating product is determined. This is established by applying to the value of the import goods in the totality of the specific compensating products, the percentage which the value of the compensating products for which a customs debt is incurred bears to the total value of the compensating products of that kind.[114]

The value of each of the different compensating products used in applying the value scale is to be the ex-works price in the Community, or the recent selling price in the Community of identical or similar products, provided that these have not been influenced by the relationship between the buyer and the seller.

12. *Discharge of the procedure*

Certain provisions in the Implementing Regulation which specified when the inward processing procedure should be discharged have been repealed.[115] It is still the case, though, that acceptance of certain declarations discharges the inward processing arrangements.[116] Frequently, it is the exportation of compensating products which leads to the discharge of the procedure.[117] Where the suspension system is in operation, however, it is the assignment of goods for any customs-approved treatment or use that leads to discharge. Where the prior exportation system is used, it is the declaration in respect of the import goods which leads to discharge. There are specific provisions in relation to the situation where import goods have been entered under two or more declarations for the arrangements by virtue of one authorization.[118]

---

[112] Implementing Regulation, Art 518.3, first sub-para.
[113] Ibid, Art 518.3(a).   [114] Ibid, Art 518.3(b).
[115] See the former Art 577 of the Implementing Regulation.
[116] See the Implementing Regulation, Art 545, particularly at .2 and Art 520.1, particularly the first indent.
[117] See, eg, Case 437/93 *Hauptzollamt Heilbronn v Temic Telefunken Microelectronic GmbH*, in n 9 above, para 20. For what counts as exportation for discharge purposes or for the purposes of a claim for repayment of import duties see Implementing Regulation, Art 544.
[118] Ibid, Art 520.1.

The bill of discharge is to be supplied to the supervising office within thirty days of, at the latest, the expiry of the period for discharge, irrespective of whether or not aggregation is used. Where the drawback system is used, the claim for repayment or remission of import duties must be lodged with the supervising office within not thirty days but six months.[119] The customs office may extend the period even if it has expired. The supervising office may make out the bill of discharge which must contain certain specified particulars unless otherwise determined by the supervising office.[120]

The discharge of the inward processing procedure by declaration for another customs-approved treatment or use has been considered by the Court of Justice. A customs authority sought to place, in an authorization, quantitive limits in respect of products which were to be placed under the procedure of processing under customs control by way of discharge of the inward processing procedure. The trader appealed against these quantitive limits and the Court decided that they were not justified. It said that:

> if the customs authority finds that . . . ways of discharging the inward processing relief arrangements . . . are not likely to lead to abuse by, for example, conferring an unjustified customs advantage on the beneficiary, it must grant the authorization; if not, it can only refuse it.[121]

13. *Administrative co-operation*

The customs authorities are obliged to communicate to the Commission the authorizations for inward processing which have been issued and applications which have been refused and authorizations which have been annulled, or revoked, on the grounds of the economic conditions not being fulfilled. The Commission is then to make these particulars available to the customs administrations.[122] It should also be noted that, at the request of the person concerned, various information sheets may be issued in order to make available pertinent information to other customs offices involved in the application of the relevant inward processing arrangements.[123]

B. OUTWARD PROCESSING

1. *What it is and why it is necessary*

'Outward processing' means 'the Customs procedure under which goods which are in free circulation in a Customs territory may be temporarily exported for

---

[119] Ibid, Art 521.1. [120] Ibid, Art 521.2 and 3.

[121] Case C–437/93 *Hauptzollamt Heilbronn v Temic Telefunken Microelectronic GmbH*, n 9 above, at para 26.

[122] Implementing Regulation, Art 552.

[123] See ibid, Art 523 and Annex 71, which refers to 'INF1', INF5', 'INF7', and 'INF9'.

manufacturing, processing or repair abroad and then re-imported with total or partial exemption from import duties and taxes'.[124] As the introduction to Annex E8 to the original Kyoto Convention makes clear, the relief is available when goods are declared for home use and is usually partial. It may, though, be total where repairs have been carried out abroad free of charge. The availability of the procedure may also be made subject to the condition that the processing operations envisaged are regarded by the competent authorities as not detrimental to national interests. Like inward processing, it is a procedure which takes account of the international division of labour in the modern world.[125]

2. Outward processing: a Community procedure

As was the case with inward processing, outward processing was first dealt with by means of a Council Directive,[126] passed a few years after the creation of the customs union. It permitted a certain degree of divergence between the Member States. Much later, outward processing, as 'an essential instrument of the Community's commercial policy'[127] was the subject of a harmonizing regulation.[128] Turning to the current legislation, CCC, Article 145 provides that outward processing allows Community goods to be temporarily exported from the Community customs territory in order to undergo processing operations and the products resulting from those operations to be released for free circulation, with total or partial relief from import duties.[129] The total relief from import duty of goods exported from the EC has been described as the 'primary aim' of the outward processing regime.[130] The temporary exportation of Community goods entails, however, the application of export duties, commercial policy measures, and other formalities for the exit of Community goods from the customs territory.[131] Generally speaking, goods are excluded from the procedure where their export gives rise to repayment or remission of import duties. So too are

[124] Specific Annex F, Chapter 2, Definitions in the Revised Kyoto Convention. The definition contained in Annex E8 to the original Kyoto Convention is the same.
[125] See the first recital to Council Regulation (EEC) 2473/86 of 24 July 1986 [1986] OJ L212/1.
[126] (EEC) 119/76 of 18 Dec 1975 [1976] OJ L24/58.
[127] See the final recital of Council Regulation (EEC) 2473/86, in n 125 above.
[128] Ibid.
[129] The outward processing procedures are not relevant to customs duty only, but apply also for the purposes of implementing non-tariff common commercial policy measures: CCC, Art 160.
[130] Case 142/96 Hauptzollamt München v Wacker Werke GmbH & Co. KG ('Wacker Werke II') [1997] ECR I–4649 at para 21.
[131] CCC, Art 145.2. Commercial policy measures are applicable on entry for the arrangements of non-Community goods only to the extent that they refer to the entry of goods into the customs territory of the Community. Commercial policy measures applicable on release for free circulation do not apply to compensating products released for free circulation following outward processing: (i) if the products have retained Community origin within CCC, Arts 23 and 24; (ii) involving repair including the standard exchange system; (iii) following successive processing operations in accordance with CCC, Art 123: Implementing Regulation, Art 509.1 and 4.

those which, before export, were released for free circulation with total relief from import duties by virtue of their end use and in respect of which the conditions for total relief still apply, and those the export of which gives rise to the granting of export refunds, or, where the Common Agricultural Policy applies, a financial advantage.[132]

3. *The standard exchange and prior importation systems*

3.1 *The standard exchange system*

The inward processing procedure permitted some deviation from the fundamental principles which govern it by allowing compensating products[133] to be derived from goods other than the import goods pursuant to the equivalent compensation system. The outward processing procedure also permits some deviation from its basic rules by permitting an imported product, known as a replacement product, to replace a compensating product produced by the outward processing. The system under which such replacement is permitted is known as the standard exchange system.[134] The customs authorities are to allow the standard exchange system to be used where the processing operation involves the repair of Community goods, except those subject to the Common Agricultural Policy, or to specific arrangements applicable to certain goods resulting from the processing of agricultural products.[135] Such goods cannot, of course, be repaired. Unlike authorization for outward processing generally, authorization for the standard exchange system is issued only at the request of the person who arranges for the processing operations to be carried out.[136]

In order for the standard exchange system to be operated it must be possible to verify the fulfilment of two conditions.[137] The first is that replacement products are to have the same tariff classification, be of the same commercial quality, and possess the same technical characteristics as the temporary export goods would have had if they had undergone the repair in question.[138] The second is that where the temporary export goods have been used before export, the replacement products must also have been used and may not be new products.[139] Derogations from the rule may be permitted by the customs authorities

---

[132] CCC, Art 146.

[133] That is, all products resulting from processing operations: CCC, Art 145.3(c).

[134] See CCC, Art 154.1. By virtue of CCC, Art 154.3 provisions governing compensating products apply to replacement products except as provided by CCC, Art 159, referred to at n 136 below.

[135] Ibid, Art 154.

[136] Ibid, Art 159. Art 159 also removes the need to establish that compensating products have resulted from processing temporary export goods, which is obviously inappropriate in this context.

[137] Ibid, Art 156.

[138] Ibid, Art 155.1. Temporary export goods means the goods placed under the outward processing procedure: ibid, Art 145.3(a).

[139] Ibid, Art 155.2 first para.

if the replacement product has been supplied free of charge either because of a contractual or statutory obligation arising from a guarantee, or because of a manufacturing defect.[140]

3.2 Prior importation system

Within the standard exchange system there is a prior importation system, which may be contrasted with the prior exportation system which operates under the inward processing procedure. The prior importation system permits replacement products to be imported before the exportation of the temporary export goods, but these goods must be exported within two months from the date of acceptance of the declaration relating to the release of the replacement goods for free circulation.[141] The period for exportation may, on request, be extended within reasonable limits where exceptional circumstances warrant it.[142] Like the prior exportation system, the operation of the prior importation system is subject to the provision of security.[143]

Where prior importation is effected, and relief is given pursuant to the provisions of CCC, Article 151 discussed below, the amount of the relief obtained by way of deduction from import duties is determined, on the basis of the items of charge applicable to the temporary export goods, on the date of acceptance of the declaration placing them under the outward processing procedure.[144]

4. Triangular traffic system

A triangular traffic system is permitted in relation to the outward processing procedure, just as it is in relation to the inward processing procedure. 'Triangular traffic' is defined in the same way for all customs procedures with economic impact as being traffic where the office of discharge is not the same as the office of entry.[145] Specific limitations on the use of the triangular traffic system have been repealed.[146]

---

[140] CCC, Art 155.2 second para.
[141] Ibid, Art 157.1.
[142] Ibid, Art 157.2 and Implementing Regulation, Art 588 which permits extensions even after expiry of the original period.
[143] CCC, Art 154.4 and Art 157.
[144] Ibid, Art 158.
[145] Implementing Regulation, Art 496(h).
[146] See Commission Regulation (EC) 993/2001, n 2 above, Art 1.26 and the former Art 777 of the Implementing Regulation which provided, amongst other things, that it could not be used under the standard exchange system with prior importation.

5. *Permitted processing operations*

The operations which are permissible under the outward processing procedure are the same as those permitted under the inward processing procedure, except that they do not extend to the use of certain goods not found in the compensating products, but which allow or facilitate the production of them, even if they are entirely or partially used up in the process. Accordingly, the following are permitted:

(i) the working of the goods, including the erecting or assembling of them or fitting them to other goods;
(ii) the processing of the goods;
(iii) the repair of the goods, including restoring them and putting them in order.[147]

6. *Authorization and entry*[148]

6.1 *The form of the application*

Authorization to carry out outward processing is to be issued at the request of the person who arranges for the processing operations to be carried out.[149] Authorization may be granted to another person in respect of goods of Community origin, according to the rules in the CCC governing non-preferential origin, in certain circumstances. The processing operation must consist in incorporating those goods into goods obtained outside the Community and imported as compensating products. Furthermore, the use of the procedure must help to promote the sale of export goods without adversely affecting the essential interests of Community producers of products identical or similar to the imported compensating products.[150] The Implementing Regulation provides that, where an application for authorization is made by a person who exports the temporary goods but does not arrange the processing operations, the customs authorities must conduct a prior examination of these conditions.[151]

The application, which may be for a single authorization (ie one involving different customs administrations[152]) is to be made in accordance with the rules governing applications for authorizations for customs procedures with economic impact dealt with in Chapter 10.[153]

---

[147] CCC, Art 145.3(b).
[148] The reader is referred to Ch 10, section C, where the general rules governing customs procedures with economic impact are referred to.
[149] CCC, Art 147.1.
[150] Ibid, Art 147.2.
[151] Implementing Regulation, Arts 585.2, 503, and 504 which apply *mutatis mutandis*.
[152] Ibid, see Art 496(c), for the full definition.
[153] See pp 299–302.

6.2 Conditions for authorization

As with the inward processing procedure, authorizations for the outward processing procedure is granted only if three conditions are met.[154] First, the authorized person must be established in the Community. Secondly, it must be considered possible to establish that the compensating products have resulted from the processing of the temporary export goods, ie the goods placed under the outward processing procedure. Indeed, the authorization must specify the means and methods to establish that the compensating products have resulted from the processing of the temporary export goods or to verify that the conditions for using the standard exchange system are met.[155] Where the procedure is used to enable the repair of goods the customs authorities must be satisfied that the temporary export goods are capable of repair. Outward processing arrangements must not be used to improve the technical performance of goods.[157] Thirdly, the authorization to use the procedure must not be liable to harm seriously the essential interests of Community processors. This requirement is concerned with what are called the economic conditions.[157]

6.3 The content of the authorization

As we noted above, the authorization is to specify the means and methods to establish that the compensating products have resulted from the processing of the temporary export goods or to verify that the conditions for using the standard exchange system are met.[158] It is also to specify the rate of yield[159] and the period for discharge.[160] The period for discharge is defined as the time by which the goods or products must have been assigned a new permitted customs-approved treatment or use.[161]

---

[154] CCC, Art 148 (a)–(c).

[155] Implementing Regulation, Art 586.1. The means and methods may include the use of the information document set out in Annex 104 and the examination of records: ibid, Art 586.1, second sub-para. Where the nature of the processing operations does not allow it to be established that the compensating products have resulted from the temporary export goods, the authorization for the procedure may still be granted in duly justified cases, provided that the applicant can offer sufficient guarantees that the goods used in the processing operations share the same eight-digit CN code, the same commercial quality, and the same technical characteristics as the temporary export goods. The authorization is to lay down the conditions for using the arrangements: ibid, Art 586.2.

[156] Implementing Regulation, Art 587.

[157] CCC, Art 148(c). Implementing Regulation, Art 585.1 provides that the essential interests of Community producers are deemed not to be seriously harmed except where contrary indications exist. An examination of the conditions is, therefore, unnecessary in plain cases.

[158] Implementing Regulation, Art 586.1.

[159] Ibid, Art 517.1.

[160] Ibid, Art 588.

[161] Ibid, Art 496(m). The definition includes the time by which a new customs-approved treatment or use is to be assigned in order to obtain total or partial relief from import duties upon release for free circulation after outward processing.

6.4 *Entry of goods for the arrangements*

The declaration entering the temporary export goods for the arrangements is to be made in accordance with the provisions governing exportation.[162] Where the prior importation system is used, the documents which accompany the declaration for free circulation are to include a copy of the authorization. This is not the case, however, where the authorization is applied for in accordance with Article 497.3 of the Implementing Regulation.[163] So far as outward processing is concerned, this states that the application for authorization may be made by means of a customs declaration in writing, or by means of a data processing technique using the normal procedure, in certain situations. The first of these is where the processing operation concerns repairs, including the standard exchange system without importation.[164] The others arise in relation to release for free circulation after outward processing (i) using the standard exchange system with prior importation or (ii) without prior importation where the existing authorization does not cover such a system and the customs authorities permit its modification and (iii) where the processing operation concerns goods of a non-commercial nature.[165]

7. *The duration and yield of the procedure*

7.1 *The duration of the procedure*

The customs authorities must specify the period within which the compensating products are to be re-imported into the Community customs territory and may extend the specified period if the holder of the authorization submits a duly substantiated request.[166] As noted above, the period for discharge is to be set in the authorization and may be extended.[167]

7.2 *The rate of yield*

Customs authorities must also set either the rate of yield of the operation or, where necessary, the method of determining that rate.[168] The rate of yield is defined as the quantity or percentage of compensating products obtained from the processing of a given quantity of temporary export goods.[169] The provisions of the Implementing Regulation which governed the setting of the rate

---

[162] Ibid, Art 589.1.

[163] Implementing Regulation, Art 589.2. This states that ibid, Art 220.3, applies *mutatis mutandis*. Art 220.3 enables the customs authorities to allow the written authorization or a copy of the application for authorization to be kept at their disposal instead of accompanying the declaration. See also Ch 10, p 300, n 61.

[164] Ibid, Art 497.3(d), first sub-para.   [165] Ibid, Art 497.3(d)(i)–(iii).

[166] CCC, Art 149.1.

[167] See Implementing Regulation, Art 588 and under 'Prior Importation system' above.

[168] CCC, Art 149.2.   [169] Ibid, Art 145.3(d).

of yield for inward processing largely apply also in relation to outward processing. These specify that the rate, including an average rate, is to be established
in the authorization at the time the goods are entered for the arrangements.
The rate must be determined, as far as possible, on the basis of production or
technical data or, where these are not available, data relating to operations of
the same type.[170] The customs authorities may establish the rate of yield after
the goods have been entered for outward processing but not later than when
they are assigned a new customs-approved treatment or use.[171]

8. Relief from import duty

The relief from import duty which is at the heart of the outward processing
procedure is granted only where the compensating products are declared for
release for free circulation in the name of, or on behalf of, the holder of the
authorization (or any other person established in the Community provided
that the person has obtained the consent of the holder of the authorization
and the conditions of authorization are fulfilled[172]). No relief is available if one
of the conditions or obligations of the authorization have not been fulfilled,
unless it is established that the failures have no significant effect on the correct
operation of the procedure.[173]

9. The method of relief

CCC, Article 151.1 provides that the relief is effected by making a deduction
from the import duty applicable to the compensating products released for free
circulation. The amount of the deduction is to be equal to the amount of the
import duties that would have been applicable, on the same date, to the temporary export goods had they been imported into the Community customs territory from the country in which they were processed, or in which the last
processing operation took place. Article 151 is subject to the terms of any
agreement between the Community and a third country on relief from import
duties for compensating products.[174] Certain charges which would have been
applicable to the importation of the temporary export goods are not to be taken
into account, namely anti-dumping duties and countervailing duties.
Secondary compensating products that constitute waste scrap, residues,
offcuts, and remainders are deemed to be included.[175]

In order to ascertain the necessary deduction it is, inevitably, necessary to
value both the compensating products and the temporary export goods. The
compensating products are to be valued according to the transaction value. The

---

[170] Implementing Regulation, Art 517.1.   [171] Ibid, Art 517.2.
[172] CCC, Art 150.1.   [173] Ibid, Art 150.2.
[174] Ibid, Art 151.5. See further n 186 for the circumstances in which the cost of a processing
operation is to be the basis of the value for duty for the purposes of relief.
[175] Implementing Regulation, Art 590.1.

temporary export goods are to be valued as required by the relevant legislation.[176] This states, first of all, that the import duties to be deducted are to be calculated on the basis of the quantity and nature of the temporary export goods in question, on the date of the acceptance of the declaration placing them under the outward processing procedure, and on the basis of the other charges applicable to them on the date of acceptance of the declaration relating to the release for free circulation of the compensating products.[177] That being established, the legislation then provides that the value of the temporary goods is to be the value attributed to them and taken into account in determining the value of the compensating products (adding to the price actually paid or payable for products, the value of the materials, components, parts and similar items incorporated in them as required by CCC, Article 32.1(b)(i)).[178] Where the value of the temporary export goods cannot be determined in this way, then their value is to be the difference between the customs value of the compensating products and the processing costs determined by reasonable means.[179]

9.1 *Reasonable means*

Taking account of the transaction value of the temporary export goods, without any adjustment pursuant to CCC, Article 32.1(b)(i), by deducting it from the transaction value of the compensating products may be a reasonable means of determining processing costs.[180] This is so even if, as a result, a higher rate of customs duty is applicable in relation to the temporary export goods than in relation to the compensating products, thus ensuring that the trader achieves a customs duty advantage. As the ECJ has said: 'The customs advantages and disadvantages which may arise in individual cases must be tolerated provided there is nothing to indicate that the prices charged by the two traders respectively were influenced by the business links between them.'[181]

---

[176] Case 16/91 *Wacker Werke GmbH & Co. KG v Hauptzollamt München-West* ('*Wacker Werke I*') [1992] ECR I–6821 at para 27.   [177] CCC, Art 151.2, first sub-para.

[178] Ibid, Art 151.2. Note that the loading, transport, and insurance costs for the temporary export goods to the place where the processing operation, or the last processing operation, took place are to be excluded from the value of the temporary export goods taken into account in determining the customs value of the compensating products in accordance with CCC, Art 32.1(b)(i). The same costs are also to be excluded from processing costs where the value of the temporary export goods cannot be determined by application of CCC, Art 32.1(b)(i). Such processing costs are, however, to include the loading, transport, and insurance costs for the compensating products from the place where the last processing operation took place to the place where they entered the Community customs territory. Loading, transport, and insurance costs include (a) commissions and brokerage, except buying commissions, (b) the cost of containers not integral to the temporary export goods, (c) the cost of packing, including labour and materials, and (d) handling costs incurred in connection with transport of the goods: Implementing Regulation, Art 590.2.

[179] Ibid, Art 151.2, second sub-para.

[180] In *Wacker Werke I*, n 176 above, at paras 9 and 26.

[181] *Wacker Werke II*, n 130 above, at para 21, where the Court also noted that the possibility of tariff anomalies arising, resulting in advantages for traders is a risk inherent in the outward processing regime.

9.2 *Reduced and zero rates of duty*

Where the temporary export goods were actually released for free circulation
at a reduced rate by virtue of their end use, prior to being placed under the
outward processing procedure, and for as long as the conditions for granting
the reduced rate apply, the amount of import duties to be deducted from the
import duties applicable to the compensating products is to be the amount of
import duties actually levied when the goods were released for free circulation.[182] If temporary export goods could qualify for a reduced or zero rate of
duty by virtue of their end use on being released for free circulation, then the
reduced or zero rate is the rate of duty which is to be taken into account for the
purposes of calculating the relief. For that rate to be applied the goods must
have undergone operations consistent with such an end use in the country
where the processing operation, or the last processing operation, took
place.[183]

9.3 *Preferential rates of duty*

The amount to be deducted takes account not only of reliefs applicable to the
temporary export goods by virtue of end use, but also of preferential tariff
measures contained in agreements with third countries and autonomous
measures. Where compensating products qualify for such measures and the
measure also exists for goods falling within the same tariff classification as the
temporary export goods, the rate of duty to be taken into account in determining the amount to be deducted is to be that which would apply if the
temporary export goods fulfilled the conditions for the application of the preferential measures.[184]

9.4 *Repair of temporary export goods*

Where the object of the processing operation is the repair of the temporary
export goods, then total relief from import duties may be available on their
release for free circulation. In order to obtain total relief, it must be established
to the satisfaction of the customs authorities that the goods were repaired free
of charge either as a result of a contractual or statutory obligation arising
from a guarantee or because of a manufacturing defect. This relief does not,
however, apply where the defect was taken into account when the repaired
goods were first released for free circulation.[185]

Partial relief from import duties may be available where the repair is carried
out for payment. The relief is calculated by taking as the customs value an

---

[182] CCC, Art 151.2, second indent.   [183] Ibid, Art 151.3.
[184] Ibid, Art 151.4.   [185] Ibid, Art 152.

amount equal to repair costs. The amount of duty is then established on the basis of the taxation elements pertaining to the compensating products on the date on which a release for free circulation in respect of them was accepted. The repair costs must, however, be the only consideration provided by the holder of the authorization and not be influenced by any links between the authorization holder and the operation.[186]

10. *Calculating the proportion of temporary export goods in compensating products*

As we noted above, it is essential to the proper functioning of the outward processing procedure that the value of the temporary export goods is ascertained, so that the duty attributable to them can be deducted from that incurred in relation to the compensating products. The valuation of the temporary export goods causes particular difficulty where the compensating products are not all released for free circulation at the same time. In these circumstances it is necessary to establish the proportion of the temporary export goods in the compensating products. Following the simplifications introduced by Commission Regulation (EC) 993/2001,[187] the legislative provisions which govern the methods of doing this are the same as those determining the proportion of import goods in the relevant compensating products. Accordingly, the consideration of the Implementing Regulation, Article 518 above[188] is applicable in relation to outward processing with the substitution of references to import goods with references to temporary export goods.

11. *The aggregated discharge procedure*

An aggregated discharge procedure is provided for in the Implementing Regulation, Article 592. It applies in respect of undertakings which frequently carry out outward processing operations under an authorization not covering repair. It enables the customs authorities to set an average rate of import duty applicable to all operations carried out under one authorization ('the aggregated discharge'). The rate is to be determined for a period not exceeding twelve

---

[186] CCC, Art 153. By Regulation (EC) 2700/2000, n 22 above, Art 1.10, a para is added to CCC, Art 153 by which it is provided that, by way of derogation from Art 151, the committee procedure may be used to determine when and under what conditions goods may be released for free circulation following an outward processing operation, with the cost of the processing operation being taken as the basis for assessment for the purpose of applying the customs tariff. Implementing Regulation, Art 591, inserted by Commission Regulation (EC) 993/2001, n 2 above, provides that partial relief from import duties by taking the cost of the processing operation as the basis of the value for duty is to be granted on request, except where temporary export goods, which are not of Community origin according to the non-preferential rules of origin in the CCC, have been released for free circulation at a zero rate of duty. This exception does not apply in relation to goods of a non-commercial nature as defined in the Implementing Regulation, Art 1.6.

[187] See n 2 above.　　　　　　　　　　　　　　　　　　[188] See pp 358–60.

months, rather than for six months as formerly, and applies provisionally for compensating products released for free circulation during that period. At the end of the period, the customs authorities must make a final calculation and, where appropriate, apply the provisions of CCC, Article 220.1 or Article 236.[189] CCC, Articles 29–35, which deal with the value of goods for customs purposes, are to apply *mutatis mutandis* to the processing costs, which are not to take into account the temporary export goods.

12. *Administrative co-operation*

The customs authorities are obliged to communicate to the Commission the authorizations for outward processing which have been issued in accordance with CCC, Article 147.2,[190] and applications which have been refused and authorizations which have been annulled or revoked on the grounds of the economic conditions not being fulfilled. The Commission is then to make these particulars available to the customs administrations.[191] It should also be noted that, at the request of the person concerned, various information sheets may be issued in order to make pertinent information available to other customs offices involved in the application of the relevant outward processing arrangements.[192]

---

[189] These provisions govern entry in the accounts and repayment and remission of duty and are dealt with in Chs 12 and 13.

[190] CCC, Art 147.2, which is considered at p 365 above, permits authorization to use the outward processing procedure to be granted to someone other than the person who arranges for the processing operations to be carried out.

[191] Implementing Regulation, Art 552.

[192] See ibid, Art 523 and Annex 71, which refers to 'INF2' in relation to outward processing which is to be used to communicate information on temporary export goods in triangular traffic in order to obtain partial or total relief for compensating products.

12

The Customs Debt and Reliefs from Duty

The rules governing the customs debt constitute a point at which the practical interests of all those affected by customs duty coincide. For the Community institutions the customs debt represents own resources which they need to survive. For the Member State the debt is a sum of money which it has a legal obligation to collect. For the trader, the debt represents simply a liability to be paid. No wonder then that the pre-consolidation legislation on customs debt said that:

> the rules governing the incurrence of a customs debt, the determination of its amount, when it becomes due and its extinction are so important for the proper functioning of the customs union that it is essential to ensure that such rules are implemented as uniformly as possible in the Community . . .[1]

These rules are now contained in CCC, Title VII (Articles 189–242) which is headed 'Customs Debt'. Articles 235–242, which concern repayment and remission of duty, are considered in the next chapter, but the remainder of the title is considered below, along with the rules governing the Community system of reliefs from duty. To start the chapter, though, in section A, we address an issue that has been mentioned in Chapters 10 and 11, namely the giving of security for the customs debt. In section B, the basic rules concerning the incurring of the customs debt are dealt with. Then in section C the significance of the time and place at which the customs debt is incurred are considered. Section D concerns some aspects of the recovery of the debt, particularly its calculation, its entry in the accounts, and communication to the debtor. Post-clearance recovery of debts is considered in section E, payment of the debt is dealt with in section F, and extinction of the debt in section G. Section H concerns reliefs from customs duty, and other privileges in relation to payment of customs duty debts are considered in section I.

A. SECURITY FOR THE CUSTOMS DEBT

As we have already seen, the provision of security, whether by way of guarantee or otherwise, is of great importance in relation to the operation of many Community customs procedures.[2] Some of the specific provisions relating to

---

[1] Second recital to Council Regulation (EEC) 2144/87 of 13 July 1987 on customs debt, [1987] OJ L201/15.
[2] Security is the subject of Chapter 5 of the General Annex to the revised Kyoto Convention.

particular procedures, such as transit, have been noted in earlier chapters. This section is concerned only with the general provisions relating to security in CCC, Title VII (Chapter 1, Articles 189–200) and certain provisions in the Implementing Regulation.

Where security is required it is to be provided by the person who is, or may become, liable to pay the debt or some other person.[3] Only one security is to be provided for a customs debt.[4] No security is required from public authorities and the requirement for security may be waived where the debt does not exceed 500 ECU.[5] Customs authorities may, and frequently do, allow comprehensive security to be provided at the request of the person liable for the debt or the provider of the security. Such a security is to cover two or more operations in respect of which a customs debt has been, or may be, incurred.[6] Flat-rate securities may also be provided by, for example, guarantee vouchers.[7]

1. *Compulsory security*

In relation to procedures for which it is compulsory to provide security as, for example, in the case of Community transit,[8] certain temporary importations,[9] prior exportation under the inward processing procedure,[10] and prior importation under the outward processing procedure,[11] the level of the security is to be fixed at the precise amount of the customs debt, where that amount can be established with certainty when the security is required. In other cases, the security is to be fixed at what the customs authorities estimate to be the maximum amount of the debt which has been or may be incurred.[12] It appears that, in practice, it is possible for customs authorities to take a very liberal view of the maximum amount which may be incurred. The Court of Auditors noted that one customs office took only 10 per cent of the potential customs duties.[13] It need hardly be said that such practices, if they exist, introduce a serious distortion into the customs union.

2. *Security at the option of the customs authorities*

CCC, Article 190.1 states that where the customs legislation specifies that the provision of security is optional, it is to be required at the authorities' discretion in so far as they consider that a customs debt which has been, or may be,

---

[3] CCC, Art 189.4.   [4] Ibid, Art 189.2.
[5] Ibid, Art 189.4 and 5.   [6] Ibid, Art 191.1.
[7] See, eg, the discussion of guarantees in relation to transit in Ch 10 at p 319.
[8] See CCC, Art 94.   [9] Implementing Regulation, Art 581.
[10] CCC, Art 115.5.   [11] Ibid, Art 154.4.
[12] Ibid, Art 192.1.
[13] See Special Report 8/99 of 16 Dec 1999, on securities and guarantees provided for in the Community Customs Code to protect the collection of traditional own resources together with the Commission's replies, [2000] OJ C70/1, at para 15.

incurred is not certain to be paid within the prescribed period.[14] The security must not exceed the precise amount of the customs debt or, where precision is impossible, the customs authorities' estimate of the maximum which has been, or may be, incurred.[15] Even if the provision of security is initially optional, it must be required once rules requiring security become applicable or at any subsequent time when customs authorities find that a customs debt which has been, or may be, incurred is not certain to be paid within the prescribed time.[16] Where security is not demanded, an undertaking to comply with the obligations which the person in question is designed to fulfil may be required.[17]

3. *Types of security*

Security for customs debts may be provided by means of a cash deposit or by a guarantor at the choice of the person who is required to provide it.[18] In addition to these, there are further types of security permitted pursuant to Article 857 of the Implementing Regulation which are noted below.

So far as cash deposits are concerned, these are to be made in the currency of the Member State in which the security is required.[19] Cheques guaranteed by the institution on which they are drawn in a manner acceptable to the customs authorities and any other instrument recognized by the authorities as a means of payment are equivalent to cash.[20] Cash deposits, or their equivalent, are to comply with the requirements in force in the Member State in which the security is required.[21] So far as concerns guarantees, the guarantor must be a third person, established in the Community, and approved by the customs authorities of the Member State in question. A guarantor is required to undertake in writing to pay, jointly and severally with the debtor, the secured amount of the customs debt which falls to be paid. The customs authorities may refuse to approve the guarantor, or the type of security proposed, where they do not appear certain to ensure payment of the customs debt within the prescribed period.[22]

---

[14] Note that CCC, Art 88 provides that, subject to specific rules for specific suspensive arrangements, customs authorities may make the placing of goods under a suspensive arrangement conditional upon the provision of security in order to ensure payment of the debt.

[15] CCC, Art 192.2.   [16] Ibid, Art 190.2.

[17] Ibid, Art 190.1, second indent.

[18] Ibid, Arts 193 and 196. The customs authorities may, however, refuse to accept the type of security offered, and the particular security offered, where it is incompatible with the customs procedure concerned: Art 196, second para.

[19] But this requirement is qualified as set out at p 376 (iv) below. No interest on the cash deposit is payable by the customs authorities: Implementing Regulation, Art 858.

[20] CCC, Art 194.1. The requirements set out in CCC, Art 194.1 do not need to be fulfilled (see, eg, the types of security permitted under Implementing Regulation, Article 857) but customs authorities must not accept any security where they do not consider that it is certain to ensure payment of the customs debt: CCC, Art 197.2.

[21] Ibid, Art 194.2.   [22] Ibid, Art 195.

The types of security permitted under Implementing Regulation, Article 857 are:

(i)   a mortgage or charge on land, an antichresis, or other right deemed equivalent to a right pertaining to immovable property;

(ii)   the cession of a claim, the pledging of goods, securities, claims, a savings bank book, or entry in the national debt register, with or without surrendering possession of them;

(iii) the assumption of joint contractual liability for the full amount of the debt by a third party approved for that purpose by the customs authorities and, in particular, the lodging of a bill of exchange the payment of which is guaranteed by a third party;

(iv)   a cash deposit, or security deemed equivalent to it, in a currency other than that of the Member State in which the security is given;

(v)   participation, subject to payment of a contribution, in a general guarantee scheme administered by the customs authorities.

The circumstances in which, and the conditions under which, recourse may be had to these types of security is to be determined by the customs authorities.[23] The acceptance of such security is, however, permitted only so long as it provides assurance that the debt will be paid equivalent to that provided by a cash deposit or a guarantor.[24] The security proposed by the debtor is to be rejected where the authorities do not consider that it is certain to ensure payment of the customs debt.[25]

4. *Maintenance of, additions to, and release of security*

Customs authorities may require the type of security chosen to be maintained for a specified period.[26] Additional security must be required from the provider of it where the customs authorities establish that the security which has been provided does not ensure, or is no longer sufficient or certain to ensure, payment of the customs debt within the prescribed period. Instead of providing additional security the person may replace the original security with a new security.[27]

A security is not to be released until such time as the customs debt in respect of which it was given is extinguished, or can no longer arise, but it must then be released forthwith. Where a customs debt has been extinguished in part, or may arise only in part, part of the security is to be released at the request of the person concerned, unless the amount concerned does not justify any action being taken.[28]

---

[23] See Implementing Regulation, Art 857.1 and 2.   [24] CCC, Art 197.1.
[25] Ibid, Art 197.2.   [26] Ibid, Art 196.
[27] Ibid, Art 198.   [28] Ibid, Art 199.

B. INCURRING A CUSTOMS DEBT: THE BASIC RULES

Customs debts may be incurred on importation in the ordinary way, on importation due to breach of certain provisions of customs law, on exportation in the ordinary way, and on exportation due to breach of certain provisions of customs law. Each of these situations is considered below. As we shall see more than one person is frequently liable for the customs debt which is incurred, and in such cases their liability is joint and several.[29]

Before looking at the specific rules on incurring a customs debt, it should be noted that customs debts on importation and exportation are incurred even where they relate to goods which are subject to measures of prohibition, or restriction, on importation or exportation of any kind whatsoever. No customs debt is incurred, however, on the unlawful introduction into the Community customs territory of counterfeit currency, or of narcotic drugs and psychotropic substances, which do not enter into 'the economic circuit' strictly supervised by the customs authorities with a view to their use for medical and scientific purposes. A customs debt is, nevertheless, deemed to have been incurred for the purposes of criminal law, where the criminal law of a Member State uses customs duties as the basis for determining penalties, or where the existence of a customs debt provides grounds for taking criminal proceedings.[30]

1. *The debt on importation*

There are two main ways in which a customs debt on importation may be incurred. The first is through the release for free circulation of goods liable to import duties. The second is through the placing of such goods under the temporary importation procedure with partial relief from import duties.[31] The time at which the debt is incurred is the time at which the customs declaration in question is accepted.[32] The person who is the debtor in relation to the customs debt is the declarant. Where a person makes a declaration in his or her own name on behalf of another person, ie by way of indirect representation,[33] the person on whose behalf a declaration is made is also a debtor.[34] The liability of the declarant is, of course, not removed by virtue of the fact that the

---

[29] CCC, Art 213.   [30] Ibid, Art 212.
[31] Ibid, Art 201.1(a) and (b).
[32] Ibid, Art 201.2. The debt is incurred irrespective of the fact that preferential treatment may be available. In the words of the Court of Justice: 'although the production of documents enabling a preferential zero rate to be applied may indeed result in goods being exempt from import duties under certain conditions, it cannot affect the existence of the customs debt itself': Case C–66/99 *D. Wandel GmbH v Hauptzollamt Bremen* [2001] ECR I–2579 at para 54. See also paras 55–56.
[33] See CCC, Art 5.2 and Ch 9.
[34] Ibid, Art 201.3.

person on whose behalf the declaration is made or another third party is also a debtor.[35] Those who provide information required to draw up a declaration who know, or ought reasonably to know, that the information is false may also be considered debtors in accordance with national provisions, where the information which is provided leads to all or part of the duties legally owed not being collected.[36] As one would expect, however, the exporter outside the Community customs territory is not made liable for customs duties even where his provision of false information has led to post-clearance recovery. The exporter is liable for customs duty only if he is also the declarant.[37]

There is a third way in which a debt on importation may be incurred. This arises in connection with the inward processing procedure. Goods originating in the EC, which have been obtained in the EC under the inward processing procedure, may attract favourable treatment on importation into a third country, on condition that Community import duty is paid on the non-Community goods which are incorporated into them. Where this is so, the validation of the documents necessary for preferential treatment to be obtained in the third country is to cause a customs debt on importation to be incurred.[38] The amount of the debt is to be determined under the same conditions as the customs debt resulting from the acceptance, on the same date, of the declaration for release for free circulation of the goods concerned for the purpose of terminating the inward processing procedure.[39] The time at which such a customs debt is incurred is the moment when the customs authorities accept the export declaration relating to the goods.[40] The debtor is the declarant and, in the event of indirect representation, the person on whose behalf the declaration is made is also a debtor.[41]

2. The debt on importation for breach of customs law

The imposition of a customs debt and liability for it is used as a penalty for failure to comply with the rules governing the customs system in certain situations. The failures giving rise to a customs debt are contained in CCC, Articles 202–205 and are set out below.[42]

---

[35] Case C–97/95 *Pascoal & Filhos Ld^a v Fazenda Pública* [1997] ECR I–4209, para 56 of the Opinion of Cosmas AG.

[36] CCC, Art 201.3, second indent.

[37] Case C–97/95 *Pascoal & Filhos Ld^a v Fazenda Pública* at n 35 above, paras 46–47. The Court of Justice has stated that the imposition of liability on an importer acting in good faith, where the exporter has made a fraudulent application for an EUR 1 certificate, is not contrary to the general principles of Community law, such as the prohibition of unjust enrichment, proportionality and legal certainty and the importer's good faith does not release him from liability: see paras 48–61. The position of the importer is discussed further in Chs 7 and 13.

[38] CCC, Art 216.1.   [39] Ibid, Art 216.4.

[40] Ibid, Art 216.2.   [41] Ibid, Art 216.3.

[42] When a debt on importation is incurred pursuant to any of these provisions and import duty is paid, the goods shall be deemed to be Community goods without the need for a declaration for entry into free circulation: Implementing Regulation, Art 866.

2.1 *Unlawful introduction of goods into the customs territory*

A customs debt is incurred where goods liable to import duty are unlawfully introduced into the Community customs territory or where goods located in a free zone or free warehouse are unlawfully introduced into another part of the territory.[43] For these purposes, unlawful introduction of goods occurs where it takes place in violation of the provisions of CCC, Articles 38–41 (which deal with the entry of goods into the Community customs territory and their presentation to the customs authorities[44]) or in violation of the second indent to CCC, Article 177 (which applies CCC, Articles 37–47 and 54–57 in relation to goods which leave a free zone or free warehouse and are brought into another part of the customs territory).[45] The debt is incurred at the moment the goods are unlawfully introduced.[46] The debtors are the person who introduced the goods unlawfully, any persons who participated in the unlawful introduction and who were aware, or should reasonably have been aware, that the introduction was unlawful, and any persons who acquired or held the goods in question and who were aware or should reasonably have been aware, at the time of acquiring or receiving the goods, that they had been introduced unlawfully.[47]

2.2 *Unlawful removal of goods from supervision*

A customs debt is imposed where goods liable to import duty are unlawfully removed from customs supervision.[48] The debt is incurred at the moment when the goods are removed from customs supervision.[49] The Implementing Regulation contains certain provisions on what constitutes removal.[50] The Court of Justice, for its part, has said that 'removal':

> must be understood as encompassing any act or omission the result of which is to prevent, if only for a short time, the competent customs authority from gaining access to goods under the customs supervision and from monitoring them as provided for in Article 37(1) of the Customs Code.

---

[43] CCC, Art 202.1. It follows from these provisions that, where goods are unlawfully introduced into the customs territory, the debt arises in the Member State into which the goods were introduced and it has responsibility for recovering the customs debt, even where the internal transit procedure has been used to transfer the goods elsewhere: Case 252/87 *Hauptzollamt Hamburg-St. Annen v Wilhelm Kiwall KG* [1988] ECR 4753.

[44] See Ch 9.   [45] See CCC, Art 202.1, second para.
[46] Ibid, Art 202.2.   [47] Ibid, Art 202.3.
[48] Ibid, Art 203.1.   [49] Ibid, Art 203.2.
[50] Where the presentation of a customs declaration for goods or any other act having the same legal effect or the production of a document for endorsement by the competent authorities have the effect of wrongly conferring on goods the status of Community goods, the acts shall be considered to constitute removal of goods from customs supervision within the meaning of CCC, Art 203.1: see Implementing Regulation, Art 865, which contains qualifications to this rule in relation to airline companies authorized to use the simplified transit procedure with the use of an electronic manifest. Art 865 does not, however, define removal, it merely gives examples of it.

It should also be noted that, for the purposes of Article 203(1) of the Customs Code, removal of goods from customs supervision does not require intent: it is sufficient if certain objective conditions are met, including, in particular, the absence of the goods from the approved place of storage at the time when the customs authorities intend to carry out an examination of them.[51]

In the light of these observations the Court concluded that: 'any withdrawal from authorised storage of goods subject to customs supervision without the authorisation of the customs authority constitutes removal for the purposes of Article 203(1)'.[52] The debtors are the person who removed the goods from customs supervision, any persons who participated in the removal and who were aware, or should reasonably have been aware, that the goods were being removed from customs supervision, any persons who acquired or held the goods in question and who were aware, or should reasonably have been aware, at the time of acquiring or receiving them that they had been removed from customs supervision, and, where appropriate, the person required to fulfil the obligations arising from the temporary storage of the goods or from the customs procedure under which they were placed.[53]

Where customs duty is incurred pursuant to the above rules in respect of goods released for free circulation at a reduced rate of import duty on account of their end use, the amount of duty paid on release for free circulation is deducted from the amount of the customs debt.[54]

2.3 *Failure to fulfil obligations or comply with conditions*

A customs debt is incurred in the event of certain failures to comply with obligations or conditions.[55] The failures in question, which do not include those mentioned above, are first, failures to fulfil obligations in respect of goods liable to import duty arising from their temporary storage or from the use of the customs procedure under which they are placed and, secondly, failures to comply with a condition governing the placing of the goods under the relevant customs procedure, or the granting of a reduced or zero rate of import duty by virtue of the end use of goods. A customs debt is not imposed, however, if it is established that the failures have no significant effect on the correct operation of the temporary storage or customs procedure in question. Certain failures, listed in the Implementing Regulation, Article 859, are considered to 'have no significant effect' provided that specified requirements are met. These are: that the failures do not constitute an attempt to remove the goods unlawfully from

---

[51] Case C–66/99 *D Wandel GmbH v Hauptzollamt Bremen*, n 32 above, paras 47 and 48.
[52] Ibid, at para 50.
[53] CCC, Art 203.3.
[54] Ibid, Art 208. This rule applies *mutatis mutandis* where the customs debt is incurred in respect of scrap and waste resulting from the destruction of such goods.
[55] Ibid, Art 204.1.

customs supervision, that they do not imply obvious negligence[56] on the part of the person concerned, and that all the formalities necessary to regularize the situation of the goods are subsequently carried out.[57] A customs debt is to be regarded as having been incurred unless the person who would be the debtor establishes that the conditions contained in Article 859 are fulfilled.[58]

The failures listed at 1–10 of Article 859 are as follows:

1. Exceeding the time limit allowed for assignment of the goods to one of the customs-approved treatments or uses where the time limit would have been extended had an extension been applied for in time.
2. Exceeding the time limit for presentation of goods under the transit procedure to the office of destination where presentation takes place.
3. Unauthorized handling of goods placed in temporary storage, or under the customs warehousing procedure, where authorization would have been forthcoming if sought.
4. Use of goods under the temporary importation procedure in an unauthorized manner, provided that the use would have been authorized under the procedure if authorization had been sought.
5. Unauthorized movement of goods in temporary storage or placed under a customs procedure, provided that the goods can be presented to the customs authorities at their request.
6. Removal of goods in temporary storage, or entered for a customs procedure, from the Community customs territory, or their entry into a free zone, principally based on the existence of a fence (ie of control-type I)[59] or free warehouse, without completion of the necessary formalities.
7. Transfer of goods, which have received favourable tariff treatment by reason of their end use, without notification to the customs authorities and before they have been put to their intended use, provided that the transfer is recorded in the transferor's stock records and the transferee is the holder of an authorization for the goods in question.
8. In respect of goods eligible on release for free circulation for total or partial relief from import duties under outward processing relief and while the goods are in temporary storage, or under another customs procedure, prior to such release: (i) failure to fulfil one of the obligations

---

[56] As to the nature of 'obvious negligence' see Ch 13.

[57] The fact that the failures do not give rise to a customs debt does not prevent the application of the criminal law or of provisions allowing the cancellation and withdrawal of authorizations issued under the customs procedure in question: Implementing Regulation, Art 861.

[58] Implementing Regulation, Art 860. In Case C–48/98 *Firma Söhl & Söhlke v Hauptzollamt Bremen* [1999] ECR I–7877 it was held that a national court was able to determine whether the criteria in Art 859.1 were satisfied (where a timeous application for an extension had been refused by a decision of a customs authority which became unappealable): see para 63f.

[59] See further Implementing Regulation, Art 799.

arising from their temporary storage or from the use of the customs procedure under which they are placed and (ii) failure to comply with a condition governing the placing of the goods under that procedure or the granting of a reduced or zero rate of import duty by virtue of the end use of the goods.

9. In the framework of inward processing and processing under customs control, exceeding the time limit allowed for submission of the bill of discharge, provided that the limit would have been extended had an extension been applied for in time.

10. Exceeding the time limit allowed for temporary removal from a customs warehouse, provided that the limit would have been extended had an extension been applied for in time.

The customs debt is incurred at one of two alternative times. The first alternative is the moment when the relevant obligation ceases to be met. The second is the moment when the goods are placed under the relevant customs procedure where it is subsequently established that a condition, governing either the placing of the goods under the relevant customs procedure or the granting of a reduced or zero rate of import duty by virtue of the end use of the goods, was not in fact fulfilled.[60] The debtor is the person who is required either to fulfil the obligations arising from the temporary storage of the goods or from the use of the customs procedure under which they have been placed, or is required to comply with the conditions governing the placing of the goods under that procedure.[61] The duty paid on release for free circulation is deducted from the duty which is due.[62]

2.4 *Unauthorized consumption or use of goods*

A customs debt is incurred where goods liable to import duties are consumed, or used in a free zone or free warehouse, under conditions other than those laid down by the legislation in force.[63] In the event that such goods disappear and their disappearance cannot be explained to the satisfaction of the customs authorities, the authorities may regard the goods as having been so consumed or used.[64] The debt is incurred at the moment when the goods are consumed, or are first used under conditions other than those laid down.[65] The debtor is the person who consumed or used the goods and any person who participated in the consumption or use and who was aware, or should reasonably have been aware, that the goods were being consumed or used under conditions

---

[60] CCC, Art 204.2.
[61] Ibid, Art 204.3.
[62] Ibid, Art 208.
[63] Ibid, Art 205.1, first para.
[64] Ibid, Art 205.1, second para.
[65] Ibid, Art 205.2.

other than those laid down by the legislation in force.[66] Where goods which have disappeared are regarded as having been consumed or used, the person liable for payment of the customs debt is the last person known to the customs authorities to have been in possession of them.[67]

2.5 *Two situations in which there is no debt on importation*

Notwithstanding the provisions of CCC, Articles 202 and 204 discussed above, there are two situations in which no customs debt on importation is deemed to be incurred in respect of specific goods. They are, first, where the person concerned proves that the non-fulfilment of certain obligations[68] results from the total destruction, or irretrievable loss, of the goods as a result of their actual nature, ie natural wastage, unforeseeable circumstances, *force majeure*, or as a consequence of authorization by the customs authorities.[69] Goods are regarded as irretrievably lost when they are rendered unusable by any person.[70] The customs authorities must, when asked by the person concerned, take account of quantities of goods missing wherever it can be shown that the losses observed result solely from the nature of the goods and not from any negligence or manipulation on the part of the person in question.[71] It is provided that negligence or manipulation means, in particular, any failure to observe the rules for transporting, storing, handling, working, or processing the goods in question, imposed by the customs authorities or by normal practice.[72] The obligation to show from what the losses resulted rests on the person concerned. Nevertheless, the obligation to show that goods were irretrievably lost for reasons inherent in their nature, ie by reason of natural wastage, may be waived by the customs authorities where they are satisfied that there is no other explanation for the loss.[73] Where the person concerned cannot show that the level of irretrievable loss due to the nature of the goods exceeds that produced by the application of standard rates established under the national law of Member States, then the national provisions governing standard rates are to be applied.[74]

The second situation in which no customs debt on importation arises is where goods, released for free circulation at a reduced or zero rate of import

---

[66] CCC, Art 205.3, first para.   [67] Ibid, Art 205.3, second para.

[68] The obligations in question are those which arise from CCC, Arts 38–41 and the second indent of CCC, Art 177 or from keeping the goods in question in temporary storage and from the use of the customs procedure under which the goods have been placed: ibid, Art 206.1.

[69] Ibid, Art 206.1, first para. Note that where no customs debt is deemed to be incurred in respect of goods released for free circulation at a reduced or zero rate of import duty on account of their end use, any scrap or waste resulting from the destruction is deemed to be non-Community goods: ibid, Art 207.

[70] Ibid, Art 206.2, second para.   [71] Implementing Regulation, Art 862.1.

[72] Ibid, Art 862.2.   [73] Ibid, Art 863.

[74] Ibid, Art 864.

duty by virtue of their end-use, are exported or re-exported with the permission of the customs authorities.[75]

2.6 *Reliefs and exemptions*

In relation to customs debts on importation which are incurred on a breach of conditions or obligations,[76] exemption, relief or favourable treatment,[77] remains available so long as the behaviour of the declarant implies neither fraudulent dealing nor manifest negligence and evidence is produced that the other conditions for the application of relief or exemption have been satisfied.[78]

3. *The debt on exportation*

A customs debt on exportation is incurred by reason of the exportation from the customs territory, under cover of a customs declaration, of goods liable to export duties. The debt is incurred at the time when the customs declaration is accepted. The debtor is the declarant. In the event of indirect representation, the person on whose behalf the declaration is made is also a debtor.[79]

4. *The debt on exportation for breach of customs law*

As with the debt on importation, the debt on exportation can be incurred by virtue of a breach of customs law. The breaches which give rise to a debt are set out below.

4.1 *Removal of goods from the customs territory without a declaration*

A customs debt is incurred by reason of the removal from the customs territory of goods liable to export duties without a customs declaration. The time at which the debt is incurred is the time at which the goods leave the territory, and the debtor is the person who removed the goods and any person who participated in the removal and who was aware, or should reasonably have been aware, that a customs declaration had not been lodged but should have been.[80]

---

[75] CCC, Art 206.2.

[76] ie pursuant to CCC, Arts 202–205 and 210–211.

[77] ie pursuant to CCC, Arts 21 (favourable treatment by reason of nature or end-use), 82 (release of goods at reduced or zero rate by reason of end-use), 145 (outward processing), or 184–187 (reliefs from customs duty).

[78] CCC, Art 212a as introduced pursuant to Regulation (EC) 2700/2000, of the European Parliament and the Council of 16 Nov 2000 [2000] OJ L311/17.

[79] CCC, Art 209.1–3.

[80] Ibid, Art 210.1–3.

4.2 *Failure to comply with conditions*

The debt on exportation is also incurred through failure to comply with the conditions under which the goods were allowed to leave the customs territory with total or partial relief from export duties. The debt is incurred at the time when the goods reach a destination other than that for which they were allowed to leave the territory with total or partial relief from duty. If the customs authorities are unable to determine that time, the debt is incurred on the expiry of the time limit set for production of evidence that the conditions entitling the goods to relief have been fulfilled. The debtor is the declarant. In the event of indirect representation it is also the person on whose behalf the declaration is made.[81]

4.3 *Reliefs and exemptions*

The same provision, namely CCC 212a, applies in relation to reliefs and exemptions as applies in relation to the debt on importation dealt with above.

C. THE SIGNIFICANCE OF THE TIME AND PLACE AT WHICH A CUSTOMS DEBT IS INCURRED

As we have seen, the time at which a customs debt is incurred is specified in relation to each means by which the debt is incurred. The time at which the debt is incurred is of importance for at least three reasons. The first of these is that the three-year limitation period applicable to the collection of customs duty runs from the date on which the liability was incurred.[82] Secondly, except where otherwise expressly provided in the CCC, the amount of customs duty due is to be determined on the basis of the rules of assessment appropriate to the goods in question at the time when the customs debt is incurred.[83] Where it is impossible to determine this time precisely, the time by reference to which due duty is to be determined is the time when the customs authorities conclude that the goods are in a situation in which a customs debt is incurred.[84] If the information available to them enables them to establish that the debt was incurred prior to the time of such conclusion, the requisite time is the earliest time at which the existence of a customs debt may be established from the information available.[85] Delay by Member States cannot, therefore, lead to a loss of resources by the Community. Protection of Community resources is also achieved because compensatory interest is payable in order to prevent the

---

[81] CCC, Art 211.1–3.   [82] Ibid, Art 221.1.
[83] Ibid, Art 214.1.
[84] Ibid, Art 214.2, first para.
[85] Ibid, Art 214.2, second para.

wrongful acquisition of a financial advantage by deferment of the date on which the customs debt was incurred or entered in the accounts.[86] The third reason the time at which the customs debt is incurred is important is that it is inextricably linked to the place where the debt is incurred, and the customs authorities of the place where the customs debt is incurred, or is deemed to have been incurred, are the customs authorities charged with calculating and collecting the customs debt.[87]

The place at which a customs debt is incurred is to be determined, primarily, by reference to three rules. The first one specifies that a customs debt is incurred at the place where the events from which it arises occur.[88] If that place cannot be determined, then it is incurred at the place where the customs authorities conclude that the goods are in a situation in which a customs debt is incurred.[89] If the location at which the debt is incurred cannot be determined by these two rules within ten months from acceptance of a transit declaration,[90] and the goods in question have been entered for a customs procedure which has not been discharged, then a third rule applies. This provides that the place at which the customs debt is incurred is the place where the goods were either placed under the procedure concerned, or where they were introduced into the Community customs territory under that procedure.[91] The customs authorities may be able to establish that the customs debt had already been incurred when the goods were in another place at an earlier date. If so, the customs debt is deemed to have been incurred at the place which may be established as the location of the goods at the earliest time when the existence of the customs debt may be established.[92]

D. RECOVERING A CUSTOMS DEBT

We noted in the section above that the customs authorities of the place where the customs debt is incurred, or is deemed to have been incurred, are the authorities responsible for calculating and collecting the customs debt. In this

---

[86] CCC, Art 214.3.
[87] Ibid, Art 215.3.
[88] Ibid, Art 215.1, first indent.
[89] Ibid, Art 215.1, second indent.
[90] Implementing Regulation, Art 450a.
[91] Ibid, Art 215.1, third indent.
[92] Ibid, Art 215.2. Under Regulation (EC) 2700/2000, n 78 above, new provisions on customs debt and recovery have been inserted into the Implementing Regulation. In addition to Art 450a, referred to at n 90 above, there are Arts 450b–d. These govern relations between customs authorities and between customs authorities and guarantors. See further Ch 10 at p 320. In addition, para 4 is added to CCC, Art 215. It provides that if a customs authority finds that a customs debt, lower than EUR 5,000, has been incurred under CCC, Art 202 in another Member State, the debt shall be deemed to have been incurred in the Member State in which the finding was made.

section we turn to consider the procedures which have to be adopted in order for recovery to be effected. There are three preliminary stages to recovery. First, the debt must be calculated; secondly, it must be entered in the accounts; and, thirdly, it must be communicated to the debtor. Each of these stages is dealt with below. Having been communicated, the debt is then to be paid. If it is not paid collection must, of course, be enforced, subject to any appeal there may be. The role of Member States and of national law in the collection process has been noted in Chapter 4, and the national character of the appeals processes is considered in Chapter 13.

1. *Calculating the debt*

Except in certain special cases, customs debts, whether of import or export duty, are to be calculated by customs authorities 'as soon as they have the necessary particulars' and must then be entered by them in accounting records or on any other equivalent medium.[93] There are three exceptions to this rule.[94] It does not apply where, first, a provisional anti-dumping or countervailing duty is introduced; secondly, it does not apply where the amount of duty legally due exceeds that determined on the basis of binding information;[95] and, thirdly, it does not apply where customs authorities are permitted to waive entry into the accounts for amounts of duty below a given level (considered below). In addition, customs authorities may discount amounts of duty which could not be communicated to the debtor within three years from the date on which the customs debt was incurred.[96]

2. *Entry in the accounts*

As we saw in Chapter 1, Member States must keep an account of the Community's own resources and CCC, Article 217.1 imposes an obligation on the Member States to enter amounts of duty in the accounts. The Member States are to determine the practical procedures for such entry, and the procedures may vary depending upon whether or not the customs authorities are satisfied that the amounts of duty will be paid.[97] There are a number of situations in which entry into the accounts is, however, not to take place. These are considered below. For the moment it is enough to note that, unsurprisingly,

---

[93] CCC, Art 217.1.
[94] Ibid, Art 217.1(a)–(c), second sub-para. See Ch 13, pp 412f.
[95] See Ch 5, p 151, re the issue of binding information.
[96] CCC, Art 217.1, third sub-para.
[97] Ibid, Art 217.2. A recent reference to the Court of Justice, concerning legislation prior to the CCC, raises issues such as the nature of entry in the accounts, the precise time at which customs duty becomes payable etc: see Case C–203/01 *Fazenda Pública v Antero & CCᵃ, Ldᵃ* [2001] OJ C227/9.

there is no obligation on Member States to enter in the accounts amounts of duty less than ECU 10, and there is no post-clearance recovery of duty where the amount of duty per recovery action is less than ECU 10.[98] The phrase 'recovery action' refers to each individual import or export transaction. Were it otherwise the ECU 10 limit could nearly always be circumvented by adding together amounts of duty due. Actions for recovery of amounts exceeding ECU 10 can, however, be combined.[99]

2.1 *Time limits for entry in the accounts*

Just as the calculations of duty are to be made as soon as the necessary particulars are available, the entry of the amounts of duty in the accounts is, generally, also to be effected 'as soon as it has been calculated' or, at the latest, on the second day following that on which the goods were released. These rules apply where a customs debt is incurred as the result of the acceptance of the declaration of goods for a customs procedure, other than temporary importation with partial relief from import duties, or of any other act having the same effect as the acceptance.[100] In respect of customs debts which are otherwise incurred, entry into the accounts is to be made within two days of the date on which the customs authorities are in a position to calculate the amount of duty in question and determine the debtor.[101] Where it is provided that goods may be released subject to meeting certain conditions laid down by Community legislation, governing either the determination of the amount of the debt or its collection, entry in the accounts is to take place no later than two days following the day on which the amount of the debt, or the obligation to pay the duties resulting from that debt, is determined or fixed.[102]

Where payment of duty has been secured, a single entry in the accounts may be made in respect of the total amount of duty relating to all goods released to the same person during a period, fixed by the customs authorities, not exceeding thirty-one days. Any such single entry must be made within five days of the expiry of the period in question.[103] Where the customs debt relates to a provisional anti-dumping or countervailing duty, it is to be entered in the accounts no later than two months following publication, in the *Official Journal*, of the regulation establishing a definitive anti-dumping or countervailing duty.[104]

---

[98] Implementing Regulation, Art 868.
[99] See Case 214/84 *Stinnes AG v Hauptzollamt Kassel* [1985] ECR 4045 at paras 10–14 which was decided on the pre-consolidated legislation, but the reasoning in which is equally applicable to the current legislation.
[100] CCC, Art 218.1, first sub-para. See also Implementing Regulation, Art 546, second sub-para.
[101] Ibid, Art 218.3.   [102] Ibid, Art 218.2, first para.
[103] Ibid, Art 218.1, second sub-para.
[104] Ibid, Art 218.2, second para.

The time limits applicable to the entry of duty in the accounts are designed 'to ensure rapid and uniform application by the competent administrative authorities of the technical procedures for the entry in the accounts of amounts of import or export duties'.[105] Failure to observe the time limits does not give rise to rights on the part of traders and failure of the customs authorities to observe them does not nullify their right and duty to collect customs duty, although it may result in a liability on the part of the Member State to pay interest on own resources to the Communities.[106]

2.2 Extension of time periods

The time periods for entry in the accounts which are set out above may be extended for reasons relating to the administrative organization of the Member States and, in particular, where accounts are centralized. The periods may also be extended where special circumstances prevent compliance with them. Except in respect of unforeseeable circumstances, or in cases of *force majeure*, the time limits are not to be extended by more than fourteen days.[107]

2.3 Subsequent entry into the accounts

Specific provision is made for situations in which the time limits for entry into the accounts have not been observed and those where the amount of duty entered is lower than the amount actually owed. In these circumstances, the amount of duty owed, or the amount which remains to be recovered, must be entered in the accounts within two days of the date on which the customs authorities became aware of the situation and are in a position to calculate the amount legally owed and determine the debtor. The time limit of two days may be extended in accordance with the rules discussed above.[108]

This 'subsequent entry in the accounts', as it is known, is not to occur in three situations.[109] The first is, where the original decision not to enter duty in

---

[105] Case C–370/96 *Covita AVE v Elliniko Dimsoio* [1998] ECR I–1771, para 36.

[106] See ibid, which was concerned with the periods now appearing in CCC, Art 218.1 first para, 218.2 first para and 218.3. The principle that traders obtain no rights for breach of the time periods applies also to the requirement that the debt shall be communicated to the debtor '[a]s soon as' it has been entered in the accounts in CCC, Art 221.1: see Case C–61/98 *De Haan Beheer BV v Inspecteur der Invoerrechten en Accijnzen te Rotterdam* [1999] ECR I–5003 at paras 34 and 35. See also Ch 2 at 'The financial context of customs duty: own resources'.

[107] CCC, Art 219.1 and 2.

[108] Ibid, Art 220.1.

[109] See ibid, Art 220.2(a)–(c). The prohibitions on entry in the accounts are stated to apply except in the cases referred to in the second and third sub-paras of CCC, Art 217.1 discussed at p 387. By stating that 'subsequent entry in the accounts *shall* not occur' (emphasis added) Art 220.2 makes clear that the person concerned is entitled to a waiver of customs duty where the conditions apply. Under the previous legislation, namely Art 5.2 of Council Regulation (EEC) 1697/79 of 24 July 1979 [1979] OJ L197/1, the position was not so clear and it was left to the

the accounts, or to enter it in the accounts at a figure less than the amount of duty actually owed, was taken on the basis of general provisions invalidated at a later date by a court decision. The second is where the failure to enter in the accounts the amount of duty legally owed (i) was the result of an error on the part of the customs authorities, (ii) which could not reasonably have been detected by the person liable for payment, and (iii) that person has acted in good faith and complied with all the provisions laid down by the legislation in force as regards the customs declaration.[110] The third situation where the customs authority is exempted from subsequently entering in the accounts amounts of duty less than a certain figure.[111]

The second situation in which entry in the accounts is prohibited, namely where there has been an error on the part of the customs authorities which could not reasonably be detected by the person concerned who has acted properly and in good faith, frequently founds a claim for remission or repayment of a customs debt in respect of which the authorities are seeking post-clearance recovery. The case law on it is, therefore, considered in the next chapter. It should be noted, however, that it has been the subject of much debate and important additions to the legislation have recently been made.[112]

3. Communication to the debtor

As soon as the amount of duty has been entered in the accounts, it is to be communicated to the debtor in accordance with the appropriate procedures.[113] It is specifically provided that communication to the debtor is not to take place after the expiry of a period of three years from the date on which the customs debt was incurred.[114] Unlike the time limits applicable for entry in the

---

Court of Justice to state it: see, eg, Case 314/85 *Foto-Frost v Hauptzollamt Lüebeck-Ost* [1987] ECR 4199 at para 22. See also Ch 13, n 21.

[110] The Court of Justice has emphasized that, in order to fall within this situation, all three requirements specified must be met: Case 161/88 *Friedrich Binder GmbH & Co KG v Hauptzollamt Bad Reichenhall* [1989] ECR 2415 para 15. See also Joined Cases T–10/97 and 11/97 *Unifrigo Gadus Srl and CPL Imperial 2 SpA v Commission* [1998] ECR II–2231 at para 54 (Case C–299/98 P [1999] ECR I–8683 appeal manifestly inadmissible and manifestly unfounded), Case C–348/89 *Mecanarte-Metalúrgica da Lagoa Ldᵃ v Chefe do Serviço da Conferência Final da Alfândega do Porto* [1991] ECR I–3277at para 12, Case C–250/91 *Hewlett Packard France v Directeur Général des Douanes* [1993] ECR I–1819, para 12 and 13, Joined Cases C–153/94 and C–204/94 *The Queen v Commissioners of Customs and Excise, ex p Faroe Seafood Co Ltd, Føroya Fiskasøla LF and another* [1996] ECR I–2465, para 83, and Case C–370/96 *Covita AVE v Greece* at n 105 above, at paras 24–28, Case C–61/98 *De Haan Beheer BV v Inspecteur der Iuvoerrechten en Accijnzen te Rotterdam,* n 106 above, at para 39 and Case C–15/99 *Hans Sommer GmbH and Co KG v Hauptzollamt Bremen* [2000] ECR I–8989, para 35.

[111] See Implementing Regulation, Art 868.

[112] See the discussion in Chs 4 and 13.

[113] CCC, Art 221.1.

[114] Ibid, Art 221.3. A proposal that this period be reduced to two years has been rejected. It was made on the basis that the customs authorities be permitted to enter into the accounts, and

accounts, failure to observe the three-year period will result in the customs debt being unenforceable.

As we have seen, it is possible for a number of debts to be recovered by means of a single action. If one of these debts is irrecoverable because it has been communicated to the debtor in breach of the three-year period, national law is to be applied in determining whether or not the entire recovery action fails.[115] In England and Wales, whilst a debt communicated to the debtor outside the three-year period is unenforceable, any other debts demanded pursuant to a single demand will be recoverable.[116]

The main qualifications to the requirement of communication within the three-year period are made in relation to appeals and criminal proceedings. So far as appeals are concerned, the three-year period is suspended, from the time that an appeal, within CCC, Article 243, is lodged, for the duration of the appeal proceedings.[117] So far as criminal court proceedings[118] are concerned, it is now provided that where the customs debt is the result of an act which, at the time it was committed, was liable to give rise to criminal court proceedings, communication to the debtor may take place after the expiry of the three-year period, under the conditions set out in the provisions in force.[119] In one case, however, there is no need to communicate the amount of the debt to the debtor at all. This is where the duty due is entered in the customs declaration for guidance and the amount so entered corresponds to the amount of duty due. In these circumstances, customs authorities may specify that the amount is not to be communicated.[120] Where they do so, the release of the goods by the authorities is equivalent to communication to the debtor of the amount of duty entered in the accounts.[121]

communicate to the debtor, a provisional amount of duty and be allowed three years from the date of communication to establish the correct amount: see Art 1.21–22. Proposal for a European Parliament and Council Regulation (EC) amending Council Regulation (EEC) 2913/92 establishing the Community Customs Code at 3 June 1998 [1998] OJ C228/8.

Note that the date of communication is important in determining the time period within which an application for repayment or remission of duty may be made: see CCC, Art 236.2.

[115] Joined Cases C–153/94 and C–204/94 *The Queen v Commissioners of Customs and Excise, ex p Faroe Seafood Co. Ltd, Føroya Fiskasøla LF and another*, at n 110 above, at para 71.

[116] *Nortrade Foods Ltd v CCE* [1998] V&DR 133 at 155.

[117] Art 221.3 introduced by Regulation (EC) 2700/2000, n 78 above, Art 1.17.

[118] It was said in relation to the predecessor of the present provisions that the criminal court proceedings referred to are those in the country which is seeking to effect post-clearance recovery. The Court of Justice has acknowledged that this can lead to different results in different Member States but noted that this arises from the fact that the classification of offences is not harmonized under Community law: see Case C–273/90 *Meico-Fell v Hauptzollamt Darmstadt* [1991] ECR I–5569 para 12.

[119] Art 221.4, introduced by Regulation (EC) 2700/2000, n 78 above, Art 1.17. See too the reference in Case C–203/01 *Fazenda Pública v Antero & CCᵃ Ldᵃ*, see n 97 above

[120] This is without prejudice to the operation of the five-day time limit for entry into the accounts where a single entry is to be made in respect of goods released over a period of time: CCC, Art 221.2 second para and Art 218.1, second para.

[121] Ibid, Art 221.2.

E. POST-CLEARANCE RECOVERY

Since 1 July 1980 the Community has made provision for post-clearance recovery[122] and, under the CCC, the obligations imposed on Member States to calculate duty, enter it into in the accounts, communicate it to the debtor, and recover it are applicable to duty which is discovered to be due after, as well as before, clearance.[123]

Post-clearance recovery becomes necessary in a variety of circumstances. The most well known of these is, probably, where certificates of origin which have been relied upon to ensure that goods are preferentially treated have been subsequently found to be invalid for some reason. Of course, it is not just the invalidity of certificates of origin which may give rise to post-clearance recovery. It may be that the rules of origin have been discovered to have been incorrectly applied.[124] Post-clearance recovery may, naturally, become necessary for a number of other reasons unconnected with origin. For example, the rules for the valuation of the goods in question may have been improperly applied,[125] the wrong tariff classification may have been adopted,[126] or the calculations of duty may have been wrongly made.[127]

There is no doubt that post-clearance recovery and the ability of traders to resist it is of major economic significance both to the trader, who frequently faces severe financial difficulty as a result of post-clearance demands, and to the Community at large. In a report presented by the Commission on 'The Recovery of Traditional Own Resources in Cases of Fraud and Irregularities (Sample 98)',[128] the Commission considered nine cases in which fraud or

---

[122] By virtue of Council Regulation (EEC) 1697/79 of 24 July 1979 [1979] OJ L197/1. See also Council Regulation (EEC) 1430/79 of 2 July 1979 [1979] OJ L175/1, which was concerned with the repayment and remission of duties. Prior to these regulations the matter was governed by national law: see Case 265/78 *H Ferwerda BV v Produktschap voor Vee en Vlees* [1980] ECR 617, paras 9 and 10.

[123] A specific obligation to make post-clearance recovery of customs duty, as appeared in Council Regulation (EEC) 1697/79, see n 122 above, Art 2.1 is not necessary in the CCC. CCC, Art 217.1, requires calculation and entry into the accounts of '[e]ach and every amount of import duty or export duty resulting from a customs debt' and Art 232, obliging customs authorities to take action to ensure payment of duty, applies, '[w]here the amount of duty has not been paid'. The obligation of the Member States to undertake post-clearance recovery has been noted in, among other cases: Joined Cases T–10/97 and 11/97 *Unifrigo Gadus Srl and CPL Imperial 2 SpA v Commission* at n 110 above, para 38 and Joined Cases C–153/94 and C–204/94 *The Queen v Commissioners of Customs and Excise, ex parte Faroe Seafood Co Ltd, Føroya Fiskasøla LF and another*, para 16 and Case C–21/92 *Criminal Proceedings against Edmond Huygen* [1994] ECR I–6381, para 17.

[124] See, eg, Case C–26/88 *Brother International GmbH v Hauptzollamt Gießen* [1989] ECR 4253, which concerned anti-dumping duty.

[125] See, eg, Case 357/87 *Firme Albert Schmid v Hauptzollamt Stuttgart-West* [1988] ECR 6239. See also Case C–15/99 *Hans Sommer GmbH and Co KG v Hauptzollamt Bremen* at n 110 above.

[126] See, eg, Case 387/78 *Top Hit Holzvertrieb GmbH v Commission* [1989] ECR 1359.

[127] See, eg, Case 214/84 *Stinnes AG v Hauptzollamt Kassel* [1985] ECR 4045 para 3.

[128] See COM(1999)160 Final, 21 Apr 1999.

irregularity had arisen in which a total of 136 million ECU was in issue. The nine cases concerned a wide variety of goods from around the world; clothing from Laos, textiles from Cambodia, tuna from Costa Rica, car radios from Indonesia, bicycles from Vietnam, and beef from Argentina. The possibility of post-clearance recovery and the prospects for repayment or remission are of concern, therefore, to importers whatever their trade.

Clearly, in any situation in which post-clearance recovery is commenced, a trader may wish to demonstrate that the provisions of CCC, Article 220.2(b) are met, so that a right to repayment or remission of the duty may be established.[129] Under CCC, Article 236.2, the customs authorities themselves are to repay or remit duty on their own initiative where they discover, within three years of communication of the debt to the debtor, that the debtor is entitled to such repayment or remission under CCC, Article 236.1.[130] It should also be noted, however, that proceeding with post-clearance recovery, where a trader has not established that he has satisfied the requirements of Article 220.2(b), is not in contravention of the right to property contained in Article 1 to Protocol 1 of the European Convention on Human Rights and Fundamental Freedoms of 1950. Neither is it contrary to the principle of proportionality. The fact that the duties cannot be recovered from the importer, who will be exposed to insolvency if recovery proceeds, and that the sum at stake is large, does not alter the position.[131]

1. National authorities, post-clearance recovery, and non-entry in the accounts

National customs authorities are to decide not to enter uncollected duties in the accounts in three limited situations.[132] The first of these is where preferential tariff treatment has been applied, in the context of a tariff quota, a tariff ceiling, or other arrangements, when at the time of acceptance of the customs declaration, entitlement to such preferential treatment had been terminated. The termination must either not have been published in the *Official Journal* before the release for free circulation of the goods in question or, the termination not being published, must not have been made known in an appropriate manner in the Member State concerned. The person liable for payment must have acted in good faith and complied with all the provisions laid down by the legislation in force as regards the customs declaration. The second situation in

---

[129] Pursuant to CCC, Art 236.1, first sub-para CCC, Art 220.2(b) concerns an undetectable error by the authorities: see Ch 13, pp 412f.

[130] Compare the position under Council Regulation (EEC) 1697/79, in 122 above, as stated in Joined Cases C–153/94 and C–204/94 *The Queen v Commissioners of Customs and Excise, ex p Faroe Seafood Co Ltd, Føroya Fiskasøla LF and another* at n 110 above, para 76.

[131] Joined Cases C–153/94 and C–204/94 *The Queen v Commissioners of Customs and Excise, ex p Faroe Seafood Co Ltd, Føroya Fiskasøla LF and another* at n 110 above, para 116. See also Case C–97/95 *Pascoal & Filhos Ld^a v Fazenda Pública*, in n 35 above, at para 55.

[132] Implementing Regulation, Art 869 (a)–(c).

which national authorities are to decide not to enter a debt in the accounts, is where the customs authorities consider that the provisions of Article 220.2.(b) are fulfilled, provided that the amount not collected from the operator concerned in respect of one or more import or export operations but in consequence of a single error, is less than ECU 50,000. The third situation is where the Member State in question has been authorized by the Commission not to enter uncollected duty in the accounts.[133] Member States are required to keep a list of the cases in which they do not enter duty in the accounts on one of these three grounds which is to be at the disposal of the Commission.[134]

2. *The Commission, post-clearance recovery, and non-entry in the accounts*

The procedure whereby the Commission decides whether or not duty should be entered in the accounts comes into operation where customs authorities consider that the conditions laid down in Article 220.2(b) are fulfilled or are in doubt about the precise scope of the criteria in regard to a particular case. Where this is so the customs authorities must submit the case to the Commission so that it can take a decision.[135] The case submitted to the Commission must contain all the information required for a full examination. It must also contain a signed statement from the person concerned, certifying that he has read the statement and has nothing to add, or listing the additional information which he considers should be included.[136] The Commission must inform the Member State as soon as it receives the case and may request the provision of additional information if it is found that the information supplied is not sufficient to enable a decision to be taken in full knowledge of the facts.[137] It must also forward a copy of the case to the Member States within fifteen days of receipt of it. Consideration of the case is then to be included on the agenda of a meeting of the Customs Code Committee as soon as possible.[138] The Commission is to decide whether the circumstances are such that duty should be entered in the accounts, after consulting a group of experts composed of representatives of all Member States meeting within the framework of the Committee.[139] The decision is to be taken within nine months of the date on which the case is received by the Commission. In cases where additional information has been sought, the nine-month period is extended by a

[133] In accordance with Implementing Regulation, Art 875.
[134] Ibid, Art 870.
[135] Delay in doing so will not affect the liability of the trader to pay duty which is found to be due. Neither will the lapse of a significant period of time between the date of the importation and the date of the adoption of a decision by the Commission: Joined Cases T–10/97 and 11/97 *Unifrigo Gadus Srl and CPL Imperial 2 SpA v Commission* at n 110 above, para 44.
[136] Implementing Regulation, Art 871, para 1.
[137] Ibid, Art 871, second and third paras.
[138] Ibid, Art 872.
[139] Ibid, Art 873, first para.

period equivalent to that which passed between the date on which the request for additional information was sent and the date on which the information was received.[140]

As a result of recent amendments to the CCC, where at any point in the procedure described, the Commission intends to take a decision which is unfavourable to the person concerned, it must communicate its objections to the person in writing, together with all the documents on which the objections are based. The person concerned then has one month from the date on which the objections were sent to express a point of view. Failure to do so means that they are deemed to have waived their right to express a position.[141] Where the Commission has communicated its objections to the person concerned in accordance with this procedure, the nine-month period, referred to above, is to be extended by a period equivalent to that between the date on which the Commission sent the objections and the date on which it received the answer, or the expiry of the period permitted for provision of an answer.[142]

The powers which are conferred on the Commission are designed to ensure that Community law is uniformly applied.[143] It follows that the Commission is not required to agree with the national authorities which submitted the case to it. Neither, however, is it entitled to disregard the right of the trader to waiver of post-clearance recovery where the necessary conditions are satisfied.[144] It should also be noted that the Commission's powers are limited to deciding whether or not the requirements of Article 220.2(b) are satisfied. They do not extend to determining whether or not the demand by the national authorities for post-clearance recovery is lawful, or whether default interest is improperly demanded.[145]

Until a decision is taken, the debtor's obligation to pay duty is to be suspended, provided that where the goods are not under customs supervision

---

[140] Implementing Regulation, Art 873, second para.

[141] Ibid, Art 872a. This provision was introduced by Commission Regulation (EC) 1677/98 [1998] OJ L212/18, Art 1, para 6. See in particular Case T–42/96 *Eyckeler & Malt AG v Commission* [1998] ECR II–401 at para 80 (appealed by the Commission, see [1998] OJ C258/14 as Case C–163/98 P but removed from the register on 19 May 2000) and Case T–50/96 *Primex Produkte Import-Export GmbH & Co KG, Gebr. Kruse GmbH, Interporc Im- und Export GmbH v Commission* [1998] ECR II–3773 (appealed by the Commission, see [1999] OJ C1/11 as Case C–417/98 P, but removed from the register on 10 May 2000) at paras 63–70 which deals with the right to be heard. The matter is further considered in Ch 13.

[142] Implementing Regulation, Art 873, para 3.

[143] Joined Cases T–10 and 11/97 *Unifrigo Gadus Srl and CPL Imperial 2 SpA v Commission* at n 110, para 29. See also Case C–64/89 *Hauptzollamt Gießen v Deutsche Fernsprecher GmbH* [1990] ECR I–2535, para 13, Case C–348/89 *Mecanarte—Metalúrgica da Lagoa Ld^a v Chefe do Servico da Conferencia Final da Alfandega do Porto* at n 110 above, at para 33, and Joined Cases C–153/94 and C–204/94 *The Queen v Commissioners of Customs and Excise, ex p Faroe Seafood Co. Ltd, Føroya Fiskasøla LF and another* at n 110, para 80.

[144] Joined Cases T–10 and 11/97 *Unifrigo Gadus Srl and CPL Imperial 2 SpA v Commission* at n 110 above, at paras 30 and 31.

[145] Ibid at paras 81–84 and para 87.

security is lodged for the amount of the duties.[146] There are, however, three other conditions which must be met for suspension to be effective.[147] First, in cases where a request for invalidation of a declaration has been presented, this request must be likely to be met. Secondly, in cases where a request for remission has been presented, pursuant to CCC, Article 236 in conjunction with CCC, Article 220.2(b) or pursuant to CCC, Article 238 or 239,[148] the customs authorities must consider that the conditions laid down in the relevant provision may be regarded as having been fulfilled. Thirdly, in other cases where a request has been presented for remission pursuant to CCC, Article 236, the conditions referred to in the second paragraph of CCC, Article 244 must have been fulfilled, ie the customs authorities must have good reason to believe that the disputed decision is inconsistent with customs legislation or that irreparable damage is to be feared for the person concerned. The obligation to pay duty is also to be suspended if the customs authorities consider that the conditions for confiscation may be regarded as having been fulfilled and the conditions in Article 233(c) or (d) apply.[149]

A Member State is to be notified as soon as possible after a decision on entry into the accounts has been taken and in any event within thirty days of the expiry of the nine-month period (subject to extensions) which the Commission has in which to take a decision. A copy of the decision is also to be sent to the other Member States.[150] Where it is decided that duty is not to be entered in the accounts, the Commission may, under conditions which it is to determine, authorize one or more Member States to refrain from post-clearance entry in the accounts, in cases involving comparable issues of fact and law. Where this occurs, the original decision not to enter duty in the accounts is to be notified to each of the Member States which are so authorized.[151] If the Commission does not take a decision within the prescribed period, or fails to notify a decision to a Member State within the thirty-day period, then the Member State in question is not to enter the duties in question in the accounts.[152]

F. PAYMENT OF THE CUSTOMS DEBT[153]

Amounts of duty which are communicated to the debtor in accordance with

---

[146] Implementing Regulation, Art 876a.1, first para. Security is not necessary where its provision would be likely, owing to the debtor's circumstances to cause serious economic or social difficulties: see ibid, Art 876a.1, second para.

[147] See ibid, Art 876a.1(a)–(c).   [148] Considered in Ch 13.

[149] Ibid, Art 876a.2. The conditions in CCC, Art 233 are considered in section G below dealing with extinction of the customs debt.

[150] Implementing Regulation, Art 874.

[151] Ibid, Art 875.   [152] Ibid, Art 876.

[153] Payment of the customs debt is one of the matters dealt with in Chapter 4 of the General Annex to the revised Kyoto Convention.

CCC, Article 221 are to be paid within specified periods.[154] Payment of the debt is to be made in cash 'or by any other means with similar discharging effect' in accordance with the relevant provisions. Payment may also be made by way of an adjustment to a credit balance.[155] A third person, instead of the debtor, may pay the duty which is due.[156] Where payment of the debt is not made within the prescribed period, the customs authorities must avail themselves of all options open to them under the legislation in force, including, of course, enforcement, to secure payment of the debt. Special provisions may be, and indeed are, adopted in respect of guarantors within the framework of the transit procedure.[157]

1. *The obligation to pay, and the prescribed periods*

The obligation to pay customs duty may be deferred or suspended[158] or subject to other payment facilities granted to the debtor. Where payment is deferred or subject to payment facilities,[159] then payment is to be made no later than the end of the period relevant to the deferral or facility in question.[160] Where payment is not deferred, suspended, or subject to facilities, it must be made within the prescribed period. This is not to exceed ten days following communication to the debtor of the amount of the duty. Where a single entry in the accounts covers goods released to a person over a period of time, the prescribed period must not enable the debtor to obtain a longer period for payment than if he had been granted deferred payment. The prescribed period may be extended in two circumstances. First, an automatic extension is given where it is established that the person concerned received the communication too late to enable him to pay within the prescribed period. Secondly, an extension may be granted by the customs authorities where the amount of duty to be paid results from action for post-clearance recovery. Such extensions are not, however, to exceed the time necessary for the debtor to take appropriate steps to discharge his obligation.[161]

[154] CCC, Art 222.1. The length of the prescribed periods is dealt with below.
[155] Ibid, Art 223.
[156] Ibid, Art 231.1.
[157] Ibid, Art 232.1(a).
[158] According to CCC, Art 222.2, suspension may be provided for, in accordance with the committee procedure, where an application for remission of duty is made in accordance with ibid, Art 236, 238, or 239, or where goods are seized with a view to subsequent confiscation in accordance with the second indent of ibid, Art 233 point (c) or (d), or where the customs debt was incurred under ibid, Art 203, and there is more than one debtor. Note that the last situation was introduced by Regulation (EC) 2700/2000, n 78 above, Art 1.18.
[159] In accordance with CCC, Arts 224–229.
[160] Ibid, Art 222.1(b).
[161] Ibid, Art 222.1(a).

2. *Deferment of payment*

As a general rule, the customs authorities must grant deferment of payment of the duty for a thirty-day period, on request, provided that the duty relates to goods declared for a customs procedure which entails the obligation to pay it, subject to the conditions laid down in CCC, Articles 225–227 which are considered below.[162] Where, however, duty is entered in the accounts on the basis of an incomplete declaration by virtue of the fact that the declarant has not provided the information necessary for the valuation of the goods,[163] or has not supplied particulars or a document which was missing when the incomplete declaration was accepted,[164] payment may be deferred only if certain conditions are satisfied. The amount of duty to be recovered must be entered in the accounts before the expiry of thirty days from the date on which the amount originally charged was entered in the accounts or, if it was not so entered, from the date on which the declaration relating to the goods was accepted. Furthermore, the period of deferment is not to extend beyond the expiry of the period for which deferment was originally granted under CCC, Article 227, or which would have been granted had the amount of duty legally due been entered in the accounts when the goods were declared.[165] Of course, a debtor may pay all or part of the duty due without waiting for the expiry of the period granted for payment.[166]

2.1 *Methods of deferment*

There are three methods by which deferment of duty may be granted and the customs authorities may choose which method is to be adopted.[167] Whichever one is adopted, however, deferment will always be conditional on the applicant providing security. Deferral may also give rise to charges in respect of the incidental expenses for opening files or for services rendered.[168] Turning to the three methods of deferral, first,[169] it may be given separately in respect of each amount of duty (i) entered in the accounts under the conditions laid down in the first sub-paragraph of CCC, Article 218.1, ie in respect of customs debts incurred as a result of the acceptance, or its equivalent, of a declaration of goods for a customs procedure other than temporary importation with partial relief from import duty, or (ii) entered in the accounts late pursuant to Article 220.1.[170] Secondly, it may be granted globally in respect of all amounts of duty within (i) above entered in the accounts during a period fixed by customs authorities not exceeding thirty-one days.[171] Thirdly, it may be granted glob-

---

[162] CCC, Art 224.
[164] See, eg, ibid, Art 254.
[166] Ibid, Art 230.
[168] Ibid, Art 225.
[170] CCC, Arts 218.1 and 220.1 are considered at pp 388–9 above.

[163] See, eg, Implementing Regulation, Art 178.
[165] CCC, Art 228.1 and 2.
[167] Ibid, Art 226(a)–(c).
[169] See ibid, Art 226(a).
[171] Ibid, Art 226(b).

ally in respect of all amounts of duty forming a single entry in the accounts in accordance with the second sub-paragraph of CCC, Article 218.1. This permits, provided payment is secured, a single entry in the accounts in respect of duty attributable to goods released to one and the same person over a period not exceeding thirty-one days.[172]

2.2 Periods of deferment

As we noted above, the period for which payment is to be deferred is thirty days.[173] There are, however, specific rules governing the period depending upon the method of deferment used. Where it is granted under the first method noted above, the period is calculated from the day following the date on which the amount of duty is entered in the accounts.[174] If the time period for entry into the accounts has been extended under CCC, Article 219, the deferment period must be reduced by the number of days taken to enter the amount in the accounts, less two.[175] Where deferment is granted globally, under the second method referred to above, the period of deferment is to be calculated from the day following the date on which the aggregation period expires and is then reduced by half the number of days in the aggregation period.[176] (Where, however, the number of days in the period is an odd number, one is to halve the next lowest even number.[177]) If deferment is granted globally, under the third method mentioned above, the period is to be calculated from the day following the expiry date of the period during which the goods in question were released. It is then reduced by half the number of days in that period.[178] Once again where the number to be halved is an odd number, the next lowest even number is to be taken.[179] Where, in relation to the second and third methods of deferment, the aggregation period or the period during which goods are released, as the case may be, is a calendar week, Member States are given the option of providing that deferred duty is to be paid on the Friday of the fourth week following that calendar week. Where the period is a calendar month, Member States may provide that deferred duty shall be paid by the sixteenth day of the month following the calendar month.[180]

[172] CCC, Art 226(c).
[173] Ibid, Art 227.1.
[174] Ibid, Art 227.1(a), first sub-para.
[175] Ibid, Art 227.1(a), second sub-para.
[176] Ibid, Art 227.1(b).
[177] Ibid, Art 227.2.
[178] Ibid, Art 227.1(c).
[179] Ibid, Art 227.2.
[180] Ibid, Art 227.3.

3. Payment facilities other than deferment

Customs authorities may grant a debtor payment facilities other than deferred payment. Like deferment, these are conditional on security being provided. Security need not be required, however, where to require it would create serious economic or social difficulties because of the situation of the debtor.[181] Interest or, as the CCC says, 'credit interest', is to be charged where facilities are granted. It is to be calculated in such a way that it is equivalent to the amount which would be charged on the national money or financial market of the currency in which the amount is payable.[182] The customs authorities need not claim interest where claiming it would, because of the situation of the debtor, create serious economic or social difficulties.[183] Whatever the facilities granted to the debtor, he may, of course, pay all or part of the duty owed prior to the expiry of the period granted to him for payment.[184]

4. Interest

Where duty is not paid within the prescribed period, interest is to be charged on the arrears. The rate may be higher than the rate applicable to credit interest, referred to above, but it may not be lower than that rate.[185] In three situations the customs authorities may waive collection of interest on arrears. These are, first of all, where, because of the situation of the debtor, charging interest would be likely to create serious economic or social difficulties; secondly, where the amount of arrears does not exceed a level fixed in accordance with the Committee procedure[186] and, thirdly, if the duty is paid within five days of the expiry of the period prescribed for payment.[187] The customs authorities may also fix minimum periods for the calculation of interest and minimum amounts payable as interest on arrears.[188]

The UK's domestic legislation providing for interest to be charged on customs duty is contained in the Finance Act 1999, s 126 and SI 2000/631.[189] By virtue of the statutory instrument, which came into force on 1 April 2000, the rate of interest is 8.5 per cent subject to variation.[190] The minimum interest charge is set at £25. Section 126(6) of the Act provides that interest is not recoverable from any person at any time more than three years after the end of the period prescribed by the CCC for payment of the customs duty in question, unless a written notice that arrears of customs duty attract

---

[181] CCC, Art 229(a).

[182] Ibid, Art 229(b).

[183] Ibid, Art 229, second sub-para.

[184] Ibid, Art 230.

[185] Ibid, Art 232.1(b).

[186] No such level has been fixed.

[187] CCC, Art 232.2(a)–(c).

[188] Ibid, Art 232.3.

[189] The Air Passenger Duty and Other Indirect Taxes (Interest Rate) (Amendment) Regulations 2000, SI 2000/631, regs 4 and 5. Note that the UK's VAT and Duties Tribunals do not have an inherent power to order the payment of interest: Murray Vernon Ltd v CCE [1997] V&DR 340.

[190] See SI 2000/631 reg 4(2) and (3).

interest was given to that person at, or after, the time when the duty first became payable and before the end of the three-year period.

G. EXTINCTION OF A CUSTOMS DEBT

There are five categories of situations in which a customs debt may be extinguished. As one would expect, it is extinguished, first, by payment and, secondly, by remission of the duty.[191] Thirdly, it is extinguished where, in respect of goods declared for a customs procedure entailing an obligation to pay duties, the customs declaration is invalidated and the goods, prior to their release, are seized and simultaneously or subsequently confiscated, destroyed on the instructions of the customs authorities, destroyed or abandoned in accordance with CCC, Article 182 CCC,[192] or destroyed or irretrievably lost as a result of their actual nature, unforeseeable circumstances, or *force majeure*.[193] Fourthly, extinction occurs where goods, in respect of which a customs debt on importation is incurred because the goods are unlawfully introduced into the Community customs territory, or into a part of it, from a free zone or free warehouse,[194] are seized upon their unlawful introduction and confiscated whether simultaneously with the introduction or subsequently.[195] In the event of any seizure or confiscation the debt is to be deemed not to have been extinguished, for the purposes of the criminal law applicable to customs offences, if under that law customs duties provide the basis for determining penalties, or if the existence of a customs debt is a ground for taking criminal proceedings.[196] The fifth and final situation in which a customs debt is extinguished occurs in relation to the debt on importation arising on the validation of documents necessary to enable goods, originating in the Community, to attract preferential tariff treatment in a third country.[197] Extinguishment occurs where the formalities, carried out in order to facilitate preferential tariff treatment by third countries, are cancelled.[198]

---

[191] CCC, Art 233(a) and (b).
[192] Ibid, Art 182 deals with re-exportation, destruction, or abandonment of goods: see Ch 10.
[193] Ibid, Art 233(c). Confiscation of goods pursuant to this provision does not affect the customs status of the goods in question: Implementing Regulation, Art 867.
[194] ie pursuant to CCC, Art 202, discussed above.
[195] CCC, Art 233(d). Confiscation of goods pursuant to this provision does not affect the customs status of the goods in question: Implementing Regulation, Art 867.
[196] CCC, Art 233, final sub-para.
[197] See ibid, Art 216.
[198] Ibid, Art 234.

H. RELIEFS FROM DUTY

Reliefs from customs duties may be obtained under a considerable variety of international agreements, for example, the Vienna Convention on Diplomatic Relations of 18 April 1961 and the Vienna Convention on Consular Relations of 24 April 1963 to name but two. Turning to Community measures, the CN itself makes certain references to reliefs from customs duty. Section IIB provides, subject to certain conditions, for relief from customs duties in respect of civil aircraft and goods for use in them. Section IIC provides for relief from customs duty in respect of certain pharmaceutical products. Furthermore, according to Section IID, the standard rate of duty (3.5 per cent *ad valorem*) is charged on goods contained in consignments sent by one private individual to another, or goods contained in a traveller's personal luggage provided that the importations are not of a commercial nature as subsequently defined.[199] The Community's own system of reliefs from customs duty is contained, however, in a Council Regulation of 28 March 1983 ('the Relief Regulation').[200] It will be obvious that the objective of this regulation, is 'to eliminate differences in the field of exemptions from customs duties'.[201] Nevertheless, complete uniformity is not demanded. The Member States retain the power to impose import or export prohibitions or restrictions which are justified on grounds of public morality, public policy, public security, and protection of health and life of individuals, ie those grounds on which freedom of movement of goods may be restricted under EC Treaty, Article 30.[202]

It is not proposed to consider the Relief Regulation in any detail but the heads of relief are set out below. So far as the domestic legislation of the United Kingdom is concerned, the power to relieve goods from customs duty so as to ensure compliance with Community obligations and the basis of the reliefs which are granted are found in the Customs and Excise Duties (General Reliefs) Act 1979 and the statutory instruments made under it.[203] There are also

---

[199] See, however, the reliefs in relation to personal importations considered below.
[200] (EEC) 918/83 [1983] OJ L305/1.
[201] Case C–394/97 *Criminal Proceedings against Sami Heinonen* [1999] ECR I– 3599 at para 24.
[202] Ibid, paras 26–29. It should also be noted that the Relief Regulation does not preclude certain reliefs being given by Member States. The special status accorded to Mount Athos pursuant to Art 105 of the Greek constitution is unaffected, as are reliefs resulting from the Conventions of 13 July 1867 and 22 and 23 Nov 1867 between Spain and Andorra and France and Andorra, respectively, as well as certain relief for merchant navy seamen involved in international travel: see Art 135. Member States' reliefs relating to foreign armed forces serving on their territories and to workers returning to their country after having resided for at least six months outside the customs territory of the Community, on account of their occupation, are also not precluded by the Relief Regulation until the establishment of Community provisions in the field. At the moment no such provisions exist: see the Relief Regulation, Art 136.
[203] See the Customs Duty (Community Reliefs) Order 1984, SI 1984/719, Customs and Excise Duties (Personal Reliefs for Goods Permanently Imported) Order 1992, SI 1992/3193 and Customs and Excise (Personal Reliefs for Special Visitors) Order 1992, SI 1992/3156.

certain limited domestic extra-statutory concessions. The Customs and Excise Commissioners publish information on the reliefs available.

1. *Heads of relief from import duty*

The heads of relief from import duty are set out below.

(i)   Certain personal property imported by natural persons transferring their normal place of residence from a third country to the Community Customs Territory (CCT). Personal property means any property intended for the personal use of the persons concerned or for meeting their household needs. No relief is granted for tobacco and alcoholic products amongst other things.[204]

(ii)   Trousseaux and household effects, whether new or not, imported on the occasion of marriage so long as certain conditions are satisfied.[205]

(iii) Personal property, subject to certain exceptions, acquired by inheritance, by a natural person having his normal place of residence in the CCT.[206]

(iv)   Certain household effects for furnishing a secondary residence by a natural person who has a normal place of residence outside the CCT.[207]

(v)   Outfits, scholastic materials, and household effects representing the usual furnishings for a student's room and belonging to pupils or students coming to stay in the CCT, for the purpose of studying here, and intended for their personal use during their studies.[208]

(vi)   Consignments of goods of negligible value dispatched direct from a third country to a consignee in the Community. Goods are of negligible value if their intrinsic value does not exceed ECU 22 per consignment. Alcoholic products, perfumes and toilet waters, tobacco and tobacco products are excluded.[209]

(vii) Non-commercial importations, as defined, of goods up to a value of 45 ECU, consigned from one private individual in a third country to another in the CCT. Certain goods including tobacco products and alcoholic drinks are subjected to specific quantitive limits.[210]

---

[204] See the Relief Regulation, Arts 2–10. It should be noted that these Arts give the Member States a certain amount of discretion. Eg, Art 3 states that they may make relief conditional upon property having borne, either in the country of origin or in the country of departure, the customs and fiscal charges to which it is normally liable.

[205] The Relief Regulation, Arts11–15.   [206] Ibid, Arts 16–19.

[207] Ibid, Arts 20–24.   [208] Ibid, Arts 25–26.

[209] ibid, Arts 27–28.   [210] Ibid, Arts 29–31.

(viii)   Certain capital goods and other equipment belonging to undertak-
           ings which definitively cease their activity in a third country and
           move to the CCT in order to carry on a new and similar activity
           there.[211]

(ix)   Certain agricultural, stock-farming, bee-keeping, horticultural,
           and forestry products, brought into the CCT by, or on behalf of, the
           agricultural producer from properties located in a third country
           adjoining the CCT, operated by agricultural producers having their
           principal undertaking within the CCT and adjacent to the third
           country in question.[212]

(x)   Seeds, fertilizers, and products for treatment of soil and crops
           intended for use on a property within the CCT, operated by agri-
           cultural producers having their principal undertaking in a third
           country adjacent to the CCT.[213]

(xi)   Goods contained in the personal luggage of travellers coming from
           a third country provided that the importations are of a non-
           commercial nature. Certain products such as cigarettes and alco-
           holic drinks are subject to quantitive limits.[214]

(xii)   Educational, scientific, and cultural materials listed in Annex I to
           the Relief Regulation and scientific instruments and apparatus,
           whoever the consignee may be and whatever its intended use.[215]

---

[211] The Relief Regulation, Arts 32–38.   [212] Ibid, Arts 39–42.
[213] Ibid, Arts 43–44.

[214] Ibid, Arts 45–49. The scope for action by Member States in relation to exemptions and reliefs
has proved particularly significant in relation to this exemption. Finland has preserved its laws
imposing restrictions on importations of alcohol where the person's journey to Tallin, Estonia,
lasted for 20 hours at most: see Case C–394/97 *Criminal Proceedings against Sami Heinonen*, n 201
above. Someone who, during a cruise departing from a port of a Member State, does not call at a
third country or makes only a token call there, and does not remain there for a period during
which he has the opportunity of making purchases, is not a traveller coming from a third country: see Case C–158/80 *Rewe Handelsgesellschaft Nord mbH and Rewe-Markt Steffen v Hauptzollamt
Kiel* [1981] ECR 1805 at para 14. The case related to the so-called 'butter-buying cruises' which
enabled passengers to buy goods such as spirits, butter, meat, tobacco, and perfume outside
German territorial waters. The extent to which the non-commercial nature of the goods is to be
determined by reference to subjective factors is to be considered by the Court of Justice: see the
reference for a preliminary ruling in Case C–99/00 *Kenny Roland Lyckeskog v Public Prosecutor's
Office, Uddevalla*, [2000] OJ C149/26.

[215] The Relief Regulation, Arts 50 to 59b. See also Commission Regulation of 29 July 1983
(EEC) 2290/83 [1983] OJ L220/20. This regulation provides that it is for the competent authorities of the Member States to give decisions on the reliefs with which it deals, not the Commission.
In the UK, the decision is made by the National Import Reliefs Unit of HM Customs and Excise
based in Eniskillen, Northern Ireland. Where relief is sought for duty-free importation of equipment as defined in Art 59a (which concerns importations by or on behalf of a scientific research
establishment or organization based outside the Community) information is sent to the
Commission for consideration, prior to a decision by the Member State: see Art 18b of Regulation
2290/83. Note that the Commission itself was charged with taking a decision as to the availability of certain reliefs in difficult cases under earlier legislation see: eg Case 269/90 *Technische
Universität München v Hauptzollamt München-Mitte* [1991] ECR I–5469.

Annex I contains lists of books, publications, documents, visual and auditory materials.

(xiii) Animals specially prepared for laboratory use and biological or chemical substances intended for research.[216]

(xiv) Therapeutic substances of human origin and blood-grouping and tissue-typing reagents.[217]

(xv) Instruments and apparatus intended for medical research, establishing medical diagnoses or carrying out medical treatment.[218]

(xvi) Reference substances for the quality control of medicinal products.[219]

(xvii) Pharmaceutical products used at international sports events.[220]

(xviii) Certain goods for charitable or philanthropic organizations and articles intended for the blind, and other handicapped persons, and disaster victims.[221]

(xix) Honorary decorations or awards provided the operations in question are non-commercial.[222]

(xx) Presents received in the context of international relations.[223]

(xxi) Gifts to and goods to be used by monarchs, or heads of state, on official visits.[224]

(xxii) Certain goods imported for trade promotion purposes, including samples and printed matter and advertising material.[225]

(xxiii) Goods imported for examination, analysis, or tests, to determine their composition, quality, or other technical characteristics, for information or industrial and commercial research purposes.[226]

(xxiv) Consignments sent to organizations protecting copyrights or industrial and commercial patent rights.[227]

(xxv) Importations of tourist information literature.[228]

(xxvi) Miscellaneous documents and articles.[229]

(xxvii) Ancillary materials for the stowage and protection of goods during their transport.[230]

(xxviii) Litter, fodder, and feedstuff for animals during their transport.[231]

---

[216] The Relief Regulation, Art 60.   [217] Ibid, Arts 60–63.

[218] Ibid, Arts 63a and 63b. See also Commission Regulation (EEC) 2290/83, Title VA, in n 215 above.

[219] The Relief Regulation, Art 63c. See also Commission Regulation of 15 Dec 1988, (EEC) 3915/88 [1988] OJ L347/55.

[220] The Relief Regulation, Art 64.

[221] Ibid, Arts 65–85. See also Commission Regulation of 29 July 1983, (EEC) 2289/83 implementing Arts 70 to 78 of the Relief Regulation [1983] OJ L200/15.

[222] The Relief Regulation, Art 86.   [223] Ibid, Arts 87–89.

[224] Ibid, Art 90.   [225] Ibid, Arts 91–99.

[226] Ibid, Arts 100–106.   [227] Ibid, Art 107.

[228] Ibid, Art 108.   [229] Ibid, Art 109.

[230] Ibid, Art 110.   [231] Ibid, Art 111.

(xxix) Fuel and lubricants present in land motor vehicles and special containers.[232]

(xxx) Materials for the construction, upkeep, or ornamentation of memorials to, or cemeteries for, war victims.[233]

(xxxi) Coffins, funerary urns, and ornamental funerary articles.[234]

2. *Heads of relief from export duty*

(i) Consignments of negligible value dispatched by post and containing goods of a total value not exceeding 10 ECU.[235]

(ii) Domesticated animals exported at the time of transfer of agricultural activities from the Community to a third country.[236]

(iii) Agricultural or stock-farming products obtained by agricultural producers farming on properties located in the CCT, adjacent to a third country, operated by specified persons having their principal undertaking in a third country adjoining the CCT.[237]

(iv) Seeds exported for use on properties located in third countries adjacent to the CCT and operated by specified persons having their principal undertaking in the CCT, in the immediate proximity of the third country in question.[238]

(v) Fodder and feedstuff accompanying animals during their exportation.[239]

I. OTHER PRIVILEGES

In addition to reliefs from duty there are two other groups of customs privileges dealt with in the CCC under the headings of 'Returned Goods' and 'Products of Sea-fishing and other Products taken from the Sea'. These are dealt with below.

1. *Returned goods*

According to CCC, Article 185, Community goods which have been exported from the CCT and are then returned, in the state in which they were exported,[240] and released for free circulation within a period of three years

---

[232] The Relief Regulation, Arts 112–116.   [233] Ibid, Art 117.
[234] Ibid, Art 118.   [235] Ibid, Art 119.
[236] Ibid, Art 120.   [237] Ibid, Arts 121–123.
[238] Ibid, Arts 124 and 125.   [239] Ibid, Art 126.
[240] See CCC, Art 186. Derogations from this rule are given in the Implementing Regulation, Art 846. So, eg, goods are exempt from import duty if they have received no treatment other than that necessary to maintain them in good condition, or handling which alters only their condition: ibid, Art 846.1(a).

are, at the request of the person concerned, to be granted relief from import duties. The three-year period may be exceeded in special circumstances. If, before their exportation from the CCT, the goods had been released for free circulation at reduced or zero rates of duty because of their use for a particular purpose, the relief from import duty is to be given only if the goods are re-imported for the same purpose. If the goods are re-imported for a different purpose then the duty charged in respect of their original importation is set off against the amount chargeable on subsequent importation. There is to be no refund, however, if the duty already paid exceeds that on subsequent importation.[241]

In order to obtain the relief it is necessary to identify the goods in question as goods which have been exported and are, therefore, returned goods. It is possible to obtain from the customs authorities a document identifying goods in the event of their being returned to the CCT. Other documentation which will usually satisfy the customs authorities that the goods are returned goods include, with certain exceptions, a copy of the export declaration either returned by the customs authorities to the exporter or certified as a true copy by them, the information sheet known as INF 3,[242] or an ATA Carnet issued in the Community even if it has expired.[243] An exporter who declares that it is probable that goods will be returned via a customs office other than the customs office of departure may request the issue of an INF 3 at the time of completion of export formalities, or afterwards, so long as the customs authorities can establish that the formalities in the request relate to the exported goods.[244] Provision is made for the customs office of exportation and that of importation to co-operate in the identification of goods.[245]

No relief on re-importation is to be granted where goods have been exported under the outward processing procedure unless those goods remain in the state in which they were exported.[246] Relief is also denied where goods have been the subject of a Community measure involving their exportation to third countries.[247] Relief is not, however, denied in certain situations set out in the Implementing Regulation where goods have been previously exported from the CCT and in respect of which customs export formalities have been completed, with a view to obtaining refunds or other amounts, or financial advantages, provided for on exportation under the Common Agricultural Policy. The conditions to be satisfied for relief to be given include requirements that the sums paid out have been repaid, that the financial advantages have been cancelled,

---

[241] CCC, Art 185.1.

[242] A specimen of this form is provided in Implementing Regulation, Annex 110.

[243] Implementing Regulation, Art 848. The relief will be unavailable, however, where no evidence as to the identity of the goods is available: see, eg, *Shaneel Enterprises Ltd v CCE* [1996] V&DR 23 at 37–40.

[244] Implementating Regulation, Art 851.

[245] Ibid, Art 856.

[246] CCC, Art 185.2(a).

[247] Ibid, Art 185.2(b).

and that the goods enter back into free circulation in the CCT within twelve months of the completion of the formalities relating to their exportation.[248]

The provisions governing the relief for returned goods are available, *mutatis mutandis*, to compensating products originally exported or re-exported subsequent to an inward processing procedure. The amount of import duty is to be determined according to the rules applicable under the inward processing procedure with the date of re-export being regarded as the date of release for free circulation.[249]

2. *Products of sea fishing*

Certain products of sea fishing are to be exempt from import duties when they are released for free circulation. They are defined as (i) products of sea-fishing and other products taken from the territorial sea of a third country by vessels registered, or recorded, in a Member State and flying the flag of that state, and (ii) products obtained from products referred to in (i) on board factory-ships which are registered, or recorded, in a Member State and flying the flag of that state.[250] In order to obtain the relief it is necessary to present a certificate in support of the declaration for release for free circulation relating to the products in question. A model of the certificate appears in Annex 110a of the Implementing Regulation.[251] It should be noted that the rules of non-preferential origin provide that products of sea-fishing are regarded as originating in the country in which the vessels which take them from the sea are registered. Comparable rules apply in relation to goods obtained on board factory-ships. The rules of preferential origin are similar.[252]

---

[248] See Implementing Regulation, Arts 844 and 845.
[249] CCC, Art 187.
[250] Ibid, Art 188. The provisions of this Art are expressed to be without prejudice to the definition of goods originating in a country in ibid, Art 23.2(f).
[251] See Implementing Regulation 856a.
[252] See CCC, Art 23 and Ch 7 above.

Repayment, Remission and Appeals

The repayment and remission of customs duty and appeals against decisions of customs authorities are dealt with in different chapters of the CCC. The former are considered in Title VII chapter 5[1] and the latter in the last title of the CCC, Title VIII. Nevertheless, traders frequently appeal with a view to seeking remission or repayment of a customs debt and the issues are appropriately dealt with together. Section A provides an introduction to repayment or remission of customs duty, outlining the groups of situations in which it is available. Section B deals with repayment or remission under CCC, Article 236 and considers the requirements in CCC, Article 220.2(b) to which it refers, namely, that duty should not be entered in the accounts where there is an error by the customs authorities which could not reasonably have been detected by the person concerned, and that person has acted properly and in good faith. Section C considers repayment or remission under CCC, Articles 237 and 238 where a customs declaration is invalidated and where there are defective goods. Then section D looks at repayment or remission in other situations pursuant to CCC, Article 239. Section E discusses the general fairness clause in the Implementing Regulation, Article 905 and section F goes on to consider the procedure governing applications made under CCC, Article 239. Section G addresses procedural matters which are generally relevant to applications for repayment or remission of duty, and section H identifies the situations in which repayment or relief is prohibited. The chapter concludes by discussing briefly, in section I the topic of appeals.

A. REPAYMENT OR REMISSION: AN INTRODUCTION

For the purposes of the CCC, repayment means, as one would expect, the total or partial refund of import or export duties which have been paid. Remission, on the other hand, refers to a decision to waive all or part of the amount of a customs debt, and to a decision to render void an entry in the accounts of all or part of an amount of import or export duty which has not been paid.[2] The CCC specifies a number of situations in which import or export duties are to be remitted or repaid, and these are considered below. As the Court of Justice has

---

[1] Part IV, Title IV of the Implementing Regulation (Arts 877–912) is also concerned with Repayment and Remission of Import or Export Duties.

[2] CCC, Art 235.

said, Council Regulation (EEC) 1430/79,[3] the provisions of which are now
contained in CCC, Article 239.1, aimed 'to establish a Community system
for the repayment of import or export duties, which is designed to replace
the corresponding rules under national legislation'.[4] The regulation
frequently had to be considered together with Council Regulation (EEC)
1697/79 on the post-clearance recovery of import duties or export duties,
which have not been required of the person liable for payment, on goods
entered for a customs procedure involving the obligation to pay such duties.[5]
The provisions of this measure are now contained in CCC, Article 236 and
Article 220.2. It also entered into force on 1 July 1980.[6] As the Court of
Justice noted, it made plain in its recitals, that it was intended 'to provide a
body of rules covering the post-clearance recovery of import and export
duties, resulting from the application of the common agricultural policy or
from the provisions of the Treaty on the customs union replacing the relevant national provisions with Community provisions'.[7] An obligation to
repay or remit customs duty can arise only in respect of amounts exceeding
ECU 10, although customs authorities may, if they wish, repay or remit duty
of a lower amount.[8] As a general rule, repayment or remission is to take
place on presentation of goods. Clearly in many situations this will be impossible. Repayment or remission may also be given, therefore, where the decision-making customs authority has information showing unequivocally
that the certificate or document produced in support of an application
applies to the goods in question.[9] Repayment or remission of duty is generally available irrespective of the nature of the goods in question. It is limited,
however, in respect of goods within the Common Agricultural Policy in
certain circumstances.[10]

---

[3] 2 July 1979 [1979] OJ L175/1. By virtue of Art 27, it entered into force on 1 July 1980.
Denmark was allowed a derogation from the regulation. Prior to its entry into the EEC it had abolished a system of customs warehousing which it had to re-introduce by 31 Dec 1982 at the latest:
see ibid, Art 26.

[4] Case 386/87 *Bessin et Salson v Administration des douanes et droits indirects* [1989] ECR 3551
para 8. The reference to repayment, rather than to repayment and remission is, no doubt, because
the case concerned a requested repayment.

[5] 24 July 1979 [1979] OJ L197/1.

[6] See ibid, Art 11.

[7] Joined Cases 212/80 to 217/80 *Amministrazione delle Finanze dello Stato v Srl Meridionale
Industria Salumi and others* [1981] ECR 2735 at para 11.

[8] CCC, Art 240 and Implementing Regulation, Art 898.

[9] Implementing Regulation, Art 890, second para. See below for the documents which are to
support an application for repayment or remission.

[10] Ibid, Art 896. The customs office of entry (defined in Implementing Regulation, Art 496)
must be satisfied that the necessary steps have been taken by the competent authorities to cancel
the effects with regard to the certificate under which the importation took place.

1. *Four groups of situations in which repayment or*
remission is made

There are four groups of situations in which repayment or remission is required. These are: (i) where import or export duties are not legally owed or the amount of duty has been entered in the accounts in contravention of CCC, Article 220.2;[11] (ii) where a customs declaration is invalidated and duty has been paid;[12] (iii) in respect of import duty, where the imported goods are defective or do not comply with the terms of the importation contract;[13] and finally (iv) in respect of both import and export duties where there are situations, outside those in (i) to (iii) above, specified in the Implementing Regulation ('special situations').[14] These are dealt with below. At the outset, though, it should be noted that it may often be desirable for a trader to put forward alternative bases for remission or repayment. In particular, a trader may wish to allege that (i) above is applicable and alternatively that a special situation exists.[15]

B. DUTY NOT OWED OR IMPROPER ENTRY IN THE ACCOUNTS:
CCC, ARTICLE 236

Import and export duties are to be repaid or remitted to the extent that it is established that, when paid or entered in the accounts as the case may be, they were not legally owed. They are also to be repaid or remitted when an amount has been entered in the accounts in contravention of CCC, Article 220.2. No remission or repayment is permitted, however, where the facts leading to the payment or entry are the result of deliberate action by the person concerned.[16] Repayment or remission of duty under this head is generally effected pursuant to an application by the person concerned. Just as the customs authorities have three years in which to communicate the amount of the debt to the debtor, so the debtor has three years from that communication in which to apply for repayment or remission. The latter period is to be extended if the person concerned provides evidence that he was prevented from submitting his application in time as a result of unforeseeable circumstances or *force majeure*.[17] Repayment or remission under this head is,

---

[11] See CCC, Art 236.1.   [12] See ibid, Art 237.
[13] See ibid, Art 238.1.
[14] See ibid, Art 239. The term 'special situation' is used both in Council Regulation (EEC) 1430/79, ibid, Art 13, n 3 above and Implementing Regulation, Art 905.
[15] See Case C–253/99 *Firma Bacardi GmbH v Hauptzollamt Bremerhaven*, Opinion of Jacobs AG of 25 Jan 2001 at para 96 and the Judgment of 27 Sept 2001 at para 54.
[16] CCC, Art 236.1.
[17] On the meaning of *force majeure* see Case C–97/95 *Pascoal & Filhos Ldª v Fazenda Pública* [1997] ECR I–4209 at para 63 and Case C–12/92 *Criminal Proceedings against Edmond Huygen*

however, to be effected without an application by the person concerned, and on the customs authorities' own initiative, where they discover within the period for applications that, when the duty was paid or entered in the accounts as the case may be, it was not legally owed or that an amount has been entered in the accounts in contravention of Article 220.2.[18]

1. *CCC, Article 220.2(a)–(c)*

As we saw in Chapter 12, Article 220.2(a)–(c) specifies three situations in which subsequent entry in the accounts is not to occur.[19] The first situation is where the original decision not to enter duty in the accounts, or to enter it in the accounts at a figure less than the amount of duty actually owed, was taken on the basis of general provisions invalidated at a later date by a court decision. The third situation is where the debt is less than 10 ECU.[20] The second situation, in Article 220.2(b), has attracted the most attention. It contains three conditions which must be satisfied if entry in the accounts is to be prohibited.[21] These are, first, that the amount of duty legally owed was not entered in the accounts as the result of an error on the part of the customs authorities. Secondly, it must be shown that the error could not reasonably have been detected by the person liable for payment. Thirdly, it must be established that the person liable has acted in good faith and has complied with all the provisions laid down by the legislation in force as regards the customs declaration. These three conditions, which the Court of Justice has emphasized must all be met,[22] are considered further below.

2. *CCC, Article 220.2(b): Error on the part of the customs authorities*

So far as this first requirement is concerned, the Court of Justice has indicated that it is imposed in order to protect a trader's legitimate expectation that the decision to collect, or forego, post-clearance customs duty is based on correct

---

[1994] ECR I–6381 at para 31. In *Pascoal & Filhos Ldª v Fazenda Pública*, n 17 above, at para 63 the Court of Justice said: 'In the absence of specific provisions this concept must be understood as covering abnormal and unforeseeable circumstances beyond the control of the trader concerned, whose consequences could not have been avoided despite the exercise of all due care, so that conduct of the public authorities may, according to the circumstances, constitute a case of force majeure.' See also Ch 7, n 172.

[18] CCC, Art 236.2.

[19] By virtue of ibid, Art 236.1 and save where the second and third sub-paragraphs of Implementing Regulation, Art 217.1 apply: see Ch 12, p 393.

[20] See Implementing Regulation, Art 220.2(c) and Art 868.

[21] Case law concerning the legislation in place prior to the CCC stated that where the conditions were satisfied the trader had a right to remission or repayment: see, eg, Joined Cases C–153/94 and C–204/94 *The Queen v Commissioners of Customs and Excise, ex parte Faroe Seafood Co Ltd, Føroya Fiskasøla LF and another* [1996] ECR I–2465, para 84. This is now explicit in the wording of Art 236.1 which states that 'duties shall be repaid' in the circumstances it sets out. See also Ch 12, n 109.

[22] See the authorities referred to in n 110 in Ch 12.

information or criteria.[23] Consequently, the errors which are referred to in the legislation are not merely errors of calculation or copying. The concept of error 'includes any kind of error which vitiates the decision in question, such as, in particular, the misinterpretation or misapplication of the applicable rules of law'.[24] Therefore, the error may, for example, consist in continually accepting an inaccurate tariff classification on a trader's declaration, particularly where the declarations have contained all the facts needed to apply the rules, so that subsequent checks would not disclose any new relevant fact, and have taken place over a long period of time without the tariff classification being challenged.[25] To give a further example, an error may also be committed if, at previous on-the-spot inspections, the customs authorities have raised no objection to the exclusion of certain expenses from the customs value of goods purchased pursuant to similar transactions.[26]

Article 220.2(b) plainly stipulates that the error must be 'on the part of the customs authorities'. The phrase 'customs authorities' is defined in CCC, Article 4(3) as meaning 'the authorities responsible *inter alia* for applying customs rules'. It follows that the error may be committed by authorities other than those which are responsible for implementing the post-clearance collection of duty, including those in the country of exportation outside the Community.[27] (Indeed, CCC, Article 220.2(b), in its current form, specifically acknowledges that the issue of a certificate by the authorities of a third country is to constitute an undetectable error in certain circumstances.) Generally speaking, however, an error by the authorities not responsible for recovery must be relevant to post-clearance recovery of duty and so cause the person

[23] Case T–42/96 *Eyckeler & Malt AG v Commission* [1998] ECR II–401 para 139 (appealed by the Commission: see [1998] OJ C258/14, as Case C–163/98 P but removed from the register on 19 May 2000); and Joined Cases C–153/94 and C–204/94 *The Queen v Commissioners of Customs and Excise, ex p Faroe Seafood Co Ltd, Føroya Fiskasøla LF and another*, n 21 above, para 87.

[24] Case C–348/89 *Mecanarte-Metalúrgica da Lagoa Ldª v Chefe do Serviço da Conferência Final da Alfândega do Porto* [1991] ECR I–3277 para 21.

[25] Case C–250/91 *Hewlett Packard France v Directeur Général des Douanes* [1993] ECR I–1819, paras 19 and 20. See also Case 314/85 *Foto-Frost v Hauptzollamt Lübeck-Ost* [1987] ECR 4199 para 24.

[26] Case C–15/99 *Hans Sommer GmbH v Hauptzollamt Bremen* [2000] ECR I–8989, para 40. The Court of Justice went on to say that if it does not appear that the trader could have been in doubt about the correctness of the results of the inspection and had complied with all of the provisions laid down by the rules in force as far as the customs declaration is concerned, then the Member State must refrain from post-clearance recovery.

[27] So in Joined Cases C–153/94 and C–204/94 *The Queen v Commissioners of Customs and Excise, ex p Faroe Seafood Co Ltd, Føroya Fiskasøla LF and another*, n 21 above, it was decided that the authorities of the Faroes were authorities which could make a relevant error: see, ibid, para 90. In Joined Cases T–10/97 and 11/97 *Unifrigo Gadus Srl and CPL Imperial 2 SpA v Commission* [1998] ECR II–2231 it was accepted that the Norwegian authorities could make a relevant error, although on the facts they did not do so. See also Case C–348/89 *Mecanarte-Metalúrgica da Lagoa Ldª v Chefe do Serviço da Conferência Final da Alfândega do Porto* [1991] ECR I–3277 at para 22.

concerned to entertain legitimate expectations.[28] That condition is not fulfilled where erroneous information about tariff classification which is not binding on, recognized, or endorsed by the collecting authority, is given by another authority.[29] Another situation in which no error is committed arises where authorities fail to tell a principal of the fact that they suspect the Commission of a fraud, in which the principal is not implicated.[30]

Article 5.2 of Regulation 1697/79, which, as we noted above, was the forerunner of the current legislation, referred to 'an error made by the competent authorities themselves'. It will be apparent that the pronoun has been excluded in the process of codification. The pronoun was relied upon in *Mecanarte* as indicating that the error had to be by the customs authorities alone.[31] An error into which they were led by an incorrect declaration of origin, when they did not have to check the statement, was not an error upon which a trader could rely. Notwithstanding the absence of the pronoun, this has remained the position and the Court of Justice has repeatedly made clear that the reason that customs authorities are not liable for those errors into which they are led by an incorrect declaration is that the accuracy of the declaration is the trader's responsibility, and he must bear the commercial risks of relying on documents which are subsequently found to be inaccurate.[32]

The principle that the error must be one for which the customs authorities are solely responsible is unchanged, in relation to the issue of certificates, by

---

[28] Case C–250/91 *Hewlett Packard France v Directeur Général des Douanes*, n 25 above, para 15. Note that a person cannot have a legitimate expectation that a certificate of origin is valid merely because it has been accepted by customs authorities, because such acceptance does not prevent subsequent checks being carried out: see Joined Cases T–10/97 and 11/97 *Unifrigo Gadus Srl and CPL Imperial 2 SpA v Commission*, n 27 above, at para 60; Case C–97/95 *Pascoal & Filhos Ld⁴ v Fazenda Pública*, n 17 above, at para 40 and Joined Cases C–153/94 and C–204/94 *The Queen v Commissioners of Customs and Excise, ex p Faroe Seafood Co Ltd, Føroya Fiskasøla LF and another*, n 21 above, at para 93.

[29] Case C–250/91 *Hewlett Packard France v Directeur Général des Douanes*, n 25 above, at para 16. The two authorities in question were both within the Community.

[30] Case C–61/98 *De Haan Beheer BV v Inspecteur der Invoerrechten en Accijnzen te Rotterdam* [1999] ECR I–5003 para 41, but the principal may be able to take advantage of CCC, Art 239.1: discussed below.

[31] See Case C–348/89 *Mecanarte-Metalúrgica da Lagoa Ld⁴ v Chefe do Serviço da Conferência Final da Alfândega do Porto*, n 24 above, at para 23; Joined Cases C–153/94 and C–204/94 *The Queen v Commissioners of Customs and Excise, ex p Faroe Seafood Co. Ltd, Føroya Fiskasøla LF and another*, n 21 above, para 91 and Joined Cases T–10/97 and 11/97 *Unifrigo Gadus Srl and CPL Imperial 2 SpA v Commission*, n 27 above, para 58.

[32] See Joined Cases C–153/94 and C–204/94 *The Queen v Commissioners of Customs and Excise, ex p Faroe Seafood Co Ltd, Føroya Fiskasøla LF and another*, n 21 above, at para 97; Case C–348/89 *Mecanarte-Metalúrgica da Lagoa Ld⁴ v Chefe do Serviço da Conferência Final da Alfândega do Porto*, n 24 above, at para 24 and Case 827/79 *Amministrazione delle Finanze v Ciro Acampora* [1980] ECR 3731 at para 8. In Joined Cases T–10/97 and 11/97 *Unifrigo Gadus Srl and CPL Imperial 2 SpA v Commission*, n 27 above, para 59. The English High Court applied this principle in *CCE v E Reece Ltd, The Times*, 11 Oct 2000. Before the VAT and Duties Tribunal Decision No C00107.

the terms of Article 220.2(b) in its latest form.[33] As we have seen in Chapter 4, it provides that the issue of an incorrect certificate does not constitute an error where the certificate is based on an incorrect account of the facts provided by the exporter, except where the issuing authorities were aware that the goods did not satisfy the conditions laid down for entitlement to preferential treatment. As well as being consistent with the approach of the Court of Justice to the narrow question of responsibility for the error, the legislation is also consistent, more generally, with the Court's decisions in cases concerning inaccurate certificates of origin. The Court had made clear, prior to the amendments to CCC, Article 220.2, that the fact that certificates of origin had been wrongly provided by the exporting authority could not be relied upon by a trader.[34] It had gone on to provide, however, that where the exporter had made a declaration of origin, in reliance on the exporter's customs authorities actual knowledge of all the facts necessary for applying the rules of origin and those authorities had raised no questions over the declaration, then the authorities of the exporting state had made an error upon which the trader could rely.[35]

3. *CCC, Article 220.2(b): Detectability*

Of course, even if an error is established and the error is one which has been committed by the customs authorities, it must also be established that the trader could not reasonably have discovered it. In considering the issue of detectability two preliminary matters should be borne in mind. First, the rules governing repayment or remission of duty in special situations, in CCC, Article 239, pursue the same aim as those in CCC, Article 236, namely that of limiting post-clearance recovery of duty to cases where payment is justified and is compatible with a fundamental principle such as that of the protection of legitimate expectations. In view of this, whether or not there is a detectable error within CCC, Article 220.1(b), to which Article 236 refers, is linked to whether there is 'deception or obvious negligence' within CCC, Article 239.1, and the conditions set out in Article 239.1 are to be assessed in the light of Articles 236 and 220.2.[36] Secondly, a trader has, as we noted in Chapter 4, an

---

[33] Introduced by Regulation (EC) 2700/2000 of the European Parliament and Council of 16 Nov 2000 [2000] OJ L311/17.

[34] Joined Cases T–10/97 and 11/97 *Unifrigo Gadus Srl and CPL Imperial 2 SpA v Commission*, n 27 above, at para 61 and Joined Cases C–153/94 and C–204/94 *The Queen v Commissioners of Customs and Excise, ex p Faroe Seafood Co Ltd, Føroya Fiskasøla LF and another*, n 21 above, at para 94.

[35] Ibid, at para 97.

[36] Case C–48/98 *Firma Söhl & Söhlke v Hauptzollamt Bremen* [1999] ECR I–7877 at para 54; Case T–290/97 *Mehibas Dordtselaan BV v Commission* [2000] ECR II–15 at para 85; Case T–42/96 *Eyckeler & Malt AG v Commission*, n 23 above, at paras 136 and 137; Case T–75/95 *Günzler Aluminium v Commission* [1996] ECR II–497 paras 51–55 and Case C–250/91 *Hewlett Packard France v Directeur Général des Douanes*, n 25 above, para 46. Special situations within CCC, Art 239 are discussed below.

obligation to know the applicable Community customs law. Indeed, from the date of publication in the *Official Journal*, the relevant Community provisions constitute the only applicable rules of customs duty law and everyone is deemed to be aware of them.[37] This means that, as a general rule,[38] all traders, whether experienced in the import/export business or not, must read and act in accordance with the law as printed in the *Official Journal*.[39] In this context it is important to note that there is a rebuttable presumption that the date of publication of an issue of the journal is the date which it bears.[40] Where the presumption is rebutted regard must, of course, be had to the actual date of publication.[41] It should also be noted that it is not possible to rely on national compilations of law, general guidance from national authorities, or even specific guidance sought from the authorities on a daily basis.[42] Such sources

[37] Case T–75/95 *Günzler Aluminium v Commission*, n 36 above, at para 50.

[38] For an exception see Case C–160/84 *Oryzomyli Kavallas OEE v Commission of the European Communities* [1986] ECR 1633 discussed under special situations at p 431 below.

[39] See generally Case 161/88 *Friedrich Binder GmbH & Co KG v Hauptzollamt Bad Reichenhall* [1989] ECR 2415, para 19 and Case C–80/89 *Erwin Behn Verpackungsbedarf GmbH v Hauptzollamt Itzehoe* [1990] ECR I 2659 which followed it. In *Erwin Behn* the Court of Justice rejected the submission that, as Hauptzollamt Itzehoe did not have the OJ at its disposal, traders should not have to be better informed than it was: see para 17. The need to be aware of the OJ is now much less onerous because at any one time the OJ for the last three months is available free on the Europa web-site: see http://europa.eu.int/eur-lex/en/oj/index.html. Buxton LJ, upholding a decision of the High Court, noted that the trader 'ignores the Journal at his peril'and held that the error in question was reasonably discoverable: see *CCE v Invicta Poultry Ltd* [1998] V&DR 128 p 130. The tribunal decision is reported at [1996] V&DR 291 and the decision of Lightman J, overturning it, at [1997] V&DR 56.

For an example of a case in which the relevant decisions of an association council were not published at all in the OJ: see Joined Cases T–186/97, T–187/97, T–190/97–T–192/97, T–210/97, T–211/97, T–216/97–T218/97, T–279/97, T–280/97, T–293/97 and T–147/99 *Kaufring AG and others v Commission*, 10 May 2001, in particular at paras 286–287.

[40] Case 98/78 *Racke v Hauptzollamt Mainz* [1979] ECR 69, para 15. All regulations, and most directives and decisions, take effect on the date specified in them or, in the absence of such a date, on the twentieth day following that of their publication: See EC Treaty, Art 254.

[41] For an example of a situation in which the presumption was rebutted see Case C–122/95 *Germany v Council* [1998] ECR I–973 at para 28 of the judgment which notes that the issue of the OJ containing the Council Decision of 22 Dec 1994 approving the Marrakesh Agreement did not appear until 13 Feb 1995. Another example is given in Case T–115/94 *Opel Austria GmbH v Council* [1997] ECR II–39 in which was established that the Council backdated an issue of the OJ (see para 131). The backdating led to an infringement of the principle of legal certainty which, in the circumstances, appeared to provide an additional reason for annulling the regulation in question. Generally speaking, however, the belated publication of a Community measure in the OJ does not affect its validity: See Case 149/96 *Portugal v Council* [1999] ECR I–8395 at para 54.

[42] See Case C–370/96 *Covita AVE v Elliniko Dimsoio* [1998] ECR I–1771 para 26. So far as the UK is concerned, one cannot rely, eg, on the CHIEF noticeboard see: *CCE v Invicta Poultry Ltd*, n 39 above, nor on inadequate Notices produced by Customs and Excise: see *Nacco Material Handling (NI) Ltd v CCE* [1998] V&DR 115 at 126–7. 'CHIEF' stands for Customs Handling of Import and Export Freight and is a computerized system for import entry processing. It is planned to extend the system to control and clear declarations for export under the 'New Export System', which at the time of writing is intended to be fully operational by 31 Dec 2001.

cannot give a trader a legitimate expectation that the law will be applied as if it were embodied in them.

In determining whether or not an error could reasonably have been detected by a trader three elements must be addressed. These are, first, the nature of the error, secondly, the professional experience of the trader, and, thirdly, the degree of care which the trader took.[43] In cases in which requests for preliminary rulings are made, these matters are all to be considered by the national court which has the responsibility for determining whether or not an error is discoverable by a trader.[44]

So far as the nature of the error is concerned, it is clearly relevant to establish whether or not the rules in question are complex, whether or not a simple examination of the facts discloses the error, and the period for which the authorities persisted in their error.[45] In *Faroe Seafood* for example it was noted that the applicable rules of origin did not exclude the possibility of relying on bookkeeping principles to distinguish between prawns of differing origins.[46] Where the trader has relied upon certificates from the customs authorities confirming a position, that may prove to be evidence of complexity as well as a lack of negligence on the trader's part.[47] If it has been necessary to make a regulation to resolve certain difficulties, for example, in relation to classification, that too is evidence of complexity.[48] In one case in which the authorities persisted in their error of classification over a period of three years and in

---

[43] See Joined Cases C–153/94 and C–204/94 *The Queen v Commissioners of Customs and Excise, ex p Faroe Seafood Co Ltd, Føroya Fiskasøla LF and another*, n 21 above, at para 99, Case C–250/91 *Hewlett Packard France v Directeur Général des Douanes*, n 25 above, at para 22, and Case C–371/90 *Beirafrio–Indùstria de Produtos Alimentares Ldª v Chefe do Serviço da Conferência final da Alfandega do Porto* [1992] ECR I–2715, para 21. See also Case C–187/91 *Belgium v Société Coopérative Belovo* [1992] ECR I–4739 paras 17–19 and Case 64/89 *Hauptzollamt Gießen v Deutsche Fernsprecher GmbH* [1990] ECR I–2535 at para 19.

[44] See, eg, Joined Cases C–153/94 and C–204/94 *The Queen v Commissioners of Customs and Excise, ex p Faroe Seafood Co Ltd, Føroya Fiskasøla LF and another*, n 21 above, at para 106.

[45] See Joined Cases T–186/97, T–187/97 and others *Kaufring AG and others v Commission*, n 39 above, at paras 282–283. In this case in order to detect the authorities' error it would have been necessary not only to know the complex legislation in question but to appreciate that it had not been transposed into Turkish law. A fact which the Commission was unaware of for 20 years (para 293). the period of error in question in the case was three years.

[46] Joined Cases C–153/94 and C–204/94 *The Queen v Commissioners of Customs and Excise, ex p Faroe Seafood Co Ltd, Føroya Fiskasøla LF and another* at n 21 above, para 103. Furthermore the use of bookkeeping rules had apparently been approved in relation to imports from Faroes to Denmark.

[47] In Case 64/89 *Hauptzollamt Gießen v Deutsche Fernsprecher GmbH*, n 43 above, at para 20, the Court accepted that where the customs authorities twice confirmed a position, that was evidence of complexity. In Case C–187/91 *Belgium v Société Coopérative Belovo*, n 43 above, at para 18, it accepted that where the customs authorities, in the course of several operations and over a long period of time, confirmed the position nine times that was evidence of complexity and the absence of negligence. In Joined Cases C–153/94 and C–204/94 *The Queen v Commissioners of Customs and Excise, ex p Faroe Seafood Co Ltd, Føroya Fiskasøla LF and another*, n 21 above, receipt of repeated certificates and the continued contention of the customs authorities in the exporting country that the goods originated there, was considered relevant: see para 104.

[48] Case C–250/91 *Hewlett Packard France v Directeur Général des Douanes*, n 25 above, at para 23.

relation to forty-six transactions, there was terminological confusion arising in relation to the usual names of a fish and from the fact that 'cod', 'stockfisch' or 'baccalà' are not used to designate species of fish but families of species or even preservation treatment applied to certain species. Furthermore, a change in nomenclature was apparent only from the addition of a scientific name. All these matters indicated that the error was not discoverable by the trader.[49] In another case in which a Member State wrongly excluded fish from the definition of the term 'agricultural products', the Court of Justice took note of the unusual nature of the definition in question, the terms in which the objective of the legislation had been expressed, the recurrence of the same error in other measures in the Member State concerned, and a divergence of opinion between Member States as to the proper interpretation of the relevant provisions.[50]

The second element to be considered in determining whether or not an error was detectable within the legislation is the professional experience of the trader concerned. In this regard it is necessary to determine whether or not the trader involved is one whose activity essentially consists in import and export operations, whether he had some experience of trading in the goods in question and, particularly, whether he had in the past carried out similar transactions on which customs duties had been correctly calculated.[51]

In relation to the third element, the care taken by the trader, the Court of Justice has emphasized that as soon as doubts arise the trader must seek 'the greatest clarification possible'.[52] It is not the case, however, that only inexperienced or small-scale traders can make errors and still satisfy the requirements of this element. Large and experienced corporations may, for example, properly but wrongly regard a customs declaration as correct where they have relied on information provided by a customs authority, even if it was not the collecting authority, where that information has been unchallenged for a long period of time.[53] Where a company has relied on information provided by a customs authority to another member of its corporate group then it may be regarded as

---

[49] Case C–38/95 Ministero delle Finanze v Foods Import Srl [1996] ECR I–6543 paras 29–32.

[50] Joined Cases C–47/95, C–48/95, C–49/95, C–50/95, C–60/95, C–81/95, C–92/95 and C–148/95 Olasagasti & C Srl, Comarcon SNC, Ghezzi Alimentari Srl, Fredo Srl, Cateringros Srl, Intercod Srl, Nuova Castelli SpA and Igino Mazzola SpA v Amministrazione delle finanze dello Stato [1996] ECR I–6579 at paras 33–36.

[51] Case C–250/91 Hewlett Packard France v Directeur Général des Douanes, n 25 above, para 26 and Case C–64/89 Hauptzollamt Gießen v Deutsche Fernsprecher GmbH, n 43 above, at para 21.

[52] Joined Cases C–153/94 and C–204/94 The Queen v Commissioners of Customs and Excise, ex p Faroe Seafood Co Ltd, Føroya Fiskasøla LF and another, n 21 above, at para 100. In Case C–48/98 Firma Söhl & Söhlke v Hauptzollamt Bremen, n 36 above, the Court said that it was necessary for a trader to 'make inquiries and seek all possible clarification to ensure that he does not infringe [the] provisions'. See also Case C–250/91 Hewlett Packard France v Directeur Général des Douanes, n 25 above, para 24 and Case C–64/89 Hauptzollamt Gießen v Deutsche Fernsprecher GmbH, n 43 above, at para 22.

[53] Case C–250/91 Hewlett Packard France v Directeur Général des Douanes, n 25 above, para 28.

having satisfied the requirement to act diligently in relation to its declaration.[54] A trader does not act diligently, however, if it relies on a statement by the customs authorities that duty is due and pays the customs duty prior to receipt of an assessment, in circumstances where the import contract stated that the purchase price was to be paid after the issue of an assessment notice, so that duty paid by the importer could be deducted from the contract price.[55]

4. *CCC, Article 220.2(b): Good faith*

So far as the third requirement in CCC, Article 220.2(b) is concerned, ie that the trader must have acted in good faith and complied with the law relating to its declaration, plainly, the more complex the area of law in issue the easier it is likely to be for a trader to show that it acted in good faith. Although the requirement of good faith and the detectability of an error are distinct matters, the more obscure the error the more likely it is that the trader has acted in good faith.[56] The Court of Justice has summarized its position as follows:

> It is settled case-law that the person making the declaration must supply the competent customs authorities with all the necessary information as required by the Community rules, and by any national rules supplementing or transposing them, in relation to the customs treatment requested for the goods in question . . ..[T]his obligation may not go beyond production of the information that the person making the declaration may reasonably be expected to possess and obtain, with the result that it is sufficient for such information, even if incorrect, to have been provided in good faith . . .[57]

The fact, therefore, that an experienced trader wrongly classifies goods in its declaration does not mean that it has failed to comply with its obligations.[58] Neither does the fact that a trader fails to take precautions to ensure that the

---

[54] Ibid.

[55] Case T–75/95 *Günzler Aluminium GmbH v Commission*, n 36 above, at para 48.

[56] For an example of a case in which the complexity of rules was material to good faith see Case C–292/91 *Gebrüder Weis GmbH v Hauptzollamt Würzburg* [1993] ECR I–2219. The facts were that goods which originated in Portugal did not originate in the Community for the purposes of the agreement between the EC and Yugoslavia even after Portugal's accession to the Community. The Court said: 'that was far from being detectable from a mere reading of the provisions in force by a trader such as Weis. The condition of good faith must therefore be regarded as being satisfied.' (para 17). The above case was relied upon by the Court of First Instance in Joined Cases T–186/97, T–197/97, and others *Kaufring AG and others v Commission*, at n 39, para 282.

[57] Joined cases C–153/94 and C–204/94 *The Queen v Commissioners of Customs & Excise, ex p Faroe Seafood Co Ltd, Føroya Fiskasøla LF and another*, n 21 above, at paras 108 and 109. In relation to the first proposition the Court relied upon Case 378/87 *Top Hit Holzvertrieb v Commission* [1989] ECR 1359 para 26. In relation to the second it relied upon Case C–348/89 *Mecanarte v Chefe do Serviço da Conferência Final da Alfândega, Oporto*, n 24 above, at para 29 and Case C–250/91 *Hewlett Packard France v Directeur Général des Douanes* at n 25 above, para 29.

[58] Case C–250/91 *Hewlett Packard France v Directeur Général des Douanes*, n 25 above, at paras 29–31.

origin of goods could be easily ascertained. This has been said to show the trader's good faith.[59] The presence of good faith has also been inferred from the fact that a trader who bought goods with forged certificates of authenticity paid the appropriate price for goods bearing a valid certificate of authenticity and conducted the transaction in accordance with the customary requirements of international trade.[60]

C. RELIEF WHERE DECLARATION INVALIDATED OR DEFECTIVE GOODS

1. *Customs declaration invalidated: CCC, Article 237*

Import and export duties are to be repaid where a customs declaration is invalidated. An application for repayment must be made within the periods laid down for submission of the application for invalidation of the customs declaration.[61]

2. *Defective goods: CCC, Article 238*

All importers will, at some time, have had to reject goods because they are defective or because they do not comply with the terms of the contract on the basis of which they were imported. Where an importer does this because the goods were defective[62] or non-compliant at the date on which the customs declaration in question was accepted, then import duties are, as a general rule, to be repaid or remitted.[63] There are, however, a number of limitations on repayment or remission in these circumstances. The Implementing Regulation provides two cases in which no repayment or remission is permitted. The first of these is where the defective nature of the goods was taken into consideration in drawing up the terms of the contract, and in particular the price, under which the goods were entered for a customs procedure involving an obligation to pay duties. The second is where the goods are sold by the importer after it has been ascertained that they are defective or do not comply with the terms of the contract.[64] Repayment or remission is also unavailable in respect of defec-

---

[59] See Joined Cases C–153/94 and C–204/94 *The Queen v Commissioners of Customs and Excise, ex p Faroe Seafood Co Ltd, Føroya Fiskasøla LF and another*, n 21 above, para 105. The precaution in question consisted of the physical separation of goods in factories in the state of the exporter.

[60] Case T–42/96 *Eyckeler & Malt AG v Commission*, n 23 above, at paras 156 and 159.

[61] CCC, Art 237. The specified period for invalidation where goods have been released is usually three months from the date of acceptance of the declaration: Implementing Regulation, Art 251. For invalidation of a customs debt see CCC, Art 66 and Ch 9.

[62] Defective goods includes those damaged before their release: see CCC, Art 238.1, second para.

[63] Ibid, Art 238.1.

[64] Implementing Regulation, Art 892.

tive or non-compliant goods which, before being declared to customs declaration, were imported temporarily for testing. Repayment or remission is not, however, prohibited where it is established that the fact that the goods were defective or non-compliant could not normally have been detected in the course of the tests.[65]

The repayment or remission is made to the extent that the amount of duty entered in the accounts relates to defective or non-compliant goods placed under the procedure in question and subject to certain conditions.[66] The first of these is that the goods have not been used, except for such initial use as may have been necessary to establish that the goods were defective or did not comply with the terms of the contract.[67] The second condition[68] is that the goods are exported from the Community customs territory or, at the request of the person concerned, destroyed or placed 'with a view to re-export' under the external transit procedure, or the customs warehousing procedure, or in a free zone or free warehouse instead of being exported.[69] The phrase 'with a view to re-export' has been the subject of some discussion, and it is understood that the EC Commission and Member States have agreed to interpret it so that goods placed in a customs warehouse or free zone do not have actually to be re-exported on every occasion.[70] In the event that the goods are placed under one of these procedures, or in a free zone or warehouse, they are to be treated as non-Community goods.[71] In order to obtain repayment or remission in the circumstances set out above an application must be submitted to the appropriate customs office within twelve months from the date on which the amount of the duty was communicated to the debtor. The time limit may be extended in duly justified exceptional cases.[72]

[65] CCC, Art 238.3.
[66] Ibid, Art 238.1.
[67] Ibid, Art 238.2(a).
[68] Ibid, see Art 238.2(b). Waste or scrap produced by the authorized destruction of the goods is to be regarded as non-Community goods once a decision has been taken accepting the application for repayment or remission: Implementing Regulation, Art 894.
[69] Where only components of an article are so treated, the amount to be repaid or remitted is to be the difference between (i) the amount of import duty on the complete article and (ii) the amount which would have been chargeable on the remainder of the article, if it had been entered in the unaltered state for a customs procedure involving the obligation to pay duties on the date on which the complete article was entered: Implementing Regulation, Art 897.
[70] See the Joint Customs Consultative Committee Paper (00)05—'Goods rejected by importers as not being in accordance with contract etc: change in procedures when the rejected goods are placed in a customs warehouse or free zone'.
[71] CCC, Art 238.2. The customs authorities are to take all necessary steps to ensure that goods placed in a customs warehouse, free zone, or free warehouse may subsequently be recognized as non-Community goods: Implementing Regulation, Art 895.
[72] Ibid, Art 238.4. The time limits for communication to the debtor are dealt with in Ch 12.

D. REPAYMENT AND REMISSION IN OTHER SITUATIONS:
CCC, ARTICLE 239

According to CCC, Article 239, remission or repayment may be made in situations other than those referred to in CCC, Articles 236–238, within two broad categories: first, where the circumstances of the case fall within situations specified in Implementing Regulation, Articles 900–903; secondly, where the circumstances constitute a special situation within the general fairness provision of Implementing Regulation, Article 905, considered in the next section. In both situations it is necessary that there be no deception or obvious negligence attributed to the person concerned[73] and this requirement is considered below. The person concerned means the person or persons referred to in Implementing Regulation, Article 878.1,[74] or their representatives, and any other person who was involved with the completion of customs formalities in relation to the goods concerned, or gave instructions necessary for the completion of the formalities.[75] As in the case of repayment or remission of duty in relation to defective goods, repayment or remission under CCC, Article 239 is made following an application submitted, within twelve months from the date on which the amount of duty was communicated to the debtor, to the appropriate customs office. The customs authorities may permit this time limit to be exceeded in duly justified exceptional cases.[76]

Before considering the requirement of no deception or obvious negligence, it should be noted that CCC, Article 239.1 states that import or export duties may be repaid or remitted in certain circumstances, whereas CCC, Articles 236–238 state that 'duties shall be repaid'.[77] It has, however, long been established that where the trader satisfies the conditions contained in Article 239, it has a right to the repayment or remission. If it did not have such a right the provision would be deprived of effectiveness.[78]

1. *No deception or obvious negligence*

The requirement that there be no deception or obvious negligence and the other requirements of the Implementing Regulation are plainly cumulative.

[73] CCC, Art 239.1 and Implementing Regulation, Art 905.1.

[74] Implementing Regulation, Art 878 requires that applications for repayment or remission are to be made by the person who has paid, or is liable to pay, the customs duty or the person who has taken over that person's rights and obligations.

[75] Ibid, Art 899.

[76] CCC, Art 239.2.

[77] See ibid, Arts 236.1, 237 and 238.1.

[78] Case T–42/96 *Eyckeler & Malt AG v Commission*, n 23 above, at para 134. The Court of Justice had taken the same approach in relation to the forerunner of Arts 236–238. As we have seen these articles, however, now state clearly that the duties to which they apply 'shall be' repaid or remitted.

This is apparent from the wording of CCC, Article 239 and Implementing Regulation, Article 899. As the Court of Justice has made clear, it is not possible, therefore, to regard the requirement of no deception or obvious negligence as being satisfied merely because a situation specified in the Implementing Regulation as giving rise to repayment or remission of duty, for example, such as that in Article 900.1(o), is satisfied.[79]

Not only is the requirement of no deception or obvious negligence a distinct requirement, it is also one which is strictly construed because the right to repayment or remission which it facilitates is an exception to the normal import/export procedure. It must, therefore, be construed in a way which ensures that cases of repayment or remission remain limited.[80] It should also be noted that the meaning of 'obvious negligence' is indistinguishable from 'obvious negligence' in Implementing Regulation, Article 859. This provides that a customs debt within CCC, Article 204.1[81] does not arise where, amongst other things, there is no obvious negligence on the part of the person concerned. It is also indistinguishable from 'manifest negligence' in CCC, Article 212a which denies favourable tariff treatment where there is 'fraudulent dealing and manifest negligence'.[82]

As we noted in 'CCC, Article 220.2(b): Detectability' above, in construing the phrase 'no deception or obvious negligence' in CCC, Article 239, the requirements of CCC, Article 220.2(b), as introduced by CCC, Article 236 have to be borne in mind. Therefore, in determining whether there is no deception or obvious negligence within Article 239, it is necessary to have regard to the matters dealt with in that section, such as the complexity of the provisions in question and the professional experience of, and care taken by, the trader.

It should be emphasized that the mere fact that irregularities have occurred in relation to a particular importation is no ground for asserting obvious negligence. There must be grounds for attributing the deception or obvious negligence to the importer. Clearly, the misbehaviour of parties outside an importer's control cannot, in the ordinary case, be so attributed. In one case, for example, the Court of First Instance observed that a failure to detect the falsification of certificates of authenticity by the exporter did not constitute obvious negligence because the importer did not know of the falsifications and was unable to carry out any checks which would have revealed them.[83]

Finally, in relation to the burden of proof, it should be noted that, in the ordinary case, the burden of proving obvious negligence will rest on those alleging it. In one case, the Court of First Instance said 'Since the manner in

---

[79] Case C–48/98 *Firma Söhl & Söhlke v Hauptzollamt Bremen*, n 36 above, paras 93– 97.
[80] Ibid, para 52.
[81] For more details see Ch 12.
[82] Case C–48/98 *Firma Söhl & Söhlke v Hauptzollamt Bremen*, n 36 above, paras 48 and 49. Art 212a is considered in Ch 12.
[83] Case T–42/96 *Eyckeler & Malt AG v Commission*, n 23 above, at paras 142 and 151.

which [the importer] entered into purchase contracts and carried out the importations at issue formed part of standard trade practice, it was for the Commission to prove that the applicant was guilty of obvious negligence'.[84]

2. *Situations giving rise to repayment or remission under Article 900*

The Implementing Regulation, Article 900 lists situations giving rise to repayment or remission at paragraphs (a)–(o). Except in situations (a), (b), (d), (e), and (n), repayment or remission is conditional upon goods being re-exported from the Community customs territory under the supervision of the customs authorities. The goods must neither have been used nor sold before being exported.[85] These requirements do not apply, however, where the goods are destroyed by order of a public authority or are delivered free of charge to charities carrying out their activities in the Community. Furthermore, one can, in most cases, request that instead of being exported the goods are destroyed or placed with a view to export under the external transit regime, under customs warehousing arrangements, or in a free zone or free warehouse.[86] In relation to cases within (g), (i), and (l) below, the options of destruction or placement under the external transit regime are not available. Goods placed under one of the treatments referred to above are treated as non-Community goods, and customs authorities are to take all requisite measures to ensure that the goods placed in a customs warehouse, free zone, or free warehouse may later be recognized as such.[87] The situations set out in Article 900 (a)–(o) refer to circumstances, set out below, as follows:

(a)   where specified goods are stolen, provided that the goods are recovered promptly and placed again in their original customs situation in the state they were in when they were stolen. The specified goods are non-Community goods placed under a customs procedure involving total or partial relief from import duties, or goods released for free circulation with favourable tariff treatment by reason of their end use.

(b)   Where non-Community goods are inadvertently withdrawn from the customs procedure involving total or partial relief from import duties under which they had been placed, provided that, as soon as the error is found, they are placed again in their original customs situation in the state they were in when they were withdrawn.

(c)   Where it is impossible to unload goods which are in free circulation,

---

[84] Case T–42/96 *Eyckeler & Malt AG v Commission*, n 23 above, at para 159.
[85] Implementing Regulation, Art 900.2 and 4.
[86] Ibid, Art 900.2.
[87] Ibid, Art 900.2.

on their arrival at their destination, because it is impossible to operate the mechanism for opening the means of transport on which the goods are located, provided that the goods are immediately re-exported.

(d) Where a non-Community supplier decides to keep goods, in free circulation, which are returned to it under outward processing arrangements so as to enable it to eliminate, free of charge, defects existing prior to the release of the goods, or to bring them into conformity with the contract under which they were released for free circulation, because it is unable to eliminate the defects in question or because it would be uneconomic to do so. It does not matter for these purposes if the defects in the goods were found after their release.

(e) Where it is found that goods, released for free circulation with full relief from import duties have been re-exported from the Community without customs supervision, when the customs authorities decide on post-clearance entry in the accounts of import duty due. It must be established, however, that the substantive conditions laid down in the CCC for repayment or remission would have been met at the time of re-exportation if the duty had been levied when the goods were released for free circulation.

(f) Where goods, previously entered for a customs procedure, are re-exported from the Community customs territory or are destroyed under the control of the customs authorities, where a judicial body has forbidden the marketing of the goods and so obliged the person concerned to pay import duties under normal conditions. It must be established that the goods have not been used in the Community.

(g) Where it has not been possible, through no fault of the declarant, to deliver goods to the consignee, and the goods have been entered for a customs procedure involving the obligation to pay import duties by a declarant empowered to do so on his own initiative.

(h) Where the goods have been addressed to the consignee in error by the consignor. The goods must be re-exported to the original supplier or to another address specified by him.[88]

(i) Where the goods are found to be unsuitable for the use for which the consignee intended them because of an obvious factual error in his order.

(j) Where the goods cannot be used for the purpose intended by the consignee because they are found not to have complied, at the time of their release, with the rules in force concerning their use or marketing and they have been released for a customs procedure involving an obligation to pay customs duties.

---

[88] Implementing Regulation, Art 900.3.

(k)   Where the consignee's intended use of the goods is prevented, or substantially restricted, because an authority or body, having the appropriate power of decision, has taken measures of a general scope, after the date of release for a customs procedure involving an obligation to pay import duties.

(l)   Where total or partial relief from import duty, applied for by the person concerned in accordance with existing provisions, cannot be granted through no fault of the person concerned and the customs authorities must enter in the accounts the amounts of the import duties that have become due.

(m)   Where the goods have reached the consignee after binding delivery dates, which have been stipulated in the contract under which they were entered for a customs procedure involving an obligation to pay import duties.

(n)   Where it has not been possible to sell the goods in the Community customs territory and they are delivered free of charge to charities which are either (i) represented in the Community but carrying out their activities in a third country, or (ii) carrying out their activities in the Community customs territory provided they are eligible for relief from duty in the case of importation for free circulation of similar goods from third countries.

(o)   Where the customs debt has not been incurred as a customs debt on importation under CCC, Article 201,[89] and the person concerned is able to show that if the imported goods had been entered for free circulation they would have been eligible for Community treatment or preferential treatment. The person concerned must show this by producing a certificate of origin, a movement certificate, an internal Community transit document, or other appropriate document. The conditions referred to in the Implementing Regulation, Article 890, which is outlined below, must also be satisfied. (Neither the Implementing Regulation, Article 890 nor Article 900.1(o) applies where goods would have been subject to favourable treatment by reason of their nature or end use, for example, by way of complete or partial exemption from import duties on goods reimported following outward processing, or goods returned following repair.)[90]

---

[89] See Ch 12. Art 201 imposes a debt on release for free circulation of goods liable to import duties and on the placing of such goods under the temporary importation procedure with partial relief from import duties.

[90] See C–48/98 *Firma Söhl & Söhlke v Hauptzollamt Bremen*, n 36 above, at para 84. See also Case C–253/99 *Firma Bacardi GmbH v Hauptzollamt Bremerhaven*, Opinion of Jacobs AG of 25 Jan 2001. A mistranslation of the German version appeared erroneously to suggest the contrary: see para 79 of the Opinion. See now the Judgment of 27 Sept 2001, particularly at para 45.

3. *Situations under Article 901*

Article 901 specifies three further situations in which repayment or remission of duty is to be made. The situations in question are set out below.

(i) Goods have been entered in error for a customs procedure, involving an obligation to pay import duties, and have been re-exported from the Community customs territory without having been previously entered for the customs procedure under which they should have been placed. In addition, the other requirements of CCC, Article 237, considered above, must be satisfied.

(ii) The goods have been re-exported or destroyed in accordance with CCC, Article 238.2(b) without customs supervision and the other provisions of CCC, Article 238 are met.

(iii) The goods have been re-exported or destroyed without customs supervision in accordance with the requirements of Article 900.1(c) and (f)–(n) outlined above, and the other conditions set out in the Implementing Regulation, Article 900.2 and 4 have been met.[91]

Repayment or remission under Article 901 is conditional on two general requirements being satisfied.[92] First, the applicant must produce all the evidence needed for the decision-taking authority to be satisfied that the goods in question have actually been re-exported from the Community customs territory,[93] or have been destroyed under the appropriate authorities' supervision.[94] Secondly, there must be returned to the decision-making authority any

---

[91] These conditions are dealt with at the beginning of 'Situations giving rise to repayment or remission under Article 900'.

[92] Implementing Regulation, Art 901.2.

[93] Ibid, Art 902.1(a), states that the necessary evidence consists of the original, or a certified copy, of the declaration for export and certification by the customs office through which the goods actually left the Community customs territory. Where this cannot be produced, certification by the customs office in the third country that the goods have arrived or the original, or a certified copy, of the customs declaration for goods made in the country of destination may be presented. Also to be presented are the administrative and commercial documents showing that the goods exported from the customs territory are the same as those declared for a customs procedure involving an obligation to pay duties, namely, the original or a certified copy of the declaration for that procedure and, where the decision-making authority considers it necessary, certain commercial or administrative documents containing a full description of the goods and giving their trade description, quantities, marks, and other identifying particulars. These must have been presented with the declaration for that procedure, or the export declaration or the customs declaration made for the goods in the third country, and may be invoices, dispatch details, transit documents, or health certificates. Where the evidence referred to above is insufficient to allow a decision to be taken in full knowledge of the facts of the case, or where certain evidence is unavailable, it may be supplemented by any other documents considered necessary by the decision-taking authority: see ibid, Art 902.2.

[94] Ibid, Art 902.1(b) states that the necessary evidence consists of the original, or a certified copy, of a report or declaration of destruction drawn up by the authorities under whose authority the destruction was supervised, or a certificate by the person authorized to certify destruction, accompanied by evidence of his authority. The documents must contain a sufficiently full descrip-

document certifying the Community status of the goods in question, under cover of which the goods may have left the Community customs territory. Alternatively, there must be presented whatever evidence the authority considers necessary to satisfy itself that the document cannot be used subsequently in connection with the importation of goods into the Community.

4. *Returned goods: Article 903*

As we saw in Chapter 12, where goods are returned under certain conditions, relief from import duties is available under CCC, Article 185 and the Implementing Regulation, Article 844. Where the relief is available, the Implementing Regulation, Article 903, provides for a right to repayment of the export duties levied when the exported goods, or a proportion of them, are returned and entered for free circulation within the Community customs territory.[95] In order to obtain the relief it is necessary for one of the situations referred to in the Implementing Regulation, Article 844 to apply.[96] This provision specifies certain situations in which exemption from import duties is available, in respect of returned goods which have been the subject of a Community measure involving their exportation to third countries, pursuant to CCC, Article 185.2(b). The application of CCC, Article 185.2(b) to the goods in question must be proved to the satisfaction of the customs office where the goods are declared for free circulation.[97]

E. THE GENERAL FAIRNESS CLAUSE: ARTICLE 905

The Implementing Regulation, Article 905 has been described as 'a general fairness clause intended to cover exceptional situations which, in themselves, do not fall within any of the cases provided for in Articles 900 to 904 of the Regulation'.[98] The provision applies in cases in which a decision on an appli-

---

tion of the goods, giving their trade description, quantities, marks, and other identifying particulars. This is to be provided so as to enable the customs authorities to satisfy themselves that the destroyed goods are those declared for the customs procedure involving the obligation to pay import duties in question, by comparing the description with the particulars given in the declaration and the accompanying commercial documents, namely, invoices, dispatch details, and so on. Where the evidence referred to above is insufficient to allow a decision to be taken in full knowledge of the facts of the case, or where certain evidence is unavailable, then it may be supplemented by any other documents considered necessary by the decision-taking authority: see ibid, Art 902.2.

[95] Ibid, Art 903.1 and 3.
[96] Ibid, Art 903.2, first para.
[97] Ibid, Art 903.2, second para.
[98] Case C–86/97 *Reiner Woltmann v Hauptzollamt Potsdam* [1999] ECR I–1041 para 18. Implementing Regulation, Art 904 specifies those situations in which no repayment or remission of duty is permitted and is considered below.

cation for repayment or remission, under CCC, Article 239.2 cannot be taken on the basis of Articles 900–904, but is supported by evidence which might constitute 'a special situation' resulting from circumstances in which no deception or obvious negligence may be attributed to the person concerned.[99] It replaces Article 13 of Regulation 1430/79[100] but the comments of the Court of Justice in relation to this earlier provision are applicable in relation to the later one. It has said that Article 13 was 'A general equitable provision designed to cover situations other than those which had most often arisen in practice and for which special provision could be made when the regulation was adopted'.[101] It is a provision that is designed to take account of the particular circumstances of specific traders and:

> is intended to be applied when circumstances characterising the relationship between a trader and the administration are such that it would be inequitable to require the trader to bear a loss which he normally would not have incurred.[102]

Given the role of the general equitable or fairness provision, it is not surprising that one is not to import into it a stipulation that the requirements of, what is now, Article 220.2(b) are to be met before repayment or remission is available.[103] Whether or not relief is available is to be determined by reference to all the facts on a case-by-case basis.[104]

---

[99] 'The person concerned' is construed as in Implementing Regulation, Art 899, referred to above: see ibid, Art 905.1, second para.

[100] See n 3 above. Inserted by Council Regulation (EEC) 3069/86 of 7 Oct 1986 [1986] OJ L286/1.

[101] Joined Cases 244 and 245/85 *Cerealmangimi SpA et Italgrani SpA v Commission* [1987] ECR 1303 paras 10 and 11. See also Case T–290/97 *Mehibas Dordtselaan BV v Commission*, n 36 above, at para 76; Case T–50/96 *Primex Produkte Import-Export GmbH & Co KG, Gebr Kruse GmbH, Interporc Im- und Export GmbH v Commission* [1998] ECR II–3773 at para 74: case appealed see [1998] OJ C258/14 as Case C–163/98 P but removed from register on 19 May 2000; Case T–42/96 *Eyckeler & Malt AG v Commission*, n 23 above, at para 132; Case C–446/93 *SEIM— Sociedade de Exportação e Importação de Materiais Ld^a v Subdirector-Geral das Alfândegas* [1996] ECR I–73 at para 41; Case T–346/94 *France-aviation v Commission* [1995] ECR II–2841 para 34; Case 160/84 *Oryzomyli Kavallas OEE and others v Commission* [1986] ECR 1633 para 10; Case 283/82 *Papierfabrik Schoellershammer Heinrich August Schoeller & Söhne GmbH & Co KG v Commission* [1983] ECR 4219 para 7, and Joined Cases T–186/97, T–187/97, and others, *Kaufring AG and others v Commission*, at n 39 above, at paras 216–220. In the latter case the Court of Justice took note of the seventh recital to Regulation 1430/79 which states that 'only those special situations most frequently encountered in practice may at the present stage be covered by regulations relating to repayment or remission of import duties; whereas it is advisable to make provision for the use of a Community procedure in order to define, where appropriate, other situations which also warrant repayment or remission of import duties'.

[102] Case T–290/97 *Mehibas Dordtselaan BV v Commission*, n 36 above, at para 77, Case T–50/96 *Primex Produkte Import-Export GmbH & Co KG, Gebr Kruse GmbH, Interporc Im- und Export GmbH v Commission*, n 101 above, at para 164; Case T–42/96 *Eyckeler & Malt AG v Commission*, n 23 above, at paras 132 and 190, and Case 58/86 *Coopérative agricole d'approvisionnement des Avirons v Receveur des douanes de Saint-Denis and directeur régional des douanes, Réunion* [1987] ECR 1525 at para 22.

[103] Case T–42/96 *Eyckeler & Malt AG v Commission*, n 23 above, at para 135f.

[104] Case C–61/98 *De Haan Beheer BV v Inspecteur der invoerrechten en accijnzen te Rotterdam*, n 30 above, at para 44.

1. *What is a special situation?*

As we have seen, Article 905, like Article 13 of Regulation 1430/79, applies in 'special situations' where there is no deception or obvious negligence attributable to the person concerned. The absence of deception and obvious negligence has already been considered. Now we turn to examine the nature of a special situation. Two general propositions can be derived from the judgments of the Court of Justice. First, a situation which is generally applicable to traders cannot be a special situation. Secondly, a special situation arises only in relation to circumstances in which relief to the trader is unavailable unless they constitute a special situation.

So far as the first proposition is concerned, the Court of Justice has made clear that, by definition, a special situation will not apply to an indeterminate number of operators.[105] Consequently, the geographical and economic circumstances of a particular area do not constitute a special situation;[106] neither do commercial risks which are common to traders, such as the possibility that partners or agents may go into liquidation or that documents such as invoices or certificates of origin, presented in good faith, are falsified or inaccurate.[107] The fact that Member States take different approaches to identical circumstances or have different laws in respect of aspects of customs law within their remit also cannot constitute a special situation.[108] Traders in similar situations in different countries may, therefore, be treated differently, for example, where the matter falls within the ECU 50,000 limit which applies in relation to the Member States' ability to decide on repayment or remission applications.[109] Although this may produce unfairness commercially, it is the correct approach in principle. If it were otherwise one would need only one customs authority to make a mistake about what constitutes a special situation for duty to be lost from the rest of the Community.

The fact that a special situation cannot apply to an indeterminate number of operators inevitably involves the Court in comparing the trader alleged to be

---

[105] Case T–290/97 *Mehibas Dordtselaan BV v Commission*, n 36 above, para 80 and Case 58/86 *Coopérative agricole d'approvisionnement des Avirons v Receveur des douanes de Saint-Denis and Directeur Régional des Douanes, Réunion*, n 102 above, at para 22.

[106] See Case 58/86 *Coopérative Agricole d'Approvisionnement des Avirons v Receveur des douanes de Saint-Denis and Directeur Régional des Douanes, Réunion*, n 102 above. As will be apparent from the name of the case, the comments of the Court were made in relation to the island of Réunion.

[107] Case T–290/97 *Mehibas Dordtselaan BV v Commission*, n 23 above, at para 81. See also Case 827/79 *Amministrazione delle Finanze v Ciro Accampora* [1980] ECR 3731 para 8; Case 230/83 *Van Gend & Loos and Expeditiebedrijf Wim Bosman v Commission* [1984] ECR 3763 at para 16; Case C–97/95 *Pascoal & Filhos Ldª v Fazenda Pública* [1997] ECR I–4209 at paras 57–60. Case T–42/96 *Eyckeler & Malt AG v Commission*, n 23 above, para 162. Nevertheless, where matters in addition to the common risks are relied upon, a special situation may exist.

[108] Joined Cases 244 and 245/85 *Cerealmangimi SpA et Italgrani SpA v Commission of the European Communities*, n 101 above, at para 15.

[109] See Implementing Regulation, Art. 905.2, fourth para, considered again below.

in a special situation with others. This was expressly acknowledged recently by Advocate General Jacobs who said

> a special situation within the meaning of Article 905(1) of the implementing regulation exists where, having regard to the objective of fairness underlying Article 239 of the Customs Code, there are circumstances liable to place the applicant in an exceptional situation as compared with other operators engaged in the same business. It is for the national authorities to make the necessary findings and, if need be, to forward the file to the Commission which will on the basis of the information placed before it make the definitive assessment whether a special situation exists such as to justify the repayment of the import duties paid.[110]

So far as the second proposition is concerned, the Court of Justice has said that:

> Errors or omissions on the part of administrative authorities cannot give rise to the application of the general equitable provision provided for in the first paragraph of Article 13 of Regulation No 1430/79 unless such errors or omissions imposed upon a trader a financial obligation which he had no legal means of contesting.[111]

Consequently, where a national authority changes its mind about the existence of a special situation that does not itself constitute a special situation. The matter may be litigated before the domestic courts. Similarly, the existence of grounds for challenging decisions of the Commission may be used to mount challenges in the ordinary way. They do not give rise to a special situation.[112]

2. *Examples of situations giving rise to special situations*

2.1 *Access to the* Official Journal

Many traders have attempted to establish the existence of special situations and few have succeeded. One case in which the Court of Justice found such a situation to have arisen was in *Oryzomyli Kavallas OEE*.[113] The traders concerned were Greek and the facts of the case related to a time soon after the entry of Greece into the EEC. The Court of Justice accepted that the traders did not have available to them the Greek language text of the relevant regulations.

---

[110] Case C–253/99 *Firma Bacardi GmbH v Hauptzollamt Bremerhaven*, Opinion of Jacobs AG of 25 Jan 2001 at para 103. The Court's Judgment (27 Sept 2001) also emphasizes that it is the Commission alone which is empowered to decide whether or not a special situation exists (para 57). See also Case C–86/97 *Reiner Woltmann (trading as Trans-Ex-Import) v Hauptzollamt Potsdam*, n 98 above, at para 21. See also Joined Cases T–186/97, T–187/97 and others *Kaufring AG and others v Commission*, n 39 above, at para 218. The court emphasized at para 218 that it must be shown that in the absence of the circumstances in question, the trader would not have suffered the disadantage caused by *a posteiori* entry of duty in the accounts. See further Case T–330/99 *Spedition Wilhelm Rotermund GmbH v Commission*, 7 June 2001 at para 54.

[111] Joined Cases 244 and 245/85 *Cerealmangimi SpA et Italgrani SpA v Commission*, n 108 above, at para 17.

[112] Ibid, at paras 16–19.

[113] Case 160/84 *Oryzomyli Kavallas OEE v Commission*, at n 38 above.

Even the competent section of the Ministry of Agriculture had not received the Greek language edition of the *Official Journal* and used texts in other language versions or translations, made by Greek officials intended for internal use. No instructions or circulars had been issued explaining to officials the basic principles of the Community rules. Furthermore, the applications in question were received by a newly-appointed official who did not have the experience to explain the difference between a single import licence and an advance-fixing certificate. The Court of Justice went on to hold that the traders had not been negligent and had established a special situation. Traders, particularly small traders without access to EC documentation centres, have frequently complained about the difficulties of gaining access to the *Official Journal*, but the Greek traders in *Oryzomyli Kavallas OEE* were in a most unusual situation which is unlikely to be replicated. As we noted above, the general rule is that traders have a responsibility to be aware of the contents of the *Official Journal* and act accordingly.[114]

2.2 Mistakes by traders

The fact that traders are obliged to be aware of the relevant law does not mean that their mistakes can never constitute a special situation. For example in *Papierfabrik*,[115] the fact that a trader mistakenly declared for free circulation goods which had been brought into the Community solely for labelling before being exported, and paid customs duties accordingly, was held by the Court of Justice to be capable of constituting a special situation. The Commission could not, therefore, refuse to consider the trader's application for repayment. Another situation which has been regarded as special is one where the trader concerned has wrongly classified goods in reliance on incorrect information, supplied, to a company belonging to the same group as the company liable, by the competent customs authorities of a Member State other than that competent to effect recovery. The reason is that the information may induce the trader to entertain a legitimate expectation that the tariff classification he has adopted is correct.[116]

2.3 Fraud by commercial operators and official investigations

As we have noted before, the importer cannot rely exclusively on the fact that the exporter has acted fraudulently to escape post-clearance recovery, although recent amendments to CCC, Article 220.2(b), in relation to the issue

---

[114] See 'Article 220.2(b): Detectability' at pp 415–17 above.

[115] Case 283/82 *Papierfabrik Schoellershammer Heinrich August Schoeller & Söhne GmbH & Co KG v Commission*, n 101 above.

[116] Case C–250/91 *Hewlett Packard France v Directeur Général des Douanes*, n 25 above, at paras 42–44.

of certificates by the customs authorities in the third country of export, give protection to a trader where the issuing authorities are, or should have been, aware that the goods in question did not qualify for preferential treatment. The customs authorities of a Member State, however, may also possess knowledge which proves to be material in relation to post-clearance recovery. The Court of Justice held that a special situation existed where the Netherlands' customs authorities knew that a fraud was being effected and, for operational reasons, decided not to inform those who would suffer a liability to customs duty as a result, and who were consequently denied the opportunity to prevent a future liability from arising. In such circumstances, the demands of the investigation by the customs authorities or the police, of which a person is ignorant, may constitute a special situation for the trader affected. In the words of the Court of Justice:

> Although it may be legitimate for the national authorities, in order better to dismantle a network, identify perpetrators of fraud and obtain or consolidate evidence, deliberately to allow offences or irregularities to be committed, to place on the person liable the burden of the customs debt arising from the choices made in connection with the prosecution of offences is inimical to the objective of fairness which underlies Article 905(1) of Regulation No 2454/93 in that it puts that person in an exceptional situation in comparison with other operators engaged in the same business.[117]

2.4 *Mistakes by customs authorities, the Commission, and others*

It will be apparent from the previous section that the actions of customs authorities may give rise to special situations. In an appropriate case errors by customs authorities, such as delays in issuing certificates of authenticity,[118] may be capable of constituting special situations. In the light of the circumstances which the Court of Justice has held constitute special situations, it may be thought that a special situation existed in *Reece*.[119] In this case the various

---

[117] Case C–61/98 *De Haan Beheer BV v Inspecteur der Invoerrechten en Accijnzen te Rotterdam*, n 30 above, at para 53. Such action may, equally, leave national authorities open to official criticism. In the UK, the Comptroller and Auditor General has reported to Parliament on the conduct of HM Customs and Excise in relation to 'excise diversion frauds' which have cost the government about £836m, of which £500m has been written off. The matter will be the subject of a further report, but the Comptroller and Auditor General has recently noted that: 'There has been a serious breakdown of controls within Customs which has led to a substantial loss of revenue. Although Customs became aware of the threat of outward excise diversion frauds as early as 1994 they did not take effective action to curtail these frauds until 1998. About half the revenue could have been protected if fraudulent consignments had been intercepted rather than letting the investigations continue in order to obtain sufficient evidence to prosecute those involved or if effective action had been taken earlier.': *Appropriation Accounts 1999–2000, Vol 16: Class XVI, Departments of the Chancellor of the Exchequer: HM Customs and Excise, Report of the Comptroller and Auditor General* HC 25 XVI, 9 Feb 2001, para 5.15, published by the National Audit Office.

[118] See Case C–253/99 *Firma Bacardi GmbH v Hauptzollamt Bremerhaven*, Judgment of 27 Sept 2001 at para 60.

[119] *CCE v E Reece Ltd*, *The Times*, 11 Oct 2000.

Vietnamese authorities had between them information showing that the agreement between the Community and Vietnam was being abused. They failed, however, to share information or even to develop a system for sharing information. Had they done so it would have been apparent to them that the exporter in question was acting fraudulently. The English High Court held that no special situation arose on the facts of that case. Even if that decision is beyond criticism, which may be questioned, it should be borne in mind that whether or not a special situation exists is to be decided on a case-by-case basis. The case should not be regarded, therefore, as establishing that the conduct of the authorities of an exporting country can never give rise to a special situation. Indeed, in one recent case the Court of Justice has reaffirmed that the conduct of authorities in the exporting country can constitute a special situation. In *Kaufring AG*,[120] the Court concluded that certain failures of the Turkish authorities in implementing the association agreement between Turkey and the EC, and a protocol to it, contributed to irregularities in connection with the export of goods from Turkey to the Community and to the creation of a special situation.[121] The Association Council created under the association agreement also played a part in creating a special situation. The Court noted that the Council's main task was to adopt measures necessary to ensure both the smooth functioning of the association agreement and compliance with it by the contracting parties. For over twenty years, however, it took no measures to ensure that Turkey complied with certain provisions in the agreement.[122]

So far as the Commission is concerned, as we noted in Chapter 4, it performs its role in the customs duty system subject to a duty of good administration. The Court of Justice has held that this imposes on the Commission an obligation to ensure that tariff quotas are properly administered and are not exceeded, and that failure to comply with these duties amounts to a special situation.[123] In its view, the falsified certificates of authenticity which the trader relied upon, made it possible for the Hilton quota to be exceeded to a significant extent only because the Commission had failed to discharge its duty of supervising and monitoring application of the quota in 1991 and 1992. In those circumstances, the falsifications, which, moreover, were carried out in a very professional way, exceeded the normal commercial risk which must be

---

120 Joined Cases T–186/97, T–187/97 and others *Kaufring AG and others v Commission* at n 39.
121 Ibid at paras 256 and 302. See also Case T–330/99 *Spedition Wilhelm Rotermund GmbH v Commission*, n 110 above, in which it was held that fraud by a national customs official gave rise to a special situation with the Implementing Regulation, Art 905.
122 Joined Cases T–186/97, T–187/97 and others *Kaufring AG and others v Commission* at n 39 above, paras 274 and 275.
123 Case T–50/96 *Primex Produkte Import-Export GmbH & Co KG, Gebr Kruse GmbH, Interporc Im- und Export GmbH v Commission*, n 101 above, at para 143, Case T–42/96 *Eyckeler & Malt AG v Commission*, n 23 above, para at 191; and Case 175/84 *Krohn v Commission* [1987] ECR 97, para 15. It appears that the Commission's failure to inform a trader of irregularities, which it allegedly

borne by the applicants.[124] The duty of good administration is imposed on the Commission in a wide range of circumstances and not just in relation to customs duty, as was noted in Chapter 4. So far as customs duty is concerned, the duty is applicable to a wide range of activities, including, for example, the supervision of the regime of preferential tariffs. It should not be understood, however, as limited to narrow areas of activity. As the Court of First Instance made clear in *Kaufring AG*,[125] the Commission has a general duty to monitor the proper implementation of an association agreement and to ensure its proper application. In coming to this conclusion the Court noted, amongst other things, that the relevant association agreement imposed obligations on the EC and that the Commission was represented on the association council in question. The Commission failed in its duty because relevant legislation was not published in the *Official Journal*, because it took years to react to problems of implementation of which it was made aware and because it failed to inform Community importers: 'at the earliest possible date of the potential risks they incurred in importing colour television sets from Turkey'.[126] Furthermore, it failed to contact the association council in good time and to make use of the dispute settlement procedure in the association agreement.

F. APPLICATIONS UNDER CCC, ARTICLE 239.2

Repayment or remission of duty under CCC, Article 239 is made following an application to the appropriate customs office, submitted within twelve months from the date on which the amount of the duties was communicated to the debtor. The customs authorities may permit this time limit to be exceeded in duly justified exceptional cases.[127] Where the national customs authority cannot determine the application on the basis of Articles 900–903 of the Implementing Regulation, is not obliged to refuse the application in conformity with the Implementing Regulation, Article 904 (as to which see section

suspected or was aware of, in the conduct of the customs authorities of an exporting country, is relied upon as a special situation in a recent reference to the Court of Justice: see Case C–251/00 *Ilumitrónica-Illumação e Electrónica Lda v Chefa da Divisã o de Procedimentos Aduaneiros* [2000] OJ C233/24.

[124] Case T–50/96 *Primex Produkte Import-Export GmbH & Co KG, Gebr Kruse GmbH, Interporc Im-und Export GmbH v Commission*, n 101 above, at para 163. Case T–42/96 *Eyckeler & Malt AG v Commission*, n 23 above, at para 189. The errors committed by the Commission in the above cases included failure to check properly and regularly information supplied by the authorities of the exporting country, failure to use computer analysis of the information available, failure to circulate specimen signatures, failure to react to an established excess of imports over the quota and to alter the applicable administrative arrangements timeously. For an example of a case in which the Commission succeeded in rebutting an attempt to impugn its conduct see: Joined Cases T–10 and 11 *Unifrigo Gadus Srl and CPL Imperial 2 SpA v Commission*, n 27 above.

[125] Joined Cases T–186/97 and T–187/97 and others *Kaufring AG and others v Commission* at n 39 above.

[126] Ibid, para 268.   [127] CCC, Art 239.2.

H), and the application is supported by evidence which might constitute a special situation resulting from circumstances in which no deception or obvious negligence may be attributed to the person concerned, the customs authority must transmit the case to the Commission for decision in accordance with the Implementing Regulation, Articles 906–909. It has been frequently said that the procedure which has been established is a two-stage procedure, requiring, first, the involvement of national authorities and then the involvement of the Commission, before which traders now have greater rights than formerly.[128] The introduction of the Commission into the procedure is clearly designed to ensure that the notion of a special situation is uniformly applied throughout the Community. While the Commission is able to ensure uniformity in relation to cases referred to it, in relation to cases which are rejected by the national authorities the Court of Justice may, ultimately, ensure uniformity pursuant to the reference procedure.[129]

Notwithstanding the importance of uniformity, a national customs authority may grant repayment or remission of duty itself if it is not in doubt about the matter and the amount concerned per operator, in respect of one or more import or export operations and arising from one and the same special situation, is less than ECU 50,000.[130] It may also permit customs formalities, relating to re-export or destruction of the goods in question, before obtaining the Commission's ruling, without prejudice to the final decision of the application.[131] In those cases in which the customs authority does not grant repayment itself but does not reject the claim, its duty is simply to verify '. . . whether the circumstances relied on are liable to place the applicant in an exceptional situation as compared with other operators engaged in the same business'.[132] It must then transmit the case to the Commission. As will be apparent, the customs authority must reject all applications which it does not either grant or refer to the Commission.[133]

1. *The case to the Commission and the Commission's role*

The case which is sent to the Commission by the national authorities must include all the facts necessary for a full examination of it. It must also include

---

[128] See, eg, Implementing Regulation, Art 906a introduced by Commission Regulation (EC) 1677/98 [1998] OJ L212/18, Case T–42/96 *Eyckeler & Malt AG v Commission*, n 23 above, paras 74 and 75 and Case T–346/94 *France-aviation v Commission*, n 101 above, para 30f.

[129] Joined Cases C–153/94 and C–204/94 *The Queen v Commissioners of Customs and Excise, ex p Faroe Seafood Co Ltd, Føroya Fiskasøla LF and another*, n 21 above, at paras 79–80; Case C–348/89 *Mecanarte-Metalúrgica da Lagoa Ldª v Chefe do Serviço da Conferência Final da Alfândega do Porto*, n 24 above, at para 32 and 33 and Case C–64/89 *Hauptzollamt Gießen v Deutsche Fernsprecher GmbH*, n 43 above, at paras 12 and 13.

[130] Implementing Regulation, Art 905.2, fourth para.   [131] Ibid, Art 905.3.

[132] Case C–86/97 *Reiner Woltmann (trading as Trans-Ex-Import) v Hauptzollamt Potsdam*, n 98 above, at para 21.

[133] Implementing Regulation, Art 905, third para.

a statement, signed by the applicant, certifying that he or she has read the case and either has nothing to add, or listing all the additional information that should, in the applicant's view, be included.[134] The Commission is to inform the Member State concerned as soon as it receives the case. It may ask for additional information if there is not sufficient for it to take a decision in full knowledge of the facts of the case.[135] Within fifteen days of receiving the case, the Commission is to forward a copy to all the Member States and the case is to be placed on an agenda of the Customs Committee as soon as possible.[136] The Commission must decide whether or not a special situation exists, after consulting a group of experts representing all Member States, within nine months of the date on which it received the case.[137] The nine-month period is extended in cases where additional information has been sought, by a period equal to that between the date on which the Commission sent the request for additional information and the date on which the additional information was received. Where the Commission has informed the applicant of its objections, according to the procedure set out below, the nine-month period is extended by a period equal to that between the date on which the Commission sent its objections and the date on which it received an answer, or where no answer was given, the period for providing one expired.[138]

If the Commission, at any time in the procedure provided for in the Implementing Regulation, Articles 906 and 907 (effectively at any time after it has received the case) intends to take a decision which is unfavourable to the applicant it must communicate its objections to him or her in writing providing all the documents on which the objections are based. An applicant then has a period of one month from the date on which the objections were sent, not received, to express his or her point of view. Failure to do this results in the waiver of the right to express a position.[139]

1.1 *Representations to the Commission*

The right of the person concerned to make representations to the Commission directly, rather than indirectly via the national authorities, was given by Commission Regulation (EC) 1677/98, Article 1, paragraph 9.[140] It was not,

---

[134] The requirement that a statement be added to an application was contained in Commission Regulation (EC) 12/97 of 18 Dec 1996 [1997] OJ L9/1. It could not be applied retrospectively to defeat applications made prior to 20 Jan 1997: see Case T–290/97 *Mehibas Dordtselaan BV v Commission*, n 36 above, paras 42 and 43.

[135] Implementing Regulation, Art 905.2, third para.

[136] Ibid, Art 906.

[137] Ibid, Art 907, first para. The Commission alone may decide whether or not a special situation exists: see n 110 above.

[138] Ibid, Art 907, third para.

[139] Ibid, Art 906a.

[140] Of 29 July 1998 [1998] OJ L212/18.

perhaps, easily obtained.[141] The Court of First Instance had decided in, *France-aviation v Commission*,[142] that 'respect for the right to be heard must be guaranteed in procedures for the repayment of customs duty'.[143] After the judgment in this case, Commission Regulation (EC) 12/97 was passed,[144] making provision for a statement by a trader to be sent to the Commission along with the case sent by the national authorities to the Commission. No provision was made, however, for direct representations by a trader to the Commission in response to its views, until Commission Regulation 1677/98[145] came into effect, following the judgment in *Eyckeler and Malt*.[146] Before this latter regulation came into effect, the Court of First Instance in *Primex* had repeated its view that the inability of the traders in question to state their case directly, under the then applicable procedure, infringed the traders' rights of defence.[147] This was considered to be particularly significant, given the Commission's margin of appreciation in relation to the determination of whether or not a special situation exists.[148] Issues of lack of care or obvious negligence on the part of a trader are clearly matters on which it should be able to comment and in the case in question the trader had been unable to do so.[149]

The rights of defence not only give a trader the right to make his views known to the Commission and to have an independent tribunal, they also enable him to put his case having regard to the documents taken into account in making the case against him, such as reports of missions carried out by Commission officials and all non-confidential documents concerning its decision.[150] To the extent that the rights of defence or rules of procedure do not

---

[141] As a review of the case-law in this area by the Court of First Instance in Case T–290/97 *Mehibas Dordtselaan BV v Commission*, n 36 above, makes clear: see paras 41–47.

[142] Case T–346/94, n 101 above.   [143] Ibid, para 34.

[144] Judgment in Case T–346/94 *France-aviation v Commission* at n 101 above, was given on 9 Nov 1995. The provisions of Commission Regulation (EC) 12/97 of 18 Dec 1996 came into force 7 days after their publication in [1997] OJ L9/1 on 13 Jan 1997.

[145] See n140 above.

[146] Case T–42/96 *Eyckeler & Malt AG v Commission*, n 23 above. Judgment in this case was given on 19 Feb 1998 and the relevant provisions of Commission Regulation (EC) 1677/98 on 30 July 1998, took effect 7 days following their publication in the OJ.

[147] Case T–50/96 *Primex Produkte Import-Export GmbH & Co KG, Gebr Kruse GmbH, Interporc Im-und Export GmbH v Commission*, n 101 above, at paras 63–70. See also Joined Cases T–186/97, 1187/97 and others *Kaufring AG v Commission*, n 39 above, at paras 151–153.

[148] See Case T–50/96, *Primex Produkte Import-Export GmbH & Co KG, Gebr Kruse GmbH, Interporc Im- und Export GmbH v Commission*, n 101 above, at para 60.

[149] See ibid, at para 70.

[150] See ibid, at paras 63 and 64. The Court founded itself on the competition cases of Joined Cases T–10/92, T–11/92, T–12/92 and T–15/92 *Cimenteries CBR v Commission* [1992] ECR II–2667, para 38, and Case T–36/91 *ICI v Commission* [1995] ECR II–1847, para 69. See also Case T–42/96 *Eyckeler & Malt AG v Commission*, n 23 above, at paras 80 and 81; Case T–124/96 *Interporc Im-und Export GmbH v Commission* [1998] ECR II–231, in which the Court annulled a decision by the Commission refusing access to documents relating, amongst other things, to the administration of a quota; and Joined Cases T–186/97 and T–187/97 and others *Kaufring AG v Commission*, n 39 above, at para 179 onwards and para 226.

give a person documents it may be possible to rely upon the general law regarding access to documents to obtain them.[151]

2. *The Commission's decision*

The Member State which referred the case to the Commission is to be informed of its decision as soon as possible and, in any event, within thirty days of the expiry of the period during which the Commission must take a decision on the case. A copy of the decision is to be sent to all other Member States. The decision-making authority is then to decide whether to grant or refuse the application on the basis of the Commission's decision. The decision-making authority must not substitute its own determination for that of the Commission but must follow it.[152] Where the Commission has decided that the circumstances justify repayment or remission, it may authorize other Member States to repay or remit duty in other cases involving comparable issues of fact and of law. When it does this, it must also notify the authorized Member States of the decision taken on the case originally referred to it.[153]

Not all decisions given by the Commission have concluded the application in question. The Court of Justice has said that:

> when the Commission, after consultation with the Customs Code Committee, have delivered a decision addressed to a Member State holding that there was, in a specific case, no justification for granting remission of import duties . . . and when that decision does not contain any legal or factual indication relating to the legal basis for effecting post-clearance recovery of the import duties concerned under the regulation in issue, a national court may rule on the latter question, having recourse, if appropriate, to the procedure under Article 177 of the Treaty.[154]

Consequently, where such a Commission decision, reached pursuant to the procedure contained in Implementing Regulation, Articles 905–908, states that there was no special situation, the Member State can proceed to consider whether or not the post-clearance recovery is permitted under Article 236 without the decision first being annulled.[155]

On occasions a trader will wish to apply for the annulment of the Commission's decision pursuant to the EC Treaty, Article 230.4. In order to facilitate the review by the Courts of a decision, and for the benefit of the trader, the Commission must give reasons for its decision pursuant to EC

---

[151] Case T–92/98 *Interporc Im- und Export GmbH v Commission* [1999] ECR II–3521 para 44. Note that the case has been appealed: See Case C–41/00 [2000] OJ C149/17 which is pending.

[152] Case C–61/98 *De Haan Beheer BV v Inspecteur der Invoerrechten en Accijnzen te Rotterdam*, n 30 above, para 48.

[153] Implementing Regulation, Art 908.3.

[154] See Case C–413/96 *Skatteministeriet v Sportgoods A/S*, [1998] ECR I–5835, para 43 cited in Case C–15/99 *Hans Sommer GmbH & Co KG v Hauptzollamt Bremen*, at n 26 above, para 31.

[155] Case C–15/99 *Hans Sommer GmbH & Co KG v Hauptzollamt Bremen*, at n 26 above, para 32.

Treaty, Article 253.[156] Whether or not the requirement is satisfied is to be
determined by reference to the wording and context of the measure as well as
all legal rules governing the matter in question. It is not necessary though that
all relevant facts and points of law be gone into.[157] It should be noted that
although the Court of Justice may annul a decision it cannot require the adoption of a different decision.[158] To do that is to encroach upon the prerogatives
of the Commission. Furthermore, a decision will not be annulled on the
ground of irregularities unless it is established that without them the procedure might have had a different outcome.[159]

The time limits within which the Commission must take a decision on the
case, and within which the Commission must notify a decision to a concerned
Member State, must be strictly observed. In the event that they are not
complied with, the application for repayment or remission must be granted by
the decision-making authority.[160]

3. *The Commission's discretion*

It will be apparent that in determining whether or not a special situation exists
the Commission exercises a significant discretionary power. This is exercisable
within a margin of assessment and requires the Commission to balance the
Community interest in ensuring that customs rules are respected, against the
interest of the importer acting in good faith not to incur loss beyond the
normal commercial risk.[161] It is not, though, just the importer's behaviour
which must be considered. The conduct of the Commission must also be taken
into account,[162] as must all relevant facts.[163] In *France-aviation* the Court of
First Instance commented on the Commission's discretion as follows:

[156] This states: 'Regulations, directives and decisions adopted jointly by the European Parliament and the Council, and such acts adopted by the Council or the Commission, shall state the reasons on which they are based and shall refer to any proposals or opinions which were required to be obtained pursuant to this Treaty.'

[157] Case T–209/97 *Mehibas Dordtselaan BV v Commission*, n 36 above, para 92 where the Court of First Instance relied upon Joined Cases C–121/91 and C–122/91 *CT Control (Rotterdam) and JCT Benelux v Commission* [1993] ECR I–3873, para 31, and Case T–195/97 *Kia Motors and Broekman Motorships v Commission* [1998] ECR II–2907, para 34. See also Joined Cases T–10/97 and 11/97 *Unifrigo Gadus Srl and CPL Imperial 2 SpA v Commission* at n 27 above, paras 71 and 72.

[158] Case T–75/95 *Günzler Aluminium GmbH v Commission* at n 36 above, para 18 and Case T–346/94 *France-aviation v Commission*, at n 101 above, para 42, to which it refers.

[159] See Case T–209/97 *Mehibas Dordtselaan BV v Commission*, at n 36 above, at para 47 in which the Court of First Instance found that the decision would not have been different. It relied upon Joined Cases 209/78–215/78 and 218/78 *Landewyck v Commission* [1980] ECR 3125, para 47, Case C–142/87 *Belgium v Commission* [1990] ECR I–959, para 48, and Case T–266/94 *Skibsvaerftsforeningen v Commission* [1996] ECR II–1399, para 243.

[160] Implementing Regulation, Art 909.

[161] Case T–290/97 *Mehibas Dordtselaan BV v Commission*, n 36 above, at para 78. The Court relied upon Case T–346/94 *France-aviation v Commission*, n 101 above, para 34 quoted below and Case T–42/96 *Eyckeler & Malt AG v Commission*, n 23 above, para 133.

[162] Case T–42/96 *Eyckeler & Malt AG v Commissions*, n 23 above, at para 133.

[163] See Case T–346/94 *France-aviation v Commission*, n 101 above, at paras 34 and 36; Joined

On the one hand, [Article 13] covers 'special situations', which necessarily presupposes that the Commission should take into consideration, and weigh in the balance, those of a multitude of factual and legal data which are likely to be relevant to its final decision. On the other hand, the Commission has to check whether the person concerned is guilty not simply of negligence, but of 'obvious negligence'. Lastly, before it takes its decision, the Commission has to consult a group of experts under Article 907 of Regulation No 2454/93, which implies that it has a choice whether or not to follow the opinion of that group. In the light of all those factors, the Court considers that, in a procedure under Article 13, the Commission has a discretion at least equivalent to that which the Court of Justice recognized it as having in the judgment in *Technische Universitaet Muenchen*, . . .[164]

The Court went on to conclude that it followed that respect for the right to be heard must be guaranteed in procedures for the repayment of customs duty. Failure to respect the right in that case led inevitably to the Commission's decision in issue being annulled.[165] In view of the annulment, the Court had no need to consider whether or not a special situation existed.[166]

Now that the Court of Justice has held that failures by the Commission may give rise to a special situation, the Commission may find itself in a somewhat uncomfortable situation not of its making. It will now have to determine whether or not it has failed in the conduct of its duties so that a special situation arises.[167] The Commission would undoubtedly carry out such an analysis fairly, but it is thought that it could not in such a case be an independent tribunal of the kind, for example, that the European Convention for the Protection of Human Rights and Fundamental Freedoms, Article 6[168]

Cases T–186/97 and T–187/97 and others *Kaufring AG and others v Commission*, n 39 above, at para 222f, and Case T–330/99 *Spedition Wilhelm Rotermund GmbH v Commission*, n 110 above, para 53.

[164] Case T–346/94 *France-aviation v Commission*, n 101 above, para 34. If the Commission concludes that there is no special situation it has no obligation to proceed to determine whether or not there is any obvious negligence or deception: Case T–290/97 *Mehibas Dordtselaan BV v Commission*, n 36 above, at para 87 and Case T–75/95 *Günzler Aluminium v Commission*, n 101 above, at para 54. The Commission's exercise of discretion and Case C–269/90 *Technische Universität München v Hauptzollamt München-Mitte* [1991] ECR I–5469 are considered further in Ch 4.

[165] Case T–346/94 *France-aviation v Commission*, n 101 above, at para 40.

[166] The alleged special situation was that a customs agent found itself liable for additional duty as a result of duty being charged in the first instance on forged invoices.

[167] As the Court noted in Joined Cases T–186/97 and T–187/97 and others *Kaufring AG and others v Commission*, n 39 above, at para 225.

[168] It is important to emphasize that: 'In contrast to the position in relation to Article 6 of the European Human Rights Convention, the requirement of effective judicial protection, in the Community sphere, is not limited merely to "civil rights" but extends to all rights deriving from the provisions of Community law.' Joined Cases C–111/95 and C–65/1995 *The Queen v Secretary of State for the Home Department, ex p Mann Singh Shingara and ex p Abbas Radiom* [1997] ECR I–3343 at para 75 of the Opinion of Ruiz-Jarabo Colomer AG. The scope of the limitation of Art 6 of the Convention is in any event diminishing. Some commentators on the Convention have suggested that 'a principle appears to be emerging to the effect that, in general, all rights of a pecuniary

guarantees. In appropriate cases, therefore, traders may contend that decisions reached by the Commission should be annulled for breach of Article 6.
The right to a fair trial has already led to traders being able to make representations to the Commission. The requirement that a tribunal must be independent may also prove to be significant.[169]

G. GENERALLY APPLICABLE PROCEDURAL MATTERS

Some procedural matters, such as time limits, have been referred to where
appropriate in the course of the text on substantive law and particular attention has, of course, been paid to the procedure governing applications raising
the possibility of a special situation in the last section. There are, however a
number of generally applicable procedural considerations and these are dealt
with below.

1. *Applications for repayment or remission*

1.1 *The form and nature of the application*

The application must be made by the person who paid or is liable to pay the
duties, or the persons who have taken over the rights and obligations of such
person or their representatives.[170] A specimen application form and provisions
relating to it are set out in the Implementing Regulation, Annex 111.[171] An
application may, however, be made on plain paper, provided that it contains the
information required in Annex 111.[172] In addition to containing the
prescribed information, the application must be accompanied by all the information and documentation required by the authorities to take a decision.[173]
In certain circumstances, the application must be accompanied by an import
or export licence or advance fixing certificate.[174] Specific requirements exist in
relation to a claim for repayment or remission of duty in relation to returned

---

nature are civil rights within the meaning of the article'. Lord Lester QC and D. Pannick QC (gen.
eds.), *Human Rights Law and Practice* (Butterworths, London, 1999), para 4.6.10.

[169] It is noteworthy that the existence of a discretion in the Commission also led to difficulties
in the context of reliefs from duty. These have now largely been removed. See further Ch 4 pp
101 f.

[170] Implementing Regulation, Art 878.1.

[171] Ibid, Art 878.2, first para.

[172] Ibid, Art 878.2, second para.

[173] It may be possible for an application to be accepted without all the necessary information
accompanying it so long as this is provided within time limits set by the customs authorities.
Failure to observe the time limit will result in the application being considered to be withdrawn:
ibid, Art 881.

[174] Ibid, Art 880.

goods.[175] The original and one copy of the application form, together with accompanying information, must be lodged with the customs office of entry in the accounts unless the customs authorities designate another office. If the office which receives the application is not the same as the one where the decision is made, then it must transmit the application immediately after acceptance to the decision-making customs authority, ie the customs authority competent to decide on the application in the Member State where the duties concerned were entered in the accounts.[176]

1.2 *The grounds of the application*

If an application for remission or repayment is made by a trader and it does not specifically mention CCC, Article 239.1, the authorities may, nevertheless, consider whether or not the circumstances in question fall within it.[177] Furthermore, even if an application is expressly placed upon a specific basis, the customs authorities must consider whether or not there is any other ground upon which repayment or remission may be claimed.[178]

2. *Decision pending*

Until a decision has been taken on an application for repayment or remission, the goods in question may not be transferred to a location other than that specified in the application, unless the applicant notifies in advance the customs office of entry, which must in turn inform the decision-making authority. The latter authority may, however, authorize completion of the customs formalities to which any repayment or remission may be subject before it has ruled on the application and without prejudice to its decision on it.[179]

  In those cases where supplementary information must be obtained in relation to an application, or where goods must be examined, it is for the decision-making authority to adopt the necessary measures. If necessary, it is to request the assistance of the supervising customs authority which is to comply promptly with its requests.[180] Sometimes, the application will relate to goods situated in a Member State other than that in which the import or export

---

[175] Ibid, Art 882.
[176] Ibid, Art 879.1 and CCC, Art 6.1.
[177] Case C–446/93 *SEIM - Sociedade de Exportação e Importação de Materiais Ld^a v Subdirector-Geral das Alfândegas*, n 101 above, paras 52–54.
[178] See Case C–48/98 *Söhl & Söhlke v Hauptzollamt Bremen*, n 36 above, at paras 88–92, in which the fact that a trader placed his claim on Art 900.1(o) did not enable the customs authorities to limit their examination to that provision. The Court also relied upon Case C–86/97 *Waltmann (Reiner) (trading as Trans-Ex-Import) v Hauptzollamt Potsdam*, n 98 above, at para 19, which states that where an authority cannot remit on the basis of Implementing Regulation, Art 899, it must verify whether there is evidence of a special situation within Art 905 and if need be forward the case to the Commission.
[179] Implementing Regulation, Arts 883 and 884.   [180] Ibid, Art 885.

duties were entered in the accounts. A specific procedure is applicable for cross-border cooperation in these circumstances.[181]

3. *The decision*

When the decision-making authority possesses all the necessary particulars it must give a written decision on the application and the decision is to be taken and notified to the applicant at the earliest opportunity.[182] Where a request for a decision is made in writing, the decision is to be made within a period set out in accordance with the existing provisions, starting on the date on which the request is received by the customs authorities. The decision must be notified in writing to the applicant. The period may, however, be exceeded 'where the customs authorities are unable to comply with it'. In such cases the applicant must be informed of the grounds for exceeding the time limit and be informed of the further period of time which is necessary for a decision to be given.[183]

If the decision rejects the application then it must set out the grounds for doing so and notify the applicant of the right to appeal.[184] The decision must contain all the particulars necessary for its implementation and, depending on the circumstances, must contain some or all of the following,[185] namely:

(i)   the information necessary for identifying the goods to which it applies;

(ii)   the grounds for repayment or remission and a reference to the corresponding Article of the CCC and, where appropriate, of Part IV Title IV (Articles 877–912g) of the Implementing Regulation;

(iii) the use to which the goods may be put or the destination to which they may be sent;

(iv)   the time limit for completion of the formalities to which repayment or remission is subject (see below 'Loss of entitlement to repayment or remission');

(v)   a statement indicating that the duties in question will not be repaid or remitted until the implementing customs office has informed the decision-making customs authority that the formalities to which repayment or remission is subject have been completed;

---

[181] Implementing Regulation, Arts 885.2 and 910–912.

[182] Ibid, Art 886.1and CCC, Article 6.2.

[183] CCC, Art 6.2. The requirement that a decision be given in accordance with existing provisions is likely to lead to the passage of a statutory instrument in the UK. It has not been possible to review the domestic law of Member States, but it appears that provisions governing time limits are not in place in all Member States and that where they do exist they differ widely from 6 months to 8 weeks.

[184] Implementing Regulation, Art 886.1, and CCC, Art 6.3.

[185] See ibid, Art 886.2.

(vi) particulars of any requirements to which the goods remain subject pending implementation of the decision;[186]

(vii) a notice informing the recipient that he or she must give the original of the decision to the implementing customs office of his or her choice when presenting the goods.

The implementing customs office is obliged to satisfy itself that any requirements to which goods remain subject pending the implementation of the decision are met and that, in all cases, the goods are actually used in the manner, or sent to the destination specified in the decision to repay or remit duty. When it has done so, it is to send a certificate to that effect to the decision-making authority.[187] A decision-making authority may only repay or remit duty once it has received this certificate.[188]

4. *Interest on repayments*

The CCC, Article 241.1, provides that no interest is payable where the competent authorities repay import or export duties, or credit interest, or interest on the arrears of import or export duties.[189] Interest is paid, however, where a decision to grant a request for repayment is not implemented within three months of the date on which the decision was adopted, and where national provisions stipulate that it shall be paid.[190] The amount of the interest paid is to be calculated so that it is equivalent to the amount which would be charged for this purpose on the national money or financial market.[191]

5. *Loss of entitlement to repayment or remission*

It is possible to lose an entitlement to repayment or remission of duties. This occurs where the person concerned fails to complete the customs formalities, to which the repayment or remission is subject, within the time limit set by the decision-making customs authority. The time limit must be no later than two

[186] Where the decision specifies that goods may be placed in a customs warehouse, a free zone, or a free warehouse the necessary formalities must be carried out. Where the decision specifies a use to which the goods are to be put, or a destination to which they are to be sent, which can be established only in a Member State other than that in which the implementing customs office is located, proof of compliance is to be furnished by production of a Control Copy T5 containing specified information: Implementing Regulation, Art 887.2 and 3.
[187] Ibid, Art 887.1 and 5.
[188] Ibid, Art 888.
[189] For 'credit interest' see Ch 12 p 400.
[190] For the UK see the Finance Act 1999, ss 127–129. These provisions came into force on 1 Apr 2000 by virtue of the Finance Act 1999 Part VII, (Appointed Day) Order 2000, SI 2000/632. S 127 is amended by the Interest on Repayments of Customs Duty (Applicable Period) Order 2000 SI 2000/633. The rate payable is 5 per cent: the Air Passenger Duty and Other Indirect Taxes (Interest Rate) (Amendment) Regulations 2000, SI 2000/632 ref 5.
[191] CCC, Art 241.1 second sub-para.

months from the date of notification of the decision to repay or remit duty. Breach of the time limit will be disregarded only if the person concerned can establish that he or she was prevented from complying with it by unforeseeable circumstances or *force majeure*.[192]

6. *Repayment or remission in error*

Where a customs debt is remitted or repaid in error, the original debt is to become payable again and any interest paid by the competent authorities must be reimbursed.[193]

7. *Repayment or remission where quotas and other arrangements apply*

Applications for repayment or remission of duty are not infrequently based upon the application of a zero or reduced rate of duty, at the date on which the declaration for release for free circulation was accepted, by virtue of quotas, tariff ceilings, or other preferential tariff arrangements. In these cases, repayment or remission is granted only if the quota has not been exhausted, or the normal rate of duty has not been re-imposed, at the time the application was lodged, accompanied by the necessary documents. The only exception to this rule is where the failure to apply the reduced or zero rate of duty was the result of an error by the customs authorities themselves, and the declaration for release for free circulation contained all particulars and was accompanied by all documents necessary for the application of that rate.[194]

A certificate of origin, internal Community transit document, or other document may be produced in support of a claim for repayment or remission indicating that the goods in question were eligible, at the time the declaration for release for free circulation was accepted, for preferential tariff treatment or Community treatment. The application is to be granted, however, only where it is established that the document refers specifically to the goods in question and that all the conditions relating to acceptance of the document are fulfilled, together with all other conditions for preferential tariff treatment.[195]

---

[192] Implementing Regulation, Art 893.

[193] CCC, Art 242. See also the Finance Act 1999, s 129.

[194] Implementing Regulation, Art 889. See Case C–413/96 *Skatteministeriet v Sportgoods A/S*, n 154 above, paras 23–25. The Court of Justice decided, in relation to pre-consolidation legislation, that tariff ceilings had to be strictly adhered to. Ceilings reimposed after the acceptance of the declaration, and prior to the discovery of an error in the classification of goods, nevertheless applied to those goods on post-clearance recovery, paras 26–34, of the Judgment.

[195] Implementing Regulation, Art 890. In Case C–253/99 *Firma Bacardi GmbH v Hauptzollamt Bremerhaven*, Judgment 27 Sept 2001, it was said that Art 890 may be applied only if the goods could have been eligible for Community treatment or preferential tariff treatment within CCC, Art 20.3(d) and (e): see para 42. Note that an application will not be granted where a certificate for the advance fixing of levies is presented in support of the application: Implementing Regulation, Art 891.

H. SITUATIONS WHICH DO NOT GIVE RISE TO RELIEF

To conclude this section on repayment or remission of duty, we turn to CCC, Article 904 which sets out three situations in which remission or repayment is not to be made. The situations are as follows:[196]

(i)   where goods which have previously been entered for a customs procedure involving an obligation to pay import duty are re-exported from the Community customs territory (for reasons other than those referred to in CCC, Articles 237 or 238 or the Implementing Regulation, Articles 900 or 901) notably failure to sell them;

(ii)   where, for any reason whatsoever, goods which have been entered for a customs procedure involving an obligation to pay import duty are destroyed after their release by the customs authorities, except where expressly provided for in Community legislation;

(iii) where documents which have been presented for the purpose of obtaining the preferential tariff treatment of goods declared for free circulation are subsequently found to be forged, falsified, or not valid for the purpose, even where the documents were presented in good faith. The Court of Justice has held that post-importation verification of documentation would be largely deprived of its usefulness if forged certificates could give rise to a claim for repayment or remission.[197] Nevertheless, this provision does not restrict the general fairness clause, discussed above, more than necessary. It is possible, therefore, for a special situation to arise where a trader has innocently relied upon forged, falsified, or invalid documentation in circumstances where the trader has not been guilty of deception or obvious negligence.[198]

I. APPEALS

An efficient and comprehensive appeals procedure for customs duty is essential in any jurisdiction. It is required under the revised Kyoto Convention[199] and also by GATT, Article X.3(b) which provides that:

[196] See also Implementing Regulation, Art 899, second indent.

[197] Joined Cases 98/83 and 230/83 *Van Gend & Loos v Commission*, n 107 above, at para 13 and Case C–446/93 *SEIM - Sociedade de Exportação e Importação de Materiais Ldᵃ v Subdirector-Geral das Alfândegas*, n 101 above, at para 44. See further Ch 7.

[198] Case C–446/93 *SEIM - Sociedade de Exportação e Importação de Materiais Ldᵃ v Subdirector-Geral das Alfândegas*, n 101 above, paras 47.

[199] See chapter 10 of the General Annex. The appeals procedure it requires is a two-stage one, with appeals being dealt with internally and by an independent body subsequently. The CCC permits a two-stage procedure: see Art 243.2.

Each contracting party shall maintain, or institute as soon as practicable, judicial, arbitral or administrative tribunals or procedures for the purpose, *inter alia* of the prompt review or correction of administrative action relating to customs matters. Such tribunals or procedures shall be independent of the agencies entrusted with administrative enforcement . . .

Community law reflects these requirements in the CCC which provides that any person shall have a right to appeal against decisions, taken by customs authorities, which relate to the application of customs legislation and which concern them directly and individually. It also provides a right of appeal for those who have applied to customs authorities for a decision relating to the application of customs legislation and who have not received a ruling within the applicable time limits. The appeal is to be lodged in the Member State where the decision has been taken or has been applied for.[200] As we shall see, however, Community law does not regulate precisely the manner in which the right of appeal is exercised. The reason for a very general approach on the part of the Community in this area has been said to be:

> not only the differences between national procedures, which in some cases are considerable, but also the fact that they often apply uniformly to the whole field of national administrative and tax law so that the harmonisation of rights of appeal for the purposes of customs law only will fragment hitherto uniform national appeals procedures.[201]

1. *Decisions*

A decision in respect of which an appeal may be made is any official act by the customs authorities pertaining to customs rules, giving a ruling on a particular case, such act having legal effects on one or more specific or identifiable persons. The definition states expressly that a 'decision' includes the provision of binding tariff information within CCC, Article 12.[202] Naturally, the concept of a decision must be uniformly understood throughout the Community. Advocate General Fennelly has said that a decision is:

> an act manifesting the exercise of a judgment or of a discretion. It is an act taken after consideration of various factors and under Community law, such an act would have to set out the grounds or reasons which led to that exercise of discretion in

---

[200] CCC, Art 243.1.

[201] See Opinion 91/C 60/03 on the proposal for a Council Regulation (EEC) establishing the Community Customs Code and the proposal for a Council Regulation (EEC) determining the cases and the special conditions under which the temporary importation arrangements may be used with total relief from import duties, adopted by the Economic and Social Committee on 18 Dec 1990 [1991] OJ C60/5, at para 2.50, cited by the Court of Justice in Case C–1/99 *Kofisa Italia Srl v Ministero delle Finanze*, 11 Jan 2001, at para 41.

[202] CCC, Art 4(5).

order that its addressee be in a position to mount an effective challenge to its validity.[203]

In many cases this statement will prove unexceptional. It should not, however, replace the primary definition contained in the CCC which in some respects may be wider. For example, it may be that rulings are given without proper consideration. Such rulings may, of course, be subject to challenge.

A person who requests the customs authorities to take a decision relating to the application of customs rules must supply all the information and documents required by them in order to take a decision.[204] So far as the customs authorities are concerned, where they adopt written decisions which either reject requests or are detrimental to the persons to whom they are addressed, they must set out the grounds on which they are based and must refer to the right of appeal given under CCC, Article 243.[205] Decisions are to be taken and notified to the applicant at the earliest opportunity. A written request for a decision must be answered with a written decision within a period, starting on the date on which the request is received, laid down in accordance with existing provisions.[206] The period may be exceeded where the authorities are unable to comply with it, and in such a case they are to inform the applicant before the relevant period has expired.[207] They must also state the grounds which justify the period being exceeded and indicate the period of time which they consider necessary in order to give a ruling.[208] Once given, decisions are to be immediately enforceable unless suspended in accordance with CCC, Article 244 referred to below. Decisions may, though, be annulled, revoked, or amended.

1.1 *Annulment, revocation, and amendment*

The provisions in the CCC dealing with these matters are without prejudice to national rules which stipulate that decisions are invalid or become null and void for reasons unconnected with customs legislation.[209]

A decision which is favourable to the person concerned is to be annulled,

---

[203] Case C–213/99 *José Teodoro de Andrade* v *Director da Alfândega de Leixões*, 7 Dec 2000, para 55 relying on Case 24/62 *Germany* v *Commission* [1963] ECR 63 at 69. Applying this reasoning, the Advocate General went on, understandably, to conclude that the imposition of an automatic financial penalty as a matter of law was not a decision of which the importer needed notification: see paras 56 and 57. He considered, however, that a sale of property at the discretion of the authorities would be a decision, as would a refusal to extend the deadline for assignment of a customs-approved use or treatment: see para 59.

[204] CCC, Art 6.1.

[205] CCC, Art 6.3. CCC, Art 6.4 provides that the requirement that a decision sets out the grounds on which it is based may be extended to other decisions.

[206] The UK has yet to pass a statutory instrument providing for the necessary time limits.

[207] CCC, Art 6.2, first para.

[208] Ibid, Art 6.2, second and third paras.　　　　　　　　　　　[209] Ibid, Art 10.

from the date on which it was taken, if it was issued on the basis of incorrect or incomplete information and the applicant knew, or should reasonably have known, that the information was incorrect and incomplete and the decision could not have been taken on the basis of correct or complete information.[210] Where a decision is annulled, the person to whom the decision was addressed must be notified of its annulment.[211] In cases where a decision which is favourable to the person concerned cannot be annulled, it must be revoked or amended where one or more of the conditions laid down for its issue were not, or are no longer, fulfilled.[212] A favourable decision may be revoked where the person concerned fails to fulfil an obligation imposed on him under it.[213] The person to whom a decision is addressed must be notified of its revocation or amendment.[214] The revocation or amendment is usually to take effect from the date of notification. In exceptional cases, however, where the legitimate interests of the person to whom the decision is addressed so require, the customs authorities may defer the date when the revocation or amendment takes effect.[215]

2. *The appeal, suspension of the decision, and the provision of security*

The right of appeal may be exercised initially before the customs authorities designated for that purpose by the Member States.[216] Subsequently, it may be exercised before an independent body which may be a judicial authority, or an equivalent specialized body, according to the provisions applicable in the Member State concerned.[217] A Member State is not obliged, however, to establish a two-stage appeal procedure and may provide for a hearing directly before the independent body.[218] The UK has adopted a two-stage approach and the Finance Act 1994 provides that an appeal to the VAT and Duties Tribunal occurs after a departmental review.[219]

Generally speaking, the lodging of an appeal does not cause the suspension of the implementation of the disputed decision. It is, however, to be suspended by the customs authorities, either wholly or partly, where they have good reason to believe either that the decision is inconsistent with the customs legislation or that irreparable damage is to be feared for the person concerned.[220]

[210] CCC, Art 8.1 and 3.   [211] Ibid, Art 8.2.
[212] Ibid, Art 9.1.   [213] Ibid, Art 9.2.
[214] Ibid, Art 9.3.   [215] Ibid, Art 9.4.
[216] Ibid, Art 243.2(a).   [217] Ibid, Art 243.2(b).
[218] See Case C–1/99 *Kofisa Italia Srl v Ministero delle Finanze*, n 201 above, at paras 34–43.
[219] See the Finance Act 1994, ss 15 and 16.
[220] CCC, Art 244, first and second paras. It is clear that there are two alternative situations in which the decision must be suspended: see Case C–130/95 *Bernd Giloy v Hauptzollamt Frankfurt am Main-Ost* [1997] ECR I–4291 at paras 30–34. Art 244 gives the power of suspension exclusively to the customs authorities and not to the judicial authorities of the Member State in question. The judicial authorities do, however, have a power of suspension exercisable in order to comply with

The Court of Justice has indicated that 'irreparable damage' is irreversible damage and that financial damage is not irreparable unless the loss concerned could not be wholly recouped in the event of the appellant's success. However, where the decision may lead to the winding up of a company or the sale of an individual's flat, the damage is irreparable.[221] So far as the likelihood of the damage occurring is concerned '[i]t is sufficient that the harm in question, particularly when it depends on the occurrence of a number of factors, should be foreseeable with a sufficient degree of probability . . . '.[222]

2.1 *The provision of security*

Where the decision in question has the effect of causing import or export duties to be charged, its suspension, on whichever ground, is to be subject to the existence or lodging of security.[223] Security need not be required, however, where its requirement would be 'likely' owing to the debtor's circumstances, to cause serious economic or social difficulties.[224] The UK's VAT and Duties Tribunal has said in this regard that the appellant must show on a balance of probabilities that the requirement of security would be likely to cause such difficulties, but that 'likely' itself does not import a balance of probabilities test. It concluded:

> it is sufficient for the Appellant to establish that there is a real prospect, that in the Appellant's circumstances, a higher level of security would cause economic or social difficulties at any time in the period up to the final determination of the appeal in question.[225]

Clearly, the precise circumstances which may constitute serious economic or social difficulties are many and varied. The Court of Justice has said, however, that:

> to require a debtor, who does not have sufficient means, to lodge security would cause him 'serious economic difficulties'. . .[and] where the debtor cannot provide

---

their obligation to ensure the full effectiveness of Community law: see Case C–1/99 *Kofisa Italia Srl v Ministero delle Finanze*, n 201 above, at paras 48 and 49 and Case C–226/99 *Siples Srl v Ministero delle Finanze and others* [2001] ECR I–277, paras 19 and 20. It has been said that the two situations set out in the second para of Art 244, in which suspension of a decision is compulsory are not the only situations in which a suspension *may* be effected: see *Customs and Excise v Mitsui & Co UK plc* [2000] CMLR 85 at para [19] discussed further below.

[221] Case C–130/95 *Bernd Giloy v Hauptzollamt Frankfurt am Main-Ost*, n 220 above, paras 35–38.
[222] Ibid, para 39.
[223] See ibid, at paras 46 and 47 and CCC, Art 244, third para.
[224] See CCC, Art 244, third para, which has been considered by the English Court of Appeal in *CCE v Broomco (formerly Anchor Foods Ltd)*, *The Times*, 17 Aug 2000 (transcript available from Butterworths Taxation Service) considered below.
[225] *Anchor Foods Ltd v CCE* [1999] V&DR 1 at 25 para 158. See also para 157.

security, the customs authorities are entitled not to make suspension of implementation of a disputed decision subject to provision of security.[226]

Where security is required in an ordinary case in which serious economic or social difficulties are not in point, the level of the security is determined by reference to CCC, Article 192. This requires that where security is compulsorily provided, as in the case where a decision is to be suspended, then the level of the security is to be the precise amount of the customs debt in question, where the amount can be established with certainty at the time when the security is required. Where the amount cannot be so established then the level of security is to be the maximum amount of the customs duty debt which has been, or may be incurred, as estimated by the customs authorities. Where serious economic or social difficulties may be caused by the provision of such a level of security, then the requirement to provide security may be waived or the security set, taking into account all the relevant circumstances including the debtor's financial situation, at a level which does not exceed that required under Article 192.[227]

It should also be borne in mind that the level of security to be provided has to be established bearing in mind general principles of Community law including the right to a fair trial. It is clear that the right of access to a court is part of the right to a fair trial and that a request for provision of security for costs which impairs the essence of the right infringes Article 6 of the European Convention on Human Rights.[228]

3. *The UK's appeal procedure*

As this book is concerned with the law which applies throughout the Community, it is not proposed to consider the UK's appeal procedure, except in relation to one or two issues of general interest related to EC law, which arise out of the UK's creation of a customs duty appeal system. Of course, the fact that the UK and other Member States have a role to play in creating an appeals system arises because, in the words of the Court of Justice:

> although Article 243 of the Customs Code grants all traders a right to appeal against decisions taken by the customs authorities which relate to the application of customs legislation, and which concern them directly and individually, Article 245 of the Customs Code leaves it to the Member States to determine the provisions for the implementation of the appeals procedure.[229]

---

[226] Case C–130/95 *Bernd Giloy v Hauptzollamt Frankfurt am Main-Ost*, n 220 above, at para 53.
[227] Ibid, at paras 60–62.
[228] See eg, *Tolstoy Miloslavksy v UK* (1995) 20 EHHR 442, particularly at para 59. See also n 168 above.
[229] C–48/98 *Firma Söhl & Söhlke v Hauptzollamt Bremen*, n 36 above, para 65.

It went on to re-state well-known principles as follows:

> in the absence of Community rules governing a matter, it is for the domestic legal system of each Member State to designate the courts and tribunals having jurisdiction and to lay down the detailed procedural rules governing actions for safeguarding rights which individuals derive from the direct effect of Community law, it being understood that such rules must not be less favourable than those governing similar domestic actions nor render virtually impossible or excessively difficult the exercise of rights conferred by Community law.[230]

As is well known, the provisions governing appeals in the CCC, Title VIII, were not applied to the United Kingdom until 1 January 1995, one year after they applied in all other Member States. The reason for this delay was that, in providing for rights of appeal in customs matters,[231] the CCC provided for entirely new rights in UK law and led to the Value Added Tax Tribunal being re-named the Value Added Tax and Duties Tribunal.[232] The UK sought to fulfil its responsibility to implement appeal procedures by enacting the Finance Act 1994, sections 14–17. As we noted above, CCC, Article 243.2(a) permits, but does not require, a two-tier appeal process. The UK chose to adopt a two-tier procedure and the Finance Act 1994, section 14, and the Customs Reviews and Appeals (Tariff and Origin) Regulations 1997,[233] provide for a review of specified decisions. Section 15 of the Act sets out the Commissioners' duty to review decisions and gives them various powers in relation to the review. Section 16 then gives a right of appeal in respect of decisions. It does not, though, give a right of appeal where a decision is not given within the specified time, notwithstanding that such a right is specifically given by CCC, Article 243.1, as we noted earlier.[234]

3.1 *Ancillary and non-ancillary matters*

Although CCC, Title VIII, does not distinguish between different types of appeal, the Finance Act 1994, section 16 does. It differentiates between decisions on ancillary matters and other decisions.[235] 'Ancillary matters' are

---

[230] Ibid, at para 66. See Ch 4 for further references to the case law in this area. The application of these principles in the above case meant that a national court was able to determine whether the criteria in Implementing Regulation, Art 859.1, were satisfied where a timeous application for an extension had been refused by a decision of a customs authority which was then unappealable: see para 67 of the judgment.

[231] Appeals lodged with a view to the annulment or revision of a decision taken by customs authorities on the basis of the criminal law are outside the scope of CCC, Title VIII: see Art 246.

[232] See Finance Act 1994, s 7(3).

[233] SI 1997/534 made on 27 Feb 1997 and applicable from 24 Mar 1997.

[234] It is understood that the Lord Chancellor's Department is aware of the issue.

[235] Whatever the nature of the appeal the burden of proof rests on the appellant. This follows from the Finance Act 1994, s 16(6). The standard of proof is, in general, the balance of probabilities.

defined to exclude those affecting liability for customs duty or entitlement to repayment or remission of duty.[236] The phrase covers many decisions which the Commissioners of Customs and Excise need to take in the management and administration of the customs duty regime, for example, decisions on the requirement of security for a customs duty liability,[237] decisions on whether the entry, unloading, or transhipment of goods is to be allowed,[238] whether permission is to be granted for the taking of samples from goods presented to the Commissioners,[239] decisions about the route to be used for the movement of goods,[240] and about various matters relating to customs procedures and warehouses.[241] Having drawn the distinction, the Finance Act 1994, s 16(4) then states that in relation to any decision about an 'ancillary matter', or to any review of such a decision, the powers of the tribunal are to be:

> confined to a power, where the tribunal are satisfied that the Commissioners or other person making that decision could not reasonably have arrived at it, to do one or more of the following, that is to say-
>
> (a) to direct that the decision, so far as it remains in force, is to cease to have effect from such time as the tribunal may direct;
> (b) to require the Commissioners to conduct, in accordance with the direction of the tribunal, a further review of the original decision; and
> (c) in the case of a decision which has already been acted on or taken effect and cannot be remedied by a further review, to declare the decision to have been unreasonable and to give directions to the Commissioners as to the steps to be taken for securing that repetitions of the unreasonableness do not occur when comparable circumstances arise in future.

In relation to matters which are not ancillary matters, however, the powers of the tribunal are much wider. They are set out in the Finance Act 1994, s 16(5) which states: 'In relation to other decisions, the powers of an appeal tribunal on an appeal under this section shall also include power to quash or vary any decision and power to substitute their own decision for any decision quashed on appeal.'

It will be apparent that an appeal in non-ancillary matters is one by way of re-hearing, but in ancillary matters the tribunal's jurisdiction is merely super-

---

[236] The Finance Act 1994, s 16(8) provides that a decision on an ancillary matter is a decision of a description specified in Sch 5 to the Act which is not comprised in a decision falling within s 14(1)(a)–(c) of the Act. These paras include decisions on the time of charge, its rate, and amount, the person liable and the amount of his liability, and entitlement to relief, repayment, remission, or drawback, and the extent of the entitlement. The 1997 Regulations referred to on p 453 above, exclude from the class of ancillary decisions; decisions such as those relating to binding tariff and origin information and to origin in relation to preferential tariff measures. S 16(9) of the Finance Act 1994 provides that a decision on an ancillary matter does not include a decision of a description specified in the 1994 Act, Sch 5, para 9(e), which refers to decisions with respect to the amount of interest specified in an assessment.
[237] Finance Act 1994, Sch 5, para 1(m).   [238] Ibid, para 1(a).
[239] Ibid, para 1(b).   [240] Ibid, para 1(c).
[241] Ibid, para 1(e) and (g).

visory, determining whether or not a decision was reasonable.[242] Whether this distinction is justifiable and consistent with the terms of CCC, Article 243 was raised in *Shaneel Enterprises Ltd v CCE*[243] but the tribunal found it unnecessary to deal with the point. Were the point to arise now, the Human Rights Act 1998 would have to be borne in mind in construing the Finance Act 1994, as the President of the VAT and Duties Tribunal has pointed out.[244] Given the wide range of issues affected by the distinction between ancillary and other matters, the compatibility of the present legislation with the European Convention for the Protection of Human Rights and Fundamental Freedoms, Article 6, establishing the right to a fair trial, should be considered on a case-by-case basis, rather than generally. It is not, therefore, proposed to consider the issue here.[245]

3.2 *The provision of security prior to an appeal*

We have already noted that, in its first paragraph, CCC, Article 244 states that an appeal against a decision does not result in the suspension of it. According to its second paragraph, suspension must be effected, however, where the customs authorities have good reason to believe that the decision is inconsistent with customs legislation or that irreparable damage is to be feared for the person concerned. The third and final paragraph of Article 244 then requires the existence, or lodging, of security where a decision causing import or export duties to be charged is suspended. It concludes by noting that security is not required where its requirement 'would be likely, owing to the debtor's circumstances, to cause serious economic or social difficulties'.

---

[242] The VAT and Duties Tribunal has applied the test set out in *Customs and Excise Commissioners v J H Corbitt Numismatists) Ltd* [1980] STC 23, in which Lord Lane said that a tribunal reviewing the exercise of the Commissioners' decision 'could only properly [review the discretion] if it were shown that the Commissioners had acted in a way in which no reasonable panel of Commissioners could have acted; if they had taken into account some irrelevant matter or had disregarded something to which they should have given weight' (at 239j). By way of an early example see *Revilo Shipping Ltd* C00008, 15 Jan 1996. Where the appeal concerns the issue of whether or not the Commissioners of Customs and Excise were correct in refusing to refer a claim for repayment or remission of duty to the Commission, the tribunal will, of course, consider only whether the Commissioners should have referred the matter. It will not of itself order the remission or repayment of duty: *South Lodge Imports Ltd v CCE* [1999] V&DR 411.

[243] [1996] V&DR 23.

[244] 'The Human Rights Act in Prospect: Some Reflections' [2000] BTR 199. Of course in Community matters fundamental rights must always be borne in mind: see eg case T–50/96 *Primex Produkte Import-Export GmbH & Co KG. Gebr. Kruse GmbH, Interpore Im- und Export GmbH v Commission*, n 101 above, at para 46.

[245] The European Court of Human Rights has, of course, had to consider whether an appeal by way of judicial review may satisfy Art 6 of the Convention. See, eg, *Bryan v United Kingdom*, (1995) 21 EHHR 342, which concerned the UK's planning procedures. The fact that the Court found judicial review adequate in that case should not, however, be thought necessarily to limit the scope for debate in the very different circumstances which may arise in relation to customs duty.

The Finance Act 1994, section 16(3) enshrines the requirement for security in domestic legislation. Broadly speaking, it provides that an appeal which relates to any decision falling within the Finance Act 1994, s 14(1)(a)–(c) (which refers amongst other things to decisions about the time, rate, and amount of charge) is not to be entertained if any amount is outstanding from the appellant in respect of any liability of his to pay duty to the Commissioners, unless two alternative requirements are satisfied. The first of these is that the Commissioners have issued a certificate stating either that security, which appears to them to be adequate, has been provided, or that the Commissioners do not require security, or have accepted such lesser amount as they consider appropriate, on the grounds of the hardship that the appellant would otherwise suffer.[246] The second alternative is that the tribunal to which the appeal is made decides that the Commissioners should not have refused to issue a certificate and is satisfied that such security (if any) as it would have been reasonable for the Commissioners to accept in the circumstances, has been given to the Commissioners.[247]

As we noted above, Collins J has construed the second paragraph of CCC, Article 244 as merely setting out the two situations in which decisions must be suspended by the customs authorities, rather than as limiting the situations in which they may be suspended. Consequently, he was able to conclude in *Mitsui* that the Finance Act 1994 s 16(3) requires the Commissioners of Customs and Excise to consider whether adequate security has been provided and, if it has, to provide a certificate[248] so that the appeal may proceed with the decision in question suspended.[249]

3.3 *Security and unconditional rights of appeal*

CCC, Article 243 says clearly that '[a]ny person shall have the right to appeal'. It imposes no qualifications on that right. Furthermore, CCC, Article 244.3 links the provision of security to the suspension of the decision appealed against, not to the right to appeal. In contrast, the Finance Act 1994 s 16(3) provides that an appeal which relates to any decision within the specified categories 'shall not be entertained' if any duty is outstanding unless one of the two conditions relating to security, discussed above, is satisfied. It appears that

---

[246] See Finance Act 1994, s 16(3)(a)(i) and (ii). The UK legislation refers to 'hardship' rather than 'serious economic or social difficulties' which appears in CCC, Art 244, third para.

[247] See Finance Act 1994, s 16(3)(b). In *CCE v Broomco (formerly Anchor Foods Ltd)*, n 224 above, the English Court of Appeal decided that the effect of s 16(3)(b) was to give appellants a right of appeal, not only in respect of the amount of security, but also in respect of the issue of irreparable damage under CCC, Art 244, second para, and that both matters were within the exclusive jurisdiction of the tribunal: see para 21.

[248] Under the Finance Act 1994, s 16(3)(a).

[249] See *Mitsui & Co UK plc*, n 220 above, at para [28]. See also *Anchor Foods Ltd v CCE* [1999] V&DR 1.

an unconditional right to appeal, with a conditional right to suspension of the decision appealed against in the CCC, has been transposed into UK law as a conditional right to appeal. Whatever the reasons for this change, it cannot be justified by reference to the need to protect the Community's own resources. If an appeal is commenced and no security is provided then collection of the duty will continue.[250]

It should be emphasized that it is not just in relation to the UK that there have been concerns over the compatibility of the appeals system with the CCC. The Court of Auditors has noted that not all Member States have properly implemented the appeals procedures for customs duty and recommended that the Commission review national law to determine to what extent it is inconsistent with Community law.[251] It may be that the prospect of such a review will encourage national legislatures to make any necessary changes.

3.4 *Production of documents*

On occasions traders seek assistance from the Value Added Tax and Duties Tribunal in obtaining documents which are material for their case, including documents in the possession of the Commission. The Tribunal has, on occasions, made a direction to the effect that the UK Commissioners of Customs and Excise should use their best endeavours to procure the production of relevant documents from the Commission.[252] On occasions they may well assist without such an order. It is, however, impossible for the tribunal to compel the Commission to produce documents to which the trader is entitled.

In *Anchor Foods*[253] the tribunal noted that it had not been addressed on the issue of whether or not it could make an order for the production of documents against the Commission on the basis that it was a legal person present in the United Kingdom by virtue of its representative office within rule 22(2) of the VAT Tribunal Rules 1986.[254] In fact, the Commission itself does not have legal personality. It is an institution of the Community which it represents.[255] It, therefore, does not fall within the terms of rule 22 of the VAT Tribunal Rules as a person over which the tribunal has jurisdiction. Furthermore, the Community, which is a legal person by virtue of EC Treaty, Article 282, benefits from wide immunities given to it by the Protocol on the privileges and immunities of the European Communities to the Treaty

---

[250] In *Anchor Foods Ltd v CCE* [1999] V&DR 1 at 26, para 165, the tribunal indicated that it would have been willing to seek a reference to the European Court of Justice on the compatibility of s 16(3) with the CCC had that proved necessary.

[251] Special Report 8/99 of the Court of Auditors on securities and guarantees provided for in the Community Customs Code to protect the collection of traditional own resources together with the Commission's replies: [2000] OJ C70/1, para 45.

[252] See *Anchor Foods Ltd v CCE* [1998] V&DR 108.

[253] Ibid.

[254] SI 1986/590, as amended.

[255] EC Treaty, Art 282.

establishing a Single Council and a Single Commission of the European Communities. Article 1 of the Protocol states that 'The property and assets of the Communities shall not be the subject of any administrative or legal measure of constraint without the authorization of the Court of Justice'. Article 2 provides that the archives of the Communities shall be inviolable, while Article 6 provides that, for their official communications and the transmission of all their documents, the institutions of the Communities shall enjoy, in each Member State's territory, the treatment accorded by that state to diplomatic missions. So far as concerns the decision of the Commission not to produce information, this is a matter which may be taken to the Court of First Instance. Jurisdiction to determine whether or not any decision relating to the production of documents should be annulled lies with it, not the courts of Member States.[256]

It may be thought that it would be desirable for a Member State's court or tribunal hearing a customs duty appeal to have jurisdiction over every aspect of the proceedings before it. That, however, would necessitate a very different system of appeals; one which is uniform throughout the Community. Uniformity in relation to the appeals system may be desirable for much the same reasons as it is desirable for the customs authorities of the Member States to act as one. Progress towards the latter is being made, not least pursuant to the Customs 2002 programme. Progress toward a uniform appeals procedure is, though, unlikely, at least at the present stage of the Community's development.

---

[256] See EC Treaty, Art 240.

14

Planning for the Future

The creation of the EC's customs union ahead of schedule in 1968 was a great achievement, but over the subsequent years more work had to be done to ensure that the customs union was fully effective. Indeed, it was not until 1985 that a regulation establishing the Community's inward processing regime was passed[1] and the regulation governing the outward processing regime was not passed until the following year.[2] The process of development is still continuing, as the Commission has made clear in its most recent Communication on customs matters.[3] This is, in part, because the commercial environment has changed greatly since 1968. The establishment of capitalist economies in Eastern Europe, the process of globalization, the development of e-commerce, and the need for traders to move goods more quickly to their destinations have all had their impact on customs services. On the one hand, traders' activities need to be faster and more efficient than ever before. This may imply lighter regulation and a greater use of information technology. On the other hand, the changes have led to opportunities for fraudsters and organized criminal activity. Combating these may imply more rigorous regulation. Balancing the requirements of these conflicting objectives will, no doubt, continue to be a difficult task.

A. PLANNING FOR THE FUTURE BY THE COUNCIL, THE COMMISSION, AND MEMBER STATES

The Communication acknowledges that, so far as the Community's customs duty regime is concerned, the legal framework is largely in place.[4] It is in relation to operational matters that some of the more intractable difficulties are faced, as we noted in chapter 10.[5] This is, as the Communication says 'the main area where efforts will need to be concentrated over the coming years'.[6] This is likely to be particularly true bearing in mind the planned enlargement of the Community.

---

[1] See Council Regulation (EEC) 1999/85 of 16 July 1985 [1985] OJ L188/1.

[2] See Council Regulation (EEC) 2473/86 of 24 July 1986 [1986] OJ L212/1.

[3] Communication from the Commission to the Council, the European Parliament, and the Economic and Social Committee concerning a strategy for the Customs Union COM(2001)51 final. I have drawn heavily on this document in writing this chapter.

[4] It is not, of course, complete. There remains considerable work to be done, eg, in relation to harmonization of penalties throughout the Community, as we noted in Ch 4.

[5] See Ch 10 at A, 'National customs controls in a customs union', and section 2 of the Communication.

[6] See para 4 of the Introduction to section 2 of the Communication, n 3.

Against this background the Commission has identified three strategic objectives for the customs union for the future. It describes them as follows:

1. providing a framework for the development of international trade based on transparent and stable rules, applied coherently,
2. providing the Community and Member States with budgetary resources,
3. protecting society from unfair international trade and damage, notably in terms of financial, commercial, public health, cultural and environmental interests.[7]

In pursuit of these objectives the Commission has outlined specific proposals for action in five main areas: legislation, operations, service to the business community, training, and the international role of customs, so that, for example, the Community is appropriately represented in international fora dealing with customs such as the WCO, the WTO, and G7. So far as legislation is concerned, there are, first, a number of specific proposals for 'fraud-proofing' work on existing and new legislation. These include initiatives to improve the coherence between customs legislation and rules for indirect taxes, along with improved administrative co-operation between customs and tax authorities. Secondly, there are proposals to adapt legislation to reduce the burdens on economic operators. These cover the introduction of generally applicable simplified procedures, increasing the use of electronic submissions, continuing the simplification and rationalization of the CN and customs procedures, such as transit, and further work on the harmonization of sanctions. Thirdly, there are proposals for training, guidelines, and manuals for traders and administrators working with customs legislation.[8] Turning to proposals in relation to operations, these include increasing the standardization of customs controls, improving the application of those that exist, completing the introduction of the New Computerized Transit System referred to in Chapter 10, and developing a new information technology strategy in customs administration.

1. *Customs 2000 and Customs 2002*

The strategy for the customs union contained in the Communication referred to above, has to be read in conjunction with the action programmes of the Commission known as Customs 2000 and Customs 2002.[9] The Customs

---

[7] See ibid, section 7, para 1.
[8] Guidelines concerning customs procedures with economic impact were published on 24 Sept 2001: [2001] OJ C–269/1.
[9] Customs 2000 was established pursuant to Decision (EC) 210/97 of the European Parliament and Council of 19 Dec 1996 [1997] OJ L33/24. Customs 2002 was established pursuant to Decision (EC) 105/2000 of the European Parliament and Council of 17 Dec 1999 [2000] L13/1. See also Report from the Commission to the Council and the European Parliament on the implementation of the Customs 2000 programme, COM(1998)471 final, 24 July 1998.

2000 Programme set out a course of action to be take over a five-year period from 1 January 1996 to 31 December 2000. It was designed to be implemented by the Member States and the Commission working in partnership in the Customs Policy Committee. This consists of the Directors General of the Member States' and Commission's customs services. After providing that Member States' customs officials at the border of the customs territory could wear the twelve-star symbol of the Community, the programme moves on to matters of substance. Article 4 of the relevant decision, noted above, sets out the common framework of objectives underlying the programme in seven points. The first aim is that Community law is applied with equivalent results at every point of the Community customs territory so as, amongst other things, to avoid distortions. Other aims include increasing the efficiency and openness of customs services, improving the training of customs officials within the Community and third countries, and providing assistance to the officials of countries which propose to accede to the Community. Further provisions of the decision deal with matters such as the application of customs controls, the monitoring and adjustment of procedures, post-clearance recovery, the fight against fraud, and improvements in working methods, including increased use of risk analysis. Article 13 deals with the difficult and important area of administrative customs penalties, in respect of which it gives the Commission the task of putting forward proposals to ensure that penalties are such that Community legislation is enforced with equal effect and the Community's financial interests are effectively protected.[10]

The Customs 2002 Programme extends the period of activity to 31 December 2002 and specifies that the New Computerized Transit System is to be fully operational by 30 June 2003.[11] It includes special provisions relating to information exchange, communication systems, manuals, and guides and deals with matters such as the exchange of officials. Importantly, it provides that the applicant countries of Central and Eastern Europe may take part in the programme in accordance with the Europe Agreements, together with Cyprus, Malta, and Turkey so far as customs law permits.[12] A final report on the implementation of the programme is to be forwarded to the Commission by the Member States by 31 December 2002. The Commission, for its part, is to submit to the European Parliament and the Council an interim report and a communication on the desirability of continuing the programme by 30 June 2001, and a final report by 30 June 2003.

One of the practical results of Customs 2002 is the creation of RALFH. This

---

[10] See R Condon, '*Customs 2000*: Taking European Customs Towards the 21st Century' [1995/96] *EC Tax Journal* 1. The author notes that, in the past, the Commission has acted in this area with the encouragement of some Member States 'but against considerable opposition from others' (see 11).

[11] Art 8.3.

[12] Art 13a.

is a contact group of the northern European ports of Rotterdam, Antwerp, Le Havre, Felixstowe, and Hamburg. It is designed to ensure closer co-operation between the customs authorities in these ports. Co-operation is planned in relation to matters such as risk analysis, working methods, the frequency and depth of inspection, inspection tools, and training and supervision of officials. As the statement of the customs managers of the northern ports says:

> it cannot be the case that every country has different points of emphasis during inspections . . . it must not be the case that companies arrange for their customs handling to be carried out in a particular port because there are less stringent, quicker or more flexible inspections. Nor can it be the case that some consignments or ocean-going vessels are inspected successively in two countries, one time right after the other, whilst others are not inspected for years. Nor can it be the case that customs in country A have information which is important for customs handling in country B, and fail to pass this information on.[13]

2. *The Council Resolution on a strategy for the customs union*

The need for co-operation between the customs authorities of Member States and indeed those of third countries, particularly those neighbouring the EU, and acceding states, has recently been emphasized by the Council in its Resolution of 30 May 2001 on a strategy for the Customs Union.[14] It endorses the general thrust of the commission's Communication referred to above and looks forward to receiving concrete planning proposals. Among other things, it highlights the role of customs authorities in fighting cross-border crime and the need to co-operate pursuant to the framework of Title VI of the Treaty on European Union, referred to in Chapter 2. The quality of drafting of customs legislation was considered in Chapter 4. In this regard the Council resolution notes that: 'a clear and unambiguous legislation that is known to the users and applied by adequately trained officials is of fundamental importance, not only for legitimate trade to flow smoothly but also for the combat against fraud to be efficient'[15] The Council goes on to invite the Commission to propose more simplification, modernization, and rationalization of customs regulations and procedures. It also seeks the development of a broad-based programme for computerization of customs procedures and exchange of customs information. It welcomes the Commission's intention to extend the Customs 2002 programme and invites the Member States to join in supporting the strategy, to participate with the Commission in actions against criminal activities and to ensure the necessary co-operation between national customs authorities.

It will be apparent that although the customs union may have been in exis-

---

[13] See the RALFH Newsletter, first edn 3.
[14] See [2001] OJ C171/1.
[15] Ibid, at para 5.

tence a long time, its development continues, with the Council and Commission agreed on the strategy which has to be pursued. Inevitably, the strategy must be subject to review and in its resolution, the Council calls for it to be evaluated within five years.

B. PLANNING FOR THE FUTURE BY TRADERS

If the authorities for their part have to do a considerable amount of planning for the future, traders also have to exercise some forethought in relation to the application of the customs duty regime. If they do not, then they may well pay more customs duty than is required. Some traders may find that they are subjected to charges having equivalent effect to a customs duty which are prohibited under the EC Treaty, as we discussed in Chapter 3. Assuming that the charge which is imposed is legal, there are a wide range of factors to be considered which may result in the impact of the duty being reduced. There is room to highlight only a few considerations here.

The classification of various products may influence precisely what is imported. It may also be that the product can be obtained from a third country, imports from which enjoy preferential treatment. The origin of the product is, therefore, a matter which should be carefully considered. This is particularly true where the product is to be subjected to processing of some kind and the nature and location of any proposed processing may very well need to be considered with the rules of origin and inward and outward processing in mind. Turning to valuation, we have seen that a trader may have some choice concerning the sale which is to be relied upon for valuation purposes. Furthermore, the drafting of a sale contract can have a significant effect on the relevant transaction value. Payments made as a condition of sale, for example, have the effect of increasing the transaction value in question.[16]

Of course, while there is considerable scope for sensible planning by the trader, there is no room for abuse of the customs system. Community law has at its disposal the tools to negate any abuse there may be. Sometimes a purposive construction of the relevant provisions may be enough to counter abuse. This proved to be the case, for example, in *Commission v UK*[17] in which a purposive construction of 'taken from the sea' ensured that fish caught in the nets of Polish boats were taken from the sea by them and not by the British boats which lifted them from the water. As a result the fish were of Polish origin and liable to duty. Arrangements to avoid customs duty were, accordingly, defeated. On other occasions it may be necessary for the Court of Justice to have recourse to the concept of abuse. The true nature of this concept is a

---

[16] See the discussion of CCC, Art 29.3(a) in Ch 8.
[17] Case 100/84 [1985] ECR 1169.

matter of serious debate and, at the time of writing, there is litigation on foot
in the UK which explores its applicability in the context of value added tax. So
far as concerns customs duty, however, there can be no doubt of its significance, and the Court of Justice treats it as axiomatic that traders should not be
permitted to abuse customs procedures. In one case concerning the discharge
of inward processing the Court said that:

> if the customs authority finds that . . . ways of discharging the inward processing
> relief arrangements . . . are not likely to lead to abuse by, for example, conferring an
> unjustified customs advantage on the beneficiary, it must grant the authorization; if
> not, it can only refuse it.[18]

This quotation shows, however, that whilst abuse is to be defeated, the
genuine activities of traders are not easily challenged. There is insufficient
room here to discuss the concept of abuse in any detail, but its inapplicability
to bona fide commercial transactions was implicitly acknowledged by the
Court[19] in a case concerning the availability of export refunds in agricultural
law. It said that:

> it is clear from the case-law of the Court that the scope of Community regulations
> must in no case be extended to cover abuses on the part of a trader.[20] The Court has
> also held that the fact that importation and re-exportation operations were not
> realised as bona fide commercial transactions but only in order wrongfully to bene-
> fit from the grant of monetary compensatory amounts, may preclude the applica-
> tion of positive monetary compensatory amounts.[21]

The Court went on to outline the requirements which must be met if the
existence of an abuse is to be established.[22] First of all there must be objective circumstances which constitute formal observance only of the conditions laid down by Community rules, as a result of which they fail to achieve
their purpose. Secondly, a subjective element must be present, in that there
must be an intention to obtain an advantage from Community rules by
creating artificially the conditions laid down for obtaining the advantage.
This subjective element may be established by, for example, evidence of
collusion between the exporter and importer. The national court in question
has to establish the existence of these two elements, in a hearing governed
by national rules of evidence provided that the effectiveness of Community

---

[18] See Case C–437/93 *Hauptzollamt Heilbronn v Temic Telefunken Microelectronic GmbH* [1995]
ECR I–1687 at para 26.
[19] In Case C–110/99 *Emsland-Stärke GmbH v Hauptzollamt Hamburg-Jonas*, 14 Dec 2000, para
51.
[20] The Court here relied upon Case 125/76 *Enterprise Peter Cremer v Bundesanstalt für land-
wirtschaftliche Marktordnung ('BALM')* [1977] ECR 1593 at para 21.
[21] The Court here relied upon Case C–8/92 *General Milk Products v Hauptzollamt Hamburg-Jonas*
[1993] ECR I–779 at para 21.
[22] See Case 110/99 *Emsland-Stärke GmbH v Hauptzollamt Hamburg-Jonas*, n 19 above, at paras
52–54.

law is not consequently undermined.[23] Although the national customs administration is likely to bear the initial burden of establishing abuse, it may, in the most serious cases, be reversed by the production of admissible evidence establishing a *prima facie* case.[24] As with planning in relation to other fiscal impositions, the facts of the particular case will prove to be of the utmost importance and the trader must be able to establish them with convincing evidence.

CONCLUSION

For the Commission, the customs authorities, and traders, planning for the future is essential. To some extent, given the huge changes and possibilities brought about by e-commerce, the challenge is as much to adapt to the present as to prepare for the future. In doing that there are many new challenges to be met and the traditional aims of reducing tariffs and eliminating quotas in respect of goods appear somewhat dated in comparison with them. The traditional aims have not, however, become irrelevant, even assuming a global trading environment in which tariffs are not imposed as negotiating weapon. The introduction of new high-technology goods into world markets has raised new and difficult questions of a traditional nature—such as how to classify the Pentium III microprocessor. As Charlene Barshefsky, US Trade Representative in the administration of President Clinton, has said:

> Classification will become even more difficult as new products continue to flood the market. Given that many countries maintain high tariffs on products considered to be consumer electronics, the ITA[25] will need to be widened to include new categories of products and ensure that existing high-tech products do not slip out of the duty-free category.[26]

The focus of attention may have moved from trade in goods but, clearly, trade in goods continues to present challenges for the customs lawyer. So far as the Community is concerned, the customs union has proved itself a fundamental

[23] Ibid, para 54. The Court here relied upon Joined Cases 205/82 to 215/82 *Deutsche Milchkontor v Germany* [1983] ECR 2633, paras 17–25 and 35–39; Case 222/82 *Johnston v Chief Constable of the Royal Ulster Constabulary* [1986] ECR 1651, paras 17–21; Case C–212/94 *FMC plc and Others v Intervention Board for Agricultural Produce and Ministry of Agriculture, Fisheries and Food* [1996] ECR I–389, paras 49–51; and Joined Cases C–418/97 and C–419/97 *ARCO Chemie Nederland Ltd and Others v Minister van Volkshuisvesting* [2000] ECR I–4475, para 41.

[24] See Case 110/99 *Emsland-Stärke GmbH v Hauptzollamt Hamburg-Jonas*, n 19 above, at para 39.

[25] The Information Technology Agreement of 13 Dec 1996 which entered into force on 1 Apr 1997. It was approved on behalf of the Community by Council Decision (EC) 359/97 of 24 Mar 1997 concerning the elimination of duties on information technology products [1997] OJ L155/1. The text of the Convention is annexed to the Decision.

[26] C Barshefsky, 'Trade Policy for a Networked World', *Foreign Affairs* Mar/Apr 2001, Vol 80 No 2, 134 at 143 (The Council on Foreign Relations).

and enduring element of the European Community since its creation in 1968 and continues to do so. Its budgetary significance for the Community remains considerable despite a general reduction in tariffs. Its significance so far as global trade is concerned cannot be underestimated.

Selected Reading

Amand, C., 'Cross-Border Warehousing' *EC Tax Review* 1996/1 28.
—— and Noone, D., 'The origin of goods muddle: For a defence of the Community importers' *EC Tax Review* 1998/3 187.
Bourgeois, J. H. J., 'The EC in the WTO and Advisory Opinion 1/94: An Echternach Procession (1995) 32 CMLRev 763.
Condon, R., 'Customs 2000: Taking European Customs Towards the 21st Century' [1995/96] *EC Tax Journal* 1.
Eeckhout, P., 'The Domestic Legal Status of the WTO Agreement: Interconnecting Legal Systems' (1997) 34 CMLRev 11.
Emilou, N., and O'Keefe, D. (eds), *The European Union and World Trade Law: After the GATT Uruguay Round* (John Wiley & Sons, Chichester, 1996).
Forrester, I. S., 'EEC Customs Law: Rules of Origin and Preferential Treatment' [1980] *ELR* 173.
Jackson, J. H., *The World Trading System: Law & Policy of Economic International Relations* (2nd edn, MIT Press, Cambridge, Mass, 1997).
—— and Sykes, A.O. (eds) *Implementing the Uruguay Round* (Clarendon Press, Oxford, 1997).
Jerram, E., 'Customs value: what is a sale for export?' 1996/3 *EC Tax Review* 189.
Lasok, D., *The Trade and Customs Law of the European Union* (3rd edn, Kluwer Law International, London, 1997).
Macfarlane, G., *Customs and Excise Law and Practice* (Longman Law, Tax and Finance, London, 1993).
Molle, W. T., *The Economics of European Integration: Theory, Practice, Policy* (in particular ch 5, 'Customs Union Theory') (3rd edn, Ashgate Publishing Ltd, Aldershot, 1997).
Pescatore, P., 'Opinion 1/94 on "Conclusion" of the WTO Agreement: Is there an escape from a programmed disaster?' (1999) 36 CMLRev 387.
Preiss, H-J, and Pethke, R., 'The Pan-European Rules of Origin: The beginning of a new era in European Free Trade' (1997) 34 CMLRev 771.
Schuren, Van der P., 'Customs Classification: One of the Cornerstones of the Single European Market but one which cannot be exhaustively regulated' (1991) 28 CMLRev 855.
Snyder, F., *International Trade and Customs Law of the European Union* (Butterworths, London, 1998).
Swann, D., *The Economics of the Common Market: Integration in the European Union* (8th edn, Penguin, London, 1995).
Terra, B. J. M., *Community customs law: a guide to the customs rules on trade*

468 *EC Customs Law*

between the (enlarged) EU and third countries (Kluwer Law International, The Hague, 1995).

WEILER, J. H. H. (ed.), *The EU, the WTO and the NAFTA: Towards a Common Law of International Trade?* (Oxford University Press, Oxford, 2000).

WHITE, J. (consultant ed.), *Customs Duties Handbook 2001* (Butterworths, London, 2001).

WORLD TRADE ORGANIZATION, *The Results of the Uruguay Round of Multilateral Trade Negotiations: The Legal Texts* (GATT Secretariat, 1994, Reprinted WTO, Geneva, 1995).

ZAIMIS, N. A., *EC Rules of Origin* (Chancery Law Publishing, London, 1992).

Index

abandonment 344
abuse of dominant position 38–9
action plans,
  Commission 85
Africa,
  customs union 3
agriculture 13
  common agricultural policy 27–8
  Community Customs Code (CCC) 92
alteration,
  customs duties 118–19
anti-dumping,
  common commercial policy 44–5
  imposition of duty 45
appeals,
  amendment 450
  ancillary matters 454–5
  annulment 450
  Community Customs Code (CCC) 91
  decisions 449–50
  documents, production of 457–8
  exercise of right 450–1
  need for procedure 448
  non-ancillary matters 454–5
  revocation 450
  right 448
  security 451–2
    prior to appeal 455–6
    unconditional rights of appeal 457
  suspension of the decision 450–1
  UK procedure 452–3
artistic merit,
  tariff 137
ATA carnet 6–7, 336
Austria 2
authorization,
  inward processing procedure 351–3
    conditions 351
    content 353
    economic conditions 352–3
    form of application 351
  outward processing,
    conditions for authorization 365–6
    content 366
    entry of goods for the arrangements
      366–7
    form of application 365
  procedures, customs 298–302
    applications 299–300
    decisions on 301–2
    examination of economic conditions
      301
    general provisions 298–9

    period for which effective 302
    single 300–1
    where to apply 300
  processing under customs control 328–9
  release for free circulation 303–4
    contents 304–5
    duration 304–5
  warehousing, customs 326–7

Benelux,
  Economic Union 3
binding information,
  invalidity 154–6
  issue 151–3
  reliance 153
  UK and 156–7
  uses 154
  validity 154–6
breeding methods,
  tariff 138
Bretton Woods conference 6

CAP see common agricultural policy (CAP)
CARICOM 4
CCC see Community Customs Code (CCC)
CIS 46, 47
clothing 13
CN see Combined Nomenclature (CN)
Combined Nomenclature (CN),
  basis 113–14
  classification regulations 128–30
  Commission's discretion to apply 126–30
  customs duties 116–18
  digits used to identify product 115
  function 113–14
  generally 112
  harmonized system 114, 115
  history 113–14
  interpretation,
    general rules 142–6
  sub-divisions 115
  sub-headings 115
  Tariff Regulation 114, 115
  updating 115
  uses 113
  what it is 114–16
  see also tariff; tariff classification
Commission,
  abuse detected by 101
  action plans 85
  administration of customs duty regime
    100
  audi alteram partem 102